W9-CCN-855

MOSCOW &
ST. PETERSBURG

JENNIFER CHATER & NATHAN TOOHEY

Contents

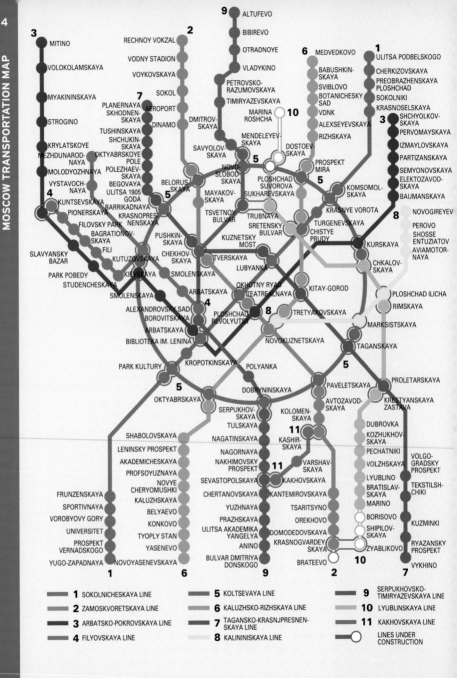

MOSCOW TRANSPORTATION MAP

	1 SOKOLNICHESKAYA LINE		5 KOLTSEVAYA LINE		9 SERPUKHOVSKO-TIMIRYAZEVSKAYA LINE
	2 ZAMOSKVORETSKAYA LINE		6 KALUZHSKO-RIZHSKAYA LINE		10 LYUBLINSKAYA LINE
	3 ARBATSKO-POKROVSKAYA LINE		7 TAGANSKO-KRASNJPRESNEN-SKAYA LINE		11 KAKHOVSKAYA LINE
	4 FILYOVSKAYA LINE		8 KALININISKAYA LINE		LINES UNDER CONSTRUCTION

© MOSCOW METRO

Moscow Maps

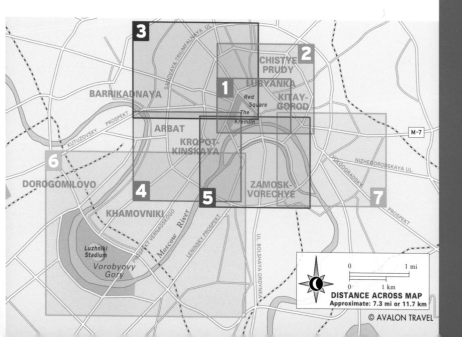

DISTANCE ACROSS MAP
Approximate: 7.3 mi or 11.7 km

© AVALON TRAVEL

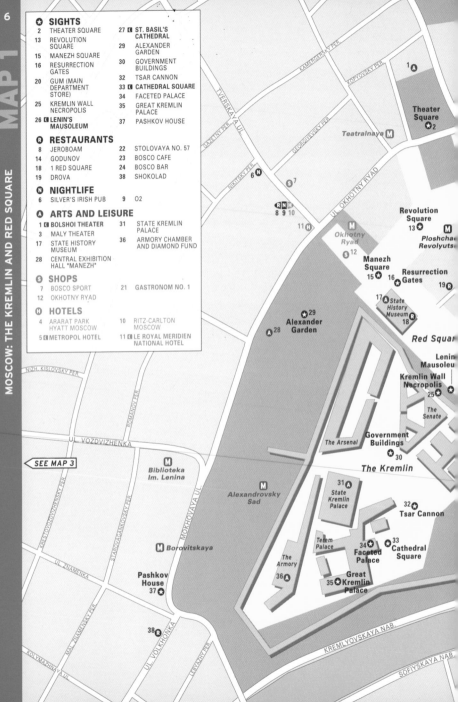

SIGHTS
2 THEATER SQUARE
13 REVOLUTION SQUARE
15 MANEZH SQUARE
16 RESURRECTION GATES
20 GUM (MAIN DEPARTMENT STORE)
25 KREMLIN WALL NECROPOLIS
26 LENIN'S MAUSOLEUM
27 ST. BASIL'S CATHEDRAL
29 ALEXANDER GARDEN
30 GOVERNMENT BUILDINGS
32 TSAR CANNON
33 CATHEDRAL SQUARE
34 FACETED PALACE
35 GREAT KREMLIN PALACE
37 PASHKOV HOUSE

RESTAURANTS
8 JEROBOAM
14 GODUNOV
18 1 RED SQUARE
19 DROVA
22 STOLOVAYA NO. 57
23 BOSCO CAFE
24 BOSCO BAR
38 SHOKOLAD

NIGHTLIFE
6 SILVER'S IRISH PUB
9 O2

ARTS AND LEISURE
1 BOLSHOI THEATER
3 MALY THEATER
17 STATE HISTORY MUSEUM
28 CENTRAL EXHIBITION HALL "MANEZH"
31 STATE KREMLIN PALACE
36 ARMORY CHAMBER AND DIAMOND FUND

SHOPS
7 BOSCO SPORT
12 OKHOTNY RYAD
21 GASTRONOM NO. 1

HOTELS
4 ARARAT PARK HYATT MOSCOW
5 METROPOL HOTEL
10 RITZ-CARLTON MOSCOW
11 LE ROYAL MERIDIEN NATIONAL HOTEL

SEE MAP 3

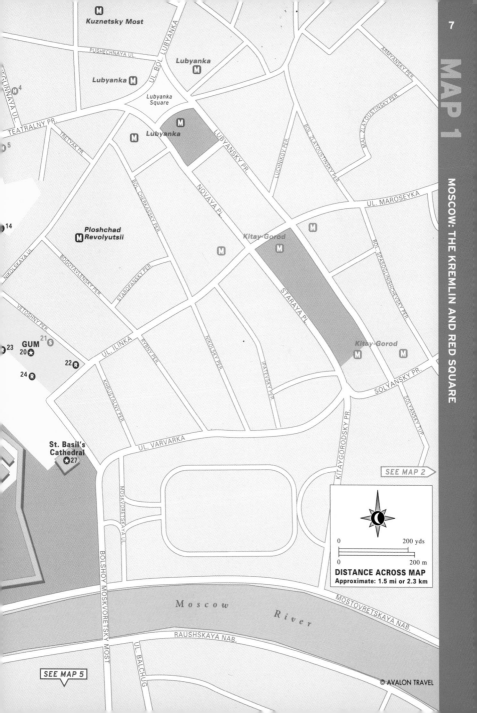

Kuznetsky Most

PUSHECHNAYA UL

UL. BOL. LUBYANKA

Lubyanka

Lubyanka

Lubyanka
Square

Lubyanka

LUBYANSKY PR.

MAL. ZLATOUSTINSKY PER.

ARMYANSKY PER.

BOL. ZLATOUSTINSKY PER.

LUCHNIKOV PER.

UL. MAROSEYKA

Ploshchad
Revolyutsii

NIKOLSKAYA UL.

BOGOYAVLENSKY PER.

BOL. CHERKASSKY PER.

STAROPANSKY PER.

NOVAYA PL.

Kitay-Gorod

STARAYA PL.

BOL. SPASOGLINISHCHEVSKY PER.

MAL. SPASOGLINISHCHEVSKY PER.

Kitay-Gorod

SOLYANSKY PR.

SOLYANSKY TUP.

GUM

VETOSHNY PER.

UL. ILINKA

RYBNY PER.

NIKITSKY PER.

IPATIEVSKY PER.

KHRUSTALNY PER.

St. Basil's
Cathedral

UL. VARVARKA

KITAYGORODSKY PR.

SEE MAP 2

MOSKVORETSKAYA UL.

BOLSHOY MOSKVORETSKY MOST

UL. BALCHUG

RAUSHSKAYA NAB.

Moscow   River

MOSTOVRETSKAYA NAB.

SEE MAP 5

TEATRALNY PR.

TRETYAK PR.

TEGININAYA UL.

0   200 yds

0   200 m

DISTANCE ACROSS MAP
Approximate: 1.5 mi or 2.3 km

MAP 2

MOSCOW: KITAY-GOROD, LUBYANKA, AND CHISTYE PRUDY

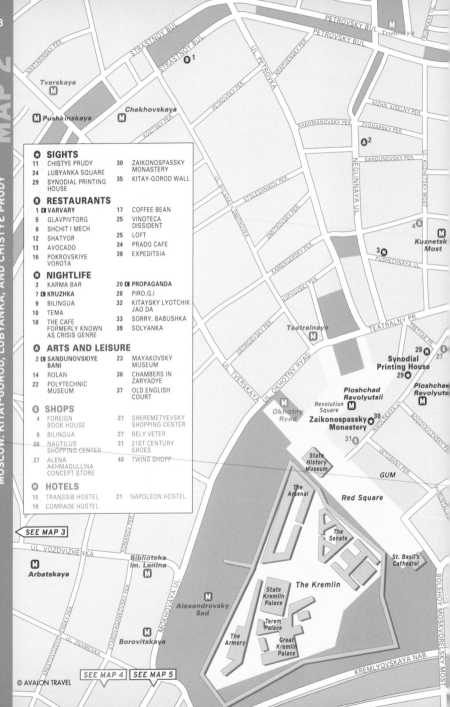

○ SIGHTS

11	CHISTYE PRUDY	30	ZAIKONOSPASSKY MONASTERY
24	LUBYANKA SQUARE		
29	SYNODIAL PRINTING HOUSE	35	KITAY-GOROD WALL

○ RESTAURANTS

1	VARVARY	17	COFFEE BEAN
5	GLAVPIVTORG	25	VINOTECA DISSIDENT
6	SHCHIT I MECH		
12	SHATYOR	25	LOFT
13	AVOCADO	34	PRADO CAFE
16	POKROVSKIYE VOROTA	38	EXPEDITSIA

○ NIGHTLIFE

3	KARMA BAR	20	PROPAGANDA
7	KRUZHKA	28	PIRO.G.I
9	BILINGUA	32	KITAYSKY LYOTCHIK JAO DA
10	TEMA		
18	THE CAFE FORMERLY KNOWN AS CRISIS GENRE	33	SORRY, BABUSHKA
		39	SOLYANKA

○ ARTS AND LEISURE

2	SANDUNOVSKIYE BANI	23	MAYAKOVSKY MUSEUM
14	ROLAN	36	CHAMBERS IN ZARYADYE
22	POLYTECHNIC MUSEUM	37	OLD ENGLISH COURT

○ SHOPS

4	FOREIGN BOOK HOUSE	27	SHEREMETYEVSKY SHOPPING CENTER
8	BILINGUA	27	BELY VETER
26	NAUTILUS SHOPPING CENTER	31	21ST CENTURY SHOES
27	ALENA AKHMADULLINA CONCEPT STORE	40	TWINS SHOPP

○ HOTELS

15	TRANSSIB HOSTEL	21	NAPOLEON HOSTEL
19	COMRADE HOSTEL		

SEE MAP 3

SEE MAP 4   SEE MAP 5

© AVALON TRAVEL

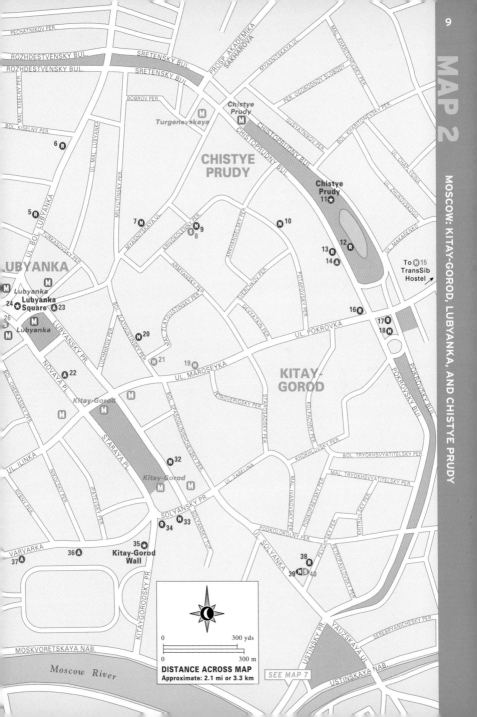

PECHATNIKOV PER.

ROZHDESTVENSKY BUL.

ROZHDESTVENSKY BUL.

SRETENSKY BUL.

SRETENSKY BUL.

PROSP. AKADEMIKA SAKHAROVA

MAL. KHARITONYEVSKY PER.

MYASNITSKAYA UL.

BOL. KISELNY PER.

BOBROV PER.

Turgenevskaya

Chistye Prudy

CHISTOPRUDNY BUL.

PER. OGORODNOY SLOBODY

RUSTAVNIKOV PER.

BOL. KHARITONYEVSKY PER.

UL. CHAPLYGINA

6 R

CHISTYE PRUDY

Chistye Prudy
11

UL. MAKARENKO

UL. ZHUKOVSKOGO

5 R

7 N

9

8

10

13 R

12 R

14 A

To 15
TransSib
Hostel

LUBYANKA

Lubyanka

24

Lubyanka
Square 23

26
3

Lubyanka

20

16 R

17 R

18 N

UL. POKROVKA

21

22

Kitay-Gorod

19

UL. MAROSEYKA

KITAY-
GOROD

POKROVSKY BUL.

32

Kitay-Gorod

BOL. TRYOKHSVYATITELSKY PER.

MAL. TRYOKHSVYATITELSKY PER.

35

34

33

SOLYANKA

UL. ILINKA

VARVARKA

36 A

37 A

Kitay-Gorod
Wall

38 R

39 N 40

MOSKVORETSKAYA NAB.

Moscow River

0   300 yds

0   300 m

DISTANCE ACROSS MAP
Approximate: 2.1 mi or 3.3 km

SEE MAP 7

USTINSKAYA NAB.

SEREBRYANICHESKY PER.

To N 1 Help

⊙ SIGHTS

15 HERMITAGE GARDEN
22 VYSOKOPETROVSKY MONASTERY
31 PUSHKIN SQUARE
37 TVERSKAYA STREET
39 TVERSKAYA SQUARE

53 PATRIARCH'S PONDS
60 MOSCOW ZOO
63 THE WHITE HOUSE (GOVERNMENT HOUSE)
66 CHURCH OF THE GREAT ASCENSION

⊙ RESTAURANTS

12 ◖ METRO
19 GALEREYA
20 LA MAREE
25 FILIMONOVA & YANKEL
28 SCANDINAVIA
33 ◖ CAFE PUSHKIN
34 ◖ TURANDOT
35 MENZA
43 SLUZHEBNY VKHOD
46 GOGOL
50 THE MOST

52 JAGANNATH
54 MARGARITA
56 SHAFRAN
57 NEDALNY VOSTOK
61 PROSTYE VESHCHI
68 MAYAK
69 KVARTIRA 44
71 BELAYA RUS
73 COFFEEMANIA
75 JEAN-JACQUES ROUSSEAU

N NIGHTLIFE

1 HELP
8 B2
8 COOL TRAIN CLUB
13 BLUE BIRD
29 VINOSYR
40 12 VOLT

44 DENIS SIMACHEV BAR
55 GRAND CRU BLACK
59 TIKI BAR
70 ◖ RYUMOCHNAYA
72 PROSTYE VESHCHI

⊙ ARTS AND LEISURE

7 BULGAKOV HOUSE CULTURAL CENTER
9 TCHAIKOVSKY CONCERT HALL
14 NYM YOGA & SPA
16 HERMITAGE GARDEN
16 NOVAYA OPERA
18 NIKULIN CIRCUS
21 MOSCOW MUSEUM OF MODERN ART
24 PLANET FITNESS

26 CONTEMPORARY HISTORY OF RUSSIA MUSEUM
42 CHEKHOV MOSCOW ART THEATER
48 GULAG HISTORY MUSEUM
62 VYSOTKA
65 GORKY HOUSE MUSEUM– RYABUSHINSKY MANSION
74 TCHAIKOVSKY MOSCOW STATE CONSERVATORY

⊙ SHOPS

3 REPUBLIKA
10 MODNAYA TOCHKA
27 L'ETOILE
30 NOVODEL
32 ◖ YELISEYEVSKY GASTRONOM
36 MINISTRY OF GIFTS
38 MOSKVA

41 TRANSYLVANIA
45 ◖ DENIS SIMACHEV
49 PETROVSKY PASSAGE
51 TSUM
58 HEDIARD
64 EXPAT SALON
67 BUKBERI

N HOTELS

2 DOROTHY'S BED & BREAKFAST
4 YELLOW BLUE BUS HOSTEL
5 MAYAKOVSKAYA B&B
6 PEKIN
11 FLAMINGO BED & BREAKFAST

11 KITA INN BED & BREAKFAST
17 GODZILLAS HOSTEL
23 GOLDEN APPLE
47 MARRIOTT ROYAL AURORA

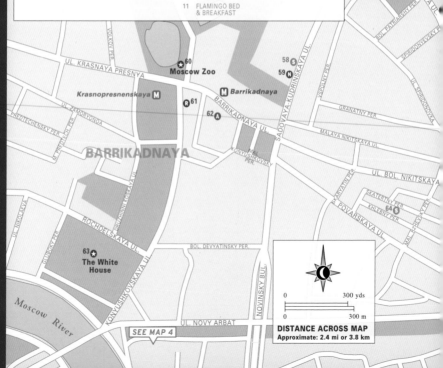

R 60 Moscow Zoo

58 S
59 N

Krasnopresnenskaya M

M Barrikadnaya

R 61
62 A

BARRIKADNAYA

53 ⊙ Patriarch's Ponds
54

64 S

63 ⊙ The White House

Moscow River

SEE MAP 4

UL. NOVY ARBAT

0   300 yds
0   300 m

DISTANCE ACROSS MAP
Approximate: 2.4 mi or 3.8 km

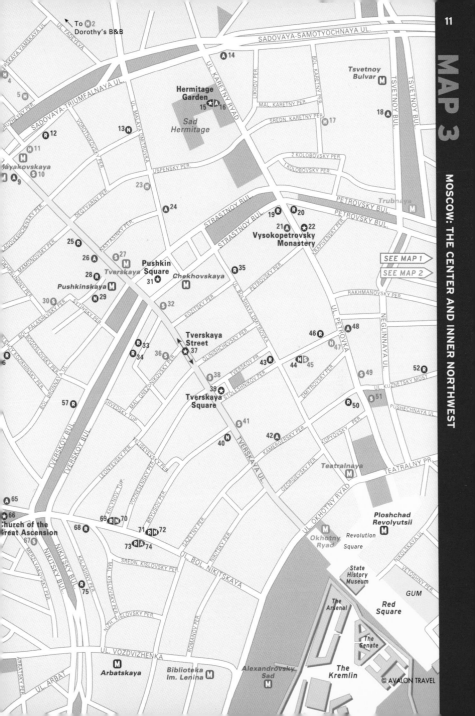

To 2
Dorothy's B&B

SADOVAYA-SAMOTYOCHNAYA UL.

Tsvetnoy
Bulvar

TSVETNOY BUL.

4

5

14

Hermitage
Garden

15 16

Sad
Hermitage

BOL. KARETNY PER.

MAL. KARETNY PER.

SREDN. KARETNY PER.

17

18

12

11

13

Mayakovskaya

10

9

23

24

2 KOLOBOVSKY PER.

3 KOLOBOVSKY PER.

Trubnaya

PETROVSKY BUL.

PETROVSKY BUL.

19 20

21   22

Vysokopetrovsky
Monastery

SEE MAP 1

SEE MAP 2

25

26

27

Tverskaya

Pushkin
Square

31

Chekhovskaya

35

RAKHMANOVSKY PER.

28

Pushkinskaya

29

30

32

33

34

36

Tverskaya
Street

37

46

48

47

44 45

43

49

52

51

50

57

38

39

Tverskaya
Square

40

41

42

Teatralnaya

TEATRALNY PR.

65

66

Church of the
Great Ascension

67

68

69 70

71   72

73   74

75

UL. OKHOTNY RYAD

Okhotny
Ryad

Revolution
Square

Ploshchad
Revolyutsii

State
History
Museum

GUM

The
Arsenal

Red
Square

The
Senate

Arbatskaya

Biblioteka
Im. Lenina

Alexandrovsky
Sad

The
Kremlin

UL. VOZDVIZHENKA

UL. ARBAT

© AVALON TRAVEL

SEE MAP 3

UL. NOVY ARBAT

Smolenskaya

Arbat Str
(The Old Arb

Smolenskaya

ARBAT

Moscow River

BORODINSKY MOST — SMOLENSKAYA UL.

GLAZOVSKY PER.

SMOLENSKY BUL.

UL. PRECHISTENKA

ZUBOVSKY BUL.

Skver
Devichego
Polya

PR. DEVICHEGO POLYA

UL. ROSSOLIMO

✪ SIGHTS
9	MOROZOV'S MANSION	30	CHRIST THE SAVIOR CATHEDRAL
13	ARBAT STREET (THE OLD ARBAT)		

⊘ RESTAURANTS
2	BARASHKA	17	MU-MU
4	OM CAFE	18	PLOTNIKOV PUB
8	YOLKI PALKI	22	TINKOFF
10	PRAGA	25	CANTINETTA ANTINORI
14	WAYNE'S COFFEE	32	GENATSVALE
16	SHASHLYK-MASHLYK	33	TIFLIS

⊘ NIGHTLIFE
5	VISION	31	RAI
15	FLORIDITA	36	VODKA BAR

✪ ARTS AND LEISURE
12	VAKHTANGOV THEATER	28	PUSHKIN STATE MUSEUM OF FINE ARTS
20	PUSHKIN APARTMENT-MUSEUM	29	ILYA GLAZUNOV GALLERY
21	BIBABO	35	CHAYKA
		37	TOLSTOY MUSEUM

⊘ SHOPS
1	LOTTE PLAZA	11	ARBATSKAYA LAVITSA
3	GLOBUS GOURMET	27	BYURO NAKHODOK
6	KIRA PLASTININA		
7	BOOKS HOUSE		

⊘ HOTELS
19	SWEET MOSCOW HOSTEL	26	MOSCOW HOME HOSTEL
23	BELGRAD	34	KEBUR PALACE
24	GOLDEN RING		

© AVALON TRAVEL

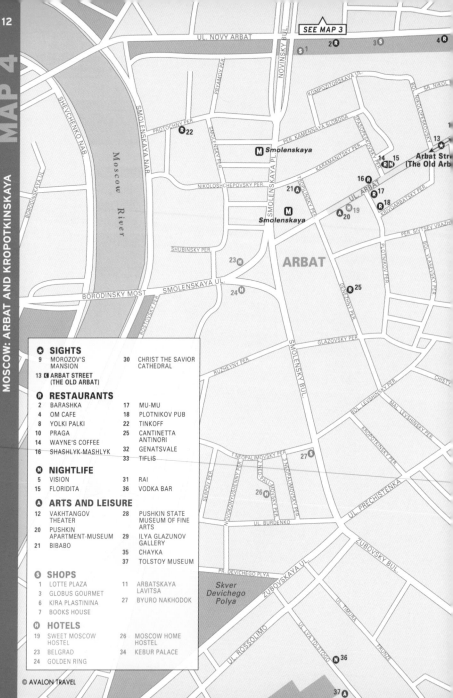

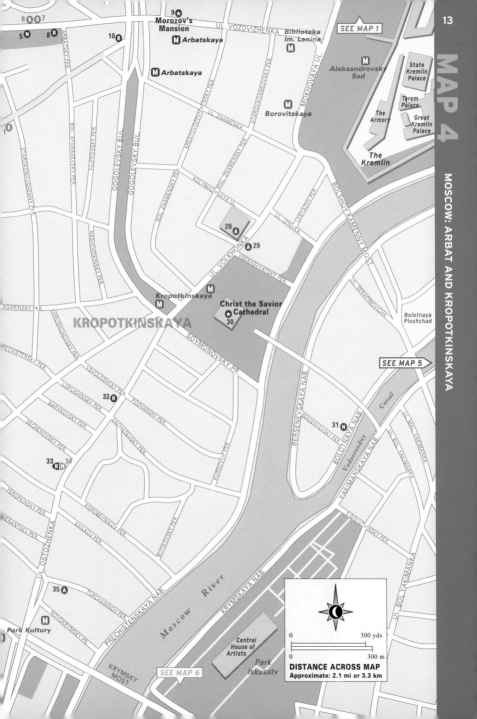

6 **S S** 7

5 **N** 8 **S**

9 ✪ Morozov's Mansion

10 **R**

UL. VOZDVIZHENKA

M Arbatskaya

M Arbatskaya

Biblioteka Im. Lenina

M

SEE MAP 1

Aleksandrovsky Sad

M

State Kremlin Palace

Terem Palace

The Armory

Great Kremlin Palace

The Kremlin

M Borovitskaya

UL. ZNAMENKA

28 **A**

29 **A**

UL. VOLKHONKA

Kropotkinskaya **M**

M

KROPOTKINSKAYA

✚ Christ the Savior Cathedral
30

SEE MAP 5

Bolotnaya Ploshchad

32 **R**

31 **N**

Canal

SOYMONOVSKY PR.

33 **R M** 34

Central House of Artists

Park Iskusstv

35 **A**

M
Park Kultury

Moscow River

KRYMSKY MOST

SEE MAP 6

DISTANCE ACROSS MAP
Approximate: 2.1 mi or 3.3 km

0   300 yds

0   300 m

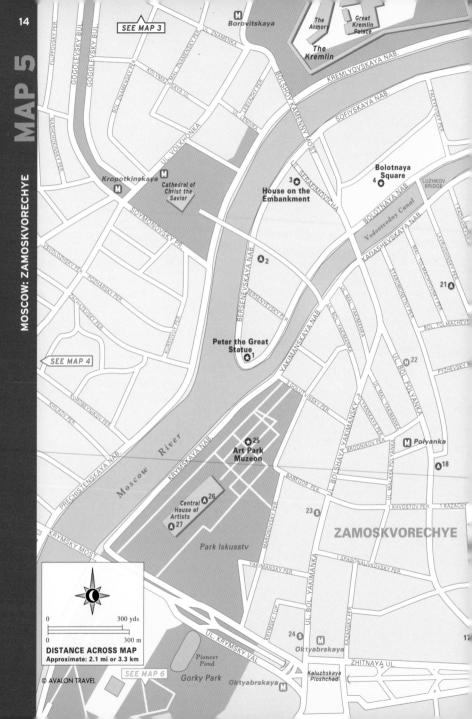

SEE MAP 3

Borovitskaya

The Armory

Great Kremlin Palace

The Kremlin

KREMLYOVSKAYA NAB.

SOFIYSKAYA NAB.

Bolotnaya Square
4

LUZHKOV BRIDGE

House on the Embankment

3

Kropotkinskaya

Cathedral of Christ the Savior

SOYMONOVSKY PR.

Vodootvodny Canal

BOLOTNAYA NAB.

KADASHEVSKAYA NAB.

21

2

SEE MAP 4

Peter the Great Statue
1

BOL. TOLMACHEVS

Polyanka
22

PYZHEVSKY

Moscow River

Art Park Muzeon
25

BABEGON PER.

Polyanka
M

18

Central House of Artists
26

27

23

ZAMOSKVORECHYE

Park Iskusstv

24

Oktyabrskaya
M

DISTANCE ACROSS MAP
Approximate: 2.1 mi or 3.3 km

0   300 yds
0   300 m

Pioneer Pond

Gorky Park

Oktyabrskaya

Kaluzhskaya Ploshchad

ZHITNAYA UL.

UL. KRYMSKY VAL

SEE MAP 6

KRYMSKY MOST

© AVALON TRAVEL

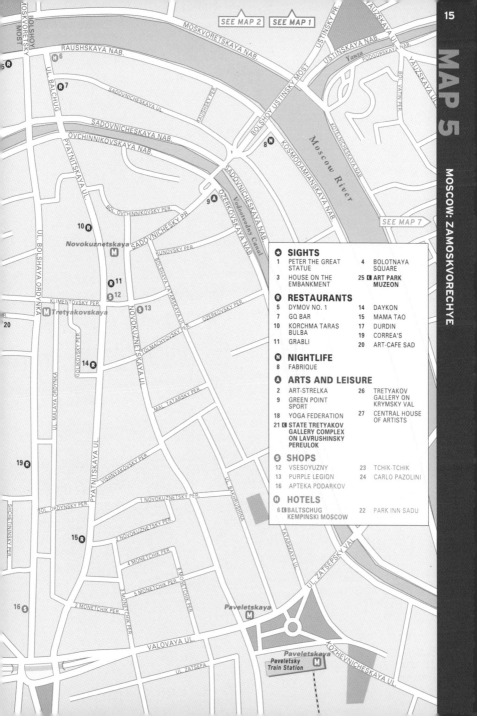

SIGHTS

- 1 PETER THE GREAT STATUE
- 3 HOUSE ON THE EMBANKMENT
- 4 BOLOTNAYA SQUARE
- 25 ◧ ART PARK MUZEON

R RESTAURANTS

- 5 DYMOV NO. 1
- 7 GQ BAR
- 10 KORCHMA TARAS BULBA
- 11 GRABLI
- 14 DAYKON
- 15 MAMA TAO
- 17 DURDIN
- 19 CORREA'S
- 20 ART-CAFE SAD

N NIGHTLIFE

- 8 FABRIQUE

A ARTS AND LEISURE

- 2 ART-STRELKA
- 9 GREEN POINT SPORT
- 18 YOGA FEDERATION
- 21 ◧ STATE TRETYAKOV GALLERY COMPLEX ON LAVRUSHINSKY PEREULOK
- 26 TRETYAKOV GALLERY ON KRYMSKY VAL
- 27 CENTRAL HOUSE OF ARTISTS

S SHOPS

- 12 VSESOYUZNY
- 13 PURPLE LEGION
- 16 APTEKA PODARKOV
- 23 TCHIK-TCHIK
- 24 CARLO PAZOLINI

H HOTELS

- 6 ◧ BALTSCHUG KEMPINSKI MOSCOW
- 22 PARK INN SADU

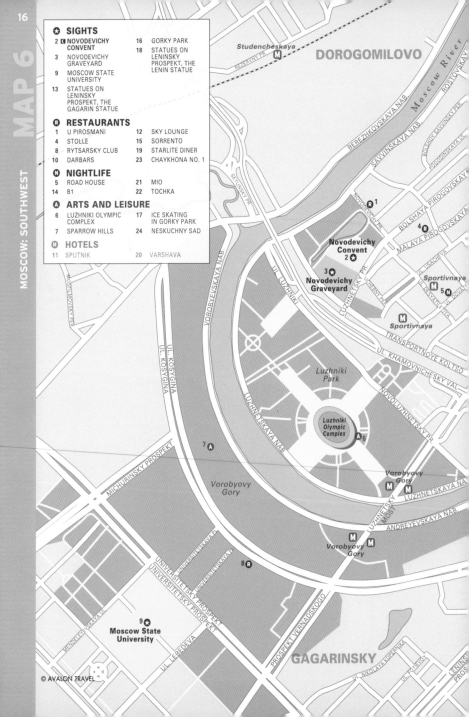

© AVALON TRAVEL

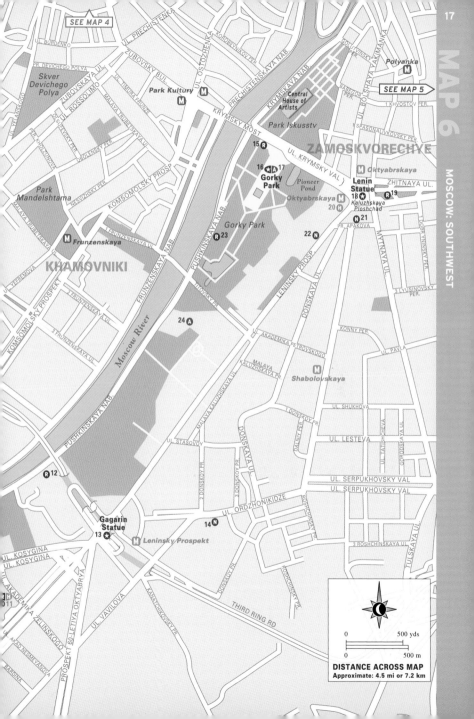

SEE MAP 4

UL. BURDENKO

PR. DEVICHEGO POLYA UL.

Skver
Devichego
Polya

ZUBOVSKY BUL.

UL. PRECHISTENKA

UL. OSTOZHENKA

KOROBEYNIKOV PER.

PRECHISTENSKAYA NAB.

KRYMSKAYA NAB.

GOLUTVINSKY PER.

BOLSHAYA YAKIMANKA

Polyanka

SEE MAP 5

ZUBOVSKY BUL.

UL. TIMURA FRUNZE

Park Kultury

KRYMSKY MOST

Central
House of
Artists

BABIGOR PER.

1 KHVOSTOV PER.

N SPASONALIVKOVSKY PER.

UL. ROSSOLIMO

Park
Mandelshtama

MALAYA TRUBETSKAYA UL.

KOMSOMOLSKY PROSP.

NESVIZHSKY PER.

Park Iskusstv

UL. KRYMSKY VAL

ZAMOSKVORECHYE

Oktyabrskaya

ZHITNAYA UL.

15

Gorky
Park

16 17

Pioneer
Pond

Lenin
Statue

18

Kaluzhskaya
Ploshchad

19

Frunzenskaya

I. FRUNZENSKAYA UL.

PUSHKINSKAYA NAB.

Oktyabrskaya

20

21

KHAMOVNIKI

FRUNZENSKAYA NAB.

Gorky Park

ILINSKY PER.

22

PR. APAKOVA

MYTNAYA UL.

3 TYUSINOVSKY PER.

3 FRUNZENSKAYA UL.

23

LENINSKY PROSP.

DONSKAYA UL.

KOMSOMOLSKY PROSPEKT

Moscow River

24

UL. AKADEMIKA PETROVSKOGO

KONNY PER.

UL. PAVLA

3 FRUNZENSKAYA UL.

MALAYA
KALUZHSKAYA PR.

Shabolovskaya

UL. STASOVOY

MALAYA KALUZHSKAYA PR.

DONSKAYA UL.

1 DONSKOY PR.

DALNIY PER.

UL. SHUKHOVA

UL. TATISHCHEVA

GORODSKAYA UL.

UL. LESTEVA

PUSHKINSKAYA NAB.

2 DONSKOY PR.

3 DONSKOY PR.

ROSHCHINSKY PR.

UL. SERPUKHOVSKY VAL

UL. SERPUKHOVSKY VAL

12

3 ROSHCHINSKAYA UL.

TULSKAYA UL.

Gagarin
Statue

13

14

UL. ORDZHONIKIDZE

Leninsky Prospekt

UL. KOSYGINA

UL. KOSYGINA

3 DONSKOY PR.

KAVATCHKOVSKY PER.

ROSHCHINSKY PR.

PROSPEKT 60-LETIYA OKTYABRYA

UL. VAVILOVA

THIRD RING RD

UL. AKADEMIKA ZELINSKOGO

UL. AKADEMIKA NESMEYANOVA

DISTANCE ACROSS MAP
Approximate: 4.5 mi or 7.2 km

0   500 yds

0   500 m

SEE MAP 2

SEE MAP 5

© AVALON TRAVEL

POLUYAROSLAVSKAYA NAB.
NIKOLOYAMSKAYA NAB.
KOSTOMAROVSKAYA NAB.
KOSTOMAROVSKY PER.
SRED. ZOLOTOROZHSKY PER.
VOLOCHAYEVSKAYA UL.

N 2

Andronnikov
Monastery
3

Ploshchad
Ilicha
M

PR. OZHELSKY

UL. PRYANIKOVA

UL. ZEMLYANOY VAL

R 1

NIKOLOYAMSKY PER.
BOL. DROVYANOY PER.
MAL. DROVYANOY PER.
PESTOVSKY PER.
SHELAPUTINSKY PER.

ANDRONYEVSKAYA NAB.

UL. SERGIYA RADONEZHSKOGO

Rimskaya M

Rimskaya
M

UL. SOLZHENITSYNA

SHKOLNAYA UL.

MAL. ANDRONYEVSKAYA UL.

RABOCHAYA UL.

BIBLIOTECHNAYA UL.

DOBROVOLCHESKAYA UL.

UL. SOLZHENITSYNA

TOVARISHCHESKY PER.
NIKOLOYAMSKY PER.
BOL. FAKELNY PER.
BOL. ROGOZHSKY PER.

ANDRONYEVSKAYA UL.
BOL. ANDRONYEVSKAYA UL.

MAL. ROGOZHSKY PER.

NOVOROGOZHSKAYA UL.

TRUDOVAYA UL.

Marksistskaya M

MARKSISTSKAYA UL.

TAGANSKAYA UL.

MARKSISTSKY PER.

NIZHEGORODSKAYA UL.

UL. ROGOZHSKY VAL

BOL. KALITNIKOVSKAYA UL.

KOVROY PER.

MARKSISTSKY PER.

MAL. KALITNIKOVSKAYA UL.

UL. TALALIKHINA

UL. BOL. KAMENSHCHIKI

PER. MAZAYKOVSKOGO

UL. GVOZDEVA

NOVOSELENSKY PER.

ABELMANOVSKAYA UL.

BROSHEVSKY PER.

MORLEVSKY PR.

SPARTAKOVSKY PROYEZOD

JERUSALIMSKAYA UL.

SIBIRSKY PR.

Novospassky
Monastery
4

LAVROV PER.

NOVOSPASSKAYA UL.

DINAMOVSKAYA UL.

Krestyanskaya
Zastava M

M

VOLGOGRADSKY PROSPEKT

KRUTITSKAYA UL.

KACHALINSKAYA UL.

R 5

KRUTITSKY PER.

Proletarskaya
M

SAJINSKY PER.

NOVOSPASSKY PROYEZD

KRUTITSKY PROYEZD

DUBROVSKAYA UL.

SOSINSKAYA UL.

Krutitskoye
6 Podvorye

DISTANCE ACROSS MAP
Approximate: 2.4 mi or 3.8 km

0   300 yds

0   300 m

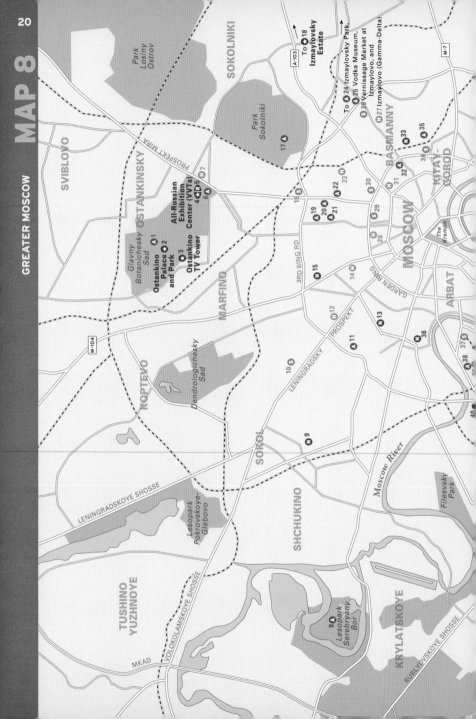

Park
Losiny
Ostrov

SVIBLOVO

SOKOLNIKI

To 18
Izmaylovsky Park,
Izmaylovsky
Estate

A-103

To 24 Izmaylovsky Park,
25 Vodka Museum,
26 Vernissage Market at
Izmaylovo, and
27 Izmaylovo (Gamma-Delta)

M-7

Park
Sokolniki

BASMANNY

35

33

34

31 32

MOSCOW

KITAY-
GOROD

OSTANKINSKY

PROSPEKT MIRA

All-Russian
Exhibition
Center (VVTs)

7

6 5
4

23

22

30

The
Kremlin

Glavny
Botanichesky
Sad

Ostankino
Palace 2
and Park

Ostankino
TV Tower

1

3

16

19

20

21

29

28

ARBAT

MARFINO

3RD RING RD

GARDEN RING

15

M-104

KOPTEVO

Dendrologichesky
Sad

12

PROSPEKT

14

13

36

38
37

11

LENINGRADSKY

10

SOKOL

9

Moscow River

Filevsky
Park

LENINGRADSKOYE SHOSSE

TUSHINO
YUZHNOYE

Lesopark
Pokrovskoye-
Glebovo

SHCHUKINO

8

Lesopark
Serebryany
Bor

KRYLATSKOYE

MKAD

VOLOKOLAMSKOYE SHOSSE

RUBLYOVSKOYE SHOSSE

MAP 8

GREATER MOSCOW

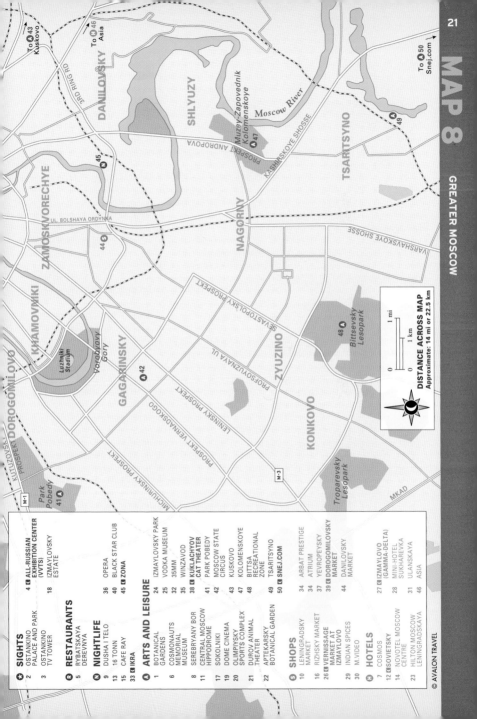

DISTANCE ACROSS MAP
Approximate: 14 mi or 22.5 km

0   1 mi
0   1 km

SIGHTS
- 2   OSTANKINO PALACE AND PARK
- 3   OSTANKINO TV TOWER
- 4   ALL-RUSSIAN EXHIBITION CENTER (VVTS)
- 18   IZMAYLOVSKY ESTATE

RESTAURANTS
- 5   RYBATSKAYA DEREVNYA

NIGHTLIFE
- 9   DUSHA I TELO
- 13   16 TONN
- 15   CAFE RAY
- 33   IKRA
- 36   OPERA
- 40   BLACK STAR CLUB
- 45   ZONA

ARTS AND LEISURE
- 1   BOTANICAL GARDENS
- 6   COSMONAUTS MEMORIAL MUSEUM
- 8   SEREBRYANY BOR
- 11   CENTRAL MOSCOW HIPPODROME
- 17   SOKOLNIKI
- 19   DOME CINEMA
- 20   OLIMPIYSKY SPORTS COMPLEX
- 21   DUROV ANIMAL THEATER
- 22   APTEKARSKY BOTANICAL GARDEN
- 24   IZMAYLOVSKY PARK
- 25   VODKA MUSEUM
- 32   35MM
- 35   WINZAVOD
- 39   KUKLACHYOV CAT THEATER
- 41   PARK POBEDY
- 42   MOSCOW STATE CIRCUS
- 43   KUSKOVO
- 47   KOLOMENSKOYE
- 48   BITTSA RECREATIONAL ZONE
- 49   TSARITSYNO
- 50   SNEJ.COM

SHOPS
- 10   LENINGRADSKY MARKET
- 16   RIZHSKY MARKET
- 26   VERNISSAGE MARKET AT IZMAYLOVO
- 29   INDIAN SPICES
- 30   M.VIDEO
- 34   ARBAT PRESTIGE
- 34   ATRIUM
- 37   YEVROPEYSKY
- 39   DOROGOMILOVSKY MARKET
- 44   DANILOVSKY MARKET

HOTELS
- 7   COSMOS
- 12   SOVIETSKY
- 14   NOVOTEL MOSCOW CENTRE
- 23   HILTON MOSCOW LENINGRADSKAYA
- 27   IZMAYLOVO (GAMMA-DELTA)
- 28   MINI-HOTEL SUKHAREVKA
- 31   ULANSKAYA
- 46   ASIA

© AVALON TRAVEL

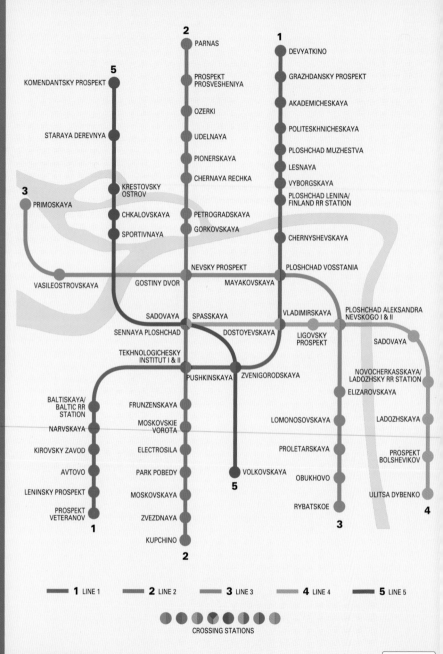

KOMENDANTSKY PROSPEKT 5

PARNAS 2

DEVYATKINO 1

PROSPEKT PROSVESHENIYA

GRAZHDANSKY PROSPEKT

OZERKI

AKADEMICHESKAYA

STARAYA DEREVNYA

UDELNAYA

POLITESKHNICHESKAYA

PIONERSKAYA

PLOSHCHAD MUZHESTVA

CHERNAYA RECHKA

LESNAYA

3
PRIMOSKAYA

KRESTOVSKY OSTROV

VYBORGSKAYA

PLOSHCHAD LENINA/ FINLAND RR STATION

CHKALOVSKAYA

PETROGRADSKAYA

SPORTIVNAYA

GORKOVSKAYA

CHERNYSHEVSKAYA

NEVSKY PROSPEKT

PLOSHCHAD VOSSTANIA

VASILEOSTROVSKAYA

GOSTINY DVOR

MAYAKOVSKAYA

SADOVAYA

SPASSKAYA

VLADIMIRSKAYA

PLOSHCHAD ALEKSANDRA NEVSKOGO I & II

SENNAYA PLOSHCHAD

DOSTOYEVSKAYA

SADOVAYA

LIGOVSKY PROSPEKT

TEKHNOLOGICHESKY INSTITUT I & II

NOVOCHERKASSKAYA/ LADOZHSKY RR STATION

PUSHKINSKAYA

ZVENIGORODSKAYA

ELIZAROVSKAYA

BALTISKAYA/ BALTIC RR STATION

FRUNZENSKAYA

LOMONOSOVSKAYA

LADOZHSKAYA

NARVSKAYA

MOSKOVSKIE VOROTA

KIROVSKY ZAVOD

ELECTROSILA

PROLETARSKAYA

PROSPEKT BOLSHEVIKOV

AVTOVO

PARK POBEDY

VOLKOVSKAYA
5

LENINSKY PROSPEKT

MOSKOVSKAYA

OBUKHOVO

ULITSA DYBENKO

PROSPEKT VETERANOV
1

ZVEZDNAYA

RYBATSKOE
3

4

KUPCHINO
2

1 LINE 1   **2** LINE 2   **3** LINE 3   **4** LINE 4   **5** LINE 5

CROSSING STATIONS

NOT TO SCALE

St. Petersburg Maps

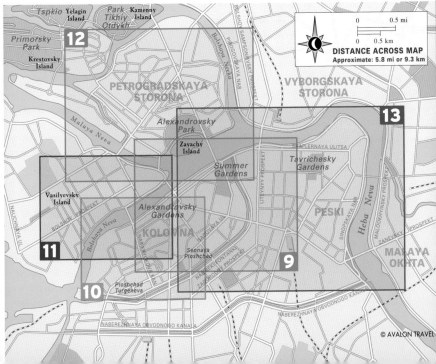

© AVALON TRAVEL

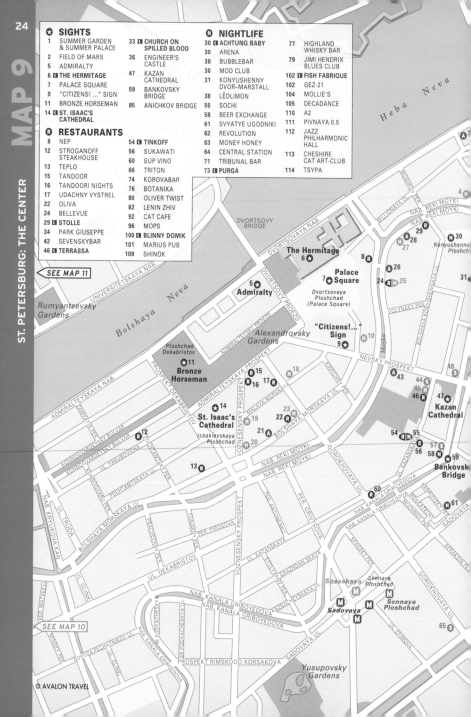

SIGHTS

1	SUMMER GARDEN & SUMMER PALACE	33	CHURCH ON SPILLED BLOOD
2	FIELD OF MARS	36	ENGINEER'S CASTLE
5	ADMIRALTY	47	KAZAN CATHEDRAL
6	THE HERMITAGE	59	BANKOVSKY BRIDGE
7	PALACE SQUARE	85	ANICHKOV BRIDGE
9	"CITIZENS! ..." SIGN		
11	BRONZE HORSEMAN		
14	ST. ISAAC'S CATHEDRAL		

RESTAURANTS

8	NEP	54	TINKOFF
12	STROGANOFF STEAKHOUSE	56	SUKAWATI
13	TEPLO	60	SUP VINO
15	TANDOOR	66	TRITON
17	TANDOORI NIGHTS	74	KOROVABAR
17	UDACHNY VYSTREL	76	BOTANIKA
22	OLIVA	80	OLIVER TWIST
24	BELLEVUE	82	LENIN ZHIV
29	STOLLE	92	CAT CAFE
34	PARK GIUSEPPE	96	MOPS
42	SEVENSKYBAR	100	BLINNY DOMIK
46	TERRASSA	101	MARIUS PUB
		109	SHINOK

NIGHTLIFE

30	ACHTUNG BABY	77	HIGHLAND WHISKY BAR
30	ARENA	79	JIMI HENDRIX BLUES CLUB
30	BUBBLEBAR	102	FISH FABRIQUE
30	MOD CLUB	102	GEZ-21
31	KONYUSHENNY DVOR–MARSTALL	104	MOLLIE'S
38	LĒDLIMON	105	DECADANCE
55	SOCHI	110	A2
58	BEER EXCHANGE	111	PIVNAYA 0.5
61	SVYATYE UGODNIKI	112	JAZZ PHILHARMONIC HALL
62	REVOLUTION	113	CHESHIRE CAT ART-CLUB
63	MONEY HONEY	114	TSYPA
64	CENTRAL STATION		
71	TRIBUNAL BAR		
73	PURGA		

SEE MAP 11

SEE MAP 10

© AVALON TRAVEL

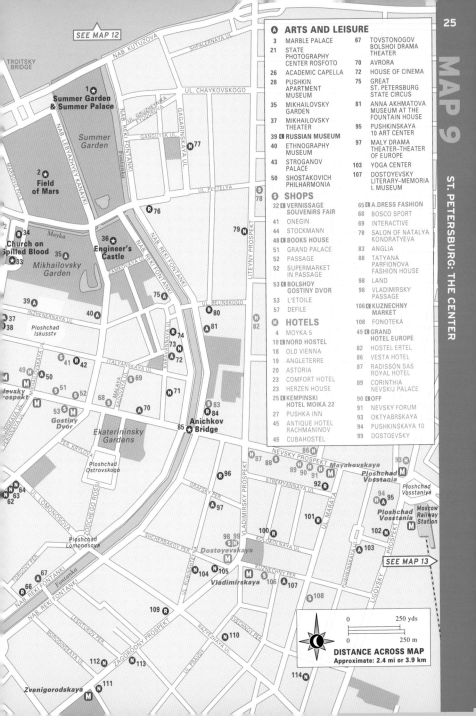

SEE MAP 12

TROITSKY BRIDGE

Summer Garden & Summer Palace

Summer Garden

Field of Mars

Church on Spilled Blood

Engineer's Castle

Mikhailovsky Garden

Ploshchad Iskusstv

Nevsky Prospekt

Gostiny Dvor

Ekaterininsky Gardens

Ploshchad Ostrovskogo

Anichkov Bridge

Ploshchad Lomonosova

Vladimirskaya

Dostoyevskaya

Nevsky Prospekt

Mayakovskaya

Ploshchad Vosstania

Ploshchad Vosstaniya

Ploshchad Vosstania

Moscow Railway Station

SEE MAP 13

Zvenigorodskaya

A ARTS AND LEISURE

3	MARBLE PALACE
21	STATE PHOTOGRAPHY CENTER ROSFOTO
26	ACADEMIC CAPELLA
28	PUSHKIN APARTMENT MUSEUM
35	MIKHAILOVSKY GARDEN
37	MIKHAILOVSKY THEATER
39	RUSSIAN MUSEUM
40	ETHNOGRAPHY MUSEUM
43	STROGANOV PALACE
50	SHOSTAKOVICH PHILHARMONIA
67	TOVSTONOGOV BOLSHOI DRAMA THEATER
70	AVRORA
72	HOUSE OF CINEMA
75	GREAT ST. PETERSBURG STATE CIRCUS
81	ANNA AKHMATOVA MUSEUM AT THE FOUNTAIN HOUSE
95	PUSHKINSKAYA 10 ART CENTER
97	MALY DRAMA THEATER-THEATER OF EUROPE
103	YOGA CENTER
107	DOSTOYEVSKY LITERARY-MEMORIAL MUSEUM

S SHOPS

32	VERNISSAGE SOUVENIRS FAIR
41	ONEGIN
44	STOCKMANN
48	BOOKS HOUSE
51	GRAND PALACE
52	PASSAGE
52	SUPERMARKET IN PASSAGE
53	BOLSHOY GOSTINIY DVOR
53	L'ETOILE
57	DEFILE
65	A.DRESS FASHION
68	BOSCO SPORT
69	INTERACTIVE
78	SALON OF NATALYA KONDRATYEVA
83	ANGLIA
88	TATYANA PARFIONOVA FASHION HOUSE
98	LAND
98	VLADIMIRSKY PASSAGE
106	KUZNECHNY MARKET
108	FONOTEKA

H HOTELS

4	MOYKA 5
10	NORD HOSTEL
18	OLD VIENNA
19	ANGLETERRE
20	ASTORIA
23	COMFORT HOTEL
23	HERZEN HOUSE
25	KEMPINSKI HOTEL MOIKA 22
27	PUSHKA INN
45	ANTIQUE HOTEL RACHMANINOV
45	CUBAHOSTEL
49	GRAND HOTEL EUROPE
82	HOSTEL ERTEL
86	VESTA HOTEL
87	RADISSON SAS ROYAL HOTEL
89	CORINTHIA NEVSKIJ PALACE
90	OFF
91	NEVSKY FORUM
93	OKTYABRSKAYA
94	PUSHKINSKAYA 10
99	DOSTOEVSKY

0   250 yds
0   250 m

DISTANCE ACROSS MAP
Approximate: 2.4 mi or 3.9 km

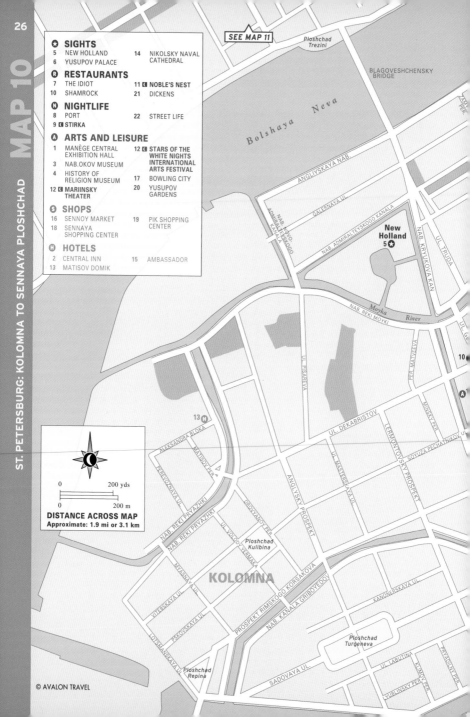

✪ SIGHTS
5 NEW HOLLAND
6 YUSUPOV PALACE

14 NIKOLSKY NAVAL CATHEDRAL

⑧ RESTAURANTS
7 THE IDIOT
10 SHAMROCK

11 Ⓒ NOBLE'S NEST
21 DICKENS

Ⓝ NIGHTLIFE
8 PORT
9 Ⓒ STIRKA

22 STREET LIFE

Ⓐ ARTS AND LEISURE
1 MANÈGE CENTRAL EXHIBITION HALL
3 NAB.OKOV MUSEUM
4 HISTORY OF RELIGION MUSEUM
12 Ⓒ MARIINSKY THEATER

12 Ⓒ STARS OF THE WHITE NIGHTS INTERNATIONAL ARTS FESTIVAL
17 BOWLING CITY
20 YUSUPOV GARDENS

Ⓢ SHOPS
16 SENNOY MARKET
18 SENNAYA SHOPPING CENTER

19 PIK SHOPPING CENTER

Ⓗ HOTELS
2 CENTRAL INN
13 MATISOV DOMIK

15 AMBASSADOR

SEE MAP 11

Ploshchad Trezini

BLAGOVESHCHENSKY BRIDGE

Bolshaya Neva

ANGLIYSKAYA NAB.

GALERNAYA UL.

NAB. ADMIRALTEYSKOGO KANALA

NAB. NOVO-ADMIRALTEYSKOGO KANALA

New Holland
5 ✪

NAB. KRYUKOVA KAN.

UL. TRUDA

NAB. REKI MOYKI

Moyka River

UL. GE

10

Ⓐ

UL. PISAREVA

UL. DEKABRISTOV

LERMONTOVSKY PROSPEKT

MINSKY PER.

SOYUZA PECHATNIKOV UL.

13 Ⓗ

ALEKSANDRA BLOKA

MATISOV PER.

BEREZOVAYA UL.

ANGLIYSKY PROSPEKT

DROVYANOY PER.

UL. MASTERSKAYA

NAB. REKI PRYAZHKI

NAB. REKI PRYAZHKI

UL. VOLGO. TERMAKA

MYASNAYA UL.

Ploshchad Kulibina

KOLOMNA

VITEBSKAYA UL.

PSKOVSKAYA UL.

LOTSMANSKAYA UL.

PROSPEKT RIMSKOGO KORSAKOVA

NAB. KANALA GRIBOYEDOV

KANONERSKAYA UL.

Ploshchad Turgeneva

UL. LABUTINA

PRYAZHINY PER.

KLIMOV PER.

Ploshchad Repina

SADOVAYA UL.

YUBLINSKY PER.

0   200 yds
0   200 m

DISTANCE ACROSS MAP
Approximate: 1.9 mi or 3.1 km

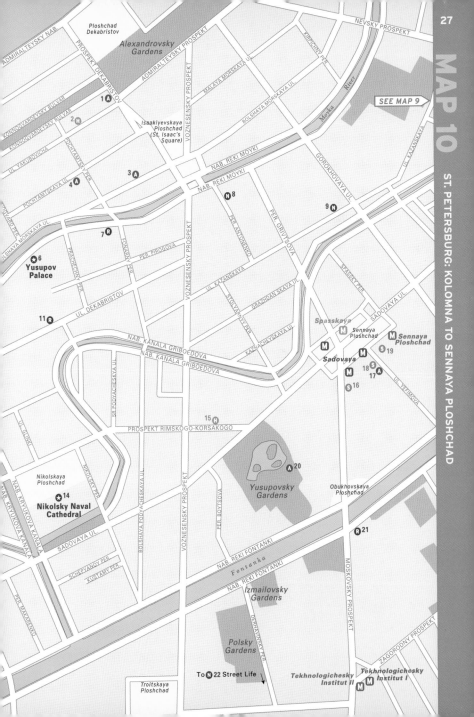

NEVSKY PROSPEKT

Ploshchad
Dekabristov

Alexandrovsky
Gardens

ADMIRALTEYSKY NAB.

ADMIRALTEYSKY PROSPEKT

PROSPEKT DEKABRISTOV

KIRPICHNY PER.

Moyka River

SEE MAP 9

1 A

VOZNESENSKY PROSPEKT

MALAYA MORSKAYA UL.

BOLSHAYA MORSKAYA UL.

UL. KAZANSKAYA

2 N

Isaakievskaya
Ploshchad
(St. Isaac's
Square)

KONNOGVARDEYSKY BULVAR

NAB. REKI MOYKI

GOROKHOVAYA UL.

UL. YAKUBOVICHA

KONNOGVARDEYSKY BULVAR

POCHTAMTSKY PER.

3 A

NAB. REKI MOYKI

4 A

POCHTAMTSKAYA UL.

8 N

9 N

BOLSHAYA MORSKAYA UL.

7 R

PER. ANTONENKO

PER. PIROGOVA

PER. GRIVTSOVA

★6
Yusupov
Palace

PRACHECHNY

FONTANNY

UL. KAZANSKAYA

SPASSKY PER.

UL. DEKABRISTOV

STOLYARNY PER.

GRAZHDANSKAYA UL.

KAZNACHEYSKAYA UL.

SADOVAYA UL.

11 R

NAB. KANALA GRIBOEDOVA

Spasskaya
M
Sennaya
Ploshchad

M Sennaya
Ploshchad

NAB. KANALA GRIBOEDOVA

M
Sadovaya

S 19

SR. PODYACHESKAYA UL.

M 18
S 16

17 A

UL. YEFIMOVA

15 N

PROSPEKT RIMSKOGO-KORSAKOGO

UL. GLINKI

BOLSHAYA PODYACHESKAYA UL.

VOZNESENSKY PROSPEKT

A 20

Nikolskaya
Ploshchad

NIKOLSKY PER.

Yusupovsky
Gardens

Obukhovskaya
Ploshchad

★14
Nikolsky Naval
Cathedral

PER. BOYTSOVA

R 21

NAB. KRYUKOVA KANALA

SADOVAYA UL.

MOSKOVSKY PROSPEKT

SCHEPYANOY PER.

NAB. REKI FONTANKI

KUSTANY PER.

Fontanka

NAB. REKI FONTANKI

PER. MAKARENKO

Izmailovsky
Gardens

DERZHAVINSKY PER.

ZAGORODNY PROSPEKT

Polsky
Gardens

Tekhnologichesky
Institut I

To N 22 Street Life

Tekhnologichesky
Institut II

M M

Troitskaya
Ploshchad

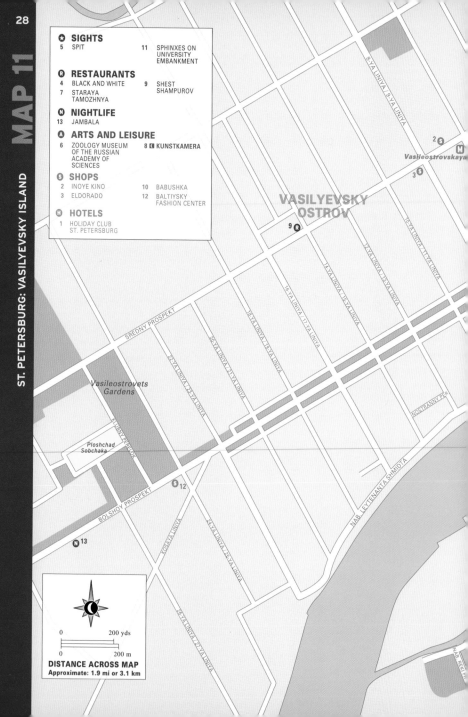

SIGHTS
5   SPIT
11 SPHINXES ON UNIVERSITY EMBANKMENT

RESTAURANTS
4   BLACK AND WHITE
7   STARAYA TAMOZHNYA
9   SHEST SHAMPUROV

NIGHTLIFE
13 JAMBALA

ARTS AND LEISURE
6   ZOOLOGY MUSEUM OF THE RUSSIAN ACADEMY OF SCIENCES
8   KUNSTKAMERA

SHOPS
2   INOYE KINO
3   ELDORADO
10 BABUSHKA
12 BALTIYSKY FASHION CENTER

HOTELS
1   HOLIDAY CLUB ST. PETERSBURG

Vasileostrovskaya

VASILYEVSKY OSTROV

SREDNY PROSPEKT

Vasileostrovets Gardens

Ploshchad Sobchaka

BOLSHOY PROSPEKT

DISTANCE ACROSS MAP
Approximate: 1.9 mi or 3.1 km

0   200 yds
0   200 m

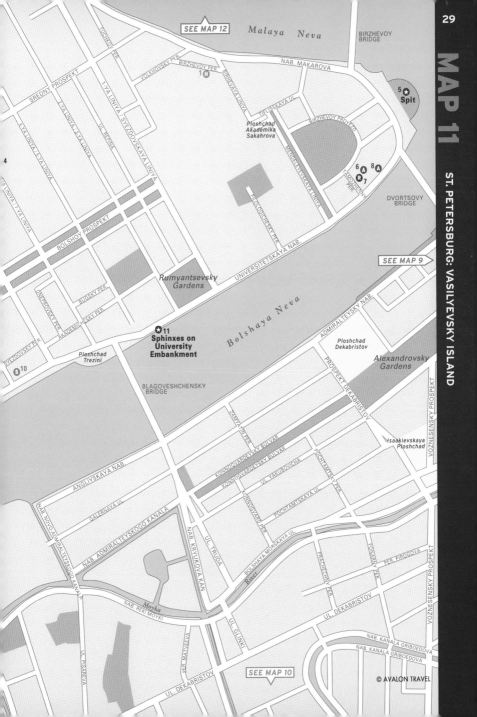

SEE MAP 12

Malaya   Neva

BIRZHEVOY
BRIDGE

NAB. MAKAROVA

5 ✪ Spit

SREDNY PROSPEKT

Ploshchad
Akademika
Sakahrova

6 Ⓐ 8 Ⓐ
Ⓡ 7

DVORTSOVY
BRIDGE

BOLSHOY PROSPEKT

SEE MAP 9

*Rumyantsevsky
Gardens*

UNIVERSITETSKAYA NAB.

Bolshaya   Neva

Ploshchad
Dekabristov

*Alexandrovsky
Gardens*

✪11
Sphinxes on
University
Embankment

Ploshchad
Trezini

Ⓢ10

BLAGOVESHCHENSKY
BRIDGE

*Isaakievskaya
Ploshchad*

ANGLIYSKAYA NAB.

GALERNAYA UL.

PROSPEKT DEKABRISTOV

VOZNESENSKY PROSPEKT

VOZNESENSKY PROSPEKT

NAB. NOVO ADMIRALTEYSKOGO KANALA

NAB. ADMIRALTEYSKOGO KANALA

UL. TRUDA

UL. KRYUKOVA KAN

BOLSHAYA MORSKAYA UL.

PER. PIROGOVA

PONARIY PER.

Moyka
River

NAB. REKI MOYKI

UL. GLINKI

UL. DEKABRISTOV

NAB. KANALA GRIBOEDOVA

NAB. KANALA GRIBOEDOVA

UL. PISAREVA

PER. MATVEEVA

UL. DEKABRISTOV

SEE MAP 10

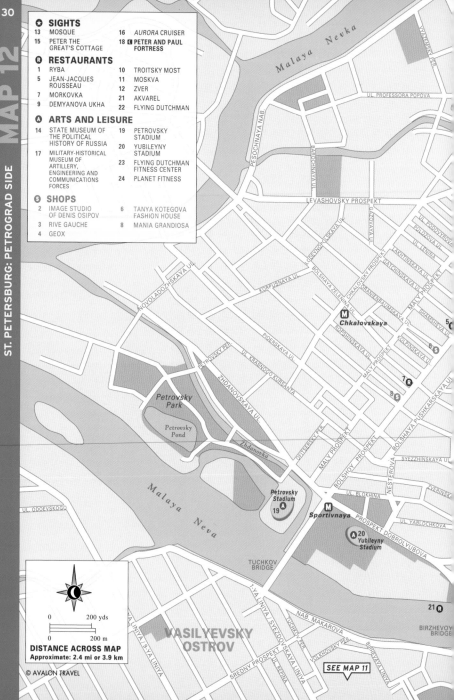

DISTANCE ACROSS MAP
Approximate: 2.4 mi or 3.9 km

© AVALON TRAVEL

SEE MAP 11

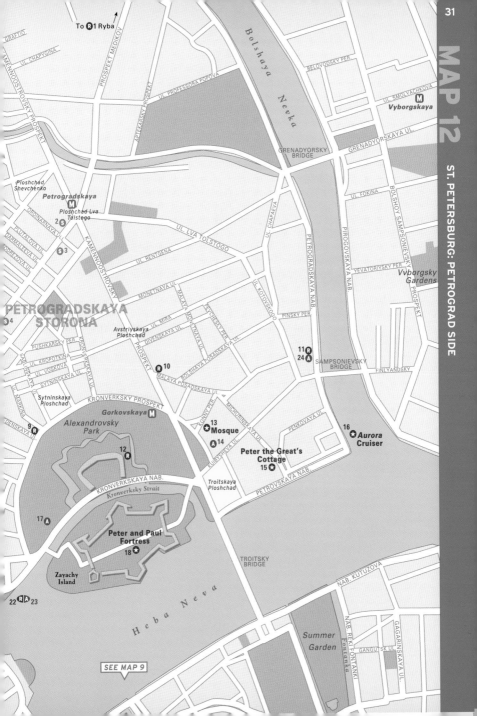

To 1 Ryba

GRAFFIC

UL. CHAPYGINA

PROSPEKT MEDIKOV

APTEKARSKY PROSPEKT

UL. PROFESSORA POPOVA

Bolshaya Nevka

BELOVODSKY PER.

UL. SMOLYACHKOVA

Vyborgskaya

GRENADYORSKY BRIDGE

GRENADYORSKAYA UL.

KAMENNOOSTROVSKY PROSPEKT

Ploshchad Shevchenko

Petrogradskaya

Ploshchad Lva Tolstogo

2

3

UL. LVA TOLSTOGO

UL. CHAPAEVA

UL. FOKINA

BOLSHOY SAMPSONIEVSKY PROSPEKT

PIROGOVSKAYA NAB.

YEVATORIVSKY PER.

Vyborgsky Gardens

ORDYNARNAYA UL.

PLUTALOVA UL.

ODREZKAYA

UL. BLENTGENA

KAMENNOOSTROVSKY

MONETNAYA UL.

UL. MIRA

MALAYA

PETCHESKY PER.

UL. KOTOVSKOGO

PINSKY PER.

PETROGRADSKAYA NAB.

PETROGRADSKAYA STORONA

4

Avstriyskaya Ploshchad

DIVENSKAYA UL.

BOLSHAYA POSADSKAYA UL.

11

24

SAMPSONIEVSKY BRIDGE

FINLYANDSKY

PUSHKARSKY PER.

UL. KROPOTKINA

UL. VOSKOVA

SYTNINSKAYA UL.

PROSPEKT

10

MALAYA POSADSKAYA UL.

GONNY PER.

MICHURINSKAYA UL.

PENKOVAYA UL.

MARKINA

Sytninskaya Ploshchad

KRONVERKSKY PROSPEKT

DENSKAYA UL.

9

Alexandrovsky Park

Gorkovskaya

13

Mosque

14

16

Aurora Cruiser

12

KUYBSHEVA UL.

Peter the Great's Cottage

15

17

KRONVERKSKAYA NAB.

Kronverksky Strait

Troitskaya Ploshchad

PETROVSKAYA NAB.

NAB. KUTUZOVA

Peter and Paul Fortress

18

TROITSKY BRIDGE

Zayachy Island

22 23

Heba Neva

Summer Garden

NAB. REKI FONTANKI

GANGUTSK UL.

GAGARINSKAYA UL.

SEE MAP 9

MAP 13

ST. PETERSBURG: SMOLNY AND OLD NEVSKY

Gorkovskaya

Alexandrovsky Park

SEE MAP 12

PENKOVAYA UL.

Finland Railway Station

Ploshchad Lenina

UL. KOMSOMOLA

Ploshchad Lenina

Troitskaya Ploshchad

PETROGRADSKAYA NAB.

ARSENALYNAYA NAB.

LITEYNY BRIDGE

Zayachy Island

TROITSKY BRIDGE

Neva

Heba Neva

NAB. KUTUZOVA

NAB. ROBESPYERA

SHPALERNAYA UL.

1

ZAKHARYEVSKAYA UL.

UL. CHAYKOVSKOGO

UL. CHAYKOVSKOGO

FURSHTATSKAYA UL.

Chernyshevskaya

Summer Garden

Fontanka

GAGARINSKAYA UL.

NAB. REKI FONTANKI

UL. PESTELYA

KIROCHNAYA UL.

2

MANEZHNY PER.

UL. RYLEEVA

LITEYNY PROSPEKT

NAB. REKI MOYKI

NAB. REKI MOYKI

Konyushennaya Ploshchad

Moyka

Mikhaylovsky Gardens

SAPYORNY PER.

BASKOV PER.

3

UL. NEKRASOVA

UL. KOROLENKO

KOVENSKY PER.

Dvortsovaya Ploshchad

SEE MAP 9

BOLSHAYA KONYUSHENNAYA UL.

INZHENERNAYA UL.

Ploshchad Iskusstv

UL. BELINSKOGO

UL. ZHUKOVSKOGO

SEE MAP 10

Nevsky Prospekt

ITALYANSKAYA UL.

10 11

Gostiny Dvor

Ekaterininsky Gardens

NEVSKY PROSPEKT

VLADIMIRSKY PROSPEKT

STREMYANNAYA UL.

Ploshchad Vosstania

GOROKHOVAYA UL.

PER. GRIVTSOVA

UL. KAZANSKAYA

NAB. KANALA GRIBOEDOVA

NAB. KANALA GRIBOEDOVA

PER. KRYLOVA

Ploshchad Ostrovskogo

ROSSI

Fontanka

GRAFSKY PER.

Mayakovskaya

Ploshchad Vosstar

SADOVAYA UL.

UL. LOMONOSOVA

ZODCHEGO

Ploshchad Lomonosova

KOLOKOLNAYA UL.

Ploshchad Vosstania

LIGOVSKY PER

Moscow Railway Station

Dostoevskaya

KUZNECHNY PER.

APRAKSIN PER.

TORGOVY PER.

Seonaya Ploshchad

23

Vladimirskaya

Spasskaya

Sadovaya

Sennaya Ploshchad

UL. EFIMOVA

NAB. REKI FONTANKI

GOROKHOVAYA UL.

BORODINSKAYA UL.

LESHUKOV PER.

ZAGORODNY PROSPEKT

RAZEZZHAYA UL.

SVECHNO

UL. PRAVDY

DOSTOEVSKOGO

MESCHANSKAYA UL.

KOLOMENSKAYA UL.

LIGOVSKY PROSPEKT

S 17

Yusupovsky Gardens

Obukhovskaya Ploshchad

Fontanka

VVEDENSKOGO KANALA

Zvenigorodskaya

SOTSIALS

Pushkinskaya

Pionerskaya Ploshchad

MARATA

BORODAY UL.

KONSTANTINA ZASLONOVA

TRANSPORTNY PER.

Ligovsky Prospekt

S 21

20

S 22

ROMENSKAYA UL.

© AVALON TRAVEL

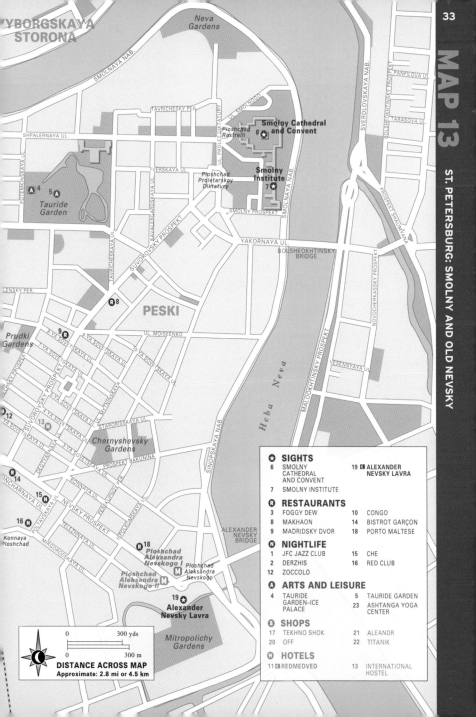

YBORGSKAYA STORONA

Neva Gardens

SMOLNAYA NAB.

TAVRICHESKY PER.

UL. SMOLNOGO

Ploschad Rastrelli

Smolny Cathedral and Convent
6

SHPALERNAYA UL.

TVERSKAYA UL.

Smolny Institute
7

Ploshchad Proletarskoy Diktatury

POTEMKINSKAYA UL.

Tauride Garden
4 5

SVERDLOVSKAYA NAB.

PANFILOVA UL.

TARASOVA UL.

BOLSHEOKHTINSKY PROSPEKT

PROSPEKT SHAUMANA

SMOLNY PROSPEKT

YAKORNAYA UL.

BOLSHEOKHTINSKY BRIDGE

KAVALERGARDSKAYA UL.

SUVOROVSKY PROSPEKT

TAVRICHESKAYA UL.

LENSKY PER.

8

PESKI

NOVOCHERKASSKY PROSPEKT

MALOOKHTINSKY PROSPEKT

VESENNYAYA UL.

Prudki Gardens
9

UL. MOISEENKO

2-YA SOVETSKAYA UL.

3-YA SOVETSKAYA UL.

Heba Neva

12 13

STARORISSKAYA UL.

Chernyshevsky Gardens

PROSPEKT BAKUNINA

SINOPSKAYA NAB.

14

15

KONNAYA UL.

NEVSKY PROSPEKT

TELEZHNAYA UL.

16

Konnaya Ploshchad

MIRGORODSKAYA UL.

POLTAVSKAYA UL.

GONCHARNAYA UL.

Alexander Nevsky Bridge

18

Ploshchad Aleksandra Nevskogo I

Ploshchad Aleksandra Nevskogo II

Ploshchad Aleksandra Nevskogo

M

19 **Alexander Nevsky Lavra**

Mitropolichy Gardens

0   300 yds
0   300 m

DISTANCE ACROSS MAP
Approximate: 2.8 mi or 4.5 km

✪ SIGHTS
6   SMOLNY CATHEDRAL AND CONVENT
7   SMOLNY INSTITUTE
19 ◪ ALEXANDER NEVSKY LAVRA

ⓡ RESTAURANTS
3   FOGGY DEW
8   MAKHAON
9   MADRIDSKY DVOR
10 CONGO
14 BISTROT GARÇON
18 PORTO MALTESE

ⓝ NIGHTLIFE
1   JFC JAZZ CLUB
2   DERZHIS
12 ZOCCOLO
15 CHE
16 RED CLUB

ⓐ ARTS AND LEISURE
4   TAURIDE GARDEN–ICE PALACE
5   TAURIDE GARDEN
23 ASHTANGA YOGA CENTER

ⓢ SHOPS
17 TEKHNO SHOK
20 OFF
21 ALEANDR
22 TITANIK

ⓗ HOTELS
11 ◪ REDMEDVED
13 INTERNATIONAL HOSTEL

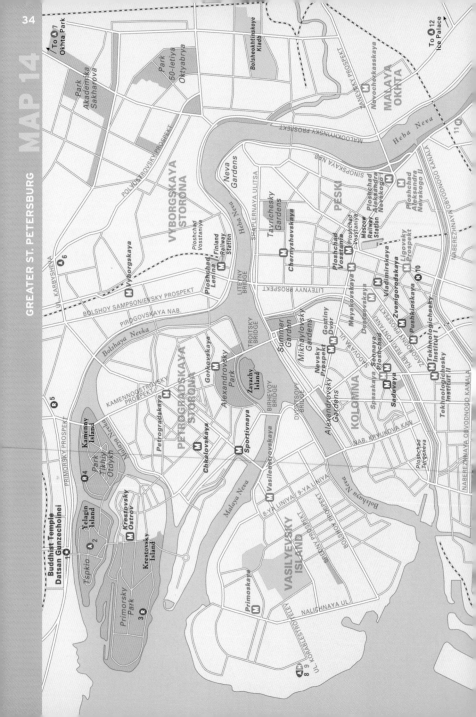

MAP 14 GREATER ST. PETERSBURG

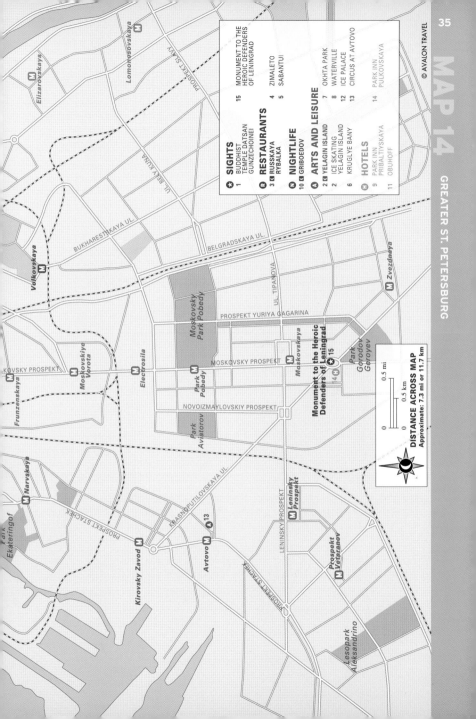

SIGHTS
1 BUDDHIST TEMPLE DATSAN GUNZECHOINEI
15 MONUMENT TO THE HEROIC DEFENDERS OF LENINGRAD

RESTAURANTS
3 RUSSKAYA RYBALKA
4 ZIMALETO
5 SABANTUI

NIGHTLIFE
10 GRIBOEDOV

ARTS AND LEISURE
2 YELAGIN ISLAND
8 ICE SKATING YELAGIN ISLAND
6 KRUGLYE BANY
7 OKHTA PARK
8 WATERVILLE
12 ICE PALACE
13 CIRCUS AT AVTOVO

HOTELS
9 PARK INN PRIBALTIYSKAYA
11 OBUHOFF
14 PARK INN PULKOVSKAYA

© AVALON TRAVEL

DISTANCE ACROSS MAP
Approximate: 7.3 mi or 11.7 km

0   0.5 mi
0   0.5 km

Discover Moscow & St. Petersburg

Russia. No other country is quite so provocative, so evocative – and so misunderstood. Closed to the Western world for some 70 years, it has retained its air of mystery even two decades after the collapse of the Soviet Union and the lifting of the Iron Curtain. Russia still entices, with its onion domes, lithe ballerinas, gilded palaces, and socialist relics.

Now, having emerged from their Soviet past, the two major cities – Moscow and St. Petersburg – offer travelers modern comfort and convenience, making their history and grandeur much more accessible.

In dazzlingly decadent Moscow – second only to New York in the number of billionaires calling it home – the "big village" side of the city still exists, with quaint side streets, romantic parks, and colorful markets. Of course, the city also has world-class attractions, such as St. Basil's Cathedral, Lenin's mausoleum, and the Bolshoi Theater.

With a population of more than 10 million people, Moscow is a true 24-hour city. Don't be surprised if you find yourself in a midnight traffic jam or discover you're not alone at the tanning salon at 3 A.M. While Western Europe sleeps, Muscovites are out walking their dogs, buying cell phones, and eating sushi.

And then there's St. Petersburg – arguably the most beautiful

city in the world. Home to artists and intellectuals, poets and musicians, St. Petersburg offers completely different values and culture, all set against a backdrop of tsarist splendor. Ornate baroque palaces, grand statues, royal gardens turned public parks, and long, straight avenues . . . in contrast to Moscow's chaotic evolution, Petersburg's meticulous design demonstrates its imperial origins down to the most minute detail.

In recent years the pace of change in these two cities has picked up tremendously. Dining and nightlife scenes have overtaken many Western cities' offerings, and physically the cities are transformed beyond belief. Moscow enjoys a building boom as St. Petersburg's once crumbling facades and rundown roads are being rejuvenated.

Russia is vast and varied, but a visit to just these two cities offers a chance to see two hugely different aspects of this amazing country. It is an experience that you will never forget.

Planning Your Trip

► WHERE TO GO

Moscow

THE KREMLIN AND RED SQUARE

The very heart of the city, the Kremlin is the fortified complex from which the city originated; it boasts numerous architectural and historical landmarks that serve as museums, as well as the president's official residence. Right beside it, outside the walls, is Red Square, where a number of the city's premier sights are clustered: St. Basil's Cathedral, Lenin's mausoleum, State History Museum, and GUM (Main Department Store).

KITAY-GOROD, LUBYANKA, AND CHISTYE PRUDY

Kitay-Gorod is one of the oldest neighborhoods, dating back to the 11th century. It has an abundance of onion-domed churches and hilly, narrow streets with plenty of stores, bars, and eateries. Kitay-Gorod flows into Lubyanka—famous for the former KGB headquarters and now secret services

territory—and Chistye Prudy, one of the loveliest parts of Moscow, with a graceful boulevard encircling a pretty pond. This is quite a bohemian neighborhood, with hip cafés, bars, and stores.

THE CENTER AND INNER NORTHWEST

Moscow's main road, Tverskaya Ulitsa, is a busy artery with lots of pedestrian and vehicular traffic. There are countless stores and coffee shops, side streets lined with restaurants, and monuments to the great and glorious. Hidden nearby is the quiet oasis of Patriarch's Ponds, where readers of *The Master and Margarita* can pay tribute to author Mikhail Bulgakov.

ARBAT AND KROPOTKINSKAYA

Old Arbat is a pedestrian street lined with souvenir stores, cafés, restaurants, and bars in beautiful old houses—the most touristy part of Moscow outside Red Square. A few

a view of the Kremlin from across the Moscow River

This summer café at the back of Gorky Park is a popular alfresco beer and barbecue spot.

blocks away, Ulitsa Novy Arbat, or New Arbat, flaunts high-rise 1960s Soviet architecture. Nearby Kropotkinskaya is home to Christ the Savior Cathedral and the posh area called the Golden Mile. Throughout, you'll find all manner of eateries and watering holes, from the ultra-elite to the quirkily down-market.

ZAMOSKVORECHYE

Zamoskvorechye—literally, "Beyond the Moscow River"—is located across the river from the Kremlin. Here, you'll find charming streetscapes with beautiful churches and low-rise pre-Revolutionary houses. This old artisans' settlement, with streets still named after the professions of the original inhabitants, is home to lavish mansions turned embassies. Other highlights include State Tretyakov Gallery Complex and Art Park Muzeon.

SOUTHWEST

Southwest Moscow boasts a lengthy strip of parkland running along the bank of the Moscow River. It starts with the amusement park Gorky Park, and continues via Neskuchny Sad (Not-Boring Garden) to the nature reserve Sparrow Hills. In winter

Gorky Park has ice skating and Sparrow Hills has skiing and snowboarding. There's a huge ski jump and a lookout platform at the top of the hill, with the best views over the city.

SOUTHEAST

The main reason to come here is to see Moscow's oldest monasteries. From the late 15th century, Novospassky Monastery was part of a network of fortified monasteries protecting the city. Nearby stands the fascinating, romantically run-down Krutitskoye Podvorye. On a bank of the Yauza River is the ancient white-walled Andronnikov Monastery, founded in 1357 and featuring fragments of Andrey Rublyov's frescoes.

GREATER MOSCOW

Moscow has a wealth of parkland in its outer suburbs, including Izmaylovsky Park, Sokolniki, Kolomenskoye, and the Botanical Gardens. The most impressive sight, however, is the All-Russian Exhibition Center, a Stalin-era monument to the achievements of the Soviet peoples, with pompous pavilions, grandiose statues, and amazing fountains. It's also a popular spot to inline skate, drink beer, and eat barbecued kebabs.

Excursions from Moscow

Moscow is close to a number of Golden Ring towns that offer a glimpse into the Russia of folklore. Among them is the immaculately preserved museum-town of Suzdal, industrial Vladimir, ecclesiastical Sergiyev Posad, and endearingly untouched Rostov Veliky.

St. Petersburg
THE CENTER

St. Petersburg's old center is like a stunning architecture museum, with gorgeous cityscapes enhanced by curving canals. The city is quite low-rise, so the churches' domes rise

a hydrofoil returning from Peterhof, with St. Petersburg's Peter and Paul Fortress and mosque in the background

embankment and the Rostral Columns on the tip of the Spit. The views across the water are spectacular.

PETROGRAD SIDE

Catch some rays at Petersburgers' favorite sunbathing spot at the site of the city's first citadel, Peter and Paul Fortress. Inside the fortress are fascinating museums and graves of the Romanov royals. Other sights on the Petrograd Side include Peter the Great's cottage, the Aurora Cruiser associated with the Bolshevik Revolution, a beautiful mosque, and the city's premier high-fashion shopping street, Bolshoy Prospekt.

SMOLNY AND OLD NEVSKY

This area is home to two historic riverside monasteries. Smolny Cathedral looks like a baroque whipped-cream cake and is surrounded by a convent. Alexander Nevsky Lavra, situated in a dense residential district, is a functioning monastery with beautiful old churches and star-studded cemeteries. Dostoyevsky, Tchaikovsky, and Stravinsky, among other famous names, can be seen on the headstones.

GREATER ST. PETERSBURG

The highlight of the greater St. Petersburg area is the Kirovskiye Islands north of the Petrograd Side: Yelagin, Kamenny, and Krestovsky, with tranquil parkland, a stadium, recreation areas, summer cafés, and entertainment. Across the river is the impressive Buddhist Temple Datsan Gunzechoinei.

above like they're intended to. The center bustles with tourists and locals. It's small enough to explore on foot, and there are sights galore—not the least of which are the Church on Spilled Blood and The Hermitage. It's also a major shopping district with restaurants, cafés, and bars.

KOLOMNA TO SENNAYA PLOSHCHAD

Criss-crossed by canals, this is a picturesque quarter. Kolomna is much quieter than the center, with old streets that will take you back in time. The renowned Mariinsky Theater is often the destination that spurs on a visit deep into this neighborhood. Sennaya Ploshchad was for centuries a sleazy market square, now spruced up and boasting modern malls. The market's still there, but it's now inside a renovated building.

VASILYEVSKY ISLAND

St. Petersburg State University and a number of museums give this neighborhood an academic atmosphere. Among the museums, the Kunstkamera has an amazing collection of natural abnormalities preserved in glass jars (not for the squeamish). You can also see genuine ancient Egyptian sphinxes on the

Excursions from St. Petersburg

Some of St. Petersburg's most famous and most brilliant sights are about 30 kilometers away: the beautiful palace estates of Peterhof, Pavlovsk, and Pushkin. Also close by is Kronshtadt and farther away is the majestic centuries-old city of Novgorod.

► WHEN TO GO

The most popular time to visit Moscow and St. Petersburg is in summer. Both cities have long daylight hours mid-year, particularly St. Pete with its "white nights." Summer means barbecues, beer gardens, scenic river and canal cruises, and the chance to enjoy lush parks and palace estates at their best. The temperature is pleasant and the cities have a more relaxed feel than at other times of the year—they are less crowded, with many locals away on vacation, and those remaining take a break from their usual frenzy to make the most of the sunshine.

Summer's downsides include higher hotel rates and larger numbers of tourists, as well as some perhaps surprising disappointments: The major theaters tend to close, so visitors with their heart set on seeing the Bolshoi's brightest stars should choose a different season.

In the fall, September and October are a good time to visit, with beautiful golden landscapes and usually mild temperatures; by November the autumn leaves have fallen and the cold starts to bite—but without the snow to add beauty. For the same reason, December is the least attractive of the winter months, compounded by the fact that it is also the darkest.

Winter is worth considering, especially January and all of February (but remember that the entire first week of January is public holidays). In the snow, Russia looks more exotic, the Golden Ring towns are at their most magical, and the cultural scene is in full swing. Winter sports fans can enjoy cross-country skiing and ice skating. It's also the most suitable time of year to enjoy vodka and traditional Russian cuisine. Daylight hours are longer in January and February than in December, and the skies are more often blue and sunny, making for some enchanting scenes.

Spring is best avoided, particularly from mid-March through April—a gloomy, slushy extension of winter. May is pleasant, however, with flowers blooming and leaves seemingly growing before your eyes, as the entire season of spring runs its course in just one month. May also means Victory Day, the May 9 holiday celebrating the end of World War II, with spectacular fireworks displays and bemedaled veterans on parade.

a lazy summer afternoon in Kronshtadt, an excursion from St. Petersburg

▶ BEFORE YOU GO

Passports and Visas

It should go without saying that you need a valid passport for international travel. Citizens of Canada, Australia, New Zealand, the United States, and the European Union are among those who need visas to travel to Russia. To get a visa, you need an invitation, which can be organized by the travel agent, hotel, hostel, tour company, or educational institution with whom you make advance reservations. After arriving, you need to register your visa, a service that is usually offered by the inviting organization.

Vaccinations

There are no special vaccinations required for visiting Moscow and St. Petersburg, but health organizations recommend staying up to date with routine vaccines such as influenza, chicken pox, polio, measles/mumps/rubella, and diphtheria/pertussis/tetanus. Hepatitis A and B vaccinations are also a good idea. If you plan to spend time in the countryside, it's advisable to get vaccinated against tick-borne encephalitis.

Travel Insurance

Before your trip, buy a comprehensive travel insurance policy valid in Russia, with full medical, dental, hospital, and emergency evacuation coverage, as well as money and baggage loss/theft coverage.

Getting There and Around

Moscow's international tourists usually arrive by airplane, most often flying into Sheremetyevo-2 or Domodedovo airports (the city's third international airport, Vnukovo, mostly takes flights from other areas of the former Soviet Union). All three airports are linked to the city center and the metro system by express railway services, which are the most convenient way to get into town, although there are also buses, minibuses, taxis, and car rental options.

Petersburg's one international airport, Pulkovo-2, does not have a train line connecting it to the city, so those arriving at the airport take buses, minibuses, or taxis to the metro or right into the center. The city's proximity to Finland and the Baltic states means that some international visitors arrive by bus and train as well.

Public transport is well developed, inexpensive, safe, fast, and efficient, so there is no real need to rent a car. For the inexperienced, driving is not recommended anyway, given the traffic jams in the cities, the state of country roads, and the peculiarities of local driving culture. (The locals have a saying, "Russia has two problems: fools and roads.") Those who are nervous about taking public transport should not imagine that driving is the answer—they'd be better off taking a guided bus tour. The metro is unbeatable for getting around the larger cities.

Train is the best way to get between Moscow and St. Petersburg, but in summer you'll need to book your tickets about two weeks in advance. All the main excursions beyond these two cities can be reached by train or bus.

Hotel Reservations

Unlike transport, accommodation can be a problem. A general shortage of hotel beds, particularly at the lower end of the price spectrum, means you should book well in advance. If you're on a budget, don't let an outlying location put you off if the price is right and the accommodation is within walking distance of a metro station.

Explore Moscow & St. Petersburg

▶ THE BEST OF MOSCOW & ST. PETERSBURG

Two weeks is ideal for a trip to Moscow and St. Petersburg, one week to explore each city. Aim for at least a 10-day visit, with five days in each. If it's your first visit and you have less than a week in total, consider focusing on just one city. At the minimum, a long weekend in either will give you a taste and whet your appetite for more. While St. Petersburg's picturesque center is quite compact and walkable, Moscow is a huge, sprawling metropolis and its great distances mean you may achieve less each day than you had planned.

Although these two cities are as different as vodka and champagne, neither reveals much of the "real Russia." For that, you need to go farther afield, to the villages and provincial towns, so try to take a full-day excursion out of each city, or even better, an overnight trip. From Moscow, be sure to see at least one Golden Ring town, Sergiyev Posad is the closest and can be seen in a day, but Suzdal is truly the ultimate Golden Ring experience and well worth overnighting, combined with a stop in Vladimir. In St. Petersburg, a jaunt to a palace estate is mandatory and easily accomplished in a single afternoon.

Day 1

Begin at Red Square, Moscow's top attraction. In one morning you can accomplish

St. Basil's Cathedral on Red Square

VODKA, BORSCH, AND SHASHLIK: EAT AND DRINK WITH THE SEASONS

WINTER
Vodka and *Zakuski*

Winter is the season for vodka, but it needs good company. Make sure you have a spread of tasty *zakuski* (Russian-style hors d'oeuvres) to accompany it: salted herring with boiled potato and onion; caviar on buttered white bread; marinated wild mushrooms; smoked sturgeon, salmon, trout, halibut, and mackerel; salami and cold cuts; and, most important of all, pickles, especially salted cucumbers. Chase each vodka shot with a bite of pickle.

- Best Brand: Russky Standart vodka

Hearty Soup

Good winter choices include meaty *solyanka*, with olives, capers, and sliced lemon; *shchi* made with cabbage; and naturally borsch, with garlic *pampushki* buns on the side.

Dumplings

For your next course, try *pelmeni*, delicious dumplings filled with pork, beef, and lamb. Salmon *pelmeni* are also popular. Vegetarians opt for Ukrainian-style dumplings, called *vareniki*, filled with cabbage or potato and mushroom. *Smetana* (sour cream) is the traditional accompaniment.

SPRING

The arrival of Orthodox Lent sees many Russians switching over to a mostly vegetarian or even vegan diet, and restaurants usually offer special Lenten (Postny) menus. This is when Russian food is at its healthiest and meat-free diets are happily accommodated in most eateries.

- Best Lenten Menu: Korchma Taras Bulba, Moscow

SUMMER
Light Beer and Shashliks

Summer is the time for light beer and shashliks – pieces of meat, fish, or vegetables grilled on skewers. Shashlik barbecue stands pop up everywhere.

Kvass

Summer is also the season for kvass, a fermented rye-bread drink that's surprisingly tasty and unbeatably refreshing. It's sold on the street, poured from giant yellow tanks on wheels or you can buy it in bottles or cans.

- Best Brand: Ochakovo kvass
- Go To: Teremok bliny fast-food stands

Cold Soup

Kvass is the main ingredient in *okroshka*, a refreshing cold soup with cucumber, radish, herbs, onion, and sausage, although the other variety of *okroshka* based on kefir, a sour milk drink, is also tasty. Try cold summer borsch, and the cold beet soup called *svekolnik*.

FALL

Autumn is a gastronomic highlight, as the markets are at their best, full of fresh seasonal produce, including melons, pumpkins, and mushrooms. Feast on ceps, or porcini, known locally as *beliye griby* (white mushrooms).

- Best Food Market: Dorogomilovsky Market, Moscow; Kuznechny Market, St. Petersburg

a lot: Lenin's mausoleum, St. Basil's Cathedral, the Kremlin walls, Spasskaya Tower, the State History Museum, and the GUM department store. Have a snack in one of the Bosco cafés facing Red Square.

Enter nearby Alexander Garden to see the Eternal Flame to the Unknown Soldier and the hourly changing of the guard. From here head into the Kremlin to see the stunningly beautiful church museums of Cathedral Square.

Have lunch on Kamergersky Pereulok, a picturesque pedestrian lane lined with cafés and restaurants. After lunch, soak up the vibe on Tverskaya Ulitsa, the city's main street. Don't miss Yeliseyevsky Gastronom, with its lavish interior and fine selection of delicacies.

a shot of horseradish-flavored vodka, complemented with pickles wrapped in pork fat

Dark Beer and Rye Toast

Colder weather means it's time to start moving on to dark beers, which go perfectly with *chesnochniye grenki* – rye toasts with garlic.

- Look For: Baltika's sweet and strong Imperial Porter; Ochakovo's drier and less alcoholic Chyronoye Lyogkoe (Black Light beer)

- Go To: Tinkoff microbrewery, Moscow and St. Petersburg

Armenian Brandy

Pair Armenian brandy with nuts and dried fruits from the Caucasus – look out for them in the markets. It's best to buy the oldest variety of brandy you can afford: 20-year-old is sublime, and 10-year-old is also delicious, but don't go younger than seven-year-old.

- Best Brand: Ararat brandy

End the day with two essential Moscow experiences, Russian-style dinner at nearby Cafe Pushkin and a ballet or opera at the Bolshoi Theater.

Day 2

This morning visit the Kremlin's Armory museum to see exquisite jewelry and centuries-old royal treasures. Follow up with lunch at 1 Red Square, specializing in authentic historical aristocrat menus.

After lunch walk to Christ the Savior Cathedral (but if you're short of time or low on energy, go directly to Moskvoretskaya Naberezhnaya to catch a boat to Vorobyovy Gory). Admire the cathedral from inside and out, then walk over the pedestrian bridges and along the embankment, enjoying amazing views.

Sergiyev Posad's spectacular church, Trinity-Sergius Lavra

Next, check out the exceptional collection of Kandinsky, Chagall, and others at the Tretyakov Gallery on Krymsky Val.

Art Park Muzeon next door is a wonderfully diverse sculpture garden with both contemporary works and old Soviet statues.

Across the road, Stalin-era theme park Gorky Park beckons. Exiting from the back gate of the park, board the next riverboat to Vorobyovy Gory and then ride the chairlift up the hill. At the top, the Sparrow Hills lookout offers great views of the city, ideally paired with shashliks from the outdoor café, or a refined French meal in the Rytsarsky Club.

Later, if you're still kicking, Sandunovskiye Bani offers the ultimate Russian bathhouse experience.

Day 3

Become an expert on Russian art by taking in the vast collection at the State Tretyakov Gallery Complex, then head to VDNKh to visit the incredible All-Russian Exhibition Center (VVTs). Possibly the ultimate in Stalinist grandeur, VVTs has to be seen to be believed. Its fountains, unique cinema, amusement rides, and many summer cafés can entertain for hours. The nearby Cosmonauts Memorial Museum is topped by a soaring silver statue of a rocket blasting off into the cosmos.

Later, cruise pedestrian-only Ulitsa Arbat. Eat, drink, shop, and ponder your evening's entertainment: the Conservatory, the circus, or the Cat Theater?

Day 4

Take the express train to Sergiyev Posad, the Golden Ring sight closest to Moscow. Visit Trinity-Sergius Lavra, a stunning ensemble of ecclesiastical architecture.

Later, visit Konny Dvor's museums of local artifacts, or head straight to Dachnaya Zhizn for lunch, then back to Moscow.

If money is no object, consider dinner (with a reservation) at Varvary or if the budget's tight, try Yolki Palki.

Day 5

Stock up on souvenirs at the Vernissage Market at Izmaylovo. Afterwards, tour nearby Vodka Museum, vodka-tasting session included.

To visit the Novodevichy Convent and Graveyard, hop the metro to Sportivnaya. Walk around the park beside the convent's walls, watching the ducks in the pond and searching for the ducklings sculpture that was a gift from Barbara Bush.

For dinner, try some Georgian food at U Pirosmani. Finish up early and head to the station for an overnight train to St. Petersburg.

Day 6

Having arrived early in the northern capital, drop your bags at your hotel, grab a coffee and bliny for breakfast, and head to Palace

Square, the city's main square. Enter through the monumental archway via Bolshaya Morskaya Ulitsa, it spectacularly frames the square; you'll see the Alexander Column and the Winter Palace.

Cross the road to the Admiralty, stroll through its gardens and snap a photo of the famed *Bronze Horseman* at Dekabristov Square. Behind the *Horseman* is the enormous St. Isaac's Cathedral: Admire its interior and climb to the lookout for a panoramic view.

Next, walk along the city's main street, Nevsky Prospekt. Beside Griboyedov Canal you'll see Kazan Cathedral and the amazing Bankovsky Bridge with its gilded griffins. Stop for lunch with a view at Terrassa.

On the other side of Griboyedov Canal, you'll pass the Church on Spilled Blood and behind it, the outdoor Vernissage Souvenirs Fair.

Dine at the Soviet-themed Lenin Zhiv! on the Fontanka Embankment, then take a canal cruise from the dock beside the Anichkov Bridge, yet another symbol of the city.

Day 7
Rise at the crack of dawn, have breakfast, and set off to *do* the Hermitage. There's more art here than you can see in one day, so don't even bother trying, just spend a half day on the highlights. Touch-screen computers help locate specific works and plot your path.

Exit the Hermitage and take the hydrofoil to Peterhof, reminiscent of France's Versailles. Be sure not to miss the last hydrofoil back to St. Petersburg, and go for drinks before staying up late to watch the bridges opening (mid-Apr.–Nov.).

Day 8
Begin your day on the Petrograd side. On University Embankment, visit the Kunstkamera to gawk at Peter the Great's collection of unusual natural wonders.

From here, it's a short walk to Peter and

the Church on Spilled Blood in St. Petersburg

Paul Fortress, where St. Petersburg began in 1703. Explore the fortress, beach, and museums, then cross the road to lunch in one of Alexander Garden's restaurants.

After lunch take the metro to the elegant old monastery, Alexander Nevsky Lavra. Don't miss the Tikhvin cemetery, with the graves of Dostoyevsky and Tchaikovsky.

Go for dinner at Stolle, their Russian pies will hit the spot. After dinner, go to the ballet or opera at the Mariinsky Theater, finishing up with beers at Shamrock pub across the road.

Day 9

There are two palaces to see today, so get up early. Take the "Palaces, Fountains" minibuses first to Pushkin. Explore the palace's extravagant interiors and gardens.

When you've had your fill, catch the next minibus to nearby Pavlovsk, a leafy little town with the Neoclassical palace and English-style gardens of Emperor Paul I's estate. In a former ballroom is the Grand Column Hall Restaurant: Grab lunch at the cheap buffet, then head back to the city by bus or rail.

For casual dining, try Blinny Domik in the Dostoyevskaya/Vladimirskaya neighborhood.

Day 10

The Russian Museum has the world's largest collection of Russian fine art, from the 10th century to the present and is especially popular for its collection of early-20th-century avant-garde Russian art. While you're there, buy some artsy souvenirs.

Afterwards, lunch at Tinkoff microbrewery, or go to SevenSkyBar and enjoy the panoramic views, a memorable finish to your visit.

▶ SOVIET FLASHBACK: MOSCOW

Day 1

For the full retro-Soviet experience, it's obvious where to stay: the Hotel Sovietsky, offering a taste of the Soviet era as experienced by the elite.

Ride the metro to Teatralnaya station and admire the gilded figures in the national costumes of Soviet republics. Exit onto Theater Square. Dominating Theater Square is the Bolshoi Theater; opposite, you'll see a statue of Karl Marx, with the inscription "Proletarians of All Countries, Unite!"

It's a short walk to Red Square. If the timing's right, pay Lenin a visit, then walk through the Kremlin wall necropolis, where numerous Soviet heroes are buried.

Next, cross Red Square to the GUM department store to visit Gastronom No. 1, a re-creation of an old but very ornate and well-stocked Soviet store. Lunch Soviet-style at Stolovaya No. 57 canteen on the 3rd floor.

The Kremlin's Spasskaya Tower is a prominent landmark on Red Square.

GUM (Main Department Store) on Red Square

After lunch, walk to the monumental Ploshchad Revolyutsii metro, featuring brilliant Socialist Realist statues of soldiers, sailors, students, and metro-builders. Take the green line to Tverskaya metro and go to the Contemporary History of Russia Museum via Pushkin Square. In addition to the museum's fascinating exhibits on the Soviet era, its store is one of the best places to buy Soviet propaganda posters.

Afterwards, head to Triumfalnaya Ploshchad, where an impressive statue of poet Mayakovsky marks a cluster of architectural landmarks. Follow the Garden Ring to the Metro microbrewery for excellent beer, good food, and a fun metro theme.

Day 2

If you didn't manage to see Lenin yesterday, pay him a morning visit if he's receiving guests today.

Ride around the metro ring line *(koltsevaya liniya,* Кольцевая линия), getting out at each stop to admire some of the most spectacular metro stations, such as Komsomolskaya, with its excess of gold and ornate mosaics. Disembark at Oktyabrskaya and exit onto Kaluzhskaya Ploshchad where there's a very photogenic Lenin statue.

Next, walk downhill around the right-hand side of the Garden Ring road to the Central House of Artists and Tretyakov Gallery on Krymsky Val. Pop into the "New Tretyakov" and see some Socialist Realist, avant-garde, and other brilliant Soviet-era art before exploring the next-door Art Park Muzeon, with dozens of statues of Soviet figures and other propaganda pieces.

Ride to Okhotny Ryad for dinner at Sluzhebny Vkhod, a restaurant-cum-museum of Soviet nostalgia.

HOLIDAY TRADITIONS

NEW YEAR'S

New Year's is the most important night of the whole year in Russia, the most fun celebration of all. It's like Western Christmas and New Year's rolled into one, with feasts and gifts. The decorated trees aren't Christmas trees, but New Year's trees; likewise, the Russian version of Santa Claus, Ded Moroz, and his right-hand woman Snegurochka, the Snow Maiden, make their appearances in honor of New Year's, not Christmas. It can be eerily quiet on the streets just before midnight, however. By tradition, everybody greets the new year at home with their family and friends, sitting at a lavishly laden table and watching the president's traditional New Year's speech on television, just before the Kremlin clock is shown chiming the countdown to the New Year. Fireworks fill the skies, and with champagne toasts, the festivities spill out onto the streets.

After New Year's, the public holidays continue for a week, until Orthodox Christmas (January 7), while the festivities continue for two weeks, until **"Old New Year,"** (Orthodox New Year, January 13-14). Over this entire period there's much merrymaking in the main parks and squares. You can warm up under festively decorated fir trees with hot mulled wine, folk singing and dancing, ice sculptures and slides – and, of course, greetings from Ded Moroz and Snegurochka.

MASLENITSA

Another fun time to visit is during Maslenitsa, a weeklong bliny (pancake) festival dating back to pagan times as a celebration to welcome spring. Now Christianized, the holiday precedes the 40-day Lenten fast and falls seven weeks before Orthodox Easter – somewhere between mid-February and early March. There are outdoor public festivities, where you can stuff yourself with bliny, enjoy folk song and dance shows, and take part in playing centuries-old games. Suzdal is an ideal place to go for Maslenitsa, with its wooden architecture museum being the perfect setting. There are dozens of Maslenitsa fairs all over Moscow and St. Petersburg. One of the best is the annual celebration just off the capitals' Red Square on Vasilyevsky Spusk.

Day 3

Take the metro to VDNKh station, where top-class Soviet sights are clustered nearby. You'll pass the Cosmonauts Memorial Museum on your way to VVTs. It's located under the striking silver Conquerors of the Cosmos monument; inside are hundreds of items of historical space significance.

A short distance away are the monumental gates of the All-Russian Exhibition Center (VVTs), with its collection of elaborate pavilions, fountains, and statues. Don't miss the People's Friendship Fountain, with 16 gilded women in the national costume of the former Soviet republics, and the Circular Cinerama, playing Soviet-era films.

Ride the metro to Turgenevskaya station and walk to Ploshchad Sretenskiye Vorota. Facing the square is a statue of Lenin's wife Nadezhda Krupskaya, one of the city's few statues of a woman.

From here, walk to Lubyanka Square, home of the old KGB headquarters, a KGB museum (call ahead), and a monument to victims of political oppression.

Also at Lubyanka Square is the Mayakovsky Museum, where Mayakovsky lived and worked from 1919 to 1930.

Dine in the secret services–themed Shchit i Mech, followed by drinks in the retro-Soviet beer restaurant Glavpivtorg.

▶ IMPERIAL GRANDEUR: ST. PETERSBURG

Day 1

Your first stop is Palace Square. The Hermitage's main complex is in six palatial 18th- and 19th-century buildings on Palace Embankment; the most important is the Winter Palace. The palace interiors are a sight in themselves, and there's a wealth of tsarist treasures to gawk at.

By the time you've seen the Hermitage's emperors' carriages, ostentatious jewels, and a mind-boggling array of masterpieces of world art, you'll have an appetite; head to nearby Kempinski Hotel Moika 22's 9th-floor Bellevue, with superb views of Palace Square.

After lunch, walk to the Summer Garden, its lanes are lined with 17th- and 18th-century Italian sculptures. As St. Petersburg's oldest garden, it contains one of the city's oldest buildings, Peter the Great's Summer Palace.

Next, cross the bridge to the Engineer's Castle (a branch of the Russian Museum). Unusually austere for St. Petersburg, it was built 1796–1800 for Emperor Paul I. Beside the palace is a statue of an equestrian Peter the Great styled as a Roman Emperor.

Have dinner at Noble's Nest, which is so fancy it's like dining in the Winter Palace.

Day 2

Start with an elegant continental breakfast in the Hotel Astoria's Rotonda Lounge, located right on St. Isaac's Square, your next stop. Standing more than 100 meters high, St. Isaac's Cathedral has amazing views from the lookout around the colonnade beneath its dome. The cathedral is open as a museum with a can't-miss ornate interior.

The park in front of the cathedral holds one of the city's most iconic symbols: the *Bronze*

St. Isaac's Cathedral

one of the Anichkov Bridge's four statues

Horseman, depicting a heroic Peter the Great on horseback.

Walk towards the Winter Palace to the hydrofoil station where you can board the boat to Peterhof, the ultimate in St. Petersburg's imperial excess.

Day 3

Today, either go to Pushkin and Pavlovsk, or, if you don't have the energy for another excursion, stay in the city and see other tsarist-era treasures, such as Smolny Cathedral, a baroque wonder that looks like an iced blue-and-white wedding cake. It's the centerpiece of the Smolny Convent, built 1748–1757 for Empress Elizabeth I.

Your next stop is the 18th-century Yusupov Palace, most famous as the site of Rasputin's murder, with magnificent interiors and treasures (by tour only).

From Nevsky Prospekt's intersection with the Fontanka River, admire the 19th-century Anichkov Bridge, a symbol of St. Petersburg, with four Neoclassical statues, each depicting a naked young man taming a wild steed. River and canal cruises depart from beside the bridge, a perfect way to finish your visit to this imperial city.

MOSCOW

SIGHTS

One of the world's most iconic cities, Moscow is a must-see destination. The Kremlin, Red Square, St. Basil's Cathedral, Lenin's mausoleum, Stalin's "wedding cake" skyscrapers, the metro—Russia's capital has some solid, world-famous attractions that need no introduction. There are countless architectural landmarks, impressive monuments, and sites of great historical significance.

Moscow's sights can be divided into a few broad categories: medieval marvels, imperial splendor, Soviet monumentalism, and post-Soviet renewal. And as diverse as these genres might be, in their Moscow manifestation they tend to have one thing in common: a sense of grandeur characteristic of a city asserting its status as a capital.

Although Moscow is a huge city with some astoundingly busy and dauntingly wide multi-lane boulevards, it also has its fair share of quiet quarters that are beautifully designed, with many green parks, flower gardens, and landscaped squares. There are quaint little backstreets where it seems time has stood still; it's fascinating to just wander about with no set route in mind. Moscow is a city of amazing diversity, a city where just about anybody can find something to suit their taste.

Given how large and spread-out the city is, it makes sense to focus each day of your itinerary on a relatively small area. Your first day should obviously be spent around the Kremlin and Red Square, perhaps followed by a wander around one of the nearby neighborhoods—take a walk up Tverskaya Ulitsa, explore the Arbat, or go for a roam around Kitay-Gorod. Another day could be spent in the city's north, checking out the All-Russian Exhibition Center, the Cosmonauts Memorial Museum, and the space monument—as well as the Ostankino estate and television

© NATHAN TOOHEY

HIGHLIGHTS

LOOK FOR (TO FIND RECOMMENDED SIGHTS.

(Most Glorious Golden Domes: The Kremlin's **Cathedral Square** will take your breath away with its stunning ensemble of white-walled cathedrals and bell towers under gilded cupolas (page 58).

(Most Morbid Sight: Lenin's Mausoleum brings you face-to-face with a legend – but there's been talk of burying him, so pay him a visit while you can (page 63).

(Most Iconic Sight: St. Basil's Cathedral, on Red Square, is the internationally recognized symbol of the city – and the whole country (page 64).

(Street with Most Character: Arbat Street has a bohemian vibe, and swarms with interesting personalities (page 74).

(Best Open-Air Art: The Art Park Muzeon is a final resting place for the city's old Soviet statues, as well as a contemporary sculpture garden (page 78).

(Most Beautiful Monastery: The Novodevichy Convent is a stunning beauty with formidable red walls and gorgeous churches, all set beside an idyllic park and duck pond (page 80).

(Best Retro-Soviet Sight: The All-Russian Exhibition Center is like a USSR theme park, with elaborate fountains and a full cast of communist heroes in its grandiose statues (page 86).

© NATHAN TOOHEY

St. Basil's Cathedral

tower, if you've got the time and energy, perhaps with a ride on the monorail thrown in for fun. Zamoskvorechye would fit well with the southwest, so in one day you could visit both or either of the Tretyakov galleries followed by the Art Park Muzeon, Gorky Park, and the parks beyond—Neskuchny Sad and Sparrow Hills. Alternatively, a return visit to the Kremlin area could be combined with a riverboat cruise to Gorky Park or the Sparrow Hills chairlift, where you can ride up to the top for views over the city and a look at Moscow State University. Novodevichy Convent

and graveyard are well worth a visit, but are not located near other sights; they are, however, on the same metro line as Sparrow Hills and Christ the Savior Cathedral, which means these sights could be combined in one day.

The size and scope of Moscow can be overwhelming, but the efficient public transport system—especially the magnificent metro, a sight in itself—makes sightseeing manageable. Just about every sight is within walking distance of a metro station, and it's surprising how quickly and inexpensively one can get around.

The Kremlin and Red Square   Map 1

THE KREMLIN

Kreml

Кремль

The Kremlin is Moscow's geographical and historical core. It's the oldest part of the city, with a tumultuous centuries-long history. Here, succession to the throne was decided from medieval times, and coronations continued even after the capital moved to St. Petersburg. After Moscow became the capital once again, the Kremlin resumed its position as the center of political life and seat of the highest state institutions. It never stopped being the heart of the nation, however, and still remains headquarters of the Russian Federation's head of state.

History

The Kremlin originated with a fortified Vyatich Slav settlement on Borovitsky Hill at least as early as the 11th century. In 1156, Prince Yury Dolgoruky ordered the construction of a new fortress with moat and ramparts, about a third of the present Kremlin's size. The fortress was destroyed during the Mongol-Tartar attack in 1237, and rebuilt in oak in 1339–1340; the first stone churches were also built around this time. New walls were built in white stone in 1367, expanding the fortress's territory almost to the Kremlin's current size.

By the late 15th century, Moscow had risen to become the capital of a centralized Russian state. To build a new Kremlin and city center befitting of Moscow's new status, Italian architects and engineers were brought in, as well as the best craftsmen from Pskov, Tver, and Rostov.

The currently existing Kremlin wall was built 1485–1495, by Italian architects, incorporating Russian architectural traditions with the most up-to-date Western European achievements in fortification. The Cathedral Square ensemble and a number of other remaining

a view of the Moscow Kremlin from Bersenevskaya Naberezhnaya

© NATHAN TOOHEY

TOWER POWER

The Kremlin's most important tower is **Spasskaya Bashnya** (Savior Tower), the square-based giant towering over Red Square near St. Basil's Cathedral. Standing 71 meters high (including its red star), it has a gate right onto Red Square – the Savior Gate, through which tsars, patriarchs, and other important people would pass with much pomp and ceremony on festive occasions. The tower's clock shows precise Moscow time thanks to underground cables linking it to control clocks at the city's Shternberg Astronomy Institute. This is the clock shown on television chiming midnight every New Year's, right after the president's speech. The tower was built in 1491 by Italian architect Pietro Antonio Solari. A tent roof, white stone carvings, statues, and other decorations were added in the 17th century.

Orientation

The UNESCO World Heritage–listed Moscow Kremlin contains an outdoor museum area that's open to the public, as well as off-limits areas including the official residence of the Russian president—which is why the term "The Kremlin" is often used in the news media to refer to the presidency or the government.

The Kremlin complex is a 27.5-hectare irregular triangle with Red Square to the east, Alexander Garden to the west, and the Moscow River running along the south. The wall is more than 2 kilometers long, ranging from 5–19 meters in height, and 3.5–6.5 meters thick. It has 20 towers, the tallest being Troitskaya Tower, which stands 80 meters high counting its red star. Facing Alexander Garden, it is the gate tower through which tourists enter the Kremlin after first passing through the Kutafya Tower—the complex's only bridgehead watchtower.

Apart from walls and towers, you can't see much of the Kremlin from Red Square or Alexander Garden. To get a good view, walk onto Bolshoy Moskvoretsky Most (bridge), which crosses the Moscow River behind St. Basil's Cathedral on Red Square, or Bolshoy Kamenny Most, near Borovitsky Tower at the end of Alexander Garden. Even better, walk a circuit crossing both bridges, linking via Sofiiskaya Naberezhnaya, the embankment directly across the river from the Kremlin.

From this side, you will see how the Kremlin stands high over the Moscow River on Borovitsky Hill, a stunning composition of gold and silver cupolas atop snow-white churches, amid stately ornate palaces and forested parkland, all inside tall redbrick walls with soaring towers and swallowtail-shaped "teeth."

constructions were also built at this time; others arose in later construction booms with the Romanov ascent in the 17th century and post-Napoleon rebuilding after 1812.

A 36-meter-wide moat had been built around the Kremlin walls in 1508–1516, but in the 19th century it was filled in. Around the same time, the Neglinka River, which had run along the western wall and into the Moscow River, was buried in an underground pipe. A bridge that crossed it remains—you can walk under it in Alexander Garden or over it to enter the Kremlin via the Kutafya and Troitskaya tower gates.

Tragically, a number of beautiful and historically significant objects were destroyed by the Soviets, including the Kremlin's oldest church, Church of the Savior on the Bor (Spas na Boru), which had survived since 1380 and had been one of the earliest stone buildings in the Kremlin—its foundations were said to have been laid by Prince Ivan Kalita in 1330.

The Kremlin was closed to the public from 1918 to 1955, and in 1961 the Kremlin Museum was founded.

Planning Your Time

Any tourist coming to Moscow for the first time should, on their very first day, head straight to the heart of the city: Take a look at Red Square, and then go inside the Kremlin (495/203-0349, www.kreml.ru, Fri.–Wed. 10 A.M.–5 P.M., ticket office 9:30 A.M.–4 P.M., adults 300R, students and children 50R, metro Borovitskaya/Alexandrovsky Sad).

A first day at the Kremlin is best spent just wandering around the grounds, admiring the architecture and looking inside the church-museums. Those on a tight schedule might want to squeeze in a look at the Armory Chamber and Diamond Fund (covered in the *Museums* section of the *Arts and Leisure* chapter) on the first day as well, but those in less of a rush will probably enjoy that experience more if it's left to be the highlight of another day.

Ticket offices to enter the grounds and museums are located in Alexander Garden beside the Kutafya Tower, which is the main entrance for tourists. The entry ticket includes visiting the five church-museums on Cathedral Square, as well as the Patriarch's Palace and Assumption Belfry. Those going to the Armory Chamber and Diamond Fund need to pay extra for separate tickets and can enter via the Borovitskaya Tower.

C CATHEDRAL SQUARE
Sobornaya ploshchad
Соборная площадь

The most stunningly beautiful sight within the Kremlin walls is Cathedral Square. In addition to its impressive bell tower and the Tsar Bell, it includes five churches and a palace that are open to the public.

The square's compositional center, the 81-meter-high **Ivan the Great Bell Tower** (Kolokolnya Ivana Velikogo), used to be the Kremlin's main watchtower. It was built 1505–1508 but was extended upwards and given a new dome in 1600—so says the Old Church Slavonic text that you can see just below the dome.

Standing in front is an enormous broken bell—the **Tsar Bell** (Tsar-kolokol). The world's largest bell, it has never been rung: In 1737, while it was still in its pit, a fire caused an 11.5-ton chunk to crack off. Nobody could get the 200-ton bell out of its pit until 1836, when it was placed on a pedestal.

A symphony of nine golden cupolas, the 15th-century **Annunciation Cathedral** (Blagoveshchensky sobor) was the domestic church of Moscow princes, hosting weddings and baptisms. Inside you can see Russia's oldest multi-tiered iconostasis, dating to the 14th–16th centuries, and including icons by Andrey Rublyov and Theophanes the Greek.

The 16th-century **Archangel Cathedral** (Arkhangelsky sobor) stands out thanks to its Italian Renaissance–style decorations. The necropolis of princes and tsars, it contains the graves of Ivan Kalita, Dmitry Donskoy, Ivan the Terrible, and many others, as well as a 13-meter-high iconostasis.

The **Assumption Cathedral** (Uspensky sobor), a 15th-century limestone wonder with five golden domes, was Russia's most important church for hundreds of years, hosting all coronations right up to Nicholas II's in 1896. It contains relics of saints, the Nail of Christ, a necropolis, a large collection of icons, and Ivan the Terrible's wooden praying seat.

Hidden behind the Assumption Cathedral, the small 15th-century **Church of the Deposition** (Tserkov Rizopolozheniya) might look modest, but inside you can see a magnificent four-tiered, silver-framed iconostasis, superb frescoes, and an ancient candelabrium. It houses a permanent exhibit of wood carvings from the 15th–19th centuries.

Built 1653–1655, the **Cathedral of the Twelve Apostles** (sobor Dvenadtsati Apostolov) and the adjoined **Patriarch's Palace** (Patriarshy dvorets) are recognizable by five helmeted domes and two archways leading from Cathedral Square to the Patriarch's courtyard. The complex commissioned by Patriarch Nikon contained the patriarch's living quarters and ceremonial chambers. Damaged by Bolshevik bombardment in 1917, it was later restored to become a museum, now exhibiting icons in the cathedral and 17th-century domestic and ecclesiastic objects in the palace.

On Cathedral Square, at noon on Saturday from April to October, you can watch the ceremonial equestrian and pedestrian procession of the Presidential Regiment.

FACETED PALACE
Granovitaya palata
Грановитая палата

Built 1487–1491 by Italian architects Marco Ruffo and Pietro Solario, the Faceted Palace is said to be the oldest surviving stone civilian architectural monument in Moscow. The diminutive, boxy construction with an unusual faceted limestone facade is what remains of a larger palace built for Ivan III. The 500-square-meter main hall—a spectacular setting with vaulted ceilings covered in frescoes and gilded carvings—was used for tsars' banquets and now hosts high-level receptions. Ivan the Terrible, Peter the Great, Ronald Reagan, Margaret Thatcher, and Queen Elizabeth II are just some of the leaders who have feasted here; you have to be in their league to get an invitation to go inside and take a look.

The reception hall's anteroom is reached by a grand staircase on the southern side called the Krasnoye Kryltso (Red or Beautiful Porch), along which tsars passed on their way to their coronation. It was destroyed in the 1930s and rebuilt in the 1990s.

GOVERNMENT BUILDINGS
The yellow building that you'll see in the Kremlin's northern corner, on your left after you enter via the Troitskaya Tower gate, is the **Arsenal,** which now serves as an administrative building. It was intended to be a weaponry museum, and was constructed 1701–1736 on orders from Peter the Great, in place of royal barns that had burnt down. Along its facade are 875 guns captured from Napoleon's army, and along the southern wall there are 20 cannons made by the best Russian gunsmiths of the 16th and 17th centuries.

The yellow-and-white triangular Neoclassical building facing the Arsenal is called the **Senate,** and it currently houses the presidential administration. Viewed from Red Square, it's the dome-and-flag-topped building visible above the Kremlin walls behind Lenin's mausoleum. It was constructed 1776–1788 by architect Matvey Kazakov on the orders of Catherine II (the Great) to house the

Governing Senate, the highest national judiciary and legislative office. In 1918 the new Soviet government offices moved in, including Vladimir Lenin's apartment and office; later it housed Josef Stalin's study and conference hall. Since then it has always been the residence of the head of state.

Beside the Senate and Spasskaya Tower gate is a yellow Neoclassical building with white columns. Known as **Building 14,** it houses some departments of the presidential administration and one of the president's offices. It was constructed 1932–1934 as a military school and housed the Presidium of the Supreme Soviet 1938–1991.

GREAT KREMLIN PALACE
Bolshoi Kremlyovsky dvorets
Большой Кремлёвский дворец

Some of the Kremlin's most beautiful and interesting buildings can only be admired from the outside, unless you're a VIP. One that you can't miss is the Great Kremlin Palace, part of the **president's official residence.** Viewed from the Moscow River, it is the Kremlin's most predominant building—a huge yellow-and-white palace with a green roof and golden spike. It was built in the 19th century to be the royal family's main Moscow residence.

Nearby is another eye-catching building, the **Terem Palace.** Also closed to the public as part of the president's official residence, it is an unusual, brightly colored building modeled on a traditional log cabin, with a red-and-white-checked roof. It was built in the 15th–16th centuries and was the tsars' main residence in the 17th century. Try to spot the 14th-century **Church of the Virgin's Nativity on the Anteroom**—the oldest surviving stone building in the Kremlin, now overbuilt but visible as part of the palace's ground floor. There are four 17th-century churches adjoined on the eastern side—particularly striking is the **Verkhospassky Cathedral,** topped with 11 gilded cupolas.

Nearby you are likely to spot a bright red-and-yellow building topped with a turret and several golden cupolas. This is the **Amusement**

Palace (Poteshny dvorets), the Kremlin's only surviving example of boyar chambers. It was built in the 17th century for the tsar's father-in-law and turned into a theater after his death, which is why it is called the Amusement Palace. For the average tourist, however, the only amusement here is in taking photos from the outside.

TSAR CANNON
Tsar-pushka
Царь-пушка

Standing near the Cathedral of the Twelve Apostles is one of the world's largest antique weapons, the Tsar Cannon. It was commissioned by Tsar Fyodor—whose portrait it bears—and created by the eminent cannon-caster Andrey Chokhov in 1586. Intricate friezes and inscriptions are carved on the barrel, which is fixed to a specially cast carriage decorated with a lion's head. Although it was designed to defend the Kremlin and not serve a purely ornamental function, it has never been fired. The cannon is 5.34 meters long, with a caliber of 890 millimeters, and weighs 39,312 kilograms. Beside it are four hollow decorative cannonballs that are bigger than the diameter of its barrel; the Tsar Cannon was designed to shoot pellets.

RED SQUARE
Krasnaya ploshchad
Красная площадь

It's just 1980s pop, but the Human League were right. To "march, march, march across Red Square" really is one of "the things that dreams are made of." It's a must-see sight, a must-have experience, up there with the Eiffel Tower, the Taj Mahal, and Tiananmen Square.

Whether you associate it with grim-faced Soviet leaders watching parades of military might, or the cheerfully colorful swirling domes of St. Basil's Cathedral, Red Square has an alluring mystique.

At 330 meters long and 70 meters wide, Red Square is not small. But, as is often the case with major sights with iconic status that makes them larger than life in the collective imagination, some first-time tourists say Red Square is smaller than they expected. And still they are impressed.

Although the name, Krasnaya Ploshchad, is translated as Red Square, in old Russian it also means Beautiful Square. Both names are a good fit. The redbrick Kremlin wall runs along one side, with red stars atop red towers, complemented by the reds of St. Basil's Cathedral, the Resurrection Gates, Kazan Cathedral, and the red-brown History Museum. All this is contrasted by revolutionary leader Vladimir Lenin's austere mausoleum of red and black granite, sternly facing the fancy GUM department store that stands opposite flaunting its frivolous boutiques. It adds up to a magnificent panorama—one that can excite and awe even when seen for the hundredth time.

History
Red Square has both looks and personality—and a past to boot. Starting as a jumble of traders outside the Kremlin wall's main gates, its first recorded mention was in 1434, but it is believed to have existed from the second half of the 14th century. After a fire in 1493, Ivan III cleared the area as a fire-safety precaution and the new open space, initially called Pozhar (Fire), was to evolve into Red Square. Trading revived, but without the construction of any permanent structures.

In 1508–1516, a 36-meter-wide moat was built around the Kremlin walls, with bridges from the tower gates to the square. The Church of the Intercession on the Moat—now widely known as St. Basil's Cathedral—appeared in the mid-16th century, along with numerous smaller wooden churches that were later removed due to the risk of fire.

Red Square's moats were filled in and trees planted along the Kremlin wall as part of post-Napoleonic rebuilding in 1814–1815, after which it became less a market square and more a place for festive occasions. Tram tracks were laid in 1909 and a tram route ran across the square, along the Kremlin wall, until 1930.

The Soviets brought a more somber, memorial air to Red Square: the first funeral parade for fallen comrades was held on the square on November 10, 1917, within days of the start of the Bolshevik Revolution. These rank-and-file revolutionaries were the first to be buried along the Kremlin wall.

With Lenin's death in 1924, a mausoleum was erected, becoming the compositional center of the square's architectural ensemble. The focus of idolization of the late revolutionary leader, it turned Red Square into the symbolic Soviet heart, and also came in handy as a podium for leaders to stand upon when appearing in public.

Red Square is famed as a stage for military parades, and one of the most significant was during World War II, on November 7, 1941, the 24th anniversary of the Bolshevik Revolution, when German forces had advanced to just 70–100 kilometers from the Soviet capital. Stalin rallied Soviet soldiers "onward to victory" before they marched straight from Red Square to trains that would take them to the front. No less significant was the Victory Parade that followed on June 24, 1945, marking the Allies' defeat of Nazi Germany.

May 9 Victory Day parades on Red Square then became an annual event and have remained an institution in the post-Soviet era, although scaled back from their heyday. Parades of weaponry ceased from 1991 until the 2008 parade, which was the first time in 18 years that tanks and missiles would roll out in a display of military muscle.

Still, Red Square has relaxed quite a bit since Soviet times. Most days, it revels in the lighter side of its personality. In winter it invites you to skate on its ice rink and occasionally hosts rock concerts. The fearsome revolutionary leader's mausoleum has slid to the status of tourist attraction.

Planning Your Time

Red Square should be at the top of any first-time tourist's list of sights to see, along with the Kremlin. Just walking around taking photos is usually enough fun on the first day, perhaps adding a look inside St. Basil's and GUM. Lenin's mausoleum is worth a look, but has

limited opening hours—most first-day tourists usually find it has already closed and have to return early in the morning on another day. The Historical Museum is another optional sight for another day, for those who are interested in that sort of thing.

If you're in Moscow between April and October, on the last Saturday of each month at 2 P.M. you can watch the ceremonial equestrian and pedestrian procession of the Presidential Regiment on Red Square, free of charge.

Unfortunately, a visit to Red Square isn't guaranteed for every tourist, as it is often closed for official events and for various other reasons. Also, access is restricted on Victory Day and New Year's, so don't count on getting anywhere near the action of these major events on the square.

And a word of warning: Given that Red Square is the most touristy spot in the whole of Russia, the usual rules for such places apply here. You need to be on your guard against pickpockets and con artists, and don't talk to strangers. That way, visiting Red Square can be a dream come true, and not turn into a nightmare.

GUM (MAIN DEPARTMENT STORE)

GUM (Glavny universalny magazin)

ГУМ (Главный универсальный магазин)

3/2 Red Square, 495/788-4343, www.gum.ru

HOURS: Daily 10 A.M.–10 P.M.

METRO: Okhotny Ryad or Ploshchad Revolyutsii

Red Square was a place of trade from its very earliest days but the first stone shopping arcades were built only in 1595: the Upper, Middle, and Lower Trading Rows, lining Red Square's eastern side directly opposite the Kremlin Wall.

The Upper Trading Rows, between Nikolskaya and Ilinka streets, have been rebuilt several times and are now called GUM, or the Main Department Store. This has long been Moscow's most famous retail complex and an obligatory stop in every tourist's itinerary.

Constructed 1890–1893 by architect Alexander Pomerantsev and engineer Vladimir Shukhov, the building was progressive in its

© NATHAN TOOHEY

GUM (Main Department Store)

use of steel and glass. It followed the then-fashionable Russian Revival style, incorporating 17th-century architectural motifs and graced by towers harmoniously repeating those of the Historical Museum on the square's northern side. Its three interior passages housed thousands of small shops.

In 1953, it was renamed as the State Department Store. The first word has been changed from Gosudarstvenny (State) to Glavny (Main), but the GUM acronym remains. The quirky shops of Soviet times have been replaced by big-name international boutiques, but in a nod to the past Gastronom No. 1 opened in 2008, a copy of an ornate Soviet grocery store that was previously in the row closest to Red Square. GUM's diminutive fountain is considered by locals to be its main sight and, underwhelming as it might be, it still makes a pleasant setting for a coffee break.

Meanwhile, the Middle Trading Rows' graceful 1901–1902 building has been hidden behind scaffolding as it undergoes a radical makeover. Located opposite St. Basil's, on the corner of Ulitsa Varvarka at No. 5 Red Square,

its central blocks were demolished in 2006–2007 to make way for redevelopment as the "Kremlyovsky" multifunctional complex, including a hotel, an eight-story residential block, and three levels of underground parking.

The Lower Trading Rows stood on the other side of Varvarka but were destroyed in the 1930s as part of major Red Square renovations that also wiped out a number of other historical and architectural treasures.

KREMLIN WALL NECROPOLIS
Nekropol u Kremlyovskoy steny
Некрополь у Кремлёвской стены
Along the Kremlin wall on Red Square
METRO: Okhotny Ryad or Ploshchad Revolyutsii

Just days into the 1917 Bolshevik Revolution, 238 fallen comrades were buried in two common graves in Red Square beside the Kremlin wall. Soon this honor was reserved for only the most distinguished people—among them the American communist journalist John Reed, author of *Ten Days That Shook the World,* and Lenin's mistress Inessa Armand, who took their place in the Kremlin Wall necropolis in 1920. After Lenin's mausoleum became the centerpiece of the necropolis in 1924, the rows behind him gradually filled with a whole galaxy of stars: Soviet leaders from Josef Stalin to Konstantin Chernenko, secret police founder Felix Dzerzhinsky, cosmonaut Yury Gagarin, politicians, statesmen, military leaders, and other outstanding people of science and the arts. Usually a walk through the necropolis is incorporated into visits to Lenin's mausoleum.

◖ LENIN'S MAUSOLEUM
Mavzoley V.I. Lenina
Мавзолей В.И. Ленина
Red Square, 495/923-5527
HOURS: Tues.-Thurs. and Sat.-Sun. 10 A.M.-1 P.M.
COST: Free
METRO: Okhotny Ryad or Ploshchad Revolyutsii

Ideology aside, architect Alexei Shchusev's ziggurat-like tomb for the revolutionary leader Vladimir Lenin is considered a masterpiece— some even regard it as Russia's greatest architectural achievement of the 20th century. The monumental red and black granite mausoleum, built in 1930, is actually the third—two similar wooden versions, also by Shchusev, preceded it. The first was hastily put together within a week of Lenin's January 1924 death, and more than 100,000 people came to see his embalmed body in the first six weeks that it was on display. An upgraded version replaced the original mausoleum after six months, and by the end of the first year, half a million mourners had been through it. Popular demand meant a more permanent solution had to be found for preserving his body as well as accommodating it.

An obligatory, if perhaps gruesome, stop in every Moscow visitor's itinerary, Lenin's mausoleum is said to have had 10 million visitors between 1924 and 1972. For a while, Stalin had a berth beside him before being relegated to the Kremlin Wall necropolis.

In the post-Soviet era there has been an ongoing debate about removing Lenin from the mausoleum and burying him, as an act of closure. Although Communists have been fighting to keep him there and the embalmed body remains a popular tourist attraction, Lenin himself would probably prefer to be buried. At the time of his death, his wife Nadezhda Krupskaya opposed the idea of embalming him and putting him on display. She argued that he wanted to be buried in a Leningrad cemetery with his relatives and would have hated the idea of a mausoleum.

Note the mausoleum's limited working hours and be aware that it closes to give the waxen-looking body a touch-up and rebalming every 18 months or so. Also, the changing of the guard, once one of the main attractions, has moved to the Tomb of the Unknown Soldier and Eternal Flame in the Alexander Garden.

RESURRECTION GATES
Voskresenskiye Vorota
Воскресенские ворота
Btwn. Manezh Square and Red Square
METRO: Okhotny Ryad or Ploshchad Revolyutsii

The best way to enter Red Square is through the redbrick Resurrection Gates. If you're approaching from Okhotny Ryad metro station or Manezh Square, look for the redbrick structure with double archways and twin towers topped by golden double-headed eagles.

The Resurrection Gates, also known as the Gates of the Iberian Virgin or Iverskiye Vorota, were built in 1680 but demolished in 1931 to clear the way for tanks to enter Red Square for the annual May 9 Victory Day parades. What you see now is a 1994–1996 replica, albeit with a color change: The original gates were predominantly white, but now they're red with white trim. In the 18th century the gates housed a laboratory of the mint, a pharmacy, and a print house.

Between the gates' two archways is a small blue-domed chapel topped by a golden figure of Archangel Michael holding a cross. This is a 1990s reconstruction of the chapel built here in 1781 to house a copy of the miracle-working Icon of the Iberian Virgin, hence the gates' other name.

Before you go through the gates, you might spot a plaque on the ground marking the geographic center of Moscow. It's a local custom to

© NATHAN TOOHEY

the Resurrection Gates on Red Square

stand at this point and toss a coin over your head while making a wish. If beggars rush to grab your coin before it even hits the ground, just take consolation from the thought that one of their wishes is coming true even if yours doesn't. Also near this point you can pay to have your photo taken with some fairly convincing professional look-alikes of Lenin and Tsar Nicholas II.

Once you've entered Red Square via the gates, you will see a small church on your left. This is **Kazan Cathedral** (Kazansky sobor) or the Church of the Kazan Mother of God. It was originally built in 1633–1637, commissioned by Prince Dmitry Pozharsky to mark his and Kuzma Minin's 1612 victory over Polish invaders. It is named after the Our Lady of Kazan icon, credited by Pozharsky for helping in battle. Along with the Resurrection Gates, it was destroyed in the 1930s to clear the way for military parades, and rebuilt in the 1990s. It's a working church, so don't waltz inside talking loudly and snapping wildly with your camera. If you're an Orthodox Christian and appropriately dressed, you might like to go inside

and light a candle. There is an ecclesiastical store selling candles, small icons, crosses, and prayer rings.

◖ ST. BASIL'S CATHEDRAL

Khram Vasiliya Blazhennogo

Храм Василия Блаженного

2 Red Square, 495/698-3304, www.shm.ru

HOURS: May-Oct. Wed.-Mon. 10 A.M.-6 P.M., Nov.-Apr. Wed.-Mon. 11 A.M.-5 P.M.; closed last Mon. of month

COST: Adults 100R, children, students, and seniors 50R, amateur photo permit 130R, amateur video permit 150R; combined ticket including entry to the State History Museum—adults 230R, students 90R, seniors 85R, children 80R

METRO: Okhotny Ryad or Ploshchad Revolyutsii

Le Corbusier likened it to the delirious ravings of a drunken confectioner. Legend has it that Ivan the Terrible blinded the architect so he'd never outdo it. With its multi-colored onion domes, variously reminiscent of pineapples, soft-serve ice cream, and fairytale temples from *One Thousand and One Nights,* St. Basil's Cathedral is truly a sight to behold.

Built 1555–1561, it was commissioned by Ivan IV (the Terrible) to commemorate the defeat of the Tatar khanate of Kazan. The story about the architect's blinding is probably untrue: historical records say the two most likely architects, Postnik Yakovlev and Barma, subsequently worked on other projects including the Kazan Kremlin.

Although St. Basil's is the most commonly used name, it's more correctly called the Cathedral of the Intercession on the Moat (sobor Pokrova chto Na Rvu, or Pokrovsky sobor). Previously there was a moat between the cathedral and the Kremlin wall.

Another misconception about St. Basil's is that it is one church. Actually, it is a cluster of nine on a single foundation, with the Cathedral of the Intercession being the tallest one with the smallest dome. A chapel dedicated to the holy fool St. Basil and housing his grave was added in 1588, hence the popular name.

The UNESCO World Heritage–listed complex has renewed its religious function but is also a branch of the State History Museum.

THE KREMLIN AND RED SQUARE **65**

It is well worth going inside it to see the wonderfully atmospheric interiors with their splendid icons, floral-painted walls, and vaulted ceilings.

The State History Museum itself (covered in the *Museums* section of the *Arts and Leisure* chapter) is the red-brick building at the opposite end of Red Square from St. Basil's. The building was constructed 1874–1883 to a design by the architect Vladimir Osipovich Sherwood, son of an English engineer hired to build canals in Russia. Sherwood, a Russian whose name is often transliterated back from Cyrillic as Shervud, was a leading exponent of the Russian Revival style, of which the State History Museum is a good example.

The **Minin and Pozharsky statue** near St. Basil's is of Prince Dmitry Pozharsky and Kuzma Minin, who heroically rallied a volunteer army to liberate Moscow from Polish invaders in 1612. Built in 1818, it originally stood nearer to Kazan Cathedral. The statue was moved to the other end of the square in the 1930s as part of the renovations that saw the church and Resurrection Gates removed completely.

The circular stone platform with cast-iron gates near St. Basil's, called **Lobnoye Mesto,** is often said to have been an execution platform, but this is disputed. The platform dates from the early 17th century (and was originally in a slightly different spot), but there was a Lobnoye Mesto on the square as early as the 1520s and its main function was as a tribune for leaders to address the masses.

KREMLIN AND RED SQUARE SURROUNDS
ALEXANDER GARDEN
Alexandrovsky sad
Александровский сад
Btwn. the Kremlin's western wall and Manezhnaya Ulitsa
METRO: Alexandrovsky Sad

An ornate set of cast-iron gates, beside the Kremlin wall on Manezh Square, is the entrance to Alexander Garden, a verdant refuge in the city center. The gates symbolize the 1812

victory over Napoleon. Running all the way along the Kremlin's 865-meter-long western wall, the garden is abundantly furnished with ice-cream and soda stands, park benches and flower beds, and draws tourists and locals alike. In the warmer months, the Okhotny Ryad mall's restaurants open their verandas, which face the garden and Kremlin walls across a series of waterfalls decorated with fairy-tale sculptures by Zurab Tsereteli.

One of the city's first public parks, it was designed by architect Osip Bove and built 1819–1822 on the former bed of the Neglinka River, now underground. It includes a grotto by Bove (1841) and a steep hillside that's a popular place for sledding in winter.

Beside the Kremlin wall inside the garden is the solemn **Tomb of the Unknown Soldier** (Mogila Neizvestnogo soldata), a memorial to Soviet soldiers who died in World War II. It was unveiled in 1967, after ashes of an unknown soldier killed in 1941's Battle for Moscow were brought from a common grave

Alexander Garden

You'll find the ticket office and entrance to the Kremlin in Alexander Garden.

© NATHAN TOOHEY

in the city's north and buried at the Kremlin wall. The Eternal Flame, inside a bronze star, was lit by a torch with a flame brought from the memorial in St. Petersburg's Field of Mars. A granite slab on the gravestone reads, "Your name is unknown, your deeds are immortal." Every year on Victory Day, May 9, it is a tradition to lay flowers on the grave. Every day on the hour between 8 A.M. and 8 P.M. the **changing of the guard** provides a great photo op; the uniformed, high-kicking spectacle formerly took place outside Lenin's mausoleum on Red Square.

MANEZH SQUARE
Manezhnaya ploshchad
Манежная площадь
Btwn. Mokhovaya Ulitsa and Red Square
METRO: Okhotny Ryad

Manezh Square is a lively car-free expanse surrounded by a number of important landmarks, smack bang in the very center of the city. Moscow's main street, Tverskaya Ulitsa, begins at one end; opposite is the State History Museum, a statue of the legendary Soviet general Georgy Zhukov on horseback, and the Resurrection Gates onto Red Square. To one side is the reconstructed Moskva hotel, and on the other is Alexander Garden and the Manezh (manège—an indoor equestrian center) after which the square is now named. The square's friendly layout makes it a popular meeting spot and it's particularly pleasant on warm summer evenings when it seems half the city is hanging out here.

In the 17th century, the Moiseyevsky Convent and graveyard occupied this spot, but they were removed in 1789—clearly, Moscow's knock-down-and-rebuild habit goes back a long way. In the early 18th century, Peter the Great had ordered that the bird and game stalls of Okhotny Ryad (Hunters' Row) be moved to the area, hence the present name of a nearby street and the closest metro station. A trading hub called Moiseyevsky Square formed, with densely built little houses and alleys between them, but all this was wiped out with the creation of Manezh Square in 1932–1937. The

Neglinka River, which used to run between the present square and the Kremlin wall, was buried in a pipe underground in 1819.

A busy traffic intersection until the 1990s, Manezh Square was transformed into a pedestrian zone as part of a major redevelopment that included construction of the underground Okhotny Ryad mall. Digging to build the mall turned up a wealth of archaeological treasures, including chronological layers from the 12th–14th centuries, remains of Moiseyevsky Convent and graveyard, and the 16th–17th century Resurrection Bridge, which previously connected Red Square's Resurrection Gates with Tverskaya Ulitsa. It can all be seen in the square's underground **Moscow Archaeology Museum** (1A Manezhnaya Ploshchad, 495/692-4171, Tues.–Sun. 11 A.M.–9 P.M., 20–50R).

Manezh Square's name comes from the yellow-and-cream temple-form Neoclassical building at one end, beyond the underground Okhotny Ryad mall. It was originally constructed 1817–1825 to an innovative structural design by Spanish engineer Agustin de Betancourt, with its exterior by architect Osip Bove. Intended as a manège or indoor equestrian academy, it has been an exhibition hall since 1831. It was rebuilt after a fire in 2004.

PASHKOV HOUSE
Dom Pashkova
Дом Пашкова
26 Mokhovaya Ulitsa
METRO: Borovitskaya

The grandiose Pashkov House, standing high on a hill facing the Kremlin's Borovitskaya tower, has been considered one of the city's most beautiful buildings ever since its construction to a design by architect Vasily Bazhenev in 1784–1786. The classical-style palace, replete with columns and urns, was

© NATHAN TOOHEY

Pashkov House

commissioned by the rich landowner Pyotr Pashkov. Heavily damaged by fire during Napoleon's 1812 invasion, it was later acquired by the government, renovated and turned into a school, then a library, then a museum, then a library once again. Regular visitors are said to have included writers Leo Tolstoy and Mikhail Bulgakov. Designated an architectural landmark, it houses the Russian State Library's rare books collection and has been undergoing renovations for several years. The house features in Bulgakov's novel *The Master and Margarita;* this is where Woland and Azazello are described as having been "at sunset, high over the city, on the stone terrace of one of the most beautiful houses in Moscow"—a vantage point from where nobody could see them but they could see practically the whole city.

Other sights close by include the **Russian State Library** (3/5 Ulitsa Vozdvizhenka, 495/202-5790, www.rsl.ru), the largest library in the country and one of the largest in the world. The tall building with a seated statue of writer Fyodor Dostoyevsky is the library's new building; its old building is Pashkov House. Boasting a 19-story book depository, the new library building was constructed 1928–1958. The closest metro station, Biblioteka imeni Lenina, is Russian for Lenin Library, its Soviet-era name.

REVOLUTION SQUARE
Ploshchad Revolyutsii
Площадь Революции
Btwn. Manezh Square and Theater Square
METRO: Ploshchad Revolyutsii

It's hard to picture it now, but the Neglinka River used to run through this square. Back in the 16th century there was a dike, a mill, flour stores, and a bridge with fruit and vegetable stalls clustered around it. On the river's left bank was an earthen rampart and the Kitaigorod wall—some of the wall's few remaining fragments can still be seen here. The square really only formed in the 19th century, after the river was buried and the ramparts were removed.

Now the square is paved and landscaped, merging seamlessly into Theater Square. A row of restaurants faces across towards the Bolshoi Theater, and their summer verandas are perfectly placed to catch the last sun rays in the evening.

THEATER SQUARE
Teatralnaya ploshchad
Театральная площадь
Beside Ulitsa Okhotny Ryad and Teatralny Proyezd, btwn. the Bolshoi Theater and Revolution Square
METRO: Teatralnaya

Divided into two parts by a busy road, Theater Square's northern half is dominated by the renowned Bolshoi Theater and an attractive garden with fountains and benches. The road—a transitional point between Ulitsa Okhotny Ryad and Teatralny Proyezd—can be crossed safely via a pedestrian underpass beside the Metropol Hotel. Attempting an over-ground crossing could be fatal; at the very least it would attract the attention of an angry whistle-blowing policeman. The southern half of the square, which actually seems more like a part of the surrounding Ploshchad Revolyutsii, has the reconstructed Moskva hotel to its west, the Metropol hotel to its east, and a **statue of Karl Marx** in the middle, unharmed by Russia's more recent revolution back to capitalism.

Marx leans determinedly out of a tribune-like granite block inscribed with the words "Proletarians of All Countries, Unite!" This Marx monument is the work of the renowned Socialist realist sculptor Lev Kerbel, whose other creations include the Vladimir Lenin statue near Moscow's Oktyabrskaya metro station, and the Karl Marx bust in the German city of Chemnitz, formerly Karl Marx Stadt. The festive unveiling of this statue in 1961 was attended by leading Communists and Socialists from all over the world.

Across the road, the Bolshoi Theater has been at this site since 1825. The grand classical-style building, by architects Osip Bove and Andrey Mikhailov, required rebuilding after a fire just 10 years after its construction. It has been under scaffolding since 2005, undergoing renovations scheduled to be completed by November 2009.

Kitay-Gorod, Lubyanka, and Chistye Prudy Map 2

CHISTYE PRUDY
Чистые пруды
Around the Boulevard Ring btwn. Bolshaya Lubyanka and Pokrovka Streets
METRO: Chistye Prudy

Chistoproudny Bulvar is a spacious strip of the Boulevard Ring graced by a large, attractive pond where ducks and swans swim in the summer and skaters take to the ice in the winter. It's the most popular part of the boulevard for hanging out, particularly among goths, who promenade on weekends in all their funereal finery. Rockers and other subcultures are also drawn to the park benches, where they hang out drinking beer and playing guitars. But anybody can join the scene— families with small children and local babushkas alike come here to stroll under the trees.

The name Chistye Prudy means Clean Ponds but you will only see one pond. It used to be called Pogany Prud or Foul Pond because the nearby slaughterhouses and meat traders used to dump waste in it. In 1703 it was cleaned up and the name changed.

KITAY-GOROD WALL
Kitaygorodskaya stena
Китайгородская стена
Revolution Square and Kitaygorodsky Proyezd
METRO: Ploshchad Revolyutsii or Kitay-Gorod

Kitay means China and *gorod* means city or town, but you won't find a Chinatown here. There are various theories to explain the name—for example, that it's because Kitay is Mongolian for wall, or that it comes from the Italian word *citta,* meaning city. Italians were involved in construction here from the 14th century and built the fortress wall that was erected around Kitay-Gorod in the 1530s. The Kitay-Gorod Wall was six meters high and six meters wide, with impressive gates and towers—but sadly it was mostly destroyed in the 1930s. What remains can be seen beside Ploshchad Revolyutsii metro station and along Kitaygorodsky Proyezd, which runs from the end of Varvarka Ulitsa towards the Moscow River. If you go down the stairs into the pedestrian underpass to Kitay-Gorod metro station at the corner of Kitaygorodsky Proyezd and Ulitsa Varvarka, you can spot a fragment of the wall's white stone Varvarskiye Gates.

LUBYANKA SQUARE
Lubyanskaya ploshchad
Лубянская площадь
At Lubyanka metro station
METRO: Lubyanka

The square is no longer named after Soviet secret police founder Felix Dzerzhinsky and his monumental statue is long gone from its center, but Lubyanka Square remains strongly associated with the security services. The ocher-colored building that dominates the square—formerly KGB headquarters and the notorious Lubyanka Prison—now houses offices of the Federal Security Service, or FSB, one of the KGB's successors and Russia's main domestic intelligence agency. In the courtyard of the FSB buildings across the road, you might spot the small yellow Church of St. Sofia of God's Wisdom—the FSB's own church, ironic as that might be given the service's origins in the atheist USSR. This is well and truly secret services territory: In addition to the former KGB headquarters, the FSB also has offices in neighboring buildings and up Ulitsa Bolshaya Lubyanka, which comes off the square.

Protesters toppled the "Iron Felix" statue from its pedestal in 1991, and the controversial, iconic work by Socialist realist sculptor Yevgeny Vuchetich found a new home in the Art Park Muzeon sculpture garden opposite Gorky Park. Now Lubyanka has a memorial to victims of political repression in the Soviet Union—a stone from the Solovetsky Islands in front of the Polytechnic Museum.

SYNODIAL PRINTING HOUSE
Sinodalnaya tipografiya
Синодальная типография
15 Nikolskaya Ulitsa

METRO: Ploshchad Revolyutsii

Although Nikolskaya Ulitsa has acquired gleaming new malls and boutiques in recent years, it was traditionally a street of spiritual and intellectual enlightenment: This is where Russia's first book and newspaper were printed and where Russia's first institute of higher learning opened; in the 19th century it boasted 26 of the city's 31 bookstores. Look out for No. 15, an ornate light-green-and-white building with a lion, unicorn, sundial, and hammer and sickle on the facade. Moscow's first state print house, Pechatny Dvor (Printing Courtyard), was founded at this site in the mid-16th century; Ivan Fyodorov printed Russia's first book, *The Acts of the Apostles,* here in 1564. The first public newspaper followed in 1703. The original buildings burned down in the 17th century and what you see now is the Synodial Printing House building, dated 1811–1815, inhabited by the Russian State Humanitarian University. It's not open to the public as a museum but is interesting to look at from the outside.

ZAIKONOSPASSKY MONASTERY
Zaykonospassky monastyr
Заиконоспасский монастырь
7-9 Nikolskaya Ulitsa
METRO: Ploshchad Revolyutsii

One of the main sights on Nikolskaya Ulitsa is this fascinating monastery. Nikolsky Monastery was founded here in the 14th century, and it became Nikolo-Grechesky Monastery after the arrival of Greek monks in the 16th century. In 1600, Tsar Boris Godunov founded Spassky Monastery on its territory; later Spassky was renamed Zaikonospassky because of its icon stalls. Moscow's first institute of higher education, the Slavic Greek Latin Academy, was founded in the courtyard in 1687. If you go through the gateway you can see the four-tiered red-and-white 17th-century Spassky Cathedral. Other remaining buildings include the 17th-century teachers' corpus and an 1822 school building. Although worship has resumed in the cathedral and there's a Sunday School on the territory, some unrelated institutions occupy some of the buildings. There are plans to revive full monastic functions.

The Center and Inner Northwest   Map 3

CHURCH OF THE GREAT ASCENSION
Bolshoye Vozneseniye Church
Церковь Большое Вознесение
Ploshchad Nikitskiye Vorota
METRO: Pushkinskaya or Barrikadnaya

The poet Alexander Pushkin married the beautiful Natalya Goncharova in this then-unfinished church in 1831. Ominously, the wedding ring was dropped during the ceremony, eliciting whispers of "bad sign"—and six years later he died in a duel defending her honor. All the same, the rotunda out front with a fountain and a statue of the couple is a popular spot for romance. Stop by and admire the ensemble from the outside.

The church's construction began in the 1790s under Matvey Kazakov but it was only finished in 1840, with its design amended along the way by Osip Bove. The bell tower was built in 2003, in place of a late-17th-century one

that had been part of an earlier church but that was demolished in the anti-religious 1930s. It is said that the original bell tower didn't match the style of the newer Bolshoye Vozneseniye anyway, and the new bell tower follows previously unrealized early-19th-century designs. Neither the church nor the bell tower are open to casual visitors.

HERMITAGE GARDEN
Sad Ermitazh
Сад Эрмитаж
3 Ulitsa Karetny Ryad
METRO: Mayakovskaya

A popular spot to ice skate in winter or stroll in the summer, Hermitage Garden has been a theatrical center since the late 19th century. The garden contains several theaters, including Novaya Opera, as well as restaurants, bars, and clubs. Hermitage Garden claims a number of firsts: Moscow's first cinema screening was held here in 1896, and Stanislavsky and Nemirovich-Danchenko's Moscow Art Theater debuted here in the Hermitage Theater in 1898. A series of super-elite nightclubs occupied the Shchukinskaya Stage building until a fire put an end to all that decadence in 2008.

MOSCOW ZOO
Moskovsky zoopark
Московский зоопарк

1 Bolshaya Gruzinskaya Ulitsa, 495/252-3580,
www.moscowzoo.ru

HOURS: Tues.-Sun. 10 A.M.-8 P.M. in summer,
10 A.M.-5 P.M. in winter

COST: Adults 150R, children and students free,
amateur video permit 25R

METRO: Krasnopresnenskaya or Barrikadnaya

Founded in 1864, the Moscow Zoo has been beautifully renovated and extended, and is likely to exceed visitors' expectations. Decorated with animal statues by the city's favorite sculptor, Zurab Tsereteli, and nicely landscaped with several ponds, it has two sections, with the bridge between them featuring a winding staircase around an open-roofed macaque enclosure. The zoo has kept polar bears since 1889 and continues to successfully breed them—the baby polar bears are a particularly popular attraction. The wild cat collection is also strong, with white tigers, snow leopards, leopards, cheetahs, jaguars, lynxes, and more. Other animals you can see include orangutans, gorillas, gibbons, kangaroos, emus, flamingos, and elephants. There is a special children's zoo section, with rides and amusements, as well as farmyard animals plus a special selection of creatures that the little ones may have heard about in their bedtime stories: a wolf, a fox, goats, and a stork.

PATRIARCH'S PONDS
Patriarshiye Prudy
Патриаршие пруды

Malaya Bronnaya Ulitsa, btwn. Yermolayevsky
Pereulok and Bolshoy Patriarshy Pereulok

METRO: Pushkinskaya or Barrikadnaya

Patriarch's Ponds has cult status among those who've read Mikhail Bulgakov's fantastical novel *The Master and Margarita,* since the opening scene is set here and the author lived nearby. There's a Margarita restaurant on the square, and the Bulgakov House Cultural Center is nearby on the Garden Ring. But even if you're not familiar with Bulgakov, it's worth exploring this peaceful oasis, which seems far from the traffic even though it's right in the city center. In the winter, skaters take to the ice. In the summer, teenagers flirt on the park benches and children fill the playground. Near the playground is a statue of poet Ivan Krylov and sculptures of animal characters from his fables.

In any season, it's soothing to stroll around this elegant pond surrounded by mature linden trees and some of the inner city's most desirable (and expensive) real estate. But this area wasn't always so classy; it used to be called Goat's Swamp. Then, in the 17th century, the Patriarch's residence was established here and three ponds created out of the swamps to supply fish. Over the years the ponds slid into a state of neglect, until the early 19th century when two were filled in, one was cleaned up and reinforced, and the graceful square was created around it.

PUSHKIN SQUARE
Pushkinskaya ploshchad
Пушкинская площадь

Intersection of Tverskaya Ulitsa and the Boulevard Ring

METRO: Pushkinskaya

Pushkin Square is a symbol of Moscow. While Red Square is unquestionably the city's most important square and its geographical center, it's too touristy and official for the locals. For Muscovites, Pushkin Square is the city's true heart.

The main landmark on Pushkin Square is—you guessed it—a statue of the great poet Alexander Pushkin. As natural as he looks in this setting, he was actually moved here in 1950 from his original position on the opposite site of the square. Literary greats including Fyodor Dostoyevsky and Ivan Turgenev gave speeches at the statue's festive opening in 1880.

MOSCOW RIVER CRUISES

For a perfect introduction to the Russian capital, cruise the Moscow River on a riverboat. The best route starts at the pier near the Kievskaya metro station, where boats depart every 20 minutes from 11 A.M.–9 P.M. daily in the warmer months, roughly from early May through October. The 90-minute journey passes such sights as the Kremlin, Moscow State University, Gorky Park, and Christ the Savior Cathedral. There are several stops along the way, including one at the chairlift that takes you up to the lookout at Vorobyovy Gory, another at the back gate of Gorky Park, and one near the Kremlin. The final stop is at Novospassky Bridge, near Novospassky Monastery. Of course, you can also ride in the opposite direction, or between any of the stops along the route. There's a café on board, so you can grab a beer to sip as you sun yourself on the deck. If the weather is wet, you can sit inside. There are toilet facilities for your convenience.

For more information contact Stolichnaya Sudokhodnaya Kompaniya (495/225-6070, 499/257-3484, www.cck-ship.ru). Ticket prices change each season; in 2008 the fare was 400R for adults and 150R for children 5-12 (under 5 are free) for a single ride. If you get off, you need to buy a whole new ticket to get back on again, unless you buy a full-day pass for roughly 650R.

A riverboat cruise is the perfect way to see Moscow's sights.

The area around the statue is a favorite meeting point for Muscovites.

Where Pushkin now stands there used to be a tall bell tower, part of the 17th-century Strastnoy Monastery, which was destroyed in 1934. Behind Pushkin, in place of the monastery, there is now a fountain and the Pushkinsky Movie Theater. The small white church near the cinema is the Tserkov Rozhdestva Bogoroditsy v Putinkakh, considered a 17th-century masterpiece. Another sight on the square is the Izvestia newspaper building, a striking asymmetrical Constructivist creation from 1927 that now boasts a Benihana among other eateries in its new restaurant "multicomplex."

You might spot a memorial plaque and

flowers in the Pushkin Square pedestrian underpass on the corner of Tverskaya Ulitsa and Strastnoy Bulvar—they mark the site of a horrific bomb blast in August 2000 that killed 13 people and injured more than 100.

TVERSKAYA SQUARE
Tverskaya ploshchad
Тверская площадь
Halfway up Tverskaya Ulitsa btwn. the Kremlin and the boulevard
METRO: Tverskaya or Okhotny Ryad

You can identify this square by the giant statue of Prince Yury Dolgoruky on horseback. Dolgoruky could be translated as "the Long-Armed" and here he commandingly gestures with a suitably lengthy limb. The city's first written mention was when he met another prince here in 1147; he is considered to be Moscow's founder. The statue was erected in 1954, replacing an obelisk to the Soviet Constitution and a Statue of Liberty in the form of a Greek goddess.

Dolgoruky faces City Hall across the road at No. 13 Tverskaya Ulitsa, a 1778–1782 building by architect Matvey Kazakov with a 1946 addition by Dmitry Chechulin—the city powers have ruled from here since the late 18th century. On Dolgoruky's left-hand side is the green-topped Church of Kosma and Damian in Shubin, built in 1625. Behind Dolgoruky is a fountain and square that was a hangout for *stilyagi,* or Soviet mods, in the 1950s, and hippies in the 1970s; now it usually has a beer garden in the summer and is a lovely spot to stop for a cold brew.

TVERSKAYA STREET
Tverskaya ulitsa
Тверская улица
From the Kremlin to Triumfalnaya Ploshchad
METRO: Pushkinskaya

Tverskaya Ulitsa is Moscow's main street, its equivalent of Paris's Champs Élysées. You haven't really been to Moscow until you've taken a walk along this bustling street to feel the Russian capital's unique vibe.

Tverskaya Ulitsa dates back to the 12th century as the road to the city Tver. In the 18th century it gained status as the road to the new capital in the north, St. Petersburg, and became an important trading street. Its wooden houses were replaced with stone ones after the 1812 fire and most of its medieval churches were destroyed in the 1920s and '30s. From 1935 to 1990 it was called Ulitsa Gorkogo (Gorky Street).

In 1938–1939, the street was widened. Old buildings were either knocked down and replaced with new Stalinist ones, or, in an incredible feat of engineering, picked up and moved back. If you go into the courtyard behind the Stalinist block at No. 6 you can see one that was moved—**Savvinskoye Podvorye.** Built in 1907, it stands out with its colorfully tiled facade combining old Russian elements with art nouveau. Previously this graceful house faced right onto the narrower Tverskaya, but in a single night in 1939 the 23,000-ton structure was shifted to new foundations in the courtyard without any of the residents even having to move out.

Tverskaya Ulitsa has more fascinating objects than can be listed here; likewise the lanes that run off it all have their points of interest. The street is lined with restaurants, cafés, and boutiques and other stores, as well as architectural landmarks and major monuments, so you can shop, grab a snack, and do some sightseeing at the same time.

VYSOKOPETROVSKY MONASTERY
Vysoko-Petrovsky monastyr
Высоко-Петровский монастырь
28/2 Ulitsa Petrovka, 495/209-1310, 495/923-7580
HOURS: Daily 9 A.M.-7 P.M.
COST: Free
METRO: Chekhovskaya

The hilltop red-brick walls and gold-domed bell tower that stand out as Ulitsa Petrovka's main landmark belong to Vysokopetrovsky Monastery, first mentioned in 1377. The Naryshkin boyars, family of Peter the Great's mother, established their burial vault here in the late 17th century, and the monastery was mostly rebuilt in so-called Naryshkin

Baroque style. This former monastery was closed in 1929 but returned to the church in 1992 and is now a patriarchal estate. A diagram on the wall by the entrance shows what's to see inside: a picturesque collection of a half-dozen churches and cathedrals dating from the 16th–18th centuries. The oldest remaining structure is the Cathedral to St. Peter, a modest-looking red rotunda built 1514–1517. The multi-tiered, gold-domed bell tower over the gates dates to 1690, as do the red walls containing the monastic cells and Naryshkin chambers.

THE WHITE HOUSE (GOVERNMENT HOUSE)

Bely dom (Dom pravitelstva)

Белый дом (Дом правительства)

12 Krasnopresnenskaya Naberezhnaya

METRO: Krasnopresnenskaya

Commonly referred to as the White House, this iconic building is the government headquarters. Previously it housed the Supreme Soviet, and later the parliament. Many will recognize it from the dramatic images broadcast around the world at two key moments in Russia's recent history. In August 1991, the White House was the headquarters of resistance during Communist hardliners' attempted coup against Soviet president Mikhail Gorbachev. Boris Yeltsin, the new president of the Russian republic, famously climbed onto a tank in front of the White House to rally the crowds and the military to resist the coup-plotters. And in October 1993, after parliament members barricaded themselves inside to protest then president Boris Yeltsin's decree disbanding the Communist-dominated parliament, tanks loyal to Yeltsin fired at the building, and soldiers stormed it. More than 100 people died in associated clashes and a memorial to them can be seen behind the White House on Druzhinnikovskaya Ulitsa.

Arbat and Kropotkinskaya   Map 4

🌒 ARBAT STREET (THE OLD ARBAT)

Ulitsa Arbat

Улица Арбат

From Ploshchad Arbatskiye Vorota to Smolenskaya Ploshchad

METRO: Arbatskaya or Smolenskaya

Ulitsa Arbat is informally referred to as Old or Stary Arbat, to distinguish it from New or Novy Arbat. The two Arbats couldn't be more different from each other.

The old Arbat is a pedestrian street that starts a short walk from the Kremlin and leads all the way to the Garden Ring at Smolenskaya Ploshchad, where the Foreign Affairs Ministry's Stalin skyscraper looms Gotham City–like overhead. Lined with shops, cafés, restaurants, and bars in beautiful old houses, Ulitsa Arbat has for many years been the most touristy part of Moscow outside Red Square. It was famed for being crowded with stalls selling every souvenir you might dream of taking home from Russia, but in 2008 city authorities decided to kick out the souvenir sellers and replace them with book stalls. The indoor souvenir stores along the street remain.

But the Arbat is more than just a kitschy tourist trap. It's a symbol of Moscow, with a cultish bohemian image. It has its own scene—in fact, more than one. There's a rock scene. There's a break-dancing scene. There are street performers and musicians. There are dozens of artists who will paint your portrait, a funny caricature, or something saccharine in romantic pastels, just take your pick.

Ulitsa Arbat has a long history. The street formed in the 14th–15th centuries as the way to the city of Smolensk, but earlier the name Arbat referred to a whole area stretching from the Kremlin to the present Garden Ring. The first written mention in 1493 was associated with a terrible fire that started in a church here and destroyed much of the city.

The origins of the name are a mystery, since

Arbat is not a Russian word and there is no agreement about which language it comes from. It is often said to come from *rabad* or *rabat,* Arabic for "the suburbs." Another theory says it's from *arba,* a Turkic word for a carriage.

Although it's touristy, a walk up the Arbat and around its alleys is worth fitting into your Moscow itinerary. It's a colorful street with good architecture and some interesting sights. You can check out the souvenir stores and stop for lunch or a drink—the eateries are not bad value for Moscow, there are plenty of cheap spots, and the summer terraces are great for people-watching.

CHRIST THE SAVIOR CATHEDRAL
Khram Khrista Spasitelya
Храм Христа Спасителя
15-17 Ulitsa Volkhonka, 495/203-3823, 495/924-8058, 495/924-8490, www.xxc.ru
HOURS: Tues.-Sun. 10 A.M.-5 P.M., Mon. 1-5 P.M.; museum daily 10 A.M.-6 P.M.; closed last Mon. of month
COST: Entrance to the lookout tower 170R, amateur photo permit 560R, amateur video permit 900R
METRO: Kropotkinskaya

Christ the Savior Cathedral stands beside the Moscow River a short distance from the Kremlin, a 1990s reconstruction of a 19th-century cathedral that was blown up in 1931 to make way for the grandiose—but never built—Palace of Soviets.

The original Neo-Byzantine–style cathedral was constructed 1839–1883 by architect Konstantin Ton. The project had been initiated by an 1812 manifesto from Tsar Alexander I calling for a cathedral to be built to thank God for saving Russia from Napoleon's attack, but the location, design, architect, and tsar all changed before work finally began.

At 102 meters tall, it was Moscow's tallest ecclesiastical structure. Among many significant events to have taken place in its ornate interior was the debut of Pyotr Ilich Tchaikovsky's *1812 Overture* on August 20, 1882.

The cathedral was dynamited on December 5, 1931, and work began on the colossal Palace of Soviets that was supposed to take its place. The planned 400-meter-high tower topped by an 80-meter-high statue of Vladimir Lenin was not to be, however: World War II interrupted construction, and the huge hole where the cathedral once stood became the Moskva swimming pool instead.

A popular movement to rebuild the original Christ the Savior Cathedral gained support and donations in the late 1980s and early 1990s. It was finally approved by the Moscow city

ARBAT'S TSOI AND PEACE WALLS

As you stroll along Ulitsa Arbat, pause near No. 37, on the corner of Krivoarbatsky Pereulok, to take in an icon of popular culture. The unfading popularity of the 1980s Soviet rock idol Viktor Tsoi is palpable at the graffiti-covered wall at the beginning of the lane, a mecca for fans of the charismatic star who was killed in a car crash in 1990. Tsoi, born in Leningrad, was the singer and songwriter for the hugely popular rock group Kino, whose songs became anthems of glasnost- and perestroika-era youth. He died at the peak of his career at the age of 28, just two months after Kino's legendary last concert for an audience of 62,000 in Moscow's Luzhniki stadium. An unofficial memorial, the Viktor Tsoi wall has been painted over but always comes back. Moves to make it official and erect a Tsoi statue were thwarted by local residents who complained that it was already attracting more than enough noisy youths.

Another noteworthy wall on the Arbat is the Peace Wall, located opposite No. 23. The Peace Wall is a wall of tiles painted by Soviet and U.S. children as a symbol of friendship back in 1990, a time of optimism, perestroika, glasnost and "Gorby-fever." About 7,000 young people aged 10-18 took part in the year-long project to create the wall, which is a block long and about two meters high. The passions of those days may have faded, but the love keeps spreading around the globe thanks to the World Wall for Peace project.

ARBAT AREA ALLEYS: FAMOUS INHABITANTS AND NOTABLE HOUSES

The lanes around the Arbat are fascinating – detailing all the objects of potential interest would require an encyclopedic tome. Here are some selected highlights.

At 10 Krivoarbatsky Pereulok (the same lane that boasts the Tsoi wall), you can see an architectural landmark known as the **Melnikov House.** It's not open to the public, but those with an interest in architecture should take a look through the fence. This strikingly original house was built by the prominent avant-garde architect Konstantin Melnikov in 1927-1929 as his family home and studio – the only private house built in Soviet Moscow. Seeking to create the greatest amount of internal space inside walls of minimal external height, he came up with an innovative design that takes an experimental approach to living space. Behind its flat, glassed facade, the house consists of two interlocking cylindrical towers decorated with a geometrical pattern of vertically stretched hexagonal windows. Melnikov's son lived in the house until his death in 2006, after which surviving relatives fought over ownership of the property. The new owners have said they intend to turn it into a museum.

Wander through Arbat's lanes and you might spot such oddities as the wooden **Porokhovshchikov House** (26 Starokonyushenny Pereulok), built in the style of an old-style peasant hut in 1870 for the Society of Russian Doctors. Or, you might spot the **"house with erotic authors"** (4/5 Plotnikov Pereulok) – reputedly a former bordello, decorated with a frieze depicting men who inexplicably resemble various great writers cavorting with young women. See if you can spot anyone you know, such as Nikolay Gogol, Alexander Pushkin, or Leo Tolstoy.

Parallel to the Arbat is **Sivtsev Vrazhek Pereulok,** where you can visit the house museum of 19th-century socialist philosopher Alexander Herzen (27 Sivtsev Vrazhek Pereulok, 495/241-5859, 11 A.M.-6 P.M. Tues., Thurs., and Sat.-Sun., 1 P.M.-6 P.M. Wed. and Fri., 40R). Writer Sergei Yesenin and American dancer

Isadora Duncan lived at No. 42; Leo Tolstoy lived at No. 34 and depicted it in *War and Peace;* Nobel Prize-winning author Mikhail Sholokhov lived at No. 33; and poet Marina Tsvetayeva lived at No. 19.

On the other side of the Arbat, on Spasopeskovsky Pereulok, is the 17th-century **Church of the Transfiguration on the Sands** (Tserkov Spasa Preobrazheniya na Peskakh), immortalized in Vasily Polenov's 19th-century painting *Moscow Courtyard* – though naturally the surrounding landscape was dramatically different then. On the same street is a New Empire-style mansion, **Spaso House** (10 Spasopeskovskaya Square), built in 1914 for a wealthy merchant, and the residence of U.S. ambassadors in Moscow since 1933. Nearby is the **house museum of the composer Alexander Scriabin** (7 Nikolopeskovsky Pereulok, 495/241-1901, 495/241-1900, Wed. and Fri. noon-7 P.M., Thurs., Sat., Sun. 10 A.M.-5 P.M., closed Mon., Tues. and last Fri, of each month, 30R).

the "house with erotic authors"

government and construction began in 1994, completed in 1999. Although it was initially supposed to be a replica, a number of changes were introduced, such as bronze sculptures on the outside instead of the original marble reliefs. It is the Russian Orthodox Church's largest cathedral, standing 103 meters tall, with space for 10,000 people.

Inside you can admire the intricately frescoed walls rising up to the soaring high ceiling, where images of biblical beings look down from the heavens inside the dome. The lookout tower is worth buying tickets to, given the church's height and its impressive location beside the Moscow River; it towers over the old center, close to major sights such as the Kremlin. This is one of the churches where visitors are nothing out of the ordinary, and even during services the presence of tourists is unlikely to surprise the worshippers, but do dress appropriately if you are going to a service (daily 8 A.M. and 5 P.M.). The biggest services of the year are when the Patriarch leads Moscow's main midnight mass here for Orthodox Christmas and Easter, as well as Christmas Day and Easter Sunday services—but you're unlikely to get much of a glimpse of the goings-on, given their massive popularity and the presence of television crews as well as countless VIPs.

MOROZOV'S MANSION
Dom Morozova
Дом Морозова
16 Ulitsa Vozdvizhenka
METRO: Arbatskaya

One of Moscow's most unusual buildings stands opposite Arbatskaya metro station on Ulitsa Vozdvizhenka, between the Kremlin and the Arbat. A white castle-like mansion decorated with stylized shells, it was commissioned by the eccentric millionaire Arseny Morozov and built 1894–1899 by architect Viktor Mazyrin. Its Moorish styling was inspired by Morozov and Mazyrin's architectural research trip, in which they were particularly struck by the Castle of the Moors in Sintra outside Lisbon, Portugal, and the Casa de

© NATHAN TOOHEY

Christ the Savior Cathedral

las Conchas in Salamanca, Spain. After the 1917 Revolution it housed the Proletkult theater, where Vsevolod Meyerhold and Sergei Eisenstein staged radical performances and Vladimir Mayakovsky read his poetry. Later it served as the embassy of various countries before becoming the House of Friendship with the Peoples of Foreign Countries. In 2006 it was renovated to become the Reception Building of the Russian Government, and hosted high-profile meetings during Russia's presidency of the Group of Eight. The mansion is not open to the general public, but there's plenty to admire from the outside.

Zamoskvorechye
Map 5

✪ ART PARK MUZEON
Park Iskusstv Muzeon
Парк Искусств Музеон
10 Krymsky Val Ul., 495/238-3679, 495/238-3396,
www.muzeon.ru
HOURS: Daily 9 A.M.–9 P.M.
COST: Russians 20R, foreigners 100R
METRO: Oktyabrskaya

Park Iskusstv Muzeon is a sculpture garden that punches well above its weight. Regularly cited by tourists as one of the more memorable highlights of their time in the capital, it is nonetheless often overlooked by locals when compiling a "must-see" list for Moscow. Originally conceived as an extension of Gorky Park with a stadium, it later went on to be a contender as a site for the Palace of the Soviets, the Soviet Academy of Sciences, the Trade Ministry and an international banks complex. It wasn't until the 1970s that it was finally settled upon to build the Central House of Artists and the New Tretyakov at this location.

At first glance the garden might seem simply like an afterthought—a leftover green space that surrounds the block-like Central House of Artists. It has, however, been displaying sculpture since the early 1980s and in 1990 it was designated as a sculpture garden. Yet it was the revolutionary events of the early 1990s that led to its becoming a major drawing card for foreign tourists. Statues of various notorious Soviet figures who had fallen out of favor were dismantled from around town and sent into retirement at the Park Iskusstv Muzeon. Among the statues put out to pasture are Dzerzhinsky, Kalinin, Stalin, and lots of Lenins (to see a Lenin in its natural habitat, head a short distance up the road to Kaluzhskaya Square near Oktyabrskaya metro station, where he still reigns in all his splendor).

Besides being a glorious graveyard for fallen monuments, the garden also displays a wonderful collection of contemporary sculptures. Hidden among the collection is one of Moscow's finest outdoor beer gardens, a perfect place to rehydrate after a long stroll on a warm summer's day.

BOLOTNAYA SQUARE
Bolotnaya ploshchad
Болотная площадь
Beside Bolotnaya Naberezhnaya
METRO: Tretyakovskaya

Literally Swamp Square, this was once a marshy meadow. From the 15th to 17th centuries, it was a market square where public fistfights took place, as well as public punishments and executions. The last execution here was in January 1775, when Yemelyan Pugachyov, leader of a Cossack rebellion and pretender to the throne, was beheaded and quartered. At his execution site there is now a fountain with metal details made from trophy weapons captured from German soldiers.

Now, the square is a landscaped park with colorful flower beds, fancy fountains, and some interesting statues. At the end of the park is an interesting sculpture by émigré artist Mikhail Shemyakin called *Children, Victims of Adults' Sins*. It depicts two gilded, blindfolded children surrounded by 13 bronze figures representing deadly sins such as ignorance, theft, and drunkenness.

A sculpture of artist Ilya Repin stands near the Luzhkov Bridge, which leads to Lavrushinsky Pereulok and the Tretyakov Gallery. On the bridge is a metal tree, where couples hang padlocks marked with their initials on their wedding day. Usually the area is crowded with brides in white and their wedding parties, as well as busloads of tourists on Tretyakov Gallery excursions.

HOUSE ON THE EMBANKMENT
Dom na naberezhnoy
Дом на набережной
2 Ulitsa Serafimovicha/20 Bersenevskaya Naberezhnaya
METRO: Borovitskaya

An imposing gray apartment building topped with an enormous Mercedes Benz logo can be seen across the Moscow River from the Kremlin. This is the infamous House on the Embankment, a symbol of Stalinist terror.

Designed by architect Boris Iofan and completed in 1931, the oppressively monumental block was built especially to house the elite. The 500 apartments were endowed with such luxuries as year-round hot water, central heating, and telephones at a time when there were only 1,000 other working numbers in the whole city. Living in the 11-story house was a dubious honor, however: Having fallen out of favor, hundreds of its 1930s residents were either executed or sent to the gulag. For Muscovites, the mere mention of this house conjures images of midnight arrests and walls with ears. The place was crawling with agents and one apartment was specially wired to monitor every phone line. Some residents said they could hear voices behind the walls—and after Stalin's death, secret corridors were found between apartments. Plaques dedicated to its illustrious residents, many of whom died during Stalin's purges, adorn its walls.

With stunning views of the Moscow River, the Kremlin, and Christ the Savior Cathedral, the gloomily grandiose Constructivist building remains a prestigious address. Besides apartments, it houses a theater, a cinema, a couple of restaurants, and a supermarket. In the first entryway is an apartment converted into a **museum about the building's history,** open Wednesday 5–8 P.M. and Saturday 2–5 P.M., but only if arranged in advance (495/959-0317, www.museum.ru/m427).

PETER THE GREAT STATUE
Pamyatnik Petry I
Памятник Петру I
On the Moscow River, across from Art Park Muzeon, on the tip of Bolotny Island
METRO: Kropotkinskaya

Standing at 96 meters, this Peter the Great statue ranks as the sixth-tallest statue in the world—taller than the Statue of Liberty, and the tallest outside of Asia. Its creator, Zurab Tsereteli, is a prolific sculptor who has produced many works both inside and out of Russia, including his 2006 10-story-high *Tear of Grief,* a memorial to September 11 victims located at the Peninsula at Bayonne Harbor in New Jersey.

This statue, which was made to mark 300 years of the Russian fleet, depicts an oversized Peter I clutching a scroll in his outstretched arm while standing atop an undersized frigate. To say that the statue has some detractors would be an understatement. It came close to never being finished: Seven plastic explosive devices wired around its base were discovered and disarmed only months before its completion. A Communist splinter group later claimed responsibility, citing revenge for plans to remove Lenin from his tomb. To this day people criticize it for its inappropriate location and Disney-like styling.

GORKY PARK

Park Gorkogo

Парк Горького

9 Ulitsa Krymsky Val, 495/237-0707

HOURS: Daily 24 hours

COST: 80R

METRO: Oktyabrskaya

Gorky Park, or Park Kultury i Otdykha imeni Gorkogo as it's officially known in Russian, is perhaps better known in the West than it is in Russia itself following the success of Martin Cruz Smith's eponymous book and the film that followed. Opened in 1928, it was originally called a rather revolutionary "Combine of Culture in the Fresh Air" and only in 1932 was it renamed after Soviet author Maxim Gorky.

Facing onto Ulitsa Krymsky Val are Gorky Park's grand gates, which were added in 1955. Tickets to enter the park are sold from small windows located in the wings of these gates. Just inside the gates is the Strobe Light Fountain, a large rectangular pool with jets of water

© NATHAN TOOHEY

paddleboating in Gorky Park

shooting up from its center. Come August 2, Paratrooper Day, the fountain serves as a meeting point for inebriated veteran paratroops to trade tales, and fisticuffs, while cooling off in its waters—a sight probably worth missing.

Past the fountain, and the cafés that surround it, are the amusement rides and shooting galleries. By the river, there is a test unit from the Buran space shuttle program, now serving as an amusement ride itself. Beyond the fun park is arguably the most pleasant part of the park—the duck ponds. This is Gorky Park's greenest area and during summer numerous outdoor cafés open around the ponds providing cheap draft beer, shish kebabs, and views of the paddle boats cruising about. The summer café by the old fountain at the back gate does a particularly fine kebab.

◾ NOVODEVICHY CONVENT

Novodevichy monastyr

Новодевичий монастырь

1 Novodevichy Proyezd, 499/246-5607

HOURS: Daily summer 10 A.M.–5:30 P.M., ticket office until 5 P.M., winter 10 A.M.–5:15 P.M., ticket office until 4:45 P.M.

COST: Russians 100R, foreigners 150R

METRO: Sportivnaya

The spectacular Novodevichy Convent has remained largely intact since the 17th century and in 2004 was listed as a UNESCO World Heritage site. The convent was founded in 1524 by Grand Prince Vasily III to commemorate the seizure of Smolensk from the Lithuanians. It is well known for having accepted many noble ladies who had fallen out of favor, such as Fyodor I's wife, Irina Godunova, and Peter the Great's sister Sofia Alexeyevna along with his first wife, Yevdokiya Lopukhina. It featured in numerous examples of 19th-century fiction, such as the site of Pierre's proposed execution in Tolstoy's *War and Peace,* and as the place where Lyovin and Kitty meet in *Anna Karenina.* After a long history of sheltering orphans and abandoned children, in 1922 it was

© NATHAN TOOHEY

Beside Novodevichy Convent is a duckling sculpture that then U.S. First Lady Barbara Bush presented to then Russian First Lady Raisa Gorbachev in 1991. It is a replica of a bronze statue in Boston Public Garden, *Make Way for Ducklings* by Nancy Schon.

closed by the Communists and turned into a women's emancipation museum. The renowned Constructivist artist Vladimir Tatlin was granted its bell tower to use as a studio, where he created his *Letatlin* sculpture. In various stages over the subsequent decades, it slowly resumed religious functions and from 1994 it once again held religious services.

The convent is surrounded by a formidable wall, which is punctuated by 12 red-and-white towers. The classically Moscow Baroque Gate Church of the Transfiguration serves as the entrance. Inside, the grounds are dominated by the large five-domed Our Lady of Smolensk Cathedral (1524–1525), which was built to resemble the Kremlin's Assumption Cathedral. Other notable buildings include the red-and-white Church of the Assumption and the refectory, the 72-meter-high bell

tower, and the south gate church, all of which demonstrate variations of the same Moscow Baroque style found in the Gate Church of the Transfiguration.

NOVODEVICHY GRAVEYARD
Novodevichye kladbishche
Новодевичье кладбище
Luzhnetsky Proyezd, 499/246-5607
HOURS: Daily 10 A.M.–5 P.M.
COST: Free
METRO: Sportivnaya

Opened in 1898 after the graveyard inside the convent's walls was deemed too crowded, the Novodevichy Graveyard located next door is one of Russia's most prestigious burial sites with a truly impressive list of luminaries laid to rest here, among the first of which was writer Anton Chekhov. Other famous graves include those of writer Nikolay Gogol, Soviet leader Nikita Khrushchev, poet Vladimir Mayakovsky, and Russia's first president, Boris Yeltsin. Besides celebrity-spotting, the verdant graveyard is worth visiting for its fantastic collection of all manner of artistic gravestones, some of which are truly avant-garde in their execution.

MOSCOW STATE UNIVERSITY
Moskovsky gosudarstvenny universitet
Московский государственный университет
Leninskiye Gory, 495/939-1000, www.msu.ru
METRO: Universitet

There's a view from the Sparrow Hills lookout that's hard to beat, but then again directly behind it is the main building of Moscow State University, which certainly gives it a run for its money. The world's tallest university building at 240 meters, it is by far the largest of the seven Stalin skyscrapers. The building's first stone was laid in 1949 and by 1953 the first classes were held. Its elaborate facade includes a variety of sculptures and ornaments, clocks and thermometers. Not only is the building itself impressive, the lawns and promenades that surround it are meticulously maintained and make for a pleasant stroll.

STATUES ON LENINSKY PROSPEKT
Pamyatniki na Leninskom Prospekte
Памятники на Ленинском проспекте
Lenin statue: Kaluzhskaya Ploshchad; Yury Gagarin
statue: Ploshchad Gagarina
METRO: Oktyabrskaya or Leninsky Prospekt

Running parallel along the length of Gorky Park and Neskuchny Sad, Leninsky Prospekt is most notable for two reasons—both of them statues. At the beginning of the avenue on Kaluzhskaya Ploshchad, near Oktyabrskaya metro station, stands Moscow's largest remaining **Lenin statue.** Created by the renowned Soviet sculptor Lev Kerbel, it was built in 1985 to commemorate the 70th anniversary of the Revolution.

Farther down Leninsky Prospekt, on Gagarin Square stands a **monument to Yury Gagarin,** the first man in space. Constructed from titanium in 1980, its futuristic design features a stylized figure standing atop a 40-meter-high pedestal, with the end effect resembling a cosmonaut rocketing toward the heavens. At its base is a copy of the Vostok spacecraft that took Gagarin on his history-making journey.

Southeast
Map 7

ANDRONNIKOV MONASTERY
Spaso-Andronnikov monastyr
Спасо-Андронников монастырь
10 Andronyevskaya Ploshchad, 495/678-1467,
www.rublev-museum.ru/abby/abby_hist.htm
HOURS: Thurs.-Tues. 11 A.M.-6 P.M., ticket office until
5:45 P.M., closed last Fri. of month
COST: Russian adults 50R, Russian students 30R,
foreign adults 150R, foreign students 75R, photo
permit 45R, video permit 80R
METRO: Ploshchad Ilicha

High on a bank of the Yauza River is the white-walled Spaso-Andronnikov Monastery, founded in 1357. The great iconographer Andrey Rublyov lived and worked here, and fragments of his frescoes remain in the monastery's **Spassky sobor** (Cathedral of Our Savior)—his life's last work before his death in 1427. The monastery was ransacked repeatedly over the centuries, suffered fires, destruction and "renovations," and was turned into a penal colony in Soviet times. Rublyov's grave and others were destroyed in the 1930s, along with the monastery's grandiose bell tower. In 1947 the former monastery was recognized as a national monument and in 1985 it became the **Andrey Rublyov Museum of Ancient Russian Culture and Art.**

Spassky Sobor is noteworthy not only for its architectural qualities, but also as one of the oldest surviving buildings in Moscow.

© NATHAN TOOHEY

Spassky sobor is one of the oldest surviving buildings in Moscow, built between 1420 and 1427.

Opinions of its age vary; it was likely built between 1420 and 1427. It is considered the brightest, most significant, and most perfect creation of early Moscow architecture.

Other sights here include the 16th-century refectory, the 17th-century walls, towers, and

MOSCOW'S MAGNIFICENT METRO

The Moscow Metro is not only fast and convenient, but also architecturally brilliant, one of the world's few urban public transport networks that is a sight in and of itself. It may not be the world's largest subway system – London's tube claims that title – but it is certainly the prettiest. Its spacious marble-clad halls, elaborate murals, and grand chandeliers give the metro more the look of a museum than a mass transit system, which is all the more impressive given that it transports over 9.5 million passengers a day. This makes it one of the busiest metros in the world – by comparison, the New York subway transports 5 million people a day.

The metro first opened in 1935, then consisting of just the red **Sokolnicheskaya line,** with a branch leading to **Smolenskaya** station – the grand old Stalin-era stations on these lines are among those most worth seeing. Others with particularly stunning stations include the **ring line,** and the green **Zamoskvoretskaya line,** but any of the centrally located stations are impressive.

Take some time (preferably at a quiet time, such as a Sunday, and not during weekday rush hour) to ride around exploring some of the stations. Tickets are sold at the *kassa* (cashier) in the entrance vestibule, and a single 22R ticket allows you to ride as far as you like for as long as you like, provided you don't actually pass through the exit gates.

The **Mayakovskaya** metro station is one of the most beautiful, with elegant columns of pink rhodonite and stainless steel, and artist Alexander Deyneka's *24 Hours in the Country of Soviets* ceiling mosaics depicting parachutists, divers, skiers, high-jumpers, and aircraft flying through the sky. It was opened in 1938 and used as a bomb shelter during WWII; Stalin gave a speech at a meeting inside the station in 1941.

Be sure to check out the monumental **Ploshchad Revolyutsii** metro station. More than 30 meters underground, it opened in 1938, designed by architect Alexey Dushkin and featuring brilliant Socialist Realist statues by sculptor Matvey Manizer. Bronze figures of soldiers, sailors, students, and metro builders strike Renaissance-style mannerist poses under heavy arches along platforms clad in multicolored marble and granite. Look out for the statue of a border guard with a dog whose nose shines thanks to a local student tradition of rubbing it for good luck.

During your journey, at each stop you will hear an announcement, "Ostorozhno, dveri zakrivayutsya. Sleduyushchaya ostanovka..." which translates as "Careful, the doors are closing. Next stop..." followed by the name of the next station. The gender of the announcer signifies the train's direction: on the ring line, there's a male voice for clockwise travel, and a female voice for counter-clockwise, and on the radial lines, you will hear a male voice when riding toward the center, and a female voice on the way out.

Two things that usually strike first-timers are the speed and length of the escalators, and the fact that a clock at the end of each platform shows how long since the last train left. Usually there's a train approximately every two or three minutes. Different stations have different opening and closing times, but in general the metro is open 5:30 A.M.-1 A.M.

People obey the no-smoking rule, and courteously give up their seats for the elderly, women (especially if pregnant), and small children. Passengers no longer have to worry about missing calls when on the metro because cell phones now work throughout the system.

To learn more, check out the **metro museum** located near the southern vestibule in Sportivnaya metro station (495/622-7309, 495/622-7833, 11 A.M.-5 P.M. Mon., 9 A.M.-4 P.M. Tues.-Sun.).

Moscow Baroque Archangel Michael Church, and the museum exhibits. The collection presents several thousand icons, fresco fragments, items of applied art, and examples of hand-written and early printed books. Aiming to present "a complete and exhaustive picture of the art of Old Russia," they include works by renowned Moscow, Tver, and Rostov iconographers of the 15th–17th centuries. A memorial statue to Andrey Rublyov can be seen in the garden in front of the gates.

You can find the monastery by walking down Ulitsa Sergeya Radonezhskogo from Ploshchad Ilicha/Rimskaya metro station. As this is primarily a museum, Orthodox dress rules do not apply.

KRUTITSKOYE PODVORYE
Крутицкое подворье
10 Krutitskaya Ul., 495/292-3731, 495/276-9256
HOURS: Wed.–Mon. 10 A.M.–5 P.M., closed first Mon. of month
COST: Free
METRO: Proletarskaya

If you're in the Novospassky Monastery neigh-

borhood, take a short walk to the other cluster of onion domes visible nearby, up a lane on the other side of the busy 3rd Krutitsky Pereulok. This redbrick ensemble is a historically and architecturally significant estate of the Russian Orthodox Church, Krutitskoye Podvorye, or the Krutitsky Patriarchal Metochion. It was founded in 1272 after Prince Daniil of Moscow gave the land to a diocese based in the Golden Horde's capital, Sarai. During the Time of Troubles in the early 17th century, when Poles occupied the Kremlin, Krutitskoye Podvorye gained stature, housing the main cathedral of Moscow Orthodoxy. Later it was gradually downgraded and in the 18th century the monastery was turned into army barracks.

Although fires, looting, and fresco-overpainting have destroyed much, restoration work began in the 1960s. Krutitsky was listed as a memorial in the mid-1960s, became a branch of the State Historical Museum in the early '80s, and was returned to the Orthodox Church in the 1990s. Restoration work continues. Visitors can see a number of 17th-century

Krutitskoye Podvorye

buildings, notably the colorfully tiled tower chamber with Sacred Gates, the two-story metropolitan's chambers, Uspensky Church and bell tower, and the gallery connecting the chambers to the cathedral, as well as the 16th-century Resurrection Cathedral.

Although it's a functioning Orthodox estate, Krutitskoye Podvorye usually seems deserted and dress rules are not enforced.

NOVOSPASSKY MONASTERY

Novospassky monastyr

Новоспасский монастырь

10 Krestyanskaya Ploshchad, 495/676-9570,
www.spasnanovom.ru

METRO: Proletarskaya

If you ride the riverboat from Kievsky Station past the Kremlin and all the way to the very last stop, you'll come to a landing station beside Novospassky Monastery.

Novospassky Monastery is said to be Moscow's oldest monastery, founded in the 13th century, but at a different location. It has been at its present site since the late 15th century, when it was moved here to become part of a network of fortified monasteries protecting the city from the south and southeast. Many great and noble people were buried here, including more than 70 boyars of the Romanov family, which had its burial vault in Novospassky until Mikhail Romanov ascended to the throne in 1613.

Novospassky Monastery's original wooden fortifications were replaced in the 17th century with the existing brick walls topped by five towers. Most of the other buildings to be seen inside the monastery walls also date from the 17th century, including the functioning five-domed Spaso-Preobrazhensky Cathedral, dating to 1645. The yellow four-tiered bell tower appeared in the 18th century.

If you want to enter the monastery, you need to be appropriately dressed—that means a long skirt and headscarf for women, long pants and no hats for men, and sleeves for everybody. The strict dress code is because this is a working monastery, having resumed service in 1991. The Soviets had closed it in 1918, destroyed the necropolis, and used the monastery grounds as a prison and alcoholic rehabilitation center, among other functions.

Between the river and the monastery is a picturesque park with Novospassky Pond in its center, a lovely spot for strolling or bench-sitting at any time of year, despite its grim past. Somewhere in the banks there is said to have been a mass grave for victims of the Soviet secret police.

Besides arriving at Novospassky by riverboat, which isn't an option in the cooler months, you can come on foot from Proletarskaya or Krestyanskaya Zastava metro stations. Alternatively, approach from Paveletskaya Ploshchad, walking down Kozhevnicheskaya Ulitsa and over the Novospassky Bridge. From the bridge you'll get a great view of the monastery as well as up the Moscow River to some interesting new developments—Moscow International House of Music, Riverside Towers business center and Swissotel Krasnye Holmy, a tall tower topped by the UFO-like City Space Lounge & Bar.

Greater Moscow Map 8

◖ ALL-RUSSIAN EXHIBITION CENTER (VVTS)

Vserossiysky vystavochny tsentr (VVTs)

Всероссийский выставочный центр (ВВЦ)

119 Prospekt Mira, 495/544-3400, www.vvcentre.ru/eng/

HOURS: Grounds daily 8 A.M.-10 P.M., pavilions daily 10 A.M.-7 P.M.

COST: Free

METRO: VDNKh

The All-Russian Exhibition Center (VVTs) is certainly a highlight of any sightseeing tour. It may not be centrally located, but if time permits only one excursion out of the very center, then this monumental attraction should definitely top the list. Its collection of elaborate pavilions, fountains, and statues is in itself a grandiose architectural museum, reflecting the ambitious undertakings of the Soviet people.

Like many places in Russia, VVTs has seen its fair share of name changes over its history. Originally conceived as a primarily agricultural fair, it opened in 1939 and was named

© NATHAN TOOHEY

the meat pavilion at the All-Russian Exhibition Center

the All-Union Agricultural Exhibition. In its original incarnation it occupied some 140 hectares, consisted of more than 250 buildings, and contained the now iconic statue the Worker and Collective Farm Girl together holding aloft their hammer and sickle.

The center closed due to the war, but reopened in 1954 and was then renamed in 1959 to the Economic Achievements Exhibition or VDNKh, as was the nearby metro station, which to this day retains the name. It was briefly named the All-Union Exhibition Center from 1989; with the collapse of the Soviet Union finally took on its present-day name. It has grown in this time to occupy 237.5 hectares and runs for a length of roughly 3.5 kilometers.

Although created to serve as an educational exhibition center, throughout its history it has attracted crowds who come simply to relax and stroll around its wide boulevards and sit by the impressive fountains. During the 1990s it assumed the role of a giant shopping center, with its pavilions handed over to retail operations and alleys jammed with tacky kiosks. In the last several years the kiosks have been removed and appliance retailers chased out, and it has regained some of its original dignity. On a warm summer day expect to see thousands of Muscovites converge here to ride, skate, and stroll or simply enjoy a cold drink with grilled kebabs in one of its numerous outdoor cafés.

As you walk through the impressive main gates, the first building that catches the eye is **Central Pavilion No. 1.** Located opposite the gates at the far end of the first boulevard, the huge spire-topped Neoclassical building reaches almost 100 meters in height. Built in 1954, it currently is home to the Russian People's Assembly.

Located behind the Central Pavilion, the **People's Friendship Fountain** is a symbol of the former Soviet Union. Depicted in full gilded glory are 16 women, each clad in the national costume of a former Soviet state. In the center of the fountain, surrounded by the young ladies, is an enormous sheaf of wheat. Every

MONORAIL REVIVAL

Running past the All-Russian Exhibition Center in the city's north is Moscow's monorail. With just six stops and running a brief 4.7 kilometers, it is quite modest in comparison with Moscow's other public transport systems. Due to its initially short working hours, infrequent runs, and hefty ticket prices (nearly three times the price of a metro ride) locals rarely used it, and most passengers were tourists. In early 2008 all of this changed: the hours were extended, frequency was increased, and ticket prices were brought in line with those of the metro. This created a surge in popularity. It is an enjoyable ride that provides great views of the area, especially Ostankino Tower. The monorail connects with two metro stations – VDNKh and Timiryazevskaya.

pioneering space flight. In its place once stood a large statue of Stalin, which was given the boot in favor of the rocket during in the mid-1960s. Behind the rocket and several examples of domestic passenger planes is the **Cosmos Pavilion.** Since it was formerly called the Mechanization Pavilion, statues of tractors and the like can still be spotted. In 1964, it was given its current name and reconstructed, housing all manner of satellites, space ships and rockets. In the 1990s it held one of Russia's first and probably most famous raves—the Gagarin Party. It later went on to become a makeshift retail center and has recently been closed for repairs.

VVTs has dozens of outdoor cafés that, with the exception of the odd Italian eatery, serve a variety of tasty grilled meats, fresh flatbread, and inexpensive draft beer. Some of the most pleasant can be found behind the Cosmos Pavilion, where there is a series of ponds, the largest of which contains the **Kolos Fountain** designed to look like a sheaf of wheat. Be warned, however, these grill cafés sell their meat by weight, are known to give you more than you asked for, and expect you to pay for it—so make sure you specify exactly how much you want and pay for it when you order, rather than waiting until after you've eaten.

The exhibition center is also home to a large collection of amusement park rides, the most prominent being a huge **Ferris wheel.** Built in 1995 to mark the 850th anniversary of Moscow's founding in 1147, the 73-meter-high Ferris wheel was for several years the highest in Europe.

second, 1,200 liters of water passes through its 800 water spouts.

Located to the right of the People's Friendship Fountain as you enter from the main gate is the **Circular Cinerama.** This innovative cinema was constructed in 1959 and offers a cool retro experience. The circular cinema consists of 11 screens positioned in a full circle with 11 projectors displaying synchronized films to create a full 360-degree panorama. Don't expect Spielberg, but the Soviet-era films will show you a long-forgotten Moscow before it was taken over by advertising billboards and fancy international stores.

Further into VVTs, the **Stone Flower Fountain** is a favorite with the general public who, on a hot day, like to cool off in the clouds of mist it generates. It is an impressive fountain in fairy-tale style, due in no small part to the numerous bronze birds and fish all squirting jets of water from their upturned mouths.

At the far end of the exhibition center is a large square with several particularly noteworthy sights. In its center stands a rocket, a copy of the **Vostok** that took Yury Gagarin on his

IZMAYLOVSKY ESTATE
Usadba Izmaylovo
Усадьба Измайлово
12 Gorodok imeni Baumana, 495/367-5661,
www.shm.ru/izmailovo.html
HOURS: Museum Wed.-Mon. summer 10 A.M.-6 P.M., winter 11 A.M.-4 P.M., ticket office until 5 P.M., closed first Mon. of month
COST: Russian adults 30R, Russian seniors 10R, foreigners 40R
METRO: Partizanskaya

Known since the late 14th century, this area was an estate of Ivan the Terrible in the late

16th century. It is probably best known, however, as a place where Peter the Great spent time in his youth, honing his sailing skills on its ponds. In the late 17th century, Izmaylovsky Island saw the construction of a tsar's residence. A handful of buildings from the 17th century remain to this day. The Bridge Tower (1671–1679) is a three-level construction that served not only as part of the bridge to the estate, but also as main gates and a bell tower. The impressive five-domed Intercession Cathedral (1671–1679) also remains, as well as the eastern Ceremonial Gates and the western gates (1679–1682). The other buildings are more recent constructions. There is a museum devoted to the estate on the grounds.

OSTANKINO PALACE AND PARK

Muzey-usadba Ostankino

Музей-усадба Останкино

5 1st Ostankinskaya Ulitsa, 495/683-4645, www.ostankino-museum.ru

HOURS: May 18-Sept. 30 Wed.-Sun. 11 A.M.-7 P.M., ticket office until 6 P.M., closed in heavy rainfall and when air humidity exceeds 80 percent

COST: Adults 80R, park only 5R

METRO: VDNKh

This is an extremely well-preserved palace and park estate. Its founding started with the picturesque grounds and pond in the 16th century, followed by the Trinity Life Church (1678–1692). It blossomed in the 18th century with the building of Ostankinsky Palace Theater (1792–1798)—Russia's only 18th-century theater remaining with its stage, seating area, changing rooms, and some stage mechanics still left intact. Live performances are held in summer. The Sheremetyev Seasons in Ostankino festival, which runs from June through September, continues the estate's musical and theatrical traditions, with 18th-century operas, ballets, and a classical music concert program. There is a museum inside the palace, where you can see the Sheremetyev family's collection of paintings, graphics, antique musical instruments, furniture, china, fans, and lamps.

OSTANKINO TV TOWER

Ostankinskaya televizionnaya bashnya

Останкинская телевизионная башня

8 Ulitsa Akademika Korolyova, 495/602-2234, www.tvtower.ru

METRO: VDNKh

Standing at a height of 540 meters and completed in 1967 to mark the 50th anniversary of the 1917 October Revolution, this remains among the world's tallest structures. Ostankino TV Tower is the third-tallest freestanding structure in the world. To this day, it remains the tallest structure in Europe—a record it will cede upon the completion of Russia Tower, which is to stand at 612 meters in the downtown Moskva City development. Upon the Ostankino TV Tower's completion, it overtook the Empire State Building as the world's tallest freestanding structure on land, only to relinquish this record eight years later with the construction of the CN Tower in Toronto. A fire in August 2000 killed three people, knocked out TV transmissions, and led to it being closed to tourists through 2008. Its viewing deck and revolving restaurant, located at 334 meters, were due to begin functioning once again in 2009.

RESTAURANTS

Moscow's dining scene is thoroughly world class and constantly reinventing itself. Here you can find almost every international cuisine and a broad price spectrum. While Moscow has a reputation for being expensive, there are some real bargains to be had, especially in the Russian buffet- or smorgasbord-style eateries, which are often chains. By chains, we don't mean fast food: The trend in recent years is to make multiple copies of successful medium-priced restaurants. These small networks are a relatively new phenomenon and provide quality dining for the newly emerged middle class, who like and trust a familiar brand. For a long time, there were only super-elite super-expensive restaurants and cheap canteens, with very little in between, but now there is active development of the mid-range niche.

Cuisines that are usually cheap in the West are not necessarily affordable here, however. If you're looking for a mom-and-pop ethnic restaurant, your best bet is one of the countless Caucasus restaurants to be found around town, and not something like Chinese or Italian, which tend to be more upscale.

The city does not have neighborhoods associated with any particular cuisines or types of food—instead, it's all mixed up and spread out. But there are some eat streets with a high concentration of restaurants of various kinds, such as Kamergersky Pereulok, Bolshaya Nikitskaya Ulitsa, Ulitsa Maroseyka, Spiridonyevsky Pereulok, and Dologorukovskaya Ulitsa–Novoslobodskaya Ulitsa.

The lines are blurred between restaurants, cafés, pubs, bars, and nightclubs—almost

© NATHAN TOOHEY

HIGHLIGHTS

LOOK FOR ☾ TO FIND
RECOMMENDED RESTAURANTS.

☾ **Most Innovative:** Maestro chef Anatoly Komm has given Russian cuisine the molecular treatment at **Varvary,** and the results are sure to shatter your preconceptions of local food (page 95).

☾ **Most Opulent:** Rococo and chinoiserie reign at **Turandot,** a heavily gilded restaurant that was more than six years in the making (page 96).

☾ **Best Theme:** Moscow is famous for its metro, and now there are even two beer restaurants called **Metro** that celebrate this iconic transport system (page 97).

☾ **Best Russian: Cafe Pushkin** is sure to impress, with its fine Russian cuisine, pre-Revolutionary-design, and multi-level interior (page 100).

☾ **Easiest Access to Beer:** At **Beryozka,** the beer taps are right on your table, so you can pour yourself as much as you want, when you want it — which might be a lot, very often, since the microbrewed beers are delicious and go perfectly with the specialty sausages (page 109).

© NATHAN TOOHEY

Beryozka has beer taps at each table.

every establishment has food, and you can dine well at 4 A.M. in a disco, or even in a restaurant—there is a vast number of 24-hour eateries in Moscow, a true city that never sleeps. And many others don't have set closing times, advertising themselves as being open "until last guest," which usually means they tend to close at midnight but will stay open if there are enough people still spending enough money.

The overwhelming majority of restaurants allow smoking, although some have nonsmoking sections.

In general, all but the very cheapest restaurants in Moscow are likely to have some English-speaking staff and either English translations on the menu, or a separate English-language menu, which the staff are usually quick to offer when they realize you are foreign.

RESTAURANTS

PRICE KEY

$ Main courses less than 250R

$$ Main courses between 250-500R

$$$ Main courses more than 500R

(Even if they can't understand you, they will understand what you want if you point to your choices, using sign language to indicate how many portions, and so on.)

Usually reservations aren't necessary, unless your group is more than four people or it's a Friday or Saturday night. But even other times can be problematic, because wedding parties, corporate events, and other large banquet groups often book out a whole restaurant. Of course, there's no harm in calling ahead regardless of the day, time, and group size, though you might find that some restaurants won't take reservations for peak times because they don't want to hold a table and then find nobody shows up. Some restaurants will only take a reservation for a large group if you pay a deposit in advance. The amount is then deducted from your final bill.

The Kremlin and Red Square Map 1

EUROPEAN
BOSCO BAR $$$

3 Red Square, 495/627-3703, www.bosco.ru/restoration

HOURS: Daily 10 A.M.-10 P.M.

METRO: Okhotny Ryad

This hip fashion café-bar-restaurant has a groovy 1970s styling, but perhaps its strongest drawing card is its location. It's on the 1st floor of the GUM shopping center, facing onto Red Square, where there's a superb outdoor dining area. The menu lists a range of sandwiches as well as sophisticated Italian, Russian, and other European dishes. The prices are not for paupers—but what do you expect when there's a million-dollar view?

FUSION
JEROBOAM $$$

3 Tverskaya Ulitsa, 495/225-8888

HOURS: Daily noon-midnight

METRO: Okhotny Ryad

This is one of Moscow's most expensive restaurants, located inside one of Moscow's most expensive hotels—and that's in a town with no shortage of either. Jeroboam's kitchen is overseen by Heinz Winkler, renowned as the youngest chef to have headed a restaurant when it was awarded three Michelin stars. Winkler, who is German, specializes in what he calls "cuisine vitale," which is his own take on haute cuisine, incorporating medicinal herbs. Perusing the menu, you might be tempted by such creations as anise sea bass, pigeon soufflé, or chanterelle gnocchi. Naturally, the Ritz-Carlton's flagship restaurant's interior is no less impressive than the chef himself, and the wine list is simply stellar.

INTERNATIONAL
SHOKOLAD $$
Шоколад

6 Ulitsa Volkhonka, 495/697-2515

HOURS: Daily 24 hours

METRO: Borovitskaya

Here you'll find a small café with a typical Moscow-style fashionable design, including wall-sized photographs at each end of the room—one of an elegant lady's arm donning a long glove, and the other of a luscious-looking strawberry being dipped in chocolate. The best thing, however, is the view across to the Kremlin from the large front windows. The menu is a mixture of Asian and European, and perhaps surprisingly, there are even some bargains to be had. Local beer goes for a reasonable price.

ITALIAN
BOSCO CAFE $$$

3 Red Square, 495/620-3182, www.bosco.ru/restoration

RESTAURANTS

alfresco dining at Bosco Cafe

HOURS: Daily 10 A.M.-10 P.M.
METRO: Okhotny Ryad

While their menus and styles differ, the two separate Bosco eateries in GUM have something in common—fabulous outdoor dining areas directly on Red Square itself. Run by the same restaurateur, these fashionable spots are separated by about 100 meters, but otherwise offer near identical settings as both are situated on the 1st floor of the GUM shopping center that faces onto the square. The so-called café is really a sophisticated restaurant, with a wide choice of Italian classics, pasta, risotto, grilled meats, and fish.

RUSSIAN

DROVA ⑤
Дрова
5 Nikolskaya Ulitsa, 495/698-2484, www.drova.ru
HOURS: Daily 24 hours
METRO: Okhotny Ryad

A stone's throw from Red Square, this is one of several all-you-can-eat restaurants in the Drova chain. There are dozens of mostly Russian dishes available from the smorgasbord, including hot and cold options. For those with more modest appetites, there is also a range of breakfast and lunch specials, where diners can mix and match various combinations for discounted prices. Right next door is an all-you-can-eat Japanese version of Drova.

GODUNOV ⑤⑤⑤
Годуновъ
5 Teatralnaya Ploshchad, 495/698-4480, 495/698-4490, www.godunow.ru
HOURS: Daily noon–midnight
METRO: Ploshchad Revolyutsii

Designed with tourists in mind, this restaurant is elaborately decorated in a traditional Russian style. Its arched ceilings and walls are painted with intricate vine-like patterns, and it's furnished with carved wood. The restaurant provides entertainment in the form of artists and musicians in national costumes who perform folk dances and songs. The menu, naturally, consists of traditional Russian offerings.

1 RED SQUARE ⑤⑤⑤
Krasnaya Ploshchad, dom 1
Красная Площадь, дом 1
1 Red Square, 495/692-1196, 495/692-1016, www.redsquare.ru
HOURS: Daily noon–midnight
METRO: Okhotny Ryad

It's hard to imagine a restaurant better suited to tourists' needs. For starters, it's located right on Red Square, inside the State History Museum building, with a suitably historical interior. Moreover, it specializes in serving dishes prepared according to traditional recipes from tsars' banquets and other ceremonial events. The recipes have all been sourced from the museum's archives. Several times a year, the restaurant holds themed banquets, where the set menu is an authentic re-creation of a particular historical feast.

STOLOVAYA NO. 57 ⑤
Столовая No. 57
3 Red Square, 3rd floor, 3rd line, inside GUM, 495/788-4343

HOURS: Daily noon-midnight
METRO: Okhotny Ryad
A super-retro canteen hidden away inside the GUM department store, this place is non-stop nostalgia, with starched white tablecloths, old-fashioned soda dispensers, and reproductions of posters from Soviet yesteryears. Savor quality renditions of old Soviet canteen classics for prices as low as you'll find anywhere downtown. There's even seating out on the internal balcony with views right across the department store's atrium.

Kitay-Gorod, Lubyanka, and Chistye Prudy   Map 2

BEER RESTAURANTS AND PUBS
GLAVPIVTORG ⑤⑤
Главпивторг
5 Ulitsa Bolshaya Lubyanka, 495/628-2591,
495/626-0022, 495/626-0303, 495/624-1996,
www.glavpivtorg.ru
HOURS: Daily noon-midnight
METRO: Lubyanka
Designed to resemble a Soviet ministerial restaurant, this place is all dark wood and leather, although the enormous floor-to-ceiling windows across the main hall keep it light and airy. Several smaller rooms are designed to resemble high-ranking Soviet officials' offices, with old maps on the walls and Bakelite telephones. In the evenings, there is live lounge music in the main hall. The house beer is decent and the food is primarily retro-Soviet, featuring plenty of dishes well suited to accompany beer.

COFFEE SHOPS
COFFEE BEAN ⑤
18/3 Ulitsa Pokrovka, 495/623-9793,
www.coffeebean.ru
HOURS: Mon.-Sat. 8 A.M.-11 P.M., Sun. 9 A.M.-10 P.M.
METRO: Chistye Prudy
A trendy and popular café, this is the place for real coffee lovers. Founded by an American, it's the sort of spot that makes Westerners feel at home. Not only can you enjoy a wide range of coffee drinks, including some with alcohol, you can also buy beans to go. There are some mouth-watering desserts, such as lime pie, cheese cake, strudels, and meringues. The menu includes a range of tea and chocolate drinks, freshly squeezed juices, and liqueurs.

INTERNATIONAL
LOFT ⑤⑤⑤
Лофт
25 Nikolskaya Ulitsa, 495/933-7713, 495/933-7714,
www.cafeloft.ru/index1.php
HOURS: Daily 9 A.M.-midnight
METRO: Lubyanka
Located on the 6th floor of a shopping center, this café has undergone a complete overhaul and is now lighter and brighter than ever. It offers lovely views of Lubyanka Square, which are even better from its open-air balcony—perfect for lazy Sunday breakfasts. The menu offers a fashionable mix of all that's popular at present—a little arugula salad, some Thai soup, carpaccio, and even some tuna ceviche. The special breakfast menu is served until midday on weekdays and until 2 P.M. on weekends.

PRADO CAFE ⑤⑤⑤
2 Slavyanskaya Ploshchad, 495/784-6969,
www.prado-cafe.ru
HOURS: Daily noon-6 A.M.
METRO: Kitay-Gorod
The restaurant describes its target audience as "socially active, financially independent people who value luxury and know the fashionable trends." And while trendy Moscow restaurants come and go in the bat of an eye, this restaurant has been around for quite some time, which must say something. Perhaps it's because, as the restaurant puts it, "people don't just come here to eat, they come for the fashionable, glamorous atmosphere." So, what's on the menu? For starters, there's prawn tempura, crab teriyaki, and foie gras with red onion marmalade. There are

ANNUSHKA TRAM-CAFÉ

For a fun meal while watching the changing cityscape out the window, take a ride on the Annushka tram-café. This cute old tram, named after the "A" tram route known colloquially by the diminutive form of "Anna," usually runs a circuit around the boulevard at Chistye Prudy – you can catch it at the tram stop right outside the Chistye Prudy metro station. On weekends, when full, it runs on a two-hour tour across the city. It's also possible to reserve the entire tram for a private party cruising around town.

The charmingly old-fashioned interior has just seven tables, with seating space for up to 25 people, plus a cloakroom and a bathroom. There's a complete menu of food and drinks, including a full range of alcoholic beverages, a children's menu, and Russian cuisine. You can also hop on just for tea, coffee, or beer.

The home base stop is at the far end of Chistoprudny Bulvar (17 Ulitsa Pokrovka, 495/236-0677, 495/507-5770, metro Chistye Prudy, website tramvai-annushka.narod.ru). There's a 100R entrance fee, and the tram-café is open and running daily from 1 P.M. until the last guest leaves.

also various soups, salads, hot dishes of fish and meat, pasta, risotto, sushi, and desserts.

SHATYOR ❸❸❸
Шатёр
12A Chistoprudny Bulvar, 495/505-6946
HOURS: Daily 24 hours
METRO: Chistye Prudy, Turgenevskaya, Sretensky Bulvar
Built on a deck floating on the pond in Chistye Prudy, this upmarket restaurant has a design that's vaguely Middle Eastern, with low divans for lounging on. It has an open plan and is open around most of the sides, which is particularly nice when there's a cool breeze coming off the water on a hot summer's night. The menu is mixed, with an emphasis on Mediterranean and Japanese dishes.

VINOTECA DISSIDENT ❸❸❸
Винотека Dissident
25 Nikolskaya Ulitsa, 495/230-5848, 495/230-5849, www.dissident.msk.ru
HOURS: Daily 11 A.M.–midnight
METRO: Lubyanka
Located one floor below Loft Cafe, Vinoteca Dissident is a small restaurant with a big collection of wines—in fact, there are some 200 varieties available by the glass alone. The interior is laid-back with racks and boxes of wine all over the place. Besides the good range of wines

by the glass, the restaurant also regularly offers various set degustation menus with several glasses of wine matched with tasty tidbits.

RUSSIAN

EXPEDITSIA ❸❸❸
Экспедиция
6 Pevchesky Pereulok, 495/775-6075, www.expedicia.ru
HOURS: Daily noon–last guest
METRO: Kitay-Gorod
This is certainly not your average Russian restaurant. For starters, it actually serves what the restaurant describes as "northern cuisine," which in this case means traditional dishes and ingredients all sourced from Russia's northernmost regions around the Arctic Circle. The menu lists such exotic delicacies as thinly sliced frozen *muksun* whitefish and cured Northern deer meat. Given the expedition theme, it should come as no surprise that there is an entire helicopter sitting in the main dining room.

POKROVSKIYE VOROTA ❸❸
Покровские ворота
19 Ul. Pokrovka, 495/917-3985, 495/621-4340
HOURS: Daily 11 A.M.–11 P.M.
METRO: Kitay-Gorod
This is a retro restaurant named and styled after a 1950s Soviet classic comedy movie, and the interior is decorated like the inside of an apartment

in the film. There are photos from the movie, and other memorabilia including genuine props that were used in the filming. The menu offers classic Russian dishes, such as the trusty salads *olivye* and *vinegret*, as well as marinated mushrooms, assorted pickles, potatoes with herring, and bliny stuffed with salmon caviar. Meaty main courses include lamb ribs and chicken kebabs.

SHCHIT I MECH ✪

Щит и меч

13 Ulitsa Bolshaya Lubyanka, 495/667-4445

HOURS: Mon.-Sat. noon-midnight

METRO: Kuznetsky Most

It's as if you've wandered into a museum dedicated to the nation's security services by mistake. But this is no museum; rather it's a grandly decorated eatery with just about every imaginable curio and collectable to do with spies and the military on display, ranging from collections of medals to portraits of KGB bosses. Given the effort that has gone into the restaurant's design, the prices for the food and drink are surprisingly low. The head chef is said to have worked in the Kremlin's special kitchen for 30 years and cooked for such leaders as Brezhnev and Andropov. His menu spans the former Soviet Union, including Caucasus-style shashliks or kebabs, Ukrainian borsch, and Uzbek *plov,* a rice dish like pilaf. There's a fabulous 15R special of black bread with herring accompanied by a shot of vodka—now that's good value!

◖ VARVARY ✪✪✪

Варвары

8A Strastnoy Bulvar, 495/229-2800,

www.anatolykomm.ru/Barvary/barvary_eng.htm

HOURS: Mon.-Sat. 7:30 P.M.-last guest

METRO: Chekhovskaya

Varvary is Moscow's answer to Spain's El Bulli or Britain's Fat Duck. Anatoly Komm, or "the maestro" as he's commonly called, has created a uniquely Russian take on molecular cuisine. Komm will shatter your preconceptions about flavor and texture with such creations as liquid bread with sunflower oil in the form of a crispy spiral, and beet ice cream. Guests must book in advance and set aside several hours for the "culinary performance." The meal consists of a fixed set of some dozen or so dishes presented one after another. In summer, there's an open outdoor terrace, which has a wonderful view across the boulevard, although you don't come here for the view. Keep in mind that the fixed meal will cost you somewhere in the range of several hundred dollars per person.

VEGETARIAN

AVOCADO ✪✪

Авокадо

12 Chistoprudny Bulvar, 495/988-2656, 495/506-0033

HOURS: Daily 10 A.M.-11 P.M.

METRO: Chistye Prudy or Turgenevskaya

One of the city's few vegetarian restaurants, this cute spot is simple, light, and bright, with large windows that look across to the Chistye Prudy pond. There is a large variety of vegetarian dishes including Japanese, Italian, and other cuisines, as well as a wide selection of freshly squeezed juices. It's also nonsmoking inside.

RESTAURANTS

The Center and Inner Northwest   Map 3

ASIAN

MENZA $

Мензa

32 Ulitsa Bolshaya Dmitrovka, 495/650-3240,
www.vci.ru/ru/front_end_vci/pages/menza

HOURS: Daily 11 A.M.–11 P.M.

METRO: Chistye Prudy or Turgenevskaya

"Noodle territory" is how this modern-styled eatery describes itself, and Japanese noodles is what it serves. Besides the various noodles, there's a handful of other vaguely Japanese dishes, but no sushi. The food here is hardly super-authentic, and this isn't the kind of place to linger for hours (the chairs are simple benches without back supports), but then again, it offers some of the lowest prices in town for some pretty tasty noodles. The house beer is also a bargain.

☾ TURANDOT $$$

Турандот

26/5 Tverskoy Bulvar, 495/739-0011

HOURS: Daily noon–midnight

METRO: Pushkinskaya

Brace yourself for simply the most outrageously over-the-top interior of any restaurant in Moscow. The design looks like something you'd expect to find in a rococo-styled hall of a tsar's palace. Given that this massive 12-room restaurant serves a modern take on Chinese cuisine, there is even a vaguely Asian theme mixed in with the gild and glitz. If it all seems a little overwhelming, there is a more modest outdoor section in summer. The food is refined Chinese and other Asian cuisine adapted to Russian tastes. You can try delicacies ranging

---

BEST BAKERY CAFÉS

Whether you're craving a brioche for breakfast or a quiche with afternoon tea, you don't have to look far. Bakery-confectionery stores with attached cafés have been multiplying across Moscow.

BALTIYSKY KHLEB

Baltiysky Khleb (www.baltic-bread.ru), or Baltic Bread, is a St. Petersburg-based company with two bakery cafés in Moscow. They offer an amazing selection, including more than 50 kinds of bread, and about 80 different cakes, pastries, sweets, and other desserts, as well as tea, coffee, juice, and cocktails.

- Both open 9 A.M.–10 P.M. daily

- 3/10 Ul. Malaya Dmitrovka, 499/699-4873, Pushkinskaya metro

- 4 Nizhny Susalny Per., 499/261-2635, Kurskaya metro

CAFÉ PUSHKIN

Some of the city's most exquisite sweets

are to be found in the confectionery café attached to the restaurant Café Pushkin. A unique feature here is the French chef's special selection of light, low-calorie, and sugar-free desserts.

- 26a Tverskoy Bulvar, 495/739-0033, Pushkinskaya metro, 11 A.M.–11 P.M. daily

KHLEB I KO

Khleb i Ko (www.eatout.ru) is a growing chain of upscale bakeries, with a range of fine and fancy breads and pastries. You can either buy sweet treats to take out or enjoy them on site with a cup of tea or coffee (although unlike the other bakery cafés listed here, these are less cafés than bakery stores).

- All open 8 A.M.–11 P.M. daily

- 12 1st Tverskaya-Yamskaya Ulitsa, 495/250-8324, Mayakovskaya metro

- 3/14 Ul. Ostozhenka, 495/695-2731, Kropotkinskaya metro

from Shanghai-style vegetable fried rice, to lobster baked in miso with sea urchin caviar. The menu is seriously expensive.

BEER RESTAURANTS AND PUBS
Ⓒ METRO ❸❸
Метро

10/13 Sadovaya-Triumfalnaya Ulitsa, Bldg. 1, 495/230-6208, www.metrostation.ru

HOURS: Daily noon-midnight
METRO: Mayakovskaya

The theme here is the metro, and this beer restaurant is designed like the Moscow underground, right down to the smallest detail. You descend a metro escalator to reach the dining room, where you can sit inside an actual metro carriage and order from a menu designed to look like the metro map. It's all good fun, and the house beer is tasty and reasonably priced.

The food is pretty good, too—a beer-compatible selection of Russian and European cuisine, from Caesar salads to venison cutlets. Another larger Metro is near Taganskaya metro station, at 2/1 Verkhnaya Radishchevskaya Ulitsa, Bldg. 5.

BELORUSSIAN
BELAYA RUS ❸❸
Белая Русь

14 Bolshaya Nikitskaya Ulitsa, 495/629-4176, www.belaiarus.ru

HOURS: Daily 11 A.M.-11 P.M.
METRO: Biblioteka imeni Lenina

Outside Belarus itself, Belorussian restaurants are a rarity, even in Moscow—but this is one place where you can try this little-known cuisine. One of the cuisine's most popular dishes is *dranniki,* or patties, with the choices including potato, meat, mushrooms, and fish.

- 12 Chistoprudny Bulvar, korpus 4, 495/623-3155, Chistye Prudy metro

- 26 Studencheskaya Ul., 499/766-1602, Studencheskaya metro

LE PAIN QUOTIDIEN

A good choice for breakfast would be any of the bakery cafés in the international chain Le Pain Quotidien (www.lpq.ru). You'll be tempted by the croissants, brioches, and muffins, as well as omelets and fresh fruits. Le Pain Quotidien is also a good lunch spot, with appealing quiches, soups, and tartines. There's also a range of gourmet fresh-baked breads, and all kinds of toppings to choose from.

- 6 Kamergersky Per., 495/937-7742, Teatralnaya metro, 7 A.M.-11 P.M. Sun.-Thurs., 7 A.M.-1 A.M. Fri.-Sat.

- 7 Novinsky Bulvar, 495/605-2056, Smolenskaya metro, 7 A.M.-11 P.M. daily

- 5/3 Zubovsky Bulvar, 499/247-1795, Park Kultury metro, 7 A.M.-11 P.M. daily

- Yevropeysky mall, 4th floor, 2 Ploshchad Kievskogo Vokzala, 495/229-6674, Kievskaya metro, 10 A.M.-11 P.M. daily

- ½ Lesnaya Ulitsa, 495/234-1785, Belorusskaya metro, 7 A.M.-11 P.M. daily

VOLKONSKY

People line up for the tasty baked treats at Volkonsky (www.wolkonsky.ru). The Maroseyka outlet has the largest café section, and it's a perfect spot for afternoon tea or coffee with dainty delicacies, which are so attractively displayed that you'll be tempted to keep going back for more.

- All open 8 A.M.-11 P.M. daily

- 2/46 Bolshaya Sadovaya Ul., 495/699-3620, Mayakovskaya metro

- 1 Stary Arbat, 580-9052, Arbatskaya metro

- 4/2 Ul. Maroseyka, 495/721-1442, Kitay-Gorod metro

There's a wide selection of hot meat and fish dishes, and some hearty soups. The home-made drinks are especially appealing, with all kinds of berry concoctions, mead, and kvass with mint. There's also a unfiltered house beer to try.

COFFEE SHOPS
COFFEEMANIA ⓢⓢ
Кофемания
13 Bolshaya Nikitskaya Ulitsa, 495/775-5188, www.coffeemania.ru
HOURS: Daily 24 hours
METRO: Biblioteka imeni Lenina
Probably Moscow's trendiest coffee shop, Coffee Mania is incredibly popular, especially in the warmer months. Its summer veranda is a real scene, often hosting hip happenings. It's right beside the Conservatory, so it attracts a fashionable artsy bohemian crowd, and not surprisingly it can be very difficult to get a table. Although it's part of a chain, it's not as cheap as you might expect. The interior is styled like a classic European café, with tempting desserts in a glass cabinet and baristas whipping up coffee drinks galore. There's a good range of breakfast food, such as oatmeal, omelets, bliny, and croissants. For lunch or dinner, the range includes pasta, wok stir fries, soups, salads, and various hot main courses. There's a full range of alcoholic drinks as well.

EUROPEAN
KVARTIRA 44 ⓢⓢ
Квартира 44
22/2 Bolshaya Nikitskaya Ulitsa, entrance from Khlynovsky Tupik, 495/291-7503, www.kv44.ru
HOURS: Daily noon-2 A.M.
METRO: Arbatskaya
This cute, bohemian piano bar and café, housed in a former two-level apartment, retains a domestic ambience with shelves stuffed with books, backgammon sets on tables, and other home-like bits and bobs scattered about the place. The food is fairly simple European fare; the cheese platter is good value, as is the wine list. There are regular jazz and classical concerts on weekend evenings. A second Kvartira

44 is located at 24/8 Malaya Yakimanka Ulitsa, near the Polyanka metro station.

MAYAK ⓢⓢ
Маяк
19 Bolshaya Nikitskaya Ulitsa, 495/291-9746, 495/291-7449, www.clubmayak.ru
HOURS: Daily noon-6 A.M.
METRO: Arbatskaya
Once a semi-private club, this artsy establishment is now open to all, but still attracts a eclectic mix of actors, artists, journalists, and the like. The interior has an Old World ambience, with its antique cabinets, dark wood furniture, and stucco moldings running around the rim of the ceiling. The menu offers good-value European cuisine, with a good range of cheese as well as pasta dishes, tasty salads, and hot meat and fish dishes with a French accent. The 350R beef steak has devoted fans, and not only for its amazingly low (for Moscow) price. In the evenings there's often live jazz and classical music performances.

SCANDINAVIA ⓢⓢⓢ
Скандинавия
7 Maly Palashevsky Pereulok, 495/937-5630, www.scandinavia.ru
HOURS: Daily noon-1 A.M.
METRO: Pushkinskaya
A true veteran on the restaurant scene, having opened in 1995, this eatery is so popular with local expats that sometimes it seems that half of Moscow's Western contingent is dining in its summer courtyard. Located just off Moscow's main street, the restaurant is right downtown, but its courtyard is secluded enough. It serves modern Scandinavian cuisine, although it often seems like it's the Scandi burger people most often come for. In winter, there's an ice bar in the courtyard.

FRENCH
JEAN-JACQUES ROUSSEAU ⓢⓢ
Жан-Жак Руссо
12 Nikitsky Bulvar, 495/290-3886
HOURS: Daily 24 hours
METRO: Arbatskaya
The original of what is now a chain of French

brasseries in both Moscow and St. Petersburg, this popular hangout has a classic French café interior—deep-red walls lined with mirrors, and chalkboards listing the day's specials. The tables are covered with plain white sheets of paper and the café provides pencils for your drawing pleasure. The menu lists simple French dishes—try the French onion soup. The wine is reasonably priced. A second Jean-Jacques can be found at 24 Tsvetnoy Bulvar.

THE MOST ❸❸❸
6/3 Ul. Kuznetsky Most, 495/660-0706, www.themost.ru
HOURS: Mon.-Thurs. 8 A.M.-midnight, Fri.-Sun. 24 hours
METRO: Teatralnaya

The rococo-style main dining hall heaves with 18th- and 19th-century paintings, trompe l'oeil murals, crystal chandeliers, and loads of gold leaf. There are heavy red-velvet curtains, and waitstaff in specially designed suits by designer Alyona Akhmadullina. This is one posh eatery, a genuine hangout of the elite; it has a nightclub on Friday and Saturday nights where oligarchs are regularly spotted. There are two menus—one is the chef's special with seasonal dishes, and the other is strictly traditional French cuisine. The food is expensive, but the restaurant also serves surprisingly affordable breakfasts 8–11:30 A.M. on weekdays and 11 A.M.–3 P.M. on weekends, with such simple staples as croissants, oatmeal, *croque madame* and *croque monsieur* sandwiches, and bliny. Notebook computers and wireless Internet are available for your use.

FUSION
GALEREYA ❸❸❸
Галерея
27 Ulitsa Petrovka, 495/790-1596, 495/937-4544, 495/937-4504, www.cafegallery.ru
HOURS: Daily 24 hours
METRO: Chekhovskaya

This super-fashionable restaurant has stood the test of time. The collection of cars that gather out front would put most Beverly Hills car dealerships to shame. The regulars are the rich and beautiful (although not necessarily at the same time) and the food is surprisingly good, given that many don't come here for food alone. On the menu, you'll find an eclectic mix that stretches from Italian and other European cuisines, to Japanese- and Chinese-style dishes, including vegetarian and low-calorie offerings.

NEDALNY VOSTOK ❸❸❸
Недальний восток
15 Tverskoy Bulvar, 495/694-0641, 495/694-0154, 495/644-9207, www.novikovgroup.ru/restaurants/east
HOURS: Daily noon-midnight
METRO: Pushkinskaya

A large restaurant with an exquisite interior created by the uber-hip Japanese design group Super Potato, "Not-Far East" has glass walls filled with dried chilies, walls seemingly created from jars of various colorful preserves, and tanks occupied by enormous live Kamchatka crabs. In the center of the restaurant is the open-plan kitchen, which prepares a fusion of pan-Asian cuisine.

INTERNATIONAL
PROSTYE VESHCHI ❸❸
Простые Вещи
32 Konyushkovskaya Ulitsa, 495/255-6362, www.gastropub.ru
HOURS: Mon.-Fri. 9 A.M.-11 P.M., Sat.-Sun. 11 A.M.-11 P.M.
METRO: Krasnopresnenskaya

It calls itself a gastro pub, but it's really a cozy and casual bar and eatery, and a really nice one at that. The food is simple—the restaurant's name means "simple things"—but at the same time innovative; for example, the starters range from tomato with red onion, to asparagus and broccoli with lightly salted salmon and a lemon-olive sauce. There is an excellent selection of reasonably priced wines by the bottle and glass, as well as a variety of special wine accompaniments and some degustation sets. The second Prostye Veshchi is a 24-hour wine bar on Bolshaya Nikitsakaya Ulitsa.

MIDDLE EASTERN
SHAFRAN $$
Шафран

12/9 Spiridonyevsky Pereulok, 495/737-9500,
www.restoran-shafran.ru

HOURS: Daily noon–last guest
METRO: Pushkinskaya

A modern take on a Lebanese restaurant, this
eatery has sleek minimal design with a pale pastel color scheme. The menu has most of your
Lebanese favorites, but many of the dishes have
been lightened up, suitable for those watching
their waistline. Located in the posh Patriarch's
Ponds neighborhood, the restaurant has large
windows to let you gawk at the local well-to-do strutting by.

RUSSIAN
☾ CAFE PUSHKIN $$$
Кафе Пушкинъ

26/5 Tverskoy Bulvar, 495/739-0033
HOURS: Daily 24 hours
METRO: Pushkinskaya

It seems to be de rigueur for local expats to
bring their visiting relatives here for a meal. This
multi-story mansion seems historic, with an ostensibly antique interior, but in fact it was built
just over a decade ago. The service is top-notch,
the refined Russian cuisine is superb, and the
overall atmosphere is wonderful. There is even a
rooftop courtyard for warm summer evenings.
Why not come for a champagne breakfast with
bliny and caviar? It's pricey, but worth it.

GOGOL $$
Гоголь

11 Stoleshnikov Pereulok, Bldg. 1, 495/514-0944
HOURS: Daily 24 hours
METRO: Pushkinskaya or Kuznetsky Most

Patrons enter Gogol through an arch and into
a large tent-like structure. Out through the
other side of the tent is a pleasant open courtyard with tables and chairs surrounded by
high walls, and a modest indoor eatery fitted
out like an old Soviet shot bar. Given the posh
street this self-called "jigger house" is located
on, the establishment is surprisingly down-to-earth and attracts artsy students and bohemian

Gogol's entrance archway

types. The prices are reasonable for the simple
Russian food. Be sure to try the homemade
flavored vodkas—especially the horseradish
one, it's sure to put hairs on your chest.

MARGARITA $$
Маргарита

28 Malaya Bronnaya Ulitsa, 495/299-6534,
495/743-3625
HOURS: Daily 1 P.M.–midnight
METRO: Mayakovskaya

This one's a real hit with tourists—come evening, it can be hard to get a table. It's a small,
cutely decorated Russian restaurant named
and themed after the Bulgakov novel *The
Master and Margarita,* much of which is set
in the surrounding neighborhood. Musicians
crank up the piano and violins in the evening,
and guests are encouraged to join in—all good
fun, but not a place for quiet conversation, and
you have to pay an extra fee for the music.

SLUZHEBNY VKHOD $$
Служебный вход

15 Ulitsa Bolshaya Dmitrovka, 495/692-8997,
495/662-2467, www.svbufet.ru

© NATHAN TOOHEY

HOURS: Daily 11 A.M.-midnight
METRO: Pushkinskaya

A retro Soviet-themed restaurant with all the requisite components, this place even has a mini museum of Soviet nostalgia housed in glass cabinets in the entryway. The main dining hall has the feel of a ministerial restaurant with starched white tablecloths, the odd Roman column, and brass chandeliers. There's a huge screen where the restaurant shows old Soviet films. The menu offers classic Russian (Soviet) dishes.

SEAFOOD
FILIMONOVA & YANKEL $$$
Филимонова и Янкель
23 Tverskaya Ulitsa, 495/223-0707, www.fishhouse.ru
HOURS: Daily noon-midnight
METRO: Pushkinskaya

This is just one in a small chain of fish restaurants offering something new for Moscow. They call themselves "fish houses," and the atmosphere is more relaxed than at most seafood restaurants around town. What's more, they offer a large selection of whole fresh fish at fixed prices, meaning no nasty surprises at the end of the meal (most other seafood restaurants sell their fish by weight, with the final price only being determined after the fish has been put on the scales—and often not revealed until you get the bill).

LA MAREE $$$
28/2 Ulitsa Petrovka, Bldg. 1, 495/694-0930, www.la-maree.ru
HOURS: Daily 11 A.M.-last guest
METRO: Chekhovskaya

This is no mere seafood restaurant, it's a "fish boutique," or that's how it describes itself in any case. The name is probably justified, as the large selection of fresh seafood on ice can be purchased for take-out and prepared at home. The restaurant itself is the epitome of refinement and should satisfy the most demanding diner who can afford the hefty prices.

VEGETARIAN
JAGANNATH $$
Джаганнат
11 Ulitsa Kuznetsky Most, 495/628-3580, www.jagannath.ru
HOURS: Daily 11 A.M.-11 P.M.
METRO: Kuznetsky Most

Located inside a large alternative-lifestyle center, Jagannath offers just what dyed-in-the-wool hippies want but which is find hard to get in Moscow—a real-deal vegetarian restaurant with all the trimmings. The waiters look like they've been teleported out of the musical *Hair,* there are plenty of brochures lying about offering aura-reading services, and the menu features more lentils than you can shake an incense stick at.

Arbat and Kropotkinskaya   Map 4

ASIAN
OM CAFE $$
Ом Кафе
15 Ulitsa Novy Arbat, Bldg. 1, 495/202-1582
HOURS: Daily 11 A.M.-last guest
METRO: Arbatskaya

Located through a golden archway and down a small flight of stairs, this eatery may be a little tricky to find, but it's probably the best value-to-price Thai café in Moscow. There are better, but they cost a bomb, and there are cheaper, but they fail to deliver—Om Cafe is the golden mean. The interior is stuffed with oriental ornaments,

the music is mellow, and the atmosphere is chilled out. There's even an outdoor veranda where it's fun to smoke a hookah in summer. Try the Tom Yum soup; just remember to ask for it spicy.

BEER RESTAURANTS AND PUBS
PLOTNIKOV PUB $$$
Плотников Паб
22/16 Plotnikov Pereulok, 495/241-8799, www.plotnikov-pub.ru
HOURS: Daily 11 A.M.-11 P.M.
METRO: Smolenskaya

Located just off Old Arbat, this place makes for a good spot to stop and rehydrate after some serious souvenir shopping. It's more large and spacious than small and cozy, but that keeps it from getting smoky, and the large windows let you easily watch the world pass by. The menu lists all the pub-grub classics, plus there's a decent draft beer selection.

TINKOFF $$
Тинькофф

11 Protochny Pereulok, 495/777-3300, www.tinkoff.ru
HOURS: Daily noon-2 A.M.
METRO: Smolenskaya

This is the second, after the St. Petersburg branch, in a chain of nationwide microbrewery restaurants. Housed in a custom-designed building opposite the British Embassy, the microbrewery sports a thoroughly modern design, with huge stainless steel vats viewable behind a glass wall, and ceiling-to-floor windows allowing in plenty of light. There are lots of German dishes on the menu, plus pizzas and sushi. The beer is some of the best brewed in Moscow.

CAUCASUS
BARASHKA $$$
Барашка

21 Ulitsa Novy Arbat, 495/228-3731, 495/228-3730, www.novikovgroup.ru/restaurants/barashka2
HOURS: Daily noon-midnight
METRO: Arbatskaya

This restaurant defies the stereotypes. There's no quaint village feel here—it's as slick and contemporary as can be, while using plenty of earthy colors to invoke the spirit of the Caucasus. The huge windows provide great views of modern Novy Arbat and its bustling shoppers. The Azeri (from Azerbaijan) cuisine has also been modernized, which in practice means lightened and presented with artistic flourish, although it's still heavy on meat, particularly lamb. Try the dolma—minced lamb, herbs, and rice wrapped in vine leaves with a garlicky yogurt sauce—or the *dushbara*, a fragrant broth containing tiny lamb-filled dumplings.

the microbrewery beer restaurant, Tinkoff

© NATHAN TOOHEY

GENATSVALE $$
Генацвале

12/1 Ulitsa Ostozhenka, 495/695-0401
HOURS: Daily noon-midnight
METRO: Kropotkinskaya

This large, traditionally styled Georgian restaurant sticks to the tried and trusted formula, both in its boisterous regular eatery and its more upscale VIP section, which has a separate entrance. The interiors evoke old Caucasus Mountains country houses, with wooden fences, vines climbing up old log posts, and hanging strings of dried produce on show. The kitchen prepares all the traditional Georgian dishes, with the shish kebabs, or shashliks, taking pride of place. If the live music doesn't get you dancing, it will certainly stop you conversing.

SHASHLYK-MASHLYK $$
Шашлык-Машлык

38/1 Ulitsa Arbat, Bldg. 1, 495/241-2107, www.arbat38.ru/shashlik
HOURS: Daily 11 A.M.-11:30 P.M.
METRO: Smolenskaya

Shashlyk-Mashlyk offers a wide range of

RESTAURANTS

© NATHAN TOOHEY

Shashlyk-Mashlyk's summer terrace on the Arbat

Caucasus cuisine on its extensive menu, which is available in English—this is the touristy Arbat, after all. Not surprisingly for a restaurant whose name refers to kebabs, its menu offers about 40 sorts of meats and vegetables on skewers, cooked on a special grill. Offal seems to be a specialty. Besides the grilled vegetables, vegetarians should take note of the non-shashlik section of the menu, where they'll find such tasty meat-free treats as *lobio*, or red beans with walnuts and spices, as well as eggplants stuffed with vegetables, walnuts, and spices. The servings come in various sizes, so take note of the weights on the menu before ordering. For dessert, there are Eastern sweets such as baklava. The interior combines stone, wood, tiles, and hand-woven rugs for an authentic ethnic atmosphere, but there's also a veranda out the front where you can combine eating with Arbat people-watching.

TIFLIS $$$
Тифлис
32 Ulitsa Ostozhenka, 499/766-9728, www.tiflis.ru
HOURS: Daily noon-midnight

METRO: Kropotkinskaya
A Georgian restaurant with a classic menu and interior, this eatery even has a small diorama of a mountain village complete with little villagers. The main draw here, however, is the fabulously verdant outdoor terrace and balcony, with bird cages and vines. On a sunny summer day this area provides some of Moscow's nicest alfresco dining.

COFFEE SHOPS
WAYNE'S COFFEE $
36/2 Ulitsa Arbat, Bldg. 1, 495/241-8694,
www.waynescoffee.ru
HOURS: Daily 11 A.M.-11 P.M.
METRO: Arbatskaya
This cute little café just off the Arbat is part of a Scandinavian chain, with coffee shops in Sweden, Finland, Estonia, Poland, and now Russia. It has a simple, modern interior, with plenty of natural light, and outdoor seating both out front and in the back courtyard. There's a full range of coffee and tea drinks, plus hot chocolate including with chili-pepper seasoning. Come for a late breakfast, and you can have

a freshly squeezed orange juice with your bagel. There's a selection of sandwiches and some hot dishes for lunch, and a house beer.

INTERNATIONAL
PRAGA 🅢🅢🅢
Прага

2/1 Ulitsa Arbat, 495/690-6171, www.praga.ru

HOURS: Daily noon–last guest

METRO: Kropotkinskaya

A local legend, this is one of the oldest restaurants in town, having been around since pre-revolutionary days. It was especially highly regarded during Soviet times for its confectionery, which remains to this day—try the sweet called Bird's Milk or Ptiche Moloko, one of the specialties. The restaurant itself is huge, with numerous differently themed halls serving different cuisines, but all opulent in their presentation.

ITALIAN
CANTINETTA ANTINORI 🅢🅢🅢
Кантинетта Антинори

20 Denezhny Pereulok, 495/241-3325, www.novikovgroup.ru/restaurants/antinori

HOURS: Daily noon–midnight

METRO: Smolenskaya

This place is considered to be one of the finest Italian restaurants in town. It's popular and pricey. It has a dedicated following of moneyed Muscovites who come regularly, so you might find it's a bit of a scene. Don't come here in your jeans looking for pizza; dress up and be prepared to spend substantial sums on handmade pasta, grilled meats and fish, antipasti or risotto.

RUSSIAN
MU-MU 🅢
My-My

45/24 Ulitsa Arbat, 495/291-5653, www.cafemumu.ru

HOURS: Daily 10 A.M.–11 P.M.

METRO: Arbatskaya

As the name might suggest, this is one in a chain of restaurants with a cow theme. The eateries are child-friendly places and the little ones really seem to like the bovine motifs found all around the restaurant—especially

© NATHAN TOOHEY

Mu-Mu on the Arbat is an inexpensive and popular place for simple Russian food.

the large black-and-white model cow out front. The restaurant offers a large buffet with dozens of reasonably priced options.

YOLKI PALKI 🅢
Ёлки-Палки

11 Ulitsa Novy Arbat, Bldg. 1, 495/291-7654, www.elki-palki.ru

HOURS: Daily 11 A.M.–11 P.M.

METRO: Arbatskaya

A good choice for vegetarians, this is part of a huge chain of inexpensive Russian restaurants. Designed to resemble a farmyard, the eateries are full of cutesy sunflowers, toy roosters, horseshoes, wicker baskets, and the like. Every restaurant has a large cart, which serves as a fixed-price smorgasbord, loaded with all manner of Russian salads and starters, plus even a few hot side dishes. There are also items that can be ordered separately off the menu, but the cart is your best bet (especially with a shot of vodka or two).

Zamoskvorechye

Map 5

ASIAN
DAYKON $$
Дайкон
36 Pyatnitskaya Ulitsa, 495/951-2972, www.daikon.ru
HOURS: Daily 24 hours
METRO: Tretyakovskaya

A sushi and noodle house is how this place describes itself, but while there is nothing wrong with the sushi here, it's the noodles and other Asian dishes that are worth the trip. The restaurant prepares a wide range of different Asian dishes, including some rarely found in Moscow, such as *laksa* and sour *assam* soups. The atmosphere is relaxed (check out the lovely fish tank) and there is an outdoor veranda suitable for summer evenings. There are also several other locations; see the website for addresses.

BEER RESTAURANTS AND PUBS
DURDIN $$
Дурдинъ
56 Ulitsa Bolshaya Polyanka, 495/953-5200, www.durdin.ru
HOURS: Daily noon-midnight
METRO: Polyanka

One of several affiliated beer restaurants with a turn-of-the-20th-century industrial design, this is a great place to sample the chain's own microbrewed beer, of which there are several varieties. The food is largely traditional Russian, German, and other European, with dishes all chosen to accompany the tasty brews. Although this is a large restaurant with several floors it can be hard to get a table on weekends, so it's worth booking in advance.

DYMOV NO. 1 $$$
Дымов № 1
34 Sofiyskaya Naberezhnaya, 495/951-7571, 495/951-3571, www.dymov1.ru
HOURS: Daily noon-midnight
METRO: Tretyakovskaya or Novokuznetskaya

Modern and bright, this restaurant has wonderful views of the Kremlin from across the Moscow River, making it the pick of the Dymov beer restaurants. Partly owned by a sausage magnate, it features a menu heavy on grilled meats and sausages. The restaurant has become a little less focused on beer recently, but there is still a good selection. They also have a deli section for take-out meats and, rather curiously, a small book shop.

CHINESE
MAMA TAO $
Мама Тао
56 Pyatnitskaya Ulitsa, 495/953-4249, www.mamatao.ru
HOURS: Daily 11 A.M.-11 P.M.
METRO: Novokuznetskaya or Tretyakovskaya

Here you'll find low prices and tasty food—such good value is a rarity in Moscow. Sure, it's not the most authentic Chinese food in town, but it's not the most Europeanized either; the food is light and simple, not greasy, and not too salty. The pictorial menu offers a trusty range of Chinese classics, the sort found in suburban Chinese eateries all over the Western world. There are various soups, spring rolls, and a selection of dim sum, noodles, and rice with extras such as meat or vegetables, and hot courses such as sweet-and-sour prawns and Peking duck. There are separate halls for smokers and non-smokers. As an extra treat, there's a special tea master who performs a tai chi–like dance, swinging around an extremely long-spouted teapot before striking a dramatic pose and pouring into your cup with surprising precision.

FUSION
ART-CAFE SAD $$
Арт-Кафе Сад
3 Bolshoy Tolmachevsky Pereulok, 499/788-9009
HOURS: Daily noon-midnight
METRO: Tretyakovskaya

Located directly opposite the Tretyakov Gallery, this cute little café is a good spot for some after-art nibbles. The endearing feature here is the lovely garden out front, which is shaded by trees—perfect for retreating to on a hot summer day. Inside there's a small gallery with some interesting exhibitions. The menu offers a mix of modern cuisines—European, Japanese, Lebanese, and grill.

GQ BAR ⑤⑤⑤

5 Ulitsa Balchug, 495/956-7775, http://bar.gq.ru
HOURS: Daily 24 hours
METRO: Novokuznetskaya or Tretyakovskaya

Named after the men's magazine, this restaurant is aimed at the man about town and is a thoroughly upmarket affair. It is huge, with an open kitchen and numerous halls including an Asian-styled room. The menu lists a mix of European, pan-Asian, and "Russian trend," a modern take on Russian classics. This is not an inexpensive restaurant.

INTERNATIONAL
CORREA'S ⑤⑤

40 Ulitsa Bolshaya Ordynka, Bldg. 2, 495/725-6035, www.correas.ru
HOURS: Mon.-Fri. 8 A.M.-11 P.M., Sat.-Sun. 9 A.M.-11 P.M.
METRO: Polyanka

Founded by a New Yorker, this eatery serves the closest thing you'll find to New York deli food in Moscow. Located on the grounds of a small business park, it is popular among the local office workers, and getting a table at lunchtime can be problematic. There are lots of sandwiches, tasty pizzas, and interesting salads on the menu, plus a large selection of other offerings on display for guests to choose from. In summer the outdoor patio is particularly nice.

RUSSIAN
GRABLI ⑤
Грабли

27 Pyatnitskaya Ulitsa, 495/545-0830, 495/545-0831, www.grably.ru

HOURS: Daily 10 A.M.-11 P.M.
METRO: Tretyakovskaya

The name means "garden rake," and this budget-priced eatery is designed to look like a country cottage and garden. The ground floor has a smorgasbord buffet, with literally hundreds of different dishes to choose from. Upstairs is a coffee shop, which has a large variety of cakes, tortes, and other such sweets. There's some outdoor seating for warmer weather.

UKRAINIAN
KORCHMA TARAS BULBA ⑤⑤
Корчма Тарас Бульба

14 Pyatnitskaya Ulitsa, 495/953-7153, www.tarasbulba.ru
HOURS: Daily noon-2 A.M.
METRO: Novokuznetskaya

This is one location in a chain of cozy Ukrainian eateries with great food, reasonable prices, a wide range of food for vegetarians and carnivores alike, and menus in every language imaginable. The menu is huge—reading it in its entirety could take about an hour—but it's well organized, so you can quickly and easily skip to the sections that interest you. Vegetarians and pescatarians should go straight to the Lenten or Postnoye menu, where they'll find a wonderfully garlicky vegetarian borsch, and *ukha* fish soup with salmon and sturgeon. Besides hearty meat dishes, there's more veggie food in the hot main courses section, such as *vareniki,* or dumplings, with such fillings as potato and mushroom or cabbage. The liquor selection is solid, with all kinds of *gorilka,* or Ukrainian-style vodka. There are many other eateries in the chain scattered all over the city—look for the logo with the profile of a fearsome-looking man with earrings and a top-knot.

Southwest

Map 6

AMERICAN
STARLITE DINER $$

Ulitsa 9A Korovy Val, 495/959-8919, www.starlite.ru
HOURS: Daily 24 hours
METRO: Oktyabrskaya

One of several eateries in a small chain of American-style diners, this one is located behind a giant Lenin statue. It is housed in an actual diner car and the interior is fitted out in a retro 1950s style, à la *Happy Days.* The menu features all those American comfort foods such as hamburgers, chili, and much-loved milkshakes. It attracts lots of expats who come for a taste of home, but you shouldn't expect U.S. diner prices. Another popular Starlite is near Mayakovskaya metro station, in the garden at 16 Bolshaya Sadovaya Ulitsa.

CAUCASUS
U PIROSMANI $$$

У Пиросмани
4 Novodevichy Proyezd, 499/246-1638, 499/255-7926, www.upirosmani.ru
HOURS: Daily noon-11 P.M.
METRO: Sportivnaya

This classical Georgian restaurant has attracted its fair share of VIPs over the years, including Presidents Clinton and Yeltsin. The large restaurant has an enclosed veranda with seating stretching around two sides of the building and providing what has to be the establishment's main appeal—fabulous views of the Novodevichy Convent and Bolshoy Novodevichy Pond in the garden beside it. It's definitely worth coming here to refuel after visiting the convent.

EUROPEAN
RYTSARSKY CLUB $$$

Рыцарский Клуб
28 Ulitsa Kosygina, 495/930-0726, www.rytclub.ru
HOURS: Daily 1 P.M.-midnight
METRO: Universitet

Here you'll find the best panoramic view in Moscow that's not from atop a skyscraper.

Sky Lounge is on the 22nd floor of the Academy of Sciences building.

Located beside the viewing deck and ski jump at the top of Sparrow Hills, this restaurant offers sweeping views clear across the city. Formerly a Georgian restaurant, it has recently reinvented itself as French. The best way to get here is via the ski lift that works all year round carrying people up from the Moscow River's banks to the viewing deck—and in summer you can reach the ski lift by riverboat.

FUSION
SKY LOUNGE $$$

32A Leninsky Prospekt, 495/938-5775, 495/781-5775, www.skylounge.ru
HOURS: Daily 1 P.M.-last guest
METRO: Leninsky Prospekt

With breathtaking views from its location on the 22nd floor of the "Golden Brains" Academy of Sciences building, this restaurant offers a top-flight experience. The interior is modern and stylish, but on warm summer days the seating on the outdoor balconies can't be beat. The modern food is excellent, but be prepared to pay a hefty sum for the privilege of eating here. There's a cheese menu, a Japanese menu, a wok menu, and an expansive European menu that includes classic pastas, risottos, and salads as well as some original creations, often with an Asian accent.

INDIAN
DARBARS $$
Дарбар

38 Leninsky Prospekt, 495/930-2925, 495/930-2365, www.darbar.ru

HOURS: Daily noon-midnight

METRO: Leninsky Prospekt

Come here for great Indian food with a simply stunning view from the top floor of the Sputnik Hotel. The hotel itself may seem a little Soviet, but the restaurant is top-notch, with good service and tasty, spicy food, including plenty of vegetarian options. It may be out of the way, but the quality of the food plus the view makes this restaurant well worth a visit, especially if you're craving some spice.

ITALIAN
SORRENTO $$$

9 Ulitsa Krymsky Val, Bldg. 2, 495/509-6000, www.sorrentoclub.ru

HOURS: Daily noon-last guest

METRO: Oktyabrskaya

This is a decent Italian restaurant located in a wing of the entrance gates to Gorky Park. There are several rooms with interiors varying from modern to formal; the menu offers modern Italian dishes with sophisticated presentation. The restaurant's most attractive feature, however, is its delightful outdoor patio located behind the restaurant on the park side of the gates.

The decked area is large and shady, and sports comfy sofas that are perfect for lounging after exploring Gorky Park.

RUSSIAN
STOLLE $
Штолле

16 Malaya Pirogovskaya Ulitsa, 499/246-0532, www.stolle.ru

HOURS: Daily 8:30 A.M.–9:30 P.M.

METRO: Sportivnaya

The wonderful chain of St. Petersburg pie shops has opened a branch in the capital and they couldn't have chosen a more appropriate location—Little Pie Street, as the street's name translates. The café follows the same formula as its northern neighbors, with a simple interior and a fantastic selection of both sweet and savory pies available to eat in or take out, all for very low prices.

UZBEK
CHAYKHONA NO. 1 $$
Чайхона No. 1

9 Ulitsa Krymsky Val, Bldg. 38 (inside Gorky Park), www.chaihona.com

HOURS: Daily 1 P.M.–1 A.M.

METRO: Oktyabrskaya or Shabolovskaya

This is a cozy eatery housed in a wooden, circular structure that's reminiscent of a nomad's tent. It's inside Gorky Park, close to the river, with great views to enjoy while lounging on the divan-style outdoor seating and puffing on a hookah with fragrant tobaccos. Inside, there are comfy cushions to recline on, DJs playing a cool mix, and a fireplace to keep you warm in the winter. Try the superb *plov*, a traditional Uzbek pilaf-style rice dish. There's an extensive tea menu. Chaykhona No. 1 has grown into a small chain; one of its nicest other eateries is located in Hermitage Garden.

Southeast
Map 7

BEER RESTAURANT
🅲 BERYOZKA 💲💲
Берёзка

29 Nikoloyamskaya Ulitsa, Bldg. 1, 495/915-5467
HOURS: Daily 11 A.M.-midnight
METRO: Taganskaya

This place is lots of fun in so many ways. For starters, there are beer taps right at the tables, where guests pour their own light or dark microbrewed beer while a meter on the wall clocks up how much beer's been quaffed. The restaurant makes its own tasty sausages, which come in several flavors. On the other hand, Beryozka is a *pelmeni* bar, so there are lots of handmade Russian dumplings to try (although you might want a shot or two of vodka to wash those down with). Finally, the whole place is decorated with birch-tree motifs—which makes sense, as its name means "little birch."

UKRAINIAN
KHATKA CHERVONA RUTA 💲
Хатка Червона Рута

Property 2, 3rd Krutitsky Pereulok, 495/988-2656, 495/506-0033
HOURS: Daily noon-midnight
METRO: Proletarskaya

If you're visiting the Novospassky Monastery and hunger pangs strike, then this is your best bet in the neighborhood. Located directly opposite the monastery, this cute little Ukrainian restaurant is in its own freestanding house. Inside it has two halls, one designed to look like a Ukrainian peasant's hut while the other is designed in a Russian style. The food is simple, but wholesome and tasty—try the berry drinks.

Greater Moscow
Map 8

SEAFOOD
RYBATSKAYA DEREVNYA 💲💲💲
Рыбацкая деревня

Selskokhozyaystvennaya Ulitsa, inside VVTs, 495/772-9072, 495/772-4768,
www.fishing-moscow.ru
HOURS: Daily 11 A.M.-11 P.M.
METRO: Botanichesky Sad

This is not just a mere restaurant, but a whole fishing "village" with ponds, pagodas, huts, a replica of a ship, a sauna, and even paintball. Guests can rent fishing tackle and choose to cast a rod for one of several varieties of fish, including carp, trout, and even sturgeon. Once you've caught something, the restaurant will prepare it and bring it out. For those feeling too lazy to fish for their dinner, the restaurant offers ready-caught fish.

RESTAURANTS

NIGHTLIFE

Moscow is rightfully known for its over-the-top glamorous excess, which manifests itself in a shamelessly decadent club scene. Elitism is the defining principle. The top-flight clubs are interested in movers, shakers, and the models who love them, although the "face controllers" let in a few artsy hipsters to add some color. Pack some serious cash if you plan on going to one of these clubs, and don't count on being let in.

Face control, or selective admittance policies, at the most democratic end of the spectrum can mean simply barring slobs and drunks—but at the elite end of the spectrum, you'll see shockingly snobby attempts at re-creating the hype of Studio 54: Desperate crowds huddle outside a club's door making sexy smiles or pleading eyes at the face controller, who ruthlessly sifts the wheat from the chaff. Usually, places with paid entry will let almost anybody in, while those with face control have free entrance for those who are deemed worthy to enter. The most elite clubs will usually let you in if you book a table, but to do that you need to put down a hefty deposit that will be deducted from your bill. Groups of males without female company are unlikely to be let in anywhere besides gay clubs.

But glamour and elitism aren't all there is to Moscow nightlife. The number and variety of clubs and bars has been growing, and now there's something for just about everyone. The cocktail bar scene has evolved in a more egalitarian direction, much to the delight of locals, who pack into new, inexpensive bars like Help and Tema to work their way through the long and varied lists of creative concoctions.

The live-music scene is huge, with an

© NATHAN TOOHEY

HIGHLIGHTS

LOOK FOR  TO FIND
RECOMMENDED NIGHTLIFE.

◖ Best Live Music Venue: Exemplary taste in its choice of live performers, as well as a cool, multi-level interior, make **Ikra** a class act (page 113).

◖ Most Enduring Mojo: While other clubs come and go, **Propaganda** is a veteran player that never falls out of favor (page 116).

◖ Weirdest Concept: Get intoxicated while incarcerated at **Zona**, a club with a bizarre prison theme (page 117).

◖ Bar with Best View: You'll really feel like you're living the high life as you sip cocktails at **City Space,** with its 360-degree views from 140 meters up (page 117).

◖ Best Bargain Brews: The **Kruzhka** chain of beer bars is like an oasis of inexpensive drinking in an otherwise expensive city (page 118).

◖ Real Retro: Nothing has changed in decades at **Ryumochnaya,** the place to go if you want an authentic blast from the past (page 118).

© NATHAN TOOHEY

the UFO-shaped City Space bar, atop a 140-meter-high tower

overwhelmingly large and diverse selection of local and international acts playing just about every night. Venues range from enormous, like B1, to intimate, like Kitaysky Lyotchik.

There has always been a hipster or bohemian scene, but recently it's been growing exponentially. Older, more bookish players like O.G.I. and Bilingua have now been joined by the trendier Solyanka, which has started spawning other affiliated projects that are always interesting, such as Lebedinoye Ozero (Swan Lake), an outdoor club-restaurant that opened at the back of Gorky Park in the summer of 2008.

Moscow's gay and lesbian club scene is well developed, with a good choice of thriving venues ranging from quiet café-bars to flamboyant discos.

If you don't tolerate smoke, you're out of luck, as smoking is allowed in Moscow's nightlife venues and nonsmoking nightclubs and bars are as rare as hens' teeth. But there is an alternative: Most restaurants have nonsmoking sections, serve alcohol, and are open late—some even have DJs. Also, there are a couple of totally nonsmoking eateries. There is also one restaurant included in the *Bars* section of this chapter—the retro Russian eatery/bar Ryumochnaya, which has a good range of booze—a good place for a drink if you'd rather avoid smoke.

There are a couple of other local peculiarities that might strike some visitors as odd. Your bag might be searched by the guards at the entrance, and you might have to walk through a metal detector. Most places won't let you wear a coat inside—you have to take it off and leave it at the cloakroom, or *garderob* (гардероб); this is a free service and the attendants don't expect a tip, but of course would be thrilled to get one.

Live Music

B1
Б1
11 Ulitsa Ordzhonikdze, 495/648-6777
HOURS: Daily 6 P.M.–6 A.M.
COST: Varies
METRO: Leninsky Prospekt
Map 6

This out-of-the-way live-music venue is located in a former warehouse. It is enormous, with space for several thousand people, and as such it tends to attract acts that aren't likely to fill a stadium, but that are too big to perform at a club. There is plenty of balcony space, so it's fairly easy to get a decent view.

B2
Б2
8 Bolshaya Sadovaya, 495/650-9909, 495/650-9918, www.b2club.ru
HOURS: Daily noon–6 A.M.
COST: Varies
METRO: Mayakovskaya
Map 3

Although affiliated with B1, B2 actually came first. It's located right downtown, so it's easier to find. One of the city's better live-music venues, it has ample space in the top-floor concert area and several other lower floors filled with bars, eateries, billiards, and even a jazz bar. There are tango dance nights, including master classes, on Tuesdays and Thursdays. In summer there is an outdoor patio.

THE CAFE FORMERLY KNOWN AS CRISIS GENRE
Kafe, Prezhde Izvestnoye
Kak "Krizis Zhanra"
Кафе, прежде известное
как "Кризис жанра"
16/16 Ulitsa Pokrovka, Bldg. 1, www.kriziszhanra.ru
HOURS: Daily 11 A.M.–6 A.M.
COST: Usually free
METRO: Chistye Prudy
Map 2

This small nightclub tends to have live acts only on weekends, with DJs spinning discs the rest of the time. It attracts a young crowd of cool kids who come for the club's progressive music policy, which tends to feature the latest indie flavor of the moment. The prices at the bar are very reasonable. The face control can be rather unpredictable so it's best to arrive early if you want to be sure to get in.

⚫ IKRA
Икра

8 Ulitsa Kazakova, 495/778-5651, www.nobullshit.ru
HOURS: Daily noon-7 A.M.
COST: Free entry to bar, concert prices vary
METRO: Kurskaya
Map 8

This is definitely one of the hippest live-music venues in town. The organizers take pride in inviting cutting-edge performers from around the world—among them Psychic TV and Roisin Murphy—which in turn draws a cool crowd of hipsters. Besides the music, there are also several groovy bars to choose from on the club's numerous floors. There's a small, intimate bar with 1960s op-art decor and cozy sofas, a larger bar with furry walls attached to the middle hall with small stage and mini dance floor, and another bar on the top floor, where there's a large stage and spacious auditorium that also serves as a dance floor.

KITAYSKY LYOTCHIK JAO DA
Китайский лётчик Джао Да

25/12 Lubyansky Proyezd, Bldg. 1, 495/624-5611, 495/623-2896, www.jao-da.ru
HOURS: Mon.-Fri. 10 A.M.-8 A.M., Sat.-Sun. noon-10 A.M.
COST: Varies for concerts, other times free
METRO: Kitay-Gorod
Map 2

Named after a fanciful Chinese pilot named Jao Da (though everyone just calls it Kitaysky Lyotchik), this bohemian club is a true veteran on the live-music scene. Located in a basement, its interior is fairly basic, with the main feature being the bar, which is designed to resemble an airplane's wing. The club attracts artists, students, and various alternative types who come to see the eclectic mix of interesting bands. The food's not bad either, and the kitchen is open till morning.

16 TONN
Shestnadtsat tonn
Шестнадцать тонн

6 Presnensky Val Ulitsa, Bldg. 1., 495/253-5300, 495/253-0530, www.16tons.ru
HOURS: Daily 11 A.M.-6 A.M.
COST: Free entry to bar, concert prices vary
METRO: Ulitsa 1905 Goda
Map 8

This long-running establishment combines an English-style pub serving microbrewed beer downstairs with a live-music space upstairs. Come for some tasty pre-concert brews before heading upstairs to catch a band. The collection of live acts is diverse, varying from Russian indie rock to European electronica. The downstairs section looks a bit like a kit pub, with its nostalgic British knickknacks. Often a sports game is playing on the large screens, and a moneyed, mature crowd of Russians and expats. Upstairs, the decor is a more of an eclectic fusion of high-tech and retro, and the clientele varies depending on who's playing.

TOCHKA
Точка

6 Leninsky Prospekt, 495/737-7666, www.clubtochka.ru
HOURS: Daily 6 P.M.-last guest
COST: Varies
METRO: Oktyabrskaya
Map 6

Hidden down a small alleyway, this club can be a challenge to find—look for a small sign on Leninsky Prospekt next to the hospital. The huge venue specializes in heavy rock, metal, industrial, and other alternative/indie styles of music. Besides numerous bars, there is a large billiards room for killing some time while waiting for the band to kick off.

NIGHTLIFE

Jazz and Blues

BLUE BIRD
Sinyaya Ptitsa
Синяя Птица
23/15 Ulitsa Malaya Dmitrovka, 495/699-2225,
www.bluebirdjazz.ru
HOURS: Daily noon-midnight, live music nightly from
7:30 P.M.
COST: Varies upwards from 200R
METRO: Pushkinskaya
Map 3

Moscow's oldest jazz club, Sinyaya Ptitsa opened in 1964, when jazz was something radical and rebellious, associated with dissidents. Back then there was a saying, "Today he's playing jazz; tomorrow he'll sell the Motherland." Nearly all of Russia's jazz stars have played in this historic club, as well as some big international names, including the Thad Jones Big Band, Pat Metheny, and Billy Taylor. The legendary venue continues its traditions with nightly shows covering the full range of jazz.

CAFE RAY
46 Novoslobodskaya Ulitsa, 499/972-4577
HOURS: Mon.-Fri. 10 A.M.-midnight, Sat.-Sun.
10 A.M.-6 A.M.
COST: Free
METRO: Mendeleyevskaya
Map 8

Jazz and pizza may seem like a strange combination, but that's just what this café and bar offers. The pizza is good and inexpensive, as is the beer. The front section's redbrick interior features large murals of jazzy characters getting down; here the jazz plays the role of background music and it's quiet enough to talk. The concerts are held in a large room out back, where the atmosphere and setting are reminiscent of a supper club.

COOL TRAIN CLUB
8 Bolshaya Sadovaya, 495/650-9909, 495/650-9918,
www.b2club.ru/jazz/
HOURS: Daily noon-6 A.M.
COST: 300-500R Thurs.-Sun. after 7 P.M.
METRO: Mayakovskaya
Map 3

Hidden deep inside the colossal B2 is this club within a club. The interior is decorated with black-and-white photos of both Western and Russian jazz stars from yesteryears. Besides the regular jazz concerts, the club provides backgammon and chess sets for whiling away the time, and there are hookahs available as well. It attracts a mixed crowd, from young boppers to jazz veterans.

ROAD HOUSE
Dom u dorogi
Дом у дороги
8 Ulitsa Dovatora, 499/245-4183, 499/245-5543,
www.roadhouse.ru
HOURS: Sun.-Tues. noon-midnight, Wed.-Sat. noon-5 A.M.
COST: Varies
METRO: Sportivnaya
Map 6

This one's a rarity in Moscow—a true down-to-earth blues bar. The interior is basic, with exposed brick and natural wood, and it's smoky—but hey, what would you expect? There's American pool, a good range of whisky and other spirits, draft beer and cocktails, plus plenty of hearty eats including chicken wings, pizzas, and a range of grilled meats. In short—everything a homesick American could want.

Dance Clubs

BLACK STAR CLUB

2 Ploshchad Kievskaya Vokzala, 495/220-5510
HOURS: Mon.-Thurs. noon-midnight, Fri.-Sat.
noon-6 A.M., Sun. noon-3 A.M.
COST: Free if you pass face control
METRO: Kievskaya
`Map 8`

Timati is Russia's most prominent R&B star and this is his latest club. Located on the top floor of the Yevropeysky mall, the club features a restaurant, the club area, and a large summer terrace. One novelty is the rooftop car park—just keep in mind that besides the regular face control, there's also "car control," so you'd better polish up the Lamborghini and leave the Lada at home if you want to get into this top nightspot.

FABRIQUE

2 Kosmodamianskaya Ulitsa, 495/953-6576,
495/540-9955, www.fabrique.ru
HOURS: Daily 9 P.M.-7 A.M.
COST: Free

METRO: Novokuznetskaya
`Map 5`

This huge nightclub boasts a large dance space with a balcony overlooking it, an upstairs dining area with a transparent floor, various lounge areas, and even an outdoor section. It gets loud and crowded. The mixed crowd is fairly down-to-earth and the door policy is more about keeping the crowd numbers manageable than maintaining the beauty quotient. Fabrique sometimes gets in some top-name DJs.

KARMA BAR

3 Pushechnaya Ulitsa, 495/624-5633, 495/789-6901,
www.karma-bar.ru
HOURS: Daily 9 P.M.-6 A.M.
COST: Free-300R
METRO: Kuznetsky Most
`Map 2`

This club, which features an exotic Asian-themed interior, is quite popular with foreign tourists and local expats, who come for its relaxed door policy and commercial Top 40–style

Mio is a cool electronic dance music nightclub.

music program. Besides its regular parties, it also attracts a crowd to its salsa events. Held earlier in the evening, they include a show and the chance to dance some salsa yourself—there are even lessons offered.

MIO
Мио

1 Kaluzhskaya Ploshchad, 495/238-5848, www.cafemio.ru
HOURS: Daily 24 hours
COST: Free except when special guest DJs play
METRO: Oktyabrskaya
Map 6

This cute little club is probably Moscow's premier electro venue. People come here for the music, which is a refreshing change from many of the other clubs around town. Besides some great DJs, the club also serves some decent Asian food and the drinks are reasonably priced. There is a small outdoor patio, which is pleasant for relaxing after a hard night's dancing.

OPERA
Опера

6 Tryokhgorny Val Ulitsa, 495/605-8900, 495/605-9822, www.clubopera.ru
HOURS: Daily 11:30 P.M.-6 A.M.
COST: Free if you pass face control
METRO: Ulitsa 1905 Goda
Map 8

Opera is another of Moscow's glamour clubs, with all the bells and whistles that you'd expect to find in such a place. Its two levels are surrounded by a circular stage where various shows and performances are held. As is typical at these clubs, the beautiful people come here more to see and be seen than for the musical program, which consists primarily of commercial house and R&B.

◖ PROPAGANDA
Пропаганда

7 Bolshoi Zlatoustinsky Pereulok, 495/624-5732, www.propagandamoscow.com
HOURS: Daily noon-6 A.M.
COST: Varies

METRO: Kitay-Gorod
Map 2

One of the oldest dance clubs in town, this place still boasts some serious mojo. It tends to attract a student crowd with its reasonably priced drinks and food. As it is fairly small it can get packed to the rafters on weekends, and so it can be hard to get in later in the evenings even though the face control is quite moderate. The club holds popular gay nights called Chinatown on Sundays. The guards vigilantly put a stop to any dancing that might break out on the stairs or balcony, so try to resist the urge to have a bit of a boogie up there.

RAI
Рай

9A Bolotnaya Naberezhnaya, 495/767-1474, 495/230-0035, www.raiclub.ru
HOURS: Fri.-Sat. 10 P.M.-7 A.M.
COST: Free if you pass face control
METRO: Kropotkinskaya
Map 4

This is a club in the style that made Moscow famous for its nightlife—an over-the-top, super-indulgent extravaganza of glamour and glitz. The huge club can hold some 3,000 people, which doesn't by any means suggest that it's any easier to get in, as the face control here is super-strict (think models and millionaires). The music here plays second fiddle, and basically consists of disco and vocal house.

SOLYANKA
Солянка

11 Ulitsa Solyanka, 495/221-7557, www.s-11.ru
HOURS: Sun.-Wed. noon-midnight, Thurs.-Sat. noon-7 A.M.
COST: Free Sun.-Wed., 300–500R Thurs.-Sat. after 11 P.M.
METRO: Kitay-Gorod
Map 2

One of the hippest clubs in town, Solyanka is located on the 2nd floor of an old house. Inside it feels somewhat like a large apartment with big windows, low-lying tables, and sofas for lounging on. It attracts a trendy crowd of artists, musicians, journalists, and the like, who come for the up-to-the-moment music mix and laid-back atmosphere. There's free wireless Internet, decent food, and a hip clothing store.

◖ ZONA

19 Leninskaya Sloboda, 495/675-6975, www.zonaclub.ru
HOURS: Daily 10 P.M.-8 A.M.
COST: Varies
METRO: Avtozavodskaya
Map 8

This far-flung club is located way out in an industrial zone, although that's not where it gets its name from. The giant club is designed to look like an enormous prison camp complete with barbed wire and prison cells. Given its location and theme, it's not surprising that it's a fairly egalitarian establishment. Its clientele seems to be mostly young clubbers from the local suburbs, as well as electronic music fans who travel across town to hear the big-name DJs who sometimes play here, such as London's Seb Fontaine.

Bars

BILINGUA

10 Krivokolenny Pereulok, Bldg. 5, 495/623-9660, www.bilinguaclub.ru
HOURS: Daily 24 hours
METRO: Turgenevskaya
Map 2

Bohemian central is the best way to describe this place. There's a bookstore on the premises, as well as a clothing store with handmade funky fashions. The bar itself is large and hosts various alternative performances and events, including film screenings. There's a good range of vodka-friendly snacks, and everything's fairly inexpensive.

◖ CITY SPACE

52 Kosmodamianskaya Naberezhnaya, Bldg. 6, 495/787-9800
HOURS: Daily 5 P.M.-2 A.M.
METRO: Paveletskaya
Map 7

You can't really appreciate just how big Moscow is until you see it from above, and that's just what you can do from this bar located 140 meters above the city on the top of the Swissotel Krasye Holmy hotel. The bar sweeps around a full 360 degrees, providing spectacular panoramic views for you to enjoy while you sip on a Singapore Sling or perhaps the barman's own version of a martini, the City Space Tini. There is food as well, such as oysters and lobster bisque, but really this is a place to come for cocktails. Prices, naturally, are also sky high.

DENIS SIMACHEV BAR

12 Stoleshnikov Pereulok, Bldg. 2, 495/629-8085
HOURS: Daily 24 hours
METRO: Pushkinskaya
Map 3

Russia's most fashionable designer, Denis Simachev, didn't just open his own boutique, he opened a boutique club. In addition to selling his fashion creations, it also sells food and drinks with an oh-so-hip vibe. Bizarrely, it has a toilet theme, with some tables styled after bathroom sinks. The club's about the size of a large closet, and everyone and his dog wants in, so get here early if you want any chance of seeing the inside.

FLORIDITA

36/2 Ulitsa Arbat, 495/626-7177, www.floridita.co.uk/moscow/ru/index.php
HOURS: Daily noon-last guest
METRO: Smolenskaya
Map 4

The legendary Havana bar, with branches around the world, opened on Ulitsa Arbat in 2008. As it's a Cuban bar, you can expect to find a good selection of rums, cocktails, and hand-rolled cigars. There's live music on Thursday, Friday, and Saturday nights, featuring Cuban musicians and various genres including salsa, reggae, and hip-hop. This isn't some kitschy themed bar, however—it's actually pretty slick and almost minimal in its presentation.

HELP

27 1st Tverskaya-Yamskaya Ulitsa, 495/995-5395, www.helpbar.ru
HOURS: Daily 24 hours
METRO: Belorusskaya
Map 3

This spot heralded a new era on the Moscow bar scene. Prior to its arrival, cocktail bars were expensive and stuck up—but Help put an end to that. It offers a huge range of inexpensive cocktails, and the crowd is fun and uninhibited—you can expect dancing on the tables once the evening warms up. One cool quirk is that the menu includes the history of each classic cocktail, as well as some of the more recent creations, which makes for fun reading and drinking.

KRUZHKA

Кружка
13 Myasnitskaya Ulitsa, Bldg. 1, 495/621-1522, 495/621-1626, www.kruzhka.ru
HOURS: Sun.-Thurs. noon-midnight, Fri.-Sat. noon-4 A.M.
METRO: Lubyanka
Map 2

Who says that Moscow's the most expensive city in the world? Kruzhka sells its house draft beers for the equivalent of a couple of dollars, making this vast chain of beer bars one of the best values in the capital. Sure, the interior is not too swish, and the menu is basically street-kiosk take-out kebabs and the like served on a plate, but hey, there's sports on TV and it's cheap, cheap, cheap. See the website for more locations, or look out around town for the orange sign depicting a beer mug between a knife and fork.

O2

3-5 Tverskaya Ulitsa, 495/225-8888
HOURS: Daily 24 hours
METRO: Okhotny Ryad
Map 1

This is probably Moscow's swankiest bar. Located on top of the city's poshest hotel, the Ritz-Carlton, the glass-covered bar provides stunning views of Red Square and the Kremlin. In summer, there's a grill on the open terrace, which is big enough to fit 200 people. Japanese chef Seiji Kusano's sushi is superb, as are the drinks—just be prepared to pay an arm and a leg for the privilege. You can order cocktails by the jug. After dark, DJs turn up the music to create a more club-like atmosphere.

PIRO.G.I

ПирО.Г.И
19/2 Nikolskaya Ulitsa, 495/621-5827
HOURS: Daily 24 hours
METRO: Lubyanka
Map 2

A bohemian joint with all the trappings, this basement has books on the shelves and plenty of artsy students who read them while stroking their pointy beards. The interior is fairly utilitarian and the menu is straightforward, with a wide range of simple Russian and European dishes for reasonable prices. There are even breakfast choices, which might appeal if your night out stretches to morning. People like to smoke here; if you don't tolerate smoke, then this is not the place for you. However, if you're a chain-smoking poet who likes to pontificate while sipping a cheap glass of wine, then this place is right up your alley.

RYUMOCHNAYA

Рюмочная
22/2 Bolshaya Nikitskaya Ul., Bldg. 1, 495/291-5474
HOURS: Daily 11 A.M.-11 P.M.
METRO: Arbatskaya
Map 3

This place is a true institution and definitely one of a dying breed. Said to have been working as a tavern on and off for over 125 years, it's a true throwback to several decades ago. The decor is simple as can be, with modest potted plants in the windows and humorous signs such as "free beer tomorrow" around the walls. The food is displayed on the counter and reheated in the microwave, but it's hardly the focus at a place where the name means "shot bar." The vodka is super cheap, and so is the beer. Unusually, it's totally nonsmoking.

FACE CONTROL

Adding an element of challenge and risk to a night out, local nightclubs have "face control." Face control – the term for selective admittance or door policies – can range from barring drunks at one end of the spectrum, right up to snobby attempts to recreate the hype of Studio-54, a legendary Manhattan nightclub frequented by celebrities in the late 1970s.

Face controllers are not bouncers, but celebrities of the nightlife world, prized by club promoters for their face recognition, memory, and fashion sense. The most famous is known as Pasha Face Control, whose renown has spread to the extent that there have been pop songs and music videos about him.

Usually places with paid entry will let just about anybody in, while those with face control have free entrance for those who are deemed worthy to enter. In the elite clubs, you can forget equality of the sexes: men need to look moneyed, and women need to be young and beautiful (the more like Barbie, the better). Shoes can be a deciding factor. The cruellest face controllers will split up groups, testing friendships by letting in some people but rejecting a few of their companions. Even "democratic" clubs have a tendency to arbitrarily turn people away, and arguing with the face controller will get you nowhere. But even in the most elite clubs, face controllers usually also let in a small quota of hip, artsy, bohemian, or alternative types, just to keep things interesting. Unless you're someone famous, the face controller knows you, or you've been personally invited by the club's management and your name is on the "door list," you can never be sure where you will get in, and where you won't.

Rejection by an all-powerful face controller can spoil a night out, while those who are accepted feel the euphoria of entering an elite, exclusive world. Though turning potential clients away might sound like a dubious business strategy, in practice face control is something that Moscow clubs boast about in their advertising. The "in crowd" knows no outsiders will get in, and the rejects only become more determined. The desperate crowds huddling at clubs' entrances only add to the hype.

SILVER'S IRISH PUB

5/6 Tverskaya Ulitsa, 495/690-4222
HOURS: Daily noon-midnight
METRO: Okhotny Ryad
Map 1

While most of Moscow's other "pubs" are really just "beer restaurants," this one's the real deal. It's a smoky, stand-at-the-bar kind of place that gets packed with expats; it's an easy place to make new friends. Late at night they serve up Irish stew. The Mexican food is good, as is the beer selection.

SORRY, BABUSHKA

2/1 Slavyanskaya Ploshchad, 499/788-0615,
www.sorrybabushka.ru
HOURS: Sun.-Wed. noon-midnight, Thurs.-Sat. noon-6 A.M.
METRO: Kitay-Gorod
Map 2

This bar features oversized photo murals of various comical characters, including the bar's namesake babushka, or grandmother. Unless you've got a friend with a discount club card, the prices are high, but that doesn't seem to stop it getting packed with college students on weekends. The music can be quite commercial, but sometimes there are interesting guest DJs and live acts.

TEMA

5 Potapovsky Pereulok, Bldg. 2, 495/624-2720,
www.temabar.ru
HOURS: Daily 24 hours
METRO: Chistye Prudy
Map 2

This bar continues the Help cocktail-bar genre and shares the same creators. It pretty much follows the same formula, with cheap cocktails and a party atmosphere, only it's a little larger and there's more room for dancing. The bar staff are adept at tossing bottles, which makes for a good show. A fun night is guaranteed, if you can get a spot.

NIGHTLIFE

TIKI BAR
Тики-Бар

3A Sadovaya-Kudrinskaya Ulitsa, 495/741-2203,
www.tiki-bar.ru
HOURS: Daily 24 hours
METRO: Barrikadnaya
Map 3

Perfect for dreary winter days, this bar injects a tropical touch into downtown Moscow. The massive cocktail bar features a Hawaiian theme with a retro '70s twist. Besides the compulsory totem poles and surfboards, there are even swinging dingy boats that serve as table seating. Naturally, there is an excellent range of tropical cocktails, some of which even come served in four-liter portions.

VISION

11 Ulitsa Novy Arbat, 495/727-3230
HOURS: Daily 11 A.M.-2 A.M.
METRO: Arbatskaya
Map 4

This is a true cocktail bar in the classic sense of the word. The bar sports a modern, minimalist interior, which doesn't seem to stop it being comfy, and there are huge windows running across the front of the bar providing excellent views down onto Novy Arbat below. Sure there's food on the menu, but it's really all about the cocktails—there are more than a hundred of them—but it's not particularly cheap here.

VODKA BAR

18B Ulitsa Lva Tolstogo, 495/246-9669,
www.vodkabar.ru
HOURS: Mon.-Fri. noon-midnight, Sat.-Sun. noon-6 A.M.
METRO: Park Kultury
Map 4

This is a large and spacious bar with high ceilings and plenty of room for dancing. The interior features some cool design work with an eclectic mix of modern Russian and Soviet motifs. As you would expect, the menu features a huge variety of vodkas, some of which have been known to have been poured gratis into customers' waiting open mouths by go-go girls dancing on the bar. There are good Russian snacks, which can be ordered by the spoonful.

Wine Bars

GRAND CRU BLACK

22 Malaya Bronnaya Ulitsa, 495/775-5553,
www.grandcru.ru
HOURS: Daily 10 A.M.-11 P.M.
METRO: Pushkinskaya
Map 3

Grand Cru is a stylish wine bar, with chic black walls, beaded curtains, and comfortable leather seating, with wine magazines strewn about for you to peruse while you savor a good drop. The wine list is extensive but not as expensive as might be expected, and since the bar doubles as a wine boutique, you can buy bottles of your favorites to take away. There are several other Grand Cru wine stores around the city, but this is the only one that's also a bar. Food-wise, there's a selection of cheeses and cold meats, such as ham and various sausages, as well as Mediterranean-style hot dishes, such as calamari risotto. The desserts menu tempts with basil ice cream and berry soup.

PROSTYE VESHCHI
Простые Вещи

14 Bolshaya Nikitskaya Ulitsa, Bldg. 2, 495/629-3494,
www.gastropub.ru
HOURS: Daily 24 hours
METRO: Biblioteka imeni Lenina
Map 3

This is a cozy and casual wine bar, and a really nice one at that. The arched brick ceilings are not red but white, keeping the place bright and cheerful. In summer, there's an outdoor terrace. There is an excellent selection of reasonably priced wines by the bottle and glass, and some degustation sets. The food is simple—the place's name means "simple things"—and the menu lists lots of tasty things that go nicely with wine, such as cheeses and giant olives. There's another location with more limited hours—it's an eatery opposite the zoo at 32 Konyushkovskaya Ulitsa.

VINOSYR
ВиноСыр

6 Maly Palashevsky Per., 495/739-1045,
www.vinosyr.ru
HOURS: Daily 3 P.M.-12:30 A.M.
METRO: Pushkinskaya
Map 3

Located just off Pushkin Square, this tiny basement wine bar offers only the smallest selection of snacks, but an enormous selection of wines by the bottle or the glass, at highly competitive prices. The selection includes French, Italian, Spanish, Argentine, Uruguayan, U.S., South African, Australian, and New Zealand labels. There are a half-dozen cured meat and sausage options, as well as a cheese selection, sold in 20-gram options or as combined platters. With seating for about 30 people, mostly around a long bench in the center of the room, it has exposed pipes, raw-brick walls painted red, and subdued lighting. Free wireless Internet is a bonus.

Gay and Lesbian

DUSHA I TELO
Душа и тело

19A Ulitsa Kuusinena, 495/943-3206,
www.clubchance.net
HOURS: Mon.-Thurs. and Sun. 11 P.M.-6 A.M., Fri.-Sat.
11 P.M.-7 A.M.
COST: Free Mon.-Thurs. and Sun., 100R Fri.-Sat.
METRO: Polezhayevskaya
Map 8

Come here if you're looking for a hot and happening nightclub with wild parties, drag shows, and performances by gay icons. This is a large venue of 1,000 square meters with two dance floors, one of which has a spacious balcony, and four bars, a restaurant, billiards, a big stage, and a large room for sitting and talking.

TRI OBEZYANI NEW AGE
Три обезьяны

11 Nastavnichesky Pereulok, Bldg. 1, 495/916-3555
HOURS: Daily 7 P.M.-7 A.M.
COST: Free-250R
METRO: Chkalovskaya
Map 7

Three bars on three levels, a large dance floor with seven-meter-high ceilings, two stages, a VIP section, karaoke, cinema, library, restaurant, summer terrace, and wireless Internet are all at your service in this club. There are drag, strip, and dance shows, DJs playing a diverse mix of music, and the club has a varied program that includes women's nights.

12 VOLT
12 вольт

12 Tverskaya Ulitsa, Bldg. 2, 495/933-2815,
www.12voltclub.ru
HOURS: Daily 6 P.M.-6 A.M.
COST: Free
METRO: Tverskaya
Map 3

This popular café-club was opened in 2003 by prominent members of the gay and lesbian community as a place for gays and lesbians to meet, eat, hang out, and find information about important issues. It has DJs and parties on Friday and Saturday nights, background music at other times, inexpensive food, low-priced drinks with special offers almost nightly, and wireless Internet.

NIGHTLIFE

ARTS AND LEISURE

Moscow is one of the world's cultural capitals and offers an abundance of arts and entertainment of the highest quality. The top museums, such as the Kremlin Armory, the Pushkin State Museum of Fine Arts, and the State Tretyakov Gallery, have collections of great wealth and scope, but there are also countless other smaller museums offering stimulating and often surprising exhibits—the vodka museum, for example, and the many apartment-museums of great writers and artists. A recent trend to create arts centers in former industrial sites has given gallery-hopping a boost at such exciting new complexes as Art-Strelka and Winzavod.

Theater is another of the city's strengths, but since drama performances tend to be in Russian they're unsuitable for visitors who don't understand the language. More accessible to spectators of all ages are the circuses and animal theaters, a genre in which Russia excels. And while a night at the ballet or opera is an obligatory part of most tourists' itineraries, don't forget about concerts—Russia has a strong musical tradition and performers of the highest international standard. A good time to catch some classical music is during one of the seasonal arts festivals, but there are less high-brow festivals worth checking out as well—from pancakes at Maslenitsa to tasty brews at the Beer Festival.

And while you might not expect it of such a huge metropolis, Moscow is quite a green city with some excellent parks that provide a great setting for skiing, skating, or just plain strolling. Some of these parks are old estates of royalty and the nobility, with historical and architectural landmarks to admire. And believe it or not, the city even has beaches where you can take a dip in the summer—or in winter, as some do.

© NATHAN TOOHEY

HIGHLIGHTS

LOOK FOR  TO FIND RECOMMENDED ARTS AND ACTIVITIES.

◖ Best Gallery: From ancient icons to modern masterpieces, the **State Tretyakov Gallery Complex** is the place to acquaint yourself with the full spectrum of Russian art (page 124).

◖ Best Show: One of the world's greatest ballet and opera institutions, the **Bolshoi Theater** needs no introduction (page 131).

◖ Most Surprising: Common wisdom says cats don't do tricks, but **Kuklachyov Cat Theater** has some pretty tricky cats (page 133).

◖ Best Fest: Everybody loves pancakes, and **Maslenitsa** gives you an excellent excuse to indulge (page 134).

◖ Most Invigorating: Steam clean in palatial surroundings at the historic **Sandunovskiye Bani** bathhouse (page 139).

◖ Best Snow in Summer: Have a full Russian winter experience any time at **Snej .com,** Europe's largest all-season indoor ski facility, also with ice skating, saunas, and other fun (page 141).

© NATHAN TOOHEY

State Tretyakov Gallery

The Arts

GALLERIES AND EXHIBITION HALLS

ART-STRELKA
Арт-Стрелка
14 Bersenevskaya Naberezhnaya, Bldg. 5
(Red October Chocolate Factory territory),
916/112-7180, www.artstrelka.ru
HOURS: Tues.-Sat. 4-8 P.M.
COST: Free
METRO: Kropotkinskaya
Map 5

Moscow's mini-SoHo, Art-Strelka is a cluster of hip modern art galleries in hangar-like former garages of the Red October Chocolate Factory, just across the pedestrian bridge from Christ the Savior Cathedral. Its opening in 2004 came at the beginning of a trend to convert downtown industrial sites into other uses including cultural and entertainment complexes.

CENTRAL EXHIBITION HALL "MANEZH"
Tsentralny vystavochny zal "Manezh"
Центральный выставочный зал "Манеж"
1/9 Mokhovaya Ulitsa, 495/540-2828,
www.manegemoscow.ru
HOURS: Vary depending on exhibit; generally Tues.-Sun. from about 10 or 11 A.M. to 8 or 9 P.M.
COST: Varies depending on exhibit
METRO: Alexandrovsky Sad
Map 1

From Rodchenko retrospectives to contemporary shows such as the annual Art Manezh and the Photobiennale, there's almost always something interesting on at the Manezh—but

ARTS AND LEISURE

the 5,000-square-meter space also hosts trade and other fairs, so you might find that there's fur or honey on display instead of art. Located right beside the Kremlin in a yellow-and-cream temple-form Neoclassical building, the Manezh was originally constructed 1817–1825 to an innovative structural design by Spanish engineer Agustin de Betancourt, with its exterior by architect Osip Bove. Intended as a manège, or indoor equestrian academy, it has been an exhibition hall since 1831. It was rebuilt after a fire in 2004.

CENTRAL HOUSE OF ARTISTS
Tsentralny dom khudozhnika
Центральный Дом Художника
10 Krymsky Val Ul., 495/238-9634, 495/238-9843, www.cha.ru
HOURS: Daily 11 A.M.–8 P.M., ticket office until 7 P.M.
COST: 50-100R
METRO: Oktyabrskaya
Map 5

The Central House of Artists, or TsDKh, is an exhibition space with constantly changing contemporary art displays, from the famous to the not so well known. There is also a large range of stores selling not only art, but handicrafts, jewelry, posters, clothes, souvenirs, and more. An onsite café provides refreshments. TsDKh is housed in a giant brick of a building that even the most avid art lover will admit is just plain unattractive. There are plans for its demolition to make way for a Norman Foster–designed 80,000-square-meter multipurpose building. The controversial project, which has been described as looking like a giant semi-peeled orange, would include a hotel and luxury apartments. The ground floor would be given back to the gallery.

ILYA GLAZUNOV GALLERY
Galereya Ili Glazunova
Галерея Ильи Глазунова
13 Ulitsa Volkhonka, 495/291-6949, www.glazunov.ru
HOURS: Tues.-Sun. midday-8 P.M.
COST: 20-60R
METRO: Kropotkinskaya
Map 4

Contemporary artist Ilya Glazunov's gallery across the road from the Pushkin Fine Arts Museum is worth a look. Although his epic works could be described as patriotic and somewhat fanciful, they are truly amazing. Large, colorful, and incredibly monumental, they encompass broad themes, such as "Eternal Russia," and significant historical events, such as the "Kulikovo Field" series, which consists of several dozen paintings on the theme of the Kulikovo Battle. Religion is another predominant theme, with Christ represented in numerous paintings.

◖ STATE TRETYAKOV GALLERY COMPLEX
Gosudarstvennaya Tretyakovskaya galereya kompleks
Государственная Третьяковская галерея
10 Lavrushinsky Pereulok, 495/951-1362, 495/238-1378, 495/230-7788, www.tretyakovgallery.ru
HOURS: Tues.-Sun. 10 A.M.-7:30 P.M., ticket office until 6:30 P.M.
COST: Russians 50-100R, foreigners 150-250R
METRO: Tretyakovskaya
Map 5

The State Tretyakov Gallery on Lavrushinsky Pereulok is the one of the world's largest and most important museums of Russian art. It is named after its founder, the wealthy merchant, entrepreneur, and art collector Pavel Tretyakov, who bought the house at this address together with his brother Sergey in 1851. He began collecting art in 1854, and had the house extensively rebuilt to house his growing collection, making it a public gallery in 1881. In 1892 he gave the property and his collection of some 2,000 artworks as a gift to the city of Moscow. It now contains about 130,000 works from the 11th to early 20th century; a second branch on Krymsky Val displays 20th-century art (see next listing). The gallery's neo-Russian facade, designed by artist Viktor Vasnetsov, was added 1900–1905, after Tretyakov's death.

TRETYAKOV GALLERY ON KRYMSKY VAL
Tretyakovskaya galereya na Krymskom valu
Третьяковская галерея на Крымском валу
10 Krymsky Val Ul., 495/230-7788, 495/951-1362, 495/238-1378, www.tretyakovgallery.ru

TOUR THE CITY

Even individual, independent travellers can benefit from taking a short guided tour as part of their trip. Sometimes it's a matter of logistics – a tour saves you the time and hassle of figuring out local public transport in a foreign language, and allows you to fit more into each day. Also, a guide's commentary can be invaluable in enhancing your understanding of what you're seeing.

In Moscow, a good local tour service offering English-language excursions is **Capital Tours** (Gostiny Dvor, 4 Ulitsa Ilinka, entrance No. 6, 495/232-2442, www.capitaltours.ru), which specializes in single-day Kremlin tours and city sightseeing tours by bus.

A broader range of excursions is offered by **Patriarshy Dom Tours** (6 Vspolny Pereulok, 495/795-0927, www.toursinrussia.com), a full-service travel agency. Its services include single-day guided tours of particular sights, including the Kremlin, the Arbat, Tsaritsyno,

Novodevichy Convent, and the metro, as well as thematic tours, such as Jewish Moscow. It also offers several-day tours to points further afield, including Novgorod and the Golden Ring, plus cooking and language classes. The full schedule and prices are listed on the agency's website.

A fun and flexible way to see the city is on the new **Hop-On-Hop-Off Moscow bus service** (www.hoponhopoff.ru). The buses run on a 60-minute circuit around the main sights, and you can get on or off at any of the 11 stops along the way. Tickets are valid for 24 hours, so you can stop anywhere for as long as you like before boarding the next Hop-On-Hop-Off bus to the next sight. On the bus you can listen to pre-recorded commentary in both English and Russian. The service's website has a map showing the location of all the stops, as well as updated price and timetable information in English.

HOURS: Tues.-Sun. 10 A.M.-7:30 P.M., ticket office until 6:30 P.M.
COST: Russians 100R, foreigners 250R
METRO: Oktyabrskaya
`Map 5`

The modern-art wing of the State Tretyakov Gallery (also called the New Tretyakov) shares a building with the more commercial Central House of Artists. It has a strong collection of Russian avant-garde art, with highlights including re-creations of Tatlin's constructions, as well as works by Kandinsky, Malevich, Filonov, Chagall, and Rodchenko. Besides the dazzling permanent collection of 20th-century modern art, it also hosts some impressive touring exhibitions. It has a small but excellent art bookstore, and a modest café serving a limited range of food and beverages.

WINZAVOD

Vinzavod
Винзавод
1 4th Syromyatnichesky Pereulok, Bldg. 6, 495/917-4646, www.winzavod.ru

HOURS: Tues.-Sun. 11 A.M.-9 P.M., most galleries close at 8 P.M.
COST: Free
METRO: Kurskaya
`Map 8`

Winzavod—which translates as Winefactory—is a new contemporary-art complex in converted former industrial buildings that once housed, as the name suggests, a wine factory, as well as a brewery. A number of the city's best and most respected small and independent galleries have moved into the 20,000-square-meter-complex, making for top-class gallery-hopping. Some of the galleries in the complex are Aidan (www.aidan-gallery.ru), XL (http://xlgallery.artinfo.ru),Regina (www.regina.ru), Proun (www.proungallery.ru), Pobeda (www.pobedagallery.ru) and the Marat Guelman Gallery (www.guelman.ru), among others. The complex includes art and design studios, a hair salon, and the conceptual boutique Cara&Co. (www.caraandco.com), where a café has opened; more cafés and bars are planned.

MUSEUMS
ARMORY CHAMBER AND DIAMOND FUND
Oruzheinaya palata i Almazny fond
Оружейная палата и Алмазный фонд
Armory Chamber 495/203-0349, 495/203-4422,
www.kreml.ru; Diamond Fund 495/629-2036,
www.gokhran.ru
HOURS: Armory can be visited in group excursions
only Fri.-Wed. 10 A.M., noon, 2:30 P.M., and
4:30 P.M.; Diamond Fund Fri.-Wed. 10 A.M.-1 P.M.
and 2-4:30 P.M.
COST: Armory 70-350R, Diamond Fund 500R
METRO: Alexandrovsky Sad
Map 1

Part of the Great Kremlin Palace complex, the
Armory includes nine exhibition halls displaying a wealth of jewels, artworks, ecclesiastical
objects, and other treasures from the 12th–19th
centuries—precious items that had been kept
for hundreds of years in the royal treasury and
the patriarch's vestry. You can see ancient state
regalia and ceremonial objects, royal carriages,
precious textiles and ornamental embroidery,
gold and silverware, and much more—even
Oriental ceremonial weapons. The building
also houses the Diamond Fund museum, which
is part of the Finance Ministry's State Fund
for Precious Stones and thus separate from
the Kremlin museum complex. The treasures
here include Catherine the Great's 190-carat
Orlov diamond, among other priceless jewels
of Russian royalty and exceptional finds of recent decades. Both the Armory Chamber and
Diamond Fund require separate entry tickets
from the main Kremlin museum complex.

BULGAKOV HOUSE CULTURAL CENTER
Kulturny tsentr "Bulgakovsky Dom"
Культурный центр "Булгаковский Дом"
10 Bolshaya Sadovaya Ulitsa, 495/775-9461,
www.dombulgakova.ru
HOURS: Daily 1-11 P.M.
COST: Free
METRO: Mayakovskaya
Map 3

Located on the Garden Ring close to Patriarch's
Ponds, the Bulgakov House Cultural Center

is another cult attraction for *The Master and
Margarita* fans. Author Mikhail Bulgakov lived
here from 1921 to 1924, first in apartment 50
and then in apartment 34. These two apartments are the prototype for the "evil apartment"
of the novel, in which the address is Apartment
50 at Sadovaya 302bis. In the 1980s, long before the present museum and cultural center
were established, the stairwell became an underground mecca for Bulgakov fans, who per-
petually hung out here and covered it in graffiti.
Now you can come and see constantly changing exhibits of Bulgakov memorabilia, *Master
and Margarita*–themed art shows, photos of the
legendary stairwell, and more—including a big
black cat called Begemot. The center offers excursions, hosts festivals, and has a cute café.

CHAMBERS IN ZARYADYE
Palaty v Zaryadye
Палаты в Зарядье
10 Ulitsa Varvarka, 495/698-3235, 495/698-1256,
www.shm.ru
HOURS: Thurs.-Mon. 10 A.M.-6 P.M., Wed. 11 A.M.-7 P.M.,
closed first Mon. of month
COST: 20-200R
METRO: Kitay-Gorod
Map 2

Here you can see how Romanov boyars lived,
in rooms with authentic 17th-century furniture and other domestic items, including a
1642 globe from Amsterdam. This fascinating museum is in the 16th-century House
of the Romanov Boyars—birthplace of the
first tsar of the Romanov dynasty, Mikhail
Fyodorovich, whose grandfather had settled
here. It passed to the Znamensky Monastery
in 1631 and then became one of Moscow's first
museums in 1859. It is now a branch of the
State History Museum.

CONTEMPORARY HISTORY OF RUSSIA MUSEUM
Gosudarstvenny tsentralny muzey
sovremennoy istorii Rossii
Государственный центральный музей
современной истории России
21 Tverskaya Ul., 495/699-6724, www.sovr.ru

HOURS: Tues., Wed., and Fri. 10 A.M.-6 P.M., Thurs. and Sat. 11 A.M.-7 P.M., Sun. 10 A.M.-5 P.M., closed last Fri. of month
COST: Russians 20-100R, foreigners 200R
METRO: Tverskaya
Map 3

Covering Russia's development from the 19th century to the present, this museum has some colorful exhibits, including 1995 puppets of Boris Yeltsin and other political figures from the TV show *Kukly*. Sad sides of the country's history are documented in displays dedicated to the Great Purge, collectivization, the gulags, and the tragic fate of the Church. The red building, with eye-catching lion statues on its gates, was home to the English Club in the 19th century. One of the museum's displays illustrates this heyday with photographs, documents, invitations, furniture, and other objects from the time. The museum's store is one of the best places to buy Soviet propaganda posters and other souvenirs.

COSMONAUTS MEMORIAL MUSEUM

Memorialny muzey kosmonavtiki
Мемориальный музей космонавтики
111 Prospekt Mira, 495/683-7914, www.cosmomuseum.ru
HOURS: Daily 10 A.M.-6 P.M.
COST: 10-30R
METRO: VDNKh
Map 8

If you're in the city's north checking out the All-Russian Exhibition Center, or staying in the Cosmos hotel, take a look at the nearby Cosmonauts Museum. The museum is located under the striking silver Conquerors of the Cosmos monument, which depicts a rocket shooting towards the heavens. The monument was unveiled October 4, 1964, on the seventh anniversary of the launch of the first satellite into orbit—the Sputnik. It was just less than two decades later, on April 10, 1981—the 20th anniversary of Yury Gagarin's first manned space flight—that the space museum opened. Inside, visitors will find a fabulous collection of hundreds of items of historical significance such as space hardware, rare documents, films and photos, and other memorabilia. In total, the

museum has a collection of some 85,000 items. Make sure you check out space dogs Belka and Strelka, both stuffed for posterity's sake. A newly built Cosmonauts' Alley leads from VDNKh metro station to the museum, with a memorial to spaceship designer Sergey Korolyov and a bronze model of the solar system.

GORKY HOUSE MUSEUM–RYABUSHINSKY MANSION

Muzey-kvartira Gorkogo—Osobnyak Ryabushinskogo
Музей-квартира Горького—Особняк Рябушинского
6/2 Malaya Nikitskaya Ulitsa, 495/690-5130, 495/690-0535
HOURS: Wed.-Sun. 11 A.M.-5 P.M., closed last Thurs. of month
COST: Free
METRO: Arbatskaya
Map 3

Just off Ploshchad Nikitskiye Vorota, at the beginning of Malaya Nikitskaya Ulitsa, is a house that some architecture buffs consider to be Moscow's finest building: the former mansion of entrepreneur Stepan Ryabushinsky, now the Maxim Gorky house museum. Architect Fyodor Shekhtel's masterpiece, built 1900–1903, is regarded as the best example of Russian art nouveau or "Style Moderne." A highlight is the much-photographed staircase, with its flowing wavelike form culminating in a jellyfish-shaped lamp. Ryabushinsky emigrated after the 1917 revolution and Stalin later gave the house to writer Maxim Gorky, who lived here 1931–1936 and thankfully didn't renovate. For most visitors, the house itself is probably more interesting than the Gorky memorabilia. Other Shekhtel works to see around Moscow include the Yaroslavsky railway station and the Moscow Art Theater building on Kamergersky Pereulok.

GULAG HISTORY MUSEUM

Gosudarstvenny muzey istorii GULAGa
Государственный музей истории ГУЛАГа
16 Ulitsa Petrovka, 495/621-7346, www.museum-gulag.narod.ru
HOURS: Tues.-Sat. 11 A.M.-4 P.M.

ARTS AND LEISURE

COST: 60R
METRO: Teatralnaya
Map 3

Through an archway opposite the Marriott Aurora hotel is this museum about the Stalin-era Main Administration of Corrective Labor Camps, known by the acronym Gulag. It includes re-creations of labor-camp barracks and investigators' offices, a map showing the extent of the Gulag network, and photographs of former prisoners as well as artworks created by them.

MAYAKOVSKY MUSEUM

Gosudarstvenny muzey V.V. Mayakovskogo
Государственный музей В.В. Маяковского
3/6 Lubyansky Proyezd, 495/621-6591, 495/628-2569, 495/621-93-87, www.mayakovsky.info
HOURS: Thurs. 1-8 P.M., Fri.-Tues. 10 A.M.-5 P.M., closed last Fri. of month
COST: Russians 50R, foreigners 90R
METRO: Lubyanka
Map 2

This museum, in the house where Vladimir Mayakovsky lived and worked from 1919 to 1930, exhibits personal belongings and photographs of the poet and his family, as well as his notebooks, letters, and graphic works such as advertisements, posters, and paintings. Works by his contemporaries are also on display, including some creations by Larionov, Tatlin, and Malevich. Mayakovsky's library holds a fascinating collection of 1920s books, both printed and handmade.

MOSCOW MUSEUM OF MODERN ART

Moskovsky muzey sovremennogo iskusstva
Московский музей современного искусства
25 Ulitsa Petrovka, 495/694-2890, www.mmoma.ru
HOURS: Daily noon-8 P.M., ticket office until 7:15 P.M., closed last Mon. of month
COST: Russian adults 100R, Russian students 80R, foreign adults 200R, foreign students 100R
METRO: Kuznetsky Most
Map 3

As you walk up Ulitsa Petrovka, the sculptures in this courtyard are sure to catch your eye. They are by Zurab Tsereteli, sculptor of the controversial Peter the Great statue on the Moscow River, and this is the Moscow Museum of Modern Art that Tsereteli founded here in 1999, in an 18th-century heritage-listed estate by architect Matvey Kazakov. Inside are various temporary exhibits and a permanent collection that was long considered to leave much to be desired, with its initial emphasis on primitivism, naïve, and folk art. Since Zurab's young grandson Vasily Tsereteli became executive director, the museum has been gaining respect with a new focus on the local contemporary art scene.

OLD ENGLISH COURT

Stary Angliysky dvor
Старый Английский двор
4A Ulitsa Varvarka, 495/698-3952, www.mosmuseum.ru
HOURS: Wed. and Fri. 11 A.M.-7 P.M., Tues., Thurs., and Sat.-Sun. 10 A.M.-6 P.M., ticket office closes about an hour earlier, closed last Fri. of month
COST: 20-35R
METRO: Kitay-Gorod
Map 2

Among the pretty churches that line Ulitsa Varvarka, a white building with a wooden roof stands out. This is the Old English Court, one of the city's oldest surviving secular buildings, dating to 1533. Ivan the Terrible gave it to English merchants in 1556 and it became England's first embassy in Moscow. Now part of the Museum of the History of Moscow, it has an exhibition about the development of diplomatic and trade relations between Russia and England. The inside has been restored to give an authentic picture of its Middle Ages interior. There are excursions in English, and costumed theatrical excursions aimed at school children.

POLYTECHNIC MUSEUM

Politekhnichesky muzey
Политехнический музей
3/4 Novaya Ploshchad, 495/623-0756, http://eng.polymus.ru
HOURS: Tues.-Sat. 10 A.M.-5 P.M., closed last Fri. of month
COST: Russians 40-100R, foreign adults 200R, students 80R

METRO: Lubyanka

Map 2

Founded in 1872, this is one of the world's oldest scientific-technical museums. It contains more than 160,000 exhibits covering everything from mining, metallurgy, and meteorology to chemistry, computing, and cosmonautics. There are fascinating collections of historical typewriters, microscopes, slot machines, automobiles, bicycles, and more. There's also an interactive section where visitors can take part in entertaining experiments; the emphasis is educational and aimed at children. The building itself is an architectural landmark, constructed 1875–1907 with wings in various styles from Neo-Russian to art nouveau.

PUSHKIN APARTMENT-MUSEUM

Kvartira A.S. Pushkina na Arbate

Квартира А.С. Пушкина на Арбате

53 Ulitsa Arbat, 495/241-9295,

www.pushkinmuseum.ru

HOURS: Wed.-Sun. 10 A.M.-5 P.M.

COST: Adults 40R

METRO: Smolenskaya

Map 4

The poet Alexander Pushkin rented the 2nd floor of this house and lived here December 1830–May 1831—this is where he first lived with his wife Natalya Goncharova after their wedding. Now a museum dedicated to Pushkin's life, it contains much memorabilia but no personal domestic items from the time when the Pushkins actually lived here. One of the oldest buildings on the Arbat, the house dates to the 18th century and belonged to the noble Khitrovo family. It was rebuilt after the 1812 fire. Romantic bronze statues of Pushkin and Goncharova now stand opposite it, the creations of sculptors Alexander and Igor Burganov.

PUSHKIN STATE MUSEUM OF FINE ARTS

Gosudarstvenny muzey izobrazitelnykh iskusstv imeni A.S. Pushkina

Государственный музей изобразительных искусств имени А.С. Пушкина

10-14 Ulitsa Volkhonka, 495/203-7998,

www.museum.ru/gmii

HOURS: Tues., Wed., and Fri.-Sun. 10 A.M.-7 P.M., Thurs. 10 A.M.-9 P.M., ticket office closes an hour earlier

COST: Guest pass to four buildings of main complex, not including temporary exhibits—Russians 60-120R, foreigners 300-500R

METRO: Kropotkinskaya

Map 4

Moscow's main gallery for foreign art, the enormous Pushkin State Museum of Fine Arts consists of six buildings, four of which comprise the main complex on Ulitsa Volkhonka: the Main Building, the Museum of Private Collections, the Gallery of European and American Art of the 19th–20th Centuries, and the Museion Educational Center. The extensive collection includes artworks of Ancient Egypt, Antiquity, the Middle Ages, the Renaissance, and modernity. Here you can see such masterpieces as Botticelli's *The Annunciation,* Matisse's *Red Fish,* Picasso's *The Girl on a Ball,* and Degas' *Blue Dancers,* as well as works by Rembrandt, Renoir, Rodin— and the list goes on and on.

STATE HISTORY MUSEUM

Gosudarstvenny istorichesky muzey

Государственный исторический музей

1 Red Square, 495/692-4019, www.shm.ru

HOURS: Sun. 11 A.M.-8 P.M., Mon. and Wed.-Sat. 10 A.M.-6 P.M., closed first Mon. of month

COST: 40-150R, amateur photo permit 80R, amateur video permit 100R, combined ticket including entry to St. Basil's—80-230R

METRO: Okhotny Ryad or Ploshchad Revolyutsii

Map 1

The imposing red-brick building facing onto Red Square at the opposite end from St. Basil's is the State History Museum, founded in 1872 as a public museum devoted to significant events in the history of the Russian state. Recent renovations completed, the museum has now fully reopened, with some new features such as wheelchair access. The museum's massive collection consists of some 4.5 million items relating to Russia's history from the Stone Age to the 20th century, as well as more than 12 million sheets of historical documents. Among the highlights is chain-mail armor worn in the Kulikovo Battle of 1380, and Peter the Great's death mask. The neighboring former Lenin Museum, which has been closed for renovations, is now a branch of the State History Museum, which intends to turn it into a museum of 20th-century history.

TOLSTOY MUSEUM
Muzey-usadba L.N. Tolstogo
Музей-усадьба Л.Н. Толстого
21 Ul. Lva Tolstogo, 495/246-9444,
www.tolstoymuseum.ru/museum
HOURS: Tues.-Sun. 11 A.M.-5 P.M.
COST: 50R
METRO: Park Kultury
Map 4

Visit the estate where the author of *War and Peace* and *Anna Karenina* spent every winter from 1882 to 1901, together with his large family. A museum since 1920, the wooden house and beautiful gardens have been preserved as they were in Leo Tolstoy's times—you can even see the desk where he wrote his last novel. Some 6,000 genuine personal belongings of the Tolstoys remain here to re-create an authentic picture of how they lived and of the era in general.

VODKA MUSEUM
Muzey istorii vodki
Музей истории водки
73 Izmaylovskoye Shosse, 499/166-5097,
www.vodkamuseum.ru
HOURS: Daily 11 A.M.-9 P.M.
COST: Russians 50R, foreigners 100R
METRO: Partizanskaya
Map 8

Conveniently located right beside the Vernissage souvenir market, the Vodka Museum offers an educational experience enhanced by Russia's famous spirit. Learn all about the drink's origins, how it is made, and its role in Russian society—then knock back a 40-percent shot of goodness. Every visitor gets a vodka shot included in the entry price, but there are also vodka-tasting sessions with three different vodka shots and three different snacks, starting from 340R, with advance bookings recommended (museum@moscow-vernisage.com).

CONCERT VENUES
MOSCOW INTERNATIONAL HOUSE OF MUSIC
Moskovsky mezhdunarodny dom muzyki
Московский международный дом музыки
52 Kosmodamianskaya Naberezhnaya, Bldg. 8,
495/730-1011, www.mmdm.ru
METRO: Paveletskaya
Map 7

This gleaming, glassy performing-arts center opened in 2003—the city's first new classical-music concert venue in a century. Headed by violinist and conductor Vladimir Spivakov, it offers a varied repertoire in its several performance spaces—the Chamber Hall, the Theater Hall, the Svetlanov Hall with Russia's biggest organ, and the open-air Music Terrace, with a restaurant. It is located next to Swissotel Krasnye Holmy hotel.

TCHAIKOVSKY CONCERT HALL
Kontsertny zal imeni P.I. Chaykovskogo
Концертный зал имени П.И. Чайковского
4/31 Triumfalnaya Ploshchad, 495/699-5353
METRO: Mayakovskaya
Map 3

This huge landmark venue dates back to the 1930s, when it was built by renowned architect Dmitry Chechulin to accommodate the theater of Vsevolod Meyerhold. The innovative producer and director's tragic 1939 arrest and subsequent shooting left the theater up for grabs, and it was given to the Moscow Philharmonia, which continues to perform about 300 concerts a year in the recently renovated space. The concert hall also hosts performances by leading soloists, organists, choirs, symphony orchestras, and folk-dance ensembles. The building also has a food hall, restaurants, and an entrance to the metro station.

TCHAIKOVSKY MOSCOW STATE CONSERVATORY
Moskovsky gosudarstvennaya
konservatoriya imeni P. I. Chaykovskogo
Московская государственная
консерватория имени П. И. Чайковского
13 Bolshaya Nikitskaya Ulitsa, 495/629-2060,
www.mosconsv.ru

METRO: Alexandrovsky Sad or Okhotny Ryad
Map 3

The Moscow Conservatory has various concert spaces, including its Great Hall, which opened in 1901 and is renowned for its superb acoustics and world-class concerts, and the Small Hall, which opened in 1898 and hosts highly regarded chamber concerts. The Conservatory is also a top music school. Founded in 1866, it boasts an alumni list that's a musical who's who: Khachaturian, Rachmaninov, Richter, Rostropovich, Schnittke, Scriabin, and more. Its teachers have been no less impressive, including Tchaikovsky himself. The four-meter bronze statue of Tchaikovsky seated in the garden outside is by the renowned Soviet sculptor Vera Mukhina, who also created the iconic *Worker and Collective Farm Girl.*

CINEMA
DOME CINEMA
Kinoteatr Pod Kupolom
Кинотеатр под Куполом
18/1 Olimpiysky Prospekt, 495/931-9873, www.domecinema.ru
METRO: Prospekt Mira
Map 8

In a space-age silver dome above a hotel's buffet hall, this is quite a spacious cinema that is rarely full—in fact, the late-night sessions are sometimes quite lonely. Usually English-language movies are screened in English with Russian-language translation over headphones, but not always—sometimes you get the Russian dubbed version with English over the headphones; sometimes the translation is even read out live with a single person doing all the voices. It's worth calling in advance to check.

ROLAN
Ролан
12A Chistoprudny Bulvar, 495/916-9412, www.5zvezd.ru/rolan
METRO: Chistye Prudy
Map 2

This trendy cinema has two halls, for 96 and 204 spectators, with state-of-the-art sound, plus a bar. It shows premieres of local and international hits, as well as art-house, animation, and festival films, sometimes but not always in the original language. It is affiliated with the Five Star (Pyat Zvyozd) chain of cinemas, which are more commercial and mass-market, but which also sometimes screens foreign films with subtitles or translation via headsets.

35MM
47 Ulitsa Pokrovka, 495/917-1883, www.kino35mm.ru
METRO: Kurskaya or Krasnye Vorota
Map 8

In a city where dubbing rules, this is one of the few remaining cinemas to still show foreign-language movies in the original language, with subtitles or translation via headsets. The repertoire goes beyond blockbusters to include art-house, experimental, and animated films, with regular festivals adding interest. There's a café-bar and a summer terrace.

BALLET AND OPERA
◖ BOLSHOI THEATER
Bolshoy teatr
Большой театр
1 Teatralnaya Ploshchad, 495/250-7317, www.bolshoi.ru
METRO: Teatralnaya
Map 1

Going to "the Bolshoi" is a highlight of most tourists' itinerary—a memorable experience not only for the performances but also for the building itself and the sense of being part of the culture that surrounds it. The Bolshoi or "Big" Theater has played a major role in the development of Russian opera and ballet since its birth in 1776. The past century has seen it consolidate its reputation as one of the world's premier opera and ballet theaters. In 2005, the main, historic building on Theater Square closed for renovations scheduled to be completed by November 2009. In the meantime, performances have been held on the Bolshoi's New Stage and in the State Kremlin Palace. If a trip to the Bolshoi is at the top of your agenda, remember also that it closes in the summer, so check the theater's online schedule before planning your trip.

NOVAYA OPERA
Новая Опера
Hermitage Garden, 3 Ulitsa Karetny Ryad,
495/694-0868, www.novayaopera.ru
METRO: Mayakovskaya or Chekhovskaya
Map 3

Novaya, or New, Opera says its artistic creed can be defined as "enthusiastic creative quest and bold innovation." Its opera soloists, orchestra, and choir are elegantly housed in a graceful building constructed just over a decade ago in the beautiful Hermitage Garden—an important theatrical center since the 19th century. With space for 700 spectators, it has sophisticated lighting and stage equipment machinery. Besides opera and orchestral concerts, it also presents ballet and other dance shows.

STATE KREMLIN PALACE
Gosudarstvenny Kremlyovsky dvorets
Государственный Кремлёвский дворец
Kremlin, 495/628-5232, www.gkd.ru
METRO: Alexandrovsky Sad
Map 1

Going here is always special: It is, after all, inside the Kremlin. One of Moscow's main venues for concerts and dance—including Bolshoi Ballet shows while its main building is undergoing renovations—the State Kremlin Palace boasts one of the largest stages in the world. Clashing with the beautiful, historical buildings that surround it, this modern block was built 1959–1961 on Nikita Khrushchev's orders and originally called the Kremlin Palace of Congresses. Extending 17 meters underground, it has a 6,000-seat hall, an acoustics system that was state-of-the-art at its time, and more than 800 rooms.

THEATER
CHEKHOV MOSCOW ART THEATER
MKhT imeni Chekhova
МХТ имени Чехова
3 Kamergersky Pereulok, 495/629-8760,
www.art.theatre.ru
METRO: Okhotny Ryad
Map 3

The Chekhov Moscow Art Theater, founded more than a century ago by the legendary Konstantin Stanislavsky and Vladimir Nemirovich-Danchenko, has been housed in architect Fyodor Shekhtel's art nouveau building since 1902. Note the sculpture by artist Anna Golubkina over the door to the New Stage, depicting a swimmer in a wave. The theater's seagull logo refers to the title of one of many Anton Chekhov plays that premiered at the theater. Chekhov, naturally, is still on the repertoire. The theater also has a museum and a drama school.

MALY THEATER
Maly Teatr
Малый театр
1/6 Teatralnaya Ploshchad, 495/623-2621, www.maly.ru
METRO: Teatralnaya
Map 1

The Bolshoi's neighbor on Theater Square is the Maly or "Small" Theater, which claims to be Russia's oldest theater, tracing its origins to 1756. It moved into its present building on Theater Square after architect Osip Bove converted a rich merchant's estate especially for it in 1824. In front of it is a statue of the 19th-century playwright Alexander Ostrovsky, bearded and solemnly seated in a heavy coat. Some think that this should be called the Ostrovsky Theater, since all 48 of his plays were performed here, and he personally would lead rehearsals. Ostrovsky's plays remain a staple at the drama theater to this day.

VAKHTANGOV THEATER
Teatr imeni Vakhtangova
Театр имени Вахтангова
26 Ulitsa Arbat, 495/241-1679, 495/241-1693,
www.vakhtangov.ru
METRO: Arbatskaya
Map 4

Founder Yevgeny Vakhtangov's breakthrough 1922 staging of Carlo Gozzi's *Turandot* led to this play becoming the theater's symbol, and it remains on the repertoire to this day. Outside the theater, you'll see a gilded statue that looks like a fairytale princess from a little girl's music box—it depicts Princess Turandot

© NATHAN TOOHEY

Vakhtangov Theater on the Arbat

and is by Alexander and Igor Burganov, who also take credit for the Arbat's monument of Pushkin and his wife. The building itself was constructed 1946–1947 in place of a late 19th-century mansion that housed the theater's performances until it was flattened by a bomb in 1941.

CIRCUS AND ANIMAL SHOWS
DUROV ANIMAL THEATER
Teatr "Ugolok dedushki Durova"
Театр "Уголок дедушки Дурова"
4 Ulitsa Durova, 495/631-3047, www.ugolokdurova.ru
METRO: Tsvetnoy Bulvar
Map 8

With a cast of cats, dogs, mice, goats, bears, raccoons, monkeys, tigers, seals, and other animals—even a hippo—several generations of the Durov family have been running this theater since 1912. It has two stages, one with 300 seats and the other with 900, a museum, and a mouse railway. On the smaller stage, mostly domestic animals perform shows aimed at the youngest spectators, who might be frightened by the larger beasts on the big stage.

☾ KUKLACHYOV CAT THEATER
Teatr koshek Kuklachyova
Театр кошек Куклачёва
25 Kutuzovsky Prospekt, 499/249-2907,
www.kuklachev.ru
METRO: Kievskaya
Map 8

Yury Kuklachyov's internationally renowned troupe of more than 100 felines gives purrfect performances in this 2,000-square-meter home-base theater. Pawstands, tightrope walks, high-flying leaps, and other acrobatic feats feature in a varied repertoire of shows, including *Nutcracker Prince,* to music by Tchaikovsky, and *Boris the Cat's Olympics,* which some say is the most interesting show, with a cast of 70 cats.

MOSCOW STATE CIRCUS
Bolshoy Moskovsky gosudarstvenny tsirk
Большой Московский государственный цирк
7 Prospekt Vernadskogo, 495/930-0272,
www.bolshoicircus.ru
METRO: Universitet
Map 8

Moscow has two circuses, but this is the one that's usually on tour itineraries. Close to Moscow State University, this 3,328-seat circus is in a custom-built circular structure with a 36-meter-high amphitheater ceiling, a venue that conveys a real sense of occasion to children and grownups alike. There are acrobats, animals—everything you'd expect.

NIKULIN CIRCUS
Moskovsky Tsirk Nikulina na
Tsvetnom Bulvare
Московский Цирк Никулина
на Цветном Бульваре
13 Tsvetnoy Bulvar, 495/625-8970, www.circusnikulin.ru
METRO: Tsvetnoy Bulvar
Map 3

Founded in 1880, this is one of Russia's oldest circuses. It was renamed the Nikulin Circus in honor of the great clown and actor Yury Nikulin, who headed it for many years—look for the statue of him in front of the building. Seating 2,000, the circus changes its theatrical, thematic shows several times a season, and often has special performances by visiting foreign-theater troupes.

Festivals and Events

WINTER
DECEMBER NIGHTS FESTIVAL
Festival "Dekabrskiye vechera"
Фестиваль "Декабрьские вечера"
Pushkin State Museum of Fine Arts, 12 Ulitsa
Volkhonka, 495/203-7998,
www.museum.ru/gmii
METRO: Kropotkinskaya
Map 4

Founded by pianist Svyatoslav Richter, this month-long annual arts festival is the most prestigious classical musical event in the capital, a cultural climax to the year. It features top performers from Russia and other countries. As part of the festival, an art exhibition with classical music as the theme is held in Moscow's main gallery for foreign art.

SPRING
EASTER FESTIVAL
Moskovsky Paskhalny festival
Московский Пасхальнвй
Фестиваль
Various locations, www.easterfestival.ru

Inaugurated by the artistic and general director of St. Petersburg's Mariinsky Theater, Valery Gergiev, the Moscow Easter Festival has become one of Russia's largest and most important musical events. It attracts top performers from all around the world, as well as Russia's best, to participate in five segments—symphonic, choral, regional, charity, and bell week, which celebrates Russia's Easter bell-ringing traditions.

◖ MASLENITSA
Масленица
Various locations; www.maslenitsa.com

Maslenitsa, also known as Butter Week, Bliny Week, or Pancake Week, dates back to pagan times as a celebration to welcome spring. Round, golden bliny (Russian-style pancakes), symbolizing the sun, were eaten as part of the festivities. After Russia converted to Christianity, it turned into a week-long bliny feast preceding the 40-day Great Lenten Fast. Maslenitsa is seven weeks before Orthodox Easter—the date varies from year to year, sometimes falling in February and sometimes in March. There are dozens of Maslenitsa celebrations all over the city for a whole week, with the two main parties usually being on Vasilyevsky Spusk (the hill sloping down towards the Moscow River behind St. Basil's Cathedral) and in the Kolomenskoye park estate. You can stuff yourself with bliny and take part in a traditional Russian fair, with singing, dancing, and centuries-old games. Most restaurants offer special bliny menus during Maslenitsa, followed by vegetarian (*postny*) menus during Lent (Veliky Post).

VICTORY DAY
Den Pobedy
День Поьеды

On May 9 every year, Russia commemorates the end of World War II in Europe with a massive celebration of Victory Day. There is a grand parade on Red Square, attended by the country's political and military leaders as well as war veterans and other specially invited guests, which in 2008 included military hardware for the first time since 1990. Veterans turn out in all their medals, and after the parade there are celebrations all over town, with concerts on the city's squares and a huge fireworks show in the evening. A good spot to watch the fireworks is the lookout beside the ski jump at Vorobyovy Gory, near Moscow State University—get there early to get a good view.

SUMMER
BEER FESTIVAL
Moskovsky mezhdunarodny festival piva
Московский международный фестиваль
пива
Luzhniki Stadium, 24 Luzhnetskaya Naberezhnaya,
www.beer-festival.ru
METRO: Sportivnaya
Map 6

Every summer since 1999, the grounds of

Luzhniki Stadium hosts one of the city's most enjoyable events—the beer festival, where major breweries, small provincial brewers, and little-known microbreweries all set up stands for you to savor their suds. There are all kinds of activities at the nine-day event, such as arm wrestling and beer-related competitions, plus live entertainment, souvenirs, and plenty of beer-friendly food. Contrary to what you might expect, this is a well-behaved and safe event, with people of all ages, including families, and surprisingly little drunkenness.

MOSCOW INTERNATIONAL FILM FESTIVAL

Moskovsky mezhdunarodny kinofestival
Московский международный кинофестиваль
Various locations; www.moscowfilmfestival.ru

Moscow's annual film festival is held each June at a number of cinemas around town, including the Pushkinsky Movie Theater on Pushkin Square—this is where filmmaker Quentin Tarantino was photographed shaking hands with Russian Communist Party leader Gennady Zyuganov at the 2004 event. The festival's president is the internationally renowned filmmaker and actor Nikita Mikhalkov.

FALL
CITY DAY

Den Goroda
День Города
`Map 1`

Moscow celebrates its birthday with City Day on the first weekend of September. Usually the main street, Tverskaya Ulitsa, is closed to vehicles and becomes a pedestrian-only party zone. There are parades, concerts, and other celebratory events all over town—join the fun at the squares along Tverskaya, as well as Teatralnaya and Lubyanskaya Squares, and Poklonnaya Gora. Security is usually high, with metal detectors and police inspecting bags at the entrance. In the evening, there are fireworks.

Sports and Recreation

PARKS
APTEKARSKY BOTANICAL GARDEN

Botanichesky sad MGU "Aptekarsky ogorod"
Ботанический сад МГУ "Аптекарский огород"
26 Prospekt Mira, 495/680-5880, 495/680-6765, 495/680-7222, www.hortus.ru
HOURS: Daily 10 A.M.-10 P.M.
COST: 50R
METRO: Prospekt Mira
`Map 8`

This is Russia's old botanical institute, having been founded in 1706 by order of Peter the Great. Originally used to provide medicinal plants, the botanical gardens now provide a true green oasis in an otherwise congested city area. As it is not just a park but a botanical garden, there is an impressive collection of flowers, shrubs, and the like. The park is quite compact and can be fully covered in an hour or so, but taking your time is certainly no waste of time.

BOTANICAL GARDENS

Botanichesky sad
Ботанический сад
4 Botanicheskaya Ulitsa, 495/977-9172, www.gbsad.ru
HOURS: Tues.-Sun. summer 10 A.M.-9 P.M., winter 10 A.M.-6 P.M., closed Apr. and Oct.
COST: 10R, free in winter
METRO: Vladykino or VDNKh
`Map 8`

Founded in 1945, N. V. Tsitsin's Botanical Gardens are one of the largest in Europe, covering an area of more than 330 hectares. Although the main gates are not located in the area, there is a gate that leads from the back of All-Russian Exhibition Center. Don't expect any cafés inside, but if you're in need of a nature fix, this is the place for you. The gardens are landscaped to create different natural-looking zones for the flora of Russia and the former Soviet Union. There's also a tropical and subtropical section, a rosarium, and even a Japanese garden.

IZMAYLOVSKY PARK
Измайловский парк

17 Narodny Prospekt, 495/166-7909, www.izmailovsky-park.ru
HOURS: Always open
COST: Free
METRO: Partizanskaya or Shosse Entuziastov
Map 8

This is a truly gargantuan park occupying 1,608 hectares, making it one of the largest in Europe. It consists of two parts. The smaller Izmaylovsky Park of Culture and Relaxation is a more typical landscaped park with amusement rides and cafés. The other part is the vast Izmaylovsky Forest Park, which despite its numerous winding paved paths is basically a picturesque wild forest with some 13 ponds scattered about its territory.

KOLOMENSKOYE
Коломенское

39 Prospekt Yu. V. Andropova, 499/612-5217, 499/612-1155, www.mgomz.ru
HOURS: Daily Apr.-Oct. 8 A.M.-10 P.M., Nov.-Mar. 8 A.M.-9 P.M.
COST: Free
METRO: Kolomenskoye
Map 8

Occupying nearly 400 hectares, the Kolomenskoye estate is one of the oldest inhabited spots in Moscow, with traces of human activity having been found dating back to the Stone Age. Kolmenskoye is famed, however, for more recent history, as home to an impressive architectural ensemble that includes the UNESCO World Heritage–listed Ascension Church built in 1532, among other landmarks. Besides the architectural attractions, the riverside museum reserve also provides lovely green expanses that are perfect for summer strolling. The site also has numerous cafés serving grilled meats and cold draft beer.

KUSKOVO
Кусково

2 Ulitsa Yunosti, 495/370-0160, www.kuskovo.ru
HOURS: Wed.-Sun. Apr.-Oct. 10 A.M.-6 P.M., Nov.-Mar. 10 A.M.-4 P.M., ticket office closes an hour earlier, closed last Wed. of month
COST: Grounds: free; palace: Russians 150R, foreigners 250R; other sights: Russians 50-150R, foreigners 100-250R
METRO: Novogireyevo or Ryazansky Prospekt
Map 8

This is a well-preserved and immaculately manicured palace estate. The summer residence of the noble Sheremetyev family, it was built in the late 18th century, and to this day, besides the palace, some 20 other architectural landmarks remain. The park is designed in French style, resembling a miniature Versailles, although the grounds also include regular parkland as well. There is a ceramics museum with a superb collection of all manner of porcelain, but it's worth coming here just for the grounds alone.

a Dutch-style house on the Kuskovo estate

EXTREME SPORTS, RUSSIAN-STYLE

Skip skydiving and forget spelunking: in Russia you can go **ice-swimming.** Survival TV shows like to spook viewers with warnings of how you'll last mere minutes if you fall overboard in sub-zero temperatures, but try telling that to the Russian pensioners whose favorite winter hobby is to swim laps in ice pools. Ice swimmers are called *morzhy*, or walruses, and even those who fear a cold draft think that there's nothing more healthy than taking a dip in freezing cold water. There are morzh clubs, whose members hack holes in the ice on rivers and lakes, and extend them into substantially sized swimming pools where they cruise about showing no signs of discomfort. A popular morzhy hangout is at Serebryanny Bor's Maloye Bezdonnoye Ozero (Little Bottomless Lake), the site of mass ice-swimming during the Epiphany holiday each January. Thousands take to the water, even at temperatures as low as minus 30 degrees Celsius – just remember that the water is warmer than the air, otherwise it would be frozen.

© NATHAN TOOHEY

cycling in Neskuchny Sad

NESKUCHNY SAD
Нескучный сад
32 Leninsky Prospekt, 495/958-5024
HOURS: Always open
COST: Free
METRO: Shabolovskaya
Map 6

Located just outside the back gates of Gorky Park is another park with a name translating literally as the "unboring garden." One of the oldest parks in Moscow, it used to include the grounds of Gorky Park before they were cut off to form the "Combine of Culture" in 1928. While Gorky is an urban amusement park, this is more of a natural park, with romantic benches under the lush trees that line the riverbank. If you're entering Neskuchny Sad from the back of Gorky Park, make sure

you climb the stairs to the top of the pedestrian bridge that divides the parks and leads across the river—the view is well worth it.

PARK POBEDY
Парк Победы
11 Ulitsa Bratyev Fonchenko, 495/148-8300
HOURS: Daily 24 hours
COST: Free
METRO: Park Pobedy
Map 8

More of an expansive WWII memorial complex than a park in the traditional sense of the word, Park Pobedy (Victory Park) nonetheless attracts hordes of cyclists, skateboarders, and in-line skaters who come to zoom about on its smooth granite surfaces. Besides the elaborate monuments, there is also an open-air display of military technology such as tanks and artillery. The nearby metro station Park Pobedy is, at 80 meters underground, the capital's deepest metro station.

ARTS AND LEISURE

SEREBRYANY BOR
Серебряный бор

1A 1st Liniya Khoroshyovskogo Serebryanogo Bora, 495/199-0970

HOURS: Daily 24 hours
COST: Free
METRO: Polezhayevskaya
Map 8

This is not a landscaped park, but a huge forested reserve largely surrounded by the Moscow River. It is located northwest of the city and as such the southeastern-flowing Moscow River is still clean enough for swimming. The park features several well-developed beaches (including a nudist beach) with change rooms, toilets, cafés, and so on. Besides the beaches there are countless long paths winding through the forest, perfect for strolling. The picnic grounds include public barbecue facilities.

SOKOLNIKI
Сокольники

1 Ulitsa Sokolnichesky Val, 495/268-5430, 495/268-6011, www.park-sokolniki.ru

HOURS: Daily 10 A.M.-8 P.M.
COST: Weekdays free, weekends adults 60R, children 10R
METRO: Sokolniki
Map 8

This is a large and pleasant park with a lot going on. There are amusement rides, tennis and table-tennis courts, sports and exercise facilities, and bicycles and in-line skates for rent. For those looking for a little less-active recreation, farther from the entrance are hectares and hectares of tranquil park land to get lost in—be sure to check out the park's wonderful rose gardens. For the completely lazy there are also numerous inexpensive restaurants and cafés serving mainly grilled meats and fresh salads. On weekends, seniors dance to their favorite old tunes at a special square near the entrance.

SPARROW HILLS
Vorobyovy Gory
Воробьёвы горы

17 Ulitsa Kosygina, 495/939-8377
HOURS: Always open
COST: Free
METRO: Vorobyovy Gory
Map 6

Extending seamlessly from the back of Neskuchny Sad is Sparrow Hills. This nature reserve, which was called Lenin Hills from 1924 to 1991, has its own eponymous metro station as well as its own chairlift, which is a pleasantly lazy way to make your way to the top of the hills. At the top of the chairlift is a lookout with some of the city's best panoramic views not atop a building. An inexpensive outdoor café is located next door, with the same impressive views. A row of souvenirs stalls sell the usual trinkets to tourists bussed in for the view, while newlyweds jostle to have their photos taken at this traditional post-wedding photo location.

TSARITSYNO
Царицыно

1 Dolskaya Ulitsa, 495/321-0743, www.tsaritsyno-museum.ru

HOURS: Grounds: daily 24 hours; Grand Palace and Bread House museums: Apr. 4-Oct. 31 Wed.-Fri. 11 A.M.-6 P.M., Sat.-Sun. 11 A.M.-7 P.M., Nov. 1-Apr. 3 Wed.-Fri. 11 A.M.-5 P.M., Sat.-Sun. 11 A.M.-7 P.M.; ticket office closes 30 minutes earlier
COST: Grounds free, Grand Palace 150R, Bread House 100R, children 20R, accompanied by a translator/guide Grand Palace 200R, Bread House 150R, Grand Palace and Bread House 300R
METRO: Tsaritsyno
Map 8

This 18th-century pseudo-Gothic palace estate is set within wonderful parkland complete with ponds and streams. Of particular note is that construction of both the Grand Palace and Bread House was begun in the late 18th century, but never completed. They stood as romantic ruins until 2006–2007, when City Hall decided to finish their construction, adding a roof among other major alterations that angered preservationists. Both buildings now serve as museums. Besides the huge Grand Palace and Bread House, there are numerous smaller buildings, bridges, and other constructions dotted around the grounds.

BANYA
◖ SANDUNOVSKIYE BANI
Сандуновские бани

14 Neglinnaya Ulitsa, Bldg. 3-7, 495/625-4631,
www.sanduny.ru
HOURS: Daily 8 A.M.-10 P.M.
METRO: Kuznetsky Most
Map 2

A *banya* is a traditional Russian bathhouse or sauna, with steam rooms, pools, showers, and usually other services, such as massage. Built in 1896, this is one of Moscow's oldest *banyas* and is widely considered to be the best in town. "Opulent" best describes this bathhouse, with the interior a masterpiece of dark wood and marble. There are various classes of men's and women's sections available for prices ranging from relatively egalitarian to over-the-top posh. Servants will provide you with your every need, from a bar of soap to cold beer and crayfish. Besides the steam rooms, there is also a beauty salon, massage, and an upmarket restaurant.

BOWLING AND BILLIARDS
BIBABO
БиБаБо

9 Karamanitsky Pereulok, 495/937-1686,
www.bibabo.ru
HOURS: Daily noon-5 A.M.
METRO: Smolenskaya
Map 4

Located right downtown, this entertainment center has seven bowling lanes and seven billiards tables (four 12-foot tables for Russian pyramid games and three nine-foot tables for American pool). Besides billiards and bowling there is also a restaurant, a sports bar, and a shop selling all kinds of bowling and billiards gear.

VYSOTKA
Высотка

1 Kudrinskaya Ploshchad, 499/252-2309,
495/605-1291, www.visotka-club.ru
HOURS: Mon.-Thurs. 3 P.M.-midnight, Fri.-Sat.
3 P.M.-5 A.M., Sun. 2 P.M.-midnight
METRO: Barrikadnaya
Map 3

This entertainment center, on a terrace of the Stalin skyscraper at Barrikadnaya, has a club-like atmosphere—there's even ultraviolet lighting on the center's eight bowling lanes. Besides the bowling, there are eight billiards tables (three for Russian pyramid games and five for American pool), a chill-out zone with soft divans, two banquet halls, and a fashionably fitted-out restaurant.

ICE SKATING
ICE SKATING IN GORKY PARK
Park Gorkogo
Парк Горького

9 Ulitsa Krymsky Val, 495/237-0707
HOURS: Daily 10 A.M.-11 P.M.
COST: 80R park entrance fee
METRO: Oktyabrskaya
Map 6

Although all year-round there is an ice skating rink inside Gorky Park, during winter Gorky Park's extensive winding paths are allowed to freeze over and the entire park becomes one huge ice skating rink, attracting no fewer visitors than it does in summer. The park's cafés are all functioning, so finding a warm-me-up is no great difficulty. Skate rentals are available.

HERMITAGE GARDEN
Sad Ermitazh
Сад Эрмитаж

3 Karetny Ryad, 495/699-9081,
495/699-0432, 495/699-0849,
www.katokermitaj.ru
HOURS: In winter when weather conditions permit
Mon.-Thurs. noon-11 P.M., Fri.-Sun. 10 A.M.-midnight
COST: Mon.-Thurs. 100R, Fri.-Sun. 150R
METRO: Mayakovskaya
Map 3

These gardens were opened in 1878 and the ice skating rink here is thought to be Moscow's oldest, although it has not been functioning continuously the whole time. The gardens that surround the open-air rink are pleasant and make for a nice place to stroll, and besides the many theaters, there are several cafés to choose between when it's time for a hot drink to warm up. Skate rentals are available.

© NATHAN TOOHEY

Moscow's expansive parks get good snow cover in winter, perfect for cross-country skiing.

ICE SKATING IN RED SQUARE
Krasnaya ploshchad
Красная площадь
Red Square, 495/788-4343, www.gum.ru/katok
HOURS: Daily 10 A.M.–11 P.M.
COST: Skating period 1.5 hours: winter weekdays 250R at 10 A.M., noon, and 2 P.M., 350R from 4 P.M.; weekends 350R at 10 A.M. and noon, 500R starting at 2 P.M.
METRO: Okhotny Ryad
Map 1

It's hard to imagine a more spectacular setting for an ice skating rink than right in the middle of Red Square. The outdoor rink is huge, at 2,700 square meters, and can accommodate up to 500 skaters at a time. Running around its sides are wooden changing cabins and cafés. The rink works in any weather conditions during the winter, and skate rentals are available.

SKIING
BITTSA RECREATIONAL ZONE
Bittsa zona otdykha
Битца зона отдыха
36th kilometer of the Moscow Ring Road, from metro station Yasenevo buses 101, 202, 165, or 710 to the Bittsa zona otdykha stop, 926/216-1727, 926/207-5639, www.bitza-sport.ru
HOURS: Always open
COST: Free
METRO: Yasenevo
Map 8

This 50-hectare park on the outskirts of Moscow provides some of the best cross-country skiing, with 21 kilometers of ski trails running through its wooded grounds. The Alfa-Bittsa sports club, located inside the park, organizes races and other sporting activities, such as cross-country running races in the warmer months. The park is enormous and ranges from wild nature to civilized areas where the ponds have beaches and cafes in the summer.

SKIING SPARROW HILLS
Vorobyovy gory
Воробьёвы горы
17 Ulitsa Kosygina, 495/939-8377
HOURS: Always open
COST: Free entry; Chairlift: Mon.-Fri. 30R, Sat.-Sun. 60R
METRO: Vorobyovy Gory
Map 6

These slopes probably provide the best city views of any skiing site in the city. In addition to a downhill run there are several cross-country trails. A chairlift serves the park's skiers, who use its slopes and occasionally the enormous Olympic ski jump. The spot also attracts snowboarders, and recently there has even been Zorbing, also known as globe-riding or sphereing—essentially, rolling downhill inside a large double-hulled transparent plastic ball. At the top of the hills you'll find a viewing deck, cafés, food kiosks, and even a posh French restaurant with panoramic views—Rytsarsky Klub—so you can warm up and refuel after your day on the slopes.

◖ SNEJ.COM
Снеж.Ком

Pavshinskaya Poyma, town of Krasnogorsk, 1 kilometer from the Moscow Ring Road, direct buses every hour from metro Tushinskaya, 495/225-2233, 498/725-0000, www.snej.com
HOURS: Daily 10 A.M.-midnight
COST: Weekdays: adults 400R/hr., children 150R/hr.; weekends and public holidays: adults 900R/hr., children 300R/hr.; equipment rental is extra
METRO: Tushinskaya
Map 8

Russia may seem like the last place in the world to need such a thing, but then again Moscow loves grandiose projects and this certainly is one. Snej.com is Europe's largest all-season indoor ski facility. The center's main ski slope is 400 meters long and 60 meters wide, with a drop of some 65 meters. Besides year-round snow, the center boasts an ice skating rink, swimming facilities, saunas, bowling, playgrounds, and stores, restaurants, and cafés.

FITNESS CENTERS
GREEN POINT SPORT
Грин Поинт Спорт

20 Ovchinnikovskaya Naberezhnaya, Bldg. 1, 495/258-8743, 495/744-4021, www.greenpointsport.ru
HOURS: Mon.-Fri. 7 A.M.-11 P.M., Sat.-Sun. 9 A.M.-10 P.M.
COST: Varies
METRO: Novokuznetskaya
Map 5

Located on the 14th floor of a business center, this glass-encased fitness center must offer some of the best views of any gym in Moscow.

Not only are there spectacular panoramas to enjoy from the various weight and cardiovascular machines, there is also a large sundeck for catching some rays after a hard workout. The café also has outdoor seating and fabulous views, and the facility offers all the usual sauna and beauty-salon services. It's one of the few gyms where single visits are possible.

PLANET FITNESS
Planeta fitnes
Планета фитнес

6 Ulitsa Malaya Dmitrovka, 495/933-1124, www.fitness.ru
HOURS: Mon.-Fri. 7 A.M.-midnight, Sat.-Sun. 9 A.M.-11 P.M.
METRO: Pushkinskaya
Map 3

A large chain of fitness centers aimed at the urban middle class, Planet Fitness offers six- and 12-month memberships as well as "clip-cards" that allow you to buy 15 visits for 10,000R. That makes it perfect for working out during a short stay in Moscow, since most other clubs only offer long memberships. Founded in 1997, by 2008 the chain had grown to a total membership of about 180,000 people, with 17 clubs in Moscow, as well as dozens more in other cities across Russia—and more under construction. It is the first Russian fitness chain to go international, opening gyms in Sweden, Ukraine and Belarus. The fitness centers offer 60 different programs, from weight training to dance and aqua aerobics, plus children's programs. They have weights rooms, cardio halls, aerobics, personal trainers, and all the other attributes of modern fitness centers. In addition to the fitness center on Malaya Dmitrovka, two other centers are centrally located: 9 Bolshoy Kislovsky Pereulok (open 24 hours a day, seven days a week); and 21 Ulitsa Pravdy (open Mon.–Fri. 7 A.M.–midnight, Sat.–Sun. 9 A.M.–10 P.M.).

SWIMMING
CHAYKA
Чайка

3 Turchaninov Pereulok, Bldg. 1, 499/246-1344, www.chayka-sport.ru/pool
HOURS: Mon.-Sat. 7 A.M.-10:30 P.M., Sun. 8:30 A.M.-7:30 P.M.

METRO: Park Kultury

Map 4

For a very Russian experience, you can come here in the middle of winter in sub-zero temperatures and take a dip in the heated pool, and feel your eyelashes and nose hairs freeze when you pop your head out of the water. But this is also a popular pool in the warmer months, and attracts serious swimmers. Like any Russian public pool, you need to visit the on-site doctor to get a medical certificate (50R; think athlete's foot) before your first dip. This is one of the few pools that allows one-off visits (600R, bring your passport)—most others require you to buy a longer-term membership.

YOGA

NYM YOGA & SPA
22 Sadovaya-Karetnaya Ulitsa, 495/699-2990, www.nymyoga.com
METRO: Mayakovskaya

Map 3

This sleek and modern center opened after its founder experienced yoga in New York and wanted to create something similar in Moscow. It offers a full schedule of hatha-based classes, primarily aimed at overworked and stressed-out office workers, but not limited to that clientele, with special classes offered for children and pregnant women. Beginners' and individual classes are also available. It's possible to come for a single visit, or buy memberships for as little as five visits or as long as 12 months. NYM has a yoga clothing and equipment store, selling American brands, and a spa center offering all manner of massages. There's another branch near the Arbatskaya metro (4/5 Plotnikov Pereulok, 495/241-7700).

YOGA FEDERATION
33/41 Ulitsa Bolshaya Polyanka, 495/514-5045, www.kundalini.ru
METRO: Polyanka

Map 5

The Yoga Federation has several centers around Moscow, but this is the most central. Its air-conditioned, ventilated hall can accommodate up to 25 people at a time. There are classes for all levels, including beginners, as well as special courses for children and pregnant women. Founded in 2003, the foundation teaches a wide range of disciplines, including hatha, kundalini, ashtanga, Iyengar, tantra, and classical yoga, plus meditation, Indian dancing, and other classes. It has a cultural-educational center that runs conferences and seminars about yoga, fitness, and health.

SPECTATOR SPORTS
CENTRAL MOSCOW HIPPODROME
Tsentralny Moskovsky Ippodrom
Центральный Московский Ипподром
22 Begovaya Ulitsa, 495/945-0437, www.cmh.ru
METRO: Begovaya or Dinamo

Map 8

Moscow's grand, if somewhat run-down, hippodrome is completely constructed in Stalinist style. It is an interesting sight in itself, with fabulous horse statues and frescoes. The track mainly holds harness races, although occasional thoroughbred races are held as well. There is a totalizator in operation and the local crowd that gathers to gamble is a colorful bunch of old characters. There are grilled meats and cold beer on sale. It's well worth a visit if you are into horse racing or just fancy a fun day at the races.

LUZHNIKI OLYMPIC COMPLEX
Olimpiysky kompleks "Luzhniki"
Олимпийский комплекс "Лужники"
24 Luzhnetskaya Naberezhnaya, 495/785-9717, www.luzhniki.ru
METRO: Spotivnaya/Vorobyovy Gory

Map 6

The complex's stadium is the largest in Russia and, since serving as the main venue for the 1980s Olympics, has held countless national and international events, including the 2008 UEFA Champions League Final. It also hosts the national hockey and football championships, national and international athletics competitions, and dance contests. Besides the huge stadium, the surrounding complex provides just about every sporting facility imaginable, offering the opportunity to take part in a huge number of different sports: aikido, aqua aerobics, badminton, bowling, volleyball, scuba diving, squash, fencing—the list goes on and on. It also functions as a concert venue and hosts the yearly beer festival, among many other activities.

OLIMPIYSKY SPORTS COMPLEX
Sportivny kompleks "Olimpiysky"
Спортивный комплекс "Олимпийский"
16 Olimpiysky Prospekt, 495/688-5322, www.olimpik.ru
METRO: Prospekt Mira
Map 8

As the name might suggest, this huge stadium and complex was built for the 1980 Olympic Games and provides an enormous range of facilities for all manner of sporting events. The complex hosts national and international championships in swimming, gymnastics, billiards, lawn hockey, tennis, volleyball, and other sports. Besides hosting various championships and competitions, it also serves as a concert venue—this is where Iron Maiden, Beyonce, Rihanna, and Nelly Furtado performed their Moscow shows. As part of the complex there is also a swimming pool, which is open to the general public, as well as a large billiards hall.

SHOPS

Shopping in Moscow is expensive—which is not surprising, given that rental prices on retail space are some of the highest in the world. Locals know this and, if possible, go abroad to shop. Russia-based expats, especially Americans, complain about the clothing situation in particular. Brands that are affordable in the United States tend to be much more expensive here. The clothing market is polarized—lots of expensive designer labels and lots of cheap Chinese knockoffs, but not much of quality or interest in the mid-price segment. Furthermore, it's hard to find cool, original designs or hip styles outside the latest fads. Muscovites love famous brand names and aren't known for taking risks in their dress style.

On the positive side, shopping hours are longer than in many other countries; it's normal for stores to be open until quite late at night, even on weekends, and there are plenty of 24-hour stores. A host of modern malls and department stores have opened, greatly expanding your options beyond Red Square's grand old GUM (covered in the *Sights* chapter).

Service standards have improved immensely in recent years, but vary enormously, not only between stores but also between salespeople in one store. The sales culture is a bit different from what Americans are accustomed to—try to remember that service without a smile isn't considered bad service here. But while you can't always expect a smile, you might find you get something better instead: honesty. Salespeople in Russia have a tendency to warn a customer if a product is no good or not fresh, and

© NATHAN TOOHEY

HIGHLIGHTS

LOOK FOR 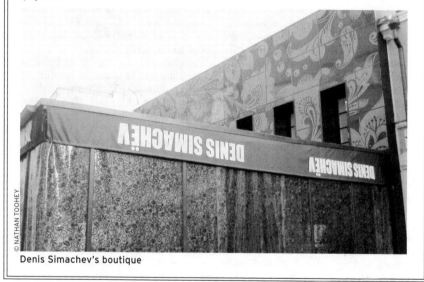 TO FIND
RECOMMENDED SHOPS.

◖ Hippest Boutique: Denis Simachev is one of Russia's most exciting designers, and his innovatively designed boutique includes a trendy restaurant and nightclub (page 151).

◖ Best Souvenir Shopping: The enormous **Vernissage Market at Izmaylovo** goes beyond the usual clichéd souvenirs, with antiques and quirky flea-market treasures to be found as well (page 157).

◖ Best Flashback: GUM's **Gastronom No. 1** re-creates a grand old Soviet food store for the elite, right down to the sales staff's uniforms (page 157).

◖ Most Amazing Supermarket: The **Yeliseyevsky Gastronom** has been Tverskaya's grandest store for more than a century and is probably still Moscow's most ornate. Its high ceilings drip with pompous chandeliers and extravagant gilt swirls (page 158).

◖ Best Market: The **Dorogomilovsky Market** has the most incredible range of goods, which makes it the shopping destination of choice for the city's chefs and foodies (page 159).

Denis Simachev's boutique

sometimes they even recommend somewhere better to buy what you're looking for.

Sales staff increasingly speak English, making things much easier for foreign tourists. But while English-speaking salespeople can be expected in souvenir stores and other businesses oriented toward tourists and foreigners, it can be hit-or-miss at stores with a primarily Russian clientele, such as shoe stores or clothing stores.

Credit and debit cards are not always accepted but ATMs are easy to find. Try to carry plenty of notes in the lower-value denominations—lots of 10R, 50R, 100R, and 500R notes—because the biggest problem when shopping in Russia is the persistent lack of change. Stores will turn you away if you present a note worth much more than your purchase, and if you present a 5,000R note for something costing less than 4,000R, they'll probably laugh you out of the store. So at the ATM it pays to withdraw, say, 4,900R, rather than 5,000R, or else you could get stuck with a fat note that's impossible to spend unless you're willing to splurge.

Moscow's main street, Tverskaya Ulitsa, is an obvious place to go shopping—here you'll find an abundance of international brand-name clothing stores, as well as cell-phone stores, bookstores, and the fabulously ornate and well-stocked Yeliseyevsky supermarket. Several other good shopping spots are described in the following *Shopping Districts* section.

If you're looking for souvenirs, the places to go are the Vernissage souvenir market at Izmaylovo, or Ulitsa Arbat, also known as Stary or Old Arbat, which is lined with souvenir stores offering every type of Russian souvenir for sale. The advantage of Izmaylovo is that it's not only a souvenir market but also a flea market, so you might find some unique and quirky treasures. On the other hand, the Arbat is more convenient, and not only because it's more centrally located. Shopping in the Arbat's stores is easier, because the prices are fixed and on display, whereas at Izmaylovo it can be difficult to know whether you're being quoted a fair price. It's true that sometimes haggling is expected, and that some market traders initially ask a much higher price than they intend to accept—but rich foreigners who make a fuss over trivial sums don't make a positive impression, especially when it's over some impoverished craftsperson's handmade wares. If you're unsure whether a market price is fair, go take a look at the price of similar items in a proper store.

Be careful what you buy: Some things, such as antiques and icons, cannot be taken out of the country without certification.

SHOPPING DISTRICTS
ARBAT STREETS—NEW AND OLD
Ulitsy Arbat—Novy i Stary
Улицы Арбат—Новый и Старый
Moscow has two Arbat Streets: Ulitsa Arbat, unofficially known as Old or Stary Arbat, and the nearby New or Novy Arbat, running

roughly parallel to it. These are both radial streets that begin in the very center of the city and lead outwards to the Garden Ring, with Novy Arbat continuing onwards to the Moscow River. The closest metro stations are Arbatskaya and Smolenskaya.

These two streets couldn't be more different from each other. The older Arbat is a pedestrian-only street lined with gorgeous old houses. It's the most touristy street in town, and unsurprisingly has an abundance of souvenir stores, as well as cafés, restaurants, bars, museums, and theaters. Previously it was covered in street stalls selling souvenirs, but in 2008 they were removed. City Hall announced the street would be rebranded as a book street, and a small number of book stalls appeared. The Arbat is still a good place to look for souvenirs, however, as the actual souvenir stores continued functioning.

Bright lights, big city—that's Novy Arbat, a surreal vision of Soviet architecture. Rows of tall buildings were constructed along the newly widened street in the 1960s, supposedly inspired by Soviet leader Nikita Khrushchev's visit to New York. On one side are five rectilinear 25-story apartment blocks, and on the other, four 26-story blocks shaped like opened books, some of which have started acquiring new blue-glass facades. The glitzy Lotte Plaza mall on the corner of Novy Arbat and the Garden Ring fits with this new blue look.

Numerous upscale boutiques, entertainment centers, bars, and restaurants have opened along Novy Arbat—too many to list here. There are countless cell-phone, camera, and electronics stores, including an outlet of the Bely Veter chain. Here you'll find Dom Knigi or Books House, which stocks English-language books and much more, and the 24-hour elite supermarket Globus Gourmet, where you can sometimes sneak a free midnight snack from the trays of complimentary samplers. There are also handbag and luggage stores, and various clothing stores.

Novy Arbat is set for a major transformation, and soon. There are plans to divert its six lanes of traffic into an underground tunnel, and turn the street into a pedestrian zone like the Old Arbat—who knows what it will look like, but one thing's for certain: New Arbat still won't look anything like Old Arbat.

Nikolskaya Ulitsa– Tretyakovsky Proyezd
Никольская улица— Третьяковский проезд

Running from the GUM department store on Red Square to Lubyanskaya Square, Nikolskaya Ulitsa is an old street with a history as a spiritual and educational center, but now it's primarily a shopping street. Besides GUM, there's the new Sheremetyevsky shopping center two-thirds of the way up, and the Nautilus center at the end, on Lubyanskaya Square. Along the way, there's a particularly large number of shoe stores, as well as clothing stores. A good spot to look for clothing is in the pedestrian passage between Nikolskaya Ulitsa and the Ploshchad Revolyutsii metro station.

Leading off Nikolskaya Ulitsa is another important shopping street, or rather, a thoroughfare—Tretyakovsky Proyezd. One of the capital's most exclusive fashion streets, it was built in the 1870s in imitation medieval style, financed by the merchants and Tretyakov Gallery founders Pavel and Sergey Tretyakov. The story goes that they were frustrated by blockages on Nikolskaya Ulitsa, so they bought the land and revived a Middle Ages thoroughfare through the Kitay-Gorod wall. On this beautiful pedestrian lane you'll find Armani, Prada, Dolce&Gabbana, and the like. Approach from the metro stations Ploshchad Revolyutsii or Lubyanka.

Petrovka–Stoleshnikov– Kuznetsky Most
Петровка—Столешников— Кузнецкий Мост

One of the city's top shopping neighborhoods is around Ulitsa Petrovka, a narrow street that begins right in the center, with the Bolshoi Theater on the left and the Maly Theater across the road on the right. Like Tverskaya Ulitsa, it's a radial street that starts near the Kremlin and leads to the Garden Ring, crossing the

Tretyakovsky Proyezd is one of Moscow's most exclusive fashion-shopping streets.

Boulevard Ring on the way. It is one of the city's oldest streets, having originated as the way to the 14th-century Vysokopetrovsky Monastery, located about halfway up. The closest metro station is Teatralnaya.

This was originally an artisans' and tradesmen's quarter—nearby street names refer to blacksmiths (Kuznetsky Most), tablecloth weavers (Stoleshnikov Pereulok), guns and cannons (Pushechnaya Ulitsa)—but in the second half of the 18th century, the elite started moving in. Princes, nobles, and merchants built palatial houses along the street. Rental houses, boutiques, and luxury-goods stores also appeared, giving the street much of the character that it has now. No. 8 was built in 1900 for Dupres, the French wine-traders mentioned in Leo Tolstoy's *Anna Karenina* and other literary works. Still functioning is the historic Petrovsky Passage, a posh mall that first opened in 1906, and TsUM, a department store that first opened in 1908 as Muir & Mirrielees. There are many other clothing and shoe stores in the section between Theater Square and the Boulevard Ring.

Elite designer-name boutiques are clustered on the charming, partly pedestrian-only Stoleshnikov Pereulok, which comes off Ulitsa Petrovka beside the Marriott Aurora hotel, leading up to the Yury Dolgoruky statue on Tverskaya Ulitsa. Here you'll find Denis Simachev, Christian Dior, Marc Jacobs, Hermes, Furla, and Agent Provocateur.

Kuznetsky Most is another important shopping street in this neighborhood. It intersects Petrovka, running between Ulitsa Bolshaya Dmitrovka and Ulitsa Bolshaya Lubyanka. Besides the Foreign Book House, there's also Jagannath, a vegetarian restaurant with a store selling health foods and hippie clothes, among other interesting stores. Approach Kuznetsky Most from the metro stations Kuznetsky Most or Teatralnaya.

Beauty

ARBAT PRESTIGE
Arbat Prestizh
Арбат Престиж
33 Zemlyanoy Val (Atrium mall), 495/777-7773, www.arp.ru
HOURS: Daily 11 A.M.–midnight
METRO: Kurskaya
Map 8

This 1,500-square-meter cosmetics store is one of the most centrally located outlets in the Arbat Prestige chain, which has more than two dozen outlets in Moscow, as well as others across Russia and in Ukraine. It stocks some affordable but high-quality Russian brands, such as Chyorny Zhemchug, or Black Pearl, and natural cosmetics from Green Mama. Familiar international cosmetics brands right across the price spectrum are also to be found, such as Gillette, Pupa, Max Factor, Neutrogena, Olay, Scholl, Sally Hansen, Shiseido, Thalgo, DKNY, and Gucci. There are fragrances for men and women alike, as well as makeup, skin-care products, and more.

EXPAT SALON
23 Skatertny Pereulok, 495/691-6467, 906/780-9774, www.expatsalon.ru
HOURS: Daily 9 A.M.–9 P.M.
METRO: Pushkinskaya
Map 3

Using sign language to explain how you want your hair cut is a risky business, but thankfully an American from South Carolina opened an English-speaking salon especially for those who haven't mastered Russian. Employing the philosophy that "the customer is always right," it has grown into a chain of two (the second is at 3 Maly Patriarshy Pereulok, 495/650-3749, 906/780-7437). There are nonsmoking salons for both men and women, with hairstylists, manicurists, cosmetologists, and massage therapists. Clients are offered a complimentary beverage, English-language magazines, DVD players and DVDs to watch (or bring your own), and assistance in arranging taxis.

L'ETOILE
L'Etual

Л'Этуаль

18 Tverskaya Ulitsa, 495/650-3684, www.letoile.ru

HOURS: Daily 10 A.M.-10 P.M.

METRO: Tverskaya

`Map 3`

Having opened its first Moscow store in 1997, by 2008 this chain of cosmetics stores had grown to 115 in the capital and more than 500 across Russia. They're visible all over the city, recognizable by their bright blue, white, and yellow wavelike logo. The chain's stores have a convenient self-service format, rather than sales counters, which makes shopping easier if you don't speak Russian. The stores stock about 150 brands of perfumes, skin-care products, and other cosmetics, including Christian Dior, Sisley, Givenchy, Estée Lauder, Clarins, and Guerlain. On the local cosmetics market, the chain is the exclusive distributor of Lulu Castagnette, Hylexin, StriVectin, Loewe, Hanae Mori, and Make Up Factory, as well as the skin-care products Virtual Laser and DermaFreeze 365.

TCHIK-TCHIK
Chik Chik

Чик Чик

32 Ulitsa Bolshaya Yakimanka, 499/238-3158, www.tchiktchik.ru

HOURS: Daily 10 A.M.-7 P.M.

METRO: Oktyabrskaya

`Map 5`

A hair salon especially for children, Tchik-Tchik is run by an American expat mother of three, who wanted to create something like the kids' salons in the United States. Brightly painted with cheerful murals on the walls, it makes getting a haircut fun. While having their hair cut, children can sit in a mini yellow Hummer, an airplane, or a Barbie Jeep, and watch television or DVDs of cartoons and children's movies in English, French, or Russian. There are also Nintendo games to help distract them from the sometimes distressing process of being combed and brushed. Prices are low, and there are various discounts on Monday, Wednesday, and Friday.

Books, Music, and Movies

BOOKSTORES

BOOKS HOUSE
Dom Knigi

Дом книги

8 Ulitsa Novy Arbat, 495/789-3591

HOURS: Mon.-Fri. 9 A.M.-11 P.M., Sat.-Sun. 10 A.M.-11 P.M.

METRO: Arbatskaya

`Map 4`

This huge bookstore occupies 4,500 square meters and stocks some 210,000 books. There's also audio and video materials, plus a huge selection of stationery items as well. The range of travel guidebooks (including English-language guidebooks) is impressive. The salespeople are helpful and you might be able to find one that speaks English, but it's a very busy store, and usually crowded, so personal service might be asking a bit much.

BUKBERI
Букбери

17 Nikitsky Bulvar, Bldg. 1, 495/202-6679, www.bookberry.ru

HOURS: Daily 8 A.M.-midnight

METRO: Arbatskaya

`Map 3`

Bukberi is a chain of modern bookstores, the kind that until fairly recently were hard to find in Russia. This store is spacious and well laid out, which makes finding what you're after easy. There is a small English-language section and a café downstairs for relaxing with your new purchases.

FOREIGN BOOK HOUSE
Dom Inostrannoy Knigi

Дом иностранной книги

8/7 Ulitsa Kuznetsky Most, 495/628-2021

HOURS: Mon.-Fri. 9 A.M.-9 P.M.,
Sat. 10 A.M.-9 P.M., Sun. 10 A.M.-8 P.M.
METRO: Kuznetsky Most
Map 2

This is Moscow's premier foreign-language bookstore. If you're looking for an English-language novel, this store is probably your best bet. The small and cozy store also stocks an excellent range of books about Russian history and culture in English. There is also a decent selection of English-language travel guidebooks.

MOSKVA
Москва
8 Tverskaya Ulitsa, 495/629-6483
HOURS: Daily 10 A.M.-1 A.M.
METRO: Tverskaya
Map 3

Moskva is a huge bookstore located right on Moscow's main street. Being so central it can get crowded, but then again it's open till 1 A.M., so come a little later in the evening and you'll find it's less cramped. Some staff speak English, and usually the salespeople are very helpful, but when they're very busy it can be hard to get their undivided attention.

RESPUBLIKA
Республика
10 1st Tverskaya-Yamskaya Ul., 495/781-3703
HOURS: Daily 24 hours
METRO: Mayakovskaya
Map 3

This is probably the grooviest bookstore in town. It's the kind of place that graphic designers and art students come to browse through the latest design magazines. Besides a great collection of coffee-table books and other such publications, there is also a large range of collector items, toys, and other useless but fun knickknacks.

MUSIC, MOVIES, AND MORE
PURPLE LEGION
Purpurny legion
Пурпурный легион
1 Novokuznetskaya Ulitsa, 495/225-1386,
www.plegion.ru
HOURS: Tues.-Sun. 10 A.M.-10 P.M., Mon. 10 A.M.-9 P.M.

METRO: Novokuznetskaya or Tretyakovskaya
Map 5

This cute little music, games, and movie store was king of its crossroads until the much larger VseSOYUZny MediaHyperMarket opened diagonally across the road. A leading player in the Moscow music retail business for more than a decade, Purple Legion offers a vastly different shopping experience from what you'll find at the bigger newcomer. This is more like a mom-and-pop music store, with a less commercial collection. There are new releases as well as old classics, and obscure alternative discs. It doesn't have all the extras that you'll find at its neighbor, but offers personal service. Don't forget to check the movie language before you buy.

TRANSYLVANIA
Transilvaniya
Трансильвания
6/1 Tverskaya Ulitsa, Bldg. 5, 495/629-8786,
www.transilvania.ru
HOURS: Daily 11 A.M.-10 P.M.
METRO: Okhotny Ryad
Map 3

Hidden away in a courtyard, through an archway just off Tverskaya Ulitsa, this is a fabulous little store, with one of Moscow's best selections of music and movies. It packs a huge collection into its relatively small space. The staff are friendly and well-informed music lovers who immensely enjoy introducing you to new sounds. You might go in there looking for one particular album, from which the staff cleverly figure out your taste, and offer a bunch of other stuff that you just must listen to. You leave as a happy customer, having bought much more than you intended to, but having discovered some new favorite artists. Books and magazines are also sold here.

VSESOYUZNY
ВсеСОЮЗный
29 Pyatnitskaya Ulitsa, 495/589-1551, www.soyuz.ru
HOURS: Daily 10 A.M.-10 P.M.
METRO: Tretyakovskaya or Novokuznetskaya
Map 5

Soyuz is an extensive chain of music stores,

and this is its biggest outlet—or rather, a MediaHyperMarket, as it calls itself. Occupying four floors, the store is enormous, with a vast range of music, games, and movies, at prices that start from very low (if you want a film in English, check the back of the case before buying, because some are dubbed while others are in a range of languages including the original). But that's not all. It also sells concert tickets, musical instruments, books, electronics such as MP3 players, digital cameras, and memory cards. There's a café, Internet terminals, digital photography services, typographic services, and much more to keep you amused for hours.

Clothing

ALENA AKHMADULLINA CONCEPT STORE

Concept Store Алены Ахмадуллиной
10/2 Nikolskaya Ulitsa, 495/621-0892, www.akhmadullina.com
HOURS: Daily 11 A.M.–10 P.M.
METRO: Lubyanka
Map 2

A leading Russian women's fashion designer from St. Petersburg, Alena Akhmadullina opened her first concept store in Moscow in September 2008. Prêt-à-porter, accessories, and a luxury fur line are showcased in this beautiful three-level boutique. There are silk printed dresses, leather printed bags, iPhone gloves, and mink overcoats. Akhmadullina's clothing has been described as resembling secretaries' outfits from old Hollywood movies, and it's an apt comparison, in the most positive sense. Pencil skirts, silk blouses with bows at the throat, creative and amusing shoes and bags—all her designs exude restrained, tasteful elegance.

BILINGUA

10 Krivokolenny Pereulok, Bldg. 5, 495/623-5718, www.bilinguaclub.ru/haberdashery.html
HOURS: Daily noon–midnight
METRO: Turgenevskaya
Map 2

This clothing store is an offshoot of the groovy Bilingua bohemian café/club. As you would expect, the clothes and other accessories are all hip and interesting. Having been created by small individual designers, many of the pieces are one-offs. Most surprisingly, the prices here are very reasonable, especially given the work

that's gone into some of the handmade items. Most of the stock is womenswear, but there is also a small selection for men.

BOSCO SPORT

4 Tverskaya Ulitsa, 495/692-1457, www.bosco.ru/olimp
HOURS: Daily 10 A.M.–10 P.M.
METRO: Okhotny Ryad
Map 1

The name Bosco di Ciliegi may sound Italian, but the company is thoroughly Russian. Bosco Sport is the fashion house's sportswear line, and is probably one of Russia's most recognizable, as it is worn by the nation's Olympic team. You'll find the full range of its sports clothes for men, women, and children, as well as adorable Cheburashka toys—Russia's Olympic mascot.

◖ DENIS SIMACHEV

Денис Симачев
12/2 Stoleshnikov Pereulok, 495/629-5702, www.denissimachev.ru
HOURS: Daily 10 A.M.–10 P.M.
METRO: Pushkinskaya
Map 3

Russia's most fashionable designer naturally has one of Moscow's most fashionable boutiques. Not only does it sell his trendy creations, it also doubles as an über-hip bar and nightclub. Simachev is a cheeky fashion renegade with an ironic sense of humor that's visible in both his men's and women's lines, which always have a playful theme: gypsies, gangsters, sailors, soldiers, bums, even *matryoshkas* (nesting dolls) are among the styles to have been

CHEBURASHKA

Cheburashka is one of Russia's most widely adored childhood characters. Originally created by the author Eduard Uspensky and first featured in his 1966 children's book *Crocodile Gena and His Friends*, Cheburashka acquired his true fame, along with his koala-like ears, when animator Leonid Shvartsman created his animated image for the stop-motion cartoon of the same name in 1970. The original story tells of how this impossibly cute little furry creature arrives from warmer climes, packed in a box of oranges. He soon makes friends with the amiable crocodile Gena, who works as a crocodile at the local zoo, and they proceed to have numerous adventures.

Cheburashka toy

Cheburashka has since gone on to become the hero of numerous anecdotes and a nickname for certain types of cars, planes, and even small-sized vodka bottles. Moreover, the Swedes borrowed his image in the 1970s to create their own children's story, *Drutten och krokodilen*, albeit with a different story line. The original animated series has found fame in Japan, where it has achieved cult status. Recently, Cheburashka became the official Russian Olympic team mascot, and he has hitched a ride to the winner's podium on more than one occasion.

Naturally, such a handsome fellow is a popular souvenir and can be found at nearly all tourist stalls and stores, ranging from original 1960s badges to modern talking stuffed toys. Bosco Sport, outfitter to the Olympic team, sells particularly high-quality Cheburashkas.

featured in his collections. One of his trademarks is to take traditional Russian motifs and incorporate them into unusual new looks. Simachev is the designer who made headlines and raised eyebrows with his iconic Vladimir Putin T-shirts, which came out in 2002 with a $200 price tag; before that he brought out retro CCCP Olympic team jackets and sold them for $500. Best not to plan your shopping visit too late in the evening or you'll be jostling to get past face control along with the other fashionistas.

KIRA PLASTININA
Кира Пластинина
10 Ulitsa Arbat, Staraya Ulitsa shopping center, 495/937-0724, www.kiraplastinina.us
HOURS: Daily 10 A.M.–10 P.M.
METRO: Arbatskaya
Map 4

Kira Plastinina is the daughter of a fruit-juice mogul and daddy bought her just what every teenage girl wants—her own international chain of fashion boutiques. Kira describes her designs as "Art-Glamour-Sporty" and the fun clothes are aimed to appeal to teenage girls.

MODNAYA TOCHKA
Модная Точка
28 Tverskaya Ulitsa, 495/937-9430, www.fashionpoint.ru
HOURS: Daily 11 A.M.–10 P.M.
METRO: Mayakovskaya
Map 3

This is one of the most centrally located stores in a small chain of boutiques that stock a select range of men's and women's apparel by some of the best Russian designers, such as Nina Donis and Denis Simachev, as well as Western designers that can be hard to find, including Ann Demeulemeester and Pinko. This store has a particular focus on Jean Paul Gaultier, so if you can't wait to get home to get a Gaultier fix, try here.

TWINS SHOPP

11 Ulitsa Solyanka, 495/221-7557,
www.s-11.ru/twins-shop
HOURS: Daily noon–10 P.M.
METRO: Kitay-Gorod
Map 2

Part of the Solyanka nightclub project, this cozy store offers hip clothing, shoes, and eyewear of little-known, up-and-coming Russian and European designers. Here, you might find something irresistible from Russia's Inshade, Sweden's Hope, or England's Garbstore. The store is run by twin sisters, who comb London stores and young designer exhibitions for interesting additions to their collection, saying their concept is to give young people the possibility to express themselves. The decor is home-like—you feel like you're in an apartment, with quirky chests of drawers decorated with cute ornaments. There are interesting items for both men and women.

SHOES

CARLO PAZOLINI

52-54 Ulitsa Bolshaya Yakimanka, 495/238-9523,
www.carlopazolini.ru
HOURS: Mon.-Sat. 10 A.M.–9 P.M., Sun. 11 A.M.–8 P.M.
METRO: Oktyabrskaya
Map 5

There's a saying among expats, "You know you've been in Russia too long when you look at a person's shoes to determine where he's from." And it's so true. Spend a bit of time in Russia, and you really can tell who's from where just by looking at what's on their feet. So if you find your feet are getting funny looks and you feel as if you're standing out like a sore thumb, you might want to buy some local shoes so that you can blend in a bit better. Or perhaps you just brought the wrong footwear for the weather—which wouldn't be surprising, given how variable it can be. If you want to blend in and look stylish, this store is a good choice. A large store with an extensive range for both men and women, it always has the most current styles being worn in the capital, and the quality is good. Most of the collection is pricey, but hidden in one corner there's a discount section with some real bargains.

21ST CENTURY SHOES

Obuv XXI veka
Обувь XXI века
5/1 Nikolskaya Ulitsa, 495/933-4518, www.shoes.ru
HOURS: Daily 10 A.M.–10 P.M.
METRO: Ploshchad Revolyutsii
Map 2

This is one store in a small chain that was established in 1998, with a mission to follow the very latest international fashions and bring ultra-fashionable footwear to the Moscow public. It sells some of the city's most interesting shoes, for both men and women, as well as some quirky clothing and accessories. It's one of the few places to find Dr. Martens boots, as well as Grinders. Catering primarily to customers who don't want to look like everybody else, it also stocks some genuinely unusual footwear, such as chunky boots and platformed sneakers by Swear. The stores also have Birkenstock boots, and women's shoes by Skechers that are at once comfortable, flat-heeled, and attractive under a skirt. The stores have an original, artistic design, and DJs providing a soundtrack to your visit. A second store is just off Tverskaya Ulitsa, near the Pushkinskaya metro station (6 Maly Palashevsky Pereulok, Bldg. 1, 495/694-5847).

Department Stores and Malls

ATRIUM
Атриум
33 Zemlyanoy Val, 495/970-1555, www.atrium.su
HOURS: Daily 11 A.M.-11 P.M.
METRO: Kurskaya
Map 8

One of Europe's largest malls, the Atrium opened in 2002 and offers four floors of shopping as well as a cinema, entertainment center, a food court, restaurants, and bars. There's a large 24-hour supermarket on the very lowest level, while the other stores have more limited working hours. The mall has a number of audio/video and electronics stores including Apple Center, Nokia, and Sony VAIO. Boutiques are numerous, with mens- and womenswear at not particularly cheap prices. The brands here include Adidas, Puma, Nike, Speedo, TJ Collection, Ecco, Zara, Russia's own Kira Plastinina, and So French.

LOTTE PLAZA
Лотте Плаза
8 Novinsky Bulvar, 495/662-8100, www.lotteplaza.ru
HOURS: Daily 10 A.M.-10 P.M.
METRO: Smolenskaya
Map 4

Luxury is what this mall is all about, occupying eight floors of a new 21-story building. Armani, Dolce&Gabbana, Bvlgari, Prada, Valentino—and that's just a small sample of what's on the 1st floor alone. Other floors have an Apple computer store, a LeFutur gift store, designer children's wear, books, and much more. The 7th floor has a food court with several eateries, as does the lower ground floor, where you'll also find an organic juice bar/café, an elite supermarket, a drugstore, and a travel agency. A new mall, it has three panoramic lifts, in which you can ride up to the very top and enjoy a meal or drinks in Kalina Bar, which has views that are spectacular whether you sit inside or out on the summer terrace.

NAUTILUS SHOPPING CENTER
Nautilus TTs
Наутилус ТЦ
25 Nikolskaya Ulitsa, 495/933-7711, www.nautilus-td.ru
HOURS: Daily 10 A.M.-10 P.M.
METRO: Lubyanka
Map 2

Designed in an eclectic style to look something like a ship of the future, this shopping center opened in 1998 and lends a different look to Lubyanskaya Ploshchad—it looks quite frivolous compared to the old KGB headquarters across the square. On its six floors are more than 40 stores and boutiques, including Pal Zileri, Dirk Bikkembergs, Trussardi, and other international brands. There's fur, clothing, footwear, accessories, jewelry, a beauty salon, and restaurants including Loft and Vinoteca Dissident.

OKHOTNY RYAD
Охотный ряд
1 Manezhnaya Ploshchad, 495/737-7393, www.oxotniy.ru
HOURS: Daily 11 A.M.-10 P.M.
METRO: Okhotny Ryad
Map 1

This mall opened in the mid-'90s in place of what was once a large traffic square. Now it is popular not only for its three underground levels of stores and boutiques, but also for its above-ground fountains and promenades, where teenagers gather to skate about and generally have fun. The lower level has a food court, which is a good option for cheap eats right by the Kremlin. The layout can be a bit disorienting, but as you roam the corridors you'll see familiar brand-name stores including Benetton, Sisley, Yves Rocher, Tommy Hilfiger, Puma, Reebok, and Mascotte. There's also a McDonald's and bowling.

PETROVSKY PASSAGE
Petrovsky passazh
Петровский пассаж
10 Ulitsa Petrovka, 495/625-3132

HOURS: Mon.-Sat. 10 A.M.-8 P.M., Sun. 11 A.M.-6 P.M.

METRO: Kuznetsky Most

Map 3

Even posher than TsUM (described later in this section) is Petrovsky Passage, a mall that first opened in 1906. It is literally a passage, taking you through a whole block to Neglinnaya Ulitsa. In the 1930s its grand halls were turned over to dirigible design. Now it's back to its original role, and with a vengeance. The stylish ladies of leisure who browse in its boutiques will erase any doubts about Moscow's newfound wealth.

SHEREMETYEVSKY SHOPPING CENTER
TK "Sheremetyevsky"
ТК "Шереметьевский"

10 Nikolskaya Ulitsa, 495/797-4718, www.rutsog.ru

HOURS: Daily 10 A.M.-10 P.M.

METRO: Lubyanka or Ploshchad Revolyutsii

Map 2

If you want to buy some new threads, take a look at this enormous retail, office, and entertainment complex. It has shopping on three levels, as well as restaurants, cafés, fast-food eateries, cinema, bowling, slot machines, and a bar. Decorated with waterfalls and statues, it has two atriums, with gallery passages on the upper levels. There are some interesting boutiques. The complex's name refers to Count Sheremetyev, who owned the Chinese House at this address in the 18th century. In the early 20th century it was reconstructed in industrial art nouveau style and was occupied by a sewing enterprise until restoration and reconstruction work began in 2003 to create the new complex.

TSUM
ЦУМ

2 Ulitsa Petrovka, 495/933-7309, www.tsum.ru

HOURS: Mon.-Sat. 10 A.M.-10 P.M., Sun. 11 A.M.-10 P.M.

METRO: Teatralnaya

Map 3

At the very beginning of Ulitsa Petrovka, opposite the Bolshoi Theater, this Gothic-styled building was an anachronistic addition to the city skyline when it appeared in 1908. Then, it was Muir & Mirrielees, a department store founded by Scotsmen Andrew Muir and Archibald Mirrielees, and created a sensation with such novelties as electric lifts. The store was nationalized and became TsUM (an acronym for Central Department Store) in Soviet times. It shed its Soviet image with a total makeover in the late 1990s and early 2000s, elite designer labels took over, and it became one of the city's poshest department stores.

YEVROPEYSKY
Европейский

2 Ploshchad Kievskogo Vokzala, 495/921-3444, www.europe-tc.ru

HOURS: Sun.-Thurs. 10 A.M.-10 P.M., Fri.-Sat. 10 A.M.-11 P.M.

METRO: Kievskaya

Map 8

This enormous shopping center opened in 2006 and provides a spacious and uncramped shopping experience. There are countless stores and boutiques, which include Britain's popular, trendy, and inexpensive Top Shop and Top Man, as well as Spain's Bershka, plus Mexx, Timberland, Nike, and Adidas. There are also lots of restaurants, some of which provide impressive city views, such as the Filimonova i Yankel fish house. The exclusive Black Star nightclub is located on the roof.

Gifts and Specialty Stores

SOUVENIRS AND GIFTS

APTEKA PODARKOV

Аптека подарков

68 Bolshaya Ordynka Ulitsa, 495/238-9374

HOURS: Mon.-Fri. 11 A.M.-9 P.M., Sat.-Sun. noon-7 P.M.

METRO: Dobryninskaya

Map 5

This gift store is not dissimilar to Byuro Nakhodok, described later in this section; in fact they stock some items produced by the same artists. There's lots of cute and kooky creations, and the store seems to stock an extra-large collection of stuffed toys, which are nice and easy to transport home without breaking. Apteka is the Russian word for drugstore, and the theme is explored in a quirky decor concept that strangely is combined with toy hares in a starring role. Prices aren't low, but they're worth it.

ARBATSKAYA LAVITSA

Арбатская лавица

27 Ulitsa Arbat, 495/290-5689

HOURS: Daily 9 A.M.-9 P.M.

METRO: Arbatskaya

Map 4

If you're looking for classical Russian souvenirs, then you'd be hard pressed to find a better place to shop for them. The store boasts a collection of some 17,000 items for sale, so if it's a nesting doll or lacquered box that you're after, no matter how large or small, you're sure to find it here. There is also a large range of amber jewelry on sale. This store stands out for its good service. The salespeople are unusually helpful and friendly, and it seems there's always an English speaker on duty—which perhaps is not surprising considering that their clientele is exclusively foreign tourists.

BYURO NAKHODOK

Бюро находок

7 Smolensky Bulvar, 495/244-7694

HOURS: Mon.-Fri. 9 A.M.-9 P.M., Sat.-Sun. noon-7 P.M.

METRO: Park Kultury

Map 4

The name means "lost and found bureau," and this store has a wonderful collection of super-quirky gifts and collectibles. Most of the items for sale are one-off creations and are put together with iconic Russian products, such as clocks made

one of the many souvenir stores on Arbat Street

© NATHAN TOOHEY

from caviar tins or samovars. It's definitely worth having a look here if you're after something a little more original than your standard nesting doll.

MINISTRY OF GIFTS
Ministerstvo podarkov
Министерство подарков
12/27 Maly Gnezdnikovsky Pereulok, 495/629-9732, www.minpod.narod.ru
HOURS: Mon.-Fri. 10 A.M.-9 P.M., Sat. 11 A.M.-9 P.M., Sun. 11 A.M.-8 P.M.
METRO: Pushkinskaya
Map 3

Artistic gifts for artsy people is what this store sells. There is all manner of creative constructions, all of which are handmade—they're not cheap, but what do you expect for original creations of such humor and flair? You'll find such gifts as special shot-glass holders designed to look like little boats, and notebooks with door handles attached to the front. Out the back is a store within a store—**Galereika** (www.galereika.ru), which specializes in gifts and toys made from felt.

NOVODEL
Новодел
9 Bolshoi Palashevsky Pereulok, Bldg. 1, 495/626-4538
HOURS: Daily noon-8 P.M.
METRO: Pushkinskaya
Map 3

This cute little two-room store, hidden away on a lane near Patriarch's Ponds, is not only a mere gift shop, but a veritable gallery of object design. Various artists have collections of different frivolous bits and bobs that include fun interior design items such as mouse pads, clocks and lamps, kitchenware such as quirky salt and pepper shakers, and wearables like slippers, T-shirts, and jewelry. You'll almost certainly find something you like.

◖ VERNISSAGE MARKET AT IZMAYLOVO
Vernisazh v Izmaylovo
Вернисаж в Измайлово
73zh Izmaylovskoye Shosse, 495/166-4118, www.moscow-vernisage.com/enmain/vernisage/shema

HOURS: Daily 9 A.M.-6 P.M.
COST: 10R
METRO: Partizanskaya
Map 8

Vernissage Market is Moscow's, and probably Russia's, largest souvenir market. It certainly is not centrally located, but if you are serious about souvenirs then this is the place for you. While Arbat stocks the standard T-shirts, nesting dolls, furry hats, and other run-of-the-mill paraphernalia, Vernissage has everything—and the Soviet kitchen sink. Not only do its hundreds of traders deal in traditional crafts and souvenirs, they also specialize in vintage collectibles: stamps, coins, jewelry, toys, old magazines, postcards, and other such items. But keep in mind that although these flea-market goods may be old, the prices are in keeping with the times—don't expect any super bargains. The market is huge and exploring it could easily fill an entire day. Luckily, there are numerous grill cafés and Chinese eateries to refuel shoppers' batteries.

FOOD AND DRINK
◖ GASTRONOM NO. 1
Гастроном № 1
3 Red Square (1st floor, GUM shopping center), 495/788-4343
HOURS: Daily 10 A.M.-10 P.M.
METRO: Ploshchad Revolyutsii
Map 1

This shop, inside the GUM shopping center beside Red Square, provides a total retro experience. The store was re-created based on historical photographs of a store that once existed in GUM. The interior design is ornate, and the staff even wear retro-styled aprons. Besides the usual gourmet foods, such as freshly made sushi, they also stock old favorites such as canned sprats, and they even have an old-fashioned soda fountain where you can savor Soviet-style pop. Prices are higher than in your average suburban supermarket, but it's not surprising when you see the location and the decor. The clientele is mostly tourists, both foreign and Russian out-of-towners.

GLOBUS GOURMET
Глобус гурмэ
19 Ulitsa Novy Arbat, 495/221-6671,
www.globusg.nichost.ru
HOURS: Daily 24 hours
METRO: Smolenskaya
Map 4

This is the spacious flagship of a chain of up-market grocery stores. The selection is huge, the produce is top of the line, and they have numerous sample counters were you can try before you buy. The prices here are high, but they often stock goods that can't be found anywhere else around town.

HEDIARD
7 Sadovaya Kudrinskaya Ulitsa, 495/254-5394
HOURS: Daily 10 A.M.-11 P.M.
METRO: Barrikadnaya
Map 3

This is a French gourmet food chain that was bought out by a Russian billionaire in 2007, so it's only appropriate that it has a prominent branch right downtown. As at Hediards the world over, you'll find a superb collection of exotic goods, especially hard-to-find spices. It's expensive, of course.

INDIAN SPICES
36/2 Ulitsa Sretenka, 495/607-1621,
www.indianspices.ru
HOURS: Daily 9 A.M.-9 P.M.
METRO: Sukharevskaya
Map 8

If it's spice that you need, then this is the place to come. The small store stocks the most impressive array of spices and condiments found anywhere in Moscow. It doesn't limit itself just to Indian, but stocks a wide range of other Asian and even Mexican goods. This is where the local Indian expats, including chefs and restaurateurs, come to buy otherwise hard-to-find ingredients.

◖ YELISEYEVSKY GASTRONOM
Елисеевский гастроном
14 Tverskaya Ulitsa, 495/650-4643
HOURS: Daily 24 hours

METRO: Tverskaya
Map 3

This store is a tourist attraction in its own right. It was founded by the Yeliseyevs, a family of wine merchants, at the beginning of the 1900s. The store itself retains its pre-revolutionary grandeur, with a massive chandelier hanging from the elaborately designed ceiling. The collection of delicacies is top notch, as is the liquor selection kept in a display room out back.

ELECTRONICS
BELY VETER
Белый ветер
10/2 Nikolskaya Ulitsa, 495/628-7394,
www.whitewind.ru
HOURS: Daily 9 A.M.-10 P.M.
METRO: Lubyanka
Map 2

This huge electronics chain has dozens of stores all over Moscow, with the most centrally located being on Nikolskaya Ulitsa (another is near the Arbatskaya metro, at 6 Ulitsa Novy Arbat, 495/730-3075, Mon.–Sat. 10 A.M.–9 P.M., Sun. 11 A.M.–7 P.M.). Bely Veter, which translates as White Wind, is a reliable choice for just about anything electronic that you might need. Its slogan is, "Your digital store." There's a wide range of photo and video equipment, including cameras, cases, printers, memory cards, stands, and batteries. The phone section has cell phones, smart phones, communicators, and accessories. The stores also have large computer sections, with notebooks and Bluetooth accessories, among many other gizmos and gadgets. They even stock music and movies on DVD and Blu-ray. Prices are competitive.

M.VIDEO
М.Видео
3 Sadovaya Spasskaya Ulitsa, Bldg. 3, 495/777-7775,
www.mvideo.ru
HOURS: Daily 24 hours (cashiers take a break nightly 11:45 P.M.-12:15 A.M.)
METRO: Krasnye Vorota
Map 8

A chain of dozens of electronics stores, M.Video outlets are located all over the city, but this one is noteworthy because it's huge, relatively central, and open 24 hours a day, seven days a week. You'll find everything in this 1,850-square-meter store: cameras and photographic equipment, MP3 players and headsets, and all manner of grooming gizmos, such as electric razors, rollers, epilators, hair dryers, and hairstyling tools. Of course, there's also all kinds of computers and associated gear, cell phones, and other communications devices. If you need automobile navigation systems, you can find them here too. Other useful things sold here include water filters and electric water boilers—which are always handy in Russia.

Markets

DANILOVSKY MARKET
Danilovsky rynok
Даниловский рынок
74 Mytnaya Ulitsa, 495/954-1272
HOURS: Mon.-Sat. 8 A.M.-7 P.M., Sun. 8 A.M.-6 P.M.
METRO: Tulskaya
Map 8

This market is particularly good for fresh fruit and vegetables, of which there is a truly impressive selection. The inside section mainly stocks imported fruit and vegetables, plus a selection of meats and seafood, but the real gems are to be found in the outdoor section, especially in late summer and early autumn when the delicious local farm produce appears.

【 DOROGOMILOVSKY MARKET
Dorogomilovsky rynok
Дорогомиловский рынок
10 Mozhaisky Val, 495/249-5553
HOURS: Daily 7 A.M.-8 P.M.
METRO: Kievskaya
Map 8

Widely regarded as Moscow's best food market, Dorogomilovsky is regularly cited as a favorite by the city's top chefs, gourmets, and food critics. The range of top-notch produce is simply stunning—there is row after row of vegetables of all shapes and sizes, from growers near and far, plus there is an impressive selection of fresh meats and seafood. The place is huge, and usually bustling. In autumn you'll find first-class wild mushrooms for sale.

LENINGRADSKY MARKET
Leningradsky rynok
Ленинградский рынок
11 Chasovaya Ulitsa, 495/151-0551
HOURS: Mon.-Sat. 7 A.M.-7 P.M., Sun. 7 A.M.-6 P.M.
METRO: Aeroport
Map 8

This market's claim to fame is its fantastic selection of cheeses, and we're not talking about your typical cheddar cheese. The handmade farmers' cheeses here come in all manner of varieties and there is a large selection of various cheese pies and pastries. There are also goods from Uzbekistan, including tea sets that are ornately painted in a distinctive national style, as well as hats and robes.

RIZHSKY MARKET
Rizhsky rynok
Рижский рынок
88 Prospekt Mira, 495/631-4295
HOURS: Mon.-Sat. 7 A.M.-7:30 P.M., Sun. 7 A.M.-6 P.M.
METRO: Rizhskaya
Map 8

Besides all your regular fruit and vegetables, meat and seafood, this market offers a fantastic selection of flowers ranging from simple daffodils to fancy irises. Check out the podmoskovskiye roses. The market is not very centrally located, however, and for foodstuffs you're better off heading to Dorogomilovsky market, which is the best by far.

HOTELS

Accommodation in Moscow is expensive. Several recent studies have ranked the city's four- and five-star hotels as the most expensive in the world, costing almost $500 a night on average. There is already an abundance of beds in this highest price bracket, yet the volume of luxury lodgings continues to grow, while the dire situation in the mid-range segment has only been worsening. All the old Soviet hotels that once offered affordable accommodation in the city center are being knocked down and replaced by flashy new five-star hotels. Although new three-stars are also appearing, they are clearly more expensive—and less central—than the Soviet-style three-stars they replaced. Practically all that remains in the medium-price segment are old Soviet hotels farther out of the center, but often Western travelers are

disappointed with them: Either they're renovated and overpriced, or unrenovated and not up to standard, and usually the staff neither speak English nor provide American-style service. Of course, these are not problems that you'll have to worry about if you can afford to stay in one of the three-, four-, or five-star hotels managed by well-known Western chains, which meet all the highest international standards.

Meanwhile, the situation with budget-priced, backpacker-style accommodation has only been improving. More and more hostels have been opening, often by Westerners or multi-lingual Russians who have traveled widely. In addition to dormitories, which are popular with independent backpacker types, these new hostels often have smaller private rooms, more suitable

© NATHAN TOOHEY

HIGHLIGHTS

LOOK FOR ◖ TO FIND
RECOMMENDED HOTELS.

◖ **Most Central:** Standing right across the road from Manezh Square, the Kremlin, and the gates to Red Square, **Le Royal Meridien National Hotel** is as central as it gets – at least until the Moskva reopens (page 163).

◖ **Grandest Hotel:** An art nouveau architectural masterpiece, the **Metropol Hotel** has some outstanding design elements, such as majolica panels by artist Mikhail Vrubel, and other mosaics, sculptural friezes, and an ornate interior furnished with antiques (page 164).

◖ **Best Kremlin Views:** It's only when you cross the Moscow River that you can really take in all the beauty of the Kremlin, and the **Baltschug Kempinski Moscow** is in a prime position for you to do just that (page 169).

◖ **Best Sky-High Views:** It doesn't claim to be the very tallest, just "one of the tallest hotels in Moscow" but **Swissotel Krasnye Holmy** is the one with panoramas to put you on top of the world (page 170).

◖ **Cheapest Non-Hostel Place to Stay:** With space for more than 3,500 guests, the enormous **Izmaylovo (Gamma-Delta)** hotel offers great views as well as some of the lowest-priced private rooms in town. Not only is it close to the metro and right beside the city's best and biggest souvenir market, it also offers a full range of extra services and entertainment (page 171).

◖ **Best Theme Hotel:** If you like the Moscow metro, you'll love the **Sovietsky,** a historic hotel offering an authentic but unashamedly non-proletarian retro-Soviet experience (page 172).

© NATHAN TOOHEY

the Metropol

PRICE KEY

$ Less than $150 per night

$$ Between $150-250 per night

$$$ More than $250 per night

Rates apply to high season and double occupancy.

for families and offering a much higher standard of accommodation at much lower prices than the cheapest hotels. Still, mid-range and budget accommodation remains inadequate, so booking well in advance is essential.

Another new trend is the so-called bed-and-breakfasts, which are mushrooming around the city, although they don't much resemble the bed-and-breakfasts found in places like Britain. Here, bed-and-breakfasts are more like serviced apartments (or apartments available for short-term stays like hotels, with no extra charges for utilities, maintenance, or housekeeping), except that usually in Moscow bed-and-breakfasts the rooms are let out separately and the kitchen and bathroom facilities are shared. They are not cheap, but tend to be centrally located, and are a good addition to the medium-range segment.

Prices vary widely depending on the month of the year and the day of the week, and the swings are different depending on the class of accommodation and its clientele. There are exceptions to the rule, but in general, cheaper tourist hotels and hostels tend to have high and low seasons dictated by the ebbs and flows in tourist numbers, like in St. Petersburg's hospitality sector: Prices fall when the tourist season dies down from October 1, and they rise again on April 1 when the tourist season begins to pick up again. While such accommodations usually have the same prices on weekends as on weekdays, there's a totally different dynamic in the more expensive hotels, perhaps because their clientele is not mostly tourists but business travelers. As a rule, the city's four- and five-star hotels charge twice as much on weekdays as on weekends. Also, for such hotels,

summer is considered low season, like winter; high season is in spring and autumn when the business season is in full swing and there are lots of trade fairs, exhibitions, and other events taking place. Also, prices can bounce back up to high-season rates on any date during the low seasons if there are special events in town. Given the unpredictability of visitor numbers and the fact that Moscow in general is considered to have a shortage of beds, it's advisable to make reservations well in advance for any type of accommodation at any time of the year.

CHOOSING A HOTEL

If you're on a budget, it pays to consider spots in outer suburbs if they are close to a metro station—you'll be surprised how fast you can zoom into the city center on Moscow's efficient underground. Some far-flung spots to stay that are conveniently close to the metro are the Izmaylovo complex at Partizanskaya, the Asia at Ryazansky Prospekt, and the Cosmos at VDNKh. From these outer suburbs, you can reach the center by metro in about 30 minutes. But it's not advisable to stay anywhere that's a whole bus, tram, or trolley-bus ride away from the nearest metro station, since this slows things down a lot. Also, the routes can be tricky to figure out, since nothing is in English on above-ground public transport.

Safety of neighborhoods is not really an issue in Moscow, as it's about the same all over the city. The only thing to consider is proximity to the metro, because even if it's not actually dangerous, you might feel uncomfortable if you have to walk very far after dark.

Take a look at the rooms on the hotel or hostel's website and read the travelers' online forums, such as www.tripadvisor.com, and you'll see that what you get for your money varies wildly. Often hotels that look cheap, in particular the old Soviet ones, are not actually as good value as the standard rooms in the newer posher-looking hotels. The Park Inn Sadu, for example, is a beautiful new Western-style hotel, where weekend prices for a double room in 2008 were as low as 6,500R a night—less than at many of the less-comfortable Soviet-era hotels in comparatively central locations. Renovation can jazz up their decor but can't do much about their cramped interiors unless major reconstruction totally changes the floor plan and number of rooms, as was done at the Hilton Leningradskaya—but naturally such a major makeover pushes a hotel up into a whole new star-rating category and a higher price bracket.

Central heating can be taken for granted in any accommodation, so you don't have to worry about freezing if you're visiting in the colder months. On the other hand, it rarely gets so hot that air-conditioning is needed, and no generalizations can be made about its availability in any kind of accommodation. Summer heat waves sometimes do happen, so if it really matters to you, check with the individual hotel or hostel before making your booking.

Double-glazed windows are the norm, so street noise isn't an issue.

Unlike in the United States, smoking is allowed in most hotels in Russia. However, hotels increasingly offer nonsmoking rooms or even nonsmoking floors, and some entirely nonsmoking hotels have started to appear.

These days, just about every hotel or hostel in Moscow has English-speaking staff, and offers visa and registration support.

There are some peculiarities to Russian hotels. What's described as a double room will often turn out to have two single beds, while a room with a double bed may be called a single, with different prices for single or double occupancy. Check-in and check-out times vary. Breakfast is usually included, but not always. Watch out for prices quoted in conditional units or *uslovniye yedinitsy,* abbreviated in Cyrillic as Y.E.—be sure to check the exchange rate that applies. The same goes for prices quoted in dollars or any other currency. Although prices within Russia are now supposed to be in rubles only, this is not always observed. Prices, particularly online, may be quoted in any currency, but you will have to pay in rubles, and some travelers have been shocked by the exchange rates used.

The Kremlin and Red Square   Map 1

ARARAT PARK HYATT MOSCOW $$$

4 Neglinnaya Ulitsa, 495/783-1234,
www.moscow.park.hyatt.com
METRO: Teatralnaya, Lubyanka, Kuznetsky Most

This is where Madonna stayed when she came to Moscow. The queen of pop took the Presidential Suite, but all the rooms are the height of luxury at this modern hotel, just five minutes' walk from the Kremlin, Red Square, the Bolshoi Theater, and other landmarks. On a lovely street surrounded by historical buildings, it offers great panoramic views of the aforementioned sights, from the rooms and also from the wonderful Conservatory Lounge & Bar on the top floor. Naturally, the hotel has all the mod-cons, services, and indulgences you'd expect of a five-star. Try authentic Armenian cuisine in the hotel's ground floor restaurant, Cafe Ararat, which replicates a legendary 1960s eatery at this site.

◖ LE ROYAL MERIDIEN NATIONAL HOTEL $$$

1 Tverskaya Ul. or 15/1 Mokhovaya Ul., Bldg. 1,
495/258-7000
METRO: Okhotny Ryad

You can't get much more central than this posh five-star hotel. Located at the very beginning of Moscow's main street, Tverskaya Ulitsa, it's right across the road from Manezh Square, the Kremlin walls and Red Square. The 179 rooms and 37 suites are decorated with antiques and objets d'art, and many offer superb views. Besides location and luxury, this hotel has also got plenty of history. Built in 1901–1903 with elements of art nouveau and eclecticism, it was turned into the 1st House of Soviets in 1918, and Lenin lived in No. 107.

HOTELS

MOSCOW'S MOST ICONIC HOTEL RECREATED

The **Moskva** hotel, Alexey Shchusev's iconic Stalinist hotel block built during 1932-1938, was dismantled in 2004, much to the outrage of preservationists, architecture aficionados, and ordinary Muscovites concerned at the loss of such a landmark building. Located on Manezh Square, a stone's throw from the Kremlin and Red Square, the Moskva has been undergoing total reconstruction that was initially supposed to be finished in 2006 but continued through 2008. Its facade was unveiled on City Day in September 2008, when the scaffolding started coming down.

A distinctive feature of the hotel's design is its outer wings, built in similar but slightly different styles. The story goes that Stalin was presented blueprints for alternative designs and signed his approval down the middle. Nobody was game to ask the dictator for a clari-

fication, so the builders went ahead with both. The new five-star Moskva, to be run by Four Seasons, has a similar exterior but a revamped interior layout.

The Moskva's iconic status in popular culture is due in part to its immortalization on the Stolichnaya vodka label. In the 1950s, the Soviet artist Andrey loganson is said to have designed the label on a paper napkin at a café in the National building (now Le Royal Meridien National Hotel), while meeting with artist friends to discuss his difficulty coming up with a concept for the brand. "There's the hotel Moskva," said a lunch companion, pointing at the Stalinist block across the square. "Why are you torturing yourself?" loganson sketched the hotel in a matter of seconds and it went straight from the napkin to the label that Stolichnaya carries to this day.

◖ METROPOL HOTEL $$$
Gostinitsa Metropol
Гостиница Метрополь
1/4 Teatralny Proyezd, 499/501-7800,
www.metropol-moscow.ru
METRO: Ploshchad Revolyutsii

A 363-room five-star located opposite the Bolshoi Theater, the Metropol is an architectural landmark in art nouveau style, built 1899–1905 to a design by British architect William Walcot. It opened with state-of-the-art technology for the early 20th century, including refrigerators, hot water, elevators, and telephones. Its rooms and restaurants drew the wealthy and the brilliant from the worlds of business and the arts, but all that changed in 1918 when it became the Second House of Soviets. By the 1930s, its hotel function returned and it served a useful propaganda function as accommodation for high-level foreign guests such as Bernard Shaw and Bertolt Brecht. It was renovated and restored 1985–1991, adding new technology while reconstructing original design elements. Furnished with antiques,

the rooms retain a sense of history while providing the most up-to-date amenities.

RITZ-CARLTON MOSCOW $$$
3 Tverskaya Ulitsa, 495/225-8888, toll-free from U.S. 800/241-3333, www.ritzcarlton.com
METRO: Okhotny Ryad

One of Moscow's newest five-stars, the Ritz-Carlton opened in 2007, in a newly constructed 11-story classical-style building. Located amid historical and architectural landmarks at the beginning of the main street, Tverskaya Ulitsa, this hotel is much more in harmony with its surroundings than its predecessor at the site, the Soviet-era Intourist high-rise hotel. The Ritz-Carlton's many luxurious amenities include a health club and spa, and it offers the services of a personal butler, shoe butler, bath butler, and even a technology butler. Among the Ritz-Carlton's restaurants is the innovative Jeroboam, with Michelin-starred chef Heinz Winkler's "cuisine vitale," and the rooftop O2 Lounge with panoramic views of the Kremlin and Red Square.

Kitay-Gorod, Lubyanka, and Chistye Prudy Map 2

COMRADE HOSTEL $

11 Ulitsa Maroseyka, 3rd fl., 495/628-3126,
www.comradehostel.com

METRO: Kitay-Gorod

Hidden away in the courtyard of a 200-year-old building, this hostel can be hard to find but is worth the effort. It offers competitive prices on beds in its two spacious eight-person dormitory rooms, with extras such as a kitchen, laundry, Internet services, and visa registration. The location puts you right in the middle of one of Moscow's loveliest old neighborhoods, close to clubs and restaurants.

NAPOLEON HOSTEL $

2 Maly Zlatoustinsky Pereulok, 4th fl.,
495/628-6695, www.napoleonhostel.com

METRO: Kitay-Gorod

Ten minutes' walk from Red Square, and two minutes from the metro, this hostel is surrounded by clubs, bars, and restaurants in a historic but hip neighborhood. It's located in a renovated pre-Revolutionary house where Napoleon is said to have stayed in 1812. It offers dorm beds only, plus a living room, a small bar, Internet-connected computers, and wireless Internet. Besides serious business such as visa support and registration, the hostel takes care of the fun side of things with escorted pub crawls, *banya* visits, and other tours.

TRANSSIB HOSTEL $

12 Barashevsky Pereulok, 495/916-2030,
www.transsiberianhostel.com

METRO: Kitay-Gorod or Kurskaya

Choose between an eight-bed mixed dorm, a six-bed mixed dorm, a four-bed female dorm, and a single double-bed room at this new hostel, in a 19th-century landmark estate building. All rooms are renovated and have air-conditioning and lockers. There's also a kitchen, satellite TV, Internet, book exchange, and garden. The hostel offers visa support, plus registration once you've arrived, and airport or railway station pick-up and drop-off services.

HOTELS

The Center and Inner Northwest Map 3

DOROTHY'S BED & BREAKFAST $$

7/3 Ulitsa Fadeyeva, Apt. 114, 926/664-4118,
919/772-4002, www.dorothysbnb.com

METRO: Mayakovskaya

A gay-friendly place to stay, Dorothy's is a Westerner-managed bed-and-breakfast affiliated with the Kita Inn and Flamingo B&Bs. It's an apartment with two rooms, one with a queen-size bed and the other with two singles. These two bedrooms are let out separately (unless, of course, you pay for the whole apartment). There's also a shared kitchen and renovated bathroom. On a residential street outside the Garden Ring, it's not quite as centrally located as the other two affiliated B&Bs, but it is nonetheless not far to Tverskaya Ulitsa and the metro station. You can use an online visa invitation ordering service, with registration support. There's no 24-hour reception desk, but the bed-and-breakfast's multilingual staff are usually around during the day, and accessible by cell phone; they can help with registration, maps, translators, guides, and whatever else you might need.

FLAMINGO BED & BREAKFAST $$

6/7 2nd Tverskaya-Yamskaya Ulitsa, Bldg. 5, Apt. 10,
919/772-4002, www.flamingobed.com

METRO: Mayakovskaya

Another Westerner-managed, gay-friendly bed-and-breakfast run by the team from Dorothy's and Kita Inn bed-and-breakfasts, this one follows the same formula. Located on a quiet street a couple of minutes' walk from Tverskaya Ulitsa and the metro, it has two double rooms, one with twin beds and one with a queen-size bed, plus a kitchen and free wireless Internet. The two bedrooms may be occupied by separate groups of people (unless, of course, you pay for the whole apartment). There's no 24-hour reception desk, but the multilingual staff are usually around during the day, and reachable by cellphone to help with registration, maps, translators, guides and the like. There's an online visa invitation ordering service, and registration support.

GODZILLAS HOSTEL $

6 Bolshoy Karetny Pereulok, Apt. 5, 495/699-4223, www.godzillashostel.com

METRO: Tsvetnoy Bulvar

Accolades in 2006 have been followed by mixed reviews in online travel forums, but affordability remains an attraction at this British-founded hostel. Located in a pre-Revolutionary building in a pleasant residential neighborhood, it's a five-minutes walk to the metro station and about 20 minutes' walk to the Kremlin. It offers double-bed rooms, twin and triple rooms, female dorms and mixed dorms, as well as kitchen, laundry, and Internet services.

GOLDEN APPLE $$$

11 Ulitsa Malaya Dmitrovka, 495/980-7000, www.goldenapple.ru

METRO: Pushkinskaya

A luxury boutique hotel with 92 individually designed rooms, Golden Apple has a trendy, avant-garde image. Praised for good service and its breakfasts, it's located right in the heart of the city, near Pushkin Square and the Boulevard, close to the boutiques of Tverskaya Ulitsa—not bad considering that prices here are significantly lower than in the five-stars around the Kremlin. The health club has cardio machines, sauna, and whirlpool tub, and the 24-hour business services center offers laptop rental, meeting rooms, and communications services.

KITA INN BED & BREAKFAST $$

6/7 2nd Tverskaya-Yamskaya Ulitsa, Bldg. 5, Apt. 9, 926/664-4118, www.kitainn.com

METRO: Mayakovskaya

Located in an apartment beside the Flamingo and run by the same people, Kita Inn's online image is more macho than the pink-hued Flamingo, but the differences would appear to be superficial—it's the same kind of gay-friendly, Westerner-managed bed-and-breakfast as its neighbor. There is no 24-hour reception desk but the multilingual staff are reachable to help with anything you need. Visa support is offered. There are two double rooms that are let out separately, one with twin beds and one with a queen-size bed, plus a kitchen and Internet access. The location is convenient, just off Tverskaya Ulitsa, amid cafés and restaurants.

MARRIOTT ROYAL AURORA $$$

11/20 Ulitsa Petrovka, 495/937-1000, www.visitmoscow.ru

METRO: Teatralnaya

This large, modern luxury hotel boasts that it's the only one in Moscow offering a personalized butler service for every guest. Other amenities include wireless Internet, in-room safes, and

The Marriott Royal Aurora is right in the center, convenient for sightseeing and shopping.

© NATHAN TOOHEY

video or DVD/CD home theater in each room. The health club and swimming pool are open 24 hours, and the restaurants are well regarded. Located on the corner of a picturesque boutique-lined pedestrian street, Stoleshnikov Pereulok, it's ideal for shopping as well as sightseeing. The Bolshoi Theater, Kremlin, and Red Square are all within easy walking distance as well.

MAYAKOVSKAYA B&B $

5/9 Oruzheyny Pereulok, 903/526-1667, 926/609-6913, www.moscow-hostel.com
METRO: Mayakovskaya

This Russian-run bed-and-breakfast is located right downtown, a couple of minutes' walk from the main street, Tverskaya Ulitsa, close to lots of restaurants, bars, cafés, and shops. The bed-and-breakfast has two parts: a 7th-floor private apartment with double bed, kitchen, bathroom, and balcony; and a 2nd-floor two-room guesthouse, one room with a double bed and balcony, and the other with twin beds, plus shared bathroom and kitchen. Wireless Internet and continental breakfast are offered, but you are welcome to prepare your own meals in the kitchen. The apartment block has such security features as video surveillance and a concierge.

PEKIN $$$

Пекин
5 Bolshaya Sadovaya Ulitsa, 495/650-2215, www.hotelpekin.ru
METRO: Mayakovskaya

Stay in a Stalin-era architectural chef d'oeuvre by Dmitry Chechulin—the acclaimed architect of the White House, the Komsomolskaya, Kievskaya, and Dinamo metro stations, and many other grandiose works. On a busy intersection where the traffic-heavy Garden Ring intersects the main road, Tverskaya Ulitsa, this is a big-city location right in the thick of things—so don't expect fresh air. In recent years this spire-topped wedding-cake building has added New York–themed bars, restaurants, and a casino, their garish signs at odds with its original hammers and sickles, and Pekin is Russian for "Beijing," so there are three corners of the world in the hotel's confusing concept. Although rated as a three-star, the 125-room Pekin boasts that its superior suites are four-star level.

YELLOW BLUE BUS HOSTEL $

5 4th Tverskaya-Yamskaya Ulitsa, Apt. 8, 495/250-1364
METRO: Mayakovskaya

The strange name of this popular hostel is supposed to sound like the Russian expression "ya lyublyu vas," or "I love you." Located right in the center of the city, in a historic building about 300 meters from the main street, Tverskaya Ulitsa, it has one eight-bed dorm room and two four-bed dorms, as well as a shared kitchen where you can prepare your own meals. There's also satellite TV and DVDs, Internet, laundry and ironing board, visa support, and a pickup service for when you arrive. The English-speaking staff are able to help out with booking plane, train, or bus tickets, among other things.

HOTELS

Arbat and Kropotkinskaya
Map 4

HOTELS

BELGRAD $$
Белград
8 Smolenskaya Ulitsa, 499/248-3125,
www.hotel-belgrad.ru
METRO: Smolenskaya

Located on the Garden Ring at Smolenskaya Square, opposite the pedestrian Arbat street and impressive Stalin skyscraper of the Foreign Affairs Ministry, this 20-floor three-star hotel offers convenience as well as panoramic views of major landmarks. The 235 rooms include higher-priced, renovated suites, as well as un-renovated lodgings at a more affordable price. It might be worth bringing a sleeping mask, as multi-colored lights flash on the hotel's exterior at night. This is one of the few restaurants where breakfast is not included in the price—the full buffet costs 580R—but you'll probably prefer to have breakfast in one of the cafés on Ulitsa Arbat.

GOLDEN RING $$$
Zolotoye Koltso
Золотое Кольцо
5 Smolenskaya Ulitsa, 495/725-0100,
www.hotel-goldenring.ru
METRO: Smolenskaya

The Belgrad's more upscale twin offers the same location with higher standards, better service, and correspondingly higher prices. There are facilities for the disabled, nonsmoking rooms, a health and beauty center, and restaurants including the classy Panorama and Winter Garden restaurants, with unforgettable views from their 22nd-floor height of 80 meters.

KEBUR PALACE $$$
32 Ulitsa Ostozhenka, 495/733-9070,
www.hoteltiflis.com
METRO: Kropotkinskaya

Still widely known by its old name, Tiflis, this 79-room four-star boasts a superb Georgian restaurant, Tiflissky Dvorik, with vine-covered verandas and excellent cuisine. But that's not the only reason to stay here. It's located in one of the city's most prestigious neighborhoods, the "Golden Mile," amid embassies, elegant architectural landmarks, and posh restaurants, just a short walk to Christ the Savior Cathedral. All rooms have wireless Internet and satellite television. There's a pool, sauna, beauty salon, and business services.

MOSCOW HOME HOSTEL $
1/12 2nd Neopalimovsky Per., 495/778-2445,
www.moshostel.com
METRO: Park Kultury or Smolenskaya

Although it's a hostel with 6-, 8-, and 10-bed dormitories, this place also has double twin rooms and luxe rooms, all at competitive prices. The location is quiet, just outside the Garden Ring, but not far to the Arbat and the metro. Comfortable and renovated, it has a common room with a terrace, a kitchen, TV, and free wireless Internet. There's a travel information desk, and airport or railway station pickup services—and no curfew!

SWEET MOSCOW HOSTEL $
51 Ulitsa Arbat, Apt. 31, 910/420-3446,
www.sweetmoscow.com
METRO: Smolenskaya

This is an ideally located hostel on the Old Arbat pedestrian street, where you'll find an abundance of architectural landmarks, historic sites, museums, souvenir stalls, restaurants, bars, and plenty of interesting characters walking about. Western-managed, with English-speaking staff, the hostel has six- and eight-bed rooms, either mixed or female-only. The reception works 24 hours and there's no curfew or lockout, so you can enjoy the surrounding nightlife as late as you like.

Zamoskvorechye

Map 5

◖ BALTSCHUG KEMPINSKI MOSCOW ⓢⓢⓢ

1 Ulitsa Balchug, 495/287-2000,
www.kempinski-moscow.com
METRO: Novokuznetskaya

The best views of the Kremlin are from across the river, and this luxurious five-star is in prime position for its guests to enjoy the superb panorama. It's a short walk across the bridge to Red Square, and not far to the Tretyakov Gallery and the metro station. The 230 rooms range from superior class to designer suites, all with every luxury and convenience demanded of hotels in this bracket. Naturally there's a health club and high-class restaurants.

PARK INN SADU ⓢⓢⓢ

17 Ulitsa Bolshaya Polyanka, Bldg. 1, 495/644-4844,
www.rezidorparkinn.com
METRO: Polyanka

This hotel opened in 2008, and is still relatively good value for its class. It's in a historical neighborhood that's full of character, with interesting architecture and some quaint little streets behind the busy artery that it's located on. It's close to some of the city's best pubs, just five minutes' walk to the Tretyakov Gallery, and a scenic 15-minute walk across a couple of bridges to the Kremlin. The 117 rooms are bright and modern, some boasting views of Christ the Savior Cathedral and the Moscow River.

HOTELS

© NATHAN TOOHEY

The Baltschug Kempinski Moscow is on the embankment opposite the Kremlin.

Southwest

Map 6

SPUTNIK $$

Спутник
38 Leninsky Prospekt, 495/930-3097,
www.hotelsputnik.ru
METRO: Leninsky Prospekt

This renovated Soviet-era hotel stands near the iconic 40-meter monument of the first man in space, Yury Gargarin, so its space-age name is fitting. It also rises high in the sky, with many of its 360 rooms having commanding views over the Moscow River and the city. Although the location is not central, it's close to the metro, shops, restaurants, and the parklands from Sparrow Hills to Gorky Park. On the top floor is an Indian restaurant, Darbars, where the views and food are both excellent.

VARSHAVA $$

Варшава
2/1 Leninsky Prospekt, 499/238-7701
METRO: Oktyabrskaya

Built in 1960, this three-star, 140-room hotel stands on a busy square graced by one of the city's few remaining Lenin statues. This is where two major roads intersect—the Garden Ring and the beginning of Leninsky Prospekt—and it's a transport hub, with both radial and ring metro lines as well as buses, trolleybuses even minibuses. There are plenty of restaurants in and around the hotel. Gorky Park is just down the road, as is the Central House of Artists and the Muzeon sculpture garden.

Southeast

Map 7

KATERINA-CITY $$$

6 Shluzovaya Naberezhnaya, 495/795-2444,
www.katerinahotels.com
METRO: Paveletskaya

Positioning itself as a business hotel, this stylish four-star is in a picturesque canal-side location, close to multinationals' offices in a major business district. Swedish-designed, it calls itself Moscow's Swedish corner, and even has a restaurant called Stockholm serving Scandinavian, European, and Russian cuisine. There are 120 rooms, including some for nonsmokers; all come with wireless Internet, soundproofing, heated floors in the bathroom, and self-regulated heating and air-conditioning.

SWISSOTEL KRASNYE HOLMY $$$

52 Kosmodamianskaya Naberezhnaya, 495/787-9800,
www.swissotel.com
METRO: Paveletskaya

A relatively new addition to the Moscow skyline, this modern hotel is in a gleaming glass tower topped with a UFO-shaped bar on its 34th floor, where the views are out of this world. Likewise, there are stunning sights to be seen out the windows of its 233 rooms, all luxuriously furnished in warm earth tones and equipped with the latest technology. There are smoking and nonsmoking floors, and special rooms for disabled guests.

Greater Moscow

Map 8

ASIA $
Азия

3/2 Zelenodolskaya Ulitsa, 495/378-0001
METRO: Ryazansky Prospekt

The Asia contains a hotel, a hostel, and a bed-and-breakfast. The bed-and-breakfast is on the 3rd–5th floors and the G&R Hostel Asia occupies the top two floors of the 15-story Hotel Asia, a hulking Soviet-style dinosaur located far, far from the center. But it's very close to the (almost-end-of-the-line) metro station, so the distance doesn't really matter, and good prices are to be had out here. This place has its fans among budget travelers. Those who want an authentic retro-Soviet experience are rarely disappointed by the unrenovated rooms; renovated rooms are also available.

COSMOS $$
Космос

150 Prospekt Mira, 495/234-1000,
www.hotelcosmos.ru
METRO: VDNKh

This fabulous silver semi-circular structure looks like something out of a Soviet sci-fi movie. Built for the 1980 Olympics, it's big—25 floors with 1,771 rooms—and includes a full range of services and amenities. There's a Russian national dance show in the restaurant. Although it's quite far from the center, the nearby metro makes it quick and easy to zoom anywhere you want to go. The location is right across the road from one of Moscow's must-see sights, the All-Russian Exhibition Center, with its amazing Soviet statues and fountains, as well as the Cosmonaut Museum with its soaring rocket monument. A monorail runs by, completing the retro-futuristic effect.

HILTON MOSCOW LENINGRADSKAYA $$$

21/40 Kalanchevskaya Ulitsa, 495/627-5550,
www1.hilton.com
METRO: Komsomolskaya

One of the "Seven Sisters," this 132-meter-high 28-story Stalin-era skyscraper looms over the square where the Leningradsky, Kazansky, and Yaroslavsky railway stations are located. Built 1949–1953, it reopened as a Hilton Hotel in 2008 after major renovations that enlarged the rooms, reducing their total number from 329 to 273. Now the hotel offers such mod cons as wireless Internet, individual climate control, and LCD televisions, but with 1950s-style furnishings to create a retro look in some suites. A couple of rooms are specially equipped for the disabled. The Stalin-era bomb shelter in the basement is now enjoying a new life as a 24-hour health club with swimming pool, sauna, and beauty salon.

IZMAYLOVO (GAMMA-DELTA) $
Измайлово (Гамма-Дельта)

71 Izmaylovskoye Shosse, korpus 4GD, 495/737-7000,
www.izmailovo.ru
METRO: Partizanskaya

This enormous two-building hotel is part of a huge high-rise five-block complex built for the 1980 Olympics, with other hotels here being the more expensive **Alfa** (korpus A, 499/166-4602, www.alfa-hotel.ru), the lower-grade **Beta** (korpus 2B, 495/792-99-13, www.hotelbeta.ru), and the reasonably priced **Vega** (korpus 3V, 495/956-0506, www.hotel-vega.ru). Altogether, they can hold 10,000 people at a time. The Gamma-Delta is the most popular among foreigners, and it alone can accommodate more than 3,500 guests. It's not likely to win any awards for its aesthetic appeal, but it's good value for the money, close to the metro, and right beside the city's best and biggest souvenir market, Vernissage at Izmaylovo. The views and breakfast are praised. The complex includes restaurants, a health center, fitness center, billiard club, bowling, and an Internet café.

MINI-HOTEL SUHAREVKA $

16/18 Bolshaya Sukharevskaya Ploshchad, Apt. 5,
910/420-3446, www.suharevkahotel.ru
METRO: Sukharevskaya

Two minutes' walk from the metro, on the Garden Ring road in the city's north, this is a convenient place to stay. It's also quite economical. Occupying the 4th floor of a historic building, it has 12 rooms—private twin and double rooms as well as mixed dorms for 6 to 10 people—with five showers and four toilets shared between all guests. There's a fully equipped kitchen, laundry, lockers, a lounge common room, 24-hour reception with multilingual staff, free high-speed and wireless Internet, and cable television. Sukharevka, aka Lenin Hostel, offers visa invitations and registration, plus guided walks, excursions, and travel information services.

NOVOTEL MOSCOW CENTRE $$$

23 Novoslobodskaya Ulitsa, 495/780-4000, www.novotel.com
METRO: Novoslobodskaya

Much praised as reasonably priced and good value for a four-star, this hotel is not only clean and comfortable but also conveniently located. It's right above a metro station, on two metro lines (radial and ring), close to the center—just 15 minutes' ride to the Kremlin. The location is also good because of the large number of restaurants along the street, with a diversity of cuisines at a good price for Moscow. About half of the 255 rooms are nonsmoking. There's ramp access for the disabled.

SOVIETSKY $$$
Советский

32/2 Leningradsky Prospekt, 495/960-2000, www.sovietsky.ru
METRO: Dinamo

Billing itself as the "Historical Hotel Sovietsky," this place is a real trip back in time—to the Soviet era as experienced by the elite. It has gone overboard to preserve and enhance its wealth of authentic furnishings and memorabilia while upgrading its amenities to contemporary standards. You'll find paintings of Lenin, Stalin, and other Soviet leaders, gilded columns, crystal chandeliers, and grand staircases. There are several "signature suites" including the Stalin Apartment with a whirlpool tub, and the Yar Apartment where Margaret Thatcher and Indira Gandhi once stayed. The hotel contains the "legendary" restaurant Yar, an amazing place with a rich history and incredible dinner shows.

ULANSKAYA $$$
Уланская

16 Ulansky Pereulok, Bldg. 1A, 495/632-9695, www.ulanhotel.ru
METRO: Turgenevskaya

Close to the picturesque boulevards of Chistye Prudy, with a wide range of restaurants and bars in easy walking distance, this little-known three-star has 61 rooms—40 are fairly basic and modestly sized singles and doubles, while the remainder are slightly larger semi-luxe suites. There's a jazz club and restaurant on the premises, but otherwise the hotel doesn't offer too many extras.

EXCURSIONS FROM MOSCOW

One of the greatest things about Moscow is the Golden Ring—a circle of old towns just outside the capital offering onion domes galore, quaint wooden houses with bright, hand-carved window frames, and real headscarved babushkas. Take a troika ride, eat a home-baked cabbage pie, and sneak a shot of vodka: This is the real Russia that you won't find in the big smoke, the fairy-tale Russia that you always imagined. Each Golden Ring town has its own personality; a visit to at least one would be a highlight for any tourist. Tiny Suzdal is the pick of the bunch—an entire museum town untouched by modern development. Nearby, Vladimir's ancient sites sit amid a modern, bustling city. Lakeside but less popular, Rostov-Veliky's old town is a trip back in time where you'll feel like you're the first to discover its charms. And closest to Moscow,

Sergiyev Posad shows the Russian Orthodox Church is thriving in the 21st century. While these are certainly not the only Golden Ring towns, they top the list as the most spectacular as well as the most accessible.

Although the scenery around the Golden Ring can't be described as spectacular, it is nonetheless pretty. Outside of the industrial hub of Vladimir and the busy highway that leads to it, most of the countryside retains its natural beauty. Forests and fields of wildflowers give way to cute villages, many with a spectacular church standing unassumingly amid humble little houses. There are dacha settlements (clusters of summer houses) beside unspoiled lakes and rivers, where you might spot fishermen and farm animals. Every now and then you'll spot onion domes on the horizon

© NATHAN TOOHEY

EXCURSIONS

HIGHLIGHTS

LOOK FOR TO FIND RECOMMENDED SIGHTS, ACTIVITIES, DINING, AND LODGING.

❰❰ Cream of the Kremlins: The **Rostov Kremlin** isn't the only kremlin with museums and a restaurant, but it beats the others by having a hotel as well – so you can sleep over, right inside the majestic white walls (page 177).

❰❰ Most Spiritual: Sergiyev Posad's **Trinity-Sergius Lavra** is Russia's real ecclesiastical center, drawing not just camera-wielding tourists but droves of Orthodox Christian pilgrims from far and wide (page 182).

❰❰ Best Bell-Ringing: Suzdal's **Savior Monastery of St. Euthymius** is absolutely stunning – visually and audibly (page 188).

❰❰ Sweetest Experience: The elaborately decorated **Mead-Tasting Hall** in Suzdal lets you try dozens of varieties of Russia's ancient honey drink, in the town that does it best (page 189).

❰❰ Most Fantastical Cathedral: Vladimir's 12th-century **Cathedral of St. Dmitry** has the most amazing walls, with 600 sculptural reliefs depicting saints and all kinds of creatures, both mythical and real (page 195).

© NATHAN TOOHEY

Pilgrims and tourists enter the gates of Sergiyev Posad's spectacularly beautiful monastery, Trinity-Sergius Lavra.

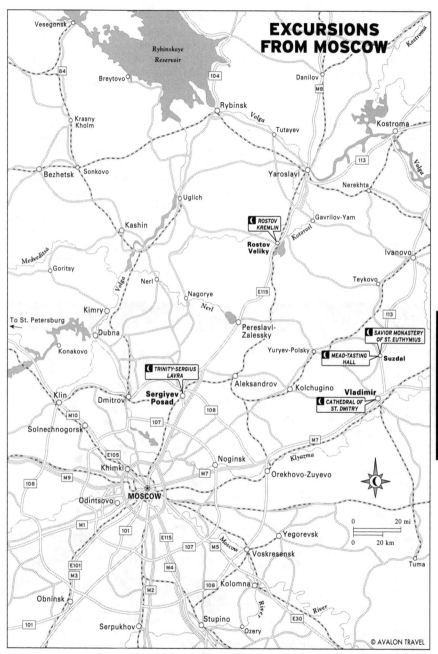

EXCURSIONS FROM MOSCOW

Vesegonsk

Rybinskoye Reservoir

Breytovo

Krasny Kholm

Rybinsk

Volga

Tutayev

Danilov

M8

Kostroma

Kostroma

84

104

Bezhetsk

Sonkovo

Yaroslavl

113

Nerekhta

Uglich

Volga

Kashin

Gavrilov-Yam

ROSTOV KREMLIN

Rostov Veliky

Kotorosl

Ivanovo

Medveditsa

Goritsy

Nerl

Nagorye

Nerl

E115

Teykovo

113

Kimry

Volga

Pereslavl-Zalessky

SAVIOR MONASTERY OF ST. EUTHYMIUS

To St. Petersburg

Dubna

Yuryev-Polsky

MEAD-TASTING HALL

Suzdal

Konakovo

TRINITY-SERGIUS LAVRA

Aleksandrov

Kolchugino

Vladimir

Klin

M10

Dmitrov

Sergiyev Posad

108

CATHEDRAL OF ST. DMITRY

Solnechnogorsk

107

M7

E105

Khimki

Noginsk

M9

M7

Klyazma

Odintsovo

MOSCOW

Orekhovo-Zuyevo

M1

101

E115

107

M5

Moscow

Yegorevsk

E101

M3

M4

Voskresensk

Tuma

Obninsk

108

M2

Kolomna

River

River

101

Serpukhov

Stupino

Ozery

E30

© AVALON TRAVEL

0   20 mi

0   20 km

EXCURSIONS

and realize Russia has an enormous wealth of undiscovered and ignored architectural and historical landmarks. There are bizarre roadside stalls selling incongruous items, and some fabulous retro-kitschy Soviet bus stops standing in the middle of nowhere—who uses them is a mystery.

PLANNING YOUR TIME

If you're only on a quick trip to Russia and want a glimpse of the Golden Ring, your best bet is to limit yourself to Sergiyev Posad. Easily accessible and "doable" in one day, it's an express Golden Ring jaunt for those on a tight schedule. Alternatively, you could take a day trip to Rostov Veliky, but more time is lost in transit to reach this more distant destination—so consider it an overnighter, unless you've got lots of energy. Given the long distance to travel between Rostov Veliky and Moscow, it doesn't really make sense to try to squeeze in a visit to Sergiyev Posad on the way, especially since the latter can be visited in a day trip from Moscow.

The undisputed highlight of the region is Suzdal, but its relative inaccessibility means it's an overnight trip, often combined with a visit to nearby Vladimir. One to two days is sufficient to see all the sights in Suzdal, which is small enough to explore on foot. An ideal trip is one-and-a-half days in Suzdal followed by a half-day in Vladimir before catching the bus or train back to Moscow.

The peak tourist season is from May through September, when the Golden Ring is at its best. Sometimes it can be difficult to find a vacant hotel room in the summer, especially in Suzdal. Large numbers of Russian tourists visit the Golden Ring towns on weekends in summer, so try to make reservations at least a week or two in advance.

Rostov Veliky

Rostov Veliky (Rostov the Great, Ростов Великий) is a town of 34,000 people located beside Lake Nero, 210 kilometers northeast of Moscow. One of Russia's oldest towns, it was first documented in 862 as being already well established and quite large for the time.

Rostov's claim to greatness goes back centuries, to the Golden Ring's heyday in the 11th–13th centuries, when it rose to become the capital of an independent principality. The birthplace of Saint Sergey Radonezhsky, it has long been an important ecclesiastical center and remained one after losing its political status. Weakened after being savagely attacked by the Mongols in the 13th–14th centuries, in the 15th century it became part of the Moscow principality. It was ransacked and burned by Polish invaders in 1608.

Now, Rostov is a sleepy provincial town of dusty streets and spectacular architecture in a picturesque lakeside setting. It's rather run down compared to Suzdal, but also a lot less touristy. There is no tourist information office. In time

© NATHAN TOOHEY

the Rostov Kremlin's mighty white walls, with towers topped by wooden fish-scale shingled cupolas

Rostov will probably start to fulfill its great potential, but for now it's endearingly untouched.

One day is long enough to explore this small town, which is compact enough to get around on foot. There's not much to do here at night. Rostov really only has two sights that are set up to receive tourists—the Kremlin and St. Jacob's Monastery. Still, it is interesting to stroll around the town and look at the many other churches and monasteries scattered about, the most notable being the Abraham Monastery on the lakeside east of the Kremlin. One of Russia's oldest monasteries, founded in the 11th century, it has unfortunately suffered heavy damage over the years and many of its structures have been lost, although it still retains a 16th-century cathedral and two 17th-century churches. It is once again functioning as a convent, and is undergoing restoration.

SIGHTS
◖ Rostov Kremlin
Rostovsky kreml
Ростовский кремль

The premier sight in Rostov is its Kremlin (48536/31-717, www.rostmuseum.ru, daily except Jan. 1 10 A.M.–5 P.M., entrance to grounds 10R, combined ticket to grounds and all exhibits 200R, individual exhibits 35R, photo permit 100R, video permit 150R). Sometimes said to be Russia's most splendid kremlin after Moscow's, the Rostov Kremlin is indeed impressive: fairytale belfries and majestic churches with green and silver domes, all inside mighty white walls with 11 towers topped by wooden fish-scale shingled cupolas. Strictly speaking, however, it's not really a kremlin—it was founded as the Rostov Metropolitan's Residence, built in the 17th

WHAT IS A KREMLIN?

Although "The Kremlin" never leaves any confusion about which kremlin is meant, Russia has many kremlins. *Kreml* is the term that has been used since the 14th century to refer to a citadel or medieval fortress around a city's oldest, central complex. The earliest Russian cities were established behind such protective walls, complete with arrow holes and lookout towers, which were necessities at the time given the constant threat of invasion and sacking from near and far. Over time, these old towns grew beyond the original citadel into new areas that were also fortified. Outside its Kremlin wall, Moscow also had Kitay-Gorod and White City walls. Such outer fortifications don't count as kremlins, and neither do monastery walls, similar looking though they may be. So, although Rostov Veliky's main sight is called the Rostov Kremlin, it's not actually a kremlin at all, as it was founded as the Rostov Metropolitan's Residence. Likewise, the walled monastery complex at Sergiyev Posad, the Trinity-Sergiyev Lavra, is not a kremlin either. The Suzdal Kremlin is a real kremlin, however, and so is the Novgorod Kremlin (Detinets).

© NATHAN TOOHEY

a church of the Rostov Kremlin

century for metropolitan Iona Sysoyevich. Now it is mostly open as a museum. There are 17th-century frescoes to see in three of the five churches (May 1–Oct. 1 only), and a wide range of exhibits in the chambers and palaces around the grounds. They include a Rostov enamel museum, with 2,500 items from the 18th–20th centuries, displays of other local applied arts and crafts wares, icons, archaeological finds, and a bell exhibit. A popular activity is the "perekhod," a walk along the walls (May 1–Oct. 1, 45R) with interesting views of the beautiful buildings in the Kremlin's pretty, landscaped grounds.

Dominating the Kremlin ensemble is the five-domed **Assumption Cathedral** (Uspensky sobor), the oldest building in Rostov, with its highest cross at 60 meters. Built 1508–1512 in place of 12th–13th century predecessors, it is just outside the museum complex's northern wall, inside the walled Cathedral Square. A working church, it is not open as a museum. Behind it is a splendid belfry, dated 1682, with silver domes and 15 bells, the largest of which weighs about 32 tons; their ringing can be heard 20 kilometers away and is considered to be incomparably beautiful.

Holy Gates lead from Cathedral Square to the Metropolitan's Courtyard, with the Gate Church of the Resurrection flanked by two fortress towers. The main entrance to the museum part of the Kremlin is from the street in front, through another 17th-century barbican church, the Gate Church of St. John the Apostle.

St. Jacob's Monastery
Spaso-Yakovlevsky monastyr
Спасо-Яковлевский монастырь

Rostov's second major sight is St. Jacob's Monastery (44 Ulitsa Engelsa, 48536/74-369, Mon.–Fri. 8:30 A.M.–7 P.M., Sat.–Sun. 8:30 A.M.–8:30 P.M., free), a beautifully restored and well-maintained complex that stands picturesquely on the banks of Lake Nero about 15 minutes' walk west of the Kremlin.

Although founded in the late 14th century, the oldest existing building in the monastery is the 17th-century blue-and-gold domed

Dmitriyevsky Cathedral in St. Jacob's Monastery

© NATHAN TOOHEY

Zachatyevsky Cathedral, or Cathedral of the Conception of St. Anna. Standing closest to the lake, it contains the ornate shrine of Saint Dmitry Rostovsky, and well-preserved 17th-century frescoes and icons.

The monastery's most grandiose building is the **Dmitriyevsky Cathedral,** a classical-styled green-domed structure built 1794–1802 on the funds of Count Nikolay Sheremetyev. The count wanted the monastery to have a cathedral worthy of Saint Dmitry and intended for his shrine to move here, but church authorities ultimately ruled that it should stay put in Zachatyevsky Cathedral. The interior is richly decorated with 19th-century paintings, icons, and sculptures.

A functioning Russian Orthodox monastery and seminary, St. Jacob's has strict rules of conduct listed in Russian on a sign at the entrance gate: no running, no shouting, no loud laughter, no displays of affection even between the married, no photography inside the churches, no photographing monks without their agreement, and so on. Although it states that it is primarily a place of residence and prayer for the monks, the monastery does welcome tourists to come inside and take a look, and staff stand at the entrance ready to supply any inappropriately dressed women with headscarves and long skirts, and shorts-wearing men with long pants.

RESTAURANTS

The restaurant and bar **Slavyansky** (8 Sovietskaya Ploshchad, 48536/62-228, Mon.–Fri. noon–midnight, Sat.–Sun. noon–4 A.M.) is a good place to go if you want fine Russian cuisine minus national costumes and bearskin rugs. It has a reputation of being prestigious, pricey, and probably the best food in town—but while it might seem swanky and expensive to the locals, it's actually not bad value. Two people can have a three-course feast here with large amounts of vodka and other drinks for about 1,500R, or just over $60. The menu includes all the classics, and the food is good. Try the fresh local Lake Nero pike-perch. The adventurous might find it interesting to taste the traditional rye bread drink, kvass, enhanced with horseradish and honey.

If you want a more touristy experience, you might prefer **Russkoye Podvorye** (9 Ulitsa Marshala Alexeyeva, 48536/64-255, daily noon–midnight), where you'll find costumed waitstaff, folk singers, and traditional fare in an old-Russian setting. This is another of the few places with Lake Nero fish on the menu, as well as all the greatest hits of local cuisine including bliny, various honey mead drinks, and kvass varieties.

For a genuine historical setting, you can't beat the **Trapeznaya Palata** (Krasnaya Palata, Kremlin, 48536/62-871, daily 9 A.M.–last guest), although it's often fully booked by large groups. The restaurant is in the Kremlin's Red Chamber, built in the 17th century and formerly the tsars' roadhouse palace. With vaulted ceilings and chandeliers, it is furnished and decorated in old-Russian style, with traditional Russian cuisine to match.

One of Rostov's oldest restaurants, **Teremok** (1 Ulitsa Moravskogo, 48536/61-648, daily noon–midnight) is the place favored by the locals, who come here to dine, drink, and dance. It's in a cute free-standing house not far from the Kremlin. The simple, old-fashioned Russian food and service won't knock your socks off, but the interior is fabulously kitschy and you are guaranteed an interesting experience.

Usadba Pleshanova (34 Leninskaya Ulitsa, 48536/76-440, www.hotel.v-rostove.ru), in the hotel of the same name, is one of those cafés where almost every dish has a creative name like "Sea Lagoon" or "Inspiration." The food is a standard assortment of Russian fare at inexpensive prices. It has a summer terrace out front and a wooden pagoda in the garden.

CRUISES AND TOURS

To see the sights of Rostov from the water, take a cruise on the lake. The ferry **Zarya** (48536/61-717, 906/631-1925) offers 50-minute Lake Nero cruises (Tues.–Sun. hourly 11 A.M.–6 P.M., 50–150R), departing from the pier close to the Kremlin's western gate.

Pleshanov-Tour (19-21/9 Ulitsa 50-Letiya Oktyabrya, office 208, 48536/66-0003, www.pleshanov-tour.ru), affiliated with hotel and restaurant Usadba Pleshanova, is a tour agency

EXCURSIONS

offering excursions, lake cruises, fishing trips, balalaika and folk-dance shows, hunting, fishing, picnics, and more.

Rostov Veliky's tour guides have a Russian-language Internet site and offer their services (www.rostov-putevoditel.narod.ru, 903/827-2728).

SHOPS

The most important souvenir to buy here is Rostov enamel, or *finift*. Enameling is a 250-year-old tradition in Rostov and the town is proud of its enamel miniatures, for which it is famed in Russia. The souvenir stores, stalls, and art galleries have a wide range of jewelry, caskets, and other enameled objects bearing colorful miniature paintings.

There's an art salon and store in the **Kremlin's Voyanaya Bashnya** (Water Tower, 48536/31-717, www.rostmuseum.ru, daily except Jan. 1 10 A.M.–5 P.M.), where you can buy Rostov enamelware and locally made handicrafts.

In a pretty wooden house by the lake just down the road from the Kremlin, **Khors Enamel Art Gallery** (31 Ulitsa Podozyorka, 48536/62-483, www.khors.org, daily 3–10 P.M.), displays and sells original enamel artworks, both in the gallery and in the garden. The gallery regularly runs artistic development projects, master classes, and symposia in both Russian and English, such as summer classes in sculpture, glass, mosaics, and enameling.

There is also a souvenir market on the street in front of the Kremlin's main entrance.

HOTELS

If you are willing to sacrifice luxury for atmosphere, you'll want to stay in the hotel inside the Rostov Kremlin, **[Dom Na Pogrebakh** (House on Cellars, 48536/61-244, www.rostmuseum.ru/hotel/hotel.html, from 2,000R s/d, advance bookings 25 percent extra for first night). It's charmingly old-fashioned and rather basic; there are standard rooms with their own bathrooms as well as cheaper rooms with just a hand basin in the room but shared bathrooms in the corridor.

For a bit more comfort, the three-star **Moskovsky Trakt** (29A Okruzhnaya Ulitsa, 48536/65-800, www.intourist-hotels.ru/rus/hotels/trakt.html, from 2,530R s, 2,750R d) has 51 rooms in a three-story building constructed in 2006. Part of the Intourist hotels group, it is close to the old center, beside a pond with a summer café. There is a range of one- and two-room suites with single or double beds, room service, a restaurant serving European cuisine, lobby bar, billiards, gym, hair salon, banquet hall, and conference hall.

More centrally located, on the road between the Kremlin and St. Jacob's Monastery, is a hotel in a restored 19th-century former merchant's estate, **Usadba Pleshanova** (34 Leninskaya Ulitsa, 48536/37-440, www.hotel.v-rostove.ru, from 2,000R s/d). The two-story house has 12 hotel rooms furnished in contemporary style, and wireless Internet (100R a day).

An affiliated hotel is the **Domik u Ozera** (Guesthouse on the Lake, corner of Ulitsa Radishcheva and Ulitsa Podozyorka, 48536/66-003, www.pleshanov-tour.ru, from 1,700R s/d), situated 70 meters from the water between the Kremlin and the monastery. The new three-story house has a fireplace, and several hotel rooms with their own bathroom facilities. Beside it is a one-story hunter's cottage, also available as accommodation.

Right across the road from the Kremlin, **Boyarsky Dvor** (4 Ulitsa Kamenny Most, 48536/60-446, from 2,000R s/d) is a three-star hotel in a restored historical architectural landmark building, with 53 rooms on its three floors. The rooms come with a minibar, hair dryer, phone, and refrigerator, and the hotel has an indoor pool and a sauna. Downstairs is a bar and restaurant with a summer terrace that's the perfect spot for a beer while enjoying the views of the Kremlin walls and cathedrals.

Right between the Kremlin and the lake, **Khors Enamel Art Gallery** (31 Ulitsa Podozyorka, 48536/62-483, www.guesthouse.khors.org, artists 400R per person per day, others 500R per person per day) has a small and cozy guesthouse offering single and double rooms at a discount for artists, with Internet access and shared kitchen and bathroom.

Lion (9/6 Ulitsa 50-Letiya Oktyabrya, 48536/64-949, www.lion-hotel.ru, from 1,300R s/d) is in an 18th-century merchant's house and is named after a hotel that existed in the same building 1913–1917. It is located close to the Kremlin and the lake, with easy access to the cruise pier. It has a restaurant, billiards, and solarium. All rooms have a bathroom, television, telephone, and desk, while the luxe and semi-luxe rooms also have cupboards, minibars, sofas, and air-conditioners.

GETTING THERE

When buying tickets, make sure you go to the right Rostov. Rostov Veliky's railway station is called Rostov Yaroslavsky—this is just another name for the same town. There is another, much larger Rostov, called Rostov on Don (Rostov na Donu)—this is a completely different city located much farther away in Russia's south.

Rostov Veliky's bus and railway stations are located together about 20 minutes' walk away from the Kremlin—to get there, walk straight ahead along Ulitsa Lunacharskogo, which is right in front of the stations and perpendicular to the train line.

By Bus

Rostov Veliky can be reached by bus from Tsentralny Avtovokzal (bus station, 75/2 Shchyolkovskoye Shosse, 495/468-0400) beside Shchyolkovskaya metro station. There are numerous buses to Rostov every day, because it is a stop on the way to several other cities including Yaroslavl, Vologda, and Kostroma. The journey takes four to five hours.

By Train

Trains to Rostov depart several times a day from Moscow's Yaroslavsky railway station (5 Komsomolskaya Ploshchad, 495/621-0817, 495/621-5914, 495/266-6300). The fastest and most comfortable is the express train to Yaroslavl, which stops in Rostov on the way. The three-hour ride costs 250–500R depending on the class of seat—and it is worth paying more for a comfy first-class spot if you can afford it. To see Rostov in a day trip by train, take the 8:24 A.M. express to get there and the 5:16 P.M. express back.

By Car

Rostov is reached by road by driving 200 kilometers along Yaroslavskoye Shosse, or the M8 motorway. There is little reason to drive, however, given how much easier it is to get there by public transport. The first 100 kilometers of highway is of good quality but the second 100 kilometers is a bit trickier, with some hilly single-lane stretches where passing is not allowed. Parking is readily available.

Sergiyev Posad

About 70 kilometers northeast of Moscow, Sergiyev Posad (Сергиев Посад) is ideal for a quick glimpse of the Golden Ring if you're on a tight schedule. Unlike the other Golden Ring towns, it is easily visited in a day trip from the capital and all its sights can easily be seen in one day, since they are mostly clustered in a single spectacularly beautiful monastery, Trinity-Sergius Lavra. That said, you could save money by staying here, since the hotels are much less expensive than in Moscow.

A city of 114,000 people, Sergiyev Posad has two symbols: the monastery, and the *matryoshka* (nesting doll), which is said to have originated here. For centuries Sergiyev Posad has been a major spiritual center of the Russian Orthodox Church, as well as Russia's toy-making capital.

The city's origins go back to 1345, when Sergiy Radonezhsky (Sergius of Radonezh) founded the monastery. Villages grew around it, and the 15th–16th centuries saw the development of local crafts, particularly wood-carving and toy-making.

Given its ecclesiastical status, Sergiyev Posad attracts scores of religious pilgrims as well as regular tourists who come to admire the magnificent monastery complex. The two groups coexist peacefully but tourists should remember this is primarily a spiritual center, and to conform to dress rules and behavioral norms (no running, no shouting, no loud laughter, no displays of affection, no photography) in the monastery.

SIGHTS
🄲 Trinity-Sergius Lavra
Troitse-Sergiyev Lavra
Троице-Сергиев Лавра
Sergiyev Posad's Trinity-Sergius Lavra (144 Prospekt Krasnoy Armii, Sergiyev Posad,

a small chapel across the road from Trinity-Sergius Lavra, which can be seen in the background

© NATHAN TOOHEY

EXCURSIONS

496/540-5942, www.stsl.ru, daily 5 A.M.–9 P.M., free; women must wear headscarves and modest skirts, not pants) is a UNESCO World Heritage site. Hundreds of people line up for hours to get inside the monastery's Trinity Cathedral—and they're not just tourists. "God is here," they say with conviction, having traveled great distances to pray inside this church where they sense special spiritual power.

In 1345, the monk Sergiy Radonezhsky established a small cell and wooden church dedicated to the Holy Trinity at this site. He lived alone as a hermit, but other monks came to join him and the monastery grew. His renown spread, and he was called upon to bless Dmitry Donskoy and the Russian army before the Battle of Kulikovo in 1380, which resulted in a landmark Russian victory over the Tatar-Mongol Golden Horde. After Sergiy's death in 1392 he was canonized. His relics are kept in the Trinity Cathedral, and remain a major attraction for Orthodox pilgrims.

The monastery was closed from 1919 until the Russian Orthodox Church's return in 1945. Although the Moscow Patriarchate moved its official residence to Moscow's Danilov Monastery in 1983, Trinity-Sergius Lavra has retained high status as a spiritual-pedagogical and monastic center.

Trinity-Sergius Lavra consists of more than 50 buildings including the **Trinity Cathedral** (Troitsky sobor, 1422)—the monastery's first stone church, with frescoes by Andrey Rublyov and Daniil Chyorny—and the spectacular blue-domed **Assumption Cathedral** (Uspensky sobor, 1559–1585), containing relics of saints, an exceptional 76-icon five-tier iconostasis, and 500 square meters of frescoes, with the burial vault of tsar Boris Godunov beside it. The 18th-century, 88.5-meter-high **bell tower** is said to be Russia's tallest.

A **holy water spring** was discovered in 1644 and a small chapel built over it in the late 17th century; the water is said to have cured many pilgrims, the first being a blind monk whose eyesight returned. Even now, people line up at the spring with cups and bottles to fill.

The towers of the monastery walls are also interesting. They include the 17th-century **Duck Tower,** decorated with a duck on its spire, and the 16th–17th century **Beer Tower,** which previously housed a monastic brewery.

Even those who are not believers feel a spiritual lift upon entering this amazing monastery, probably the most beautiful of all in Russia. Visiting the churches is awe-inspiring but can feel a little awkward for the less religious, since the people inside are having a personal spiritual experience, not putting on a show for tourists' entertainment. Just to walk around the grounds and admire the churches makes for a rewarding visit, but it's also worth seeing the vestry museum.

Museums

The **Konny Dvor** (Horse Yard, 2A 1st Udarnoy Armii, 496/549-9066, 926/152/2470, 916/926-1129, Tues.–Wed. and Fri.–Sun. 10 A.M.–5:30 P.M., closed last Wed. of the month) complex has various exhibits including local artifacts going right back to the stone age, as well as ancient texts, medieval clothing, and tsars' carriages, plus local applied arts and crafts such as carved wooden toys. The displays of local toy production are better than at the Toy Museum. For entry to individual exhibits, Russian adults pay 40R, students and children 20R; foreign adults pay 60R and students and children 30R. Get into all exhibits for 100R (50R students and children) for Russians and 150R (80R students and children) for foreigners. Photo permit 20R, video permit 50R.

See Russia's first nesting doll—made in 1890, she's a modest maiden holding a black rooster—at Sergiyev Posad's **Toy Museum** (123 Prospekt Krasnoy Armii, 496/540-2581, Wed.–Sun. 10 A.M.–5 P.M., closed last Fri. of month, Russian adults 60R, students and children 40R, foreign adults 300R, students and children 150R, photo permit 100R, video permit 300R). In the museum you can also see dolls from the early 19th century, 1930s Red Army toys, 1920s toy cars, 1970s moon mobiles, and lots of toys from China and Japan. The fee for foreigners is a bit steep considering

© NATHAN TOOHEY

Sergiyev Posad's Konny Dvor, or "Horse Yard," complex includes a historical museum and displays of local arts and crafts.

the collection's modest size and the fact that the informational signs are in Russian only. At the entrance there is a stall selling *matryoshkas* and other traditional locally made toys.

Under the patronage of princes and tsars, Trinity-Sergius Lavra became one of the wealthiest Russian monasteries. In its **vestry museum** (in the yellow vestry building beside Trinity Cathedral, 144 Prospekt Krasnoy Armii, 496/540-5942, excursion bookings 496/540-5721, www.musobl.divo.ru, Wed.–Sun. 10 A.M.–5:30 P.M., closed last Fri. of month, Russian adults 100R, children and students 60R, foreign adults 200R, children and students 100R) you can see a rich collection of treasures spanning many centuries. Marvel at icons by the greatest masters, bejewelled and elaborately embroidered robes, ancient hand-written and printed texts, donations from princes and tsars, and an abundance of silver and gold, gems and pearls. The display is quite extensive and likely to leave you feeling muse-umed-out for the rest of the day.

RESTAURANTS AND NIGHTLIFE

Located in the hotel of the same name beside the viewing platform on Blinnaya Gora (Pancake Hill), **Aristocrat** (1a Sergiyevskaya Ulitsa, 496/547-2594, www.goodhotels.ru, daily 8 A.M.–11 P.M.) overlooks the monas-tery. Some of its tables have views, although the windows aren't large enough to enjoy them easily. There's Russian and European cuisine for a reasonable price, plus a bar, billiards, and a banquet room. Set menus are available for groups. Out front there's a beer tent where you can happily while away a few hours sipping cold brews as you admire the panorama.

Across the road from the monastery, be-side the Vernissage souvenir market, the hip eatery **⟨ Dachnaya Zhizn** (134/2 Prospekt Krasnoy Armii, 496/540-5114, daily 10 A.M.–midnight) is part of the Russky Dvorik restau-rant complex. The most up-to-date restaurant in Sergiyev Posad, it offers Japanese, Russian, and barbecue menus in a bright, sunny main dining room. Alternatively, you can sit amid cushions in one of the private Eastern-style lounge rooms on the summer terrace, which surrounds a small garden with fountains.

Located in the Konny Dvor museum complex, in a 19th-century noble's estate, **Konny Dvor** (2A 1st Udarnoy Armii, 496/549-9066, daily 10 A.M.–11 P.M.) has a lovely summer terrace with wonderful views of the monastery and the White Pond with its ducks and swans. Inside is a formal dining room decorated in a nostalgic-historic style. The cuisine is a combination of modern and traditional Russian, well suited to go with vodka. Set menus are available for tour groups.

Dachnaya Zhizn and Russky Dvorik restaurants' club and bar has brought some nightlife into sleepy Sergiyev Posad, at least on weekends. **Nichego Lishnego** (134/2 Prospekt Krasnoy Armii, 496/541-3210, Fri.–Sat. 6 P.M.–5 A.M., free) advertises parties with DJs from near and far, but warns that you should book in advance if you want a table, as places are limited.

The **Pint** (140/1 Prospekt Krasnoy Armii—enter from Ulitsa Karla Marksa, 496/541-3140, daily 11 A.M.–11 P.M.) beer restaurant has a vaguely pub-like atmosphere and the best range of brews in Sergiyev Posad—German, Czech, Dutch, Russian—all at Moscow prices. To soak it up, there's hearty European and Russian beer-friendly food.

Across the road from the monastery, the touristy **Russky Dvorik** (134/2 Prospekt Krasnoy Armii, 496/540-5114, daily 10 A.M.–9 P.M.) caters exclusively for groups until 3 P.M. The decor is suitably folksy kitsch, and the menu includes all the Russian classics. Individual diners who arrive at groups-only time or who are looking for something a bit slicker should go next door to Dachnaya Zhizn.

SHOPS

A civilized souvenir market with all the requisite Russky trinkets, **Vernissage** (corner of Prospekt Krasnoy Armii and Ulitsa Mitkina, daily 10 or 11 A.M.–4 or 5 P.M.) occupies a

The souvenir market beside the walls of Sergiyev Posad's Trinity-Sergius Lavra has some eccentric flea-market odds and ends among the usual *matryoshkas* and fur hats.

specially built space that extends off the pedestrian underpass beneath Prospekt Krasnoy Armii, between the Dachnaya Zhizn/Russky Dvorik restaurant complex and the separate Russky Dvorik hotel. A less-official-looking souvenir market stretches off the other end of the underpass and runs all the way to the monastery, with some eccentric flea-market odds and ends among the usual *matryoshkas* and fur hats. Go for a browse in both sections, compare prices, and you are sure to find anything you're looking for. The traders seem friendlier and less mercenary than in Moscow.

The small **Vologda Linen** (8 Voznesenskaya Ulitsa, daily 10 A.M.–6 P.M.) located near the Aristocrat hotel and viewing platform offers fine linen and woven wares from the town of Vologda, a leader in the flax industry long renowned for its lace. Here you can find a wide range of hats, bags, shawls, shirts, and other clothing, as well as some extra surprises, at reasonable prices with personalized service (in Russian).

HOTELS

Aristocrat (1a Sergiyevskaya Ulitsa, 496/547-2594, www.goodhotels.ru, from 1,800R s, 2,400R d including breakfast) is enviably located in a three-story redbrick house high on Blinnaya Gora (Pancake Hill), boasting some rooms with monastery views, as well as a sauna, pool, solarium, bar, and restaurant. The staff is friendly and the standard double rooms come with either a double bed or two singles, plus refrigerator, television, telephone, and bathroom—and some even have a balcony. In the semi-luxe and luxe rooms you also get a hair dryer. The luxe suites have two rooms including a living room with sofas.

The newly renovated **Posadsky** (171 Prospekt Krasnoy Armii, 496/542-4226, www.hotel-sposad.ru, from 2,400R s, 2,800R d) on the top floor of a Soviet-era block has large rooms, half with monastery views. It is five minutes' walk from the monastery, amid shops in the town center. There are 34 rooms of various classes, ranging from standard singles and doubles up to two-room luxe. They come with satellite television, bathrooms, telephones, safes, and minibars. The renovation continues with a new restaurant, including tables on the roof and promising panoramic views.

On a residential street 200 meters from the monastery, **Russky Dvorik** (14/2 Ulitsa Mitkina, 496/547-5392, 496/547-5393, 495/741-0586, www.russky-dvorik.ru, from 2,100R s, 2,800R d including breakfast) looks specially built to immerse the tourist in a Disney-esque Russian experience. Thematic accommodation includes re-creations of wooden *izba* houses and blue-and-white Gzhel craft-style lodgings, in a landscaped "village" garden. There's also *banya,* billiards, barbecue, restaurant, and parking; the service is professional.

GETTING THERE

By car, drive along the M8 highway, or Yaroslavskoye Shosse, a distance of 54 kilometers from the Moscow Ring Road.

A comfortable express train to Sergiyev Posad departs Moscow's Yaroslavsky Station (5 Komsomolskaya Ploshchad, 495/621-0817, 495/621-5914, 495/266-6300) at 9:05 A.M.; the journey takes an hour. The return express train departs Sergiyev Posad at 7:55 P.M. Tickets are 288R each way. There are also local trains at least every half-hour, taking about 90 minutes. To get to the monastery from the bus/train station, walk in the same direction that the train was traveling, along Sergiyevskaya Ulitsa or Voznesenskaya Ulitsa—it's about a five-minute walk.

Express bus #388 to Sergiyev Posad departs from 2nd Poperechny Proyezd, near VDNKh metro station, every 15–20 minutes 6:50 A.M.–10:40 P.M. The journey averages 1 hour, 15 minutes and brings you to the bus station, which is right beside the railway station.

Suzdal

"The jewel of the Golden Ring" is a cliché, but it sums up Suzdal (Суздаль). Blessed with an over-supply of medieval churches and monasteries—and a lack of railway access that might have led to its modern development—it was declared a museum town in 1967 and spared the usual Soviet improvements such as factories and apartment blocks. The number and variety of stunningly beautiful churches is so great that they cease to be separate sights: The sight here is Suzdal itself.

Located 220 kilometers from Moscow, with a population of about 11,000, Suzdal retains a peaceful, provincial feel, but it has a long and rich history. Although it was settled in the 9th century, the first written mention of Suzdal was in 1024. Its heyday began in the 12th century, when it was capital of the Rostov-Suzdal principality and more important than Moscow. Status as capital of a whole series of principalities followed, but the beginning of the end came with devastating Tatar attacks in the 13th century. Suzdal began to rise again in the 14th century, rivaling Moscow for leadership, but it ended up losing its independence after being incorporated into the Moscow principality in 1392. Centuries of gloom followed, as plague, fires, and more enemy attacks decimated the population. The 16th century saw the number of monasteries multiply and Suzdal become a religious center. Only in the mid-17th century did the town begin to enjoy economic recovery.

Today, Suzdal retains the look of an ancient Russian village. Chickens and geese roam among brightly painted wooden cottages with intricately carved window frames, and the River Kamenka meanders lazily through the town and across a rolling green landscape dotted with onion domes wherever you look. It's increasingly touristy, but not yet Disney-esque.

SIGHTS
Suzdal Kremlin
Suzdalsky kreml
Суздальский кремль
Suzdal originated at its Kremlin (20 Kremlyovskaya Ulitsa, 49231/21-624, free entry to always-open grounds), with the construction

VISITING CHURCHES AND MONASTERIES: PROPER ETIQUETTE

Russia's beautiful, centuries-old churches and monasteries are among its most spectacular sights. While some of them now serve purely as museums, others are primarily places of worship and prayer, and attitudes toward tourists vary. Some working monasteries, such as Sergiyev Posad's Trinity-Sergius Lavra, are such major sights that the presence of tourists is expected, but less-famous churches might not be so welcoming. To avoid causing offense and being chased away, follow some basic rules.

- Women are asked to cover their heads – so bring along a headscarf – and to wear long skirts. Men must wear long pants and remove their hats. Both genders should wear sleeves.

It goes without saying that shorts, tank tops, and bare midriffs are inappropriate.

- Avoid visiting a church during a service if you're not an Orthodox believer.

- Be quiet and respectful. Don't talk or laugh loudly, yell, or shout. Don't run. Don't smoke.

- Displays of affection are not considered to be acceptable behavior in a church or monastery, even if you're a married couple.

- Don't take photographs of the priests, monks, or nuns. Don't take photographs inside the churches.

of the first fortress here in the first half of the 10th century. Conveniently compact—even tiny compared to the kremlins of Moscow and Novgorod—Suzdal's Kremlin has its fair share of sights.

This is where you'll see Suzdal's oldest surviving building—the blue-domed, star-spangled Rozhdestvensky sobor, or **Cathedral of the Nativity** (Wed.–Mon. 10 A.M.–6 P.M., closed last Fri. of month, Russian adults 50R, foreigners 100R). Dated to the 13th century but partially reconstructed in the 16th century, it is a UNESCO World Heritage site. Inside, besides some more recent frescoes and icons, you can see the original 13th-century golden gates and the necropolis of boyars, nobles, and royalty, including sons of Yury Dolgoruky.

Facing the cathedral are 16th- and 17th-century stone chambers known as the Archbishop's Palace, where you can visit the **Suzdal History Exhibition** (Wed.–Mon. 10 A.M.–6 P.M., closed last Fri. of month, combined ticket to all exhibits—Russian adults 150R, foreigners 300R, separate exhibits—Russian adults 30R, foreigners 60R). Consisting of nine halls, it covers the town's entire history starting with local archaeological finds from the 6th century B.C. The collection includes 13th-century Tatar-Mongol and Russian weapons and armor. There's also an exhibition of old Russian paintings, and a whole museum center especially for children.

The other main sights at the Kremlin are an impressive 17th-century belfry, and the 18th-century wooden Nikolsky Church, brought here from Yuryev Polsky district in the 1960s. After admiring them, the perfect way to complete your Kremlin visit is with a meal in the Trapeznaya restaurant, which you enter from the back of the Archbishop's Palace.

Savior Monastery of St. Euthymius
Spaso-Yevfimiyev monastyr
Спасо-Евфимиев монастырь
Suzdal's largest monastery is the astonishingly beautiful UNESCO World Heritage–listed Savior Monastery of St. Euthymius (Ulitsa Lenina, 49231/20-746, Tues.–Sun.

10 A.M.–6 P.M., closed last Thurs. of month). Founded in 1352, it occupies a commanding position high on the banks of the Kamenka River. In Stalinist times the monastery was turned into a prison; later it became a museum. You can wander around the grounds admiring the architecture, visit 10 museums with exhibits of icons, frescoes, six centuries of books, history, Prince Dmitry Pozharsky (whose was buried here), Suzdal jail, restoration, and even medicinal herbs (most single exhibits individually: Russian adults 30R, foreigners 60R, combined ticket: Russian adults 200R, foreigners 400R).

The monastery contains several 16th- and 17th-century churches, with the grandest being the 16th-century Spaso-Preobrazhensky or **Transfiguration Cathedral** (Russian adults 50R, foreigners 100R). The frescoes inside are by a renowned 17th-century painter, Gury Nikitin.

Beside the cathedral is a tall 16th-century **belfry**—and by far the most memorable part of any visit is the bell-ringing, so make sure you're there to hear them being rung at 10:30 A.M., noon, and 1:30, 3, and 4:30 P.M.

After you've seen the monastery, walk around the outside of its walls for a great view of the Intercession, or Pokrovsky, Convent, which can be enjoyed from the terrace of the café beside the monastery. You can easily combine these two sights by walking across the field between the monastery to reach the convent—with a jaw-dropping, eye-popping 360-degree panorama to enjoy on the way.

Intercession Convent
Pokrovsky monastyr
Покровский монастырь
The UNESCO-listed Pokrovsky Convent (Pokrovskaya Ulitsa, 49231/20-131) is one of the main sights to see in Suzdal, although it's not a museum as such and doesn't have specific opening hours or entry fees to the grounds. This is a working convent, but the usual monastery dress rules are not enforced, except for a ban on shorts. It's prohibited to smoke or drink alcohol on the grounds or to photograph the nuns.

The convent was founded in 1364, but nothing from that age remains—what you see is mostly from the 16th century. It has been home to many great and noble women after their fall from grace—for centuries it was a favorite spot for princes and tsars to dispose of their wives. The Moscow prince Vasily III began the trend at the beginning of the 16th century, forcing his wife Solomonia Saburova to take the veil here for failing to produce an heir. She was later canonized as Saint Sofia. Later came the second wife of Ivan the Terrible's son, the daughter of Tsar Boris Godunov, and even Peter the Great's first wife, Yevdokiya Lopukhina, who spent 20 years as a nun in this convent.

The largest church is the 16th century Pokrovsky (Intercession) Cathedral, with its 17th-century belfry and 18th-century gallery. Behind it is the 16th-century Refrectorial Immaculate Conception Church. Over the entrance is the Holy Gate Annunciation Church, also from the 16th-century. None of these are open to tourists and can only be admired from the outside.

Besides walking around the nicely landscaped grounds, admiring the stunning architecture and smelling the flowers, what remains for tourists is a museum about the convent's history, called the **Prikaznaya izba** (Fri.–Tues. 10 A.M.–6 P.M., closed last Fri. of month, Russian adults 20R, foreigners 30R).

In one of the wooden huts, there's a restaurant called **Trapeznaya** (Sun.–Thurs. 10 A.M.–10 P.M., Fri.–Sat. 10 A.M.–midnight) serving simple Russian food and beer but no wine or spirits.

The convent's cute wooden cottages used to serve as a hotel, and they were by far the most romantic place to stay in Suzdal. In a rare charitable turn for post-Soviet Russia, however, the hotel closed in mid-2008 and reopened as an orphanage, although skeptical tourist-industry locals express doubts that it will remain one forever.

It's worth seeing Pokrovsky Convent and Savior Monastery of St. Euthymius one after the other. You can walk around the walls, across the field, and over the bridge between them. On the way, you'll be surrounded by splendid views of an onion-domed landscape that takes you back centuries. Say hi to the geese on your way, and if you're lucky you might see some goats.

Museum of Wooden Architecture
Muzey derevyannogo zodchestva
Музей деревянного зодчества

Located a short walk from Suzdal's Kremlin is the Museum of Wooden Architecture (Pushkarskaya Ulitsa, 49231/20-784, daily 9 A.M.–7 P.M., entrance to the grounds: Russian adults 30R, foreigners 60R, combined ticket to all exhibits: Russian adults 100R, foreigners 200R, single exhibit: Russian adults 25R, foreigners 60R). The open-air exhibit includes a couple of 18th-century churches, mills, and peasants' houses; inside the cottages are exhibits and re-creations of peasant life. This museum was created in the 1960s by bringing wooden churches, cottages, and other buildings from other villages and arranging them here in the form of an artificial village. The grounds are used as a fitting setting for various folk festivals and holidays including the annual Cucumber Festival.

Wax Figures Museum

Suzdal's main galleries and exhibits are in the Kremlin, but the town recently gained a radically different newcomer—a Wax Figures Museum (Muzey Voskovykh Figur, 10B Kremlyovskaya Ulitsa, 985/763-8451, www.wax-museum.ru, daily 10 A.M.–6 P.M., adults 100R). Here, you can see 53 wax figures representing all the great people of Russian history, from the 9th to the 19th centuries.

◖ Mead-Tasting Hall

Around the back of the Trading Arcades is one little place that's an absolute must—the **Zal Degustatsii Medovukhi** (Mead-Tasting Hall, 63A Ulitsa Lenina, in the Torgoviye Ryady, Torgovaya Ploshchad, Kamenka River side, 49231/20-803, Mon.–Fri. 10 A.M.–6 P.M., Sat.–Sun. 10 A.M.–8 P.M.). Suzdal is renowned for making the best mead in Russia and this is the best place to try it. There are three tasting menus—traditional, berry, and herb—each consisting of 10 different types of mead in 50-milliliter shots, and you can choose to have them non-alcoholic (120R) or one of three different alcoholic strengths (150R). The tasting room is beautifully painted with colorful frescoes over its vaulted ceilings. There's also honey beer and other original drinks, plus bliny and other snacks.

RESTAURANTS AND NIGHTLIFE

Many of Suzdal's restaurants and bars are to be found in and around the Trading Arcades (Torgoviye Ryady) on Torgovaya Ploshchad (Market Square) right in the town center.

Facing onto the square is the town's trendiest café, **Losos i Kofe** (63A Ulitsa Lenina, in the Torgoviye Ryady, Torgovaya Ploshchad, 49231/24-320, www.losos-cofe.ru, daily 11 A.M.–2 A.M.). The name translates as Salmon and Coffee, and the menu has a dual focus on Norwegian salmon and Ethiopian coffee, incompatible as they might sound. Prices are high for Suzdal, with main courses at 160–640R.

On the Kremlyovskaya Ulitsa side of the Trading Arcades is **Gostiny Dvor** (63A Ulitsa Lenina, in the Torgoviye Ryady, Torgovaya Ploshchad, 49231/21-778, daily 11 A.M.–8 P.M.). This huge restaurant has numerous halls decorated in different historical Russian styles—one is like a 19th-century noble's home, one is like a tavern, another has jars of pickles on the shelves. The food is sophisticated Russian, with main courses mostly in the 300–400R range, and there's even a whole page of mushroom dishes. There are charming views from the veranda as well as from some of the dining rooms. This is one of the few places in town where you can get a good espresso.

One of Suzdal's best restaurants is **Traktir Zaryadye** (63A Ulitsa Lenina, in the Torgoviye Ryady, Torgovaya Ploshchad, Kamenka River side, 49231/24-319, daily midday–midnight). With twin halls—one smoking, one

Kremlyovskaya Ulitsa in Suzdal, with the Pogrebok restaurant on the left and the Kremlin's Cathedral of the Nativity visible at the end of the street

© NATHAN TOOHEY

EXCURSIONS

nonsmoking—it has delightful views of the river and several gorgeous churches. The service is a bit laid-back but comes with a smile, and the food is both tasty and good value, with main courses around 250R. The mead is superb, with a special fizz that makes it quite different from any of the varieties in the Mead-Tasting Hall.

The C **Trapeznaya in the Kremlin** (20 Kremlyovskaya Ulitsa, 49231/21-763, daily 11 A.M.–11 P.M., kitchen until 10 P.M.) is affiliated with the Traktir Zaryadye and is another of Suzdal's best restaurants. Entered from the river side, around the back of the Archbishop's Chambers, this is a sophisticated restaurant in an unforgettable setting serving high-quality cuisine, with main courses around the 250R mark. It's a great place to have traditional Russian *zakuski* (hors d'oeuvres) with vodka.

Across the road from the Trading Arcades is the veteran restaurant **Pogrebok** (5 Kremlyovskaya Ulitsa, 49231/21-732, daily 11 A.M.–2 A.M.). In Soviet times, and even in the 1990s, this was one of the town's few restaurants. This is where every tourist tried Suzdal's legendary mead while dining on the traditional local dish of mushrooms baked under a bread cap in a clay pot. Now the place is showing its age but makes for a fun retro experience.

FESTIVALS

The town celebrates holidays with enthusiasm, including such oddities as the **Cucumber Festival** in mid-July at the Museum of Wooden Architecture (Pushkarskaya Ulitsa, 49231/20-784), where you can taste all different kinds of pickled, salted, and fresh cucumbers, take part in eating competitions, buy cucumber souvenirs, and enjoy song and dance shows. All the regular Orthodox holidays and folk festivals are celebrated in a big way as well—at **Maslenitsa** (also at the Museum of Wooden Architecture) there's even goose-fighting to watch. For more details of festival events and exact dates for each year, contact the museum or the **Suzdal Tourist Center** (45 Ulitsa Korovniki, 49231/21-530, 49231/24-233, 49231/20-908, www.suzdaltour.ru).

RECREATION

For active leisure in the fresh air, there's **Bicycle Rent** (11 Profsoyuznaya Ulitsa, www.dvakolesa.ru, 910/092-8482, 903/545-3587, English-language inquiries by email, prokat@dvakolesa.ru). Besides offering rental of a wide range of bicycles, there are bike tours with English- or Russian-speaking guides, and a small guesthouse.

SHOPS

Suzdal has some great souvenir stores, with most of the usual knickknacks at lower prices than in the larger cities, as well as some extra treasures made by local craftspeople. There are outdoor souvenir market stalls on Torgovaya Ploshchad and outside the main sights such as the Kremlin and Museum of Wooden Architecture, but you're likely to find something better in the stores.

While in the neighborhood of the Museum of Wooden Architecture, don't miss the nearby store **Suveniry Samovary Antikvariat** (Souvenirs, Samovars, Antiques, 27A Pushkarskaya Ulitsa, 903/832-9366, daily 9 A.M.–6 P.M.). Here, *matryoshkas* start from as little as 200R and the range is better than in Moscow, with painting styles from pre-revolutionary to Soviet and contemporary. There are also samovars from about 2,000R, interesting antiques, and all sorts of locally made handicrafts.

Another good souvenir store is **Khudozhestvenny salon, Suveniry, Antikvariat** (Art Salon, Souvenirs, Antiques, 10Б Kremlyovskaya Ulitsa, 915/761-1631, daily 10 A.M.–6 P.M.), next to the Wax Figures Museum. The store is not large but has a good range of locally made handicrafts.

Nearby, halfway down Kremlyovskaya Ulitsa between Torgovaya Ploshchad and the Kremlin, there are a cluster of kitschy new wooden cottages in imitation traditional village style. Inside, among various tourist-orientated services, is a souvenir store, **Vladimirskiye Uzory** (Vladimir Patterns, 10Г Kremlyovskaya Ulitsa, 910/672-2470, daily 10 A.M.–6 P.M.), with an excellent range of wooden spoons, bowls, and other kitchenwares painted with traditional berry and floral motifs. There's also a workshop where local craftspeople demonstrate how they make the items.

An interesting range of antiques can be found in **Salon Antikvar** (63A Ulitsa Lenina, in the Torgoviye Ryady, Torgovaya Ploshchad, 905/615-2880, daily 10 A.M.–6 P.M.), including the endearing Soviet china figurines that have acquired some cult status.

HOTELS

Recent years have seen a revolution in Suzdal's hotel sector. Some large new hotel complexes have opened, as well as mini-hotels and many guest houses. The explosion in accommodation and growth in competition means that the old breed of overpriced, low-quality hotels is dying off. Many mainstays of the past have faded away, and those that remain have had to lift their game and restrain their prices.

the Holy Gates to the convent, where the Rizopolozhenskaya hotel is located

An impressive new hotel is ◖ **Pushkarskaya Sloboda** (45 Ulitsa Lenina, 49231/23-303, www.sloboda-gk.ru, www.pushkarka.ru, from 2,400R s, 2,700R d, student discounts—from 1,300R s, from 1,500R d, half-price accommodation Sun.–Thurs.; includes an hour in the spa complex but not breakfast). A huge complex on the banks of the Kamenka River, not far from the Museum of Wooden Architecture, it consists of four different styles of accommodation in a landscaped territory, including the first four-star lodgings in Suzdal and three-star wooden cottages decorated with pseudo-folksy wood carvings, a VIP building, and a 19th-century house. There are even special "youth" rooms with round double beds. All the entertainment and dining you'd ever need can be found within the complex, which includes several restaurants and bars and a spa center with saunas, pool, beauty salon, and various health treatments such as Chinese massage. It's incredible that such a place offers student and weekday discounts.

The other new mega-complex is ◖ **Goryachiye Klyuchi** (14 Ulitsa Korovniki, 49231/24-000, www.parilka.com, from 1,380R s, 2,050R d). More than just a hotel with the usual restaurants and bars, this place also has landscaped grounds, a *banya* village, a whole range of different kinds of saunas and baths, massage, fishing, and various accommodation options including a regular hotel, cottages, and a pseudo-medieval wooden tower structure. It's all located on Suzdal's outskirts, however, and would be most suitable for those with a car, although hotel staff are happy to phone a taxi (50R to the town center).

Another notable new addition is **Hotel Kremlyovsky** (5 Ulitsa Tolstogo, 49231/23-480, www.kremlinhotel.ru, from 3,950R s, 4,400R d), located close to the Museum of Wooden Architecture, which is visible from some windows, as is the Kremlin. There's an elegant main hotel building with a restaurant, plus a cedar house in a garden with wooden pagodas around a barbecue area. Tastefully fitted out with new furniture, all rooms have satellite television, a minibar, telephone, and individual electronic safe, and the luxe and semi-luxe rooms have air-conditioning.

EXCURSIONS

The most centrally located place to stay is **Sokol** (2A Torgovaya Ploshchad, 49231/20-987, www.hotel-sokol.ru, from 1,900R s, 2,480R d, including breakfast), in a yellow three-story building opposite the Trading Arcades. It's well known and popular, and is often fully booked with busloads of tourists.

Fortunately, there's now another hotel a few doors down the street from Sokol. **Zolotoy Ruchey** (72 Ulitsa Lenina, 49231/25-105, www.gold-river.ru, from 2,200R s/d, including breakfast) opened in 2008 and is a lovely hotel with clean, nicely designed rooms and friendly, competent service. It's good value for the money, and serves a good breakfast. There are 39 rooms, a restaurant, room service, a laundry, and business services such as photocopying and faxing.

If you're on a tight budget, the cheapest place in town is the centrally located **Molodyozhnaya** (104 Ulitsa Lenina, 49231/20-553, dorm beds from 600R). It has communal rooms only, and only two showers, although it can accommodate up to 80 people at a time. There are group discounts, going as low as 350R per person for a group of 30.

Another low-priced hotel is the modest **Rizopolozhenskaya** (9 Ulitsa Kommunalny Gorodok, 49231/24-314, www.hotelsuzdal.ru, from 1,100R s, 1,700R d, not including breakfast), located in the Convent of the Deposition of the Robe, or Rizopolozhensky Monastyr. Founded in 1207, this still-working but somewhat run-down convent includes a 72-meter-high bell tower, distinctive twin-peaked Holy Gates, and the 16th-century Cathedral of the Deposition of the Robe. The lodgings are basic, but centrally located.

If you'd prefer to stay in a small guesthouse, a good choice is **Traktir Kuchkova** (35A Pokrovskaya Ulitsa, 49231/20-252, from 2,800R s, 3,000R d), beside the Intercession (Pokrovsky) Convent. This was Suzdal's first private hotel, and was awarded a national "Best Small Hotel" prize in 2005. It's a really home-like place to stay, with cozy rooms and friendly service.

At the other end of the spectrum is a Soviet dinosaur, the huge old GTK or Main Tourist Complex, now rebranded as **Tourcenter Suzdal** (45 Ulitsa Korovniki, 49231/21-530, 49231/24-233, 49231/20-908, www.suzdal-tour.ru, hotel from 2,240R s, 2,440R d, motel from 1,580R s, 1,780R d, includes breakfast, pool, and gym). One of Suzdal's few modern-style buildings, it is hidden on the outskirts where it can't spoil the historical landscape. With a full range of entertainment, dining, and recreation facilities (including an indoor swimming pool and bowling), it was once state-of-the-art lodgings, but now looks left behind by the newcomers.

INFORMATION AND SERVICES

The **Post Office and Telegraph** (Krasnaya Ploshchad, 49231/21-151, 49231/20-528, Mon.–Fri. 8 A.M.–8 P.M., Sat. 8 A.M.–7 P.M., Sun. 9 A.M.–6 P.M.) offers envelopes, stamps, telephone services, Internet, and a motley collection of unrelated goods (lots of pest-control solutions) but, strangely, no postcards.

For medical help, the town has a **hospital** (1 Ulitsa Gogolya, 49231/24-211, ambulance 03).

The various tourist agencies around town exist to sell Russian-language excursions and other services, rather than to offer free consultations for confused foreigners, so your hotel's reception staff could be the best people to turn to for tourist information and answers to any other questions.

GETTING THERE

The only express bus from Moscow to Suzdal departs the bus station beside Shchyolkovskaya metro station (Tsentralny Avtovokzal, 75/2 Shchyolkovskoye Shosse, 495/468-0400) at 5 P.M. daily except Sunday. You can also take one of the many daily buses bound for Ivanovo, which stop at Suzdal on the way. The journey takes about 4.5 hours.

The most convenient way to reach Suzdal is to go via Vladimir, from where there are about two buses an hour running the 26-kilometer, 45-minute trip to Suzdal (37R). Buy your ticket inside the bus station. The bus goes from bus bay No. 10. If you go to Vladimir from Moscow by bus, that journey takes about 3.5 hours; if you go by train, that journey takes 2.5–3 hours. From Moscow to Suzdal via Vladimir can take 3.5–5 hours, depending on the wait (up to 30 minutes) for the connecting bus in Vladimir.

The bizarrely derelict and only partially functioning Suzdal bus station is about 2 kilometers from the center of town. Fortunately, buses from Vladimir now tend to continue onwards to Suzdal's center after selling all the passengers another ticket (8R). You'll have to go to the bus station to get a bus back to Vladimir, however; it can be reached on foot, by a town bus, or taxi (50R).

There is no train station in Suzdal.

By car, take the M7 Moscow–Nizhny Novgorod highway, which exits Moscow from Shosse Entuziastov. It's a 182-kilometer drive to the Ivanovo turnoff near Vladimir, from where you turn left for Suzdal. The journey takes 2.5–3 hours.

Vladimir

The classic two-in-one Golden Ring excursion is the Vladimir-Suzdal combo, and it makes good sense. The two historic towns are close together, so if you're going all the way to Suzdal—the superior destination—you might as well check out Vladimir's sights on your way, since it's tricky to get to Suzdal without going via Vladimir.

And Vladimir does have some impressive sights—three, in fact, all on the main street a short walk from the bus and railway stations, all doable in less than one day. What could be easier?

Vladimir, located 190 kilometers northeast of Moscow, is widely held to have been founded in 1108 by Prince Vladimir Monomakh. The city has been pushing for 990 to be recognized as the correct date, however, arguing that Saint Vladimir Svyatoslavich the Great founded a fortress at the location in that year. In any case, by 1157 it had become capital of the Vladimir-Suzdal principality, and the economic, political, and cultural center of northeastern Rus.

The 12th century, a time of great prosperity for Vladimir, saw the construction of its three main sights—the Golden Gates, Assumption Cathedral, and the Cathedral of St. Dmitry. The glory days came to an end with devastating Tatar-Mongol attacks and invasion in 1238, and although Vladimir retained status as the seat of the metropolitans of Kiev and All Rus from 1299 to 1328, in the mid-14th century it was superseded by Moscow as the political and spiritual center.

Despite Vladimir's proximity to Suzdal, the two couldn't be more different from each other. Vladimir has none of Suzdal's peaceful, pastoral old-Russia feel. Instead, it's a busy industrial town of about 316,000 people. The busy main street, Bolshaya Moskovskaya Ulitsa, where you'll find the sights, restaurants, and hotels, is quite attractive and pleasant to walk along. From the railway or bus station, go up the hill to the main road, turn left, and you'll soon come to Cathedral Square, or Sobornaya Ploshchad, with the Assumption Cathedral, Palaty museum, and Cathedral of St. Dmitry. After you've visited them and looked at the view over the valley behind, continue up the road as far as the Golden Gates and Troitskaya Church, check out their attractions, then head back to the station or your hotel, stopping in one of the restaurants along the way.

SIGHTS
Assumption Cathedral
Uspensky sobor
Успенский собор
Vladimir's main sight is the Assumption Cathedral (Sobornaya Ploshchad, 4922/224-263, Tues.–Sun. 7 A.M.–8 P.M., Russian adults 50R, foreigners 100R). The UNESCO World Heritage cathedral, built 1158–1160 and then rebuilt after a fire

Vladimir's Assumption Cathedral and bell tower

1185–1189, was the largest and most important cathedral of the Vladimir-Suzdal principality. Its rich interior offers much to see, including frescoes from the 12th and 13th centuries, but the real treasure is the Last Judgment by the great painters Andrey Rublyov and Daniil Chyorny, dated 1408. The bell tower beside the cathedral is dated 1810. Behind the cathedral is a panoramic lookout over the river and valley. A short distance to the left, past the Palaty (described later), is the wonderful Cathedral of St. Dmitry—another must-see.

◖ Cathedral of St. Dmitry
Dmitriyevsky sobor
Дмитриевский собор

The long-closed Cathedral of St. Dmitry has reopened as a museum (Sobornaya Ploshchad, 4922/322-467, Mon. and Thurs. 11 A.M.–5 P.M., Wed., Fri., and Sat.–Sun. 11 A.M.–6 P.M., closed last Wed. of month, Russian adults 60R, foreign adults 120R). It boasts a small collection of historical and ecclesiastical artifacts, although these are not as interesting to look at as the church itself. Inside

you can see the remains of some original 12th-century frescoes, but the real highlight is on the outside. The walls are decorated with about 600 sculptural reliefs depicting saints and all kinds of creatures, both mythical and real. Built 1194–1197, it is considered one of the best creations of the Vladimir-Suzdal school.

Golden Gates
Zolotiye Vorota
Золотые ворота

If you arrive in Vladimir by automobile, at the entrance to the city you will have to drive around a huge white structure standing in the middle of the road. With a 14-meter-high archway beneath an icon and a golden dome, these are Vladimir's Golden Gates, built 1158–1164. They are said to be Russia's only remaining preserved ancient city gates, although they were heavily restored and partially rebuilt in the 18th century. It's well worth going inside to see the impressive **Military-Historical Museum** (Zolotiye Vorota, Bolshaya Moskovskaya Ulitsa, 4922/322-559, Fri.–Wed. 10 A.M.–6 P.M., closed last Fri. of month, Russian adults 30R, foreigners 60R). Its centerpiece is a diorama illustrating the terrifying Tatar-Mongol attack on Vladimir in 1238—an event the gates survived. Besides weapons and armor from the 13th century, you can also see military artifacts from the 1812 Napoleonic War, memorial items from World War II, and—strangely enough—a cosmonautics exhibit. Getting in to see it all involves a bit of effort, however: Far from having wheelchair access, the museum is in the tower above the gates, up a long, steep, narrow staircase that could make it inaccessible for the overweight and unfit.

MUSEUMS AND EXHIBITION HALLS

To see creations of the local master craftspeople, head to the exhibit **Khrustal, Lakovaya miniatyura, Vyshivka** (Crystal, Lacquer Miniatures, Embroidery, 2 Dvoryanskaya Ulitsa, 4922/324-872, Thurs.–Sun. 10 A.M.–5 P.M., Mon. and Wed. 10 A.M.–4 P.M., closed last Fri. of month, Russian adults 30R, foreigners 60R). Located in Troitskaya Church near the Golden Gates, it displays the most interesting creations of Vladimir area, such as crystal from the town of Gus-Khrustalny. The hall's good acoustics attract visitors to its chamber choir concerts, and classical music is constantly playing in the museum.

The **Historical Museum** (64 Bolshaya Moskovskaya Ulitsa, 4922/322-284, Mon. and Thurs. 10 A.M.–4 P.M., Fri.–Sun. 10 A.M.–5 P.M., closed last Thurs. of month, Russian adults 30R, foreigners 60R) covers Vladimir's history from ancient times until 1917. It is worth a visit for its amazing display of archaeological finds from Sungir, a huge Upper Paleolithic settlement and cemetery discovered near Vladimir in 1956. The 76,000 items found at the site, estimated to be about 30,000 years old, included a mammoth, homes, storage pits, and graves filled with treasures.

A totally different kind of historical exhibit can be seen at the museum **Stary Vladimir** (Old Vladimir, Ulitsa Kozlov Val, 4922/225-451, Tues.–Sun. 10 A.M.–6 P.M., closed last Wed. of month, Russian adults 30R, foreigners 60R). Inside a red-brick tower, it displays memorabilia including books, newspapers, magazines, and posters from the late 19th and 20th centuries, but the real highlight is the viewing platform at the top.

If you've got kids in tow, you could try the museum **Palaty** (58 Bolshaya Moskovskaya Ulitsa, 4922/325-278, Thurs.–Sun. 10 A.M.–5 P.M., Tues.–Wed. 10 A.M.–4 P.M., closed last Thurs. of month, combined entry ticket for Russian adults 110R, Russian children 60R, foreigners 200R, entry to the children's museum wing 40R/25R/60R). Besides a gallery of Russian art of the 18th–20th centuries and a historical exhibit, it also has a children's museum center with about 10 different displays, from the educational to the fun.

RESTAURANTS

A cheap and cheerful place that's a must-try on the main street is the bliny café ◖ **Zakusochnaya Blinchiki** (32 Bolshaya Moskovskaya Ulitsa, 4922/326-781, daily 10 A.M.–7 P.M.). A Vladimir institution, it specializes in bliny (Russian-style crepes or pancakes) with a choice of toppings including red caviar, honey, and sweetened condensed milk (20–30R). The drinks selection includes vodka and beer.

For a more refined meal, go to ◖ **U Zolotykh Vorot** (17 Bolshaya Moskovskaya Ulitsa, 4922/323-435, www.golden-gate.ru, daily noon–midnight). This classical restaurant near the Golden Gates is the perfect place for a feast of traditional Russian foods with vodka. Get the *raznosol* pickle assortment, the herring with potatoes, and the red caviar toasts for your first few shots, then follow up with some borsch or the hearty meat soup *solyanka*. If you've still got room, the main courses are good too and start from a very reasonable 200R. The cranberry *mors* drink is not to be missed. U Zolotykh Vorot is also a hotel.

Vladimir also has a new and very popular Uzbek restaurant, **Salim** (22 Bolshaya Moskovskaya Ulitsa, 4922/421-003, daily noon–1 A.M.). The decor will make you feel like you're in the mystical East as you savor authentic cuisine such as the rice dish *plov* or the fresh and flavorsome selection from the self-serve salad bar. Main courses go for about 200R.

Another place with a vegetarian-friendly self-serve salad bar is the folksy Russian-style **Traktir Telega** (2 Bolshaya Moskovskaya Ulitsa, 4922/431-555, daily noon–11 P.M.), located opposite the Golden Gates. With all the classic Russian dishes also represented on the menu at reasonable prices (about 200R), this would be another good place for a vodka-and-pickle session, especially if you're looking for a casual nouveau-rustic setting.

For contemporary European cuisine and smiling service in a modern setting, head to **Kofeynya na Chekhova** (2 Ulitsa Chekhova, 4922/323-039, daily 8 A.M.–6 A.M.). This would be the place to go for a good cup of coffee, but prices are above average for Vladimir, especially for alcohol.

NIGHTLIFE

The Moscow concepts of "face control and dress code" have made it to the provinces, or at least to Vladimir. Trendily boasting that it has both of these restrictive entrance policies is **Club Night** (44A Bolshaya Moskovskaya Ulitsa, 4922/421-288, www.fresh44.ru, Fri.–Sat. noon–8 A.M., Sun.–Thurs. noon–6 A.M., "free for stylish people"). Positioning itself as the "only progressive club in town"—despite its humble-looking exterior—it has all the requisites, such as Japanese cuisine and hookahs. There are three floors with four bars, hosting thematic parties on Fridays and DJs on Saturdays.

Another trendy spot is **Losos i Kofe** (19A Bolshaya Moskovskaya Ulitsa—enter from Ulitsa Gagarina, 4922/451-705, www.losos-cofe.ru, Sun.–Tues. 9 A.M.–2 A.M., Fri.–Sat. 24 hours), a café with parties and DJs on weekend nights, and a nice summer terrace. The menu has a dual focus on salmon and coffee, incongruous as that might sound. Main courses go for 160–640R.

SHOPS

More and more souvenir stores are opening up along Vladimir's main road, so you won't have any trouble hunting down *matryoshkas* and the like.

But if you want to buy something uniquely Vladimirian, a good place to look is **Vladimirsky Shik** (2 Dvoryanskaya Ulitsa, 4922/324-872, Wed.–Mon. 11 A.M.–7 P.M., closed last Wed. of month). It's located in the Troitskaya Church, which also houses the Crystal, Lacquer Miniatures, Embroidery exhibit—so it would make sense to pop in here to pick up such traditional wares after seeing the best on display.

Also in Troitskaya Church, beside Vladimirsky Shik, is **Muzeiny Suvenir** (2 Dvoryanskaya Ulitsa, 4922/451-483, Wed.–Mon. 11 A.M.–7 P.M., closed last Wed. of month). Here the selection is quirkier, more original, and less traditional.

HOTELS

Vladimir's accommodation scene has finally been overtaken by Suzdal's. Before, it used to make sense to stay in Vladimir and make day trips to Suzdal, since here you could get much better value for your money. Now all that has changed and there is little reason to base yourself in Vladimir rather than Suzdal, unless you find the latter to be fully booked, too quiet and sleepy, or too far from transport links to Moscow.

One new hotel trying to lift the bar is **Monomakh** (20 Ulitsa Gogolya, 4922/440-444, www.monomahhotel.ru, from 2,100R s, 2,700R d/3,200R including breakfast). Located five minutes' walk from the Golden Gates, it boasts air-conditioners, safes, parking, and one hour of free wireless Internet (you have to pay after that). There's also a restaurant, and staff can arrange car rental and excursions on horseback or by horse-drawn carriage.

For convenience to the railway and bus stations, you can't beat the old hotel **Vladimir** (74 Bolshaya Moskovskaya Ulitsa, 4922/324-447, www.vladimir-hotel.ru, from 1,500R s, 2,200R d including breakfast). This renovated Soviet-era hotel offers all the usual services—restaurant, excursion bureau, business center, billiards, beauty salon—and remains a good-value option.

EXCURSIONS

For a more pre-Revolutionary atmosphere, you could try **U Zolotykh Vorot** (15 Bolshaya Moskovskaya Ulitsa, 4922/420-823, from 1,800R s, 2,300R d including breakfast). The name translates as "At the Golden Gates" and indeed it's located near this landmark, right on Vladimir's main road; most windows look onto the street, which gets quite a lot of traffic. The interiors are furnished in a classical style, like the superb restaurant of the same name in the same building.

INFORMATION AND SERVICES

For medical attention, go to **City Clinical Hospital for Emergency Medical Help** (1 Ulitsa Gorkogo, 4922/330-229, daily 24 hours), **Polyclinic No. 1** (4 Novoyamskaya Ulitsa, 4922/241-962, Mon.–Fri. 8 A.M.–7 P.M., Sat.–Sun. 8 A.M.–2 P.M.), or **Vladimir Region Clinical Hospital** (43 Sudogodskoye Shosse, 4922/329-711, daily 24 hours).

Internet and various computer services are offered at **Internet@Salon Na Gagarina** (1 Ulitsa Gagarina, 4922/326-471, daily 9 A.M.–9 P.M.).

For post, telecommunications, and money-wiring, go to the main **post office** (2 Ulitsa Podbelskogo, 4922/324-460, daily 8 A.M.–9 P.M.) or one of the more central branches (75b Bolshaya Moskovskaya Ulitsa, 4922/324-520, Mon.–Sat. 9 A.M.–8 P.M.).

Tourist information is available at the **Vladimir and Suzdal Museum-Reserve Excursion Bureau** (43 Bolshaya Moskovskaya Ulitsa, 4922/324-263, 4922/420-680, daily 10 A.M.–6 P.M.).

GETTING THERE
By Bus
The most comfortable and convenient way to reach Vladimir is on the commercial buses that run between 6 A.M. and 8 P.M. from in front of Moscow's Kursky station. Tickets cost 200R and cannot be purchased in advance—they are sold by the driver when all the passengers are already in their seats on the bus. The journey takes about 3.5 hours. The return express bus goes roughly twice an hour from outside Vladimir's train station, where there is a yellow sign showing the timetable.

There are also several public buses daily from Moscow's bus station (Tsentralny Avtovokzal, 75/2 Shchyolkovskoye Shosse, 495/468-0400, metro Shchyolkovskoye) at 7:45 A.M. and 6:30 and 8:30 P.M.; on Monday there is an extra bus at 1:40 P.M., and Monday–Wednesday at 7:45 P.M. The journey takes about 3.5 hours. The return public buses go from Vladimir's bus station (unlike the express, which goes from the train station beside it). On public buses, you have to buy your ticket in advance at the bus station's ticket office.

By Train
There are up to a dozen trains to Vladimir each day from Moscow's Kursky station (29 Ulitsa Zemlyanoy Val, 495/917-3152, 495/916-2003, 495/266-5310): one bound for Vladimir at 6 P.M., and a number of through trains that vary depending on the day of the week. The journey takes 2.5–3 hours. For the way back, besides the many through trains, there's a Vladimir–Moscow train departing Vladimir at 7:30 A.M. Tickets cost 165–360R.

By Car
Take the M7 Moscow–Nizhny Novgorod highway, which exits Moscow from Shosse Entuziastov. It's a 182-kilometer drive to the Vladimir turnoff.

ST. PETERSBURG

SIGHTS

Moscow's younger rival and polar opposite, St. Petersburg charms with its palaces and canals—the reason for the nickname Venice of the North. More than the actual capital, the "northern capital" has become a tourist-friendly city, with signs in English showing the way and indicating the distance to museums and other points of interest. Carefully planned and logically laid out, St. Pete is easy to navigate, with a manageable number of must-see sights. Its old center—Europe's largest—can easily be explored on foot, something helped by the fact that it is completely flat. Although its population numbers some 5 million, it feels quite compact compared to Moscow.

Peter I (the Great) and his heirs invited the world's most brilliant architects to design the city, and the result is a stunning ensemble of balance and beauty. Renowned for great ballet, art, literature, and music, St. Petersburg remains the cultural capital. But it is also a stronghold of alternative and avant-garde culture, Russia's progressive "window to the West" where new trends first emerge.

A particular attraction of St. Petersburg is its "white nights," a midsummer period when night never really falls and the city never sleeps. It peaks the last week of June, when the city is teeming with tourists, the narrow streets are jammed with giant tour buses, and long lines are a fixture outside major sights, especially the Hermitage. Spectators turn out in their thousands to witness the Neva River bridges' nighttime openings—a frustration for locals but a fun photo opportunity for visitors.

The best place to start sightseeing is Palace

© NATHAN TOOHEY

HIGHLIGHTS

LOOK FOR (TO FIND RECOMMENDED SIGHTS.

(**Most Magical Church:** The **Church on Spilled Blood** is the northern capital's dramatic answer to St. Basil's Cathedral in Moscow (page 204).

(**Must-See Sight:** The **Hermitage** is the city's premier attraction, not only for its staggering collection of artworks and historical artifacts, but also for the palatial gallery's stunning interiors (page 205).

(**Larger-than-Life:** More than 100 meters high, **St. Isaac's Cathedral** towers over the city, dominating the skyline and offering awesome views from its colonnade (page 210).

(**Most Historically Significant:** The **Peter and Paul Fortress** is the birthplace of the city, packed with historical and architectural landmarks – along with a beach to boot (page 214).

(**Best Graveyard:** Burial spot of the rich and famous for centuries, **Alexander Nevsky Lavra** has such an incredible collection of graves that it is considered a sculpture museum (page 217).

© NATHAN TOOHEY

the Church on Spilled Blood

Square, checking out the Winter Palace from the outside and then walking around to the other side of the palace to admire the views across the Neva River. You can go inside the Winter Palace and "do" the Hermitage on a different day—on the first day it's best to just take in the city itself (unless you're a dedicated art buff and just dying to see all the masterpieces). Afterwards, you could take a stroll to nearby sights such as the Admiralty, the Bronze Horseman, and St. Isaac's Cathedral, or go for a walk up Nevsky Prospekt. Or take a route from Palace Square along the Moyka Canal to the Church on Spilled Blood and Mikhailovsky Garden, then approach Nevsky Prospekt by walking along the Griboyedov Canal, which takes you close to Kazan Cathedral, Books House, and the Bankovsky Bridge. In the evening, take a canal cruise. Another day could be spent across the other side of the Neva River, on the Petrograd Side and Vasilyevsky Island, seeing the Peter and Paul Fortress and nearby museums, such as the Kunstkamera. Of course, one day should be dedicated to making an excursion to Peterhof or another palace estate, and the Russian Museum also deserves a visit. The rest depends on your own personal taste and how much time you've got—St. Petersburg has so many unforgettable sights that you won't be disappointed, whatever you choose.

The Center   Map 9

ADMIRALTY
Admiralteystvo
Адмиралтейство
1 Admiralteysky Prospekt
METRO: Nevsky Prospekt

This grand yellow Empire-style building, with a monumental tower topped with a gilded spire and weather vane shaped like a ship, is at the very heart of the city. Here three major arteries converge—Nevsky Prospekt, Gorokhovaya Ulitsa, and Voznesensky Prospekt. To its north is the Neva River, across the road to the east is Palace Square and the Hermitage, and to the southwest is another major sight, St Isaac's Cathedral.

For centuries the Admiralty building has been a symbol of St. Petersburg and of Russia as a naval power. The present building was constructed 1807–1823, but the Admiralty has been here much longer. In 1704 Peter the Great laid the foundations for a fortress wharf at the site, and the tsar himself used to work among the shipbuilders on the wharf, developing the fleet.

The admiralty is closed to the public, but it's pleasant to walk a circuit around it, admiring the sculptural reliefs that decorate its facades. There are pleasant gardens on its south and west, with fountains and statues of literary greats, and nearby is the famed Bronze Horseman at Dekabristov Square. From the embankment side there are great views of landmarks to photograph across the river, including the Peter and Paul Fortress and the Strelka. The proximity of Palace Square, St. Isaac's, and the Bronze Horseman makes these ideal to combine with a stroll around the Admiralty.

ANICHKOV BRIDGE
Anichkov most
Аничков мост
Intersection of Nevsky Prospekt and the Fontanka River
METRO: Gostiny Dvor or Mayakovskaya

Another symbol of St. Petersburg is this iconic bridge with its four Neoclassical statues, each depicting a naked young man taming a wild steed. The bridge was built in 1840, replacing earlier versions, and the horse statues by sculptor Peter Klodt were added in 1851. If you follow the statues around in a counter-clockwise direction, you can see man overpowering beast as the horse goes from rebelliously rearing to being more submissive. Some people claim to be able to make out the image of a face in the southwestern horse's genitalia.

CHIZHIK-PYZHIK

Chizhik-Pyzhik would have to be St. Petersburg's smallest sight. Perched on a stone ledge on the embankment wall by the First Engineer Bridge, where the Moyka River meets the Fontanka River, the diminutive 11-centimeter high bronze statue depicts a Siskin finch. Unveiled in 1994, the statue takes its inspiration from the rhyme "Chizhik-Pyzhik," which refers to the students of the School of Jurisprudence and their vodka drinking in a local tavern. The college students' uniforms were yellow and green, matching the colors of the Siskin (*Chizhik* in Russian). The rhyme roughly translates as follows:

Chizhik-Pyzhik where have you been?

I drank vodka on the Fontanka

Drank one shot, drank two –

Head's a ringing

Chizhik-Pyzhik has already formed its own tradition – one in which your wish will come true if you manage to land a coin on the small statue's ledge. Unfortunately, Chizhik-Pyzhik has another claim to fame: the figure has been stolen a half-dozen times, making it St. Petersburg's most stolen statue.

BANKOVSKY BRIDGE
Bankovsky most
Банковский мост
Btwn. No. 27 and No. 30 Griboyedov Canal, behind Kazan Cathedral
METRO: Nevsky Prospekt

It's one of the essential St. Petersburg experiences to walk across this pedestrian bridge suspended from the mouths of gold-winged griffins—half-lion, half-eagle creatures from ancient mythology. If you're near the intersection of Nevsky Prospekt and Griboyedov Canal—perhaps visiting the Kazan Cathedral and the Church on Spilled Blood—then a side trip to this fabulous bridge is a must. It would be worth a trip here just to see this bridge even if those other sights weren't nearby. The bridge was built 1825–1826 by engineer Wilhelm von Traitteur with the griffins by sculptor Pavel Sokolov, the same duo that created the quite similar Lions Bridge over Griboyedov Canal near the Mariinsky Theater. The name comes from the old bank beside it, now housing the Finance and Economics Academy. The griffins are one of the symbols of the city; one can be seen on the logo of the local English-language newspaper, the *St. Petersburg Times*. This diminutive pedestrian bridge is a real work of art, making for great photographs either by itself or with the canal and nearby churches in the background. But everybody wants to be photographed with the griffins, so it can be difficult to get a shot without passersby spoiling it.

BRONZE HORSEMAN
Medny Vsadnik
Медный Всадник
Ploshchad Dekabristov
METRO: Nevsky Prospekt

Yet another of St. Petersburg's symbols—some say its most important—is this pompous representation of the city's founder, Peter the Great, astride a horse rearing up over a snake. The statue by French sculptor Etienne Maurice Falconet was commissioned by Catherine the Great and erected in 1782. It bears an inscription that says "To Peter I from Catherine II" and is seen as a political ploy on her part to

During World War II the bridge was damaged but the statues were safe, having been buried in the gardens of **Anichkov Palace,** which Empress Elizabeth had built for her lover in 1741–1750—you can see it on the embankment to the southwest. Another grand landmark, the **Beloselsky-Belozersky Palace,** can be seen on the southeastern corner—a photogenic pinky-red neo-baroque confection, recognizable by its support columns in the form of muscular bearded men. It was built in 1846 by architect Andreas Stackenschneider in imitation Rastrelli style. River and canal cruises depart from beside the bridge.

legitimize her dubious position on the throne. The statue is known as the Bronze Horseman thanks to a poem about it by Alexander Pushkin. It stands on a huge boulder known as the Thunder Stone, which was brought here with great difficulty from Lakha, six kilometers away. With St. Isaac's Cathedral standing grandly behind it, the Bronze Horseman is a popular backdrop for wedding photos.

◖ CHURCH ON SPILLED BLOOD
Spas na Krovi
Спас на Крови

2A Naberezhnaya kanala Griboyedova, 812/315-1636
HOURS: Thurs.-Tues. summer 10 A.M.-8 P.M., winter 11 A.M.-6 P.M.
COST: Russian adults 100R, Russian children 50R, foreign adults 250R
METRO: Nevsky Prospekt

The northern capital's equivalent of Moscow's St. Basil's Cathedral is this shimmering beauty beside Griboyedov Canal, just off Nevsky Prospekt. Although it copies various old Russian architectural styles, it is about 350 years younger than St. Basil's. It was built 1883–1907 at the site where Tsar Alexander II was assassinated in 1881 and contains cobblestones from the embankment onto which he bled, which is why it is known as the Church on Spilled Blood—although the official name is the Resurrection of Christ Church. It is decorated inside and out with intricate mosaics by great artists of the time, including Viktor Vasnetsov and Mikhail Vrubel. It's worth going inside to marvel at the stunning bejeweled interior. The church was closed in 1930 and reopened as a museum after restoration in 1997. In the vestry behind it is a museum about the life of Alexander II; on the western side is one of Petersburgers' favorite parks, Mikhailovsky Garden (described in the *Arts and Leisure* chapter).

"CITIZENS! . . ." SIGN
Nadpis "Grazhdane! . . ."
Надпись "Граждане! . . ."

14 Nevsky Prospekt
METRO: Nevsky Prospekt

On the wall of a school at the Admiralty end of Nevsky Prospekt you can see an unusual memorial to the WWII siege of Leningrad—a genuine sign from 1943 saying "Citizens! During artillery bombardment this side of the street is most DANGEROUS" (Граждане! При артобстреле эта сторона улицы наиболее ОПАСНА). The blue-and-white stenciled sign was one of many on the northern side of streets around the city, because Nazi German bombardment was coming from the south. A memorial plaque, fixed beneath it in 1962, says: "This inscription has been preserved in memory of the heroism and courage of Leningraders during the 900-day blockade of the city."

ENGINEER'S CASTLE
Inzhenerny Zamok
Инженерный Замок

2 Sadovaya Ulitsa, 812/570-5112, www.rusmuseum.ru
HOURS: Mon. 10 A.M.-4 P.M., Wed.-Sun. 10 A.M.-5 P.M.
COST: Russian adults 100R, foreign adults 300R, foreign children and students 150R
METRO: Gostiny Dvor

With an austere elegance atypical for St. Petersburg, this palace known as the Engineer's Castle was built 1796–1800 for Emperor Paul I in a style reminiscent of a European medieval fortress. Located at the southern end of the Summer Garden, where the Moyka Canal flows out of the Fontanka River, it was originally on an artificial island, with canals built all the way around it and bridges guarded by sentries. Beside it is a statue of an equestrian Peter the Great styled as a Roman Emperor, with an inscription saying "To the Great Grandfather from the Great Grandson"—which is seen as a mockery of Paul's mother Catherine the Great's dedication to Peter I on her Bronze Horseman, as well as a refutation of the rumors that he was her illegitimate son. Plagued by palace machinations and plots, the paranoid Paul was only to live in his castle for 40 days: In March 1801 he was murdered in his bedroom by a band of dismissed officers in a palace coup. Later the palace housed an engineering college with writer Fyodor Dostoyevsky among its students; it came to be known as the Engineer's Castle,

boats on the Lebyazhy Canal, and behind them, the Engineer's Castle

although the official name was **St. Michael's Castle,** for the patron saint of the House of Romanov. Today, the castle is a branch of the Russian Museum, where visitors can see Russian art from the 12th to 21st centuries, including seven halls of 18th-century portraits depicting royalty, nobles, and other great people.

FIELD OF MARS
Marsovo polye
Марсово поле
Btwn. Moyka Canal, Millionaya Ulitsa, and Lebyazhy Canal, adjacent to the Summer Garden
HOURS: Daily 24 hours
COST: Free
METRO: Gostiny Dvor

The only real sight in this wide, bare park is a solemn memorial in its center, the Eternal Flame. This is a 1957 revamp of the Memorial to Victims of the Revolution, built 1917–1919 after 180 people who died during the February Revolution were buried in a mass grave here; later they were joined by communists who died fighting in the Civil War. The park was called the Victims of the Revolution Square from 1918 to 1944, but then reverted to its old name, Field of Mars, which dates back to the early 19th century when it was a military parade ground named after the Roman god of war. At the Neva River end of the field is Suvorov Square, where you can see an 1801 statue of the much-awarded generalissimo Alexander Suvorov depicted as Mars. The field wasn't always such a serious spot, however—in the late 18th century it was known as Amusement Square, hosting festivals and other merry-making, and before that it was Tsarina's Meadow, a park where Empress Elizabeth Petrovna liked to stroll.

◖ THE HERMITAGE
Ermitazh
Эрмитаж
2 Dvortsovaya Ploshchad (Palace Square), 812/710-9079, www.hermitagemuseum.org
HOURS: Tues.-Sat. 10:30 A.M.-6 P.M., Sun. 10:30 A.M.-5 P.M., ticket office closes one hour earlier; Treasure Gallery Tues.-Sat. 11 A.M.-4 P.M., Sun. 11 A.M.-3 P.M.

COST: Russian adults and foreigners with Russian work permits or permanent Russian residency 100R, other foreigners 350R, children and students free; free entrance for everyone on the first Thurs. of month; Treasure Galleries (Gold Rooms, Diamond Rooms) 300R; amateur photo permit 100R; amateur video permit 350R
METRO: Nevsky Prospekt

If there's one St. Petersburg sight that needs no introduction, it's the Hermitage. Like the Louvre in Paris, it's an absolute must. Everyone visiting the city should spend at least half a day in this incredible museum complex. Of course, in that time frame you can barely scratch the surface of its immense collection—one of the world's greatest, assembled over two and a half centuries.

The museum is considered to have been founded with Catherine the Great's purchase of a collection of Flemish and Dutch paintings in 1764. In full, the State Hermitage contains about three million items, including 16,783 paintings, 621,274 works of graphic art, 12,556 sculptures, 298,775 works of applied art, 734,400 archaeological monuments, over one million coins and medals, and more than 140,000 other items, comprehensively covering art and culture from the Stone Age right through to the 20th century.

The main museum complex consists of six palatial 18th- and 19th-century buildings along the Neva River on Palace Embankment (Dvortsovaya Naberezhnaya), with the most important being the Winter Palace. (Besides the main complex, other parts of the Hermitage include Peter the Great's Winter Palace, also on Palace Embankment, the General Staff Building on Palace Square, the Menshikov Palace on Vasilyevsky Island, as well as the far-flung Porcelain Museum near Lomonosovskaya metro station and the Storage Facility at distant Staraya Derevnya.)

Of greatest interest for most visitors are the exhibits in four buildings of the main museum complex: the Winter Palace, the Small Hermitage, the Old Hermitage, and the New Hermitage. These display the main collections of art and culture of the ancient world, the

one of the Hermitage museum buildings on Millionaya Ulitsa

© NATHAN TOOHEY

Orient, Europe, and Russia, the archaeological exhibits, and the coin and medal collections. The Winter Palace is your starting point; the entrance for individuals is through the courtyard off Palace Square (Dvortsovaya Ploshchad), where there is also a special entrance for the disabled. Groups enter from the river side of the Winter Palace. Internal passages lead seamlessly through to the other buildings.

Perhaps confusingly, in its English-language information the Hermitage uses the British and Continental European floor-numbering system, in which the lowest or street level is the ground floor, and the 1st story above the ground is called the 1st floor. At the same time, its Russian-language information employs the system more familiar to Americans, with the street level being called the 1st floor.

Antiquity, prehistoric, and Oriental collections are on the ground (Russian 1st) floor. But at this point you are likely to be distracted by the opulence of the interiors, which are a must-see sight in themselves. A highlight of any visit to the Hermitage is ascending to the 1st (Russian 2nd) floor via the awe-inspiring **Jordan Staircase,** two wide flights of marble stairs bedazzlingly adorned with gold, statues, and gleaming chandeliers amid granite columns, beneath an 18th-century ceiling painting of Mount Olympus.

On the 1st (Russian 2nd) floor, besides the world-class Western European and Russian art, don't miss the Winter Palace's **Malachite Room.** With columns, vases, and other fittings made of brilliant green stone embellished with lavish gilding, it was created in the 1830s as a drawing room for Empress Alexandra Fyodorovna, wife of Nicholas I. Another eye-opener is the New Hermitage's **Raphael Loggias,** an amazing fresco-encrusted corridor created for Catherine II (the Great) in the 1780s, copied from galleries in the Vatican.

Western European art alone occupies 120 rooms, spanning the Middle Ages to the present with works by the great masters of Italy, France, Holland, Spain, and other countries. Highlights of the 30-room Italian collection, located on the 1st (Russian 2nd) floor, include two works by

Leonardo da Vinci—the Benois Madonna and the Madonna Litta—as well as numerous works by other Renaissance masters such as Titian, Raphael, Giorgione, and Michelangelo.

Another of the most popular sections is on the 2nd (Russian 3rd) floor, French art of the 19th to early 20th century—here you can see such famous paintings as **Henri Matisse**'s *Dance* and *Music,* plus **Pablo Picasso**'s *Three Women* and *The Absinthe Drinker.* In total, there are 37 paintings by Matisse and 31 by Picasso, as well as seven works by Claude Monet, six by Renoir, and more by Degas, Cezanne, Gaugin, van Gogh, and many others.

The top floor is also the place to go to see the **Wassily Kandinsky** room, with six works by this early-20th-century avant-garde artist, including *Composition No. 6,* one of his most significant.

The **Treasure Galleries,** for which you'd need to buy a separate ticket, feature a wealth of jewelry and precious metals from the third millennium B.C. to the 20th century. There are fascinating animal-form items of Scythian gold, as well as ancient Greek, Byzantine, and medieval European adornments, and jewel-encrusted weapons, vases, bowls, and other supposedly functional items. The ecclesiastical collection includes icons, chalices, and altar crosses. There are also luxury goods that mostly belonged to the Russian imperial court and aristocracy, all heaving with precious stones.

The volume of treasures inside the Hermitage is too great to detail here. It's so overwhelming that a day at the museum can leave you feeling worn out and numbed with art overload—not to mention an overdose of gold, marble, malachite, and over-the-top imperial splendor. So if you want to see more than you can manage in one afternoon, consider a couple of visits on different days instead of racing along the Hermitage's lengthy corridors, ticking off your entire list of must-see masterpieces in one go.

Planning Your Visit: Depending on your level of interest in art and history, you could spend any amount of time here—it's been estimated that it would take about five years to see everything. Because there's a lot more than a tourist can possibly digest during a short visit to the city, you need to pinpoint what's of most interest to you. Thankfully, touch-screen computer information stands inside the Hermitage can help you find what you're looking for and plan your route. Operating in both Russian and English, they allow you to print out maps of the museum, showing the location of various collections and specific items. You can choose a thematic route or select your top-five masterpieces, and the program will plot your path, printing out the floor plan with a dotted line for you to follow. In addition, the information stands can provide explanatory notes with pictures, as well as updated information about which halls are closed.

If you want to plan your visit in advance, the complete floor plans are freely available on the Hermitage's user-friendly Internet site, in both Russian and English. Not only can you study which collection is in which room, on which floor and in which building, you can also check out the location of the museum's stores, cafés, ATMs, and toilets. Another option is to take a guided tour; these can be booked in advance (812/571-8446).

Also, the site offers the possibility of bypassing the long lines at the ticket office by ordering vouchers in advance. The museum's online shop sells vouchers for a one-day simple ticket to the main museum complex ($17.95) as well as a two-day combined-entry ticket to all of the Hermitage's museums ($25.95). Photo and video permits are also available via the site. When you arrive at the museum, you need to present the vouchers to the administrator and show some identification, such as a passport or drivers license, in order to exchange the vouchers for actual tickets.

Large bags, backpacks, umbrellas, and other bulky items cannot be carried around the museums and must be checked in (but are best left back at your hotel, if possible).

KAZAN CATHEDRAL
Kazansky sobor
Казанский собор
25 Nevsky Prospekt, 812/314-5856

Kazan Cathedral

HOURS: Daily 8:30 A.M.–8 P.M.

COST: Free

METRO: Gostiny Dvor

Standing proudly on Nevsky Prospekt beside Griboyedov Canal is a most atypical Russian Orthodox church, Kazan Cathedral. With a monumental semicircular colonnade of 96 Corinthian columns, its design was inspired by St. Peter's Basilica in Rome. It was built 1801–1811 and named for its copy of the Our Lady of Kazan icon, which had been obtained by Ivan the Terrible in the 16th century and brought to St. Petersburg from Moscow by Peter the Great. After 1812 the cathedral was seen as a symbol of the victory over Napoleon. Field Marshal Mikhail Kutuzov, who led the victory, is interred inside the cathedral and a memorial to him can be seen in the garden in front, along with one to another 1812 hero, Prince Michael Andreas Barclay de Tolly. In the 1930s, the cathedral was closed and turned into the Museum of the History of Religion and Atheism. Services resumed in the 1990s and the cathedral returned to the Russian Orthodox Church. Inside, besides Kutuzov's grave, you can see grandiose columns, a majestic iconostasis, and the Our Lady of Kazan icon, which returned in 2001. It remains a working cathedral. The museum dropped its atheist propaganda profile and moved to a new location near St. Isaac's.

The garden in front, with its fountains and benches, is a pleasant place to sit and people-watch. While you're in the neighborhood, walk up the canal behind the cathedral to see the amazing Bankovsky Bridge with its gilded griffins.

Across Nevsky, at No. 28 on the corner of Griboyedov Canal, you can see another iconic landmark—the **Singer Building.** An art nouveau masterpiece with a distinctive tower topped by a glass globe, it was built 1902–1904 for the Singer sewing machine company. In Soviet times, it was the House of Books, and now it is a shopping center and café. Up the canal beyond it is the Church on Spilled Blood.

PALACE SQUARE
Dvortsovaya ploshchad
Дворцовая площадь

Beginning of Nevsky Prospekt

METRO: Nevsky Prospekt

Palace Square is the first place any tourist should visit in St. Petersburg. The city's main square—and one of the world's most beautiful—it encapsulates all of St. Petersburg's splendor.

The most important sight on the square is the **Winter Palace,** a majestic green, gold, and white rococo building with 3.5-meter-high classical statues staring down from the roof. Now housing part of the Hermitage Museum's vast collection, it was built 1754–1762 by architect Francesco Bartomoleo Rastrelli and was the royal residence until 1917. The sight of all its overwhelmingly ostentatious luxury and grandeur makes more understandable why the common people would rise up in revolt. And this square has indeed been a setting for rebellion. Here, in January 1905, unarmed demonstrators marched to the Winter Palace to present a petition to the tsar, calling for reforms—and they were shot down in their hundreds by the Imperial Guard. This bloody event came back to haunt the tsar, with widespread revolutionary uprisings in 1905 ultimately leading to the February Revolution of 1917, which overthrew the tsar and saw the Winter Palace occupied by the Provisional Government until its capture by the Bolsheviks in the October 1917 Revolution that followed.

In front of the Winter Palace, the centerpiece of Palace Square is the 47.5-meter-high **Alexander Column,** designed by French-born Auguste de Montferrand and built 1830–1834 to commemorate Russia's 1812 victory over Napoleon's France. The column, made from a single piece of red granite and topped with a statue of an angel holding a cross, incredibly balances on its end without support. It is named after Emperor Alexander I, who ruled 1801–1825.

Perfectly complementing the column is the 580-meter-long **General Staff Building** curving gracefully around the square's southeastern perimeter. Designed by Carlo Rossi, it was built

SIGHTS

1819–1829, also to mark the 1812 victory. At its center is a magnificent double triumphal arch crowned by a Roman-style victory chariot with six horses—another of St. Petersburg's iconic symbols.

The best way to enter the square is through this archway—approach via Bolshaya Morskaya Ulitsa, a right turn off Nevsky Prospekt just after the Moyka Canal (if you have walked down Nevsky from the metro station). As you walk through, the monumental archway spectacularly frames a superb view of the square, the column, and the Winter Palace.

To the right of the Winter Palace, at the beginning of Millionaya Ulitsa, is an eye-catching building with giant granite statues of muscular men serving as column supports on its grand portico—this is the **New Hermitage**, built 1842–1851 to a design by German architect Leo von Klenze. It was Russia's first building constructed specifically to serve as an art gallery.

◖ ST. ISAAC'S CATHEDRAL

Isaakiyevsky sobor
Исаакиевский собор

4 Isaakiyevskaya Ploshchad, 812/314-2168, 812/315-9732

HOURS: Thurs.-Tues. cathedral 10 A.M.-7 P.M., colonnade 10 A.M.-6 P.M.; May 15-Sept. 15 also open at night: cathedral 7-10:30 P.M., colonnade 7 P.M.-4 A.M.

COST: Cathedral: daytime–Russians 120R, foreigners 300R, nighttime–Russians 150R, foreigners 300R; photo permit 50R; colonnade: daytime–Russians 70R, foreigners 170R, nighttime–Russians 150R, foreigners 300R; photo permit 25R

METRO: Gostiny Dvor or Sennaya Ploshchad

Standing more than 100 meters high, the enormous St. Isaac's Cathedral towers over St. Petersburg's low-rise skyline, its massive gold dome visible from afar. Not surprisingly, one of the main attractions here is the view from the lookout around the colonnade beneath its dome—it's quite a climb but well worth it for the spectacular panorama it provides. Built 1818–1858 at enormous expense to a design by French-born Auguste de Montferrand, St. Isaac's Cathedral is from the outside a somber giant of severe granite columns softened only

by the dozens of statues that gaze down. The cathedral has been criticized as disproportional, with an overly large dome, but nonetheless has found its place in the city's landscape. The interior is open as a museum and overwhelms with the lavish excess of its decoration. Look up into the elaborately painted dome to see a white dove at the very top. Although the cathedral feels quite sterile and devoid of spirituality, services are held on Sundays and Orthodox holidays.

Facing the cathedral on Isaakiyevskaya Ploshchad (St. Isaac's Square) is a statue of Tsar Nicholas I, and a pretty garden that's a popular spot to sit and enjoy the scenery. Souvenir sellers work the strip facing the cathedral.

SUMMER GARDEN AND SUMMER PALACE

Letny sad i Letny dvorets
Летний сад и Летний дворец

Naberezhnaya Kutuzova

HOURS: Garden: May 1-Sept. 30 daily 10 A.M.-10 P.M.; Oct. 1-Mar. 31 daily 10 A.M.-6 P.M.; closed for drying in Apr.; Summer Palace: May 10-Oct. 1 Mon. 10 A.M.-5 P.M., Wed.-Sun. 10 A.M.-6 P.M., closed last Mon. of month

COST: Garden: free; palace: Russian adults 100R, foreign adults 300R, foreign children and students 150R

METRO: Gostiny Dvor

Perhaps the most romantic place in St. Petersburg is the Summer Garden, laid out in 1704 on the instructions of Peter the Great. Here, you can stroll along alleys of grand, mature trees, lined with sculptures created by Italian artists in the late 17th and early 18th centuries. This was the first collection of secular sculptures in Russia, and 91 of the original 150 remain. St. Petersburg's oldest garden, it contains one of the city's oldest buildings—Peter the Great's surprisingly diminutive Summer Palace, constructed 1710–1713 and a rarity in that it has never been rebuilt. The palace is now open to the public as a museum of history and art. The garden is picturesquely surrounded by water: The Neva River, Fontanka River, Moyka Canal, and Lebyazhy Canal run along its sides. The best time to visit is in summer, since the sculptures are hidden in protective covers during the cooler months.

Kolomna to Sennaya Ploshchad   Map 10

NEW HOLLAND
Novaya Gollandiya
Новая Голландия
Btwn. Ploshchad Truda, Kryukov Canal, and the Moyka Canal
METRO: Sadovaya or Sennaya Ploshchad

One of St. Petersburg's most mysterious hidden treasures is this artificial island created by Peter the Great in 1721. It's named after his beloved Netherlands, where he studied shipbuilding. The 7.6-hectare triangular island does look a bit Dutch, with its 18th-century classical-styled redbrick buildings picturesquely overlooking canals. This was the city's first military port, with a shipyard, arsenal, and prison. Its most outstanding landmark is a tall redbrick archway by 18th-century French architect Jean-Baptiste Vallin de la Mothe. Closed to the public as a military complex for more than 285 years, the island is now undergoing a major transformation. It is being redeveloped to a design by Sir Norman Foster, due for completion around 2010 as a commercial and cultural center with hotels, offices, restaurants, a museum, and shopping and entertainment centers. Fortunately, the archway and other landmark buildings on the island are to be preserved. Until it's all finished, however, all you can do here is walk around the outside embankments and admire the romantic ruins.

NIKOLSKY NAVAL CATHEDRAL
Nikolsky morskoy sobor
Никольский морской собор
1/3 Nikolskaya Ploshchad, 812/114-0862
HOURS: Daily 6:30 A.M.-8 P.M.
COST: Free
METRO: Sadovaya or Sennaya Ploshchad

Some consider this the most beautiful baroque church in all of Russia. But not only is the gold-domed turquoise-and-white cathedral itself a stunning beauty—its setting is also stunning. A short distance from the Mariinsky Theater, Nikolsky Naval Cathedral and its tall bell tower rise gracefully above a leafy garden with Griboyedov Canal curving around one side and the Kryukov Canal along another. Elegant bridges cross to narrow streets that look little changed since the 19th century. Postcard-quality photos are guaranteed from just about any angle. Built 1753–1762, Nikolsky has always been a naval church—it did not close even in the Soviet era—and contains memorial plaques to sailors, including the 118 who died in the *Kursk* submarine tragedy in 2000. This is a functioning church, not a museum or a spectacle for tourists, so if you want to enter its dark, candlelit halls with their centuries-old icons and heady incense, you should be dressed appropriately. If not, just enjoy it from the outside—also an amazing experience.

YUSUPOV PALACE
Yusupovsky dvorets
Юсуповский дворец
94 Naberezhnaya reki Moyki, 812/314-9883
HOURS: Daily 10 A.M.-6 P.M.
COST: Adults 300R, students 250R, children 150R; Rasputin exhibition 100-130R
METRO: Sadovaya or Sennaya Ploshchad

This yellow classical-style palace on the Moyka Canal is most famous for the murder of the "Mad Monk" Grigori Rasputin, which took place here in December 1916. Among the various exhibits inside is one about the life and death of Rasputin, including wax figures illustrating the story of his murder.

The palace, built in 1760 by French architect Jean-Baptiste Vallin de la Mothe, was acquired in 1830 by the noble Yusupovs, one of the wealthiest families in Russia. On that fateful night in 1916, a group of nobles led by the flamboyant Prince Felix Yusupov invited Rasputin to the palace and attempted to kill him with cyanide-spiked cakes and wine, before shooting him, clubbing him, and throwing him into the river. The autopsy found cause of death to be hypothermia. As for Felix Yusupov, he successfully left Russia after the tsar's abdication and lived to a ripe old age in Paris, dying only in 1967.

SIGHTS

The palace can only be visited in group excursions, with English-language tours available by prior arrangement. There are two different excursions—besides the Rasputin tour, there is a general Yusupov Palace tour exploring the magnificent authentic 19th- and early 20th-century interiors decorated in a variety of historical styles, including a baroque theater, with sculptures and artworks from the Yusupovs' collection.

Vasilyevsky Island   Map 11

SPHINXES ON UNIVERSITY EMBANKMENT
Sfinksy na Universitetskoy naberezhnoy
Сфинксы на Университетской набережной
On the embankment in front of 17 Universitetskaya Naberezhnaya
METRO: Vasileostrovskaya or Nevsky Prospekt

St. Petersburg is a long way from Egypt, but that doesn't stop it from having sphinxes. Two authentic 3,500-year-old sphinxes can be seen on the University Embankment, in front of the Academy of Fine Arts. The oldest sphinxes in Russia, they are said to have come from the mortuary temple of Amenhotep III, and found their way onto the black market in Alexandria after having been discovered by British archaeologists during excavations at Thebes in 1829. Emperor Nicholas I bought them in 1830, after which it took two years to ship the 25-ton statues from the Nile to the Neva.

The beautiful 18th-century buildings along the University Embankment include a number of other points of interest. Many prominent artists graduated from the **Academy of Fine Arts,** and you can see some of their works in its museum (17 Universitetskaya Naberezhnaya, 812/323-3578, Wed.–Sun. 11 A.M.–6 P.M., 120R).

The **Menshikov Palace** (15 Universitetskaya Naberezhnaya, 812/323-1112, Tues.–Sat. 10:30 A.M.–6 P.M., Sun. 10:30 A.M.–5 P.M., 200R), built 1710–1727 for Peter the Great's friend St. Petersburg Governor General Alexander Menshikov, is a branch of the Hermitage museum. The fact that it was grander than Peter's palaces didn't bother the tsar—take a look inside at the restored interiors, with Chinese-style and

ST. PETERSBURG'S SPHINXES

Strange as it may seem, the genuine ancient Egyptian sphinxes on University Embankment aren't the only sphinxes in St. Petersburg.

There are bronze sphinxes by the contemporary artist Mikhail Shemyakin on Naberezhnaya Robispyera, or Rosbespierre Embankment, opposite the notorious Kresty Prison. Called the *Memorial to the Victims of Political Repression,* it consists of two sphinxes who look like beautiful women on one side of their faces, but like skulls on the other side. Shemyakin also created the statue on Moscow's Bolotnaya Ploshchad, *Children, the Victims of Adults' Sins.*

Four 19th-century sphinxes by the sculptor Pavel Sokolov can be seen on the corners of the Egyptian Bridge, which crosses the Fontanka River at Lermontovsky Prospekt. Sokolov also created the griffins of Bankovsky Bridge behind the Kazan Cathedral in central St. Petersburg, and the lions on the Lion Bridge crossing Canal Griboyedova behind the Mariinsky Theater.

maritime-themed studies as well as grandiose staircases and opulent period furniture.

St. Petersburg State University stretches along the embankment at No. 7–9—its alumni include Vladimir Lenin, Dmitry Mendeleyev, Alexander Kerensky, Alexander Blok, Dmitry Medvedev, and Vladimir Putin, among other great and famous people.

© NATHAN TOOHEY

a genuine ancient Egyptian sphinx on University Embankment

This neighborhood of science and academia also includes the Kunstkamera and Zoological museums in the old Academy of Sciences building at No. 3.

SPIT
Strelka
Стрелка

Eastern tip of Vasilyevsky Island

METRO: Vasileostrovskaya or Nevsky Prospekt

If you cross Palace Bridge (Dvortsovy Most), the bridge right in front of the Hermitage, you'll come to the Strelka, or Spit, of Vasilyevsky Island. Several interesting sights are clustered here, with the added bonus of awesome views across the river.

The square right on the spit's tip is Birzhevaya Ploshchad, which translates as Bourse Square. The pale, colonnaded building facing the square is the **Old St. Petersburg Stock Exchange.** Built 1805–1810 by French architect Thomas de Thomon, its design is inspired by an ancient Greek temple. It houses the **Central Naval Museum** (4 Birzhevaya Ploshchad, 812/328-2701, Wed.–Sun. 11 A.M.–6 P.M., 40–80R), displaying

Peter the Great's first boat, a 19th-century submarine and thousands of model ships.

In front of the Naval Museum are two eye-catching red pillars that aesthetically frame the Stock Exchange building. Called the **Rostral Columns,** they were erected in 1811, also designed by de Thomon. One of St. Petersburg's unmistakable symbols, they originally served as beacons and are still lit on special occasions. The four pairs of ship prows that decorate each column represent four rivers, the Volga, Dnepr, Neva, and Volkhov.

On the northern side of the Strelka is a colonnaded classical-style building topped with a round-dome—this is the **Russian Literature Institute,** also known as **Pushkin House** (4 Naberezhnaya Makarova, 812/328-1901, www.pushkinskijdom.ru). By prior arrangement you can take a tour of its literary-historical museum.

After you've taken in the sights on the Strelka, it's a short walk over the Birzhevoy Bridge beside Pushkin House to reach another of the city's major sights, the Peter and Paul Fortress on Petrograd Side.

SIGHTS

Petrograd Side

Map 12

AURORA CRUISER
Kreyser Avrora
Крейсер Аврора
Petrovskaya Naberezhnaya, 812/230-8440,
www.aurora.org.ru
HOURS: Tues.-Thurs. and Sat.-Sun. 10:30 A.M.-4 P.M.
COST: Free
METRO: Gorkovskaya

The *Aurora*'s fame is associated with the 1917 Bolshevik Revolution, since it is credited with firing the blank shot that was the signal to storm the Winter Palace. This event was just one small blip in its illustrious career, however. Launched in 1900, it served in the Russian Navy's Baltic Fleet from 1903, and sailed to the Far East in 1904–1905 to participate in the Russo-Japanese War, surviving the Battle of Tsushima. Its later travels around the world included participation in the King of Siam's 1911 coronation in Bangkok. After the revolutions and Civil War, it was a Navy training ship until 1940, then helped defend Leningrad during World War II.

The *Aurora* is open to the public as a museum with free entry, but for a small fee (10–25R) it also offers excursions of its deck, engine, and boiler compartments.

MOSQUE
Sobornaya Mechet
Соборная Мечеть
7 Kronverksky Prospekt, 812/233-9819
METRO: Gorkovskaya

St. Petersburg's mosque stands out in the city skyline, with its turquoise dome and twin minarets. Built 1910–1921, it was modeled on Gur-e Amir, the 15th-century mausoleum of Tamerlane in Samarkand, Uzbekistan. It is the world's northernmost mosque, and one of the largest in Europe, with space for 5,000 people. The dome stands 39 meters high and the minarets 45 meters.

The mosque was closed in 1940 and turned into a medical-equipment storehouse. It was returned to the Muslim Religious Society and worship resumed in 1956, after appeals to Soviet leader Nikita Khrushchev by Indonesia's President Sukarno and India's prime minister Jawaharlal Nehru, as well as petitions by thousands of local and international Muslims.

It remains a working mosque. Men pray on the 1st (ground) floor, women on the second, and on the third is a school with Arabic and Tatar language classes. Trying to go inside is not recommended if you're not part of the Muslim community, but for tourists the mosque is still an interesting sight from the outside, where you can admire the intricate ceramic mosaics that cover the facade, minarets, and dome.

◖ PETER AND PAUL FORTRESS
Petropavlovskaya krepost
Петропавловская крепость
Zayachy Ostrov, 812/230-6431, www.spbmuseum.ru
HOURS: Thurs.-Mon. 10 A.M.-6 P.M., Tues. 10 A.M.-5 P.M.
COST: Free entry to grounds; 50-250R for a combined ticket to all exhibits except the bell tower; tickets to individual attractions can also be bought separately
METRO: Gorkovskaya

This is where St. Petersburg began. The Peter and Paul Fortress could be called the kremlin of the northern capital, as it's the city's original citadel, founded by Peter the Great in 1703. The date Peter lay the first stone, May 27, is considered the city's birth date.

This historic fortress, intended as a defense against the Swedes but also used as a prison, the city garrison, and the royal necropolis, is situated on the Petrograd Side's little Zayachy Ostrov, or Hare Island—you can recognize it by the tall golden spire of the Peter and Paul Cathedral towering over the fortress walls, visible across the Neva River from the Hermitage.

The fortress was designed by the Swiss architect Domenico Trezzini, who was the head architect of Peter's new capital from 1703 and who takes credit for a large number of the city's earliest constructions.

You can come from Gorkovskaya metro

© NATHAN TOOHEY

the Neva River and Peter and Paul Fortress

station and walk through Alexander Park to reach the fortress or come from the center, walking over Troitsky Bridge from near the Field of Mars.

A **tourist information center** and ticket office is located in the Ioannovsky Ravelin (daily 10 A.M.–6:30 P.M.), which is right inside the gate after you cross the entry bridge. Directly in front of it is Trezzini's **Petrovsky Gate,** the only triumphal entrance remaining from Peter's time. Pass through the gates to enter the fortress's main territory, where you will find a large number of landmarks and museums as well as restaurants, cafées, and souvenir stalls.

Trezzini's **Peter and Paul Cathedral** is one of the most important sights. The angel and cross at the top of its spire are—you guessed it—another of the city's symbols. Built 1712–1733, this Petrine Baroque cathedral was the **House of Romanov necropolis** and contains the graves of tsars and emperors from Peter the Great to the last tsar, Nicholas II, among other members of the imperial family. The cathedral and necropolis are open to the public as a museum (daily 10 A.M.–8 P.M., 30–150R), as is the

bell tower (tours Thurs.–Tues. 11 A.M. and 1, 2:30, and 4 P.M., 30–100R).

Also within the fortress, you can visit the **State Museum of the History of St. Petersburg** (all Thurs.–Tues. 11 A.M.–7 P.M., 30–60R); the 18th-century buildings hold exhibitions including "The History of St. Petersburg 1703–1918," and "The History of the Peter and Paul Fortress," plus the Museum of Old Petersburg and—bizarrely—the Museum of Cosmonautics and Rocket Technology. There's also an old **print-house workshop and graphics exhibit** (daily 10 A.M.–7 P.M., free).

Several of the bastions and ravelins here were used as prisons, with an illustrious list of inmates. Among them, the writer Fyodor Dostoyevsky was held in the Alexeyevsky Ravelin. Trubetskoy Bastion was the prison and torture chamber where Peter the Great oversaw the torture and death sentence of his son, the tsarevich Alexey.

Look out for contemporary emigre sculptor **Mikhail Shemyakin's unusual Peter the Great statue.** Unlike the Roman emperor–style

SIGHTS

equestrian hero outside the Engineer's Castle or the allegorical Bronze Horseman beside the Admiralty, this 1991 version shows Peter more like he is documented to have really looked: exceptionally tall with a small head on a long body with long, skinny legs, and seated on a chair instead of a noble steed.

Another attraction in the fortress is the **Nevskaya Panorama walking route** (daily 10 A.M.–10 P.M., 30–60R), which you can find at the Gosudaryev Bastion, located between the Petrovsky Gate and the Nevsky Gate. A special pathway over the rooftops around the fortress perimeter offers amazing views of the city from a unique perspective. You can also enjoy the views by walking around the outside of the walls.

Inside the arch of the **Nevsky Gate,** which opens out onto the river, take a look at the plaques showing the levels of floods in 1752, 1777, 1788, 1824, 1924, and 1975. In front of it is the **Komandantsky Pier,** used for Orthodox water consecration ceremonies in the mid-18th century. In the late 19th and early 20th centuries, it was used to load prisoners onto boats when sending them off to carry out their death sentence.

The most amusing sight in St. Petersburg would have to be the sunbathers on the **Neva River "beach"** outside the Peter and Paul Fortress. All year round this spot seems to be blessed with sun but sheltered from the wind, because even in a frost you can see sunbathers here—perhaps the stunning views have something to do with it as well. When the sun is low, you can catch more rays standing up than reclining on the sand, and these sun-lovers demonstrate a whole repertoire of extra-exposure poses. They don't always strip right down to their bathing suits, however, sometimes just pulling their trousers down to their ankles and opening their coats. Of course you'd be crazy to swim in the polluted Neva River, but that doesn't stop the hardcore from taking a dip—even in winter.

The beach also hosts various festivals, events, and shows, such as ice- and sand-sculpture exhibits, volleyball, concerts, and more.

A blank shot is fired from a cannon in the Naryshkin Bastion every day at noon, so don't get a fright when you hear a loud bang—it's not a bomb or anything else to worry about. It has historical significance: Back in Peter's time shots would be fired to mark the start and close of the working day and other important events, and it was from the Naryshkin Bastion that the cruiser *Aurora* fired its famous shot in the 1917 Bolshevik Revolution.

Helicopter excursions depart from the grassed area behind the fortress, near the Kronverk Canal.

PETER THE GREAT'S COTTAGE
Domik Petra I
Домик Петра I
6 Petrovskaya Naberezhnaya, 812/232-4576
HOURS: Wed.-Mon. 10 A.M.-6 P.M., closed last Mon. of month
COST: Russians 20-70R, foreigners 70-200R
METRO: Gorkovskaya

The oldest house in St. Petersburg, and the only wooden building remaining from the city's earliest days, is Peter the Great's cottage near the Peter and Paul Fortress. Built in 1703 in just three days, it is made of pine logs that were painted to look like brick. The tsar lived here periodically from 1703 to 1708 while overseeing the construction of the Peter and Paul Fortress and other parts of the city—but only in the summer, as this "palace" was not heated. Later, a series of protective cases were built around it, with the current brick one built in 1844. The house is open as a museum and inside you can see some of Peter's belongings, such as a coat, a pipe, walking stick, cast of his hand, and a wooden chair that he is said to have made. Peter liked simple lodgings, and visitors often comment that this 60-square-meter, three-room cottage is rather humble for Russia's ruler; likewise the 2.5-meter-high ceilings are low considering that Peter was close to 2.1 meters (7 feet) tall. Outside you can see a 19th-century bust of Peter the Great and a garden with oak trees that were planted by the 19th-century royal family to mark special occasions.

Smolny and Old Nevsky   Map 13

⟨ ALEXANDER NEVSKY LAVRA
Svyato-Troitskaya Alexandro-
Nevskaya Lavra
Свято-Троицкая Александро-
Невская Лавра
1 Naberezhnaya reki Monastyrki, 812/274-1702,
812/274-0409, www.lavra.spb.ru
HOURS: Daily 6 A.M.–5 P.M.
COST: Free
METRO: Ploshchad Alexandra Nevskogo

Alexander Nevsky Lavra is one of the must-see sights in St. Petersburg. Whether you're interested in history, religion, the arts, sculpture, or just getting some pretty holiday snaps, there are plenty of reasons to come and see this monastery. It boasts of a number of beautiful 18th- and 19th-century churches in a picturesque island setting, but the most interesting sights here are to be found in the graveyards. The monastery was a prestigious burial spot right from its founding, and no expense was spared on the lavish sculptural headstones of great and famous people from the arts, the military, government, and royalty.

Three of Alexander Nevsky Lavra's cemeteries comprise the **State Museum of City Sculpture** (Fri.–Wed. 9:30 A.M.–6 P.M., 35R). For the foreign tourist, the most interesting is **Tikhvin Cemetery,** also known as the Necropolis of the Masters of Arts. It's a real who's who of art, music, and literature, with the graves of Dostoyevsky, Tchaikovsky, Mussorgsky, Stravinsky, Glinka, Rimsky-Korsakov, Kustodiev, and Shishkin, among many other internationally famous names. The **St. Lazarus Cemetery** is St. Petersburg's oldest, established in the 18th century as a necropolis for members of the Imperial family, the court nobility, and military and political leaders as well as the most outstanding people of science and arts. **St. Nicholas Cemetery** contains graves of important religious and political figures of the 19th–21st centuries.

Founded by Peter the Great in 1710, the monastery was supposed to be located at the site where Prince Alexander of Novgorod and his small army defeated the Swedes in 1240, but the battleground actually turned out to be elsewhere. The monastery seems keen to bury this widely held version of its history, and its website instead says the location is where Alexander's son Andrey defeated the Swedes in 1301.

In any case, the 19-year-old Prince Alexander's great feat saved Russia from invasion from the north and earned him the nickname Nevsky. He was later canonized by the Russian Orthodox Church. Peter named the monastery after Alexander and had his remains brought here from Vladimir. Along with the relics of dozens of other saints, Alexander Nevsky's remains are in the shrine of the monastery's main church, the 18th-century Trinity (Troitsky) Cathedral—having returned here in 1989 after being sent by the Soviets to the Museum of the History of Religion and Atheism, while the silver reliquary that had contained them went to the Hermitage.

In 1797 the monastery was elevated to the status of *lavra*—a monastery of the highest rank—and it remains one of just four in all of Russia and Ukraine to have this distinction. The Soviet authorities formally closed Alexander Nevsky Lavra in 1918 but it continued functioning unofficially until the 1930s, when all the monks were arrested. Trinity Cathedral was returned to the church in the 1950s, followed by St. Nicholas church in 1987. The monastery resumed operating in full in 1996.

SMOLNY CATHEDRAL AND CONVENT
Smolny sobor i monastyr
Смольный собор и монастырь
1-3 Ploshchad Rastrelli, 812/271-9182
HOURS: Thurs.-Tues. 10 A.M.–5:30 P.M.
COST: 50-200R
METRO: Chernyshevskaya

The epitome of whipped-cream baroque, Francesco Bartomoleo Rastrelli's Smolny Cathedral stands sumptuously by the Neva

SIGHTS

River, looking like an iced blue-and-white wedding cake. It is the centerpiece of the Rastrelli-designed Smolny Convent, built 1748–1757 for Empress Elizabeth I, who wanted to spend the end of her life here in peace. This breathtakingly beautiful convent is located at the former site of tar yards (in Russian, *smolny dvor*), hence its common name, although the correct name was originally the Voskresensky or Resurrection Cathedral and Convent. After Elizabeth's death in 1762 the convent housed the Smolny Institute for Noble Maidens. Founded in 1764 on Catherine the Great's orders, it was Russia's first educational institute for females, adding the yellow Smolny Institute buildings next door in the early 19th century. The cathedral itself was only completed in 1835, by another architect; it was consecrated in that year and remained a congregational church until its closure in 1923. Still not an active church, it is used as a concert hall and is said to have perfect acoustics. It also contains an exhibition hall and a souvenir/gift stall, but the best part is the viewing platform at the very top. The convent buildings surrounding the cathedral are now classrooms of St. Petersburg State University, including those of its Center of Russian Language and Culture, which offers intensive Russian-language classes for foreign students. It's absolutely the most inspiring setting a student could ever hope for (for details see the center's website, www.russian-language.org).

SMOLNY INSTITUTE
Smolny institut
Смольный институт
1 Smolny Proyezd/3 Ploshchad Proletarskoy Diktatury, 812/276-1746
HOURS: Mon.-Fri. 10 A.M.-6 P.M.
COST: Excursions: Russians 250R, Russian students 200R, foreigners 700R, foreign students 400R
METRO: Chernyshevskaya

A short walk from Smolny Cathedral is a yellow classical building with white columns across its facade and a Russian flag on the peak of its roof—this is the Smolny Institute, now housing the St. Petersburg city administration. Built to architect Giacomo Quarenghi's design in 1806–1808 for the Smolny Institute for Noble Maidens, it is famed as Bolshevik headquarters, Vladimir Lenin's residence after the October Revolution in 1917, and then Leningrad Communist Party headquarters. Sergey Kirov was murdered inside the Smolny Institute in 1934. Later the building became City Hall. It remains the residence of the St. Petersburg governor and also contains a museum with exhibits covering its entire history, including the noble girls' school, the Bolshevik era, the WWII blockade, and beyond.

Greater St. Petersburg   Map 14

BUDDHIST TEMPLE DATSAN GUNZECHOINEI
Buddiisky khram Datsan Gunzechoinei
Буддийский храм Дацан Гунзэчойнэй
91 Primorsky Prospekt, 812/430-9740
HOURS: Daily 10 A.M.-7 P.M.
COST: Free
METRO: Staraya Derevnya or Chernaya Rechka

St. Petersburg's beautiful *datsan,* located a short walk over the bridge from Yelagin Island, is an interesting combination of traditional Tibetan cathedral temple and northern art nouveau architecture. It was built for the city's Buddhist community in 1909–1915, initiated by the 13th Dalai Lama Thupten Gya and the Buryat lama Agvan Dorzhiev, funded by them and Buddhists of Buryatia and Kalmykia. In the 1930s, the temple was closed, its lamas arrested, and its objects sent to the Museum of the History of Religion and Atheism. It housed a sports center, military radio communications, and even a zoological institute until its return to the Leningrad Buddhists Association in 1990. It remains a working Buddhist temple and boasts a new Buddha made by Mongolian craftsmen as well as the returned Standing

Buddha from Siam, which had been presented to the *datsan* by the Russian consul in Bangkok in 1914. The colorful, incense-laden interior is sure to inspire and amaze, but it's probably best not to go during a service (daily 10 A.M.–noon and 3–4 P.M.). There are certain rules of conduct: Take off your hat; move from left to right in the altar hall and don't turn your back on the altar; don't chat or talk on your cell phone. There are even special slippers for guests to wear instead of their street shoes.

MONUMENT TO THE HEROIC DEFENDERS OF LENINGRAD

Monument geroicheskim zashchitnikam Leningrada

Монумент героическим защитникам Ленинграда

Ploshchad Pobedy, 812/373-6563

HOURS: Mon., Thurs., and Sat.-Sun. 10 A.M.-6 P.M., Tues. and Fri. 10 A.M.-5 P.M., closed last Tues. of month

COST: 50R

METRO: Moskovskaya

If you arrive in St. Petersburg by airplane, this is the first sight you'll see on your way from the airport to the center: a 48-meter-high red-granite obelisk with the five-meter-high *Victors* sculptural composition at its base, in front of a huge broken ring of granite and concrete framed by an ensemble of 26 bronze figures depicting snipers, soldiers, sailors, pilots, and other fighters. Opened in 1975 to mark the 30th anniversary of victory in World War II, the monument is at the center of Victory Square—just nine kilometers from the war's front line. There is a very moving museum in the bunker-like space beneath the memorial, with genuine artifacts of the time giving a vivid picture of the 900-day blockade of Leningrad and the incredible courage of soldiers and regular citizens alike in the face of cold, hunger, and enemy attack.

RESTAURANTS

The northern capital's dining scene long lagged behind Moscow's, but it has finally almost caught up, in quality, diversity, and prices too. No longer the bargain that it used to be just a few years ago, St. Pete still offers slightly better value than Moscow. Here you'll find less of the capital's slick McChic, and more original gems.

The economic recovery came to St. Pete a bit later than Moscow, but the past couple of years have seen an explosion in new openings, from cute and cozy cafés to upscale restaurants capitalizing on this beautiful city's spectacular views and the ever-increasing number of tourists. And, although this is generally a cold-climate city, restaurateurs have finally caught on that alfresco dining can be a hit in the summer.

Besides the Russian-European eateries you'd expect to find, St. Pete now has everything from Thai to Tatar. There are whole restaurants dedicated to cuisines that the capital lacks—Indonesian and Greek, for example. But as in Moscow, there are no neighborhoods known for specific types of food. There's no Chinatown or Little Italy—such a phenomenon just doesn't exist here.

English-speaking staff and menus can be found in the city's Indian restaurants, the pub-styled beer restaurants, and the more expensive establishments, especially in areas of the city where there are lots of tourists, but you're unlikely to find them in places serving Caucasus cuisine, or in cheap eateries.

As this is Russia's beer capital, the city has some great microbrewery restaurants and pubs.

© NATHAN TOOHEY

HIGHLIGHTS

LOOK FOR  TO FIND
RECOMMENDED RESTAURANTS.

Best Microbrewery: Huge and high-ceilinged with shining vats on display, **Tinkoff** brews eight delicious filtered and unfiltered beers, as well as one for each of the four seasons (page 223).

Best Outdoor Dining: St. Pete has some great alfresco restaurants and others with impressive views, but **Terrassa** combines both, to awesome effect (page 226).

Best Cheap Eats: For the Russian comfort food that everybody loves, you can't go wrong at **Blinny Domik** (page 226).

Best Takeout: When there's no time to stop for a meal, a **Stolle** pie will hit the spot (page 227).

Best Place to Impress a Date: Dine like royalty at **Noble's Nest** – it's so posh you'll feel like you're in Peterhof palace (page 229).

Best Place to Fish for Your Dinner: Cast your rod and reel to get your meal at **Russkaya Rybalka,** a restaurant beside a picturesque pond on one of St. Pete's park islands (page 234).

© NATHAN TOOHEY

that classic dish, Chicken Kiev, served with fries and peas

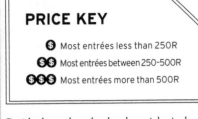

PRICE KEY

$ Most entrées less than 250R

$$ Most entrées between 250-500R

$$$ Most entrées more than 500R

Besides beer, the other local specialty is the fish *koryushka*, which is caught locally in the spring and goes perfectly with a cold brew.

Usually it's possible to get a table without a reservation, unless it's a peak time—Friday or Saturday night—or your group is of more than four people. Wedding parties, corporate events, and other large banquet groups often book out a whole restaurant, however, so it can pay to call ahead and check if you can get a table regardless of the day, time, and group size. Some restaurants won't take reservations for peak times because they don't want to hold a table, turn other people away, and then find nobody shows up for the reservation. Some places will only take a reservation for large groups that pay a deposit that will be deducted from the final bill.

The Center   Map 9

ASIAN
MOPS $$
Мопс

12 Ulitsa Rubinshteyna, 812/572-3834

HOURS: Daily 1 P.M.-1 A.M.

METRO: Dostoyevskaya

This is a tasty Thai restaurant with an innovative interior design. St. Petersburg's first Thai eatery skips a traditional decor in favor of a more modern approach—the walls are tiled and the furnishings are of simple dark wood. The menu nonetheless features all the Thai classics, such as *tom yum* and plenty of curries. There's also a good selection of cocktails and a suitably casual, friendly vibe.

SUKAWATI $$
8 Kazanskaya Ulitsa, 812/312-0540, www.sukawati.ru

HOURS: Daily noon-5 A.M.

METRO: Nevsky Prospekt

Russia's only Indonesian restaurant offers a Europeanized take on the cuisine, and adds some sushi just for good measure. Try the assorted *satay* skewers with peanut sauce, or the *nasi goreng* and *rijstaffel* rice platters. The hip decor and laid-back atmosphere makes for a nice place to unwind and relax, especially in the sexy basement lounge. Gal pals like to gather here for long lunches, à la *Sex and the City*.

BEER RESTAURANTS AND PUBS
MARIUS PUB $$
Мариус паб

11 Ulitsa Marata, 812/315-4880

HOURS: Daily 24 hours

METRO: Mayakovskaya

With its Old World interior, this thoroughly refined and elegant pub verges on feeling like a gentlemen's clubhouse. Marius aims to be St. Petersburg's first gastronomic pub and, as such, it has an extensive menu of classical European dishes. The food's fairly heavy, but that only helps soak up the house beer, which is brewed on the premises. All these various elements combine to make Marius the kind of place ideal for hunkering down on a cold winter night.

OLIVER TWIST $$
Оливер Твист

3 Ulitsa Belinskogo, 812/272-3311

HOURS: Sun.-Thurs. noon-1 A.M., Fri.-Sat. noon-2 A.M.

METRO: Gostiny Dvor or Mayakovskaya

Opened in 2006, this cozy little pub boasts all the decor features you'd expect to find in an upmarket example of the genre—plenty of dark wood, red flock wallpaper, stained glass, and leather-clad booths. Oliver Twist has a decent range of draft beers, including a few

ADVENTURES IN EX-SOVIET CUISINES

A visit to Moscow or St. Petersburg offers a rare opportunity to sample not only Russian food but also the little-known but superb cuisines of some former Soviet republics.

The most loved of them all is **Georgian** – surely one of the world's great, undiscovered cuisines. It's strong on both vegetable dishes and meats, so there's something for everyone. It's also spicy. Some must-try dishes include: *khachapuri*, a delightful cheese pie that's the ultimate comfort food and is available in regional varieties from different parts of Georgia; *satsivi*, usually chicken in a garlicky walnut sauce; eggplant rolls filled with a walnut mixture and topped with pomegranate seeds; and of course shashliks (shish-kebabs).

Armenian and **Azeri** cuisines have their similarities to Georgian but are less vegetable-focused and are heavier on meat. Both feature *shashliks* and, naturally, each nation thinks its kebabs are the best. Azeri soups are interesting, such as *piti*, with chickpeas, lamb, potatoes, and mint, and *dyushbara*, with lamb-filled mini-dumplings. Armenia dolma are well worth trying – vine leaves stuffed with meat, rice, and spices – and don't forget to try Armenia's superb brandy.

Another great ex-Soviet cuisine is **Uzbek**, and here the classic dish is *plov* (pilaf). There are regional variations, but usually this fragrant rice dish includes lamb, as well as chickpeas, carrot or saffron strips, and sometimes raisins and barberries. Another one to try is *lagman*, a hearty noodle soup with lamb and vegetables.

There's a misconception that Russian food is all meat and potatoes, but that might be a more apt description of **Belarussian** cuisine. If you visit one of the few Belarussian restaurants, be sure to try *draniki* (potato cakes) with a dollop of sour cream.

Ukrainian cuisine is stronger in the vegetable department and deserves recognition for its diversity. Lots of dishes commonly considered Russian are actually Ukrainian, most notably borshch. Try *vareniki* (dumplings), which are usually filled with cabbage, or potato and mushroom, as well as sweet varieties filled with berries. Ukrainian vodka is called *gorilka* (pronounced horilka) – the honey and pepper variety is a perfect winter warmer.

ales. As for the food, glorious food, the menu is fairly brief and includes such beer-friendly snacks as club sandwiches, chicken wings, and barbecue ribs. There's even the decidedly British fish-and-chips.

TINKOFF $$$
Тинькофф

7 Kazanskaya Ulitsa, 812/718-5566, www.tinkoff.ru
HOURS: Sun.-Thurs. noon-2 A.M., Fri.-Sat. noon-3 A.M.
METRO: Nevsky Prospekt or Gostiny Dvor

Russia's first national microbrewery chain started right here—although it could hardly be called humble beginnings. This huge, high-ceilinged restaurant sports a slick, high-tech interior, which makes for a nice change from the "ye olde" theme found in most beer-focused restaurants around town. Food-wise, the selection leans toward heavy beer-hall dishes, including a whole range of German cuisine such as various sausages and even pig's knuckle. There's also some sushi, and even pizza. The microbrewed beer is some of the city's best.

CAUCASUS

CAT CAFE $
Кэт Кафе

22 Stremyannaya Ulitsa, 812/571-3377
HOURS: Daily noon-midnight
METRO: Mayakovskaya

With only a half-dozen tables, this tiny little Georgian restaurant boasts more than a decade of satisfied customers. Every inch of spare space is crammed with quirky decorations and knickknacks. This place is popular with actors, singers, and various other artistic types, not to mention tourists. The food is good, and given the café's diminutive size, it's best to book ahead or arrive early if you want a seat.

© NATHAN TOOHEY

Hot chocolate in Russia comes thick, like melted chocolate, rather than thin and milky like cocoa.

EUROPEAN
BELLEVUE $$$

22 Naberezhnaya reki Moyki, 812/335-9111

HOURS: Daily noon-3 A.M.

METRO: Nevsky Prospekt

Located at the top of the Kempinski Hotel, this restaurant is all about the lovely view, which looks across the rooftops to Palace Square and the Winter Palace as well as out to St. Isaac's Cathedral. The view is especially nice at night when the palace is all lit up. The prices are high and the Euro-style food offers no real surprises, but then again you might not notice given the panoramic distraction. If you're on a budget, come at lunchtime when a lower-priced fixed menu is offered.

KOROVABAR $$$

8 Karavannaya Ulitsa, 812/314-7348

HOURS: Daily noon-1 A.M.

METRO: Gostiny Dvor or Nevsky Prospekt

This has to be the hippest steak restaurant in town, if not Russia. This place just oozes coolness with its super-fashionable modern interior. It's mainly minimal, with some cowskin hide to let you know what kind of restaurant you're in. There's even a secret room hidden behind wooden shelves. In summer, they open a small summer patio out front. They serve a large variety of steaks and other meaty treats.

STROGANOFF STEAKHOUSE $$$

4 Konnogvardeysky Bulvar, 812/314-5514, www.stroganoffsteakhouse.ru

HOURS: Daily noon-midnight

METRO: Sadovaya

An enormous steak house that creates an air of class without being too stuffy, Stroganoff is furnished with plenty of leather and dark wood but the brick walls are painted white, which lightens up the place. There are no surprises on the menu—it's all about the steaks. There's a children's room with amusements to

BIZNES LANCH

In the old days, local eateries used to offer a *komleksny obed* – a set lunch menu at a set price. Now such fixed-price meals are called a *biznes lanch* (business lunch), but the idea remains the same. During lunchtime, for a low price (150–300R), you get a salad, soup, hot main course, and a drink; the menu changes daily. You can find a *biznes lanch* in just about every restaurant, whether Russian, Italian, or whatever. Don't expect the same quality as you'll find ordering from the a la carte menu – but if you're on a budget, it's an unbeatable deal.

keep the little rug rats busy, but otherwise, it all adds up to the kind of place that's perfect for business meetings with important colleagues and clients.

TEPLO $$
Тепло
45 Bolshaya Morskaya Ulitsa, 812/570-1974
HOURS: Daily 9 A.M.-midnight
METRO: Gostiny Dvor or Sadovaya

Opened in early 2008, this super-cozy and relaxed café even boasts a fireplace, which is quite appropriate since its name translates as "warm." There are lots of coffee-table books and board games to keep you amused, especially on a cold winter day, but it's not a grandma's cottage kind of place—the furnishing are simple and the walls are white. Try the hot glühwein (mulled wine) and the home-baked pies and bread. In summer there is outdoor seating.

GREEK
OLIVA $$
Олива
31 Bolshaya Morskaya Ulitsa, 812/314-6563
HOURS: Daily noon-midnight
METRO: Gostiny Dvor or Sadovaya

With four halls dressed up in Greek national style—lots of sky blue and white contrasted by earthy clay cookware hanging on

the walls—this place is popular with locals, having scooped its fair share of St. Petersburg gastronomy awards. It's also child-friendly, offering special menus for the kids. In the evening, there's live Greek music and dancing.

INDIAN
TANDOOR $$
Тандур
2 Voznesensky Prospekt, 812/312-3886
HOURS: Daily noon-11 P.M.
METRO: Sadovaya, Sennaya Ploshchad, Nevsky Prospekt

St. Petersburg's oldest Indian restaurant, Tandoor has been serving up curries and kebabs since 1994. Located opposite the Admiralty, the restaurant has a rich interior with plenty of Indian carvings, weavings, and other such decorations. Keep in mind that if you want it spicy, it's best to remind the waiter—Indian restaurants in Russia tend to tone down the spice to suit the local palate.

TANDOORI NIGHTS $$
4 Voznesensky Prospekt, 812/312-8772
HOURS: Daily noon-midnight
METRO: Sadovaya, Sennaya Ploshchad, Nevsky Prospekt

Located right next door to Tandoor, this new rival offers a polar opposite approach in its interior design. Rather than an Indian enclave stuffed with ethnic ornaments, Tandoori Nights has chosen a light, white modern interior, with minimalist furniture and a long bright-orange strip depicting Indian written characters along one wall. If you ask for it spicy the chef won't let you down. The food is delicious and you can watch Bollywood movies as you dine.

INTERNATIONAL
NEP $$
Нэп
37 Naberezhnaya reki Moyki, 812/571-7591, www.neprestoran.ru
HOURS: Sun.-Tues. noon-11 P.M., Wed.-Sat. noon-1 A.M.
METRO: Nevsky Prospekt

Named after the New Economic Program,

this is a cabaret restaurant with a Soviet 1920s theme, located just around the corner from Palace Square. There are various shows that are regularly rotated, with the evening performances starting at 8:30 P.M. The cabaret show costs 270R per person (not including dinner). The menu is a mixed bag, with Russian, European, and even Thai dishes available.

SEVENSKYBAR 💲💲

15 Italyanskaya Ulitsa, 812/449-9432, www.sevenskybar.ru
HOURS: Sun.-Thurs. noon-2 A.M., Fri.-Sat. noon-6 A.M.
METRO: Gostiny Dvor

A club-like restaurant with DJs spinning tunes in its modern, minimal interior, Sevenskybar is located on the top floor of a fancy shopping center. The restaurant offers superb panoramic views to put you in Seventh Heaven, sweeping across to the Church on Spilled Blood and other landmarks. There is plenty of seating along the bar, but then you'd miss out on the view. The menu ranges from Italian to Singaporean and Japanese.

SUP VINO 💲

Суп Вино
24 Kazanskaya Ulitsa, 812/312-7690
HOURS: Daily noon-midnight
METRO: Sennaya Ploshchad or Sadovaya

A simple and small eatery with just a half-dozen tables, Sup Vino has a similarly diminutive selection of soups and salads. The variety is wide, however, ranging from Thai-style *tom yum* to Finnish-style fish soup. This is the kind of place you'd drop into for a quick lunch on the run if it weren't for one thing— its impressive wine list will have you wanting to kick back and relax over a good drop or two.

🌙 TERRASSA 💲💲💲

3A Kazanskaya Ulitsa, 812/937-6837, www.terrassa.ru
HOURS: Mon.-Thurs. 11 A.M.-midnight, Fri. 11 A.M.-1 A.M., Sat. noon-1 A.M., Sun. noon-midnight
METRO: Nevsky Prospekt

A large and fashionable restaurant, Terrassa is located on the 6th floor of a business center; its main drawing card is a spacious open-air deck with breathtaking views of Kazan Cathedral. If the weather's not right for alfresco dining, the inside space is equally bright and airy, with similar views. There's an open kitchen where the chefs prepare a full gamut of dishes from Asian to Italian. There's even a take-out deli section.

ITALIAN
PARK GIUSEPPE 💲💲

Парк Дзузеппе
2B Naberezhnaya kanala Griboyedova, 812/571-7309, 812/973-0943, www.park-restaurant.ru
HOURS: Daily 11 A.M.-3 A.M.
METRO: Nevsky Prospekt

This one's a winner. A lovely light and airy restaurant located just a stone's throw from the Church on Spilled Blood, Park Giuseppe faces directly onto the Mikhailovsky Garden. The interior is nice, but the covered veranda is better, both with views out across the park. As the name would suggest, it serves Italian cuisine, including tasty pizzas that are discounted at lunchtime, so eating here doesn't have to be as expensive as you might expect given the location and look of the place. There's an excellent wine selection, and reasonably priced beers for the lunchtime pizza crowd.

RUSSIAN
🌙 BLINNY DOMIK 💲

Блинный Домик
8 Kolokolnaya Ulitsa, 812/315-9915, 812/318-5345
HOURS: Daily 10:30 A.M.-11 P.M.
METRO: Vladimirskaya or Dostoyevskaya

The name means something like "little pancake house," although it's not pancakes that they serve but Russian crepes, or bliny. The interior is all wooden, but bright, and resembles something out of *Little Red Riding Hood*. The bliny are great and come with all manner of toppings, from sweet to savory. This cute-as-a-button place is great for kids, but be warned— it's popular and can get crowded to the point that you have to wait for a table.

LENIN ZHIV 💲💲
Ленин Жив

40 Naberezhnaya reki Fontanki, 812/275-3559,
www.lenin-jiv.ru

HOURS: Mon.-Fri. noon-1 A.M., Sat.-Sun. noon-3 A.M.

METRO: Mayakovskaya

If you have a taste for 1920s Soviet avant-garde art, propaganda posters, and Commie kitsch, then you'll love this café right near Anichkov Bridge. The name means "Lenin Lives," and the theme is expertly executed here. Besides classic propaganda posters on the walls, there are old Soviet books on the shelves, gramophones and other kinds of retro knickknacks, plus Russian-European food—from beef stroganoff and borsch to Italian-style pasta dishes. There's a good range of booze, with a dozen beers to choose from, including the Lenin house beer, Leninskoye Pivo.

█ STOLLE 💲
Штолле

1/6 Konyushenny Pereulok, 812/312-1862, www.stolle.ru

HOURS: Daily 9 A.M.-9 P.M.

METRO: Nevsky Prospekt

It's all about the pies, and what wonderful pies they are. The Stolle chain of pie stores serves freshly baked traditional Russian pies in a multitude of flavors to eat in or take out. The selection ranges from the savory, such as rabbit with mushroom or cabbage, to the sweet, such as cranberry or apricot. The prices here are unbeatable and the atmosphere relaxed, well worth a visit if you feel like some simple home cooking. See their website for other locations.

UDACHNY VYSTREL 💲💲💲
Удачный Выстрел

3 Gorokhovaya Ulitsa, 812/571-6949, www.lucky-shot.ru

HOURS: Daily noon-last guest

METRO: Nevsky Prospekt

The name of this game restaurant translates as Lucky Shot. On the menu you can find furry friends from bear, boar, and elk to raccoon, as well as some fish dishes and the odd vegetable side dish. The place is decked out like a hunter's lodge, but if you find the taxidermy spooky, you can sit in the courtyard instead. Udachny

Vystrel is well regarded, winning awards as the city's best conceptual restaurant.

SEAFOOD

TRITON 💲💲💲
Тритон

67-69 Naberezhnaya reki Fontanki, 812/666-6666, 812/310-9449, www.triton.ru

HOURS: Daily noon-2 A.M.

METRO: Gostiny Dvor

Named after the son of the Greek god Neptune, its not surprising that this is an upscale Mediterranean seafood restaurant. The posh interior re-creates an underwater world, with swimming sharks painted on the ceiling and a real aquarium acting as the floor in the entryway, as well as numerous other aquariums about the place. The menu features all manner of seafood that's flown in fresh, as well as a suitably impressive wine list.

UKRAINIAN

SHINOK 💲💲
Шинок

13 Zagorodny Prospekt, 812/571-8262

HOURS: Mon. 11 A.M.-2 A.M., Tues.-Sun. 11 A.M.-5 A.M.

METRO: Dostoyevskaya

With decor that transports you to a Ukrainian country farmhouse, and waitstaff in national costumes, this is the place to try Ukrainian cuisine in St. Pete. There's a great range of *vareniki* dumplings, including plenty with tasty vegetarian stuffings—cheese, or potato with mushroom, for example—and more kinds of borsch than you could imagine. To wash it down, there are all sorts of *gorilka* (Ukrainian vodka) and even a rare, ancient drink called *varenukha*.

VEGETARIAN

BOTANIKA 💲💲
Ботаника

7 Ulitsa Pestelya, 812/272-7091

HOURS: Daily noon-11 P.M.

METRO: Gostiny Dvor or Chernyshevskaya

Its slogan is "the science of well-being," and this trendy restaurant certainly has your well-being in mind. All the food here is not just meat free but also low in fat and sugars, ensuring it would meet the demands of the most discerning Vedic diner. The café's interior is similarly holistic, featuring a pale-green color scheme with dark-green divans. It all adds up to an experience guaranteed to keep your karma in balance.

Kolomna to Sennaya Ploshchad   Map 10

BEER RESTAURANTS AND PUBS
DICKENS ⚫⚫⚫

108 Naberezhnaya reki Fontanki, 812/380-7998

HOURS: Sun.-Mon. 8 A.M.-1 A.M., Tues.-Thurs. 8 A.M.-2 A.M., Fri.-Sat. 8 A.M.-3 A.M.

METRO: Sennaya Ploshchad

If you're looking for an English-style pub with an excellent range of draft cask ales and good pub grub, then this is the place—although neither are particularly cheap here. Dickens can get particularly crowded on weekends or when there's a big game to watch (they broadcast games from Europe and Russia). Upstairs is an upscale restaurant with posh food and nice views over the river; there's an outdoor section in front, and even an old-fashioned red telephone booth. Make sure you try the pickled egg—it's the real deal.

SHAMROCK ⚫⚫

27 Ulitsa Dekabristov, 812/570-4625, www.shamrock.spb.ru

HOURS: Daily 9 A.M.-2 A.M.

METRO: Sadovaya

This pub is a genuine institution. It seems like it's been around forever—it opened in the early 1990s, which makes it an old-timer in this town. What it lacks in polished brass and stained glass, it makes up for with a genuine vibe that's hard to find in local pubs. Sometimes there's live Celtic music. There is a

© NATHAN TOOHEY

Sausages are a popular German-style accompaniment for beer.

good range of draft beers and even Irish stew on the menu. This pub is a great place for a nightcap after an evening at the Mariinsky Theater across the road.

RUSSIAN
THE IDIOT $$

82 Naberezhnaya reki Moyki, 812/315-1675
HOURS: Daily 11 A.M.-1 A.M.
METRO: Sadovaya

This may well be the most popular restaurant among resident foreigners in St. Petersburg. It seems they all take their visiting relatives here as a matter of course. It's not surprising really, as the atmosphere's great, the cute interior is packed with quaint antiques, and every guest is given a complimentary shot of vodka—what more could you want?

There is even a comprehensive selection of vegetarian dishes.

◖ NOBLE'S NEST $$$
Dvorianskoye Gnezdo
Дворянское Гнездо
21 Ulitsa Dekabristov, 812/312-0911, www.dvgnezdo.ru
HOURS: Daily noon-midnight
METRO: Sennaya Ploshchad

If you're too dressed up to feel comfortable at the Shamrock pub after the Mariinsky Theater, then the nearby Dvorianskoye Gnezdo, or Noble's Nest, is probably what you need—it's like dining in the Winter Palace itself. Its aristocratic interior, waitstaff in fancy costumes, and modern Russian menu served in a French style are sure to create the perfect (though expensive) ending to any night at the theater.

Vasilyevsky Island   Map 11

CAUCASUS
SHEST SHAMPUROV $
Шест Шампуров
59 Sredny Prospekt, 812/321-7907
HOURS: Daily 11 A.M.-11 P.M.
METRO: Vasileostrovskaya

The name means "six skewers," and this Azeri restaurant is all about shish kebabs, or shashliks. You don't come here for the interior, but for the amazing variety of grilled meat on skewers. If it walks, crawls, swims, or flies on this earth, this restaurant has probably stuck a skewer through it and popped it on the grill. There is lamb (all parts, including the dangly bits), turkey, beef, pork, quail, salmon, trout, sturgeon, and more—all at great prices.

EUROPEAN
BLACK AND WHITE $
25 6-ya Liniya, 812/323-3881, www.blackwhite.ru
HOURS: Daily 8:30 A.M.-1 A.M.
METRO: Vasileostrovskaya

As the name would suggest, the interior of this café is decorated with geometrical patterns, zigzags, and silhouettes, all in black and white. Located on a pleasant pedestrian street, the café has a fairly limited food menu, but does offer some nice set breakfast deals as well as lunchtime specials. The main attraction here, however, is the wide selection of coffee, including the exotic and extremely expensive kopi luwak—a bean that's hand picked, as it were, by the little Asian Palm Civet.

FRENCH
STARAYA TAMOZHNYA $$$
Старая Таможня
1 Tamozhenny Per., 812/327-8980,
www.concord-catering.ru/restaurants/old-customs/
HOURS: Daily 1 P.M.-1 A.M.
METRO: Vasileostrovskaya

The name means "the old customs house," and this veteran restaurant is styled as a historical customs office, complete with wax-like figures of customs officials by the door. The restaurant's redbrick arched ceiling encloses a richly decorated interior with numerous period paintings and other antiques. The overall effect is almost theatrical. The eatery describes itself as a "restaurant of haute cuisine," and given the list of luminaries that have dined here, it's hard to argue.

Petrograd Side Map 12

EUROPEAN
ZVER $$

Зверь

5B Aleksandrovsky Park, 812/232-2062,
www.restoranzver.spb.ru

HOURS: Daily noon–midnight

METRO: Gorkovskaya

"Nature in all its forms of preparation" is the restaurant's slogan, and it's not referring to the flora part of the natural world. Zver, or "beast," is a meat restaurant. It serves venison, elk, wild boar, bear, quail, pheasant, trout and sturgeon, as well as more run-of-the-mill options. The interior is designed to look like a hunting lodge, but on a hot summer day the lovely glassed-in veranda is more appealing, especially with its view across Aleksandrovsky Park.

FRENCH
JEAN-JACQUES ROUSSEAU $

Жан-Жак Руссо

54/2 Bolshoy Prospekt, 812/323-9981

HOURS: Sun.–Thurs. 10 A.M.–midnight, Fri.–Sat. 24 hours

METRO: Petrogradskaya

A classical French brasserie, but not in a pompous way, Jean-Jacques Rousseau has an interior painted deep red, and numerous mirrors mounted around the walls add an extra sense of space. Chalkboards display the day's specials. This is the perfect place to stop by for a glass of wine and a cheese platter. There is even a small veranda out front for an alfresco snack on a warm summer day. There is a second 24-hour branch in the center, at 10 Ulitsa Marata.

FUSION
AKVAREL $$$

Акварель

14A Dobrolyubova Prospekt, 812/320-8600,
www.aquarelspb.com

HOURS: Daily noon–last guest

METRO: Sportivnaya

The original fusion-cuisine eatery in St. Petersburg, this restaurant has a lovely setting in a custom-built three-level floating pontoon. The walls are all made of glass, providing superb views out across the water, and there's an outdoor terrace for summer dining. The food is thoroughly hip, much like the interior—a good choice when you feel like something light and modern. There's a full selection of sushi and oysters, as well as Canadian lobster either as sashimi or stewed in a cream sauce with spinach and three sauces. The soup selection includes Spanish gazpacho, French bouillabaisse, a Chinese-style won-ton soup, and a Thai soup with tiger prawns and coconut milk. For your main course, you could have Peking duck, or filet mignon with glazed shallots, date puree, and chocolate demi-glace sauce.

MOSKVA $$$

Москва

18 Petrogradskaya Naberezhnaya, 812/332-0200

HOURS: Mon.–Thurs. 10 A.M.–1 A.M., Fri. 10 A.M.–2 A.M., Sat. 11 A.M.–2 A.M., Sun. 11 A.M.–1 A.M.

METRO: Gorkovskaya

Located on the 6th floor of a business center, this trendy restaurant may be a little off the beaten track, but the trip is well compensated by the panoramic views offered from its huge windows and balcony. The interior of the restaurant's three halls is slick and minimalist, while the summer balcony is more relaxed. The restaurant describes its cuisine as "cosmopolitan," and there is a special summer menu available on the balcony with more grilled dishes, cold soups, and seasonal cocktails.

INTERNATIONAL
FLYING DUTCHMAN $$$

Letuchy Gollandets

Летучий Голландец

Mytninskaya Naberezhnaya, by the Birzhevoy Bridge, 812/336-3737, 921/921-3676, www.gollandec.ru

HOURS: Daily 10 A.M.–6 A.M.

METRO: Sportivnaya

Not one but three separate restaurants are housed inside this re-creation of an 18th-century Dutch sailing ship. Each restaurant serves a slightly different menu—choose between Russian/European, Latin American (think steaks), and Japanese. The views across the Neva River to the Hermitage are magnificent and what's more, there is even a fitness center on board for burning off those excess calories after dinner.

MORKOVKA $
Морковка

32 Bolshoy Prospekt, 812/233-9635

HOURS: Mon.-Thurs. noon-midnight, Fri.-Sun. noon-last guest

METRO: Sportivnaya or Chkalovskaya

Calling itself a "Café of Healthy Food," Morkovka, or Carrot, is a celebration of vegetables and fruit—they even give each guest a complimentary glass of carrot juice. The menu has Russian-Italian and Japanese sections, and although it's mostly vegetarian there are some fish and seafood dishes to keep the carnivores happy. The trendy, modern interior design immerses you in contrasting fruity-veggie colors, such as orange, green, and eggplant.

ITALIAN
RYBA $$
Рыба

5 Ulitsa Akademika Pavlova, 812/918-6969

HOURS: Daily noon-midnight

METRO: Petrogradskaya

The name might mean "fish," but this is no seafood restaurant. In fact, it's a modern Italian eatery. Situated on top of a shopping center (its separate entrance is located around the side of the building), the restaurant has some dramatic, if somewhat industrial, views—especially of St. Petersburg's TV tower. The pizzas

and pastas are excellent and they even prepare some Asian wok dishes for good measure. Overall, it's a relaxed yet classy restaurant.

SEAFOOD
DEMYANOVA UKHA $$
Демьянова Уха

53 Kronverksky Prospekt, 812/232-8090, 812/232-4914

HOURS: Daily noon-midnight

METRO: Gorkovskaya

Opened in 1971, this is St. Petersburg's oldest seafood restaurant. It is truly a legendary establishment, with a fisherman's log-hut interior that looks like it hasn't changed in decades. The kitchen specializes in traditional local fish (there are no meat dishes on the menu), prepared according to traditional Russian recipes, which is not as common around town as you might expect. The *ukha* fish soups and pike-perch entrées come recommended.

VEGETARIAN
TROITSKY MOST $
Троицкий мост

9/2 Kamennoostrovsky Prospekt, 812/232-6693, www.t-most.ru

HOURS: Daily 9 A.M.-11 P.M.

METRO: Gorkovskaya

The first in what has now grown to become a chain of vegetarian cafés, this spot has a light and bright atmosphere and a laid-back attitude. Numerous vegetarian snacks, salads, and other tempting treats are on display in glass cabinets and the staff will serve up however much you ask for, charging for each dish by weight, though some of the hot dishes are only prepared upon ordering. There is a decent selection of desserts as well. See the website for additional locations.

Smolny and Old Nevsky Map 13

BEER RESTAURANTS AND PUBS
FOGGY DEW $$
Фогги дью

39 Ulitsa Vosstaniya, 812/273-6263,
www.foggydewpub.ru

HOURS: Daily noon-2 A.M.

METRO: Chernyshevskaya

The original of several Irish pubs in this chain, this location is small, but that only makes it all the more cozy. The design isn't breaking any new ground, but then who demands that from an Irish pub. On the menu you'll find all the usual food you'd expect to find in an establishment of this sort, such as pork ribs, chicken wings, and fried calamari. The range of draft beers is decent, and the whiskey selection even better. See the website for additional locations.

FRENCH
BISTROT GARÇON $$$
Бистро Гарсон

95 Nevsky Prospekt, 812/717-2467, www.garcon.ru

HOURS: Daily 9 A.M.-1 A.M.

METRO: Mayakovskaya or Ploshchad Vosstaniya

Designed to re-create the feel of a turn-of-the-20th-century Parisian bistro, this French eatery has fresh newspapers hanging from racks and wine crates stacked by them. Specials are written up on a chalkboard. The award-winning restaurant flies in fresh produce from France daily and changes the menu with every season. Naturally such efforts don't come cheap, and this place isn't for the faint of wallet. Breakfast provides a chance to sample its wares (try the croissants) with out breaking the bank. Drop in after arriving on the early-morning train from Moscow—it's just down the road from the station.

INTERNATIONAL
CONGO $$
Конго

57 Ulitsa Zhukovskogo, 812/275-9954

HOURS: Daily noon-midnight

METRO: Ploshchad Vosstaniya

More an Africa-themed restaurant than an African-cuisine restaurant, Congo's design features all the ethnic elements and handicrafts befitting a restaurant with such a name. Motifs include zebras and other wild safari animals, and the stools resemble large conga drums. The menu is largely devoid of any genuine African dishes, although there is couscous and fried bananas, as well as European-style dishes that have been jazzed up with the addition of exotic fruits. It makes for a nice place to come on a gray winter day.

MAKHAON $$
Махаон

43 Suvorovsky Prospekt, 812/275-2804,
www.mahaon-cafe.ru

HOURS: Mon.-Fri. 9 A.M.-11 P.M., Sat.-Sun. 11 A.M.-11 P.M.

METRO: Ploshchad Vosstaniya

This modest café-style spot is worth dropping into if you're in the area and looking for somewhere to stop for a snack or a cup of coffee. It's named after a type of butterfly, and the upper floor is decorated with butterfly motifs on its wallpaper, while the lower level is more formal in its design. The diverse menu lists some trusty classics, such as Greek and Caesar salads, some favorite Russian soups, including fish *ukha* and meat *solyanka*, as well as a few pizza choices, and various hot dishes including pepper steak and Moroccan-style kebabs.

SEAFOOD
PORTO MALTESE $$$
174 Nevsky Prospekt, 812/271-7677,
www.portomaltese.net

HOURS: Daily noon-midnight

METRO: Ploshchad Aleksandra Nevskogo

One in a chain of Serbian seafood grill houses, this restaurant's atmosphere is relaxed and the prices reasonable, all things considered. Its main claim to fame is that it flies in its seafood twice a week, after which it is laid out on ice, displayed for customers to inspect before ordering. Once you have chosen your fish, it's whisked away to be prepared

© NATHAN TOOHEY

Shashliks, or kebabs, are ubiquitous in the summer, and best eaten outdoors.

according to your wishes—grilled, steamed, fried, and so on. There are no fixed prices for the fresh fish, rather they're sold by weight, so if you're worried ask the waiter to weigh and price the whole fish before you settle on it.

SPANISH
MADRIDSKY DVOR $$$
Мадридский двор
14 8-ya Sovetskaya Ulitsa, 812/325-6500
HOURS: Daily noon-midnight

METRO: Ploshchad Vosstaniya

Here you'll find simply the most elaborate interior of any Spanish restaurant in town, if not in all of Russia. Its four halls are carefully designed right down to the last detail. Some rooms are designed to look like an old Spanish courtyard, complete with fountains, columns, and vine-covered arches, while others resemble aristocratic studies. It's perfect for impressing dates and the food is authentic—the paella is highly recommended.

RESTAURANTS

Greater St. Petersburg

Map 14

FUSION
ZIMALETO $$$
Зималето

24 Naberezhnaya reki Bolshoy Nevki, 812/320-0860,
www.zimaletobar.ru

HOURS: Daily noon-3 A.M.

METRO: Chyornaya Rechka

A super-fashionable club/restaurant located in a park on one of the Kamennoostrovsky islands, this place focuses on outdoor merriment—in winter there's an outdoor ice skating rink, and in summer the deck chairs come out and they crank up the barbecue. The menu features a large range of cocktails, modern European cuisine, sushi, and plenty of grilled goodies in summer.

RUSSIAN
SABANTUI $
Сабантуй

20 Torzhkovskaya Ulitsa, 812/492-8678,
812/492-2048

HOURS: Daily noon-midnight

METRO: Chyornaya Rechka

This one's a true rarity, a Tartar restaurant. St. Petersburg may be a long way from Russia's Muslim republic of Tatarstan, but this restaurant does its best to re-create the feel of that exotic land. A row of cozy booths is divided by intricately woven hanging rugs, complemented by various Eastern-themed decorations. The menu features dishes such as pilafs, shish kebabs, and grilled meats.

SEAFOOD
☾ RUSSKAYA RYBALKA $$$
Русская рыбалка

11 Yuzhnaya Doroga, 812/323-9813,
www.russian-fishing.ru

HOURS: Daily noon-9 A.M.

METRO: Krestovsky Ostrov

A large wooden house perched over the banks of a picturesque pond on one of St. Petersburg's park islands, this restaurant offer a novel approach to dining. Guests are given a rod so they can fish for their dinner. After something live and flipping is reeled in, the restaurant will weigh the fish (they charge by weight), prepare it, and bring it piping hot directly to the diners. Best of all, there's a lovely outdoor veranda in summer.

NIGHTLIFE

St. Petersburg has a reputation for the biggest, loudest raves, and the smallest, coziest clubs. Although it has its fair share of posh establishments, it stays in touch with its underground roots. The live music scene is thriving—this city is the birthplace of a disproportionately large number of Russia's best bands. The bars are packed, and the dance clubs are pumping. The hottest nightlife quarter is around Konyushennaya Square, where a number of happening clubs and bars are located, including Achtung Baby, Mod Club, Bubblebar, and Arena. There's not much of a gay and lesbian scene to speak of, however. Besides the gay mega-club Central Station, there are few other obvious choices. The city's only lesbian club fizzled out in 2008.

Just like in Moscow, the lines are blurred between bars, clubs, and restaurants, with many venues impossible to pigeonhole into just one category. And as in Moscow, the scene changes quickly. Clubs come and go, closing and reinventing themselves constantly or moving to new addresses, so no listing can stay up to date for very long.

In the warmer months, when the Neva River bridges open and close throughout the night, you will see a mass exodus from nightspots just before bridge-crossing time. If you get stuck on the wrong side of the bridge, be prepared to order another drink and wait for the next chance to cross—which could be in several hours.

Smoking is allowed in most clubs and bars, and the smaller venues can get very smoky indeed. Heavy drinking is tolerated only to a

© NATHAN TOOHEY

HIGHLIGHTS

LOOK FOR **⊂** TO FIND
RECOMMENDED NIGHTLIFE.

⊂ Most Legendary: Generations of Petersburg partiers have fond memories of wild nights at **Fish Fabrique** (page 237).

⊂ Most Happening: Achtung Baby is the place to be, and it's ideally located for a night of club-hopping (page 241).

⊂ Most Underground: Housed in a Stalin-era bomb shelter, **Griboedov** is underground in every sense of the word (page 241).

⊂ Most Festive: Since New Year's is always fun, and so are weddings, **Purga** re-creates the experience every night in its side-by-side clubs (page 244).

⊂ Coolest Concept: Laundromats are few and far between in St. Pete, so come to **Stirka** to wash down a beer while washing your clothes (page 244).

certain extent: Cross the line and the doormen will probably make you leave. Remember to leave your coat in the cloakroom or *garderob* (гардероб) if there is one, otherwise hang it up on a rack: Wearing coats inside is not the done thing, and sometimes it annoys the bouncers. Cloakrooms are free, and the attendants don't expect tips (but they are unlikely to refuse them).

Live Music

A2

12 Razyezhaya Ulitsa, 812/984-3690, www.a2club.su
HOURS: Sun.-Thurs. 6 P.M.-2 A.M., Fri.-Sat. 2 P.M.-6 A.M.
COST: Free-1,000R
METRO: Vladimirskaya or Dostoyevskaya
Map 9

This popular live-music venue has a lot going for it: good sound quality, a great line-up of acts, a warm atmosphere, reasonable prices. The varied program even includes poetry evenings, as well as jazz festivals, DJ-driven electro parties, and all kinds of concerts, from rock to synth-pop and hip-hop, featuring Russian and international performers. The club section is upstairs, and downstairs is a Russian-European restaurant. The woman behind it, Svetlana Surganova, is a rock star who obviously knows a thing or two about the music scene.

BUBBLEBAR

2 Konyushennaya Ploshchad, 812/314-5072, www.bubblebar.ru
HOURS: Daily 7 P.M.-6 A.M.
COST: Depends on passing face control and dress code

METRO: Nevsky Prospekt
Map 9

This popular two-level spot on the Konyushennaya Square club cluster has a varied musical repertoire—reggae one day, disco/funk the next, electro-pop the day after. Sometimes there's live music, sometimes DJs. It's popular with alternative youngsters, who consider it the best club in town. The drinks menu has all the wine, beer, and spirits that you'd expect, as well as a lengthy list of cocktails: shooters, simple mixes, long, short, and even beer cocktails.

CHE

Че
3 Poltavskaya Ulitsa, 812/717-4715
HOURS: Daily 24 hours
COST: Free
METRO: Ploshchad Vosstaniya
Map 13

A good atmosphere and tasty food are to be found in this long-running restaurant/café and bar, decorated with roses and photographs of nude beauties. Cigars, cocktails, and a varied program of live music set the tone at night, with jazz, flamenco, and sometimes even Irish music. In the day, you're more likely to hear lounge music, and late at night—house. It's pleasant here any time of day. The breakfasts are much praised.

CHESHIRE CAT ART-CLUB
Art-klub "Cheshirsky kot"
Арт-клуб "Чеширский кот"
32 Zagorodny Prospekt, 812/575-66151,
www.catartclub.ru
HOURS: Mon.-Thurs. 1 P.M.-1 A.M., Fri.-Sun. 1 P.M.-last guest
COST: Free-250R
METRO: Vladimirskaya or Dostoyevskaya
Map 9

This art-club has a varied program, with pop and rock concerts, festivals, film screenings, performance art, exhibitions, and DJs playing minimal techno. It even has *Alice in Wonderland*–themed "crazy tea-drinking" sessions with English-language practice on Sundays, for children in the afternoon and for adults later.

◖ FISH FABRIQUE
53 Ligovsky Prospekt (Pushkinskaya 10 Arts Center),
812/764-4857, www.fishfabrique.spb.ru
HOURS: Daily 3 P.M.-6 A.M.
COST: Varies
METRO: Ploshchad Vosstaniya
Map 9

One of the city's oldest underground clubs, this legendary establishment started out in a different part of the Pushkinskaya 10 center, back in the days when the arts complex was an artists' squat. Back then it was bigger, smellier, and grungier. Now it's more respectable but retains an alternative vibe and still gets packed on weekends, and is a fun spot to go for beers and live music.

GEZ-21
ГЕЗ-21
53 Ligovsky Prospekt (Pushkinskaya 10 Arts Center),
3rd fl. of wing, 812/764-5258, www.tac.spb.ru
HOURS: Mon.-Fri. 5-11:30 P.M., Sat.-Sun. 3-11:30 P.M.,
concerts at 8 P.M.
COST: Varies
METRO: Ploshchad Vosstaniya

Map 9

This neighbor of Fish Fabrique in the Pushkinskaya 10 complex is also known as the Experimental Sound Gallery, a project of the Techno-Art-Center. Come here if you want to hear local experimental music, be it sound installations, underground electronic, noise, free jazz, minimalism, ethno, or anything else. There are occasional thematic parties, including goth nights, and on Wednesday and Friday the venue screens noncommercial films.

JAMBALA
Джамбала
80 Bolshoy Prospekt, Vasilyevsky Island (Senator business center), 812/332-1077, www.jambala.ru
HOURS: Mon.-Thurs. 11 A.M.-11 P.M., Fri. 11 A.M.-6 A.M., Sat. 3 P.M.-6 A.M., Sun. 3-11 P.M.
COST: Concerts 200R
METRO: Vasileostrovskaya
Map 11

St. Petersburg's only reggae café-club says "rastaman coziness and a summer mood" are its highest priority. It combines live concerts and DJs with screenings of concerts by famous reggae performers. Not only does it have a full menu of food, it also serves the rare Vasileostrovskaya beer on tap at a low price. There's even a store at the club, where you can buy Rastafarian-themed T-shirts, hats, badges, CDs, and other accoutrements.

MOD CLUB
Клуб Мод
2 Konyushennaya Ploshchad, 812/570-4384,
www.modclub.spb.ru
HOURS: Daily 6 P.M.-6 A.M.
COST: 200R Fri.-Sat., free other nights
METRO: Nevsky Prospekt
Map 9

With two bars, a jukebox, and live indie music most nights, this student-oriented neighbor of Achtung Baby and Bubblebar attracts a similarly young clientele. It positions itself as a venue for local acts to perform, but also hosts gigs by guest musicians, sometimes foreign.

NIGHTLIFE

BRIDGES UP! DON'T GET STUCK!

From mid-April through November, it's "navigation season" in St. Petersburg, which means that 13 of the city's more than 300 bridges rise at night to let the ships through. These include all the main bridges crossing the Neva River and linking the city center with Vasilyevsky Island and the Petrograd Side.

It's important to be aware of the bridges' timetable, not only so that you can watch the spectacle of their dramatic rising and lowering, but also so that you don't get stranded on the wrong side of the river. If you do get stuck, head toward one of the bridges that rise twice during the night, and try to enjoy yourself while waiting for the interval when they go back down to let cars and pedestrians cross, before rising again. Those opening twice include the centrally located Blagoveshchensky Most, connecting Vasilyevsky Island with Angliyskaya Naberezhnaya near the Admiralty, and Tuchkov Most, connecting Vasilyevsky Island with the Petrograd Side. The other option in an emergency is to take a taxi on the long journey to cross the river via the distant Bolshoy Obukhovsky Most, which doesn't rise, but usually it's more convenient to just wait for the interval.

During the mid-summer White Nights, when the weather is warm, you will find a festive, fun atmosphere around the bridges throughout the night. Crowds line the river banks to watch the first rising, especially near the Winter Palace and Admiralty, so get there early to get a good vantage point. There are also nighttime bridge-watching river cruises, some of which depart from the boat stations right in front of the Winter Palace (Hermitage Museum). Below is the bridges' drawing schedule, but these are subject to change, so check for updates in the local press – The St. Petersburg Times, or St. Petersburg in Your Pocket.

BRIDGES' DRAWING TIMES

- Alexandra Nevskogo: 2:20-5:10 A.M.

- Birzhevoy: 2-4:55 A.M.

- Blagoveshchensky (Leytenanta Shmidta): 1:25-2:45 A.M.; 3:10-5 A.M.

- Bolsheokhtinsky: 2-5 A.M.

- Dvortsovy (Palace): 1:25-4:55 A.M.

- Finlyandsky: 2:20-5:30 A.M.

- Grenadersky: 2:45-3:45 A.M.; 4:20-4:50 A.M.

- Kantemirovsky: 2:45-3:45 A.M.; 4:20-4:50 A.M.

- Liteyny: 1:40-4:45 A.M.

- Sampsoniyevsky: 2:10-2:45 A.M.; 3:20-4:25 A.M.

- Troitsky: 1:35-4:50 A.M.

- Tuchkov: 2-2:55 A.M.; 3:35-4:55 A.M.

- Volodarsky: 2-3:45 A.M.; 4:15-5:45 A.M.

MONEY HONEY

28 Sadovaya Ulitsa, 812/310-0549, www.money-honey.ru
HOURS: Daily 10 A.M.-5 A.M.
COST: 100-200R after 7 P.M.
METRO: Gostiny Dvor
`Map 9`

Located in Apraksin Dvor, this rockabilly club opened in 1994, making it quite a veteran player. There are two levels: a saloon bar and a large concert hall, with a Wild West theme and live music every night. Sometimes you can even catch obscure genres such as Ukrainian psychobilly performing here. The slogan is "Beer & Rock 'n' Roll," and it can get rowdy.

PORT

Порт
2 Pereulok Antonenko, 812/314-2609
HOURS: Daily 6 P.M.-6 A.M.
COST: 40-400R
METRO: Sennaya Ploshchad
`Map 10`

Back when it opened in the '90s, Port was an

elite club for electronic music, and its high-tech interior was cutting edge. Now it's more democratic, with various theme parties and some big-name live acts, both international and local. It's a huge club with numerous party zones, including several dance floors, stages, and bars, plus a chill-out space and billiards.

RED CLUB

7 Poltavskaya Ulitsa, 812/717-0000, www.clubred.ru

HOURS: daily 7 P.M.-6 A.M.
COST: 400-700R
METRO: Ploshchad Vosstaniya
Map 13

This friendly two-level, multi-hall venue has good live music and DJs as well as a range of other environments for those who just want to sit, drink, and talk. There's a concert hall, two dance floors, and three bars, with space for 800 people. It attracts a mixed crowd—and gets crowded—with lots of bohemian types and foreigners, both expats and visitors. You might have to line up to get in. As well as the most interesting Russian performers, some major international acts have taken the stage, including Zombie Nation, Dead Can Dance, David Carretta, StereoTotal, Mouse on Mars, and Tiefschwarz. The club's music policy is electro/house/tech-house.

SOCHI

Сочи

7 Kazanskaya Ulitsa, 812/312-0140

HOURS: Daily 11 A.M.-6 A.M.
COST: Free
METRO: Nevsky Prospekt
Map 9

Another creation of the people behind the legendary much-loved (but now closed) Dacha bar, this newer music venue has had mixed reviews, ranging from gushing praise to criticism of the DJ's music playlist and the conduct of the staff. In any case, you can find quite different music, different kinds of people, and a different atmosphere on different nights.

ZOCCOLO

TSOKOL

ЦОКОЛЬ

2/3 3-ya Sovetskaya Ulitsa, 812/274-9467, www.zoccolo.ru

HOURS: Sun.-Thurs. 7 P.M.-midnight, Fri.-Sat. 7 P.M.-6 A.M.
COST: From 150R
METRO: Ploshchad Vosstaniya
Map 13

The successor of the legendary (and sorely missed) Moloko, this underground club features practically every sort of independent music and all kinds of performers, from obscure grind-core acts to rising stars, and dinosaurs of the local rock scene. On weekend nights there are dance parties with DJs and electronic music. Low beer prices guarantee a good time.

NIGHTLIFE

Jazz and Blues

JAZZ PHILHARMONIC HALL

27 Zagorodny Prospekt, 812/764-8565,
www.jazz-hall.spb.ru
HOURS: Daily 8-11:30 P.M.
COST: 300-800R
METRO: Vladimirskaya or Dostoyevskaya
Map 9

Founded in 1989 by veteran local jazz star and composer David Goloshhchokin, this is a conservative concert venue for serious jazz aficionados, with a repertoire emphasizing mainstream and Dixieland. There are two halls, with the larger Jazz Philharmonic Hall seating 200 people at two- to six-person tables, where supper and beverages are served during the concerts. The smaller Ellington Hall fits 40 people and is a less formal jazz bar. Tables in both halls can be booked in advance (812/164-8565).

JFC JAZZ CLUB

33 Ulitsa Shpalernaya, 812/272-9850, www.jfc-club.spb.ru
HOURS: Daily 7-11 P.M.
COST: Varies, from 200R
METRO: Chernyshevskaya
Map 13

This cozy little club is the most popular and exciting jazz venue in town, with live music nightly across the whole spectrum: Dixieland, blues, jazz-rock, funk, acid-jazz, mainstream, avant-garde, ethno, and Latin American. Just 100 square meters in size, it seats 50–60 people; a few dozen more can squeeze in to stand. There's no food as such, just nibbles like nuts to go with your beer.

JIMI HENDRIX BLUES CLUB

33 Liteyny Prospekt, 812/579-8813
HOURS: Daily noon-midnight
COST: 200-350R
METRO: Mayakovskaya or Chernyshevskaya
Map 9

This cozy brick-walled cellar has a tiny stage where local and even American blues musicians perform. At times the music program stretches to Latin American and rock 'n' roll. Besides being a concert venue and bar, it's also a restaurant, serving much-praised American, Russian, and Georgian food. Don't be surprised if you find the place packed at night. In the daytime it's more like a café, with music clips showing on its screens.

STREET LIFE

6 2nd Krasnoarmeyskaya Ulitsa, 812/575-0545,
www.street-life.spb.ru
HOURS: Daily noon-2 A.M.
COST: Varies, from 200R
METRO: Tekhnologichesky Institut
Map 10

Positioning itself as an art-restaurant, this place has a 70-seat concert hall that tries to capture the spirit and style of 1930s America, the age of jazz and swing. The spacious interior has high ceilings, and a big screen to make sure everybody can see the action on stage during the live concerts. Adjoining the concert hall is the European Terrace restaurant, with a musical-themed menu and wireless Internet.

Dance Clubs

▐ ACHTUNG BABY

2 Konyushennaya Ploshchad, www.achtungbaby.ru

HOURS: Daily 5 P.M.-6 A.M.

COST: Free-500R

METRO: Nevsky Prospekt

Map 9

One of the most popular nightspots in town, this two-hall high-ceilinged DJ bar attracts a young mixed crowd. A peaceful watering hole until 10 p.m., it heats up later when the patrons get sweaty to the sounds of pop-rock, dance rock, electro rock, electroclash, post-punk, new rave, new retro, disco, and funk. There's live music a couple of times a month, and sometimes football (soccer) matches are shown on the big screens. In summer there's a beach-bar called Dyuny (Dunes) in the courtyard, with sand to lounge about on. The location, right in the middle of the city's main nightlife hub, makes for good club-hopping. Prices are reasonable.

ARENA

Арена

2 Konyushennaya Ploshchad, 812/955-5559, www.arenaproject.ru

HOURS: Sat. midnight-6 A.M.

COST: Depends on passing face control and dress code

METRO: Nevsky Prospekt

Map 9

If you're looking for glamour, this is the place for you. Big-name international DJs play in this chic club, which is renowned as the place that attracts the city's most suntanned young ladies on the highest stiletto heels with the most successful-looking men on their arms. It has won awards as the city's best club. It started out as Arena, then closed and reopened as the even-trendier Arena-2, then once again was reborn with even more glitz as Arena-3—who knows how many more times it will reinvent itself.

DECADANCE

Декаданс

17 Shcherbakov Pereulok, 812/947-7070

HOURS: Wed.-Thurs. 6 P.M.-1 A.M., Fri.-Sat. 6 P.M.-6 A.M.

COST: Depends on passing face control, free-500R

METRO: Dostoyevskaya

Map 9

Much hype surrounds this expensive club-restaurant, which is considered the city's main "scene." Decorated with golden ceilings and a crystal bar, it oozes glamour, and is unashamedly elitist. The face control can be tough, even humiliating—only the famous can be confident they'll be allowed beyond the red velvet curtain at the entrance—but still it somehow gets quite crowded inside. Some consider the Thursday dance parties to be the best.

▐ GRIBOEDOV

Грибоедов

2A Voronezhskaya Ulitsa, 812/764-4355, www.griboedovclub.ru

HOURS: Club: daily 9 P.M.-6 A.M.; Griboedov Hill café: daily noon-6 A.M.

COST: Club: free-400R; café: free noon-8 P.M., with Griboedov tickets or club cards after 8 P.M.

METRO: Ligovsky Prospekt

Map 14

For a decade this club, located in a Stalinist bomb shelter, has managed to maintain its mojo, and it has now come up from underground by adding an above-ground café, Griboedov Hill. Founded by musicians from the group Dva Samoylota, it has an artsy interior, an interesting clientele, and an always-cool vibe. The underground section includes a bar, cushioned chill-out room, and a dance floor where DJs and live bands keep things moving. Upstairs in the café, there's free wireless Internet.

KONYUSHENNY DVOR—MARSTALL

Конюшенный двор—Marstall

5 Naberezhnaya kanala Griboyedova, 812/315-7607, www.kondvor.ru

HOURS: Mon.-Fri. 1 P.M.-6 A.M., Sat.-Sun. 4 P.M.-6 A.M.

COST: Free with foreign passport, or up to 400R

METRO: Nevsky Prospekt

Map 9

A veteran on the scene—it's been dancing for

more than a decade—this isn't really what you'd normally call a strip club, but after 11 p.m. (when it's only open to over-21s), it has creative costumed, erotic strip-dance shows, and topless dancers performing on elevated platforms. There are two levels, and the music program ranges from new music to retro. Free entry for foreign passport-holders makes it an attractive hangout for expats and tourists, especially men hoping to meet local ladies. That seems to suit the ladies who come here hoping to hook a man.

LËDLIMON

6 Naberezhnaya kanala Griboyedova, 812/438-1450, www.ledlimon.ru
HOURS: Wed.-Sat. 10 P.M.-6 A.M.
COST: 500R
METRO: Nevsky Prospekt
Map 9

This trendy, commercial club has a summer terrace, a rotating bar, a music program that includes R&B and retro, plus "sexy 'n' funky" nights, cocktail parties, matchmaking games, and karaoke. Locals describe the face-control policy as democratic, and from Sunday to Thursday there's half-price entry for those with a student ID. It's a good choice for those who don't fancy the over-the-top glamour and elitism of some of the other dance clubs around town.

REVOLUTION

28-30 Sadovaya Ulitsa, Apraksin Dvor, korpus 1, 812/571-2391

HOURS: Daily 7 P.M.-6 A.M.
COST: 150-250R
METRO: Sadovaya or Sennaya Ploshchad
Map 9

Occupying six levels, this popular dance club is one of the largest in St. Petersburg. There's a restaurant and four bars, a lounge with a DVD hall, and panoramic views over the city from the top level. DJs spin at parties with a different theme every evening, and there are live concerts on Friday and Saturday night, ranging from rock to electronic music. Come on a Thursday if you want to find it less crowded.

TSYPA

Цыпа
4 Kolomenskaya Ulitsa, 812/764-3678, www.chickybar.ru
HOURS: Fri.-Sat. 10 P.M.-8 A.M.
COST: Free if you pass face control
METRO: Dostoyevskaya/Vladimirskaya
Map 9

Not only hard to find, but also hard to get into, Tsypa has no sign on the street, just a heavy curtain—behind which stands a guard who decides who to let in. Don't be surprised if he asks you some questions or searches your bag. Inside it's very loud—too loud to talk. There are two rooms, neither with any tables; one has a bar that guests have been known to dance on, and the other has some divans along the wall. Tsypa, by the way, means "chicky."

Bars

BEER EXCHANGE
Pivnaya Birzha
Пивная Биржа

25/3 Naberezhnaya kanala Griboyedova, 812/571-5659
HOURS: Daily noon-last guest
METRO: Gostiny Dvor or Nevsky Prospekt
Map 9

This centrally located beer bar calls itself an exchange for a reason: The prices of its brews rise or fall depending on demand—you can even watch the price fluctuate on special display boards, like at a stock exchange. There are about 10 different beers to choose from, as well as German-style food, which is what people in Russia tend to think goes best with beer. There are two halls with seating for 80, and some big screens that usually show sports or music clips.

DERZHIS
Держись

56 Ulitsa Mayakovskogo, 812/272-0970,
www.derzhis.ru
HOURS: Daily 4 P.M.-2 A.M.
METRO: Chernyshevskogo
Map 13

Come here for cocktails—this bar has hundreds to choose from, all divided into separate categories to help you narrow down your choice: classic, strong, exotic, dessert, shots, and "extreme." For extra fun, the bar hosts thematic parties. Considered an ideal spot for a girls' night out, its name translates as "Hold up!"—probably because that's what your friends will be saying to you after you've had a few of the barman's "extreme" concoctions.

HIGHLAND WHISKY BAR
Visky-Bar "Khaylend"
Виски-бар "Хайленд"

20 Gagarinskaya Ulitsa, 812/272-4990,
www.whisky-bar.spb.ru
HOURS: Bar: daily 2 P.M.-last guest; coffee shop: daily 11 A.M.-11 P.M.
METRO: Chernyshevskaya or Nevsky Prospekt
Map 9

This cute little spot is a two-in-one experience.

Enter and go to the left, and you'll find a light, bright café with a modern but cozy interior. Go to the right, and you enter another world—a dark and sometimes smoky whisky bar that feels like it has been transported here from somewhere in the British Isles. The menu lists more than 100 different types of whisky (or whiskey) from three countries, right across the price spectrum, as well as Scottish food and cigars. They say they'll give you a whisky shot for free if you show up in a kilt.

MOLLIE'S

36 Ulitsa Rubinshteyna, 812/570-3768, www.mollies.ru
HOURS: Mon.-Thurs. noon-2 A.M.,
Fri.-Sat. noon-3 A.M., Sun. noon-1 A.M.
METRO: Dostoyevskaya or Vladimirskaya
Map 9

Mollie's opened in 1994, and claims to be St. Petersburg's oldest Irish pub. Located in an old house on a historic street, it has a comfy, worn-in feel. The interior is authentically pub-like, with simple wooden furniture, beer paraphernalia, Irish souvenirs, and photos of happy drinkers. There's a good range of draft beer, and a mix of Russian and Irish food on the menu. Being a popular spot, it gets loud and smoky. The clientele is a mixture of young and old Russians, expats, and tourists.

PIVNAYA 0.5
Пивная 0.5

44/2 Zagorodny Prospekt (enter from Zvenigorodskaya Ulitsa), 812/315-1038, www.piv05.ru
HOURS: Daily 11 A.M.-2 A.M.
METRO: Pushkinskaya
Map 9

With high ceilings and a warm copper-toned industrial-style interior, this is a modern beer bar with a nostalgic retro-Soviet touch. There's booth seating, and brown leather divans that stretch along the sweeping windows that span its facade, so you can either gaze out onto the street or watch the cinema classics showing on the big screens around the hall. Two smaller

POWERFUL PORTER

Russia, of course, is best known for its vodka, and few would associate the country with beer, but there is one beer that is truly Russian – the porter stout. Originally brewed in England on special order for the Russian royal court, the imperial stout is a dark and strong style of beer, quite different from any other, even its close relative, the Irish stout. Russia eventually started to produce its own version, and this style of beer is now generally referred to as the "Baltic stout." The most widely available porter is the Baltika Brewery's No. 6 Porter. The well-respected beer critic Michael Jackson described it as having a "woody aroma, with oily, creamy, fudgy, toffeeish, juicy flavors." Besides being slightly sweet and the color of ebony, it is also a strong beer with seven percent alcohol content, so you'll want to treat this one with some respect.

rooms have karaoke. Pivnaya is Russian for beer-drinking establishment, and 0.5 refers to the standard half-liter mug size. In addition to some international beers, there's a locally brewed house beer that's well worth trying. The food selection is specially chosen for its beer compatibility and includes specialty sausages.

☾ PURGA
Пурга
11 Naberezhnaya reki Fontanki, Purga-1 812/570-5123, Purga-2 812/571-2310, www.purga-club.ru
HOURS: Purga-1: daily 4 P.M.-6 A.M.; Purga-2: Wed.-Sun. 8 P.M.-last guest
COST: 100R after 8 P.M. Sun.-Thurs., 200R after 8 P.M. Fri.-Sat.
METRO: Mayakovskaya
Map 9

The two Purga bars, situated side-by-side on the Fontanka embankment, are among the most fun spots to spend an evening in St. Petersburg. In **Purga-1**, it's New Year's Eve every night, with broadcasts of past addresses by Russian and Soviet leaders on the television, countdown to midnight, champagne toasts, and much revelry; next door in **Purga-2**, people dress up as brides and grooms to celebrate fake weddings. The waitstaff dance about dressed as rabbits—that's how silly things get. In both bars you can book a table for a flat fee that is deducted from your bill at the end of the night—500R per table Sunday–Thursday and from 1,000R on Friday and Saturday; those who book don't pay the entry fee.

☾ STIRKA
Стирка
26 Kazanskaya Ulitsa, 812/314-5371, www.40gradusov.ru
HOURS: Mon.-Fri. 9 A.M.-11 P.M., Sat.-Sun. 10 A.M.-1 A.M. or later
METRO: Nevsky Prospekt or Sennaya Ploshchad
Map 10

Stirka means "wash," as in "laundry," and it's no gimmick. At this cozy café-bar you can do your laundry, sip a coffee or a beer, listen to DJs, poetry, or occasional live performances, and look at art exhibits. The place was actually opened by a German photographer as her Art & Design School graduation project. There's free wireless Internet 10 a.m.–4 p.m.

SVYATYE UGODNIKI
Святые угодники
6 Bankovsky Pereulok, 812/312-9126
HOURS: Daily 8 P.M.-6 A.M.
METRO: Gostiny Dvor
Map 9

Just like the popular Griboedov Club, this new spot is a project of members of the music group Dva Samolyotov. It is a successor to another of their clubs, Fidel, which closed in 2008 together with its neighbors, including Dacha, due to reconstruction of their building. The new bar has former Fidel DJs playing varied and unpretentious music, from Russian pop to international hits by the likes of Depeche Mode. The tiled interior features big screens showing 1970s movies, and the toilet has made waves with its two-way mirror walls.

TRIBUNAL BAR
Бар "Трибунал"
26 Karavannaya Ulitsa, 812/314-2423
HOURS: Daily 4 P.M.–6 A.M.
METRO: Gostiny Dvor
Map 9

Having moved from a long-term location near the Bronze Horseman, Tribunal has set up new digs right downtown. It has always positioned itself as "international," and remains popular with locals and foreigners alike. The menu seeks to please the foreign palate with such familiar foods as chicken wings, steaks, pasta, and pizza. But you can also just come for beer, aperitifs, absinthe, digestifs, cocktails, or wine, and watch the go-go girls dancing to pop, rock, and mainstream music.

Gay and Lesbian

CENTRAL STATION
Tsentralnaya Stantsia
Центральная станция
1/28 Ulitsa Lomonosova, 812/312-3600,
www.centralstation.ru
HOURS: Restaurant-bar: daily 11 A.M.–10 P.M.; club: daily 11 P.M.–6 A.M.
COST: Free until 11 P.M., after 11 P.M. varies depending on day and program, free–300R for men, 150–1,000R for women
METRO: Nevsky Prospekt
Map 9

The city's main gay men's club—where about a third of the clientele is said to be foreign—has three floors with seven bars, two stages, three dance floors, and lots of dark corners with cozy sofas, as well as a Japanese-European restaurant. For entertainment, there are DJs, dancers, drag shows, video art, and surprise performances. There's even a "crazy menu," from which you can order private dances and other delights. Not every floor is open all the time, but the club's Internet site reassures that "the dark staircase and men's bar are always open." From Thursday to Sunday, the club's shop is open, selling club souvenirs, gay souvenirs, and things to help you have a fun night. Besides sushi, pasta, and steaks, the restaurant section has free wireless Internet.

ARTS AND LEISURE

While Moscow feels more about money, St. Petersburg has more of an air of arts and culture. Instead of billionaire businessmen in flash automobiles, here you're more likely to see lithe ballerinas on the bus, and bohemian types walking about with musical instruments. The city's artsy nature is palpable and ingrained—going to a gallery, the ballet, or a symphony is a part of life.

Befittingly for a city that prides itself as Russia's cultural capital, St. Petersburg has world-class arts of every kind. Besides the Hermitage, which is an absolute must-see and covered in the *Sights* chapter, St. Petersburg has a number of other excellent museums, notably the Russian Museum, a solid competitor to Moscow's Tretyakov, with the world's largest collection of Russian fine art. Likewise, St. Petersburg's Mariinsky Theater is internationally recognized as one of the world's greatest, with a brilliant ballet that keeps Moscow's Bolshoi on its toes. And given the number of great artists and writers to have lived in the northern capital, there are countless fascinating memorial apartment museums where you can sense the spirit of a legend. The underground arts scene has also thrived in the northern capital, with the Pushkinskaya 10 complex being an epicenter of activity. And in every season, there are arts festivals promising Russian and foreign guest performers of the highest level.

St. Petersburg also offers ample opportunities for sports and recreation, with some elegantly landscaped parks where you can ski, skate, and row. Spectator sports are also thriving, especially since Zenit's recent successes in football (soccer). What could be more exciting than being in the thick of home-team fans roaring at the victory of the local football or hockey team? Now that's something sure to set your pulse racing.

© NATHAN TOOHEY

HIGHLIGHTS

LOOK FOR  TO FIND
RECOMMENDED ARTS AND ACTIVITIES.

◖ Strangest Collection: Some might call it weird, but for Peter the Great the **Kunstkamera** collection of abnormal bodies and body parts was all in the name of enlightenment (page 249).

◖ Most Amazing Gallery: The **Russian Museum** has the world's largest collection of Russian fine art and, along with the Hermitage, is an essential cultural component of any tourist itinerary (page 251).

◖ Best Ballet: The **Mariinsky Theater** is one of the few that can compete with Moscow's

Bolshoi – in fact, some say it's the better of the two (page 253).

◖ Finest Festival: Summer is generally a dead time for the arts, but the **Stars of the White Nights International Arts Festival** is an exception to the rule, providing a cultural climax in peak tourist season (page 255).

◖ Most Idyllic Island: In sunshine or in snow, **Yelagin Island** offers unbeatable outdoor fun – from rowing on its ponds and strolling under its trees in the summer to sledding and skating in the winter (page 256).

the Russian Museum's Mikhailovsky Palace

© NATHAN TOOHEY

The Arts

GALLERIES AND EXHIBITION HALLS

MANÈGE CENTRAL EXHIBITION HALL

Центральный выставочный зал "Манеж"

1 Isaakiyevskaya Ploshchad, 812/314-5959,
www.manege.spb.ru

HOURS: Fri.-Wed. 11 A.M.-7 P.M.

COST: Varies

METRO: Nevsky Prospekt

Map 10

Architect Giacomo Quarenghi's classical-style indoor equestrian arena, or manège, built 1804–1807, became the city's Central Exhibition Hall after restoration in the 1970s. The architectural landmark on St. Isaac's Square has an area of 4,380 square meters, providing plenty of space for the many art exhibitions, festivals, retrospectives, concerts, and presentations that it hosts.

PUSHKINSKAYA 10 ART CENTER

Art-tsentr "Pushkinskaya 10"

Арт-Центр "Пушкинская-10"

10 Pushkinskaya Ulitsa (enter through archway at 53 Ligovsky Prospekt), 812/764-5371,
www.p10.nonmuseum.ru

HOURS: Wed.-Sun. 3-7 P.M.

COST: Free

METRO: Ploshchad Vosstaniya

Map 9

The Museum of Non-Conformist Art—the first of its kind in Russia, exhibiting little-known, unofficial art of the second half of the 20th century—is just one of several galleries and museums in this alternative arts center. Its origins date back to 1989, when a group of independent artists and musicians occupied the then-condemned building. The squat thrived, acquiring cult status and eventually international fame; it has since been renovated, and the artists have registered as a non-governmental non-profit organization, the Free Culture Society. Besides galleries and museums, their center now also includes concert venues, clubs, and the studios of about 40 artists.

STATE PHOTOGRAPHY CENTER ROSFOTO

Gosudarstvenny tsentr fotografii Rosfoto

Государственный центр фотографии Росфото

35 Bolshaya Morskaya Ulitsa, 812/314-1214,
www.rosfoto.org

HOURS: Daily 11 A.M.-7 P.M.

COST: 100R, free for foreign students with student ID

METRO: Nevsky Prospekt

Map 9

Founded by the Culture Ministry in 2002, the State Photography Center is engaged in exhibitions, education, and research. Its exhibits feature Russian and foreign photographers, both well known and up-and-coming, as well as video art, animation, and experimental cinema. It also displays historical photographs and photographic installations.

MUSEUMS

ANNA AKHMATOVA MUSEUM AT THE FOUNTAIN HOUSE

Muzey Anny Akhmatovoy v Fontannom Dome

Музей Анны Ахматовой в Фонтанном Доме

34 Naberezhnaya reki Fontanki (enter through archway at 53 Liteyny Prospekt), 812/579-7239,
www.akhmatova.spb.ru

HOURS: Tues.-Sun. 10:30 A.M.-6:30 P.M.

COST: Russians 20-50R, foreigners 200R, photo permit 100R, video permit 200R

METRO: Mayakovskaya

Map 9

Poet Anna Akhmatova lived 30 years at this address, in the home of her common-law husband, the art scholar and writer Nikolay Punin. The apartment, in the southern wing of the baroque Sheremetyevsky Palace, was turned into a museum in 1989, the 100th anniversary of her birth. It gives a fascinating picture of how the couple lived in the 1920s–1940s, with photographs, personal belongings, and lots of books.

DOSTOYEVSKY LITERARY-MEMORIAL MUSEUM
Literaturno-memorialny muzey F.M. Dostoyevskogo
Литературно-мемориальный музей Ф.М. Достоевского
5/2 Kuznechny Pereulok, 812/571-4031, www.md.spb.ru
HOURS: Tues.-Sun. 11 A.M.-6 P.M.
COST: Russians 20-50R, foreigners 60-120R
METRO: Vladimirskaya
Map 9

The writer Fyodor Dostoyevsky lived at this address with his family from October 1878 until his death in January 1881. Here, in apartment 10, he wrote *Brothers Karamazov* and his Pushkin Speech. A museum was created in the great writer's former home in 1971, after it was restored and fitted out according to archival records and the recollections of his contemporaries. Not only can you see an abundance of memorabilia relating to his life and work, you can also soak up the Dostoyevskian atmosphere of the surrounding neighborhood, where the action in many of his works takes place.

ETHNOGRAPHY MUSEUM
Rossiysky etnografichesky muzey
Российский этнографический музей
4/1 Inzhenernaya Ulitsa, 812/570-5662, www.ethnomuseum.ru
HOURS: Tues.-Sun. 10 A.M.-6 P.M., closed last Fri. of month
COST: Russians 10-70R, foreigners 30-300R; guided tours in English 1,000R per group
METRO: Nevsky Prospekt
Map 9

Receive a broad picture of the traditional way of life of more than 150 peoples of Russia and the former Soviet Union from the 18th to 20th century at this fascinating museum—one of the world's largest—which was founded as part of the Russian Museum in 1895. Now independent, it has a collection of more than half a million objects, including costumes, jewelry, weapons, drums, pipes, toys, carpets, embroidery, and domestic items. Topics include Russian Wedding, Shamanism and the Peoples of Siberia and the Far East, Sea Hunters, and The Feast in Georgian Culture, among many others.

HISTORY OF RELIGION MUSEUM
Музей истории религии
14/5 Pochtamskaya Ulitsa, 812/571-0495, www.relig-museum.ru
HOURS: Thurs.-Tues. 11 A.M.-6 P.M.
COST: Adults 120R, students 50R, children 35R, seniors 30R
METRO: Sennaya Ploshchad or Sadovaya
Map 10

The History of Religion Museum—founded in the Kazan Cathedral in 1932 and notoriously renamed the Museum of Religion and Atheism in 1954—was born again with a return to its old name in 1990 and a new address in 2000. Any Soviet-era anti-religious propaganda mission is gone; instead, what you find here are exhibits illustrating the diversity and unity of human spirituality all over the world, from antiquity to the present. The collection of some 200,000 items includes archaeological finds from as early as the 6th millennium B.C.

KUNSTKAMERA
Кунсткамера
3 Universitetskaya Naberezhnaya (enter from Tamozhenny Pereulok), 812/328-0812, www.kunstkamera.ru
HOURS: Tues.-Sun. 11 A.M.-7 P.M., closed last Tues. of month
COST: Russians 50-100R, foreigners 100-200R, amateur photo or video permit 50R
METRO: Vasileostrovskaya
Map 11

This place is a real eye-opener, but its most interesting parts are not for the squeamish. Founded by Peter the Great himself, it opened in 1714 and includes the tsar's anatomical collection—human and animal bodies, body parts and fetuses preserved in alcohol and displayed in glass jars, with a particularly strong emphasis on abnormalities. It's quite surreal to see families with small children and young couples on romantic dates gazing at conjoined twins and two-faced babies. But this place is more than just a freak show—it contains more than a million

LET PETER SHOW YOU ST. PETERSBURG

An unbeatable way to explore the city is with **Peter's Walking Tours** (812/943-1229, www.peterswalk.com). An actual Petersburger named Peter started his unconventional, off-the-beaten-track tours back in 1996, and they proved to be a real hit. Now Peter has a whole team of guides and more than a dozen English-language tours to choose from. They include several different kinds of pub crawls, even one with a Dostoyevsky theme, in addition to the regular Dostoyevsky Walk. There's also a Big Night Out Tour, a Food Tour, a Slum Walk, a Rasputin Walk, a Communist Legacy Tour, a Bike Tour, and day trips to Kronshtadt and the palace estates, among others. Some require advance booking, but most do not. To see the full schedule, prices, and meeting places, take a look at Peter's website.

artifacts of many different cultures of the world. The Kunstkamera, more fully known as the Academy of Science's Peter the Great Museum of Anthropology and Ethnography, is Russia's oldest museum. It has been in its current Petrine Baroque building on the Neva since 1727.

MARBLE PALACE
Mramorny dvorets
Мрарморный дворец
5/1 Millionaya Ulitsa, 812/595-4248, www.rusmuseum.ru
HOURS: Wed.-Sun. 10 A.M.-5 P.M.,
Mon. and holiday eves 10 A.M.-4 P.M.
COST: Russians 30-100R, foreigners 150-300R; combined ticket with entrance to Mikhailovsky Palace, Stroganov Palace, and Engineer's Castle: Russians 100-300R, foreigners 300-600R; amateur photo permit 100R
METRO: Nevsky Prospekt
Map 9

This gallery is a branch of the Russian Museum, housed in an opulent 18th-century Neoclassical palace built for one of Catherine the Great's favorites, Grigory Orlov. Architect Antonio Rinaldi's monumental design employs different kinds of marble and granite both on the facade and interior, hence the name. In the courtyard is a rather pompous equestrian statue of Alexander III. In addition to some interesting temporary exhibits of contemporary Russian and foreign artists, the gallery has permanent exhibitions of foreign artists in Russia in the 18th–19th centuries and, most interestingly, the Peter Ludwig collection of 20th-century art.

MILITARY-HISTORICAL MUSEUM OF ARTILLERY, ENGINEERING AND COMMUNICATIONS FORCES
Voyenno-istorichesky muzey artillerii, inzhenernykh voysk i voysk svyazi
Военно-исторический музей артиллерии, инженерных войск и войск связи
7 Alexandrovsky Park, 812/232-0296, www.artillery-museum.ru
HOURS: Wed.-Sun. 11 A.M.-6 P.M., closed last Thurs. of month
COST: Russians 20-50R, photo permit 20R, video permit 50R; foreigners 150-200R, photo permit 50R, video permit 100R
METRO: Gorkovskaya
Map 12

Across the canal from the Peter and Paul Fortress is one of the world's largest military museums, founded in the old Arsenal in the 18th century. There's an open-air exhibit of missile-launchers, artillery, and other weaponry, and much more inside—in total, some 750,000 items from the Middle Ages to the present. Besides weapons, there are uniforms, banners, equipment, and historical relics, including armor worn by False Dmitry I.

NABOKOV MUSEUM
Muzey V.V. Nabokov
Музей В.В. Набоков
47 Bolshaya Morskaya Ulitsa, 812/315-4713, www.nabokovmuseum.org
HOURS: Tues.-Fri. 11 A.M.-6 P.M., Sat.-Sun. noon-5 P.M.
COST: Russians 40R, foreign students 20R, other foreigners 100R, photo permit 100R, video permit 200R

METRO: Gostiny Dvor or Sadovaya
Map 10

The author of *Lolita* was born and grew up in this beautiful house near St. Isaac's Square, living here until the age of 18, when he and his family emigrated soon after the 1917 Revolution. Now a museum, it displays personal belongings and photographs of the Nabokov family—highlights include Vladimir Nabokov's butterfly collection, his boots and coat, his writings, his pens, and his autographed Scrabble game.

PUSHKIN APARTMENT MUSEUM
Memorialny muzey-kvartira A.S. Pushkina
Мемориальный музей-квартира
А.С.Пушкина
12 Naberezhnaya reki Moyki, 812/571-3531,
www.museumpushkin.ru
HOURS: Wed.-Mon. 10:30 A.M.-6 P.M.,
closed last Fri. of month
COST: Russians 20-80R, foreigners 80-200R; free
Feb. 10 and June 6
METRO: Nevsky Prospekt
Map 9

This is the former home of Russia's favorite poet, Alexander Pushkin. Fatally wounded after a duel, this is where he tragically died in 1837. Authentically furnished interiors re-create how it looked in his time, with many personal belongings of Pushkin and his beautiful wife, for whom he dueled. Morbid parts of the collection include his death mask, the waistcoat he wore to the duel, and a lock of his hair, cut after his death on request of the writer Turgenev.

◖ RUSSIAN MUSEUM
Russky muzey
Русский музей
4 Inzhenernaya Ulitsa, 812/595-4248,
www.rusmuseum.ru
HOURS: Wed.-Sun. 10 A.M.-5 P.M.,
Mon. and holiday eves 10 A.M.-4 P.M.
COST: Russians 30-150R, foreigners 150-350R;
combined ticket with entrance to Marble Palace,
Stroganov Palace, and Engineer's Castle: Russians
100-300R, foreigners 300-600R; amateur photo
permit 100R

METRO: Nevsky Prospekt
Map 9

The world's largest collection of Russian fine art—some 400,000 works covering every form and genre from the 10th century to the present—is kept in several palatial buildings of the Russian Museum. Opened in 1898, the Russian Museum was the country's first state museum of Russian fine art. It was established in one of the city's main architectural landmarks, the Mikhailovsky Palace, built 1819–1825 by leading architect Carlo Rossi for Grand Duke Mikhail Pavlovich, son of Paul I. The **Mikhailovsky Palace,** together with its **Benois Wing** extension, comprises the main complex of the museum; other parts are in the Marble Palace, Stroganov Palace, and Engineer's Castle. The Benois Wing is especially popular for its collection of early 20th-century Russian art—Kandinsky, Malevich, and Filonov, among others—and can be entered either via the Mikhailovsky Palace or its own entrance (2 Canal Griboyedova). The Russian Museum's central information desk is in the Mikhailovsky Palace's ticket hall, where you can find floor plans to help you find your way around.

STATE MUSEUM OF THE POLITICAL HISTORY OF RUSSIA
Gosurdarstvenny muzey politicheskoy
istorii Rossii
Государственный музей политической
истории России
2/4 Ulitsa Kuibysheva, 812/449-2833,
www.polithistory.ru
HOURS: Fri.-Wed. 10 A.M.-6 P.M.
COST: Russians 20-60R, foreigners 100-200R,
photo permit 100R
METRO: Gorkovskaya
Map 12

This is the place to come for a dose of Soviet memorabilia, such as posters, banners, and kitschy Communist crockery—you can even see Lenin's actual office, preserved as it was when he was based here after the Bolsheviks seized the building in 1917. But that's not all—the museum's amazing collection spans

ARTS AND LEISURE

political history from the 18th century to the present. The successor to the Museum of the Revolution founded in 1919, it contains about 500,000 items. The beautiful art nouveau palace was built 1904–1906 for the Mariinsky Theater's prima ballerina Matilda Kshesinskaya, the mistress of Nicholas II before he became tsar.

STROGANOV PALACE
Stroganovsky dvorets
Строгановский дворец

17 Nevsky Prospekt, 812/571-8238, www.rusmuseum.ru
HOURS: Wed.-Sun. 10 A.M.-5 P.M.,
Mon. and holiday eves 10 A.M.-4 P.M.
COST: Russians 30-100R, foreigners 150-300R; combined ticket with entrance to Mikhailovsky Palace, Marble Palace, and Engineer's Castle: Russians 100-300R, foreigners 300-600R; amateur photo permit 100R
METRO: Nevsky Prospekt
Map 9

This baroque palace, built 1753–1756 by architect Francesco Bartolomeo Rastrelli for the Stroganov family, is now part of the Russian Museum. Besides the newly restored interiors—including the only remaining interior design by Rastrelli, a grand ballroom with the "Hero's Triumph" ceiling painting by Italian Giuseppe Valeriani—you can admire the Stroganov family's collections, including icons and minerals, as well as porcelain and other works from the Russian Museum collections.

ZOOLOGY MUSEUM OF THE RUSSIAN ACADEMY OF SCIENCES
Zoologichesky muzey RAN
Зоологический музей РАН

1 Universitetskaya Naberezhnaya, 812/328-0112, www.zin.ru
HOURS: Wed.-Mon. 11 A.M.-6 P.M., admission until 5 P.M., open daily during school breaks, closed public holidays
COST: Adults 150R, students 50R, children under school age free
METRO: Vasileostrovskaya or Sportivnaya
Map 11

See Peter the Great's horse, stuffed and preserved for posterity, as well as other stuffed beasts including a mammoth, at this enormous zoological museum—one of the world's largest of its kind—founded in 1832 and based upon the Kustkamera's original zoological collection. Some 40,000 animals are on display. There are skeletons—such as that of the world's largest blue whale at 27 meters, and of even the tiniest insects, worms, and parasites—plus educational dioramas.

CONCERT VENUES
ACADEMIC CAPELLA
Akademicheskaya Kapella Sankt-Peterburga
Академическая Капелла
Санкт-Петербурга

20 Naberezhnaya reki Moyki, 812/314-1048, www.glinka-capella.ru
METRO: Gostiny Dvor
Map 9

Russia's oldest professional musical institution, the St. Petersburg Capella traces its illustrious history back to a 15th-century choir and an 18th-century music school. Many great names are associated with it, either as students or teachers—among them are Rimsky-Korsakov and Glinka. The Capella's acclaimed symphony orchestra and choir now perform music of different ages and styles in the palatial old concert hall of the Imperial Court Capella, located not far from the Hermitage.

SHOSTAKOVICH PHILHARMONIA
Filarmonia imeni D.D. Shostakovich
Филармония имени Д.Д. Шостакович

Grand Hall: 2 Mikhailovskaya Ulitsa, 812/312-9871;
Small Hall: 30 Nevsky Prospekt, 812/312-4585;
www.philharmonia.spb.ru,
www.saintpetersburgphilharmonic.com
METRO: Nevsky Prospekt
Map 9

St. Petersburg's Philharmonia has more than 200 years of history behind it—and numerous history-making premieres in its Grand Hall, including Beethoven's Missa Solemnis in 1824 and Shostakovich's First Symphony in 1926. The prestigious 1,500-seat Grand Hall, built in 1839 and renowned for its superb acoustics, has seen performances by many great musicians, such as Lizst, Berlioz, Wagner, and Stravinsky. In 1949 the Small Hall opened for chamber music concerts. The Philharmonia is considered the city's top concert hall and continues to present world-class performances by its two resident orchestras and international guests.

BALLET AND OPERA

C MARIINSKY THEATER

Mariinsky teatr

Мариинский театр

1 Teatralnaya Ploshchad, 812/326-4141,

www.mariinsky.ru

METRO: Sadovaya or Sennaya Ploshchad

Map 10

This illustrious ballet and opera theater opened in 1860 and has seen such major world premieres as Tchaikovsky's Queen of Spades and Khachaturian's Spartacus. It continues to stay at the top of its game, led by artistic and general director Valery Gergiev. The Mariinsky's opera and ballet companies trace their origins back to the 18th century and are still known internationally by their old Soviet name, the Kirov. The ballet company—one of the world's greatest—launched the careers of such stars as Anna Pavlova, Rudolf Nureyev, and Mikhail Baryshnikov.

MIKHAILOVSKY THEATER

Mikhaylovsky teatr

Михайловский театр

1 Ploshchad Iskusstv, 812/595-4305,

www.mikhailovsky.ru

METRO: Nevsky Prospekt

Map 9

Although outshone by the Mariinsky, St. Pete's other opera and ballet theater has a proud and glorious history of its own, boasting such highlights as Johann Strauss conducting several times. One of Russia's oldest opera and ballet stages, it opened in 1833 and was a closed club for the elite until the 1917 Revolution. Having been renamed the Mussorgsky Theater in 1989, it recently returned to its old name and offers a similar repertoire to the Mariinsky.

THEATER

MALY DRAMA THEATER– THEATER OF EUROPE

Maly dramatichesky teatr—Teatr Yevropy

Малый драматический театр—

Театр Европы

18 Ulitsa Rubinshteyna, 812/713-2078,

www.mdt-dodin.ru

METRO: Vladimirskaya

Map 9

The MDT, founded in 1944, is renowned for serious psychological theater aimed at serious theater buffs. For example, one of its most acclaimed productions is artistic director Lev Dodin's day-long staging of Dostoyevsky's novel The Devils, about murder and suicide among 19th-century revolutionaries. The theater has toured internationally with many positive reviews.

TOVSTONOGOV BOLSHOI DRAMA THEATER (BDT)

Bolshoy dramatichesky teatr imeni G.A. Togstonogov

Большой драматический театр имени Г.А. Товстоногов

65 Naberezhnaya reki Fontanki, 812/310-0401,

www.bdt.spb.ru

METRO: Sennaya Ploshchad

Map 9

One of Russia's most brilliant drama theaters, the BDT was founded in 1919 by a collective that included the writer Maxim Gorky. It is considered to have become the country's best drama theater under former head director Georgy Tovstonogov, who took the helm in 1956 and steered it to ever greater heights until his death in 1989. Now named after Tovstonogov, the BDT keeps the show going, to high acclaim.

CINEMAS

AVRORA

Аврора

60 Nevsky Prospekt, 812/315-5254 (recorded message), 812/942-8020 (reservations)

www.avrora.spb.ru

METRO: Gostiny Dvor

Map 9

This grand old Neoclassical-style movie theater

opened as the 800-seat Piccadilly cinema in 1913. Its rich history includes the great composer Dmitri Shostakovich playing the piano to accompany film screenings during the age of silent movies. After being renamed Avrora in 1932, the cinema underwent major renovations that doubled its size. Further renovations for its 85th birthday in 1998 brought in new technology: Now the cinema boasts Dolby Digital and Dolby Digital—Surround EX. There's a large hall with a 100-square-meter screen, a smaller VIP hall, and soft, comfortable seating that includes love seats (loveseat tickets cost more than double the regular ticket price, which is roughly the ruble equivalent of $10). The repertoire ranges from the latest Russian films to new foreign movies that are sometimes shown in the original language.

HOUSE OF CINEMA
Dom Kino
Дом Кино
12 Karavannaya Ulitsa, 812/314-0638 (recorded message), 812/314-5614 (reservations), www.domkino.spb.ru
METRO: Gostiny Dvor
Map 9

Constructed 1914–1916 in the style of a 16th-century Italian palazzo of late Palladian style, this sure is one palace of a movie theater. It was built for a bank, but had a concert hall with a cinema right from the start. The movie theater Splendid Palace opened here in 1917. Like at the Avrora, its piano was played by a young Dmitri Shostakovich while he was a student in the 1920s. Since then, the movie theater has been upgraded and renovated several times. The city's most progressive movie theater and the place to go for newish European art-house movies, it is a favorite of local cinema buffs. The city's Cinematographer's Union is based

here, and there's a restaurant. The House of Cinema hosts numerous festivals every year, including animation, shorts, students' films, and cinema from different countries.

CIRCUS
CIRCUS AT AVTOVO
Tsirk v Avtovo
Цирк в Автово
1A Avtovskaya Ulitsa, 812/183-1501, www.avtovocircus.narod.ru
METRO: Avtovo
Map 14

It might lack a fancy theater building or enviable address, but still this far-flung circus has its fans. Some even say it's the city's favorite circus, thanks to the high standard of performances by its dedicated troupe. Expect monocyclists, monkeys, jugglers, trapeze-artists, acrobats, and even elephants.

GREAT ST. PETERSBURG STATE CIRCUS
Bolshoy Sankt-Peterburgsky Gosudarstvenny Tsirk
Большой Санкт-Петербургский Государственный Цирк
3 Naberezhnaya reki Fontanki, 812/570-5198, www.circus.spb.ru
METRO: Gostiny Dvor
Map 9

Jugglers, trapeze artists, clowns, acrobats, and performing animals keep wowing the crowds at St. Pete's main circus, which opened in 1877 in an elegant custom-built theater beside the Fontanka River. The first stone building to house a circus in Russia, it is still one of the most beautiful circus buildings anywhere. Some of the country's most famous clowns have performed here, including Oleg Popov and Yury Nikulin. The circus has its own museum (Mon.–Fri. 11 A.M.–6 P.M.).

Festivals and Events

WINTER

ARTS SQUARE INTERNATIONAL WINTER FESTIVAL

Mezhdunarodny Zimny festival
"Ploshchad Iskusstv"

Международный Зимний Фестиваль
"Площадь Искусств"

Shostakovich Philharmonia Grand Hall, 2 Mikhailovskaya Ulitsa, 812/710-4126, www.artsquarewinterfest.ru

METRO: Nevsky Prospekt

Map 9

Acclaimed conductor Yuri Temirkanov is artistic director of St. Pete's premier winter arts festival, held at the Philharmonia on Arts Square between Western and Orthodox Christmases. An annual highlight is the New Year's concert and ball. Past years have featured performances by the Bolshoi Ballet, as well as the Eifman Ballet, jazz from Igor Butman and his Big Band, a show by the Obraztsov Puppet Theater, opera soloists in concert, and the maestro Temirkanov conducting the St. Petersburg Philharmonic Orchestra.

SPRING

CITY DAY

Den Goroda

День Города

Various locations, 812/713-2501, www.st-petersburg.ru

Held the last weekend in May, the city's annual birthday celebration usually includes a carnival, street theater, a regatta, and other sporting events, orchestras, fireworks, and the festive turning-on of the city's fountains—an event that often results in swimming in the fountains if the weather is warm. Venues for the festivities include Palace Square, the Peter and Paul Fortress, Peterhof, and Nevsky Prospekt.

SUMMER

◖ STARS OF THE WHITE NIGHTS INTERNATIONAL ARTS FESTIVAL

Mezhdunarodny festival iskusstv
"Zvezdy belykh nochey"

Международный фестиваль искусств
"Звезды белых ночей"

1 Teatralnaya Ploshchad, Mariinsky Concert Hall, 3/26 Ulitsa Pisareva, 812/326-4141, www.mariinsky.ru

METRO: Sennaya Ploshchad

Map 10

The Mariinsky Theater's artistic director Valery Gergiev established this popular event in 1993 and it continues to generate much excitement. The festival runs mid-May–July and consists of classical ballet, opera, and orchestral events. It's a great way to see world-class shows if you're in Russia in summer, when the regular theater season is closed—but tickets can be expensive and sell out early.

STEREOLETO

Стереолето

Various locations, 904/333-3320, www.bestfest.ru

This hip annual contemporary music fest attracts a hot line-up of international performers—previous years have featured the likes of the Go! Team, Massive Attack, and Chicks on Speed. Usually the festival takes place in late June and consists of a series of parties with concerts, chillout zones..

FALL

INTERNATIONAL FESTIVAL OF EARLY MUSIC

Mezhdunarodny festival Earlymusic

Международный фестиваль Earlymusic

Various locations, 812/570-6660, www.earlymusic.ru

The Foundation for the Revival of Early Music has been holding its annual festival every September since 1998. Dedicated to promoting pre-19th-century music, it presents works from the Middle Ages, Renaissance, baroque, and classical eras, featuring leading international and local early-music soloists, orchestras, and ensembles.

ARTS AND LEISURE

Sports and Recreation

PARKS
MIKHAILOVSKY GARDEN
Mikhaylovsky sad
Михайловский сад
Btwn. Naberezhnaya kanala Griboyedova, the Moyka River, and Sadovaya Ulitsa
HOURS: Daily May–Sept. 10 A.M.–10 P.M., Oct.–Mar. 10 A.M.–8 P.M.
COST: Free
METRO: Nevsky Prospekt or Gostiny Dvor
`Map 9`

This lovely garden is located right in the thick of the city's sights, with Church on Spilled Blood, Engineer's Castle, the Russian Museum, and the Field of Mars all right next door. Founded in 1713, the park has undergone numerous makeovers over the years and in 1823–1825 it was incorporated into the grounds of Mikhailovsky Palace, which dominates the park. Take note of the fence with art nouveau flourishes that faces the Church on Spilled Blood—it was designed by the same architect as the church itself.

TAURIDE GARDEN
Tavrichesky sad
Таврический сад
4 Potemkinskaya Ulitsa, 812/272-6044, 812/273-6420
HOURS: Daily 24 hours
COST: Free
METRO: Chernyshevskaya
`Map 13`

St. Petersburg's largest central park is a great place to come and get away from the hustle and bustle of the big city, without having to travel too far from downtown. Besides amusements such as ice skating in the winter, the gardens simply provide for some pleasant fresh air and fine walking.

◖ YELAGIN ISLAND
Yelagin ostrov
Елагин остров
4 Yelagin Ostrov, 812/430-0911, www.elaginpark.spb.ru
HOURS: Daily summer 6 A.M.–midnight, winter 6 A.M.–11 P.M.
COST: Weekends and public holidays adults 30R

a birdhouse on Yelagin Island

METRO: Krestovsky Ostrov or Staraya Derevnya
`Map 14`

Yelagin Island is located in the north of St. Petersburg and, along with Kamenny and Krestovsky Islands, forms a group that was collectively known as the Kirov Islands from 1934 to 1993. To this day, Yelagin Island's park is known as the Central Park of Culture and Leisure S. M. Kirova. Although all three islands offer historical sights and lovely areas for summer strolling, Yelagin Island is probably the pick of the bunch if for no other reason than that it is completely car-free. There are numerous ponds with boats for rent, lots of winding paths for getting lost on, and the impressive Yelaginoostrovsky Palace, among other notable attractions.

YUSUPOV GARDENS
Yusopovsky sad
Юсуповский сад
50a Sadovaya Ulitsa
HOURS: Daily 24 hours
COST: Free
METRO: Sadovaya or Sennaya Ploshchad
`Map 10`

A pocket of green stashed among city buildings

on a busy downtown street, the park is actually a little larger than it may appear from the street. Besides the Old Yusupov Palace at one end, there is a small lake with islands crossed by cast-iron bridges. The park has always been popular among city dwellers as a place for recreating and was the site of St. Petersburg's first public ice skating rink in 1865 (but it no longer exists). The park still attracts crowds when winter festivals are held here.

BANYA
KRUGLYE BANY
Круглые Баны
29 Ulitsa Karbysheva, 812/550-0985
HOURS: Daily 24 hours
COST: Varies
METRO: Ploshchad Muzhestva
`Map 14`

Its name means "round baths," and sure enough this bathhouse's building, built 1927–1929, is shaped like a giant donut. Probably the most remarkable feature is found in the building's hole in the middle—an open-air, heated (to prevent freezing) dunking pool, perfect for a refreshing post–steam room cool-off even on the coldest winter day.

BILLIARDS AND BOWLING
BOWLING CITY
Боулинг Сити
3 Ulitsa Yefimova, 812/380-3005, www.bowlingcity.ru
HOURS: Daily 24 hours
METRO: Sennaya Ploshchad or Sadovaya
`Map 10`

This huge downtown bowling center boasts 36 lanes among its many other attractions. Besides the bowling, there's a futuristic pool hall, a traditional Russian pyramid billiards room, a restaurant complex, sports bar, coffee shop, and even two private cinema rooms, which double as karaoke halls. For those who forgot their bowling gloves, there is a sports store as well.

BANYA BASICS

A trip to the *banya*, or bathhouse, is a centuries-old Russian ritual that's well worth experiencing. Here's a primer so that you'll know what to expect and what to do.

Public *banyas* have separate sections for men and women. Inside these gender-segregated areas, people go about naked or wrapped toga-style in white sheets; bathing suits are not normally worn. Some banyas also have smaller private rooms that can be rented by coed groups – in this case bathing suits are sometimes (but not always) worn, and washing may be secondary to socializing in togas over food and drinks in the lounge area.

Sheets, towels, and other necessities such as shampoo and soap can be bought or rented when you pay at the entrance, or you can bring your own; other things you might need are some rubber flip-flops or plastic slippers, and a loofah or sponge. It's customary to wear a felt hat to protect your hair in the steam room, or you can take an extra towel to wrap around your head. You can also buy a *venik* (bough of birch or other leaves) – beatings with them are a special kind of massage in the steam room.

After undressing and leaving your belongings in a locker in the change room, wrap yourself in a sheet and head for the steam room. It's likely to get very hot. Sit or lie on a wooden bench (lower down is cooler), and work up a good sweat, then go dunk yourself in the cold pool or stand under a cold shower – this temperature contrast is what makes the *banya* so invigorating. Usually there are also big plastic tubs that you can fill up and tip over your head. Repeat the steam room-cold water sequence several times. In between, you can take a break for refreshments, a massage, or beauty treatments. Have a good scrub under a hot shower, using a loofah to remove dead skin cells.

When you're done, you're likely to hear the expression "S lyogkim parom" – a traditional saying expressing good wishes that roughly translates as "With a light steam."

ARTS AND LEISURE

ICE SKATING
ICE SKATING IN YELAGIN ISLAND
Yelagin ostrov
Елагин остров
4 Yelagin Ostrov, Bldg. 4, 812/430-0911,
www.elaginpark.spb.ru
HOURS: Mon.-Fri. 11 A.M.-10 P.M., Sat.-Sun. 11 A.M.-11 P.M.
COST: Free
METRO: Krestovsky Ostrov or Staraya Derevnya
Map 14

Located at Bolshoy Square, Yelagin Island's ice skating rink is an open-air affair. The skating is free here if you bring your own skates, although they do have skate rentals. Besides excellent skating, the island even rents out kicksleds, for scooting farther afield along the winding paths and trails.

TAURIDE GARDEN—ICE PALACE
Tavrichesky sad—Ledovy dvorets
Таврический сад—Ледовый дворец
4 Potemkinskaya Ulitsa, 812/329-5534
HOURS: Daily hours vary, but fixed sessions 2-11 P.M.
COST: Adults 300R, children 200R
METRO: Chernyshevskaya
Map 13

Completed in the mid-2000s, this indoor ice palace located in the Tauride Garden has all the features you'd expect to find in a modern ice skating center. The entrance price is for a 90-minute session with only a limited number of tickets sold; the first session starts at 2 p.m. and new sessions commence every 90 minutes thereafter. There are other special-offer session times as well, with varying prices and numbers of tickets sold. Skate rental is available.

SKIING
OKHTA PARK
Охта парк
Village of Syargi, 812/718-1870, www.ohtapark.ru
HOURS: Mon.-Fri. 11 A.M.-10:30 P.M., Sat.-Sun.
9 A.M.-10:30 P.M.
COST: Varies, start from 200R/hour
METRO: Shuttle bus leaves from Prospekt
Prosvechcheniya
Map 14

Petersburg is very flat, so if you want to go downhill skiing you'll need to head out of town to find some slopes. Okhta Park is one of the closest ski resorts to St. Petersburg, just over half an hour away. It's fairly small but well equipped, with modern facilities.

FITNESS CENTERS
FLYING DUTCHMAN FITNESS CENTER
Letuchy Gollandets Fitnes Tsentr
Летучий Голландец Фитнес-Центр
Mytninskaya Naberezhnaya, by the Birzhevoy Bridge,
812/703-3774, www.gollandec.ru/fitness
HOURS: Mon.-Fri. 8 A.M.-11 P.M., Sat.-Sun. 9 A.M.-10 P.M.
METRO: Sportivnaya
Map 12

Situated on a floating re-creation of a historical sailing ship, this sports center offers some of the best views in town from its various sports halls. It's an upmarket fitness center with all the latest whizz-bang technology, as well as a health food and fresh juice bar, a sauna, and even a children's room. What's more, there is a full-fledged restaurant on-board as well.

PLANET FITNESS
Planeta Fitnes
Планета фитнес
18 Petrogradskaya Naberezhnaya, 812/332-0000,
www.spb.fitness.ru
HOURS: Mon.-Fri. 7 A.M.-11 P.M., Sat.-Sun. 9 A.M.-9 P.M.
METRO: Gorkovskaya
Map 12

A large chain of fitness centers, Planet Fitness offers 6- and 12-month memberships as well as "clip-cards" that allow you to buy just 5 or 10 visits—perfect for working out during a short stay in St. Petersburg, since most other clubs only offer long-term memberships. Founded in 1997 and aimed at the urban middle class, by 2008 the chain had grown to 13 clubs in St. Petersburg, as well as dozens more in other cities across Russia—a total membership of about 180,000 people. It is the first Russian fitness chain to go international, opening gyms in Sweden, Ukraine, and Belarus. The fitness centers offer 60 different programs, from weight training to dance and aqua aerobics, plus children's programs. They have weights rooms, cardio halls, aerobics, personal trainers, and all the other attributes of a modern fitness center. The center on Petrogradskaya Embankment, near Gorkovskaya metro station, is open 24 hours a day, seven days a week, and has yoga classes. There are other centrally-located centers near Gostiny Dvor and Sadovaya metro stations (respectively, 1/7 Mikhaylovskaya Ulitsa in the Grand Hotel Europe, 812/329-6597; 37 Kazanskaya Ulitsa, 812/315-7175).

SWIMMING AND WATER PARKS
WATERVILLE
Вотервиль

14 Ulitsa Korablestroiteley, 812/324-4700,
www.waterville.ru
HOURS: Daily 11 A.M.–11 P.M.
METRO: Primorskaya
Map 14

This is a large indoor water park with seven water slides, a 25-meter swimming pool, plus other pools, a wave machine, rivers, lakes, and other water-related amusements. There is also a banya complex with a range of steam-room styles (Finnish, Turkish, Indian, and Russian) and a fitness center, plus a range of bars, restaurants, and shops. It's particularly convenient for those staying in the Primorskaya Hotel. Prices vary depending on the time of day—a weekend all-day pass is 990R.

YOGA
ASHTANGA YOGA CENTER
Astanga-yoga tsentr
Аштанга-йога центр

49 Gorokhovaya Ulitsa, 812/293-5755,
www.yoga108.ru
METRO: Sennaya Ploshchad
Map 12

Founded in 1999, this center has three branches in St. Petersburg (the others are at 44 Ligovsky Prospekt, 812/929-8007, Ploshchad Vosstaniya metro, and 18 Ulitsa Professora Popova, 812/293-5755, Petrogradskaya metro), offering hatha yoga group classes at different levels throughout the day, as well as individual tuition. There's introductory Ashtanga, as well as Iyengar, yoga therapy for the spine, meditation, beginner's classes, and children's classes. The spacious studios are well ventilated, and have communal mats to use if you don't have your own; mats are also sold at the studios.

YOGA CENTER
Yoga tsentr
Йога центр

16 Pushkinskaya Ulitsa, 812/764-6303,
www.yoga-spb.ru
METRO: Mayakovskaya
Map 9

Specializing in Iyengar yoga, this small chain of yoga studios offers classes at levels from beginners upwards, as well as therapeutic, anti-stress, classes for children, and various women's classes. The studios have stores selling yoga books and equipment. The center says it works on the basis of combined styles and methods of teaching, describing its approach as a synthesis of various contemporary yoga schools, ancient and contemporary philosophy and psychology, ancient medicine, Ayurveda, and the formulations of St. Petersburg State University scientists. A second center is near Petrogradskaya metro (40A Kamennoostrovsky Prospekt, 812/497-3107).

SPECTATOR SPORTS
ICE PALACE
Ledovy dvorets
Ледовый дворец

1 Prospekt Pyatiletok, 812/718-6620, 812/718-6622,
www.newarena.spb.ru
METRO: Prospekt Bolshevikov
Map 14

St. Petersburg's Ice Palace is a modern sporting arena and concert venue that was built to hold the World Hockey Championships in 2000. Besides hosting a variety of sporting events, the arena serves as a major concert venue and is a venue of choice among touring Western big-name acts. It also serves as an ice skating rink open to the general public.

ARTS AND LEISURE

PETROVSKY STADIUM

Petrovsky sportivny kompleks

Петровский спортивный комплекс

2 Petrovsky Ostrov, 812/232-1622,
www.petrovsky.spb.ru

METRO: Sportivnaya

Map 12

Come here for a full-fledged football experience, Russian-style. Petrovsky Stadium has been the site of a sporting arena for more than 80 years. It is now home to the Zenit football club, the Russian Premier League champions in 2007 and winners of the 2008 UEFA Cup.

YUBILEYNY STADIUM

Yubileyny stadion

Юбилейный Стадион

18 Prospekt Dobrolyubova, 812/498-6043, www.yubi.ru

METRO: Sportivnaya

Map 12

Yubileyny Stadium has three arenas—large, small, and training—and hosts hockey matches, basketball and volleyball games, and even acrobatic rock 'n' roll competitions. There's a children's skating school in the training arena. When it's not holding sports events, it is used to host a variety of exhibitions and other events, including rock concerts. There is an ice skating rink that is open to the public.

SHOPS

St. Pete is a more convenient place to shop than Moscow. Since the city is much more compact than the capital, everything seems to be within relatively accessible distance, and you can make the rounds on foot. Retail space is cheaper, and prices noticeably lower. Also, Petersburgers are a bit more artsy and alternative than Muscovites, making this a more interesting spot for fashion shopping.

The main area to shop for high fashion is Bolshoy Prospekt on Petrograd Side, as well as the Grand Palace mall on Nevsky Prospekt. Street fashion is best sought along Sadovaya Ulitsa, between Nevsky Prospekt and Sennaya Ploshchad—particularly in Apraksin Dvor about halfway down, which is a good place for bargain-hunting. Whatever you're looking for, Nevsky Prospekt is a good place for shopping—you

can find just about anything in Gostiny Dvor, and there are countless stores along the street, especially clothing and shoe stores. For souvenirs, you can't beat the outdoor market just off Nevsky, behind the Church on Spilled Blood, which is located on Griboyedov Canal.

Still, like Moscow, St. Petersburg can't really be called a shopping destination. In general, prices are higher and the selection worse than in Western Europe or the United States. Besides offering the chance to buy some hard-to-find Russian fashion labels, inexpensive vodka, and souvenir-type purchases like amber jewelry, lacquer boxes, fur hats, Soviet kitsch, and *matryoshka* (nesting dolls), the shopping scene isn't anything to write home about.

As in Moscow, shopping hours are quite long, and there are plenty of 24-hour stores.

© NATHAN TOOHEY

HIGHLIGHTS

LOOK FOR ◖ TO FIND RECOMMENDED SHOPS.

◖ **Most Beautiful Bookstore:** The tower and dome of **Books House** will impress as much as the range and volume of books to be found within (page 265).

◖ **Best Local Fashions:** You didn't come to Russia to buy Western labels, so head to **A.Dress Fashion** to snap up some unique local creations that you won't find back home (page 266).

◖ **Most Historic:** One of the world's oldest shopping malls, **Bolshoy Gostiny Dvor** is an impressive sight, an architectural landmark, and a handy spot to shop (page 268).

◖ **Best Souvenir Shopping:** A stunning setting and an awesome range of wares make **Vernissage Souvenirs Fair** an absolute must for any tourist (page 270).

◖ **Best Market:** The mouth-watering sights and smells of **Kuznechny Market** cook up a memorable gastronomic experience (page 272).

© NATHAN TOOHEY

a typical old-style store in the Kolomna neighborhood

Service standards have improved, and sales staff increasingly speak English, but don't judge the service by whether the salesperson smiles. Service in Russia is more genuine, fake smiles are rare, and you can usually depend on a frank answer to your questions about a product's quality or freshness.

The once-ubiquitous abacuses are now virtually extinct, and stores have switched over to using up-to-date technology. Be ready to pay with cash, because cards are not widely accepted. Also, be sure to carry plenty of smaller denomination notes, because lack of change is a constant problem, and stores frequently turn away customers who don't have the exact money or something close to it.

Market traders sometimes initially name an inflated price that can be knocked down a bit, but you'll just look mean if you try to drive too hard a bargain. Russia doesn't have the haggling culture that exists in some other countries. If you're unsure whether a market price is fair, go take a look at the price of similar items in a proper store.

Be careful what you buy: Some things, such as antiques and icons, cannot be taken out of the country without certification—see the *Essentials* chapter for more information.

SHOPPING DISTRICTS
Bolshoy Prospekt, Petrograd Side
Bolshoy Prospekt, Petrogradskaya Storona
Большой проспект, Петроградская
сторона

The Petrograd Side's Bolshoy Prospekt is the city's top fashion street, with the greatest concentration of designer boutiques along its length. There's Pal Zileri, La Perla, Paul Smith, Tru Trussardi, Baldinini, and Hugo Boss, among many others, including Russian designer Tanya Kotegova and Bosco Sport. Confusingly, St. Petersburg has two Bolshoy

SHOPS

Prospekts—one on Vasilyevsky Island and one on Petrograd Side. Local addresses need the tags B.O. (or V.O., signifying Vasilyevsky Ostrov, or Vasilyevsy Island) and П.С. (P.S., Petrogradskaya Storona or Petrograd Side) to differentiate them. The Bolshoy Prospekt in Petrograd is between Petrogradskaya and Sportivnaya metro stations.

Nevsky Prospekt
Невский проспект
St. Petersburg's main street, Nevsky Prospekt, stretches all the way from the Admiralty, near the Hermitage, to Alexander Nevsky Square. People come here to promenade, people-watch, eat, drink, and shop. Together with the neighboring streets and lanes—notably the pedestrian-only Malaya Sadovaya Ulitsa—this is the premier shopping district. Along Nevsky's length are such major malls and department stores as Gostiny Dvor and Grand Palace, and an ever-growing number of boutiques. Major international brands are well represented, as well as Russian ones including Tatyana Parfionova and Bosco Sport. The best shopping is between Ploshchad Vosstaniya and the Admiralty, accessed by metro stations Nevsky Prospekt/Gostiny Dvor, Mayakovskaya, and Ploshchad Vosstaniya.

Sadovaya–Sennaya
Садовая—Сенная
Sadovaya Ulitsa, and its surrounding area southwest of Nevsky Prospekt, was historically the city's main trading district. Starting from Bolshoy Gostiny Dvor, the landmark department store on the corner of Nevsky Prospekt, there were markets of various kinds along its length; most are now gone, but a major one remains at Sennaya Ploshchad, or Hay Square, formerly the site of the city's hay market. A bustling and chaotic square full of street traders even a decade ago, the square has been heavily reconstructed and cleaned up in recent years and is now quite orderly, with the trade shifted into new shopping centers and a renovated market building. Now, Sennoy Market sells fruits, vegetables, meat, and fish, and the shiny new malls sell shoes, clothing, electronics, cosmetics, and other consumer goods.

There is another old market halfway between Nevsky and Sennaya—Apraksin Dvor. Hundreds of years ago this was a place to buy game, fruits, berries, and mushrooms, but now it's mostly clothing stalls, with more clothing stores along the facade facing Sadovaya Ulitsa. This is where you'll find some of the lowest prices in town.

A good shopping route would be to start on the corner of Sadovaya Ulitsa and Nevsky Prospekt (near Nevsky Prospekt/Gostiny Dvor metro). Walk a circuit around the stores inside Bolshoy Gostiny Dvor, and then walk along Sadovaya Ulitsa in the direction of Sennaya Ploshchad. Stop in small stores along the way, as well as in Apraksin Dvor. When you reach Sennaya Ploshchad, you can check out Sennoy Market and the two new malls, Pik and the Sennaya Shopping Center. Hop back on the metro at Sadovaya/Sennaya Ploshchad station.

Beauty

IMAGE STUDIO OF DENIS OSIPOV
Imidzh-studiya Denisa Osipova
Имидж Студия Дениса Осипова
94 Bolshoy Prospekt, Petrograd Side, 812/497-3132,
www.denis-osipov.ru
HOURS: Daily 10 A.M.-10 P.M.
METRO: Petrogradskaya
Map 12

This is the place to go if you want a dramatic change of image. A salon for young radicals, it has four brightly and creatively decorated halls, all in different styles that are changed each year in line with the four main trends chosen by hairdressing maestro Osipov. Each client is sent to a specific hall depending on the required hairstyle, which is decided in a preliminary interview and which might ultimately turn out to be a surprise for the client. You could arrive as a classic-looking brunette and leave a punky blonde with pink bangs. Some of the staff speak English, but not all, so those who don't speak Russian should get a Russian-speaker to phone in advance and make a booking with an English-speaking hairdresser. Osipov has three other salons, all hidden in courtyards: one near metro Mayakovskaya (9 Ulitsa Marata, 812/571-9512), one near Ploshchad Vosstaniya (95 Nevsky Prospekt, 812/335-2009), and one near metro Chernyshevskaya (32–34 Kirochnaya Ulitsa, 812/327-8468). Prices vary depending on the level of the hairdresser's skills and qualifications.

L'ETOILE
L'Etual
Л'Этуаль
35 Nevsky Prospekt, 812/325-6934, www.letoile.ru
HOURS: Mon., Tues., and Fri.-Sun. 10 A.M.-10 P.M.,
Wed.-Thurs. 10 A.M.-10:30 P.M.
METRO: Nevsky Prospekt or Gostiny Dvor
Map 9

Russia's largest chain of cosmetics and perfume stores, not surprisingly, has a presence in the northern capital. There are three L'Etoile stores on Nevsky Prospekt alone (the others are at No. 19, closer to the Hermitage, and No. 64, near Mayakovskaya metro), but all over town you'll spot the chain's blue, white, and yellow wave-like logo. The stores are bright and cheerful, with a self-service format that makes it easier if you don't speak Russian. All the major international brands can be found here.

RIVE GAUCHE
Riv Gosh
Рив Гош
69 Bolshoy Prospekt, Petrograd Side, 812/346-2515
HOURS: Daily 10 A.M.-9 P.M.
METRO: Petrogradskaya
Map 12

Rive Gauche has more than three dozen cosmetics stores in St. Petersburg, selling top-of-the-line brands such as Chanel, Givenchy, Yves Saint Laurent, and Estée Lauder. The store on Petrograd Side's Bolshoy Prospekt is special not only because it's appropriately located in the heart of the city's premier high-fashion shopping district, but also because it includes a beauty salon where you can have massages, mud masks, chocolate masks, anti-cellulite treatments, and peeling. Other Rive Gauche cosmetics stores are in such central locations as Nevsky Prospekt, Sadovaya Ulitsa, and the Vladimirsky Passage mall.

SALON OF NATALYA KONDRATYEVA
Salon Natali Kondratyevoy
Салон Натальи Кондратьевой
27 Ulitsa Pestelya, 812/273-9452
HOURS: Mon.-Sat. 9 A.M.-9 P.M., Sun. 9 A.M.-8 P.M.
METRO: Chernyshevskaya
Map 9

This highly regarded beauty salon has specialists of international standard, and it's so popular that you have to make reservations well in advance. In addition to the full range of hairdressing services, the salon offers manicures, pedicures, facials, cosmetology, piercing, tattooing, and both horizontal and vertical solariums. Although the receptionist speaks some English, she says the other staff don't—it might be worth bringing a translator.

Books, Music, and Movies

BOOKSTORES

ANGLIA
Англия

38 Naberezhnaya reki Fontanki, 812/579-8284, www.anglophile.ru
HOURS: Daily 10 A.M.–8 P.M.
METRO: Nevsky Prospekt
Map 9

The wide range of English-language books in this friendly store includes plenty about Russia, but that's not all. There's fiction, with the hottest new releases of English-language literature, and all kinds of nonfiction, dictionaries, guidebooks, and handbooks. There's also a cultural and educational center, with English-language classes, certification, and teacher training.

◖ BOOKS HOUSE
Dom Knigi
Дом книги

28 Nevsky Prospekt, 812/448-2355, www.spbdk.ru
HOURS: Daily 9 A.M.–midnight
METRO: Nevsky Prospekt
Map 9

Located in an architectural landmark, the beautiful Singer building picturesquely located on the corner of Nevsky Prospekt and Griboyedova Canal, this is the city's most famous and most beloved bookstore. Besides more than 100,000 titles of every imaginable genre, there's a literary café on the 2nd floor, with views of Kazan Cathedral. There's also free Internet access in the 1st-floor audio/video section. Information desks with helpful staff are on hand to help you find anything you need.

MUSIC, MOVIES, AND MORE

FONOTEKA
Фонотека

28 Ulitsa Marata, 812/712-3013
HOURS: Daily 11 A.M.–10 P.M.
METRO: Mayakovskaya
Map 9

This audio/video store is a favorite among St. Petersburg music lovers and movie buffs, who consider it the grooviest disc shop in town. There's a diverse range of CDs and DVDs, plus rare vinyl and comics. The collection is well organized and easy to navigate, and the prices are low. The staff may speak little English, but the language of melomania is universal. Request to listen to something and then lay back on the leather sofas and enjoy.

INOYE KINO
Иное Кино

33 Sredny Prospekt, Vasilyevsky Island, 812/715-2599, www.inoekino.ru
HOURS: Daily 11 A.M.–10 P.M.
METRO: Vasileostrovskaya
Map 11

The name could be translated as "Alternative Cinema," and that aptly sums up this dream shop for dedicated cinephiles. Having started out in 1995 as a fairly standard video store, over the years it expanded its stock of classic, alternative, European, Oriental, and other foreign cinema, as well as both forgotten and unforgettable Soviet and Russian films. Now, it's renowned as the place to go for reasonably priced avant-garde, art-house, experimental, and festival films, as well as Hollywood hits and classics. The store has a club-like atmosphere—you can buy a membership card that raises the curtain for discounts, invitations to club events, and text-message notifications of new titles in stock. English-language films are available, and the sales staff understand and can speak a little English.

TITANIK
Титаник

86 Ulitsa Marata, 812/336-4762
HOURS: Daily 24 hours
METRO: Mayakovskaya
Map 13

Titanik is a chain of 18 CD and DVD stores located all over the city, and some of them are open 24 hours a day, seven days a week (46 Sredny Prospekt, Vasilyevsky Island, 812/323-1919, Vasileostrovskaya metro; 35 Bolshoy Prospekt,

SHOPS

Petrograd Side, 812/235-4885, Petrogradskaya metro; 107 Ligovsky Prospekt, 812/764-0866, Ligovsky Prospekt metro; 17 Kirochnaya Ulitsa, 812/579-9950, Ligovsky Prospekt metro). Popular primarily with twentysomethings, the stores have music and movies for all ages and tastes. There are recent releases and old classics from Russia and abroad, spanning the full spectrum of genres, as well as related literature and knicknacks. The salespeople are well informed and helpful, making this a good spot to pick up some Russian movies or music to take home.

Clothing

◖ A.DRESS FASHION
5 Gorokhovaya Ulitsa, 812/570-4899,
www.a-dressspb.ru
HOURS: Daily 11 A.M.–8 P.M.
METRO: Nevsky Prospekt
Map 9

The city's largest store specializing in Russian fashion, this boutique has three halls totaling 200 square meters, as well as a showroom. It offers some cool local labels for men's and women's apparel, including Arngoldt, Biryukov, Bukhinnik, and Terexov. The store's buyers select their stock in St. Petersburg, Moscow, and Kiev, Ukraine. While other elite fashion galleries around town specialize in haute couture, this store has a cozier but edgier, more avant-garde character.

BOSCO SPORT
54 Nevsky Prospekt, 812/363-4045, www.bosco.ru
HOURS: Daily 10 A.M.–9 P.M.
METRO: Nevsky Prospekt
Map 9

Snap up some snazzy sportswear by the outfitter of Russia's Olympic team. This brand's distinctive style gives a fresh twist to some iconic, traditional Russian motifs by incorporating them into contemporary, cutting-edge designs. The stores also sell cute Cheburashka toys—the Russian Olympic mascot, a revamped version of a classic Soviet animated character. Another Bosco Sport can be found near the Sportivnaya metro (16 Bolshoy Prospekt, Petrograd Side, 812/235-6607).

DEFILE
27 Naberezhnaya kanala Griboyedova, 812/571-9010,
www.defile.ru
HOURS: Mon.-Sat. 11 A.M.–8 P.M., Sun. noon-7 P.M.

METRO: Nevsky Prospekt or Gostiny Dvor
Map 9

Having opened in 1999, this was the first post-Soviet multi-brand boutique to specialize in fashion of Russia and other former Soviet republics. Located just off Nevsky Prospekt, behind Kazan Cathedral, it offers some interesting threads, belts, and accessories for both men and women by Masha Sharoyeva, Biryukov, Borodulin's, Lilya Pustovit, and others. The range of styles is diverse but unified by originality.

INTERACTIVE
2 Malaya Sadovaya Ulitsa, 812/312-6218
HOURS: Sun.-Fri. noon-9 P.M., Sat. 11 A.M.–9 P.M.
METRO: Nevsky Prospekt or Gostiny Dvor
Map 9

One of the city's hippest youth-oriented clothing stores, this spot is so popular that trendy-looking people line up outside on the beautiful pedestrian-only Malaya Sadovaya Street. It's a happening hangout with cool clothes and shoes, party flyers and tickets, magazines, CDs, and even a DJ. One of the local labels worth checking out is Extra. There are some treasures to be found and the prices are a real bargain.

OFF
8 Ulitsa Pechatnika Grigoryeva, 812/764-2267,
www.offoffoff.ru
HOURS: Sun.-Tues. noon-8 P.M., Wed.-Sat. noon-10 P.M.
METRO: Ligovsky Prospekt
Map 13

Creative, exclusive second-hand is what this cozy, home-like store is all about. It's a favorite among students, who even come from Moscow to shop here. Off sells genuinely original clothing, for both men and women. Not only are the clothes second hand, they're also remade into new items, with the addition of prints, badges, sewn-on decorations, and other interesting touches. Sometimes different, strongly contrasting items of clothing are merged into one: a singlet over a suit coat, for example. The store occupies two levels but feels quite cramped—it's absolutely stuffed with quirky creations. There are hats, bags, glasses, and other stuff, all one-offs. If you like to look downright weird, this is your store. It's right near the club Griboedov, so come here and get something hip to wear over there.

TANYA KOTEGOVA FASHION HOUSE

Modny dom Tani Kotegovoy
Модный дом Тани Котеговой
44 Bolshoy Prospekt, Petrograd Side, 812/346-3467, www.kotegova.narod.ru
HOURS: Mon.-Fri. 11 A.M.-8 P.M.
METRO: Petrogradskaya
Map 12

Having registered her name as her trademark and opened her own boutique back in 1991, Tanya Kotegova has established a reputation for elegant, minimalist women's clothing with clean lines, laconic silhouettes, and refined sexuality, using only natural fabrics and incorporating antique accessories into contemporary costumes. Kotegova has designed costume collections for the Mariinsky Theater (Kirov Ballet). Some of her designs look fit for Marlene Dietrich, to whom one of her collections was dedicated. Her shoes are another highlight.

TATYANA PARFIONOVA FASHION HOUSE

Modny dom "Tatyana Parfyonova"
Модный дом "Татьяна Пафёнова"
51 Nevsky Prospekt, 812/713-1415, www.parfionova.ru
HOURS: Daily noon-8 P.M.
METRO: Mayakovskaya
Map 9

Clothing by Parfionova, one of Russia's most respected and well-known designers of women's wear, is available in only a select and very small number of boutiques, but naturally the best place to look for it is in her own flagship fashion house. The award-winning designer's style has been described as elegant, fashionable, original, and artistic, with embroidered details being part of her signature style.

SHOES
ALEANDR
107 Ligovsky Prospekt, 812/939-0107
HOURS: Daily 10 A.M.-9 P.M.
METRO: Ligovsky Prospekt
Map 13

This is a good place to go for footwear that won't cost an arm and a leg. Shoes from Russia, Brazil, and China can be found on the shelves, at prices that are hard to beat. Aimed at the middle class, the store has two halls, one for men and one for women. One local women's brand worth noting is Laura Berti, which makes business, evening, and leisure shoes intended for modern women seeking a compromise between fashionable trends and comfort.

GEOX
45 Bolshoy Prospekt, Petrograd Side, 812/232-6329, www.geox.ru
HOURS: Daily 10 A.M.-10 P.M.
METRO: Petrogradskaya
Map 12

"Geox breathes" is the slogan of this Italian footwear brand, which uses waterproof, breathable fabrics. Men's, women's, children's, and even babies' shoes are sold here, and what they've all got in common is comfort. There's a wide range of designs, from formal to casual, and all the models look pretty good too, which makes Geox a good choice for those who need comfort for sightseeing by day and style for going out to dinner afterwards—and sweat-free feet the whole time.

MANIA GRANDIOSA
28 Bolshoy Prospekt, Petrograd Side, 812/232-9583, www.maniagrandiosa.com
HOURS: Daily 9 A.M.-9 P.M.
METRO: Sportivnaya
Map 9

Hiking boots just won't do if you want to pass

face control—or more precisely, shoe control—in the city's coolest clubs. What you need is a pair of stilettos, darling. But how many travelers actually think to pack some? It sounds pretty absurd until you arrive in footwear-focused Russia. Mania Grandiosa is one place where you can get some drop-dead daring heels that will have you strutting up to the velvet rope with confidence. There's a slick selection of classic and sports shoes for men too. Hussein Chalayan, John Richmond, Artioli, Casadei, and numerous other top international brands are here, and there are soft red sofas to sit on while you try them on. Belts and bags are also on display in the immaculately designed, minimalist interior. Sure, it's all quite expensive, but consider that you're buying a ticket to the social scene as well. Soon you'll be sneering at others' sneakers.

Department Stores and Malls

BALTIYSKY FASHION CENTER
TTs "Baltiysky"
ТЦ "Балтийский"
68 Bolshoy Prospekt, Vasilyevsky Island,
812/322-6976, www.fashiongallery.spb.ru
HOURS: Daily 11 A.M.–9 P.M.
METRO: Vasileostrovskaya
Map 11

The first-ever Gallery of Russian Fashion occupies the third level of this huge, modern shopping complex, which consists of some 100 boutiques selling women's, men's, and children's fashion, as well as footwear, underwear, and accessories. Some of the labels to be found here are Larissa Pogoretskaya, Leonid Alexeev, Pirosmani, Princess and Frogs, Vitamin, Mekler, Iya Yots, Alexandra Kiaby, Kogel, and Ilya Chelyshev. There are cafés specially designed for fashion shows, parties, and competitions, with free wireless Internet.

◖ BOLSHOY GOSTINY DVOR
Большой гостиный двор
35 Nevsky Prospekt, 812/710-5408, www.bgd.ru
HOURS: Fri.-Tues. 10 A.M.–10 P.M., Wed.-Thurs.
10 A.M.–10:30 P.M.
METRO: Gostiny Dvor
Map 9

Dating back to the 18th century, this elegant yellow building was one of the world's first shopping malls and remains one of the largest retail centers in town. Located on the main street, right in the center of the city, it's a prominent landmark and worth visiting even if you don't need to buy anything. Inside there is a series of stores selling a diverse range of wares along its lengthy corridors—walk the kilometer-long circuit and you'll see everything from matryoshkas, fur, and vodka to kitchenwares and shoe polish. Designer boutiques occupy the upper level's Haute Couture Gallery.

GRAND PALACE
Grand Palas
Гранд Палас
44 Nevsky Prospekt/15 Italyanskaya Ulitsa,
812/710-5504, www.grand-palace.ru
HOURS: Daily 11 A.M.–9 P.M.
METRO: Nevsky Prospekt
Map 9

This posh shopping center calls itself a "gallery of boutiques." It brings together 80 elite multibrand and mono-brand boutiques and jewelry stores under one roof. There's Escada, Burberry, Carrera y Carrera, Nina Ricci, Feraud, Joop!, Trussardi, Sonia Rykiel, and many other luxury labels. The complex includes a beauty salon and restaurants, with Sevenskybar offering superb views over the city.

PASSAGE
Passazh
Пассаж
48 Nevsky Prospekt, 812/315-5257,
www.passage.spb.ru
HOURS: Mon.-Sat. 10 A.M.–9 P.M., Sun. 11 A.M.–9 P.M.
METRO: Nevsky Prospekt
Map 9

Founded in the 19th century, this stylish shopping

arcade is an architectural landmark that's like a smaller version of Moscow's GUM. It's not a bad place to shop, especially for souvenirs or clothing needs, but even just walking through to admire the architecture is an enjoyable experience. It's popular with locals and tourists alike, but still it doesn't seem to ever get overcrowded. There's a well-stocked supermarket downstairs.

PIK SHOPPING CENTER
TK "Pik"
ТК "Пик"
2 Ulitsa Yefimova, 812/449-2003, www.tk-pik.ru
HOURS: Daily 10 A.M.-10 P.M.
METRO: Sadovaya or Sennaya Ploshchad
Map 10

One of the glitzy shopping centers to have been built on Sennaya Ploshchad during its major reconstruction in the first years of the 21st century, Pik is the new, civilized, and respectable face of this once-sleazy square. It's an enormous complex, with a solid selection of clothing and shoe shops, as well as plenty of other stores selling useful things from cell phones to tobacco. There's an Apple computer store, a Soyuz music and movie store, a Le Futur gift store, and a Russian fur store. It even has a Detsky Mir children's store, with kids' clothes, shoes, toys, stationery, books, and child-care items. Mono-brand boutiques include Karen Miller, Etam, and Savage. The six-story complex has a supermarket on the bottom level, and on higher levels there's a cinema and more than a dozen cafés, bars, and eateries, including one on the top floor with views of St. Isaac's Square.

SENNAYA SHOPPING CENTER
Torgovy kompleks Sennaya
Торговый комплекс Сенная
3 Ulitsa Yefimova, 812/740-4624, www.sennaya.ru
HOURS: Daily 10 A.M.-9 P.M.
METRO: Sennaya Ploshchad
Map 10

Besides an abundance of stores of all kinds, this huge shopping complex has countless restaurants, cafés, and bars, a bowling alley, clothing and shoe repair shops, an optician, and a dry cleaner. Clothing and footwear brands include Benetton, Calvin Klein, Adidas, Puma, Nike, Reebok, Ecco, Esprit, Levi's, and Russian teenage designer Kira Plastinina.

STOCKMANN
Стокманн
25 Nevsky Prospekt, 812/326-2637, www.stockmann.ru
HOURS: Sun.-Thurs. 10 A.M.-9 P.M., Fri.-Sat.
10 A.M.-10 P.M.
METRO: Nevsky Prospekt
Map 9

A Finnish retailer operating in St. Petersburg since 1993, Stockmann's best known local outlet is predominantly a clothing store but also sells some other goods such as housewares. There's a lovely open space in the center with a pleasant café under a high ceiling. Another much larger Stockmann is planned to open farther up the road, at No. 114 Nevsky Prospekt near Ploshchad Vosstaniya metro station, with 80 stores as well as cafés, restaurants, a fitness center, and offices over seven floors.

VLADIMIRSKY PASSAGE
Vladimirsky Passazh
Владимирский пассаж
19 Vladimirsky Prospekt, 812/331-3232,
www.vladimirskiy.ru
HOURS: Daily 11 A.M.-9 P.M.
METRO: Dostoyevskaya
Map 9

This new mall has 170 stores selling goods that range from clothing and shoes to cell phones, sporting goods, souvenirs, housewares, watches, jewelry, flowers, and toys. The stores and their wares span the spectrum in terms of price and target customer, from Barbie World to Swarovski. There's a supermarket in the basement, plus restaurants and bars, a food court, and a popular bakery café.

SHOPS

Gifts and Specialty Stores

SOUVENIRS AND GIFTS

BABUSHKA
Бабушка

33 Naberezhnaya Leytenanta Shmidta, 812/321-1477,
www.souvenirboutique.com
HOURS: Daily 8 A.M.-8 P.M.
METRO: Vasileostrovskaya
`Map 11`

This cute souvenir supermarket is packed with matroyshkas, lacquer boxes, amber, chinaware, and every other Russian souvenir imaginable, including plenty of good choices at low prices. There are lots of little trinkets that don't cost much, and won't take up much space or weigh down your luggage—perfect token gifts for colleagues at work and distant relatives.

ONEGIN
Онегин

11 Ploshchad Iskusstv, 812/570-0058,
www.onegin-gallery.com
HOURS: Daily 8 A.M.-10 P.M.
METRO: Nevsky Prospekt
`Map 9`

Jewelry, china, crystal, and artworks are just some of the souvenirs at this store near the Russian Museum. The jewelry selection includes amber, traditional Rostov-style finift enamel miniatures intricately painted with floral pictures, and semiprecious stones. Locally made crystal items, such as ornaments, with laser graphics are another specialty, and sets of decanters with matching shot glasses.

◖ VERNISSAGE SOUVENIRS FAIR
Yarmarka suvenirov Vernisazh
Ярмарка сувениров Вернисаж

1 Naberezhnaya kanala Griboyedova, 812/572-1554
HOURS: Daily 11 A.M.-7 P.M.
METRO: Nevsky Prospekt
`Map 9`

A large outdoor market located on the square right behind the Church on Spilled Blood, this is the city's most popular spot to buy souvenirs. Every kind of Russian souvenir is for sale here, and the picture-perfect setting makes shopping here an unforgettable experience. Most traders seem to speak English and have a tendency to initially name prices higher than they really expect to get.

FOOD AND DRINK

LAND
Лэнд

19 Vladimirsky Prospekt, 812/331-3232,
www.vladimirskiy.ru
HOURS: Daily 24 hours
METRO: Dostoyevskaya
`Map 9`

In the basement of the gleaming new Vladimirsky Passage mall is a premium-class supermarket that local expats rave about as one of the best spots to buy rare foreign foodstuffs that they miss from back home. The fact that it's open 24 hours is clearly another plus, especially if you're staying in the hotel Dostoevsky that's in the same building.

© NATHAN TOOHEY

drinks for sale at a kiosk

WHAT TO BUY: TOP FIVE SOUVENIRS

Souvenir-shopping in Moscow and St. Petersburg is easy: there's a range of recognizably Russian classics to suit any taste and budget, and it's all widely available at just about any souvenir store, stall, or market.

NESTING DOLLS

The **matryoshka,** or nesting doll, is a symbol of Russia that seems to embody the old "riddle wrapped in a mystery, inside an enigma" saying. However, it's not a very old tradition, having only originated in the late 19th century, and its real origins are foreign – the first *matryoshka* was inspired by a similar kind of doll from Japan. You can see the original *matryoshka* in the toy museum at Sergiyev Posad, which is also a good place to buy one. A set of hollow wooden dolls of decreasing size placed one inside the other, *matryoshkas* come in various sizes and numbers. Classic *matryoshka* dolls are colorfully painted with images of pretty, plump women, but you can also buy *matryoshkas* depicting political leaders and celebrities – and even plain ones that you can paint yourself.

FUR HATS

Nothing's more Russian than a fur hat, although they have been falling out of favor among the younger generation in Moscow and St. Petersburg. Fur hats are easy to find – both synthetic and natural, in various colors and styles. The men's classic fur hat has ear flaps that are tied together on top; untying them to keep your ears warm is a fashion faux pas associated with provincials and unhinged alcoholics. You will also look like a fool if you wear one in the wrong season, or wear an inappropriate style – a woman wearing a man's hat, for example, or wearing a military or police hat if you're not a soldier or police officer.

SOVIET MEMORABILIA

You don't have to be a communist to like Soviet memorabilia – over time it has developed an ironic, kitschy hipness. There's plenty to be found at souvenir markets, including Lenin busts, hammer-and-sickle flags, red silky banners, propaganda posters and postcards, badges, red-

© NATHAN TOOHEY

star hats, and watches. Besides the blatantly political items, there are other cool Soviet-era souvenirs, such as Yury Gagarin busts and other space memorabilia, model cars, and fabulously designed brown leather policemen's bags.

AMBER JEWELRY

Amber jewelry is beautiful, widely available, and quite inexpensive. It's also compact, lightweight, and easy to transport, so it makes a good gift or souvenir. You can find all sorts of rings, pendants, earrings, bracelets, and even pictures made of this translucent golden-brown fossil tree resin, sometimes even with insects preserved inside. About 90 percent of the world's extractable amber is in Russia's Kaliningrad region, on the Baltic Sea. The Russian word for amber is **yantar** (янтарь).

RUSSIAN CRAFTS

Certain Russian villages and towns are have developed their own unique craftwares; these wares tend to be named after their place of origin but are ubiquitous in souvenir stores all over the country. Some that make great gifts are: **Gzhel,** a style of blue-and-white painted ceramics, such as plates and figurines; **Khokhloma,** wooden tableware and utensils painted with gold, red, and black, typically in patterns of flowers, leaves, and berries; **Palekh,** shiny black lacquered wares such as boxes or brooches, brightly painted with intricate miniature pictures, usually folk legends and fairytale scenes; and **Zhostovo** metal trays painted with distinctive floral bouquets.

SUPERMARKET IN PASSAGE
Supermarket v univermage "Passazh"
Супермаркет в универмаге "Пассаж"
48 Nevsky Prospekt, 812/315-5257,
www.passage.spb.ru
HOURS: Mon.-Sat. 10 A.M.-10 P.M., Sun. 11 A.M.-10 P.M.
METRO: Nevsky Prospekt
Map 9

The supermarket downstairs from the elegant Passage department store is well stocked, and conveniently located on the main street. When it first opened in the 1990s, it was one of the few spots to buy hard-to-find foreign foodstuffs, and even now its range remains better than average, making it popular with the local expatriate population, as well as regular Petersburgers. The liquor selection is particularly good.

ELECTRONICS
ELDORADO
Эльдорадо
38 9-ya Liniya, Vasilyevsky Island, 800/555-1111,
www.eldorado.ru
HOURS: Daily 10 A.M.-9 P.M.
METRO: Vasileostrovskaya
Map 11

Eldorado is a huge nationwide chain of electronics hypermarkets, supermarkets, and communications stores. The St. Petersburg hypermarkets are all far-flung; the store near Vasileostrovskaya metro station is one of the supermarkets. They stock a full range of electronics—photo/video, computing, communications, and domestic and grooming appliances, plus all the accessories that go with them. Of the other Eldorado outlets, another centrally located one is in the Sennaya Shopping Center.

TEKHNO SHOK
Техно Шок
52 Ligovsky Prospekt, 812/764-6647, www.tshok.ru
HOURS: Daily 10 A.M.-10 P.M.
METRO: Ligovsky Prospekt
Map 13

This is the most centrally located of Tekhno Shock's 13 electronics hypermarkets in St. Petersburg. It's an enormous appliance store where you might get lost in long aisles of washing machines. The assortment includes all kinds of cameras, cell phones, and associated accessories, grooming appliances such as hair dryers, curling tongs, epilators, and trimmers—there's even vacuum pore-cleaners. If you happen to need an iron, you can get one here as well.

Markets

◖ KUZNECHNY MARKET
Kuznechny rynok
Кузнечный рынок
3 Kuznechny Pereulok, 812/312-4161,
www.kuznechrin.sp.ru
HOURS: Mon.-Sat. 8 A.M.-8 P.M., Sun. 8 A.M.-7 P.M.
METRO: Vladimirskaya
Map 9

The finest food market in town, this place is a real cornucopia, with animated salespeople crying out to attract your attention, begging you to taste their wares. The spacious market building has superb pickles, fresh and dried fruits, vegetables, honey, and cheeses, not to mention a great range of smoked fish. A visit to this market should be included in every tourist itinerary.

SENNOY MARKET
Sennoy rynok
Сенной рынок
4 Moskovsky Prospekt, 812/310-1209
HOURS: Daily 8 A.M.-7 P.M.
METRO: Sennaya Ploshchad
Map 10

Fruits and vegetables, meat and seafood—this market has it all, and it's right downtown, just off the square at Sennaya Ploshchad. There are also various half-prepared items just waiting for your oven, as well as ready-to-go salads, pickles, baked goods, and the like. This place was once a bit seedy, but renovations have spruced it up and made it quite respectable.

HOTELS

Like Moscow, St. Petersburg long suffered from a shortage of affordable beds, but fortunately the accommodation situation has been improving in the northern capital in recent years. Besides a number of new four- and five-stars, there has been quite a boom in mini-hotels, hostels, and bed-and-breakfasts. Often located in converted formerly communal apartments, they represent a whole new segment in a hospitality industry that once offered little beyond enormous Soviet hotels and the expensive, luxurious five-star establishments. Meanwhile, well-known international chains have been taking over the management of the old Soviet hotels, renovating them and transforming them into standard Western-style accommodations. Another new option is short-term apartment rental, an additional service offered by some of the hostels and mini-hotels.

Breakfast is usually included and can range from lavish buffets in the four- and five-star hotels, to buttery oatmeal with tea or instant coffee in the cheaper spots. Pay attention to your accommodation's check-in and check-out times, as they can vary.

Between autumn and spring, central heating can be expected in any hotel, hostel, or other accommodation, so you don't have to worry about being cold while in your room. On the other hand, even in mid-summer, air-conditioning is rarely needed and so it's not widespread—and no generalizations can be made about its availability in any kind of accommodation.

© NATHAN TOOHEY

HIGHLIGHTS

LOOK FOR TO FIND
RECOMMENDED HOTELS.

Grandest: The name does not mislead – the city's grandest hotel is the **Grand Hotel Europe,** with a meticulously restored 19th-century neo-baroque facade and fin-de-siecle art nouveau features inside (page 277).

Best Location: Where the city's prettiest canal curves close to Palace Square you'll find the **Kempinski Hotel Moika 22.** Stunning views from its top-floor restaurant seem to put the Winter Palace in the palm of your hand – indeed, all the best sights are practically at the doorstep (page 277).

Closest Hostel to the Hermitage: If you stay at **Nord Hostel,** you can walk out your front door and see Palace Square framed by the triumphal arch – a million-dollar view for less than 50 bucks if you bunk in the dorm (page 278).

Funkiest Decor: Run by active participants in the city's underground electronic music scene, **Off** looks like an artists' squat, with colorful walls covered in graffiti and posters, and artfully crooked pictures. They've even got turntables in the corridor (page 278).

Wildest: Not for the tame, **Redmedved** (redbear) tries to bring out the animal in you. Don't hibernate; go bar-hopping with the other cubs (page 281).

© NATHAN TOOHEY

the view from Kempinski Hotel Moika 22's top floor

CHOOSING A HOTEL

Despite the growth in the number of beds, St. Petersburg's rapidly growing popularity with tourists means that it can be difficult to find a room, especially in summer—even though prices are then at their seasonal peak—and you should make reservations well in advance. Price and availability will limit your choices, and in the summer you might just have to take what you can get.

PRICE KEY

$ Less than $150 per night
$$ Between $150-250 per night
$$$ More than $250 per night

Rates apply to high season and double occupancy.

Don't be immediately put off by locations far from the historical center, but check the proximity to the nearest metro station. Provided the metro is within walking distance, accessing the center should be quick and easy for the confident independent traveler. Safety of neighborhoods is not really a problem—like in Moscow, it's about the same all over the city. The only thing to consider is proximity to the metro, because even if it's not actually dangerous, you might not feel safe if you have to walk far after dark. And, if you've got any choice, avoid staying anywhere that's a bus, tram, or trolleybus ride away from the nearest metro station, since this is not only slow but confusing, since nothing is in English on above-ground public transport. Those who don't fancy figuring out how to use any public transport at all—even the relatively easy metro—should choose whatever they can afford as close as possible to Palace Square or Nevsky Prospekt, and book early.

Given the ubiquity of double-glazed windows, street noise is unlikely to be a problem.

Smoking is allowed in most hotels, but there is a new trend for hotels to offer nonsmoking rooms or even nonsmoking floors, and some entirely nonsmoking hotels have started to appear.

These days, practically every accommodation in St. Petersburg has English-speaking staff, and visa support is a standard service.

Watch out for prices quoted in conditional units or *uslovniye yedinitsy,* abbreviated in Cyrillic as Y.E.—be sure to check the exchange rate that applies. The same goes for prices quoted in dollars or any other currency. Although prices within Russia are now supposed to be in rubles only, this is not always observed. Prices, particularly online, may be quoted in any currency, but you will have to pay in rubles, and some travelers have been shocked by the exchange rates used.

The Center   Map 9

ANGLETERRE **$$$**
24 Malaya Morskaya Ulitsa, 812/494-5666,
www.angleterrehotel.com
METRO: Sennaya Ploshchad or Gostiny Dvor

Located right beside the five-star Astoria on St. Isaac's Square is this attractive four-star alternative, also with views of St. Isaac's Cathedral. The Angleterre is most famous as the hotel where the poet Sergey Yesenin committed suicide in 1925, hanging himself after writing a farewell note in his own blood. The hotel's interior has since been fully reconstructed, so poetry and gloom

aficionados can no longer stay in the suicide suite. Instead, they can chase away their blues in the beauty salon, sauna, pool, and gym, or if that doesn't work, try cheering up with fancy fish eggs, bliny, and vodka in the Caviar Bar.

ANTIQUE HOTEL RACHMANINOV **$$**
Antik-Otel Rakhmaninov
Антик-Отель Рахманинов
5 Kazanskaya Ulitsa, 812/571-7618,
www.hotelrachmaninov.com
METRO: Nevsky Prospekt

HOTELS

You can stay in Sergey Rachmaninoff's actual childhood bedroom in this boutique hotel, located in the house where the great composer lived in 1884–1885. Rachmaninoff's room is the "luxe" suite, decorated with his photos and genuine antique furniture. The other 25 rooms of various classes also feature antiques to evoke a cozy Silver Age ambience. Another plus is the great location, right downtown in the historic center, close to Kazan Cathedral and Nevsky Prospekt.

ASTORIA ⑤⑤⑤

39 Bolshaya Morskaya Ulitsa, 812/494-5757,
www.thehotelastoria.com
METRO: Sennaya Ploshchad or Gostiny Dvor

This five-star Rocco Forte hotel on St. Isaac's Square is considered one of the city's best. The 1912 architectural landmark with views of St. Isaac's Cathedral has been fully renovated to a level of sheer luxury that attracts world leaders and celebrities. The 213 rooms' interior design reflects the city's grandeur, with marble bathrooms and opulent furnishings. The property is also home to classy restaurants, a spa, a sauna, and a 24-hour gym.

COMFORT HOTEL ⑤⑤

Komfort otel
Комфорт отель
25 Ul. Bolshaya Morskaya, 812/570-6700,
www.comfort-hotel.spb.ru
METRO: Nevsky Prospekt

You'll be close to some of St. Petersburg's premier sights and a wide range of restaurants and shops if you stay at Comfort Hotel. It's located between the Neva River and the Moyka Canal, just a couple of minutes' walk from Nevsky Prospekt, the Hermitage, the Admiralty, and St. Isaac's Cathedral. A mini-hotel with 18 rooms, it is suitable for business travelers and tourists alike, combining classic old-fashioned interiors with up-to-date facilities (computer rental, free Internet) and high-tech security. The most expensive room has a whirlpool tub and fireplace.

CORINTHIA NEVSKIJ PALACE ⑤⑤⑤

57 Nevsky Prospekt, 812/380-2001, www.corinthia.ru

METRO: Mayakovskaya

Although housed in two restored 19th-century buildings, the Nevskij Palace lacks the pre-Revolutionary grandeur and captivating sense of history found in some of St. Petersburg's other hotels. The place feels thoroughly modern, which is perhaps fitting for a business hotel. The 285 rooms have wireless Internet, stereo systems, satellite television, and air-conditioners, among other comforts. Its award-winning rooftop Landskrona restaurant has breathtaking views and a popular Sunday brunch. Another advantage is the convenient location, right on the main street in the center of the city's retail and business district.

CUBAHOSTEL ⑤

5 Kazanskaya Ulitsa, 812/921-7115, www.cubahostel.ru
METRO: Nevsky Prospekt

Possibly the best choice for backpackers on a tight budget, Cubahostel offers a winning combination of low prices in a million-dollar location right by Kazan Cathedral. The 4th-floor hostel has mixed dorm rooms with 4–10 beds, free Internet access, a common kitchen—and no curfews or lockouts, so you can party the night away in the nearby clubs, pubs, and bars.

DOSTOEVSKY ⑤⑤⑤

Otel Dostoyevsky
Отель Достоевский
19 Vladimirsky Prospekt, 812/331-3200,
www.dostoevsky-hotel.ru
METRO: Vladimirskaya

This gleaming 207-room hotel is a bit too pristine to evoke the mood of Dostoyevsky's novels. It's at the top of a modern mall, but at least it's in the great writer's stomping grounds—a lovely old neighborhood that's full of character. Here you'll find Dostoyevsky's apartment museum, the beautiful Vladimirsky Cathedral, loads of quirky cafés and bars, as well as the cornucopia of Kuznechny Market. There's a business center, gym, sauna, restaurants, and bars within the hotel complex. The metro is across the road, but if you prefer to walk, Nevsky Prospekt is about 10 minutes away.

BRUNCH IN STYLE

Breakfast is a no-brainer since most hotels include it in the price of the room. But why not treat yourself to something extra special? The top hotels have a real treat on Sundays – a luxurious brunch with an unlimited feast of fine food and drinks for a flat fee. Such a feast doesn't come cheap, so settle in for several hours to get your money's worth.

- One of the best is in the **Grand Hotel Europe's** Europa restaurant, where you can enjoy a luxurious Jazz Brunch with caviar, crepes, seafood, and various international cuisines in a stunning art nouveau setting.

- The **Corinthia Nevskij Palace** has a Mediterranean brunch, with live music and children's entertainment to keep everyone amused while feasting on a decadent selection of delicacies – there's even a special buffet for the kids.

- **Holiday Club St. Petersburg** has a Spanish family brunch, with paella and sangria in the Sevilla restaurant.

- For a view as well as fine food, head to the **Ambassador Hotel,** where the brunch has a different theme each week – but you can be sure the tables will be heaving under the abundant meats, pancakes, and sweets.

C GRAND HOTEL EUROPE $$$
1/7 Mikhailovskaya Ulitsa, 812/329-6000,
www.grand-hotel-europe.com
METRO: Nevsky Prospekt

It doesn't get posher than this. Big, grandiose, and expensive, the Grand Hotel Europe is the epitome of luxury. Enviably located between Nevsky Prospekt and Ploshchad Iskusstv (Arts Square), it's considered the city's best hotel, a genuine five-star, fit for a king—and it does indeed attract the international elite. The visitor list is a real who's who: George Bernard Shaw, Tchaikovsky, Dostoevsky, Prokofiyev,

Shostakovich, to name just a few. Of course, all the services you'd expect are here.

HERZEN HOUSE $$
Gertsen khaus
Герцен хаус
25 Ul. Bolshaya Morskaya, 812/571-5098,
www.herzenhotel.spb.ru
METRO: Nevsky Prospekt

This 20-room mini-hotel is named after the writer and revolutionary Alexander Herzen, who is said to have lived at this address in 1840–1841. Located in the historic, cultural, and business center amid major sights (Hermitage, Admiralty, St. Isaac's Cathedral), it puts you at the center of all the action, with restaurants and bars galore right at your front door. It's an ideal choice for those who want to see the city on foot. The hotel can arrange baby-sitters and nannies, and can pick you up at the airport or station. There's free wireless Internet, as well as free computer use and Internet access for those who haven't brought their own Wi-Fi enabled gizmos.

HOSTEL ERTEL $
Хостел Эртель
46 Liteyny Prospekt, Apt. 23, 812/973-3757,
www.zimmer.ru
METRO: Mayakovskaya

A small downtown hostel, Ertel offers a range of affordable accommodation options in its 11 rooms—singles, doubles, triples, and quadruples, plus separate male and female dormitories—with a combined total capacity for 36 people. There's a kitchen, washing machine, phone, fax, and Internet, but the bathroom facilities are shared, amounting to three toilets, three showers, and six sinks. If you don't fancy waiting in line to refresh yourself, Ertel also rents out one-, two- and three-bedroom apartments.

C KEMPINSKI HOTEL MOIKA 22 $$$
22 Naberezhnaya reki Moyka, 812/335-9111,
www.kempinski.com
METRO: Nevsky Prospekt

A stunning location on the charming Moyka

Canal within spitting distance of Palace Square is a strong drawing card at this newer hotel. The expensively fitted-out interior might lack the Old World charm of the Grand Hotel Europe or the Astoria, but the setting would seem to compensate. Even if you're not staying here, it's worth dropping by for a meal or drink in the Bellevue Brasserie up top, with its drop-dead gorgeous views of Palace Square.

MOYKA 5 $$$
Мойка 5

5 Naberezhnaya reki Moyki, 812/601-0636, www.hon.ru
METRO: Nevsky Prospekt

One of the city's best addresses, this beauty on the posh Moyka Canal puts you within a few footsteps of the main sights. Part of the Nevsky Hotels Group, Moyka 5 opened in 2006. It has 18 standard rooms and six luxe-class suites with whirlpool tub and sauna. There's wireless Internet and breakfast in separate spaces for smokers and nonsmokers.

NEVSKY FORUM $$$
Невский Форум

69 Nevsky Prospekt, 812/333-0222, www.forumhotel.ru
METRO: Mayakovskaya

If you're suffering baroque burnout, then this is the hotel for you. While others in this price bracket trigger Hermitage flashbacks, this hotel provides a refuge from all that ostentation. Nevsky Forum's 29 individually designed rooms are simple yet sophisticated, minimalist and masculine, with beige and brown colors to suit the serious business traveler. The location is appropriate—right on Nevsky, in the commercial center. The hotel's very top-class room has its own gym and sauna.

NORD HOSTEL $
10 Bolshaya Morskaya Ulitsa, 812/571-0342, www.nordhostel.com
METRO: Nevsky Prospekt

A hostel near the Hermitage? Sounds too good to be true, but that's what you find here. In a lovely little street leading from Nevsky Prospekt to Palace Square, Nord Hostel has 6-, 8-, and 10-person dorm rooms as well as private double

rooms. Besides being good value, it's got a cozy home-like look.

OFF $
63 Nevsky Prospekt, 812/764-2267, www.offoffoff.ru
METRO: Mayakovskaya

Perfect for artsy bohemian types, this mini-hotel and hostel is just a few minutes' walk from the Moskovsky train station. Its colorful corridors are covered in huge murals and posters, leading to humorously decorated 2-, 3-, and 10-bed rooms, a cheerfully chaotic kitchen, and a bathroom with a bright-red toilet. More than just a hotel, Off also has a hip clothing store and a studio.

OKTYABRSKAYA $$
Октябрьская

10 Ligovsky Prospekt, 812/578-1515,
www.oktober-hotel.spb.ru
METRO: Ploshchad Vosstaniya

You can't get a bed closer to the Moskovsky railway station than this. The Oktyabrskaya is in two buildings both located directly across the road from the station, so you don't have to lug your heavy bags very far after you get off the train. This Soviet-era old-timer isn't the bargain that it used to be, but renovations have upgraded its 484 rooms to a higher standard. Still, convenience is the main drawing card.

OLD VIENNA $$
Staraya Vyena
Старая Вена

13 Ul. Malaya Morskaya, 812/312-9339,
www.vena.old-spb.ru
METRO: Nevsky Prospekt

History-themed Old Vienna seeks to take you back to the early 20th century, when a renowned bohemian restaurant was at this address right in the heart of the city—five minutes' walk from the Hermitage and Palace Square, with St. Isaac's and the Admiralty just a stone's throw away. A cozy and charming mini-hotel of just 14 rooms, it boasts a library with old Russian classics, and is decorated in a nostalgic style, complete with historical photos on the walls.

PUSHKA INN $$$

Пушка Инн

14 Naberezhnaya reki Moyki, 812/312-0957,
www.pushkainn.ru
METRO: Nevsky Prospekt

This is one of the prettiest spots to stay in all of St. Petersburg—not to mention one of the closest to the Hermitage and Palace Square. Pushka Inn is in a luxurious 18th-century architectural landmark building with views of the picturesque Moyka Canal, right next door to Alexander Pushkin's house museum. The 34-room boutique hotel includes four multi-room family suites with their own fully equipped kitchens. Besides the romantic, nostalgic furnishings and antiques, it's equipped with all the mod-cons, such as notebook computer rental, high-speed Internet access, air-conditioners, and a DVD library.

PUSHKINSKAYA 10 $

Пушкинская 10

10 Pushkinskaya Ulitsa, 812/320-0982, www.hotel10.ru

METRO: Mayakovskaya or Ploshchad Vosstaniya

The former address of a legendary artists' squat and grungy nightclub, Pushkinskaya 10 had a makeover, being reborn as a more civilized cultural center, a cleaner version of the old nightclub, and this new hotel. With just nine individually designed rooms, it's just a couple of minutes' walk from Nevsky Prospekt. Don't expect too much luxury, but there are such conveniences as high-speed Internet, laundry services, and a 24-hour bar. All within staggering distance of the nightclub, Fish Fabrique!

RADISSON SAS ROYAL HOTEL $$$

49/2 Nevsky Prospekt, 812/322-5000,
www.stpetersburg.radissonsas.com
METRO: Mayakovskaya

A few doors away from the Corinthia Nevskij Palace on St. Pete's main street is this newer five-star competitor. It offers 164 rooms in an 18th-century building with a preserved facade and reconstructed interior, complete with free wireless Internet, gym, sauna, solarium, and

© NATHAN TOOHEY

A plaque on the wall of the Pushka Inn says the Decembrist Ivan Pushchin lived there from 1823 to 1825.

massage room. No surprises, just what you'd expect from such an international brand.

VESTA HOTEL $$

92 Nevsky Prospekt, 812/272-1322,
www.vestahotel.spb.ru
METRO: Mayakovskaya

Although it boasts a Nevsky Prospekt address, this cozy three-star is hidden away from the street in a quiet courtyard. Besides the usual single, twin, and double rooms, it offers child-friendly family rooms and also studio-suites with a complete kitchen including all the requisite utensils. Business travelers are catered for, with Internet access and meeting rooms.

Kolomna to Sennaya Ploshchad   Map 10

AMBASSADOR $$$

5-7 Prospekt Rimskogo-Korsakogo, 812/331-8844,
www.ambassador-hotel.ru
METRO: Sennaya Ploshchad

With 255 luxuriously appointed rooms including a posh presidential suite, the Ambassador positions itself as prestigious, although it does offer "economy" rooms. Unusually for Russia, it seeks to cater for disabled guests with special facilities, and has nonsmoking rooms as well. There's a 24-hour gym, a swimming pool, a beauty salon, sauna, and several restaurants and bars. A good choice for ballet buffs, the Ambassador is within easy walking distance of the Mariinsky Theater. The closest sight is Nikolsky Cathedral, and there's also the lovely Yusupovsky Garden, where you can breathe some fresh air while strolling around the gorgeous pond.

CENTRAL INN $

2 Ul. Yakubovicha, Apt. 14, 812/571-4516,
www.central-inn.ru
METRO: Sennaya Ploshchad or Sadovaya

One of the attractions of this inexpensive mini-hotel is that some of the rooms have views of St. Isaac's Cathedral. But even if you opt for the lowest-priced rooms without views, you can still enjoy the cathedral, as it's located right opposite. Stay connected during your visit using the wireless Internet service or rent a computer from the hotel. There's a sauna to help you unwind after a heavy day of sightseeing.

MATISOV DOMIK $$

Отель Матисов Домик

3/1 Naberezhnaya reki Pryazhki, 812/495-0242,
www.matisov.com
METRO: Sennaya Ploshchad

If you want to stay in a totally untouristy part of town where you can experience the "real" Petersburg, then this 46-room, three-star mini-hotel might suit. Far from any metro stations or major shops, it's not a convenient location, but New Holland and the Mariinsky Theater are fairly close. The neighborhood is rich in charming canals and romantically run-down old streets where you can pretend you've travelled back in time to Dostoyevsky's era.

Vasilyevsky Island   Map 11

HOLIDAY CLUB ST. PETERSBURG $$$
2-4 Birzhevoy Pereulok, 812/335-2200,
www.holidayclubhotels.ru
METRO: Vasileostrovskaya
This five-star 278-room hotel opened in 2008, right near the Strelka. Besides its luxurious rooms and all its restaurants, a unique feature is its Spa & Wellness World, where you can take to the water in style. Who needs canal cruises when there's a pool area styled after Roman baths, but with modern whirlpool tubs? Not to mention Sauna World with seven different kinds of steamy experiences to try including some truly obscure ones; the so-called Shower World, which the hotel bills as "an adventure in itself" (the mind boggles); and a full range of spa services and a complete gym.

Smolny and Old Nevsky   Map 13

INTERNATIONAL HOSTEL $
28 3-ya Sovetskaya Ulitsa, 812/329-8018, www.ryh.ru
METRO: Ploshchad Vosstaniya
This tried-and-trusted Russian-American joint project is a long-term player, with more than a decade of experience and lots of happy customers. It's a five-minute walk from the Moskovsky railway station, which makes it super-convenient if you're traveling between Moscow and St. Pete by train. The high-ceilinged restored 19th-century house has three- and five-bed dorm rooms as well as double rooms at affordable prices. Services include laundry, Internet, airport shuttle, and visa support.

REDMEDVED $
57 Ulitsa Zhukovskogo, 812/272-2182,
www.redmedved.com
METRO: Ploshchad Vosstaniya
A suitable choice for party animals, this new hostel boasts that it's the "funniest and most eventful" in St. Petersburg. It even organizes bar crawls every Friday and Saturday night. Five minutes from the Moskovsky train station, Redmedved (read Redbear) has four rooms with a varying number of bunk beds and a maximum capacity of 26. There's a kitchen with a microwave, refrigerator, kettles, and a toaster, and a common room with a television.

Greater St. Petersburg   Map 14

OBUHOFF $$
1 Ulitsa Knipovich, 812/365-0190,
www.obuhoffhotel.ru
METRO: Ploshchad Alexandra Nevskogo
This 40-roomer is a neat, friendly, good-value place to stay. The service is good, the rooms are lovely, and they lay on a decent breakfast, but it's not in a very convenient location. It's a bit of a hike to the metro station—not the sort of walk that would be pleasant after dark, even though the route would be along the river beyond the Alexander Nevsky Lavra monastery. Staying here, you'd be taxi-dependent, which isn't easy if you don't speak Russian.

PARK INN PRIBALTIYSKAYA $$
14 Ulitsa Korablestroiteley, 812/329-2626,
www.pribaltiyskaya.parkinn.com.ru
METRO: Primorskaya
Forget quaint history—we've seen the future and it's made of concrete. This enormous 1,200-room hotel on the far end of Vasilyevsky Island is surrounded by the kind of high-rise

Soviet-era apartment blocks that can give Westerners the heebie-jeebies, but locals actually consider it quite a prestigious neighborhood. An old Intourist hotel, the Pribaltiyskaya has the full gamut of services and has been gradually upgrading to Park Inn standards in recent years. It's located right on the Gulf of Finland, with great views over the water and an Aqua Park to frolic in. The metro is a bit too far, but that doesn't matter for many of the guests, who seem to be part of large-group bus tours.

PARK INN PULKOVSKAYA $$$
1 Ploshchad Pobedy, 812/740-3900, www.parkinn.ru
METRO: Moskovskaya

Although far from the historic center, this hotel's location has its pluses. With views of Victory Square and the Monument to the Heroic Defenders of Leningrad, it is convenient to the airport and near the minibuses that run to the palace estates of Pushkin and Pavlovsk. It's also near the metro, so you can zip into the center in about 15 minutes. The 840 rooms include standard, business class, and luxe suites. Besides bars and restaurants, it offers a spa and fitness center.

EXCURSIONS FROM ST. PETERSBURG

From St. Petersburg you can take several interesting excursions that are easily accessible and reveal vastly different aspects of Russia's northwest.

A day trip to one of the palace estates in St. Petersburg's suburbs reveals the staggering wealth of Russia's tsarist rulers. The top three palace choices for a tourist on a short visit are Peterhof, Pavlovsk, and Tsarskoye Selo (aka Pushkin)—all rich enough in sights to fill a full day, but close enough to St. Petersburg not to require staying the night there. Don't just go to visit the palace museums, but also take the time to explore and admire the incredible landscaped gardens in which they are set; each has its own unique character.

In sharp contrast is Kronshtadt, a sleepy island fortress town with an interesting history and distinct naval personality. Despite its proximity to St. Petersburg, it seemingly lives in a world of its own, perhaps because it was long a closed city, off-limits to outsiders due to its strategic importance.

Vyborg, formerly part of Finland, is a border town that still retains its Finnish character. Its distinctive architecture makes it totally unlike any other town in Russia, with a 13th-century castle, fat towers, and cobblestoned streets, as well as a brilliant park museum.

If you have time to go farther afield, Novgorod, between Moscow and St. Petersburg, shows yet another face of this fascinating country. One of Russia's oldest cities, it has a wealth of well-preserved medieval churches and monasteries in a neat urban setting that shows off all the historical landmarks to their best advantage.

HIGHLIGHTS

LOOK FOR (((TO FIND RECOMMENDED SIGHTS, ACTIVITIES, DINING, AND LODGING.

(((**Most Unforgettable Fountain:** The **Grand Cascade** in Peterhof is a sensory overload of gold and gushing water that provides the most stunning welcome to this palace estate when you arrive by hydrofoil (page 287).

(((**Most Playful and Picturesque Park:** Peterhof's **Lower Park** is a real delight, featuring an incredible variety of garden landscaping with some surprises courtesy of Peter the Great (page 288).

(((**Most Palatial Palace:** The **Catherine Palace** in Pushkin is a sumptuous baroque beauty of sky blue, white, and gold – now with the Amber Room restored to its former glory (page 291).

(((**Best Castle:** The 13th-century Swedish-built **Vyborg Castle** is not just Russia's best castle, but also its only castle, with fabulous views from the lookout at the top (page 297).

(((**Coolest Kremlin:** Russia's oldest surviving kremlin is **Novgorod's Kremlin,** dating back to the 11th century and historically called Detinets. Surrounded by parkland and picturesquely located beside a river with a sandy beach, it contains Russia's oldest stone church, the Cathedral of St. Sofia, fascinating monuments and museums, and a wonderful restaurant (page 302).

EXCURSIONS

© NATHAN TOOHEY

The Catherine Palace in Pushkin is an elaborate baroque concoction.

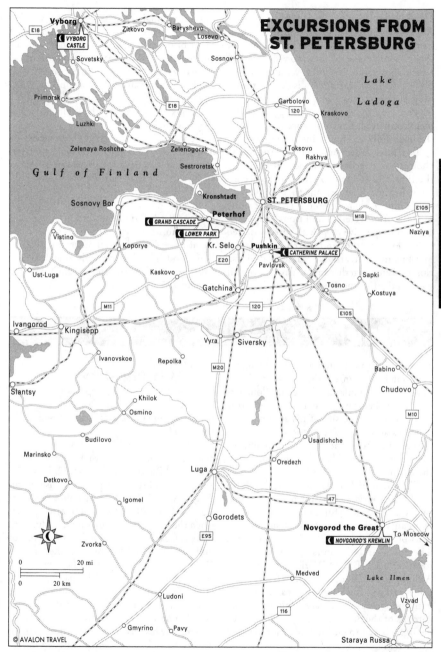

EXCURSIONS

PLANNING YOUR TIME

Anyone visiting St. Petersburg in the summer for any amount of time, no matter how short, should make the effort to visit Peterhof, Russia's answer to Versailles. With its incredible fountains and cascades, it is the most stunning of the palaces—unquestionably one of St. Pete's top sights. This is really just a summer destination, however, since that is when the hydrofoils and fountains are working.

Tsarskoye Selo and Pavlovsk are strong choices for a second excursion, if you have the time and interest to see more palace estates; in the colder seasons they would be a better choice than Peterhof. They are quite different from Peterhof and from each other, so it's not repetitive to visit all three. Located quite close together and linked by a regular minibus route, Tsarskoye Selo and Pavlovsk can be visited together in one day, but only if you're quite fit, since you have to walk a long distance through Pavlovsk's enormous wooded grounds to see anything. Tsarskoye Selo is the easier of the two, since you can take a minibus practically to the palace's front door and the garden attractions are immediately visible. Both estates are worthy of a full-day visit, however, and if you try to see both in one day you'll just be scratching the surface of what they have to offer.

Neither Kronshtadt nor Vyborg would go down as essentials, but they do make for fascinating and easy day trips. Both can be visited at any time of year, but Vyborg is especially beautiful in the winter.

Novgorod is not yet up there with Moscow and St. Petersburg as an essential Russian destination, but perhaps it's only a matter of time. Deserving of an overnight trip, Novgorod is still a relatively undiscovered treasure and rewards those who make the time to visit.

Peterhof

Translating from Dutch as "Peter's Court," Peterhof is a town on the southern shores of the Gulf of Finland, about 30 kilometers west of St. Petersburg. In 1714, Peter I (the Great) made it the site of his summer residence, establishing the palace estate as a place to stay en route to and from Kronshtadt, the island fortress, naval base, and harbor just to the north.

The town of Peterhof is quite lovely in itself, but tourists come for just one thing: the Peterhof State Museum-Preserve, where you can see the palaces and elaborate gardens of Peter the Great and his successors. The town and the museum-preserve are together a UNESCO World Heritage site. Although there is a pretty church and some other parks in the town, they can't compete with the spectacular palaces, fountains, and gardens of the museum estate, where there's enough to keep you busy for more than a whole day.

PETERHOF STATE MUSEUM-PRESERVE

Gosudarstvenny muzey-zapovednik Petergof
Государственный музей-заповедник Петергоф

Come to Peterhof and spend the whole day at its one mega-sight—the Peterhof State Museum-Preserve (2 Razvodnaya Ulitsa, 812/450-7425, www.peterhof.ru, www.peterhofmuseum.ru, daily 9 A.M.–7 P.M., Russians 50–200R, foreigners 150–300R, free entry after 5 P.M. when the fountains are turned off). This park and palace estate on the banks of the Gulf of Finland was established by Peter the Great in 1714. Over the next 11 years he oversaw the construction of many of its palaces, fountains, and gardens, which were supposed to be Russia's answer to France's Versailles. Peter's already-impressive estate was made even more elaborate by his successors on the throne, but it was destroyed by Nazi German invaders during

The boat station in front of the Winter Palace is the place to catch a hydrofoil to Peterhof.

World War II and subsequently reconstructed, temporarily being renamed to the less German-sounding Petrodvorets (Peterpalace).

This incredible estate is best approached from the water. Arriving via hydrofoil, you enter the Lower Park at the tip of the **Sea Canal**, which leads you through the immaculately landscaped gardens and past graceful bridges and ever-more-elaborate fountains, until suddenly the most spectacular sight appears before you: the Grand Cascade.

◖ Grand Cascade

The Grand Cascade, a multi-level, multi-jet fountain lined with gilded statues, rises up a steep hill, where the baroque Grand Palace lords above. The centerpiece of this absurdly ostentatious display is a giant statue of Samson ripping apart the jaws of a lion, from which shoots the tallest water-jet of all—this composition is supposed to symbolize Russia's victory over Sweden in the Great Northern War. Climb up the stairs beside the cascade and admire the view from the top.

Another sight here is the **Grottos** (Mon.–Fri. 11 A.M.–5 P.M., Sat.–Sun. 11 A.M.–6 P.M., ticket office is in Grand Palace and closes half hour earlier, Russians 50–120R, foreigners 80–150R)—caves inside the cascade, giving a closer view of the waterworks as well as yet more statues and busts hidden inside.

Grand Palace

The Grand Palace (Tues.–Sun. 10:30 A.M.–5 P.M., closed last Tues. of month, Russians 100–250R, foreigners 250–520R) is open as a museum. Inside you can marvel at the lavish royal interiors, mostly reconstructed (like the rest of the estate) after their destruction during Nazi German occupation in World War II.

Part of the Grand Palace, the **Osobaya Kladovaya** (Tues.–Sun. 10:30 A.M.–6 P.M., Russians 50–200R, foreigners 200–400R) is a museum in the private rooms of Catherine the Great. Here you can see jewelry, costumes, dresses, and personal belongings of Russian rulers from Peter I (the Great) to Nicholas II, including works of the famed Fabergés.

◖ Lower Park

The main garden attractions, including numerous fountains and several cascades, are in the formal French-styled Lower Park. Wander about and delight in Peter's **joke fountains,** of which there are several, including a cobblestone path that will shoot water jets and soak you if you step on the right (or rather, wrong) pebble, and an umbrella-shaped pagoda that showers you as you step in to take shelter. On hot days these fun fountains attract crowds of children, who scamper about getting wet and wild. On even hotter days, children and adults alike can be seen taking a dip even in the larger fountains' pools.

Located right on the banks of the Gulf of Finland is a Dutch-style villa called **Monplaisir** (summer Thurs.–Tues. 10:30 A.M.–5 P.M., Russians 50–150R, foreigners 150–300R). Peterhof's oldest building, constructed 1714–1723, this was Peter's favorite residence, even after the appearance of a grander palace at the top of the hill. Inside you can see restored Petrine interiors and some of his personal effects.

At the west of the Lower Park is the 18th-century **Marly Palace** (Tues.–Sun. 10:30 A.M.–6 P.M., Russians 50–100R, foreigners 80–150R), also with Petrine memorabilia on display. It is surrounded by ponds that used to supply the royal table with fish—now even you can try to catch a sturgeon here and eat it in one of the estate's restaurants.

Upper Garden

Behind the Grand Palace is the Upper Garden, located outside the territory of the Peterhof Museum-Preserve. It's not worth going outside to explore here if you want to return to St. Pete by hydrofoil, because you'd need to buy another ticket to get back in. But if you're taking a bus or train back, you might as well walk through on your way, although it's nothing compared to the Lower Park. Across the road from the Upper Garden, stop to admire the

© NATHAN TOOHEY

Peterhof's Lower Park

Cathedral of St. Peter and St. Paul, built in 1905 in pseudo-Russian style.

RESTAURANTS

There are several cafés and bars within the Peterhof State Museum-Preserve. Simple, inexpensive snacks and drinks can be found in the cafés at the sides of the Grand Palace as well as in several pavilions scattered around the Lower Park. A short distance inland from the Marly, at the west of the Lower Park, there's a nice little beer garden with an elevated terrace.

For something a bit fancier and more fun, try **fishing for your dinner in the Marly Palace pond** (May 14–Sept. 28 daily 10 A.M.–7 P.M.). Hook a sturgeon and receive a trout as an added bonus, all to be cooked up for you to eat in one of the park's restaurants, **◖ Shtandart** (Lower Park, 812/450-6281, www.restaurantshtandart. spb.ru, daily 11 A.M.–5 P.M.). All the necessary equipment is provided free of charge—you just pay for the fish you catch (1,800R per kilogram of

sturgeon). The Shtandart also offers an à la carte menu with Russian cuisine starting from the ruble equivalent of about $20 for a main course.

Better value is to be found outside the grounds, although those returning to St. Petersburg by hydrofoil don't really have this option. If you are returning by minibus or train, walk up the left side of the Upper Garden, outside the estate's grounds, and you'll find **Trapeza** (9 Kalininskaya Ulitsa, 812/427-9393, daily noon–10 P.M.), a good spot to try refreshing, traditional cold summer borsch (170R).

RECREATION

Baltic Airlines (7/9 Nevsky Prospekt, 2nd fl., 812/117-0084, www.balticairlines.ru) offers various **helicopter excursions,** including regular 10–15 minute scenic flights over Peterhof (weekends and public holidays only, 11 A.M.–6 P.M., 1,000R), departing from the western side of the Lower Park. In addition

EXCURSIONS

© NATHAN TOOHEY

dining alfresco at Shtandart

there are routes between Peterhof and St. Petersburg. Or if you're game you can take a tandem parachute jump (5,000R).

GETTING THERE

Absolutely the best way to reach Peterhof is by hydrofoil. Called Meteors, they depart from two jetties right in front of the Hermitage Museum on the Neva River's Palace Embankment (36–38 Dvortsovaya Naberezhnaya, 812/325-6120, 812/325-3341, www.russian-cruises.ru) every 30 minutes (400R one way, 700R round-trip); the trip takes about 40 minutes. The last returning hydrofoil departs Peterhof at 6 P.M.—if you miss it, you'll have to get back to town by minibus or train. The hydrofoil ticket price does not cover the entry fees to the estate's grounds. Those tickets are sold separately on the pier where you disembark from the hydrofoil.

A far less pleasant but much cheaper way to get between St. Petersburg and Peterhof is by minibus. Called *marshrutki* in Russian, these minibuses run regularly from the Baltiysky railway station as well as the metro stations Avtovo and Leninsky Prospekt. The advantage of the minibuses compared to the train is that they stop right opposite the Upper Garden, close to the Museum-Preserve's top entrance.

The train, running every 15–30 minutes from the Baltiysky railway station (20 Naberezhnaya Obvodnogo Kanala, 812/768-2859, metro Baltiyskaya), is less cramped than a minibus, but the disadvantage is that the spot where you get off, the fancily renovated Novy Petergof station, is not very close to the actual museum-estate. From the station you'd need to take a taxi, bus, or minibus, or walk about 15 minutes.

Minibuses and trains both cost about 50 rubles and take about 45 minutes, not counting the amount of time it takes to reach the station from which they depart. Buying tickets, finding the right minibus or train, and figuring out when to get off is much more difficult and tiring than taking the hydrofoil—especially if you don't speak Russian—and it's really not worth the hassle. The hydrofoil might sound expensive but it's well worth the price.

If, on the other hand, you're cashed up and love living the high life, you can go by helicopter. Baltic Airlines (7/9 Nevsky Prospekt, 2nd fl., 812/117-0084, www.balticairlines .ru) advertises helicopter flights between St. Petersburg's Peter and Paul Fortress and the Peterhof Museum-Preserve's Lower Park (departures from Peter and Paul Fortress weekends and public holidays only at 11:30 A.M. and 1:30 and 3:30 P.M.; returning from Peterhof at 12:30, 2:30, and 4:30 P.M., 1,000R).

Pushkin

Twenty-five kilometers south of St. Petersburg is Pushkin (Пушкин), a gorgeous town graced by an enormous tsarist estate that's almost as stunning as Peterhof. (In fact, Pushkin's palaces and gardens might be superior overall, but it's a tall order to compete with Peterhof's location on the Gulf of Finland and its spectacular gilded fountains.)

Founded in the 18th century as a summer residence for royalty, the town is still sometimes called **Tsarskoye Selo** (Tsar's Village), its pre-1918 name. From 1918 to 1937, as noble properties were turned into museums,

educational institutions, and summer camps, the town was renamed Detskoye Selo (Children's Village)—and that's still the name of the railway station, although the town is now named after the poet Alexander Pushkin, who was educated at the Imperial Lyceum here.

Just about everything had to be rebuilt after World War II, when Nazi Germany invaded the town, trashed the palace estate, and looted its treasures. The meticulously reconstructed palace and park ensemble and the town center of Pushkin are UNESCO World Heritage sites.

TSARSKOYE SELO STATE MUSEUM-PRESERVE

Gosudarstvenny muzey-zapovednik Tsarskoye Selo

Государственный музей-заповедник Царское село

Rich architecture and beautifully landscaped gardens make an indelible impression at the palace estate of Tsarskoye Selo (7 Sadovaya Ulitsa, 812/465-9424, www.tzar.ru, daily 9 A.M.–10 P.M., ticket office until 6 P.M., Russians, Russia-based foreign diplomatic staff, and foreigners permanently residing in Russia 50–90R, other foreigners 90–180R).

Alexander Palace

Catherine the Great commissioned Tsarskoye Selo's Alexander Palace, or Alexandrovsky dvorets, which has a permanent exhibit "Memories of Alexander Palace" (Wed.–Mon. 10 A.M.–6 P.M., closed last Wed. of month, ticket office until 5 P.M.; Russians, Russia-based foreign diplomatic staff, and foreigners permanently residing in Russia 50–150R, other

foreigners 150–300R). Built in the 1790s to a design by Giacomo Quarenghi, it was the favorite palace of the last tsar, Nicholas II.

◖ Catherine Palace

The main sight is the Catherine Palace, or Yekaterininsky dvorets (Wed.–Mon. 10 A.M.–6 P.M., closed last Mon. of month, ticket office until 5 P.M.; in summer, entrance may be restricted to group bookings only 10 A.M.–noon and 2–4 P.M., and individuals noon–2 P.M. and 4–5 P.M.; Russians, Russia-based foreign diplomatic staff and foreigners permanently residing in Russia 90–260R, other foreigners 280–550R). It was originally built in the 1750s for Empress Elizabeth, who had inherited the estate from her mother, Catherine I. The architect, Francesco Bartolomeo Rastrelli, also takes credit for St. Petersburg's Winter Palace and Smolny Cathedral, which similarly demonstrate his trademark opulent style. The extravagant exterior decoration is outdone by the unbelievably luxurious interiors, which include the newly restored **Amber Room,** a lavish chamber of amber,

Catherine Palace

© NATHAN TOOHEY

EXCURSIONS

gold, and mirrors that justifies the palace's pricey entry fees. Having won renown as "the eighth wonder of the world," the original Amber Room was famously lost after being looted by Nazi Germany in World War II.

Elizabeth's successors added their own touches to the palace, with one noteworthy extension being the classical-styled **Cameron Gallery,** built by Scottish architect Charles Cameron for Catherine the Great. Inside you can see an exhibition entitled "Alexander I in Tsarskoye Selo" (Thurs.–Tues. 10 A.M.–5 P.M., closed last Tues. of month; Russians, Russia-based foreign diplomatic staff, and foreigners permanently residing in Russia 50–150R, other foreigners 150–300R).

Gardens

Take some time to explore the immense gardens, ranging from the formal **Catherine Park** in front of the Catherine Palace, to English-styled landscaping around the **Great Pond,** and more overgrown woods beyond. A few hours wandering around these enchanting gardens will reveal a Chinese Village, Chinese Theater, Turkish Cascades, Gothic Gates, and all manner of statues, towers, columns, pavilions, grottos, and lovingly designed ruins. At the Great Pond you can ride in a Venetian-style **gondola** (daily noon–5:30 P.M., Russians 150–300R, foreigners 200–400R, one-hour rental 4,000R) or take a **ferry cruise** (Mon.–Fri. noon–6 P.M., Sat.–Sun. 11 A.M.–6 P.M., Russians 100–200R, foreigners 200–400R).

RESTAURANTS

On the grounds of the Tsarskoye Selo palace estate, the best restaurant is the **Admiralty** (Admiralty building, 812/4665-3549, daily noon–11 P.M.), which serves a trendy mixed menu ranging from Thai to Italian cuisine. Although it has a summer terrace picturesquely located on the banks of the Great Pond, you might find all the tables and chairs have been carried inside—the staff seem to think tourists would prefer to sit in the rather stuffy interior, which fails to exploit the sensational views. The prices are fairly substantial—expect to pay the ruble equivalent of about $20 for a main course.

Outside, there's a nice little spot called the **Grand Cafe Flora** (2 Oranzhereynaya Ulitsa, 812/466-6113, daily 11 A.M.–last guest). It's close to the palace estate, right near the spot where the minibuses stop. Prices are lower than at the Admiralty—you might even find something you fancy for about $10—and they make a decent cappuccino.

GETTING THERE

The easiest way to get to the Tsarskoye Selo Museum-Preserve is on a *marshrutka* (minibus). Dedicated "Palaces, Fountains" minibuses depart from the square adjacent to Moskovskaya metro station—look for the Lenin statue, and you'll find the bus stop is right behind him. These minibuses stop near the estate's gates before continuing onwards to Pavlovsk. Minibus route numbers 342, 286, 287, 545, and 347 also go to Pushkin. Trains run from St. Petersburg's Vitebsk Station (52 Zagorodny Prospekt, 812/768-7900, metro Pushkinskaya) to Pushkin's railway station, which is called Detskoye Selo, but this is less convenient because the railway station is not close to the palace estate. It is, however, interesting from a historical point of view—the Tsarskoye Selo–Petersburg railroad was Russia's first, built in 1837 and used to transport the royal family to their summer retreat.

Pavlovsk

About 30 kilometers south of St. Petersburg and 4 kilometers south of Pushkin is lovely, leafy Pavlovsk. The town was founded in the late 18th century, growing around the palace estate of Emperor Paul I—hence the name Pavlovsk, derived from Pavel, the Russian form of Paul. The one sight here is the UNESCO World Heritage palace estate museum-preserve. Wilder than Peterhof and Tsarskoye Selo, this is a place of more natural, subtle beauty—perfect for those who want to breathe some fresh air, meet friendly squirrels, and get lost in the woods.

PAVLOVSK STATE MUSEUM-PRESERVE

Gosudarstvenny muzey-zapovednik
Pavlovsk
Государственный музей-заповедник
Павловск

In stark contrast to the showy Peterhof and Tsarskoye Selo estates is this peaceful alternative, the Pavlovsk State Museum-Preserve (20 Sadovaya Ulitsa, 812/452-1536, www.pavlovskmuseum.ru, daily 10 A.M.–6 P.M., Russians 40–60R, foreigners 80–150R). Although the entrance is right opposite the train station and bus stop, it takes a long hike through some deep forest to reach the palace and other buildings. Walk straight ahead up the main path until you reach a stream, then follow the paths to the right up the hill to the palace.

The estate's history dates back to 1777, when Catherine II (the Great) gave hunting grounds here to her son Paul, who was later to become Emperor Paul I. In the 1780s, Scottish architect Charles Cameron designed Paul's Neoclassical palace and the surrounding **English-style gardens**—a masterpiece of landscape art. Having suffered heavy damage due to a fire in 1803, the palace was partly rebuilt by other architects; it later required further reconstruction after damage in World War II.

The **Grand Palace** (May 15–Sept. 15 daily

EXCURSIONS

© NATHAN TOOHEY

Pavlovsk's Grand Palace

10 A.M.–5 P.M.; Sept. 15–May 15 Sat.–Thurs. 10 A.M.–5 P.M., closed first Mon. of month; Russians 50–180R, photo permit 50R, video permit 100R, foreigners 250–400R, photo permit 200R, video permit 300R), now open as a museum, is relatively small, quietly elegant, and perhaps a bit more tasteful than the flashier palaces of Peterhof and Tsarskoye Selo. The Parade Halls are the most interesting part, including Charles Cameron's Egyptian-style vestibule and living quarters of Paul I, with period furniture and artworks. There are various other exhibits to see, such as "The World of Women and Their Amusements: Noble Life of the Late 19th–early 20th Century," and "The Wonderful Faces of Russian Royalty" (both open Fri.–Sun. 10 A.M.–5 P.M.).

Really it's the gardens here that are the main attraction, however. Quite natural-looking after Peterhof and Tsarskoye Selo, they are immensely varied and absolutely enormous—more than 500 hectares—so it's easy to get lost. This is a place for quiet strolling, peaceful bench-sitting, and listening to birdsong. There are elegant pagodas to admire, as well as romantic ruins, classical statues, and Paul's mausoleum. Cute red squirrels scamper among the trees—some are quite tame and will beg for food, which is something to keep in mind when you see the nut-sellers along the paths.

RESTAURANTS

In one of the palace's side wings, right on the main Palace Square, you'll find the **Grand Column Hall Restaurant** (Grand Palace, 20 Sadovaya Ulitsa, 812/957-0019, Sat.–Thurs. 10 A.M.–6 P.M.). This former ballroom is quite a posh setting for a self-serve buffet, where you can have lunch for the ruble equivalent of a couple of dollars. As you sit beneath the crystal chandeliers, amid tall columns and gracefully arching windows, you can almost picture the noble events that took place here. There's also the option of sitting at one of the tables outside on the square. The same management also runs cafés in the 18th-century **Dairy and Aviary Pavilions** (20 Sadovaya Ulitsa, 812/957-0019, Sat.–Thurs. 10 A.M.–6 P.M.), with the Dairy Pavilion being the place to go for that summertime classic, shashlik (grilled meat on a skewer).

GETTING THERE

Suburban trains to Pavlovsk run regularly from St. Petersburg's Vitebsk Station (52 Zagorodny Prospekt, 812/768-7900, metro Pushkinskaya), a 40-minute ride that costs about 50R and brings you right to the estate's gates. Another option is the *marshrutka* (minibuses), which also cost about 50R and depart from near the Moskovskaya metro station—you'll find them between the giant Lenin statue and the huge Stalinist building behind him. Emblazoned with the words "Palaces, Fountains," they stop at the Tsarskoye Selo palace estate before continuing on to Pavlovsk, so you might consider exploring that museum and its gardens first, before catching another minibus onwards to Pavlovsk. After you're done, you can catch a minibus back, or you can exit via the back gate next to the palace and catch a bus back to the Pavlovsk train station, a 10-minute ride for less than 20R. Trains depart for St. Petersburg's Vitebsky station roughly every half-hour.

Kronshtadt

Kronshtadt (Кронштадт) is a naval town on Kotlin island in the Gulf of Finland, with a history as old and as rich as St. Petersburg's—helped, no doubt, by the fact that it was founded by Peter the Great just one year later than the northern capital itself. The island was captured from Sweden in 1703, and on May 18, 1704, the first fortifications where inaugurated. The Kronshlot fort, as it was known until 1723, was rapidly constructed to prevent the return of the Swedes, and since that time it has never let an adversary sail past.

Catherine the Great ordered the admiralty to be transferred to the island after the St. Petersburg fire of 1783 and it was around this time that the Obvodny Canal that runs through the center of the old town was constructed. The fortified island's strategic positioning proved invaluable to the defense of St. Petersburg in both the Russo-Swedish War of 1788–1790 and the Baltic theater of the Crimean War from 1853 to 1856.

Kronshtadt, however, is best known as the site of the 1921 Kronshtadt Rebellion when, in March of that year, thousands of Kronshtadt sailors and their supporters revolted against the Bolsheviks. The rebellion was only subdued and the island recaptured by all-out assault from across the frozen Gulf of Finland by the Red Army. It was not until 1996 that Kronshtadt ceased to be a closed town and was once again open to foreigners.

Kronshtadt's location, just 30 kilometers west of St. Petersburg and accessible by road, makes the small town of some 45,000 people an easy day trip. With a similar architecture to its bigger brother, it feels vaguely similar and yet somehow different given its dominating naval heritage. Although there are few sights as such, it's pleasant to wander along the waterfront, along the canals, and through the leafy parks. The pleasantly green streets and quiet lanes are an attraction in themselves, especially after the hustle and bustle of busy St. Pete.

EXCURSIONS

© NATHAN TOOHEY

fishing at Kronshtadt's port

SIGHTS
Forts of Kronshtadt
Форты Кронштадта

Seventeen fortresses surround Kronshtadt—some are on islands, some are attached to Kotlin Island, and some form part of the dam across which the road runs between Kronshtadt and St. Petersburg. They are mostly abandoned and derelict, although some are used as naval warehouses, and every summer at least one of the forts plays host to the popular Fort Dance rave, among other open-air parties. Special boat tours cruise around a half-dozen of the forts, departing almost hourly between 12:30 and 7 P.M. from the Winter Pier, which is on the left side of Petrovsky Park. Tickets cost 225R; children under five years are free. For more information, contact Kronshtadt's tourist information center (1/33 Ulitsa Martynova, 812/311-9134, 812/311-9147, daily 10 A.M.–7 P.M.).

Kronshtadt Fortress Museum
Muzey Kronshtadtskaya krepost
Музей "Кронштадтская крепость"

Located in what was once a sailors club inside the Naval Cathedral, the fortress museum (2 Yakornaya Ploshchad, 812/311-4713, Wed.–Sun. 11 A.M.–5 P.M., closed last Thurs. of month, Russians 25–60R, foreigners 100–300R, photo permit 40R, video permit 60R) houses a collection of several thousand items, including 86 model ships. Besides the models, expect to see all manner of nautical materials such as historical paintings, documents, weapons, flags, medals, and awards among the many displays in the seven separate halls. Definitely one for maritime buffs.

Naval Cathedral
Morskoy sobor
Морской собор

Located on the aptly named Anchor Square (Yakornaya Ploshchad), this ornate cathedral (2 Yakornaya Ploshchad, 812/236-4713, Wed.–Sun. 11 A.M.–5 P.M., closed last Thurs. of month, Russians 25–60R, foreigners 100–300R, photo permit 40R, video permit 60R) was completed in 1913 after 10 years of construction. The neo-Byzantine cathedral, which dominates the surrounding town, was designed to resemble Hagia Sophia cathedral in Istanbul. However, given that it was dedicated to the Russian Navy and its sailors, it features maritime motifs in its facade—look for the anchors that run around the base of its huge dome as well as on its main doors.

After the Revolution it continued to hold services until 1927, when the communists converted it into a cinema. Later it served as a sailors club and theater. In 1974, a naval museum was founded in the place of the club and remains to this day as the Kronshtadt Fortress Museum. Only in 2002 did the Orthodox cross reappear atop the 70-meter-high dome, while talks have been underway to return the cathedral to the church. Not far from the cathedral burns the eternal flame for Kronshtadt's war dead, as well as a monument to Admiral Makarov. Small stalls on Yakornaya Ploshchad sell sailor shirts and other maritime souvenirs.

State Historical Architecture-Art Museum of Kronshtadt
Istorichesky arkhitekturno-khudozhestvenny muzey g. Kronshtadta
Исторический архитектурно-художественный музей г. Кронштадта

Founded with the help of local historians in 1991, the museum (2 Leningradskaya Ulitsa, 812/435-0873, daily 11 A.M.–6 P.M., 30R) only acquired its current stately housing inside a former water pumping station in 2006. The museum nicely complements the naval-related Kronshtadt Fortress Museum with a more civic collection documenting the founding and development of the city. Many of the items on display, such as family items, photographs, letters, and other heirlooms, were donated by local residents. Make sure you check out the diorama providing a bird's-eye view of the island, town, and surrounding forts.

RESTAURANTS
The fantastically retro restaurant **Austeriya v Kronshtadte** (43 Sovetskaya Ulitsa, 812/236-

0532, 812/311-0532, daily noon–midnight) may well not be intentionally old-school, but then that only adds to the charm. Its three halls are designed with a marine theme—check out the fountain designed as a cascade over seashells in the main room. There is live music on weekends. The menu offers classical Russian dishes at bargain prices—the soups are particularly good.

Zolotoy Lev (45 Prospekt Lenina, 812/439-4001, Mon.–Fri. noon–midnight, Sat.–Sun. noon–2 A.M.) translates as "golden lion," and it serves surprisingly good Chinese food. This is no Chinese takeout-style place; the interior is actually quite formal in an elegant Chinese way. The prices, however, are low as can be (the disposable chopsticks will cost you though, albeit only 5R). All around, it's a good bet.

Cafe Bastion (35 Sovetskaya Ulitsa, 921/868-8186, daily 11 A.M.–4 A.M.) is located in a recently reconstructed House of Culture. Besides the café, the entertainment complex now has a cinema, concert hall, and even a fitness center. Without a doubt, the café's main appeal is its large 2nd-floor outdoor terrace with a simply stunning view across the Obvodny Canal to the Naval Cathedral. It's worth coming here for the view alone.

TOURIST OFFICE

Kronshtadt's tourist information center (1/33 Ulitsa Martynova, 812/311-9134, 812/311-9147, 10 A.M.–7 P.M.) has friendly staff that can provide all the usual informational pamphlets and maps, as well as organize excursions around the town and boat tours of the island's outer-lying fortifications.

GETTING THERE

Bus #101 to Kronshtadt leaves every 15 minutes from metro station Staraya Derevnya, and tickets cost 16R. You can also get to Kronshtadt on minibus K-405, which leaves from metro station Chyornaya Rechka, or minibus K-407, which leaves from metro station Prospekt Prosveshcheniya—both cost 50R. The ride takes about 45 minutes, and is quite scenic and interesting, passing along the dam across the Gulf of Finland, with views of island fortresses along the way.

Vyborg

Growing from a trading point, Vyborg (Выборг) was officially founded in the late 13th century by the Swedish crown and since that time has been fought over numerous times, changing hands between the Russians, Swedes, and later the Finns over the course of its history. In the years between the two world wars, it was the second-largest city in Finland. It was only at the end of World War II that it saw its final handover, when it was captured by the Red Army. Today, it is a quaint little town of some 78,000 people, with a decidedly Nordic feel—an atmosphere created not only by the cobblestoned streets and Finnish architecture, but also by the hordes of Finnish tourists who come from across the border just 30 kilometers away to enjoy Vyborg's reasonably priced shopping, restaurants, and bars. Expect to see and hear plenty of Finnish in the market and on signs and menus. For the tourist coming from farther afield, the town holds no less appeal—its unique place in Russian history, having spent so much time developing under other nations' patronage, ensures that no other Russian town offers an experience quite like it.

SIGHTS
C Vyborg Castle
Vyborgsky zamok
Выборгский замок

The area's main landmark is this castle (81378/2-3940, 81378/2-5186, museum: Tues.–Thurs. and Sat.–Sun. 11 A.M.–7 P.M., Fri. 11 A.M.–6 P.M.; tower: 10 A.M.–10 P.M.; Russians: museum and tower each 40R;

EXCURSIONS

© NATHAN TOOHEY

Vyborg's Round Tower is known as "Fat Katerina."

foreigners: museum 80R, tower 70R/50R; photo permit 30R, video permit 60R), located on a small islet just opposite the center of town. Founded in 1293, it is the town's oldest building and Russia's only intact European castle. Today, the castle is open to the public as a museum. It has various exhibits on the history of the castle and town, its time as part of Finland, and the area's flora and fauna. Visitors to the castle can try their hand at shooting arrows from a bow, and attendants in medieval costume are on hand to help. The real attraction, however, would have to be the atmospheric grounds of the castle and the view from atop the tower, which provides a spectacular panorama of the town below.

Mon Repos
Монгеро
Монрепо
Just a half-hour walk from Vyborg Castle lies Mon Repos park (Severny Village, 81378/2-0539, daily 24 hours, 50R 10 A.M.–8 P.M., free other times). At 180

hectares, this is Eastern Europe's largest English-style park. Landscaped in a classic 18th-century romantic fashion, it flourished during the stewardship of Baron Ludwig Heinrich von Nicolai, who acquired it in 1788, and it was under his watch and that of his son that the estate received such theatrical touches as its Chinese pagoda and bridges, a Turkish chamber, and Neptune's palace. Nonetheless, the idyllic garden itself is what you come to Mon Repos for. With its setting on Zashchitnaya Bay, its hilly relief, and picturesque pond, it rivals the grounds of St. Petersburg's palace estates. Mon Repos is the perfect place for a picnic lunch on a warm summer day.

RESTAURANTS AND NIGHTLIFE
◖ **Kruglaya Bashnya** (Round Tower, Rynochnaya Ploshchad, 81378/3-1729, www .roundtower.ru, Sun.–Thurs. noon–2 A.M., Fri.–Sat. noon–midnight) is a real treasure. Located inside a genuine mid-16th-century

tower right on the Market Square, it was first used as a restaurant in 1922 and still boasts tons of atmosphere. The round tower, which has also been known as "Fat Katerina," has a fantastic historical interior and menu that features classic Russian and European cuisine, and even a vegetarian section.

Vyborg's slickest bar, **Champion** (18 Prospekt Lenina, 81378/2-0247, daily noon–2 A.M.) aims for a pub-like atmosphere with a sports theme and international beer brands—as well as lower-priced local Baltika for 70R. There is lots of dark wood and sports paraphernalia such as cricket bats on the walls. The bar's large windows provide good views across the road to Park Lenina while allowing you to watch the world pass by.

Fizalis (10–12 Leningradsky Prospekt, 81378/2-0464, 81378/2-1062, 981/745-7888, daily noon–8 P.M.) would have to be Vyborg's classiest restaurant. It has an Old World charm, with classic furnishings and a polished finish. The menu aims for a more contemporary feel, with modern dishes and even a bit of Japanese in the 250–500R range.

If it's a sunny day and heading indoors is just too hard to take, then **Russky Dvor** (Ulitsa Shurma, Porokhovoy Pogreb lit. A, 81378/26-369, daily noon–midnight) has the solution. Located at the far end of Krepostnoy Bridge, it has one of Vyborg's finest outdoor seating areas, with fantastic views of the castle. The menu offers inexpensive, conservative Russian dishes with fries on the side—you could dine here for 200–300R. If there's no space outside, either head into its cellar-like interior, or go just down the road to the yachting quay, where there is a modest beer tent by the docks.

HOTELS

Although Vyborg is just a couple of hours by train from St. Petersburg, it may still be worth your while spending a night here if you want an unhurried visit, or if St. Petersburg's hotels have no vacancies, or if you simply want to economize a little.

The **Hotel Druzhba** (5 Zheleznodorozhnaya Ulitsa, 81378/2-4924, 81378/2-5744, 81378/2-2411, from 2,660R s/d) is one of the larger hotels in town, located not far from the train and bus stations, right on the bay. Built by the Soviets, the vaguely ziggurat-like construction was overhauled in 2005. Many of the rooms provide good views across the bay to the castle.

Another big hotel housed inside a more traditional redbrick building, the ◖ **Vyborg** (18 Leningradsky Prospekt, 81378/2-5675, 81378/2-2383, from 2,100R s, 2,700R d) has more than 100 rooms plus a sauna available for use 24 hours a day. On the 2nd floor is a restaurant, which serves both Russian and Karelian cuisine.

Directly next to the train station is the rather kitschy-looking **Hotel Viking** (10 Zheleznodorozhnaya Ulitsa, 812/331-7178, www.viking-inn.ru, from 2000R s/d). Designed like a pseudo-castle, it's nonetheless thoroughly modern. It has a large range of services on offer, as well as a large selection of differently designed rooms, such as the whirlpool suite, the newlyweds suite, and the tower suite occupying the whole top (5th) floor of one of the hotel's towers. There's also guarded parking.

For something a little more cozy, the **Letuchaya Mysh** (Bat Hotel, 3 Ulitsa Nikolayeva, 81378/3-4537, 81378/2-5393, www.bathotel.ru, from 1,980R s, 2,400R d) provides a cute alternative. Located right downtown in a historical building, the hotel is located beside the castle and the town's main street. Originally housed on the attic floor when it opened in 2003, it has since expanded to the floor below with the new rooms featuring a more modern design and such extras as free Internet (also available in the semi-luxe rooms on the floor above), plasma TVs and heated floors in the bathrooms. It has a stylishly designed café on the ground floor.

Two mini-hotels that come recommended are the **Apart Hotel Ullberg** (10 Leningradsky Prospekt, 81378/5-5417, www.hotel-apart.ru, from 2,900R s, 3,200R d) and the Apart Hotel Sampo (11 Ulitsa Vasilyeva, 81378/3-1496, www.hotelapart.ru, from 1,900R s, 2,400R d).

EXCURSIONS

GETTING THERE
By Train
There are some dozen regular commuter trains to Vyborg daily, departing from Finland Station (6 Ploshchad Lenina, 812/457-7900, metro Ploshchad Lenina) with a travel time of roughly 2.5 hours. A better bet is to take one of the more comfortable express trains, of which there are three or four daily in each direction. The express trains take roughly 1.5 hours and the tickets are sold in a separate office in the front left corner inside the station, where there are often long lines, especially on weekends. Regular tickets cost about 200R, with the express costing some 30–50 percent more.

By Bus
Buses to Vyborg leave from metro stations Grazhdansky Prospekt and Parnas and stop on the way at metro station Ozerki (by which point there may not be any seats left). The buses leave every half hour or hour, and tickets cost roughly 150R.

Novgorod the Great

One of Russia's oldest cities, Veliky Novgorod (Novgorod the Great) celebrates its 1,150th birthday in 2009. Located about 180 kilometers from St. Petersburg, it's a picturesque place with more postcard-perfect views than you can point a camera at, making for a good alternative to the Golden Ring towns near Moscow.

Novgorod is more majestic than Suzdal, without the inflated prices but with all the medieval churches and monasteries; it offers more to see than in Vladimir, with none of that town's industrial development and unsympathetic Soviet buildings; and it certainly has more sights than Rostov-Veliky and Sergiyev Posad, with

© NATHAN TOOHEY

Novgorod's Kremlin sits across the river from the old marketplace arcade visible in the foreground. A pedestrian bridge links these landmarks.

NEW, OLD DISCOVERIES IN OLD NEWTOWN

Russia's oldest icon, "Apostles Peter and Paul," comes from Novgorod. It is part of the Novgorod museum collection but has spent six years in Moscow undergoing restoration work, which has for the first time been able to pinpoint its origins to the 11th century. The restorers established the date by analysing the paints, which proved to be analogous to those used in the "oldest surviving Russian manuscript, the "Ostromir Gospel of 1056-57" – also from Novgorod.

Meanwhile, archaeological digging continues in Novgorod, and keeps turning up rare treasures. Among recent finds, in 2008 archaeologists working in Yaroslav's Courtyard found a bronze heart-shaped stamp that they dated to the 15th-16th centuries. On one side there is a carving of a cross and the words "We bow down before your cross." On the other side is a bird, probably a swan, and the word "stamp." According to archaeologists, the fact the stamp bears nobody's name makes it a real rarity and reflects a superstition of the time. It was found in the necropolis by the walls of St. Nicholas Cathedral, which was built in 1113 and is Russia's second-oldest surviving church after St. Sofia's in the Novgorod Kremlin.

better accommodation, dining, and entertainment. Unlike the Golden Ring towns, a trip to Novgorod from Moscow is not a day trip.

The historic monuments of Novgorod and its surroundings are listed as a UNESCO World Heritage site. Among its other attractions is a pleasant sandy beach on the river bank, right by the walls of its impressive Kremlin. Compact enough to explore on foot, the city has leafy parks, fresh air, and a relaxed, friendly vibe.

HISTORY

The first written mentions of Novgorod, or "Newtown," date to 859. Holmgard, the Varangian prince Ryurik's settlement about two kilometers away on the right bank of the Volkhov River, was founded first—it was the "old town" relative to which the settlement in the city's present location was a "new town." Strategically located on the trade route between the Baltic and Black Seas, it was the second-most important city in Kievan Rus as early as the 9th century.

Novgorod prides itself as the cradle of Russian democracy. Having been granted independence from Kiev in 1019, Novgorod became a republic in 1136, ruled by a popular assembly called a *veche*. It would invite princes to serve, hire them on contract, and dismiss them if dissatisfied with their performance.

Birch-bark letters found by archaeologists have shown almost total literacy among Novgorodians as early as the 11th–12th centuries.

Although Novgorod was spared Tatar-Mongol attacks, the republic came to an end with defeat by Ivan III in 1478, after which it became part of the Moscow state.

World War II saw the city occupied by the German Army 1941 to 1944. The city was almost completely destroyed: of 2,532 residential buildings, only 40 semi-ruined buildings were left after the war. Of 200 churches, only 38 remained. But Novgorod has since been restored into one of Russia's most beautiful cities.

ORIENTATION

A city of about 220,000 people, Veliky Novgorod straddles the Volkhov River about six kilometers north of Lake Ilmen. Most sights are located in the center, within the earthen rampart on both sides of the river—a small enough area to explore on foot in one day. On the western side of the river are the Kremlin and the central squares; the eastern side has a cluster of sights visible across the river around the old trading area of Yaroslav's Courtyard, easily reached by a pedestrian bridge straight from the Kremlin.

There is little point in venturing beyond the earthen rampart ring except to go the short distance to the bus and railway stations, or when visiting Vitoslavlitsy Wooden Architecture Museum and St. George Monastery.

PLANNING YOUR TIME

A two-day visit is enough to see Novgorod. On one day, you can explore the Kremlin, its museums, and surrounds, and take a walk across the footbridge to see Yaroslav's Courtyard. On the second day, you can take a riverboat cruise up the river to Lake Ilmen, passing Vitoslavlitsy and St. George Monastery. Alternatively, take a bus or taxi to Vitoslavlitsy and St. George's Monastery for a closer view. If you only have one day, stick to the center, the Kremlin, and Yaroslav's Courtyard.

SIGHTS
◖ Kremlin (Detinets)
Kreml (Detinets)
Кремль (Детинец)

Novgorod's main sight is its Kremlin (8162/773-608, 8162/773-770, www.novgorod museum.ru, daily 6 A.M.–midnight, free), and a few hours walking around inside its walls, admiring its churches, towers, museums, and monuments, is an essential part of any visit. You can enter from the main square, Sofiyskaya Ploshchad, and once you're done—perhaps after lunch in the tower restaurant Detinets—exit from the opposite side, onto the embankment, beach, and bridge to Yaroslav's Courtyard.

Historically called Detinets, it is said to be the oldest surviving kremlin in Russia, dating to 1044. The fortifications were expanded and rebuilt several times; the existing walls were built in the 15th century, with 9 of 12 towers still standing. The highest tower, the 41-meter-high **Kokuy bashnya** (Apr. 1–Sept. 30 daily 11 A.M.–7 P.M.), was built in the 18th century. Climb to the top for a breathtaking view over the city and many kilometers beyond.

The most important sight within the Kremlin walls is the 38-meter-high **Cathedral of St. Sofia** (10 A.M.–6 P.M., closed last Tues. of month), also known as the Holy Wisdom of God Cathedral. This beautiful white church with gold and silver domes was built 1045–1050,

the Novgorod Kremlin's Millennium of Russia monument

© NATHAN TOOHEY

and is said to be Russia's oldest stone church. The dark, candlelit interior will take you back in time, with its superb iconostasis and frescoes all the way up to its curved ceilings. The oldest icon is the 12th-century Sign of Our Lady, believed to have saved Novgorod from Suzdalian attack in 1170. As this is a working church, women should wear headscarves and modest skirts (not pants), although this rule is not strictly enforced here. On the outside, take a look at the cathedral's western doors, the Magdeburg Gates. Covered in sculptures depicting biblical scenes, they were made in the German town of Magdeburg in the 12th century.

Next to the cathedral is the 15th-century **St. Sofia's Belfry** (Apr. 1–Sept. 30 Wed.–Mon. 10 A.M.–1 P.M. and 1:30–5:30 P.M., Russians 2–5R, foreigners 10–20R), with five arches and a silver dome rising above the Kremlin wall. Besides listening to the bells ringing, you can see a display of old Novgorod bells and climb up to the bell tower's viewing platform.

Opposite the cathedral is one of the city's symbols, the bell-shaped 15-meter-high **Millennium of Russia monument,** erected in 1862 to commemorate 1,000 years since the founding of the Ryurik Dynasty. It has three levels: an angel holding a cross at the top, a second level showing six stages in the development of the Russian state from Ryurik to Peter I (the Great), and a lower level with a frieze of 109 figures depicting outstanding people from politics, the military, the arts, and academia.

Other sights in the Novgorod Kremlin include a 40-meter bell tower that appears to be slightly leaning like the Tower of Pisa, and the tiny 15th-century **Andrey Stratilat Church,** with 16th-century frescoes preserved inside.

The main **Kremlin museum** (Wed.–Mon. 10 A.M.–6 P.M., closed last Thurs. of month, Russians 3–10R, foreigners 20–40R) is in a building called the Zdaniye Prisutsvennykh Mest, with an exhibit about the history of Novgorod as well as collections of icons, wood carvings, and artworks.

Nearby, at the **Museum of Pictorial Art** (2 Sofiyskaya Ploshchad, Tues.–Sun. 10 A.M.–6 P.M., adults 50R, students 25R, children 20R) you'll find Russian art from the 18th–20th centuries.

River Volkhov and Lake Ilmen

Reka Volkhov i ozero Ilmen

Река Волхов и озеро Ильмень

Exiting the Kremlin's eastern gate takes you to an embankment on the Volkhov River with spectacular views across to Yaroslav's Courtyard on the other side, as well as a pedestrian bridge to take you there. Beside the Kremlin walls there's also a clean, sandy **beach,** which is packed with swimmers, sunbathers, and volleyball players on warm days. The grassy slopes between the walls and the beach are ideal for picnics. Next to the bridge is the little pier from which riverboats run **cruises to Lake Ilmen** (May to Sept. weekends and public holidays, adults 200R, children 100R), passing sights including Vitoslavlitsy, St. George Monastery, and, opposite them, the ruins of the 12th-century Annunciation Church at the site of Prince

Ryurik's Holmgard settlement, now known as Ryurikovo Gorodishche. The cruises last one hour and depart every 20 minutes.

St. George Monastery

Yuryev monastyr

Юрьев монастырь

It is a short walk from Vitoslavlitsy (described next) to St. George Monastery (Yuryevskoye Shosse, daily 10 A.M.–8 P.M., free, photo permit 20R, video permit 100R) and a 15-minute trip south of the city by taxi or bus #7 or 7A. Although not worth the trip to visit all by itself, it's a good way to round out an excursion to the Vitoslavlitsy Wooden Architecture Museum.

Founded by Yaroslav the Wise in 1030, this was once Novgorod's most important monastery. To go inside, women should wear a headscarf and long skirt, which can be borrowed from the little blue store just inside the entrance.

The massive **St. George Cathedral**—32 meters high, 26 meters long, and 24 meters high—was built in 1119. Its 12th-century frescoes were overpainted in 1902 but some fragments remain, notably the gigantic saints in the staircase tower.

The monastery complex also includes a 52-meter-high belfry, five corpuses including one with prison cells, and three other churches. With five blue domes decorated in golden stars, the 19th-century **Cathedral of the Rising of the Cross** is the most striking.

After visiting the monastery, it's worth taking a walk around the walls to the beach behind it, on the banks of Lake Ilmen. There's even a little café with wooden pagodas where you can enjoy water views, sip a cold beer, and savor freshly smoked Lake Ilmen pike perch.

Vitoslavlitsy Wooden Architecture Museum

Muzei narodnogo derevyannogo zodchestva "Vitoslavlitsy"

Музей народного деревянного зодчества «Витославлицы»

For a glimpse of what Russia might have looked like centuries ago when all the houses were wooden, take a trip to Vitoslavlitsy Wooden

EXCURSIONS

Architecture Museum (Yuryevskoye Shosse, mid-Apr.–mid-Sept. daily 10 A.M.–6 P.M., mid-Sept.–mid-Apr. daily 10 A.M.–4 P.M., Russians 20–50R, foreigners 60–110R, photo permit 50R, video permit 150R), a 15-minute trip south of the city by taxi or bus #7 or 7A. Founded in the 1960s in a picturesque lakeside location close to St. George Monastery, this sight is usually visited along with the monastery in one excursion. Beautiful wooden churches, houses, and other constructions were moved here from across the region and stand scattered across a verdant 30-hectare territory. The churches, from the 16th–18th centuries, represent a variety of architectural styles. Inside the wooden *izba* houses, museum staff dressed in historical costumes play the role of villagers amid old-style domestic objects. Although it's all very artificial, it's interesting and educational. Festivals are held for occasions such as Orthodox Christmas. In winter, there are sled rides, and in summer, a craft market and traditional games, as well as folk music ensembles and bell-ringing.

Yaroslav's Courtyard and Marketplace
Yaroslavovo Dvorishche i Torg
Ярославово Дворище и Торг

The best views of the Kremlin are to be had from across the river in the historic trading quarter, where Prince Yaroslav the Wise relocated from Ryurik's Settlement in the early 11th century. The palace is no longer, but there is still much to be seen. To get there, walk across the footbridge from the embankment beside the Kremlin's eastern gate.

The old marketplace is recognizable by the 18th-century arcade, a white wall with a row of arches facing the river. Inside is an **exhibition about fresco restoration** (Wed.–Sun. summer 10 A.M.–5 P.M., winter 10 A.M.–4 P.M., closed last Fri. of month, Russians 2–6R, foreigners 17–35R).

The Yaroslav's Courtyard complex includes seven churches from the 12th–16th centuries, mostly open as museums. The oldest is the tall pink five-domed **St. Nicholas Cathedral,** built in 1113. Inside, you can see

a few remnants of the original Last Judgment frescoes and a **historical exhibition** (Wed.–Sun. 10 A.M.–1 P.M. and 2–6 P.M., closed last Fri. of month).

RESTAURANTS
Novgorod's best beer is in the **Beer Harbour bars** (8162/766-217, www.pivo-gavan.ru). There are many locations including: 3 Ulitsa Lyudogoshcha (daily 1 P.M.–last guest); a marquee on the Volkhov River embankment by the bridge near the Kremlin wall (daily noon–last guest); and a summer café in the Kremlin park (summer daily 11 A.M.–1 A.M.). The menu varies from bar to bar, but excellent microbrewed light and dark beers are poured on the embankment (great views!) and on Ulitsa Lyudogoshcha. The mead is awesome, as are the grilled meat and original sausages.

For fine European and traditional Russian cuisine at lower-than-Moscow prices, try **Beresta** (Beresta Palace Hotel, 2 Studencheskaya Ulitsa, 8162/940-910, www.fclnovgorod.ru, daily 7–11 A.M., noon–4 P.M., and 6–11 P.M.). Locals consider it the best restaurant in Novgorod.

Charodeyka (1/1 Ulitsa Volosova, 8162/730-879, daily 11 A.M.–11 P.M.) is a cozy café right near the Kremlin with a summer terrace where you can sun yourself while enjoying the competitively priced coffee and other caffeinated beverages. It offers a kids' menu, an assemble-your-own-salad menu, and a "lazy" menu for those who couldn't be bothered.

Popular with the city's trend-setters and well-to-do, **Cafe le Chocolat** (8 Ulitsa Lyudogoshcha, 8162/739-009, daily 9 A.M.–11 P.M.) is a slick café-restaurant that serves unbeatable coffee and a tempting breakfast selection, as well as innovative desserts. It's conveniently located opposite the Acron hotel.

Coffee Land (7 Ulitsa Chudintseva, 8162/766-166, daily 10 A.M.–11 P.M.) is a bright and friendly café close to the Volkhov and Acron hotels, with a great range of tasty coffee and tea drinks as well as snacks at lower prices than at Cafe le Chocolat. There's even a vegetarian menu. Visitors are invited to mark their hometown on a globe—and it's surprising to see from how far and wide they've come.

What could be more romantic than dining in the Kremlin's 17th–18th century Pokrovskaya Tower? The high-ceilinged dark, candlelit dining room at ◖ **Detinets** (in Kremlin's Pokrovskaya Tower, 8162/774-624, daily 11 A.M.–6 P.M. and 7–11 P.M.) is the perfect place to try well-prepared traditional dishes at surprisingly low prices. Try the Ilmen fish dishes, especially the *shchi* soup, and the mead and rye drink kvass. Arrive early or book ahead, as it can get busy with tour groups in the evenings. In the daytime, the enclosed balcony is a good place to dine with Kremlin views.

The Ilmen Gastronomical Complex in the Kremlin park is by Novturinvest, operator of the Sadko and Volkhov hotels. It includes the restaurant **Holmgard** (2 Gazon, 8162/777-192, www.novtour.ru, daily noon–midnight), which claims to be the only place in town cooking on an open flame, as well as the **Ilmen Bistro** (2 Gazon, 8162/777-192, www.novtour.ru, daily 10 A.M.–9 P.M., until 11 P.M. in summer), with an outdoor barbecue terrace and a deli.

Lenkom Traktir (2/13 Fedorovsky Ruchei, 8162/671-767, www.lenkom.kulturanova.ru, daily noon–3 A.M.) is a quirky retro-Soviet café, decorated with Lenin busts, hammer-and-sickle banners, and other memorabilia, which serves up old-fashioned food to a nostalgic musical soundtrack. Stop by for a drink if you're in the Yaroslav's Courtyard area or staying at the Sadko hotel.

Napoli Restaurant (21/43 Studencheskaya Ulitsa, 8162/636-307, www.napoli-restaurant. ru, daily noon–midnight, average 1,200R per person, 350R lunches), an upscale Italian restaurant near the Beresta Palace hotel, has a cozy but classy interior, good service, free wireless Internet (ask for the password), and a contemporary menu of delicious pizzas, pasta, risotto, meat, and fish dishes. It even offers takeout pizza.

PERFORMING ARTS

The **Novgorod Region Philharmonia** (6 Kremlin, 8162/773-748, 8162/772-777, www

.filarmon.natm.ru) offers a constantly varying program of ballet, concerts, international and local soloists, puppet shows, and more at varying prices.

SHOPS

Sloboda (8 Kremlin, 8162/736-498, daily 10 A.M.–6 P.M.) has Novgorodian and broadly Russian souvenirs, including birch-bark and wooden objects, lace, embroidery, dolls, jewelry, and more.

Gallery at the Marketplace (Yaroslav's Courtyard, 2 Ulitsa Ilina, 8162/664-472, daily 11 A.M.–7 P.M.) offers an excellent range of high-quality souvenirs and artworks including copies of local archaeological finds—medieval jewelry and even birch-bark letters with amusing translations.

Sennaya Ploshchad is an outdoor souvenir market selling souvenirs including plenty of birch wares just off the park beside the Kremlin, next to the Red Izba tourist office and a clean public toilet.

HOTELS

Along with its more expensive neighbor, the Volkhov, **Acron** (24 Predtechenskaya Ulitsa, 8162/736-908, 8162/736-912, www.hotel-akron.ru, from 1,200R s, 1,740R d, including breakfast, booking fee extra) is the most centrally located place to stay in Novgorod, right near the Kremlin, old center, cafés, and restaurants. The rooms are better than at the similarly priced Intourist, but the service is not quite as good and is more oriented toward Russian visitors.

The ◖ **Beresta Palace** (2 Studencheskaya Ulitsa, 8162/940-910, www.fclnovgorod.ru, from 2,800R s, 3,300R d, including breakfast, use of the pool, saunas, and gym) four-star hotel is the city's most luxurious and the one to choose if you want fully Western-standard accommodation. The only drawback is that it's located quite far from the Kremlin and other major sights, so you'd have to take buses or taxis. It has three restaurants, including the highly regarded Beresta.

A member of the International Youth Hostel

Federation, **Cruise-Big Spruce** (11 Prusskaya Ulitsa, 8162/775-487, 8162/772-283, hostel dorm beds from 300R, 600R d; hotel from 800R d; plus 100R registration fee for foreigners) is a centrally located hostel-hotel combo. It offers the cheapest beds in town.

The **Intourist** (16 Velikaya Ulitsa, 8162/775-089, 8162/774-710, www.intourist .natm.ru, from 1,420R s, 1,800R d, not including breakfast, discounts in low season) is a renovated Soviet-era three-star hotel located in a quiet riverside location about 10 minutes' walk from the Kremlin and three kilometers from the station. Although not as central as the Acron, Volkhov, and Novgorodskaya, its advantage is that it was designed for foreign tourists and remains focused on this sector. The staff speak English and provide good service. For an extra fee (about 240R), there's an all-you-can-eat buffet breakfast with live piano music.

A fully nonsmoking hotel, the **Novgorodskaya** (6A Ulitsa Desyatinnaya, 8162/777-223, 8162/772-260, www.novgorod-skaya.nov.ru, "single" rooms with one-and-a-half or double bed 1,250R, two-bed rooms from 1,320R, includes breakfast, booking fees extra) is centrally located near the Kremlin park, with views of the earthen rampart, old fortifications, and a 15th-century church. It has a sauna, café-bar, and guarded parking.

Classically Soviet-looking from the outside, the **Rossiya** (19/1 Naberezhnaya Alexandra Nevskogo, 8162/634-185, www.amaks-hotels. ru, unrenovated d from 1,200R, renovated s from 1,400R, rooms with a view from 1,800R, including breakfast) three-star hotel has the best views, and competitive prices. Located on the embankment beside Yaroslav's Courtyard, it offers rooms with balconies looking directly across the river to the Kremlin.

A three-star hotel located 15 minutes' walk from the center near Yaroslav's Courtyard, the **Sadko** (16 Fedorovsky Ruchei, 8162/663-004, 8162/661-807, www.novtour.ru, from 1,500R s, 2,200R d, including breakfast) is said by some to be the best value in its class. It has cafés, a restaurant, parking, fax, Internet, transport and excursion services, and staff who speak English, German, and French.

The **Volkhov** (24 Predtechenskaya Ul., 8162/335-505, 8162/335-507, www.novtour .ru, from 1,600R s, 2,300R d, including breakfast) boasts an unbeatable location alongside the Acron. The renovated three-star has a sauna, mini-pool, nonsmoking rooms, and staff speaking English, French, and German.

A project of the Sadko and Volkhov hotel operator Novturinvest, the **Yuryevskoye Podvorye** (6A Yuryevskoye Shosse, 8162/946-060, www .novtour.ru, from 1,800R s/d) is a new hotel, dining, and entertainment complex opposite the Vitoslavlitsy Wooden Architecture Museum, all in old-Russian style. Staff speak English and can organize guides speaking Russian, English, German, and French.

INFORMATION AND SERVICES

The **Tourist Information Center "Red Izba"** (5 Sennaya Ploshchad, 8162/773-074, www.visitnovgorod.ru, daily 10 A.M.–5 P.M.) is a friendly and helpful center with English-speaking staff, offering free information about Novgorod for tourists and tour operators: guides, excursion leaders, emergency help, hotels, tour bases, restaurants, cafés, cultural life, entertainment, leisure. The center's website includes a substantial English-language section, including some routes for sightseeing on foot. There's a 24-hour hotline at 8162/998-686.

Besides postal services, the **post office** (2 Bolshaya Dvortsovaya Ulitsa in Yaroslav's Court, 8162/631-988, Mon.–Sat. 8 A.M.–8 P.M., Sun. 10 A.M.–4 P.M.) offers telephone, telegraph, and Internet services plus Western Union and other money-wiring, pos-terminals, cash advances, and withdrawals by credit and debit cards. **North-West Telecom** (2 Lyudogoshcha Ulitsa, 8162/786-786, daily 24 hours) offers local, intercity, and international telephone services, fax, and Internet.

For medical assistance go to **Novgorod Region Clinical Hospital** (14 Ulitsa P. Levitta, 8162/642-887, 8162/642-875) or **Polyclinic Diamed** (13 Prospekt Mira, korpus 1, 8162/624-309, 8162/624-463).

GETTING THERE

Novgorod means "Newtown," and there are two Novgorods in Russia—Veliky or "Great" Novgorod, in the northwest between Moscow and St. Petersburg, which is the one described here, and Nizhny or "Lower" Novgorod, on the Volga east of Moscow. When organizing your visit and buying tickets, make sure it's clear which one you mean. Note that Veliky Novgorod's train station is called Novgorod-na-Volkhove (Новгород-на-Волхове).

The **Novgorod Train Station** (15 Oktya-brskaya Ulitsa, 8162/739-380, 8162/775-372) is conveniently located near the center of town, at the end of Prospekt Karla Marksa. It's about 1.5 kilometers from the Kremlin, or a 15-minute walk. The **Novgorod Bus Station** (13 Oktyabrskaya Ulitsa, 8162/739-979, 8162/776-186) is right beside the train station.

From St. Petersburg

Most people visit Veliky Novgorod from St. Petersburg because it's closer—a 180-kilometer journey compared to more than 520 kilometers from Moscow.

From St. Petersburg, it takes just over three hours by train, on average about four hours by bus, and just over 2.25 hours by car along the M10 highway.

There is a train from St. Petersburg's Moskovsky Station (2 Ploshchad Vosstaniya, 812/768-0111) at 8:12 A.M., arriving at Novgorod-na-Volkhove at 11:25 A.M., and another at 5:18 P.M., arriving at 8:33 P.M. Tickets cost about 670R each way.

There are about a dozen direct buses daily to Novgorod from St. Petersburg's Obvodny Canal bus station (36 Naberezhnaya Obvodnogo kanala, 812/766-5777, metro Ligovsky Prospekt and then bus #3, 26, 54, 59, or 141 to the stop "nab. Ovgodnogo kanala"), costing 290R a ticket each way. The first bus departs at about 7:30 A.M. and the last at 9:30 P.M. The time-table is on the website www.avokzal.ru.

From Moscow

If money is no object and you'd prefer a comfortable overnight sleeper train ride to an awkward sit-up day trip, then going to Novgorod from Moscow is for you. The only drawback for night owls is that the train arrives very early, but as a plus it means you get a full day of sightseeing without having to pay for a night in a hotel first.

Train #42 departs from Moscow's Leningradsky Station (3 Komsomolskaya Ploshchad, 495/262-9143) at 9:50 P.M., arriving 5:50 A.M. On the way back, train #42 leaves Novgorod at 9:20 P.M., arriving in Moscow at 5:32 A.M.

Train ticket prices vary depending on the date, rising in the summer. Traveling in a two-berth coupe costs roughly between 2,500R and 4,000R per person each way, and four-berth bunks are roughly half price. Booking well in advance is advisable.

GETTING AROUND

Whether you arrive by bus or rail, you can reach the central squares and hotels near the Kremlin by walking for 10 minutes straight down Prospekt Karla Marksa, which starts right out front. Alternatively, take bus #4 or 20, which stop near the Kremlin as well as hotels including the Volkhov, Sadko, and Beresta Palace.

Taking a taxi could be easier—try saying the name of your hotel and "pitdisyat rublyay" (50R), or "sto rublyay" (100R) for the Beresta.

In the center, all the sights are easily reached on foot.

Farther afield, St. George Monastery and the Vitoslavlitsy Wooden Architecture Museum are reached by buses 7 and 7A departing every 20 minutes from outside the railway station—a 15-minute ride costing 10R. By taxi, the fare is about 150R. On the way back, there are stops beside both these sights and the bus will be going the same direction by which you arrived.

BACKGROUND

The Setting

GEOGRAPHY
Moscow

Sprawling over an area of about 1,000 square kilometers, and with an official population of more than 10 million people, Moscow is a huge metropolis—not only the largest city of the Russian Federation, but also the largest in Europe. It is situated in the European part of the country, in the middle of the East European plain. Standing about 130 meters above sea level, the city is said to have been built on seven hills. The difference between the highest and lowest points is about 85 meters.

The city is located on the banks of the Moscow River, with the Kremlin in the very center. It has a circular structure, with several ring roads running around the central core, crossed by a number of radial roads fanning outwards. The most central ring, called the Boulevard Ring, does not completely encircle the city. It was built in the late 18th and early 19th centuries on the former site of the 16th-century White City Wall. The second ring is the Garden Ring, a busy multi-lane road built in the 19th century in place of earthen ramparts and filled-in moats. The Third Ring Road is a much newer freeway, completed in 2004. The outer ring road, about 15 kilometers from the center and called the MKAD or Moscow Ring Road, is generally considered to

define the city limits, although parts of the city do lie beyond it.

St. Petersburg

Russia's second-largest city, St. Petersburg, is the third-largest city in Europe, with a population of 4.7 million. With an area of about 600 square kilometers, it is situated in northwest Russia, on the eastern side of the Gulf of Finland, in the Neva River delta. The city is built on a series of islands on drained marshlands, amid a network of canals and rivers with the Neva River being the city's main waterway.

The city is very flat, and much of its area is barely above sea level, with the highest elevation at 42 meters, and as such floods have plagued the city throughout its history. The St. Petersburg Dam, running 25 kilometers long across the Gulf of Finland with Kronshtadt at its center, is intended to protect the city from floods and serve as part of a ring road around it.

St. Petersburg is the world's most northern major city. Its northern position results in extreme differences in day length. In mid-summer, the city enjoys "white nights," when the sky never really completely darkens and sunset merges with sunrise. Winter is long and dark.

A planned city, it has an orderly structure, with roads radiating outwards from the Admiralty in the center, and otherwise a gridlike layout elsewhere. The main road, Nevsky Prospekt, is intersected by the Moyka Canal, the Griboyedov Canal, and the Fontanka River. Other major parts of the city are located on islands on the other side of the Neva River—Vasilyevsky Island, the Petrograd Side, and Vyborg Side.

CLIMATE

Russia is famed for its winters, and in both Moscow and St. Petersburg the season is everything you'd expect: cold, with lots of snow. Broad temperature fluctuations are common— anything from 5 degrees Celsius (41°F) to -30 degrees Celsius (-22°F) can be expected, although it is more common for temperatures to sit somewhere between -5 degrees (23°F) and -10 degrees (14°F). St. Petersburg feels colder than Moscow even when the temperature is the same. January and February are the more pleasant winter months, with longer daylight hours and some glorious blue-sky sunny days.

Most years, spring doesn't bloom until early May. March and April tend to be gloomy months with gray skies, rain, wet snow, and lots of mud and slush. Summer can be hot and humid, with temperatures often above 20 degrees Celsius (68°F) and sometimes rising above 30 degrees Celsius (86°F). Rainstorms are frequent, especially in Moscow, and cool summers are common, particularly in St. Petersburg. The temperature falls quickly once autumn arrives, but the beautiful golden leaves compensate.

History

THE RYURIK DYNASTY, NOVGOROD, AND KIEVAN RUS

A trading route "from the Varangians to the Greeks" formed in the late 8th or early 9th century, passing along rivers and lakes on the territory of present-day Russia and Ukraine. Connecting the Baltic Sea with the Black Sea, it enabled trade between Scandinavia and Byzantium, and spurred the growth of settlements along the route.

One of these settlements was Veliky Novgorod, where Slavic and Finno-Ugric tribes chose a Varangian or Viking prince called Ryurik to be their ruler in 862. This was the beginning of the Ryurik Dynasty, and is considered the birth of the Russian state.

Having expanded their dominion and moved their capital to Kiev, Ryurik's descendants founded and ruled the state known as Kievan Rus, predecessor of the three modern nations of Russia, Ukraine, and Belarus. With Kievan Rus's decline from the mid-12th century, independent principalities broke away, still ruled by branches of the Ryurik Dynasty. Vladimir-Suzdal, Novgorod, and Moscow were among those that grew in status as important regional centers.

THE BIRTH OF MOSCOW

Moscow's founding is considered to have taken place in 1147, the date of the first written mention, when prince Yury Dolgoruky, ruler of the Rostov-Suzdal province of Kievan Rus, summoned another prince to meet him there.

The Moscow area was continuously inhabited from the second millennium B.C., however, initially by Finno-Ugric people. At least as early as the 11th century, there was a fortified Vyatich Slav settlement on Borovitsky Hill—site of the present-day Kremlin. The pine-forested hill was then much higher and steeper than it is now. Protected by two rivers—the Moscow (Moskva) River to the south and the Neglinka to the west—the 1.5-hectare wooden town was strategically placed as a frontier point; it was also a center of crafts and trade.

In 1156, Dolgoruky ordered the construction of a much larger fortress with moat and ramparts around the small wooden town. It became a border fortress of Vladimir principality, housing the prince's residence and court as well as churches and cemeteries. This settlement became part of the Suzdal principality at the beginning of the 12th century.

THE MONGOL INVASION

Armies of Genghis Khan's Mongol Empire had forged into Rus by 1223, when the Battle of the Kalka River, between the Mongols and a combined army of Kievan Rus principalities, resulted in Mongol victory. Fifteen years later the Mongols were back for a full-scale invasion, killing residents, and ransacking and burning a series of cities including Moscow, Vladimir, Suzdal, Rostov, and Kiev; one of the few major cities to escape destruction was Novgorod. The Mongols set up a capital on the lower Volga and were to rule parts of Rus for nearly 300 years.

The Mongol invasion of Rus dramatically changed the political landscape. Moscow had been sacked by the Mongols in 1238, but in its subsequent recovery it rose to overtake once-dominant cities like Kiev and Vladimir that had been trashed by the Mongols and were struggling to recover. In the 14th century, Moscow became the capital of an independent principality and sole tax collector for the Mongol rulers. The Moscow princes greatly expanded their wealth, influence, and lands.

In 1380, the Moscow prince Dmitri Donskoy led combined Russian armies to a crushing victory over a much larger army of the Tatar-Mongol Golden Horde at the Kulikovo Battle. The city was sacked again a few years later, before the Mongol yoke was finally cast off for good under Ivan III, in 1480. The Grand Prince of Moscow, Ivan III tripled his principality's territory, and by the late 15th century, Moscow had risen to become the capital of a centralized Russian state.

THE TIME OF TROUBLES AND THE ROMANOV DYNASTY

The Ryurik Dynasty ruled until Ivan the Terrible's son and successor, Tsar Fyodor I, died leaving no heir in 1598. There was much turmoil in the ensuing crisis of succession, and the following period, known as the Time of Troubles, saw Russia under attack by Polish and Lithuanian forces. Poles occupied the Kremlin, and thousands of people were killed in massacres, battles, and riots, until Prince Dmitri Pozharsky and Kuzma Minin heroically rallied a volunteer army to liberate Moscow from Polish invaders in 1612. The then-16-year-old Mikhail Fyodorovich Romanov, a relative of Fyodor I and son of the Patriarch Filaret, was elected tsar by a national assembly in 1613, beginning the Romanov dynasty that ruled Russia until 1917.

PETER THE GREAT AND ST. PETERSBURG

The son of Tsar Alexey I, Peter Alexeyevich Romanov was born inside the Moscow Kremlin in 1672. Upon his father's death in

the statue of Prince Dmitri Pozharsky and Kuzma Minin in front of St. Basil's Cathedral

1676, Peter's half-brother Fyodor III became Tsar, but died in 1682 with no heir. Next in line for the throne was Fyodor's brother Ivan V, but due to his physical and mental disabilities, he was deemed unfit to rule. The 10-year-old Peter I became joint tsar with Ivan V, with the real power wielded first by his half-sister and later his mother, as regents. Ivan V died in 1696, two years after Peter's mother, finally putting Peter I in the position of sole ruler.

Standing more than two meters tall, Peter "the Great" was a giant for his times. With boundless energy and an inquisitive intellect, he embarked on a modernizing program that included reforming the army and building a navy. In 1697 he set off on an 18-month journey to Western Europe, during which he studied shipbuilding in the Netherlands, observed the navy in England, learned about city building in Manchester, and generally observed Western ways. Returning to Russia, he launched a raft of Westernizing reforms, and set about expanding Russia's territory. His determination to take control of the Baltic Sea led to the Great Northern War with Sweden, which ran from 1700 to 1721 with Russia eventually victorious after earlier losses.

In 1703, Peter established the Peter and Paul Fortress on Zayachy Island on the Neva River, and thus founded his new city, St. Petersburg, on territory newly captured from Sweden. Calling it after his patron saint, he gave the city a deliberately Western European–sounding name—it was, after all, supposed to be Russia's window to the West. Peter moved the capital to his new city in 1712. After his death in 1725, the capital was moved back to Moscow in 1728 by successors who didn't share his ideals. Empress Anna made St. Petersburg the capital once again in 1732, and the city was to remain the capital until 1918.

NAPOLEON'S INVASION AND RETREAT

The French Emperor Napoleon I and Tsar Alexander I of Russia had formed an alliance by signing the Tilsit Treaty in 1807, according to which France was supposed to aid

Russia in fighting Ottoman Turkey, and Russia was to side with France in a blockade against the United Kingdom. Neither side considered the other to be fulfilling its obligations and Franco-Russian relations worsened. The Anglo-Russian war of 1807–1812 ended with Russia, Britain, and Sweden signing secret agreements against France. Napoleon, seeking to keep Russia within his Continental System, invaded Russia in June 1812, with an army of more than 600,000 men—then the largest ever assembled in Europe. Seeing the pointlessness of facing the French in battle, the much-smaller Russian army of about 240,000 men retreated, employing a scorched-earth strategy until September's bloody but indecisive Battle of Borodino, after which the Russians retreated again, leaving open the way to Moscow. The city was evacuated and stripped of food in advance of the French arrival a week later; fires burnt the city almost completely to the ground and made it difficult for the French to find shelter. Short of supplies and frustrated by Russia's refusal to surrender, Napoleon's army began its retreat in October. Returning along the scorched-earth route by which they'd come, the French fell victim to cold, starvation, disease, desertion, and Russian attacks that ultimately saw only a fraction of Napoleon's men make it back alive. French losses are estimated to have amounted to some 380,000 dead and 100,000 captured, compared to Russia's loss of 210,000 men.

DECEMBRISTS

Officers returning from Western Europe after the Napoleonic Wars brought back reformist ideals. Secret societies formed with political aims ranging from achieving a constitutional monarchy to establishing a republic. After Alexander I's death in December 1825, the eldest and more progressive son refused the throne, leaving the more conservative Nicholas I to become tsar. A group of officers led some 3,000 soldiers in a protest on Senate Square in St. Petersburg, refusing to swear allegiance to Nicholas I. The uprising was violently put down on Nicholas's orders,

with an artillery attack that killed hundreds. Leading "Decembrists" were interrogated, tried, convicted, and punished: Five were put to death and others were exiled to Siberia. The square where the uprising took place has since been renamed Decembrist Square (Ploshchad Dekabristov). Although the revolt failed, its reverberations continued to be felt, influencing prominent writers and thinkers, and inspiring a new generation of revolutionaries.

LATE 19TH CENTURY

After Nicholas I's death in 1855, the reformist Alexander II took the throne; among his reforms was the emancipation of the serfs in 1861. Peasants were to pay for the land assigned to them, however, which caused much discontent.

Meanwhile, an industrial revolution was gathering steam, and the economy was growing. Moscow and St. Petersburg were becoming major industrial centers. The cities' population changed, drawing in workers including peasants who had left the land, forming a new urban proletariat and spurring the growth of new poor neighborhoods. The dismal plight of the working class and the peasants became a focus for radical students and educated, elite revolutionaries.

There was a series of failed attempts by radical revolutionaries to assassinate Alexander II before a terrorist bomb blew him up in 1881; the Church on Spilled Blood, located beside St. Petersburg's Griboyedov Canal, marks the spot.

Alexander II's successor, Alexander III, was a conservative who put a stop to reforms that his father had initiated. His death in 1894 brought Russia's last tsar, Nicholas II, to the throne—a reign that got off to a tragic start when, on the day of his coronation in 1896, more than a thousand people died in a crush at celebrations on Moscow's Khodynskoye Field.

THE 1905 REVOLUTION

The late 19th and early 20th centuries were a time of growing political activism in Russia. With ever-louder calls for change, peasants and workers were rebelling. Discontent over military failures in the Russo-Japanese war fueled further unrest. There were mutinies, demonstrations, and strikes, and new political parties emerged, among them Vladimir Lenin's Bolsheviks.

In January 1905, a peaceful, unarmed procession of about 140,000 workers approached St. Petersburg's Winter Palace in order to present a petition to Tsar Nicholas II, calling for the establishment of a constitutional assembly. The Imperial Guard opened fire, killing and wounding at least 1,000 people, or as many as 4,600 according to some estimates. This event, known as Bloody Sunday, sparked further turmoil and a general strike. It ultimately led to Nicholas's signing of a manifesto promising civil rights and creating the country's first parliament, among other reluctant concessions that were accompanied by brutal crackdowns to crush unrest, and attacks on Jews, who were perceived as revolutionaries. December of 1905 saw fighting on the streets of Moscow, with troops firing on demonstrators to crush dissent. The revolution was put down, but not for long: The Bolsheviks saw it as a precursor to their revolution of 1917.

1917 REVOLUTIONS

At the start of World War I, St. Petersburg's name was deemed too German, and the city was renamed Petrograd. The city became a focus of revolutionary activity: Already-existing tensions were exacerbated by anger over military failures and war casualties, as well as hunger and economic hardships related to the cost of the war. There was an explosion of chaotic unrest, which culminated in two revolutions in 1917—the February Revolution, in which Tsar Nicholas II was forced to abdicate and the Romanov Dynasty came to an end, and the subsequent October Revolution, in which Lenin's Bolsheviks seized power from the Provisional Government.

As counterrevolutionary resistance led to civil war, Russia withdrew from World War I to concentrate on its battle at home. In 1918, Lenin moved the capital back to Moscow, and

the Bolshevik Party became the Communist Party. The royal family, which had been under house arrest, was executed. Following victory in the Civil War—after millions of lives had been lost and the economy devastated—the Soviet Union was founded in 1922, as a union of the Russian, Belorussian, Ukrainian, and Transcaucasian republics. Moscow became not only the capital of the Russian Soviet Federative Socialist Republic, but also of the Soviet Union.

STALINISM

Lenin died in 1924, and the "cradle of the revolution"—the former capital, Petrograd, previously St. Petersburg—was renamed Leningrad. The General Secretary of the Communist Party of the Soviet Union, Iosif Dzhugashvili, aka Josef Stalin, emerged as the new leader after a long and ruthless power struggle. Consolidating his power, he introduced a command economy and pushed forward rapid industrialization, developing Leningrad as a major industrial center. He also forced the collectivization of agriculture, confiscating farmer's land; millions starved in the ensuing famines, or were killed or sent to Siberia for resisting giving up their livelihood. The growing population in the gulag prison camps provided a captive labor force for mining and industrial projects in remote areas.

In the 1930s, a major campaign of political repression began. Known as the Great Purge or Great Terror, it saw hundreds of thousands of people executed and millions imprisoned in gulag camps as Stalin sought to wipe out real and perceived enemies and anyone seen as a political threat. In Leningrad, the terror began with the assassination of local party boss Sergey Kirov at Smolny in 1934. Ethnic minorities were expelled from the city, there were show trials, and the population was gripped with paranoia and fear as people disappeared after NKVD secret police took them from their homes at night. In Moscow, the elite House on the Embankment became a symbol of Stalinist terror, with hundreds of its 1930s residents executed or sent to the gulag.

THE GREAT PATRIOTIC WAR–WORLD WAR II

Stalin had negotiated a non-aggression pact with Adolf Hitler's Nazi Germany. Signed by Soviet and German foreign ministers in 1939, the Molotov-Ribbentropp Pact secretly divided Central Europe into spheres of influence. Thinking he had a deal, Stalin was shocked when Hitler broke the pact and invaded the Soviet Union in June 1941.

Hitler's forces were on the outskirts of Leningrad by August. Palace estates, particularly Peterhof and Pushkin, were looted and destroyed. The Nazi leader wanted not only to take Leningrad first, but to wipe the city off the face of the earth. In September, the city was encircled and its supply lines cut. More than a million people starved to death. Hundreds of thousands of soldiers died defending the city. Thousands of citizens were killed and tens of thousands wounded as Leningrad suffered heavy shelling and bombing by the Germans, but still the city did not surrender. The Siege of Leningrad, also known as the Blockade, lasted from September 1941 to January 1944, when a Soviet offensive pushed the invaders back. Leningrad became the first city to be awarded the Soviet honorary title of Hero City in 1945.

Outside Moscow, the Nazis were closing in by October 1941; the city was under siege, bombarded from the air. The Axis advance was just 70–100 kilometers from the city on November 7, the anniversary of the Bolshevik Revolution, and Stalin rallied Soviet soldiers "onward to victory" before they marched straight from Red Square to trains that would take them to the front. In the city center, metro construction continued during the war, new stations opened, and Muscovites took shelter in underground metro stations during air raids. The Battle of Moscow, which ran until January 1942, resulted in millions of casualties, but saw the Soviets successfully resist Nazi Germany's determined efforts to take the capital. Having forced the Nazis' first major retreat, it became a symbol of resistance. In 1965, on the 20th anniversary of the end of World War II, Moscow was awarded the title of Hero City.

On May 9 of each year, the Victory Day anniversary is celebrated with much pomp in both cities, as well as in practically every other population point across the whole country. The biggest celebrations are in Moscow, where parades on Red Square are a tradition.

POST-STALIN THAW

Stalin died in 1953, and a more relaxed era known as "the thaw" began under Nikita Khrushchev, the First Secretary of the Communist Party of the Soviet Union, who was relatively liberal. Having assumed full power in 1956, Khrushchev denounced Stalin and embarked on de-Stalinization, easing political and intellectual repression and opening up to the non-Communist world with reforms in foreign policy. He became Premier of the Soviet Union in 1958. The gulag system was scaled back before finally being liquidated, and prisoners were amnestied, released, and rehabilitated. There were agricultural reforms as well, and initially good harvests. Vast new housing estates relieved domestic conditions for the masses, allowing families to move from shared communal apartments into their own flats. Visible economic improvements and achievements in space buoyed Khrushchev's leadership.

Although the Cold War was escalating, U.S. vice president Richard Nixon visited the Soviet Union in 1959, meeting Khrushchev at a special American exhibition in Moscow. A discussion they had about communism versus capitalism is now famously known as the Kitchen Debate, as it took place in a model American suburban house that was decked out with all the mod-cons of the day. Disagreeing with each other on just about everything, they agreed to be more open with each other in the future. Khrushchev visited the United States a few months later; the visit wasn't an all-around success and he left offended, but the two countries were now supposedly rivals instead of enemies.

Khrushchev's policies and boorish personality had displeased some in the Communist Party leadership. There was a poor harvest and agricultural downturn, and economic problems mounted. Among his enemies' other grievances, such as alienating China, was the outcome of the Cuban missile crisis of 1962. Party bosses plotted his ouster, which came in 1964, leading to Leonid Brezhnev taking over as Soviet leader.

STAGNATION

The Brezhnev era, 1964–1982, is widely considered a time of stagnation. But to some, it was a time of political stability and economic security, climaxing with the euphoria of the 1980 Olympic Games in Moscow. The city had been enjoying an economic boom, with a surging population and a changing skyline as new housing developments and Olympics-related construction transformed the face of the Soviet capital.

Although it had been a time of détente, with visits by Soviet and U.S. leaders to each other's countries and the signing of breakthrough arms-control treaties, the Soviet invasion of Afghanistan in 1979 resulted in a boycott of the Moscow Games by the United States and some other countries.

Right from the start of Brezhnev's rule, many of Khrushchev's reforms were reversed, and more repressive cultural policies returned. The 1968 invasion of Czechoslovakia by the Soviet Union and its Warsaw pact allies had halted the "Prague Spring" political liberalization in that country, but even back in the USSR the times were a-changing. A dissident movement was emerging, as well as unofficial subcultures including the legendary Leningrad underground, which would blossom into the country's coolest rock music scene.

GORBACHEV'S PERESTROIKA

Brezhnev's death in 1982 was followed by the short rule of Yury Andropov and then Konstantin Chernenko, both of whom were elderly and ill, and died in office. Within hours of Chernenko's death in March 1985, Mikhail Gorbachev became General Secretary of the Communist Party and thus Soviet leader. He quickly launched a radical reform program with the catchwords "perestroika" (economic restructuring), and "glasnost" (openness).

Although Gorbachev's crackdown on alcohol dampened spirits, his liberalizing reforms had much of the population fired up with optimism. People enjoyed more freedom of speech and the media were less controlled. A new law on cooperatives allowed limited private ownership of business.

Internationally, the Cold War was dying down as Gorbachev struck up good relations with Western leaders and reached arms reduction agreements with U.S. president Ronald Reagan. Soviet forces withdrew from Afghanistan. The Brezhnev Doctrine was

FIRST MAN IN SPACE

Everyone knows about America's first man on the moon, but there was another first: the first man in space, cosmonaut **Yury Gagarin** of the Soviet Union.

On April 12, 1961, the handsome, ever-smiling, and likeable Gagarin blasted into space in the Vostok 1 spacecraft, becoming the first human in space and the first to orbit the earth. Besides becoming a hero of the Soviet Union, he won hearts with his down-to-earth comments during the flight – famously saying, poyekhali (let's go!) at takeoff, and his later musings on the beauty of planet Earth while gazing down on it from outer space.

From humble origins, his pioneering space flight catapulted him into celebrity status, with goodwill tours around the globe and even a dinner with England's Queen Elizabeth II. Sadly, he perished in a fighter pilot training crash in 1968 at the age of 34, but he remains to this day an iconic figure and a true national hero.

You can see a soaring, silver statue dedicated to Yury Gagarin on Moscow's Ploshchad Gagarina, near Leninsky Prospekt metro station.

abandoned, which meant a new policy of non-interference in the Eastern Bloc countries' internal affairs—a dramatic change in foreign policy, which opened the way for the collapse of Communism across Eastern Europe. The West was giddy with "Gorby mania," and the surprisingly charming Soviet leader with the birthmark on his forehead became an iconic figure.

COLLAPSE OF THE SOVIET UNION

Domestically, as economic problems bit hard, glasnost worked against itself by allowing Gorbachev's opponents to loudly voice their criticism. Likewise, democratization weakened his and the party's grip on power. The Soviet Union's future structure was under question, with new forms of union under discussion and unrest in some republics indicating that they might try to break away. Many conservatives in the Soviet government opposed the reforms.

In August 1991—just days before a new union treaty was due to be signed, transferring more power to the republics—Communist hardliners attempted a coup against Gorbachev, who by then had the title of Soviet president. On August 18 the coup leaders flew to Crimea, where Gorbachev was on vacation, and pressured him to declare a state of emergency, resign, and transfer power to the vice president; Gorbachev is said to have refused, and some versions of the story have him under house arrest. The next day, after the coup plotters returned to Moscow, they declared a state of emergency and announced that they, the State Committee for the State of Emergency, were now in charge.

With tanks on the streets of Moscow, and crowds of citizens building barricades, Boris Yeltsin—who had in June become the first popularly elected president of the Russian Soviet Federative Socialist republic—escaped arrest and led the resistance. He famously climbed onto a tank in front of the Russian parliament, the White House, to rally the crowds and the military to resist the coup-plotters. The tanks withdrew on August 21, and the coup attempt collapsed three days after it had begun. Gorbachev returned to Moscow, the coup leaders were arrested, and one committed suicide.

Now the unraveling of the Soviet Union gathered unstoppable momentum. Among other momentous changes, the Russian republic declared that its flag would now be the red, blue, and white national flag instead of the Soviet flag. In an act of symbolic significance, protesters toppled the statue of secret police founder Felix Dzerzhinsky from its pedestal on Lubyanskaya Square. Leningrad reverted back to its old name, St. Petersburg.

In quick succession, various Soviet republics declared their independence from the Soviet Union. Gorbachev resigned as Communist Party general secretary, and Yeltsin signed a decree terminating its activity in Russia. The leaders of Russia, Ukraine, and Belarus annulled the treaty that had established the Soviet Union and founded a new union, the Commonwealth of Independent States, which the other former Soviet republics (except for the three Baltic states) were later to join. Gorbachev resigned as Soviet president on December 25, 1991. With the Soviet Union now dead, the old red Soviet flag was lowered and the tricolor Russian flag rose in the Kremlin.

THE YELTSIN ERA

Boris Yeltsin and his team quickly moved ahead with a radical program of reforms to create a free-market economy and dismantle the old Soviet command economy. Their "shock therapy" approach involved rapidly liberalizing trade and prices, and slashing subsidies and welfare spending, while raising taxes and interest rates, among other dramatic changes. Hyperinflation wiped out people's life savings, incomes fell, unemployment grew, and millions plunged into poverty without the social safety nets that had protected them in the Soviet era.

With the economy in chaos, opponents in the Russian parliament fought the radical economic reforms. The stand-off escalated into a constitutional crisis, culminating in a bloody clash in Moscow in October 1993. After parliament members barricaded themselves inside the White House to protest Yeltsin's decree disbanding the Communist-dominated parliament, tanks loyal to Yeltsin fired at the building, and soldiers stormed it. More than 100 people died in associated clashes, with one of the main hotspots being at the Ostankino television tower.

A new parliament, the State Duma, was subsequently voted in, and a referendum approved expanded powers for the president.

With new presidential elections looming in 1996, and Communist leader Gennady Zyuganov appearing to be the front-runner, a new wave of privatization effectively put Russia's most valuable state enterprises into the hands of a small clique of supportive businessmen at knock-down prices. These tycoons or "oligarchs" put their resources behind Yeltsin's election campaign to ensure his victory over Zyuganov, and in return for their support, Yeltsin pushed through the so-called loans-for-shares scheme: the businessmen lent the government money, and in return they got to buy state assets cheaply in questionable auctions. As a result, the government missed out on much of the income it should have received from the privatization process.

Having won the election, Yeltsin's second term was plagued with health problems and questions about whether he was fit for office. Economic crisis continued.

The economy had been shrinking and the government had been running a budget deficit for years, when shock waves from the 1997 Asian crisis resulted in oil—the country's main source of income—plunging in price to as little as $8 a barrel.

A severe economic crisis hit Russia in August 1998, with the government's default on $40 billion worth of debt and devaluation of the ruble. A string of bank collapses followed, life savings and investments were wiped out, destroying any confidence anyone might have had in the banking system and the economy in general. As the financial system imploded, the ruble's value plummeted from 6 rubles to

the U.S. dollar to more than 20 rubles to the dollar by year's end. Unemployment surged amid mass layoffs in bankrupted companies, there were shortages of basic consumer goods, and much poverty and desperation. Consumer prices rose by 84 percent on average by the end of 1998, and adjusted salaries were about 60 percent of what they had been a year earlier. Even in relatively well-off Moscow, 20 percent of the population fell below the poverty line, while in poorer parts of the country, the figure was as high as 90 percent.

THE PUTIN ERA

Former KGB officer Vladimir Putin was a bit of a mystery when Yeltsin appointed him prime minister in 1999. "Who is Putin?" was the much-repeated catchphrase in the media. It didn't take long to find out the answer to the question. By 2000, when he was elected president, "Putinmania" was breaking out as his approval ratings soared.

When Putin came to power, the country had just been battered by a decade of agonizing economic reforms and the devastating financial crisis in 1998. There were a lot of problems to deal with, including political instability, huge foreign debt, an economy too dependent on oil, and a banking system in shambles.

With the help of a team of liberal economists in the government and senior advisory positions, he pursued a prudent fiscal policy. Among many reforms, a new tax code in 2000 slashed the personal income tax level to a flat 13 percent, a step which had a dramatic impact by reducing the rampant tax evasion and boosting tax collection rates. The European Union reclassified Russia as a market economy in 2002, the same year that the country was invited to become a full member of the Group of Eight. Putin announced the goal of doubling GDP by 2010. He also restructured agreements between the Kremlin and the oligarchs Yeltsin had been beholden to; as a result some of the biggest players went into exile or were jailed.

As oil prices soared, the creation of a stabilization fund in 2004 helped reduce the inflationary pressures of booming oil revenues while building up savings to cover any substantial fiscal gap in the future.

As Putin's second term as president drew to a close in 2008, annual GDP growth was averaging more than 7 percent, Russia had paid back its foreign debt and had accumulated the world's third-largest foreign currency reserves, as well as a large reserve fund to guard against another crisis. The budget had boasted a surplus since 2000.

While foreign media responded to Russia's growing strength by producing ever more negative reports about the country and its leadership, accusing it of "rolling back democracy," at home Putin continued to enjoy massive popularity—even to the extent that some couldn't imagine life without him in charge, and called for changes to the constitution to allow him a third term as president. The eight years of his presidency are known as the stability era, and the young people who grew up within it, the stability generation.

CONTEMPORARY TIMES

Contrary to the expectations of some observers and the wishes of a substantial segment of the population, Putin's presidency came to an end. In March 2008, Putin's chosen successor, 42-year-old Dmitry Medvedev, was elected president of the Russian Federation. Putin was appointed prime minister.

As Medvedev took over as president, the country had been enjoying stable economic growth for seven successive years. Soaring oil prices had given the country new confidence to assert its right to assume a greater international role. Still, there were many hurdles that remained on the domestic front. Russian government ministers acknowledged that the problems the country needed to overcome included an over-reliance on energy exports, a declining population, a lack of modern skills, an unhealthy way of life, corruption, and bureaucratic interference.

Medvedev, with his background as a lawyer, was seen as likely to be more liberal than Putin, partly because unlike Putin he had never served in the security services. Medvedev came into power with a modernizing agenda, focusing on combating corruption, achieving institutional reforms to allow small businesses to grow, weaning the economy off its dependence on oil profits, and building industry and the high-tech sector.

However, a series of events forced some change in focus. The conflict with Georgia following that country's attempt to retake the breakaway region of South Ossetia, and the subsequent souring of Russia's relations with countries including the United States, drew attention to other issues, including the need to upgrade and update the military. At the same time, huge sums needed to be pumped into the banking system to avert a financial crisis spreading into Russia, as bank collapses and bailouts spread from the United States to Britain and Europe.

Government and Economy

GOVERNMENT

Russia is a federal presidential republic. The president is elected to a four-year term by popular vote; the constitution limits the president to two consecutive four-year terms.

The president is the head of state, and commander-in-chief of the armed forces. Among other things, he is responsible for defining the state's domestic and foreign policy guidelines, and ensuring the concerted functioning and interaction of the bodies of state power. He is officially the guarantor of the constitution and of civil and human rights and liberties.

The government is headed by the prime minister. Unlike in some countries, its formation does not depend on the distribution of seats in parliament. The president appoints the prime minister, with the approval of the State Duma, or lower house of parliament. The president also appoints deputy prime ministers and other federal ministers, acting on proposals from the prime minister. Certain federal executive bodies are under the president's direct authority. The president has the right to give instructions to the government and power bodies responsible for defense, security, internal and foreign affairs, justice, disaster relief, and emergency situations prevention.

The legislature is called the Federal Assembly and consists of two chambers—the lower house or State Duma, and the upper house or Federation Council. There are 450 deputies in the Duma, elected for four-year terms by a system of proportional representation. Each of the country's 83 regions sends two members to the Federation Council: One senator is elected by each regional legislature, and the other is nominated by its governor and approved by the legislature. They serve four-year terms. In November of 2008, President Dmitry Medvedev submitted legislation to the State Duma to extend presidential terms from four to six years, and extend term limits for State Duma deputies from four to five years. It passed easily.

All bills are first considered by the State Duma and must pass three readings before being considered by the Federation Council. After being approved by the upper house in a single vote, a bill is sent to the president to sign into law.

The president has the right to dismiss the government. If the State Duma votes no confidence in the government or refuses its confidence twice in three months, the president either dismisses the government or dissolves the Duma. The government may hand in its resignation, but it needs to be accepted by the president in order to take effect.

As of 2008, the pro-Kremlin party United Russia was the largest political party in Russia, and the Communist Party remained the second largest, as well as the largest opposition party. United Russia and its members comprised 88 out 178 delegates in the Federation Council. United Russia had a constitutional majority in the Duma, having won 315 out of 450 seats in the December 2007 elections.

As federal cities, Moscow and St. Petersburg function as regions in themselves and have their own representatives in the Federation Council. The Moscow city government is headed by its mayor, who is also considered a governor. Moscow Mayor Yury Luzhkov, having led the city since 1992, was elected to a third four-year term in 2003 and appointed to a fourth term by Putin in 2007 (in 2004, gubernatorial elections were replaced by a system in which the president picks candidates who are then approved by local legislatures). St. Petersburg's governor, Valentina Matviyenko, was appointed and approved in 2006. Both Luzhkov and Matviyenko belong to United Russia, which also dominates the legislatures of both cities—the Moscow City Duma and the Legislative Assembly of St. Petersburg.

LEGAL SYSTEM

Russia's judiciary consists of the Constitutional Court, Supreme Court, Supreme Court of Arbitration, and lower federal courts.

Russia has had a moratorium on the death penalty since 1996, although without legally abolishing capital punishment from the Criminal Code.

Jury trials had been abolished by the Bolsheviks in 1917 but were reintroduced in 1993. Only the most serious crimes are tried by jury, and only if a defendant requests it. In 2006, jury trials numbered 700 of 1.2 million criminal cases. The acquittal rate has been much higher for defendants tried by jury than by judges. In 2007, it was reported that about two out of every 10 defendants tried by juries were acquitted, compared to less than one in 100 tried by judges.

ECONOMY

The country, which had been in economic shambles at the end of the 1990s, regained its confidence under Putin, thanks to rising oil prices, stable politics, steady economic growth, and firm control over the important natural resources industries.

Russia's impressive economic recovery had seen the country's gross domestic product increase almost nine-fold in nine years. Still, its

RUSSIAN FOLK WISDOM

Like every country, Russia has its superstitions, and it is often said that Russians are very superstitious. That said, it is not the end of the world if you choose to ignore the local superstitions – 70 years of rational Communism has seen to that. The following are some superstitions you may encounter.

- When giving flowers, make sure to give an odd number, as even numbers are for funerals.

- Birthdays should be celebrated on the day or after, but not beforehand.

- Do not shake hands or kiss over the threshold of a door.

- Newborn babies should not be shown to strangers until they are 40 days old.

- Presents for babies should be purchased after they are born.

- Knives should not be given as presents.

- Purses and wallets should not be given empty so as not to encourage poverty, a small amount of money should be included.

- Returning home for forgotten things is bad luck. If you must return, you should look in a mirror before leaving again.

- When drinking vodka and the like, empty bottles should be removed from the table.

And two further beliefs that locals will insist are not superstitious, but medical fact:

- Air moving rapidly over exposed skin, such as through an open window in a bus (no matter how hot and stuffy it is), will make the person sick.

- If it's not a hot summer day, cold beer will give you a sore throat. (But still it's okay to eat ice cream in subzero temperatures.)

per capita GDP of $12,000 was just a quarter of the level of the United States.

The Russian economy remains heavily dependent on energy exports. Russia accounts for about 12 percent of the world's oil output, making it the largest producer after Saudi Arabia. Oil and other raw materials account for about 75 percent of the Russia's exports, and diversification is one of the country's biggest challenges. Less than one million of Russia's workforce of 142 million is employed in oil-related industries, but they produce about half the country's GDP. Gazprom, the most powerful company in the country, is a major supplier of natural gas to Europe. It pays taxes equal to 20 percent of the Russian budget.

The economic situation became uncertain as financial chaos spread around the world in 2008. As the United States and other countries felt the effects of a growing economic crisis, many in Russia continued to maintain the country would suffer relatively little—that it would be "an island of stability." A repeat of the country's 1998 financial meltdown was considered to be highly unlikely. The government had created a fat financial cushion during the years of growing oil prices, and the domestic banking sector had little exposure to global security markets or the subprime crisis, and was better capitalized and better regulated than it had been a decade earlier. The economy was also more diversified than it had been then. All of these factors were expected to provide some economic stability.

Still, some commentators maintained that Russia was too interconnected to the international economy to be unaffected by the global turmoil. Exports amount to about 30 percent of its gross domestic product, and some 80 percent of the country's exports consist of commodities.

Besides the fact that the price of oil—Russia's main export—had fallen greatly, production levels were expected to fall in 2008 for the first time after years of growth, due to heavy taxes, depleting fields, and the growing costs associated with bringing new fields online.

DEMOGRAPHY

Russia's population has been shrinking: Twelve million more Russians died than were born from 1992 to 2007, and 5.5 million new immigrants weren't enough to make up for the decline. The population was expected to shrink from its 2008 level of about 142 million, to between 125 million and 135 million by 2025.

Moscow is the largest city, with an official population of 10.4 million, while the second-largest, St. Petersburg, has 4.7 million.

There are about 160 different ethnic groups and indigenous peoples in the Russian Federation. Almost 80 percent is ethnically Russian. The next largest groups are Tatars (3.8 percent) and Ukrainians (2 percent).

Russia's traditional religions are Christianity, Islam, Buddhism, and Judaism. Russian Orthodox Christianity is the most widespread religion, with about 60 percent of the population identifying as Orthodox. About 10–15 percent of the population is Muslim.

ESSENTIALS

Getting There

BY AIR
Moscow

Most of Moscow's international tourists arrive by air. A major air hub for the entire former Soviet Union as well as Russia itself, the capital has three international airports. Two, Sheremetyevo-2 and Domodedovo, handle the lion's share of international traffic, with Vnukovo more recently having widened its international services to outside the former Soviet Union.

SHEREMETYEVO-2

Built to handle Moscow's 1980 Olympic Games, **Sheremetyevo-2** (495/232-6565, 495/578-9101, www.sheremetyevo-airport.ru) is Moscow's original international airport terminal and is located north of the city. The airlines it services include Delta, Aeroflot, Transaero, Alitalia, KLM, Korean Air, Olympic, SAS, Turkish Airlines, Lot, Finnair, Air France, and JAT. It is widely disliked by air travelers for its dark, gloomy halls and long lines at passport control, although planned renovations and new terminals should help.

Difficulty in getting to and from the airport due to traffic jams are a serious problem—a problem that was only alleviated in mid-2008 by the introduction of a direct express train (Terminal "Savyolovsky–Sheremetyevo," 2

© NATHAN TOOHEY

Ploshchad Butyrskoy Zastavy, 495/266-8910, www.aero-express.ru) from Savyolovsky Station (2 Ploshchad Savyolovskogo vokzala, 495/285-9005, metro Savyolovskaya). Trains run daily 5 A.M.–1 A.M., every half-hour or hour (subject to seasonal variations); the 35-minute trip costs 250R, or 350R in business class. Another direct express train running between the airport and Belorussky Station is being added.

The taxi gang that used to have a virtual stranglehold on taxi services at the airport has thankfully been usurped (although they're still milling about) by the introduction of an official fixed-fee service (around 1,500R depending on destination) that can be booked at a booth by the exit.

DOMODEDOVO

Since its major overhaul in the mid-1990s, Domodedovo (495/933-6666, www.domodedovo.ru) has been steadily winning over international airlines, which have been switching allegiances from Sheremetyevo-2 and moving to the more modern Domodedovo. The airport services airlines including American Airlines, Lufthansa, Austrian Airlines, bmi, JAL, Malev, Emirates, Swiss, Thai, Singapore Airlines, and British Airways. Situated south of the city, it's brighter and lighter, and lines tend to be less of a problem.

The airport has long been served by an express train (www.domodedovo.ru/en/main/getting/1/aero/), which leaves from Paveletsky Station (1 Paveletskaya Ploshchad, 495/235-0522, metro Paveletskaya) to the airport daily 6 A.M.–11 P.M., every half-hour or hour, taking 40–50 minutes and costing 250R. From the airport to Paveletsky Station the service runs 7 A.M.–midnight. Three times a day a service runs from Belorussky Station (7 Ploshchad Tverskaya Zastava, 495/251-6093, metro Belorusskaya) to Domodedovo (to the airport 12:53, 3:50, and 11:24 P.M., from the airport 11:25 A.M. and 12:20 and 9:30 P.M.) and stops en route at Komsomolskaya Square and Kursky Station. Travel time is 60–70 minutes and tickets cost the same as the regular express.

Taxis can be booked at a taxi stand inside the baggage claims area; the price can be agreed in advance and it costs roughly 1,900R to travel to the center.

VNUKOVO

Although the oldest of the three airports, Vnukovo (495/436-2813, www.vnukovo.ru) is the new kid on the block, as it were, having only recently had its facilities upgraded to an international standard. Besides flights to various destinations in the former Soviet Union, the airport now services flights from farther afield, including Europe. Its terminals now rival Domodedovo's with their modern facilities and ease of use.

Vnukovo's express train service (www.aero-express.ru) leaves from Kievsky Station (2 Ploshchad Kievskogo vokzala, 499/240-7071, metro Kievskaya) to the airport daily 7 A.M.–11:09 P.M., roughly every hour (less frequently during the middle of the day); the trip takes 35 minutes and costs 250R. From the airport to Kievsky Station, trains run 7:55 A.M.–12:01 A.M. Taxis can be booked at a taxi stand inside the arrivals hall with the price agreed in advance. Average price to the city center is 1,200–1,500R.

St. Petersburg

Arriving by air in St. Petersburg is much more straightforward than in Moscow, as the city has just one international airport terminal, **Pulkovo-2** (18 Ulitsa Pilotov, 812/704-3444, www.pulkovoairport.ru), located right beside the domestic terminal, **Pulkovo-1** (18 Ulitsa Pilotov, 812/704-3822, www.pulkovoairport.ru). The airport is fairly modest, but modern, and you won't have any problems finding your way about.

Transport to and from the airport is limited to road transport. The #13 minibus runs between Moskovskaya metro station and the airport, a 15–20 minute ride, with tickets costing 22R. There is a bus roughly every 15 minutes between 6:30 A.M. and 11:30 P.M. Between 12:55 A.M. and 4:15 A.M., a bus runs roughly once an hour between the Vladimirskaya metro station and the airport. Between 2 A.M. and 5:15 A.M. a bus runs back from the airport to Vladimirskaya metro station.

There is a taxi stand in front of Pulkovo-2, and there are information boards beside both the arrivals and departure areas, with fixed prices displayed for various destinations around town. A ride to the center is set at 700R, although there are reports that the taxis are nevertheless demanding more.

BY RAIL

For information about train routes, tickets, and timetables, look on the Internet site www.rzd. ru, which is in both Russian and English, or www.tutu.ru, which is easier to use if you have functional Russian language skills.

Moscow

The vast majority of international trains that service Moscow arrive from other areas of the former Soviet Union. Direct trains do run from Berlin and Warsaw, among other cities, and in late 2007 a direct Paris–Moscow route was reintroduced after a break of 13 years. Berlin, Warsaw, and Paris trains all arrive at Belorussky Station (7 Ploshchad Tverskaya Zastava, 495/251-6093, metro Belorusskaya). Moscow's many train stations are all serviced by the metro system, buses, and taxis.

St. Petersburg

The northern capital has international train connections at Vitebsk Station (52 Zagorodny Prospekt, 812/768-7900). Russia's oldest train station, inaugurated in 1837, it services the Baltic states and Eastern Europe. Ladozhsky Station (73 Zanevsky Prospekt, 812/436-5310, www.lvspb.ru) is St. Petersburg's newest station; completed in 2003, it services Finland. It's easy to get to and from both stations, as they are well served by the metro and other public transport.

BY BUS
Moscow

For the truly brave at heart (those who don't mind a slower, less comfortable mode of transport), it is possible to travel to Moscow on an international bus. There are quite a few companies that offer this service, but be prepared for a long road trip. Moscow's main bus station is called the Tsentralny Avtovokzal (75/2 Shchyolkovskoye Shosse, 495/468-0400, metro Shchyolkovskoye), but your arrival point in Moscow will depend on where you're coming from and with which bus company. One of the leading private bus companies is **Eurolines** (3 Komsomolskaya Ploshchad, 499/975-2170, 499/975-2072, www.eurolines.ru), with a ticket office in the Leningradsky train station, on the 2nd floor of the main ticket hall. Another providing international bus transit is **Intercars Europe–Bayer Trans** (37/6 Leningradsky Prospekt, 495/950-3970, 495/950-3972, www. oldworld.ru, metro Dinamo or Aeroport), with an office inside the Aerovokzal building.

St. Petersburg

For St. Petersburg, international bus travel is much more realistic, as Finland, Belarus, and the Baltic states are all within easy striking distance, and there are many companies that run bus services from many points around town. One of the main arrival/departure points for international routes is the Avtobusny Vokzal (36 Naberezhnaya Obvodnogo Kanala, www .avokzal.ru, 812/766-5777, metro Ligovsky Prospekt). A major bus service is **Eurolines** (2/1 Mitrofanyevskoye Shosse, Admiral business center, 812/441-3757, www.eurolines.ru, metro Baltiyskaya), with tickets also sold at a number of tourism agencies around town, including Okdayl (24 Griboyedov Canal, 812/571-2994, metro Nevsky Prospekt) and Sindbad (12 2nd Sovetskaya Ulitsa, 812/332-2020, metro Ploshchad Vosstaniya).

Getting Around

TRAVELING BETWEEN MOSCOW AND ST. PETERSBURG
By Air

While certainly not the most romantic way to get between the two cities, flying does have its advantages. Aggressive competition has driven prices down in recent years and price-wise flying now compares very favorably with travel by train. At roughly 2,500R one-way including taxes, economy air tickets now cost roughly the same or less than the cost of traveling in an overnight four-berth coupe on an express train. Flights take about an hour and leave almost hourly from all three Moscow airports, and ticket availability is usually not a problem, even in peak season. Major airlines that fly between the two capitals include Aeroflot (www.aeroflot.ru), which flies from Sheremetyevo-1 terminal, reached by a regular shuttle bus from Sheremetyevo-2. The S7 airline (www.s7.ru) flies from Domodedovo, as does Transaero (www.transaero.ru). Rossiya (www.rossiya-airlines.com) flies from Vnukovo, as does the budget airline SkyExpress (www.skyexpress.ru). All these airlines offer at least some flights on Western aircraft.

By Rail

Taking the train is how most tourists would envisage an ideal journey between Russia's two largest cities. And indeed, provided that you choose the right class and have the right neighbors in your coupe, the train is by far the most pleasant way to make the journey. Most of the trains that run between Moscow and St. Petersburg leave within a couple hours of either side of midnight and arrive the following morning.

TYPES OF TRAINS

Trains offer several different classes of travel. **Platskartny** is the most basic of the classes, offering simple bunks in an open dormitory-style carriage, with sleeping spaces for 54 people.

When not too crowded, these arrangements can be quite acceptable, but when it's a full house it's a different matter.

The next class up is the four-berth coupe, or **kupe.** These carriages have nine separate compartments, each with four bunks, two up and two down. The pleasure in traveling in this class is largely dependent on the quality of those sharing the compartment with you. Be aware that it is polite to let the two upper bunk passengers sit on the lower bunks before going to bed at night and while getting ready in the morning before the train arrives.

Two-berth carriages are referred to as **SV,** and until recently were the highest-quality option. The carriages have nine compartments, as in kupe class, but each compartment has just two lower bunks. Less people in the carriage means shorter lines for the lavatory, which is also likely to be much cleaner. Many of the fancier trains offer SV with such amenities as televisions, room service, and climate control.

In the past couple of years, several innovations have occurred on Moscow–St. Petersburg railway services. SV is no longer the top-of-the-line service. New trains, such as the **Grand Express** (www.grandexpress.ru), offer such luxuries as double beds, satellite television, and showers. Another newly introduced service is single-sex carriages, which is particularly appealing for women traveling alone, who previously might have chosen to travel platskartny, but now can choose four-berth without the fear of being cooped up with three strange men.

Other options are the afternoon and evening **fast trains** that run daily between the two cities. The **Avrora** departs at 4:30 P.M. and takes five and a half hours, while the others—the **Nevsky Express** and the **ER-200**—depart at 6:30 and 7 P.M. respectively, reaching their destination four and a half hours later. Seating resembles that on an aircraft, although some carriages have cabins holding six separate seats, and there are two classes—regular and business. Tickets range roughly 2,000–4,000R.

COST OF TICKETS

Ticket prices vary greatly from low to high season. Generally speaking, low season is during the colder months and high season is during summer. Ticket prices can vary up to some 20 percent either way from the median price. On several days of the year, usually around the May holidays and January 1, tickets are discounted to a remarkable 45 percent of their normal price—a real bargain. Naturally, prices also vary greatly depending on the train. As a rule of thumb, platskartny costs 500–1,000R, kupe 2,000–3,000R, and SV 4,000–5,000R. The super-luxurious Grand Express will set you back roughly 25,000R. It's worth remembering that taking the overnight train does save you the cost of one night's hotel accommodation.

PURCHASING TICKETS

Tickets are best purchased at the *kassa* (ticket office) at the railway station from which your train is to depart. In Moscow, the vast majority of St. Petersburg–bound trains depart from Leningradsky Station (3 Komsomolskaya Ploshchad, 495/262-9143), which is sometimes confusingly referred to as "Oktyabrsky" because that's the name of the railway line running to St. Pete. In St. Petersburg, the vast majority of Moscow-bound trains go from the Moskovsky Station (2 Ploshchad Vosstaniya, 812/768-0111). Each station also has a service center where you can avoid lines and buy tickets in greater comfort, with better service, for about 200R extra per ticket. Another place to buy tickets in St. Petersburg is the centrally located ticket office called Okdayl (24 Griboyedov Canal, 812/571-2994).

Of course, you should buy your tickets in advance—about two weeks in advance is desirable, especially in summer and for weekend trips. However, last-minute purchases are possible, because people often cancel their journey and return their tickets right up to the day of departure. If you're not too fussy about the date and time of your trip, or the class of seat or berth, you can probably get tickets in the week before your planned trip.

For information about Russian train routes, tickets and timetable, look on the Internet sites www.rzd.ru, which is in both Russian and English, or www.tutu.ru, which is easier to use if you have a functional Russian.

SAFETY PRECAUTIONS

Over the years there have been stories about people being robbed while unconscious after being gassed in their coupes, or after being served spiked tea by the conductor—but in reality this seems to happen little, if at all, and so it's probably either a thing of the past or an urban myth.

The overnight train journey is not really dangerous, but to be on the safe side it's worth taking a few precautions. If you're in platskartny or in a coupe with strangers, you should probably sleep with your money, cards, passport, other documents, and valuables hidden in a money belt that's concealed under your clothing. Keep things like cameras hidden away, not lying around the place. Perhaps put your purse under your pillow or hide it under the covers. The lower bunk beds lift up, and there's a compartment underneath where you can stash your bag—it would be difficult for a thief to get to it while you're lying on the bunk. Take your valuables with you when you go to the bathroom or restaurant car, because there have been incidences of people returning to find their things missing, especially if the train stopped while they were away (and by the way, the tap water in the train bathroom is just for washing your hands—don't drink it or clean your teeth with it).

In a coupe, be sure to lock the door by flicking the knob at the top of the door, turning the other one next to the door handle, and fixing on the special lock called a blokirator that should be in the coupe or provided by the conductor—it's like a flat plastic box with a spring and it fits over the door handle lock when it's in locked position, so that the door cannot be unlocked and opened from the outside. Ask for one if you can't find one in your coupe *(Dayte, pozhaluista, blokirator)*.

Don't get drunk with strangers, whether they are your coupe mates or people you might meet in the restaurant car. It's best not to get into conversations with strangers; instead keep a low profile and don't speak loudly, especially in English.

GETTING AROUND MOSCOW AND ST. PETERSBURG
The Metro
The metro is a safe and convenient way to get around both Moscow (www.mosmetro.ru) and St. Petersburg (www.metro.spb.ru). A single ride to anywhere in the system costs 22R in Moscow and 20R in St. Petersburg. Both cities offer various discounts for a range of multi-ride tickets. A 10-ride ticket in Moscow costs 200R (valid for 21 days) and in St. Petersburg 165R (valid for seven days). Moscow's turnstile technology allows you to simply wave your ticket, which can be left in your wallet or purse, at the yellow circular ticket reader on every gate. St. Petersburg still uses a combination of tokens and magnetic cards that need to be swiped. Tickets are sold at the *kassa* inside each station's entrance hall.

Both metro systems' trains run with an impressive frequency of once every several minutes or so, with digital clocks at the end of each platform showing how long it's been since the last train departed. Unfortunately, both systems get extremely crowded at peak times, so if you can avoid using the metro 8 A.M.–11 A.M. and 5–7 P.M. on weekdays, you'll come away with a much better impression. Opening times for individual stations vary, but the Moscow system runs from around 5:20 A.M.–1 A.M., while St. Petersburg's stations open around 5:30 A.M. and close around 12:30 A.M.

Navigating the system is fairly straightforward, and displays inside the carriages have both Cyrillic and Latin names for each station indicted. The sign indicating where to go to change from one line to another is marked Переход *(perekhod)*.

Above-Ground Public Transport
Both Moscow and St. Petersburg are well serviced by a wide variety of above-ground public transport. There are buses, trams, and, rarely

© NATHAN TOOHEY

Metro stations are marked with a big M.

seen in the West, trolleybuses—a kind of bus that uses overhead power cables. Tickets can be bought from the driver (Moscow 25R, St. Petersburg 18R), but they are cheaper in Moscow if bought beforehand from dedicated kiosks (20R), which can usually be found near the stops outside metro stations, as well as other popular stops. These services tend to run on a similar schedule to the metro, but it all depends on the individual route. Both cities also have privately run *marshrutki* or minibus services, which charge about the same as public bus rates in Moscow, while they're a fraction more expensive than public buses in St. Petersburg. Compared to regular buses, the *marshrutki* tend to run more frequently, are faster, and less crowded. Passengers sitting at the back expect those in front to pass their money forward to the driver; tickets are not always issued. *Marshrutki* will stop and let you out anywhere along their route, just indicate to the driver that you want to get out.

The buses and minibuses do not offer a phone line to call for information as you might find in other countries.

Moscow has a fairly modest 4.7-kilometer-long monorail service that runs from the Ulitsa Sergeya Eisenshteina, stopping by the All Russian Exhibition Center and the Ostankino Tower, plus several other stops before it finishes its run near the Timiryazevskaya metro station. The service runs every five minutes 7 A.M.–11 P.M., and costs 22R.

Taxis

There are many companies providing taxi services in Moscow and St. Petersburg. Any of these taxis can be flagged down on the street (if they're not already booked) or ordered by phone. Most official taxis have meters and are more than happy to use them. Many locals, however, prefer to agree on a fixed price for the journey before embarking—a price lower than the meter would give. Taxi rides around the center of town in an official taxi should cost in the region of 300–700R. A taxi company with one of the largest fleets is Novoye Zholtoye Taksi, or **New Yellow Taxi** (www

.nyt.ru, Moscow: 495/940-8888, St. Petersburg: 812/600-8888); they're easily recognizable with their bright-yellow cars.

Another option in Moscow is **Pink Taxis,** or women's taxis (www.womantaxi.ru, 495/66-200-03, 495/66-200-33). This taxi firm provides bright-pink cars exclusively for use by women and children—and all the drivers are women.

A third option is the ever-present **chastniki,** or gypsy cabs, as foreigners call them. These unofficial and unmarked cars can be hailed by sticking an arm out, which is followed by haggling over a price with the drivers who stop. Such "taxis" tend to be beat-up old clunkers mostly driven by citizens of former Soviet republics, but occasionally company drivers may use the company car to earn an extra ruble or two while the boss is at lunch. Either way, while these drivers charge roughly half what official taxis do, their "service" is completely unregulated and as such comes with no guarantee of the driver's sobriety or car's roadworthiness.

Car

While hiring a car may be simple enough, driving one around town would be a monumental challenge for the average tourist. Moscow is notorious for its city-stopping traffic jams, and St. Petersburg is fast catching up. Given the super-efficient metro system, in both cities driving is simply a waste of time—literally. And there is another problem that's perhaps even worse: the local driving culture, with its disregard for road rules. Many drivers seem to think speed limits are there to be broken, and red lights are a reason to line up across an intersection, blocking the way of the traffic that has a green light. Those with fast and expensive cars will zippily zig-zag between other vehicles on multi-lane highways, rarely bothering to use their indicators.

For the brave or foolish who are determined to drive, some of the car rental agencies operating in Russia are **Hertz** (Moscow: 2 Ploshchad Tverskoy Zastavy, 495/775-8333, Sheremetyevo-2 airport, 495/578-5646,

Domodedovo airport, 495/775-8333, and Vnukovo-1 airport, 495/775-8333; St. Petersburg: 85 Nevsky Prospekt, 812/326-4505, 23 Malaya Morskaya Ulitsa, 812/326-4505, Pukovo-1 and Pulkovo-2 airports, 812/326-4505; www.hertz.ru, and **Avis** (Moscow: 7/1 Meshchanskaya Ulitsa, 495/684-1937, 495/744-0733, 39 Prospekt Mira, Bldg. 2, 495/775-3920, Sheremetyevo-2 airport, 495/578-7179, www .avis-moscow.ru; St. Petersburg: 2 Ploshchad Alexandra Nevskogo, entry 3, hotel Moskva, 812/600-1213, Pulkovo-1 and Pulkovo-2 airports, 812/327-5418, www.avis-rentacar.ru).

Tourists may drive in Russia for up to 60 days using a valid foreign drivers license and a notarized Russian translation. If you'd rather avoid the hassle of having your license translated and notarized while in Russia, your best bet is to use an international driver's license (in the United States they can be obtained from the American Automobile Association).

Drivers will also need a third-party liability **insurance policy** that is valid in Russia. This is probably easiest to acquire once inside Russia, from insurance companies such as Ingosstrakh (www.ingos.ru) and Rosno (www.rosno.ru).

Bicycle

You'd have a better chance of surviving walking blindfolded though a minefield than cycling around Moscow's chaotic roads, and cycling in St. Petersburg is banned on many streets downtown. Of course, both towns have many quieter streets and lovely parks to cycle around, but as a means of downtown transport the bike is probably better left at home. Bike rental is not readily available.

Visas and Officialdom

HOW TO APPLY FOR A VISA

Citizens of Canada, Australia, New Zealand, the United States, and the E.U. all need visas to travel to Russia (with the exception of those staying aboard a cruise ship docked in St. Petersburg for less than 72 hours).

Tourist Visas

Travel agents who specialize in tours to Russia should be able to organize a Russian visa at the same time as all other travel arrangements for an extra fee. For those looking to acquire a visa independently, the procedure is as follows. To apply for a visa, a tourist needs to first receive an "invitation." Tourist invitations can be issued by most Russian tour firms, hotels, and hostels for a fee of about $25–40. In the case of hotels and hostels, they will usually only issue an invitation valid for the period in which you're staying with them. Tour firms can be more flexible, but in any case the maximum length of a tourist visa is one month. Tourist visas can be single or double entry—double entry allows you to leave Russia and enter a second time. Many tourist agencies let you apply, pay, and receive the invitation all online, such as via www.waytorussia.net. Other visa agencies include www.visahouse.com and Liga Consultant (www.rusvisa.org).

Once you have the invitation in hand, the next step is to take it to your nearest Russian Embassy or consulate. Some restrictions have been introduced regarding applying for a Russian visa in a country other than your own—the rules vary depending on your nationality and the country you're applying in, so it's best to check in advance or simply apply in your home country. Each embassy may have slightly different application procedures, and some will accept postal applications. Besides the invitation, typical requirements include a filled-out visa application form, two passport-sized photographs, and your passport with two clear pages and six months' validity after the proposed expiry date of the visa. Application fees vary depending on your nationality and where you apply. Processing time also varies, and one-day express processing is often available for a higher fee.

Business Visas

Business visas, which have longer durations and more flexible multiple entries, can be organized in a similar fashion as tourist visas, but cost more and take longer to process. Acquiring a work visa and work permit in order to work in Russia is a long and difficult process and one that can't be done without the help of a genuine employer.

Personal Visas

Visitors who are staying with friends or relatives also have the option of obtaining a personal visa. Although these visas have the advantage of a three-month duration, they also have numerous drawbacks. The personal visa invitation can only be issued by a Russian citizen or foreigner with permanent residency. The process of acquiring the invitation is quite complicated and can take about 45 days. Furthermore, the visa will need to be registered by the migration officials of the district where the inviter is officially recorded as living and not some other district or area of Russia. For this and other reasons, personal visa invitations are not that commonly used.

Student Visas

Student visa invitations will be organized by the educational institution where the student plans to study. They are advantageous in that that they can be extended for as long as studies are continued, but have a drawback of often requiring the issuing of an exit visa each time the student wishes to leave the country. The educational institution will organize the exit visa upon request.

UPON ARRIVAL

Upon arrival in Russia, each visitor must fill in a migration card and present it to the passport control desk, along with their passport and visa. Usually migration cards are handed out aboard the plane or train before arrival, but if they are not, they can be found on tables in the arrivals hall, along with customs declaration forms. A stamped migration card is needed in order to register one's visa. The card also needs to be presented again upon leaving Russia, so be sure not to lose it.

REGISTRATION

Once inside Russia, visitors must register their visas within 72 hours, not including weekends and holidays. If you are staying at a hotel or hostel, they will register the visa for you after you provide them with your passport together with your visa and migration card. If you are staying with family or friends, then the landlord will need to take your documents to either the post office or police station and register you there. Once you are registered, you will receive a small piece of stamped paperwork. Foreigners are required to carry their passports, visas, migration cards, and registration at all times, and you may be stopped and have your documents checked by the police.

CRUISE SHIPS REGULATIONS

There is one exception to all of these visa rules: Visitors who arrive on cruise ships that dock in St. Petersburg for less than 72 hours do not require visas. There are, however, restrictions. Such tourists are not free to simply disembark from the ship and wander about as they see fit. Such visa-free visitors must sleep aboard the ship and are permitted to visit the city only on a tour conducted by a specially approved tour company. The cruise ship will usually organize such excursions, although visitors are actually allowed to choose an excursion from the approved list of tour operators independently.

CUSTOMS

Customs rules are fairly straightforward and displayed in English on large signs in the airports. There are some restrictions regarding cash and travelers checks. Visitors are allowed to bring in up to $10,000 or its equivalent in other currency without declaring it. Any amount above that should be declared on a customs declaration form and presented to the customs control officers via the "red channel" (the "green channel" is for those with nothing to declare). On departure, visitors can leave with up to $3,000 without declaring it. For sums between $3,000

EMBASSIES AND CONSULATES

MOSCOW

- **Australia:** 10a/2 Podkolokolny Pereulok, 495/956-6070, 495/956-6075, Kitay-Gorod metro

- **Canada:** 23Starokonyushenny Pereulok, 495/956-6666, 495/956-6158, Kropotkinskaya metro

- **Ireland:** 5 Grokholsky Pereulok, 495/937-5911, Prospekt Mira metro

- **Mexico:** 4 Bolshoy Levshinsky Pereulok, 495/969-2879, Smolenskaya metro

- **New Zealand:** 44 Povarskaya Ulitsa, 495/956-3579, 495/956-2642, Barrikadnaya metro

- **United Kingdom:** 10 Smolenskaya Naberezhnaya, 495/956-7200, Smolenskaya metro

- **United States of America:** 19/23 Novinsky Bulvar, 495/956-4227, 495/956-4141, Barrikadnaya metro

ST. PETERSBURG

- **Australia:** 1 Italyanskaya Ulitsa, 812/315-1100, Nevsky Prospekt metro

- **Canada:** 32B Malodetskoselky Prospekt, 812/325-8448, Tekhnologichesky Institut metro

- **United Kingdom:** 5 Ploshchad Proletarskoy Diktaturi, 812/320-3200, Chernyshevskaya metro

- **United States of America:** 15 Furshtatskaya Ulitsa, 812/331-2600, Chernyshevskaya metro

and $10,000, the money should be declared. For amounts greater than $10,000, a stamped import declaration showing that the money was brought in by the tourist will be needed. Up to two liters of alcohol, 250 grams of caviar or sturgeon, and 400 cigarettes (other tobacco products amounts vary) can all be taken out without paying export tax.

Tourists have run afoul of the law by trying to take with them items deemed of national cultural significance, such as war medals, old coins, icons, and other historical artworks. If the store did not provide you with export documents (perhaps you bought the items at a street market or were given them as a gift) and you are in any doubt about the historical nature of the souvenir, then you should have it checked by the **Cultural Heritage Committee** (Moscow: 7/2 Kitaygorodsky Proyezd, 495/623-8561; St. Petersburg: 17 Malaya Morskaya Ulitsa, 812/571-8133). It should go without saying that importing or exporting drugs, weapons (including bullets), explosives, and the like is strictly forbidden.

Conduct and Customs

SOCIAL CUSTOMS
Etiquette

On the street, Russians tend to be a reserved and rather unsmiling bunch, which is in sharp contrast to behavioral norms in private company, where they tend to be gregarious. Speaking loudly in public and animatedly gesticulating may well attract some disapproving stares. Signs of public affection, on the other hand, are well tolerated. Whistling on the street is considered uncouth, while whistling indoors is inauspicious, according to superstition (it's said you'll whistle the household's money away). It can get a bit rough-and-tumble on the metro at peak hour, and you should not expect an apology if you are bumped into; on

"NO ENTRY IN SPORTSWEAR"

CLOTHING

Forget the old Soviet-era clichés about bringing a plug for the bathroom sink and jeans to sell – those times have passed.

As a rule, at any occasion and at any time of year in Russia, there's no such thing as being too dressed up. If you don't want to stand out like a sore thumb in restaurants, theaters, galleries, or even just walking around the city, you need to be dressed presentably. Muscovites and Petersburgers favor a more dressed-up city style. Typical travel gear, including backpacks, will label you as a tourist – especially if you're not a teenager or a student – and will make you easy prey for pickpockets. Choose a more grown-up, urban style of bag, and not one that hangs on your back where you can't see it.

Even in **summer,** you should bring a light jacket. For **spring and autumn,** a leather or suede coat and a sweater is usually suitable, plus some kind of hood, cap, or hat to keep your head dry. Umbrellas come in handy but are widely available and so cheap that they are practically considered disposable.

In **winter,** the cold is nothing to fear: Indoor spaces are well-heated, even excessively so, and outdoors is comfortable if you dress appropriately. Winter temperatures can be anywhere between the relatively warm +5°C to the painfully cold -30°C and broad day-to-day fluctuations are common, so pack for the full spectrum. Petersburg feels colder than Moscow, even at the same temperature. Long underwear is worth bringing, or at least some tights to wear under long pants, if you plan on spending a substantial amount of time outdoors, but if you rug up too much you can easily overheat and get sweaty when indoors, especially on the metro – which will make you colder when you go outside again. For days in town it works better to wear a warmer coat and lighter clothing underneath, rather than compensating for an inadequate coat with multiple warm underlayers. Of course, you'll also need a warm hat that covers your ears, a scarf, gloves (lined leather works better than wool knit), warm socks, and thick-soled non-slip footwear. Affordable winter wear is easy to find in local stores.

If you want to **visit churches and monasteries,** be sure to pack some modest clothing: long pants for men, sleeves for both genders, headscarf and long skirt for women – a good choice is a light wraparound skirt that fits in your handbag, so you can whip it out and put it on over your other clothes when needed.

FOOTWEAR

Note that locals have something of a shoe fixation: Footwear must be clean, and not worn out. If doormen are sneering, your shoes are the most likely reason. If you're in hiking boots, you might as well go around with "tourist" written on your forehead. Some establishments still have a "no entry in sportswear" policy and apply it to any kind of sneaker.

Russians take off their shoes as soon as they enter any kind of living space, so slippers are handy, especially if you'll be visiting people or taking the overnight Moscow–St. Petersburg train.

the other hand it is expected that you should stand up for the elderly, the pregnant, and small children.

When **greeting,** men shake hands with each other and commonly kiss the cheek of a woman, but only if already acquainted. Women who know each other also usually greet with a kiss on the cheek. Shaking hands with women is not the done thing, and if a woman offers her hand, a man is likely to kiss it. When a woman and man meet for the first time, they smile and say *ochen priyatno* (very pleasant to meet you).

Dress Norms

Clothing customs shouldn't present any great challenges and tourists can wear pretty much what they want without any problems (except when visiting churches, which have strict dress rules, described later in this section). There are, however, a few points worth noting.

Moscow and St. Petersburg are both large and increasingly cosmopolitan cities. As such, it's a good idea to pack urban clothes if you don't want to stand out. Wearing such items as waterproof all-weather coats, strap-on water bottles, utility belts, and other such camping gear may seem like a good idea, but keep in mind that you will out of place. Shorts, which were once rarely worn by grown men, have made big inroads recent years, and now they're fine for wandering about town on a hot day, however you would probably feel more comfortable changing into long trousers before heading out to a decent restaurant. If you have a strong moral aversion to the wearing of fur you'd be better off not coming in the winter months as Russians have no such compunctions and it's open season on little furry animals. When visiting someone's home, you are likely to be given slippers to wear inside the apartment, as wearing street shoes inside is usually frowned upon—and walking around barefoot, no matter how warm the apartment, is a no-no.

When visiting any functioning church or monastery, observe the dress rules. Women must cover their heads, wear a modest top with sleeves, and most importantly of all, wear a skirt that's at least knee-length, and not jeans or any other kind of short or long pants unless they're covered by a skirt. Men must wear long pants and shirts with sleeves, and remove their hats.

Restaurants

Russia has no striking peculiarities in its restaurant and dining culture. Compared to American waiters, Russian waiters tend to be less effusive in their greetings, don't tell their names, and will assume that you realize that they are your waiter (for today). Salads are traditionally served before soups, but in disorganized restaurants, it's not unheard-of for dishes to come out in an illogical sequence, and out of sync. Very often menus list not only the price of each dish, but also the weight of each dish, broken down into its constituent parts, i.e. cabbage rolls with mashed potato and vegetable sauce might have a weight listing as 300/100/50 meaning 300 grams of rolls, 100 grams of potato and 50 grams of sauce—this can be quite handy for deciding which dishes are more or less substantial. Be aware that with whole fish and to a lesser extent steaks, the price can be listed per 100 grams, rather than per portion. The whole fish could well weigh 300, 400, 500 grams or more, and you will be charged accordingly. The menu should indicate whether the price is per 100 grams—if in doubt, ask your waiter.

The standard tip is 10 percent. It is considered polite to ask the waitstaff first if you want to slide tables together or move chairs. Remember that Russians tend to speak much more quietly than Americans. Usually, in a crowded restaurant, you won't be able to hear the Russians at the next table, but you'll be able to hear every word of the Americans at the far end of the room. Perhaps talking at such a loud volume is unnoticeable in America where everybody else is also talking loudly, but in Russia it works out that you'll be broadcasting your conversation to the whole restaurant. When leaving, offering a farewell "do svidaniya" to the staff will be appreciated and will usually be warmly reciprocated.

Lining Up

When there is a line, it is quite normal for people to approach the end of the line and ask who is the last person in line. They can ask the last person to "hold" the place behind them and then go off to conduct some business elsewhere, returning later to take up the spot that was held for them—this is not pushing in. However, if you join a line, it is polite for the last person to warn you if the spot behind them is being held. When standing in line, Russians tend to stand closer together than would be normal in some other countries.

Tipping

Tipping is not done anywhere except restaurants and bars where 10 percent of the bill is left as a tip.

SMOKING

Russia is a very smoker-friendly nation. As a smoker, you should find Russia a welcoming refuge from the ever-increasing tobacco intolerance of the West. Bars, clubs, and restaurants will all happily provide you with the best seat in the house, as it were, with the nonsmoking section (if there is one) most likely located in a small closet-sized room out back. For those sensitive to smoke who may find this arrangement unacceptable, about the only alternative is the Russian institution of the "children's café," where there is no smoking throughout the establishment—but also clowns, ice cream, and other such wholesome distractions. As tolerant to smoking as Russia may be, there are some limits: Smoking is not permitted in metro stations, on public transport, nor in public buildings—and people do not ignore this rule.

TIPS FOR TRAVELERS
Access for Travelers with Disabilities

Russia is definitely a challenging destination for travelers with disabilities. Generally, only the most modern buildings have wheelchair access, although major museums do offer good access. Many wide major streets can only be crossed via underground walkways with steep flights of stairs. Public transport is rarely wheelchair-accessible. Things are slowly changing—restaurants are adding ramps and menus in braille (Russian braille, naturally)—but all the same travelers with disabilities will still really have their work cut out for them. Russian Wonder Travel claims to be the only company specializing in travel services for people with disabilities; for more information see its very informative website, www.russiable.com, or the site of the Society for Accessible Travel and Hospitality, www.sath.org.

Traveling with Children

Children are given pride of place in all public areas in Russia. A woman with a small baby should not be surprised to be given preferential treatment, such as moving to the front of the line, offered occupied seats, and so on. Diaper-changing rooms can be found in modern shopping centers and department stores as well as in all airports and train stations. Small children can make a racket that would raise the dead and the parents will still go unreprimanded. Do expect, on the other hand, to receive plenty of stern advice from babushkas you don't know—especially regarding your child's inadequately warm clothing or absence of hat.

Women Traveling Alone

In a nation that parachuted female snipers behind enemy lines during World War II, a woman traveling alone is hardly going to raise any eyebrows. Feel free to dress as you please (except at a church). When traveling on trains, if you are not traveling in a women-only carriage, you can ask the carriage attendant to move you to a different coupe if you don't fancy sharing the compartment with three men you don't know.

Gay and Lesbian Travelers

Homosexuality was banned in Soviet times, but since then the law has been overturned and things have loosened up a bit. Nowadays, Russians' attitude to gays and lesbians is a mixed one. Gay singers and show business performers enjoy great popularity and success, but Moscow City Hall has repeatedly banned the holding of a downtown gay march, and attempts to stage one have met a homophobic reaction. Public displays of gay affection are not a good idea and will likely lead to problems. Moscow and St. Petersburg both do have gay and lesbian clubs, however. For further information about gay and lesbian issues in Russia see the website Gay.ru (www.gay.ru).

Health and Safety

EMERGENCY NUMBERS

The emergency services numbers in Russia are as follows: 01 for the firefighting service, 02 for police, 03 for ambulance, and 04 for emergency gas mains repair. There are plans to switch over to a unified emergency services number, 112, which should be functioning by 2010. The emergency number 112 can already be used from any GSM cell phone.

MEDICAL SERVICES
Hospitals and Clinics

While Moscow and St. Petersburg have some Western-standard hospitals, both cities also offer some more familiar Western-style clinics where a tourist would feel more at ease. These medical clinics offer Western doctors who speak English. The clinics can arrange hospital care at one the city's better hospitals if turns out to be necessary.

In Moscow, the **American Medical Center** (26 Prospekt Mira, Bldg. 6, enter from Grokholsky Pereulok, 495/933-7700, www.amcenter.ru, 24 hours) and the **European Medical Center** (5 Spiridonyevsky Pereulok, 495/933-6655, www.emcmos.ru, 24 hours) both offer a wide range of medical services and can arrange for hospitalization if needed. A similar level of service is provided in St. Petersburg at the **American Medical Clinic** (78 Naberezhnaya reki Moyki, 812/740-2090, www.amclinic.ru, 24 hours) and at **Euromed** (60 Suvorovsky Pereulok, 812/327-0301, www.euromed.ru, 24 hours).

Pharmacies

These days, pharmacies stock a full range of Western medicines. Problems could arise, however, given that many of the common medications may be sold under different names than what you are used to, and finding a certain product could be time consuming. For this reason it is probably a good idea to bring any specific medicines that you may need. If you find that you do need to buy some medicine,

avoid buying from kiosks and similar stands, as there is a risk of fakes. Shop in one of the more reputable chains, such as 36.6. There are numerous pharmacies all over both cities, with many open 24 hours. In Moscow, these include **36.6** (25/9 Tverskaya Ulitsa, Bldg. 2, 495/699-2459, metro Tverskaya; 25 Zemlyanoy Val, Bldg. 1, 495/917-1285, metro Kurskaya, www.366.ru), and **Doktor Stoletov** (2/15 Ulitsa Maroseyka, 495/624-8787, metro Kitay-Gorod; at the VDNKh metro station exit to VVTs, 495/648-7506), and in St. Petersburg, **36.6** (98 Nevsky Prospekt, 812/275-8189, metro Mayakovskaya; 62 Bolshoy Prospekt, Petrograd Side, 812/235-4712, metro Petrogradskaya) and **Pervaya Pomoshch** (16 Vladimirsky Prospekt, 812/275-8189, metro Dostoyevskaya), among many others.

Medical Insurance

Medical insurance is essential for traveling to Russia. Many consulates will demand to see insurance before issuing a visa. Even if this is not the case, only the foolhardy would risk traveling without it. If you do end up in an accident, carrying insurance documents with you will ensure that you receive any expensive treatments you may need without having to wait while creditworthiness is confirmed.

FOOD AND WATER

While the tap water in Moscow and its surrounding towns is widely considered potable, this is not the case with the tap water in St. Petersburg. St. Petersburg's water is known to occasionally contain the giardia lamblia parasite, which causes giardiasis, or Beaver Fever as it is sometimes known, usually characterized by an upset stomach and severe diarrhea. It is hard to treat and may require strong medications; it is known to recur, sometimes years later. As such, don't drink St. Petersburg's water straight from the tap. Bottled water is recommended, even for brushing teeth. Locals often just boil the tap water, but a good filter should really be used as well. And while Moscow's water is better, people usually don't drink it straight from the tap—first you should boil it or at least filter it.

Food hygiene is generally not a problem, although there are a couple of points worth noting. Health officers from the Consumer Protection Service regularly point to the low hygiene standards found in the preparation of *shaurma, shaverma,* or *doner* kebabs, sold from street kiosks. Although many impoverished students may disagree, it probably is a good idea to give these meat sandwiches a miss.

Other potential pitfalls are the wild berries and mushrooms sold by the harmless-looking babushkas, typically around train stations. These fruits of the forest cannot be vouched for, and may well have been gathered from polluted areas and thus contain toxins, even possibly radioactive contaminants. Such produce is safe to buy from the official markets where it has been certified safe.

CRIME

Street crime in Moscow and St. Petersburg is generally no worse than any other major capital in the West. Visitors should follow the usual common-sense guidelines as for any large city: Avoid dark alleyways late at night, avoid drunken strangers on the streets, and so on. The most common problem is pickpockets, especially in areas crowded with tourists. Remember to keep all valuables, especially hard-to-replace travel documents, well tucked away, and don't leave items such as bags and purses unattended in public places. Theft from hotel rooms is not particularly common but of course one should exercise common sense, remembering to lock up and put things away when going out.

One of the more exotic scams that tourists may encounter is the so-called "turkey drop." A person walking down the street in front of you will drop a large bundle of cash (which is usually fake) and continue on, seeming unaware. If you retrieve the money in order to return it to the original man, his colleague will step forward offering to split it with you, perhaps shuffling you off to a quiet corner or alley. The original man then returns to "reclaim" his lost money and upon counting the now-opened bundle, declares some of it missing, accusing you of taking it and leading to various demands and threats. If someone drops money in front of you, it's best simply to ignore it and walk on by.

Information and Services

MONEY

The days of the dollar being Russia's currency of choice are over. The ruble is now number one in anyone's pocketbook and all payments everywhere are now made in rubles. One hangover from less stable times is the use of the *uslovnye yedinetsy* (conditional units, У.Е.). In these situations, a price listed is in some mythical currency, usually somewhere between the dollar and the euro, but, all the same, payment will still be in rubles.

The ruble comes in the following paper-note dominations: 5,000, 1,000, 500, 100, 50, and 10 rubles, although the paper 10-ruble note is slowly being phased out in favor of a 10-ruble coin. Besides the 10-ruble coin, there are also the 5-, 2-, and 1-ruble coins. The ruble is broken down into 100 kopeks, which come in 50-, 10-, 5-, 1-kopek coins, although the 5- and 1-kopek coins are increasingly rare and there is talk of getting rid of them.

Money Exchanges

Money exchanges are more than plentiful and can be found on just about every corner, and virtually all banks exchange money as well. The most commonly accepted currencies are dollars and euros, followed by British pounds (and occasionally Swiss Francs). All other currencies are going to be problematic and can

MONEY BELT

ATMs are now commonplace, so you don't need to bring your entire travel budget in cash or travelers checks (which are not always easy to cash anyway). While credit cards can be used to make withdrawals at ATMs, not every shop or restaurant accepts them.

A money belt that you can hide under your clothing is a good spot for your cards, excess cash, and documents, especially since you need to carry your passport everywhere and pickpockets are common on crowded metro cars.

Moscow's City Hall is developing a series of touch-screen information terminals.

© NATHAN TOOHEY

be exchanged only at a couple of specialist exchange points with unattractive rates. While exchange points sometimes offer better rates than banks, banks are safer and more reliable. Exchange points have been known to be less than honest in their dealings with customers, especially tourists. Things to watch out for include good rates on display that are only available when exchanging very large sums (the regular rate may only be displayed in small type or in a hard-to-see spot). When changing cash, be sure to thoroughly check the cash drawer when collecting your money—sometimes a note may get somehow mysteriously stuck to the back far end of the drawer where you may not notice it. Always count your money before leaving the exchange window. The days of black marketers changing money on the street are over—if someone does offer this service, it is surely a con.

ATMs

Bankomats, as ATMs are referred to in Russian, are widespread in Moscow and St. Petersburg, although a little less so in the smaller towns outside of them. Besides issuing rubles, many also issue dollars and euros. Usually their menus have an English-language option. Most will add a charge for issuing cash from a card that does not match the bank that runs the ATM. The fee varies and is usually around 100R or

0.5 percent, and the machine will not always warn you in advance. There have been rare cases of fraud involving tampered ATMs—to help reduce the chance of this happening, cover the keypad with your free hand so your personal identification number (PIN) is not visible when entering it. Criminals have been known to film people entering their PINs with hidden cameras. ATMs located inside banks are also safer than ones facing onto the open street.

Credit Cards, Travelers Checks, and Money Transfers

Visa and MasterCard credit cards are growing in popularity and can be used in more and more shops and restaurants, although they are still not universally accepted, especially in smaller establishments. When paying with a credit card you may have to show your passport as identification. If you plan to pay with a credit card at a restaurant or bar, check that the establishment accepts credit cards before running up a bill—a Visa or MasterCard sticker displayed on the door or by the cash register is no guarantee it will be accepted. American Express and Diners Club cards are not widely used in Russia.

Travelers checks and credit cards can also be used to get cash over the counter at most banks. A passport will need to be provided as identification and the bank will take a commission, which varies from roughly 1 to 5 percent. Western Union money transfer services are fairly common and can be found in various banks around town (look for the logo in the bank's window), but it is a rather expensive service.

TOURIST INFORMATION CENTERS

Moscow has a small tourist information center (4 Ulitsa Ilinka, inside the Gostiny Dvor center, 2nd fl., section 311–314, 495/232-5657, www.moscow-city.ru/?lang_char_id=en, metro Ploshchad Revolyutsii), located a shortish distance from Red Square. The staff are friendly and will happily provide you with a wealth of printed materials, not only about Moscow, but

just about any city across the entire country. Moscow's City Hall is developing a series of touch-screen information terminals that can be found around town and that provide a range of information—the first such terminal is located on Ulitsa Novy Arbat. Mosinfo touch-screen terminals also provide directory service–type information.

St. Petersburg is better served with tourist information centers. Currently there are centers in both the domestic and international airport terminals, on the corner of Nevsky Prospekt and Sadovaya Ulitsa, on Palace Square, beside the Peter and Paul Fortress, near Smolny Cathedral, and on St. Isaac's Square.

POSTAL SERVICE

The Russian Post (www.russianpost.ru) service is fairly slow, but letters, postcards, and packages sent from Russia do seem to usually get to their destination eventually. International letters and postcards can be sent from any post office, but larger packages need to be sent from specially designated post offices. In Moscow,

© NATHAN TOOHEY

The sign at Paveletsky Station shows the way to the express train to Domodedovo airport.

these post offices include the **Main Post Office** at 26/2 Myasnitskaya Ulitsa, metro Chistye Prudy; the **International Post Office** at 37 Varshavskoye Shosse, metro Nagatinskaya; and the **Central Telegraph Office** at 7 Tverskaya Ulitsa, metro Okhotny Ryad. In St. Petersburg, packages should be sent from the **Central Post Office** at 9 Pochtamtskaya Ulitsa, metro Sadovaya.

When sending international packages, you should bring the items unwrapped, as the postal workers will want to see whether what you are sending matches what's written on your postal declaration. They will wrap the goods for you and then let you address it for sending. A more reliable, faster, but more expensive option is the Russian Post's **Express Mail Service,** or EMS (www.russianpost.ru/portal/en/home/postal/ ems), which is the equivalent of the United States' Express Mail International service, and is available in every post office.

Yet another option is the major international courier companies such as **DHL** (www.dhl.ru) and **FedEx** (www.fedex.com/ru), which offer their usual services, albeit at a hefty price.

INTERNET ACCESS

Both Moscow and St. Petersburg have quite a few Internet cafés, although their popularity has fallen somewhat over the last few years. On the other hand, Wi-Fi or wireless Internet has only been growing in popularity and the best bit is that it is nearly always provided for free. Another paid service is **Beeline WiFi** (www .beeline.ru), which has almost complete coverage of downtown Moscow and a more limited coverage in St. Petersburg. Registration can be done on the company's website and payment can be made using cards that can be bought around town in such places as mobile-phone stores and payment kiosks.

PHONES
Cell Phones

Nearly any GSM-standard cell phone that uses the 900 or 1800 frequencies should work in Russia if your home provider has a roaming agreement with one of Russia's three major cell-phone providers, which all international providers should. Keep in mind, however, that making calls while roaming can be prohibitively expensive, so if you need to make lots of local calls using your cell phone it might be a wise idea to purchase a local SIM chip. These chips can be purchased in any of the countless cell-phone kiosks around town and usually come with some credit already on them.

Long-Distance Calls

To call long distance within Russia, first you must dial 8, wait for the tone, and then proceed with the area code and the local number. For international calls, you dial 8, wait for the tone, then 10 for international access, followed by the country code, the area code, and local number. All the numbers in this book have been listed with their area code included. One point to keep in mind is that Moscow has grown so large that it has now been divided into two separate **area codes**—the original 495 and the new 499. To call from one area to the other, follow the procedure for making a long-distance call. The call will be charged as a local call.

MEDIA

Moscow has a reasonably healthy selection of local English-language publications. The local daily newspaper the *Moscow Times* (www.the-moscowtimes.com) does a thorough job of covering Russian news, especially business. The paper can be picked up for free at numerous bars, restaurants, hotels, and business centers around town. The paper is also included with the *International Herald Tribune,* which is printed locally and can be bought at kiosks and hotels. The recently revamped weekly newspaper *Moscow News* (www.mnweekly.ru), also free, provides news and business coverage as well as arts and entertainment, including nightlife and restaurants..

Element (www.elementmoscow.ru/main.php) is a weekly entertainment newspaper with reviews of restaurants, events calendars, and other useful information, and it can also be found for free in bars and restaurants around town. *Where* magazine is a similar publication, although it is dual language and comes out monthly in full color. *Passport* (www.passport magazine.ru) is another monthly English-language color magazine with a similar subject matter, although it more oriented towards local expats rather than tourists.

The *St. Petersburg Times* (www.sptimes.ru), the sister publication of the *Moscow Times,* comes out on Tuesdays and Fridays, and can be found for free around town in restaurants, bars, hotels, and business centers. The Friday edition includes an entertainment section with a what's on calendar listing concerts, exhibitions, and so on. Particularly useful for tourists is the local edition of the free monthly guide *In Your Pocket* (www.inyourpocket.com/russia/city/ st_petersburg.html), which has extensive listings describing hotels, restaurants, bars, and so on, as well as timetables and general tourist information—it is distributed around town in hotels, bars, and restaurants. *Pulse* (www.pulse .ru) is a monthly entertainment magazine that comes out in both English and Russian editions. It carries a large range of lifestyle articles as well as listings, events calendars, and so on. It can be found in restaurants and bars around town for free.

Weights and Measurements

TIME ZONES

Moscow, St. Petersburg, and most of western Russia use Moscow Standard Time, with is three hours ahead of Greenwich Mean Time. This means that it is usually eight hours ahead of the East Coast of the United States and 11 hours ahead of the West Coast. Russia observes Moscow Summer Time from the last Sunday in March to the last Sunday in October, when it becomes four hours ahead of Greenwich Mean Time.

ELECTRICITY

Russia uses 220V AC, 50Hz. Its sockets match the European standard found in France or Germany. To use appliances from England, an adapter will be needed. To use North American appliances, a voltage converter with a European-standard adapter will be needed (with the exception of most laptop computers and other travel appliances that come with the converter included and therefore only need the plug adapter). Adapters and voltage converters can be found in most electronic stores or international airports.

MEASUREMENTS

The metric system was adopted by the Soviet Union in 1924 and is universally used across Russia. One interesting measurement difference from the rest of the metric-using world is that although Russians use liters and milliliters to measure beer, wine, and other beverages, spirits such as vodka are traditionally measured in grams—a standard shot these days being 50 grams (nearly 55 milliliters or 1.86 fluid ounces).

RESOURCES

Glossary

avtovokzal bus station
banya bath-house, Russian-style sauna
bashnya tower
blin/y pancake/s
bolshoy, bolshaya, bolshoye big
bulvar boulevard
dacha country house/summer cottage
dom house, building
dvorets palace
gora, gory mountain/hill, mountains/hills
kolokol bell
kolokolnya belltower
koltso ring
kremlin citadel
maly, malaya, maloye small
monastyr monastery, convent
most bridge
naberezhnaya embankment
novy, novaya, novoye new
ozero lake

palata chambers, palace
pereulok lane
ploshchad square
prospekt avenue
proyezd thoroughfare
prud/y pond/s
reka river
shashlik shish kebab
shosse highway
stary, staraya, staroye old
sad garden
sobor cathedral
sredny middle
stena wall
tserkov church
ulitsa street
vokzal station
vorota gates
zakuski appetizers, hors d'oeuvres

Russian Phrasebook

PRONUNCIATION GUIDE

Russian is the official language of the Russian Federation, although more than 100 other languages are also spoken by various ethnic minorities around the country.

Although English is not as widely spoken as in Western Europe, it is fairly unproblematic to get about in Moscow and St. Petersburg with English alone. All the same, it will certainly make life easier if you learn the Cyrillic alphabet for reading maps, store and street names, and a few simple phrases and names of day-to-day objects won't go astray.

The Russian Cyrillic alphabet consists of 33 letters, which unlike English, tend to follow a consistent pronunciation. The exceptions are that some vowels sound quite different when unstressed compared to how they sound in stressed form, and the letter g (г) is pronounced as v in ego, -ego and -ogo (его, -его, -ого).

The Alphabet

А, а as 'a' in "father"
Б, б as 'b' in "boat"
В, в as 'v' in "vine"
Г, г as 'g' in "good" but as 'v' in ego, -ego, -ogo (его, -его, -ого)
Д, д as 'd' in "do"
Е, е as 'ye' in "yes" (when unstressed, 'i' in "it")
Ё, ё as 'yo' in "yore"
Ж, ж as 'g' in "genre," 's' in "pleasure," or 'zh'
З, з as 'z' in "zone"
И, и as 'ee' in "see"
Й, й as 'y' in "yes"
К, к as 'k' in "kitten"
Л, л as 'l' in "lamp"
М, м as 'm' in "moon"
Н, н as 'n' in "not"
О, о as 'o' in "obey" (when unstressed, 'a' in "along")
П, п as 'p' in "pet"
Р, р as rolled 'r'
С, с as 's' in "so"
Т, т as 't' in "tip"
У, у as 'oo' in "ooze"
Ф, ф as 'f' in "fact"
Х, х as 'ch' in "Bach"
Ц, ц as 'ts' in "sits"
Ч, ч as 'ch' in "chip"
Ш, ш as 'sh' in "shut"
Щ, щ similar to the 'sh' in "sheer" or 'sh ch' such as in "fresh cheese"
Ъ, ъ the hard sign which, placed after a consonant, indicates it is not palatalized
Ы, ы as 'i' in "sill"
Ь, ь the soft sign which, placed after a consonant, indicates a softened pronunciation
Э, э as 'e' in "met"
Ю, ю as 'u' in "use"
Я, я as 'ya' in "yard" (or, when unstressed, 'i' in "it")

COMMON WORDS AND PHRASES

Greeting and Meeting

Hello (formal or when addressing a group of people) Здравствуйте [zdrá-stvooy-tye]
Hello (informal, to one person) Здравствуй [zdrá-stvooy]
Hi (colloquial, to a friend or friends) Привет **[pree-vyét]**
Good morning! Доброе утро! [dó-bra-ye óot-ra]
Good day! Добрый день! [dó-bri dyen]
Good evening! Добрый вечер! [dó-bri vyé-cheer]
Good night! Спокойной ночи! [spa-kóy-nay nóchi]
How are things? (Very) well! Как дела? (Очень) хорошо! [kak dee-lá?] [(ó-cheen) ha-ra-shó]
My name is . . . Меня зовут . . . [mee-nyá za-vóot . . .]
What is your name? (formal) Как Вас зовут? [kak vas za-vóot . . .]
What is your name? (informal) Как тебя зовут? [kak tee-bya sa-vóot . . .]
Do you speak English? Вы говорите по-английски? [vy ga-va-rée-tye pa-an-gléey-skee?
Goodbye! До свидания! [da svee-dá-nee-ya]
See you! Пока! [pa-ká]

Being Polite

Thank you (very much)! (Большое) спасибо! [(bal-shó-ye) spa-sée-ba]
Please/You are welcome/Here you are Пожалуйста [pa-zhál-sta]
Sorry (formal)! Извините! [eez-vee-née-tye]
Sorry (informal)! Извини! [eez-vee-née]

Getting Around

Tell me, please . . . Скажите, пожалуйста, . . . [ska-zhí-tye, pa-zhál-sta . . .]
Where is . . . ? Где . . . ? [gdye . . . ?]
Repeat, please! (formal) Повторите, пожалуйста! [pav-ta-rée-tye, pa-zhál-sta]
Repeat, please! (informal) Повтори, пожалуйста! [pav-ta-rée, pa-zhál-sta]

straight on прямо [pryá-ma]
to the right направо [na-prá-va]
to the left налево [na-lyé-va]
entrance вход [fhót]
exit выход [ví-hat]
crossing переход [pe-re-hót]
metro метро [met-ró]
bus автобус [af-tó-boos]
trolleybus троллейбус [tra-lyéy-boos]
tram трамвай [tram-váy]
next stop следующая остановка
[slyé-doo-yoo-shshiya a-sta-nóf-ka]
ticket билет [bi-lyét]

Shopping

open открыт/о/а [at-krít/o/a]
closed закрыт/о/а [za-krít/o/a]
break перерыв [pere-rív]
cashier касса [ká-ssa]
How much does it cost? сколько стоит?
[skól'-ko stó-it?]
give, please дайте, пожалуйста [day'-té, pa-
zhál-sta]
**Miss! (the form of address used for
waitresses, shop assistants, and female
strangers in general)** Девушка! [Dyé-
vushka!]
**Young man! (as above, but for
men)** Молодой человек! [Mál-a-doy chel-
o-vék!]
discount, discounts скидка, скидки [skíd-ka,
skíd-ki]
credit card кредитная карта [kredít-naya
kárta]
money деньги [dyén-gi]

Stores and Services

shop магазин [ma-ga-zín]
market рынок [rí-nok]
supermarket супермаркет [sóoper-márket]
department store универмаг [univer-mág]
groceries продукты [pra-dóokti]
clothing одежда [a-dézh-da]
footwear обувь [ó-boof]
souvenirs сувениры [su-ve-ní-ri]
books книги [knígi]
pharmacy аптека [ap-téka]
bank банк [bank]

currency exchange обмен валюты [ab-mén
va-lóoti]
hotel гостиница [ga-stín-itsa]
restaurant ресторан [resto-rán]
cafe кафе [ka-fay]
toilet туалет [tu-a-lét]
women's женский [zhén-ski]
men's мужской [muzh-skóy]

Food and Beverages

drinks напитки [na-péet-kee]
vodka водка [vót-ka]
beer пиво [pée-va]
wine вино [vee-nó]
water вода [va-dá]
juice сок [sok]
tea чай [chay]
coffee кофе [kó-fe]
milk молоко [ma-la-kó]
sugar сахар [sákhar]
bread хлеб [hlyep]
butter масло [más-la]
cheese сыр [sir]
rice рис [rees]
egg яйцо [yitsó]
meat мясо [myá-sa]
beef говядина [ga-vyá-dee-na]
pork свинина [svee-née-na]
lamb баранина [ba-rá-nee-na]
poultry птица [ptée-tsa]
chicken курица [kóo-ree-tsa]
fish рыба [ri-ba]
salmon лосось [la-sós]
herring селёдка, сельдь [sel-yódka, séld]
sturgeon осетрина [a-set-réena]
pike perch судак [soo-dak]
cod треска [tree-ská]
trout форель [fa-rél]
caviar икра [ik-rá]
vegetables овощи [ó-va-shshee]
tomato помидор [pa-mee-dór]
cucumber огурец [a-goo-ryéz]
carrot морковь [mar-kóf]
cabbage капуста [ka-póo-sta]
potato картошка [kar-tósh-ka]
fruit фрукты [fróok-ti]
apple яблоко [yá-bla-ka]
pear груша [gróo-sha]

orange апельсин [a-peel-séen]
banana банан [ba-nán]
strawberry клубника [kloob-née-ka]

Numbers
0 ноль [nol]
1 один [a-déen]
2 два [dva]
3 три [tree]
4 четыре [chye-tí-rye]
5 пять [pyat]
6 шесть [shest]
7 семь [syem]
8 восемь [vó-seem]
9 девять [dyé-veet]
10 десять [dyé-seet]
11 одиннадцать [a-dée-na-tsat]
12 двенадцать [dvee-nát-sat]
13 тринадцать [tree-nát-sat]
14 четырнадцать [chee-tír-na-tsat]
15 пятнадцать [peet-nát-sat]
16 шестнадцать [shis-nát-sat]
17 семнадцать [seem-nát-sat]
18 восемнадцать [va-seem-nát-sat]
19 девятнадцать [dee-veet-nát-sat]
20 двадцать [dvát-sat]
30 тридцать [tréet-sat]
40 сорок [só-rak]
50 пятьдесят [pee-dee-syát]
60 шестьдесят [shees-dee-syát]
70 семьдесят [syém-dee-syat]
80 восемьдесят [vó-seem-dee-syat]
90 девяносто [dee-vee-nó-sta]
100 сто [stó]
1000 тысяча [tí-see-cha]

Days of the Week
Monday понедельник [pa-nye-dyél-neek]
Tuesday вторник [ftór-neek]
Wednesday среда [srye-dá]
Thursday четверг [chyet-vyérk]
Friday пятница [pyát-nee-tsa]
Saturday суббота [soo-bó-ta]
Sunday воскресенье [vas-krye-syé-nye]

Months and Seasons
January Январь [yan-vár]
February Февраль [feev-rál]
March Март [mart]
April Апрель [ap-ryél]
May Май [may]
June Июнь [ee-yún]
July Июль [ee-yúl]
August Август [áv-goost]
September Сентябрь [seen-tyábr]
October Окртябрь [ak-tyábr]
November Ноябрь [na-yábr]
December Декабрь [dee-kábr]
Winter Зима [zee-má]
Spring Весна [vees-ná]
Summer Лето [lyé-ta]
Autumn Осень [ó-seen]

Suggested Reading

HISTORY AND GENERAL INFORMATION

Bown, Matthew Cullerne. *Art Under Stalin.* New York, NY: Holmes & Meier, 1991. A good guide to art of the entire Soviet period.

Cecil, Clementine and Harris, Edmund. *Moscow Heritage at Crisis Point.* Moscow, Russia: Moscow Architectural Preservation Society (MAPS) and SAVE Europe's Heritage, 2007. A well-illustrated and thorough overview of the city's architecture, including what's been lost and what's under threat.

Cohen, Stephen F. *Failed Crusade: America and the Tragedy of Post-Communist Russia.* New York: Norton. 2000 and 2001. A New York University professor gives a harsh critique of U.S. policy to Russia.

Figes, Orlando. *Natasha's Dance: A Cultural History of Russia.* New York, NY: Metropolitan Books, 2002. This much-praised book comprehensively covers the full spectrum of the country's culture and history. It's considered essential reading for anyone who wants to understand Russia and the Russians.

Freeland, Chrystia. *Sale of the Century: Russia's Wild Ride From Communism to Capitalism.* New York, NY: Crown Publishers, 2000. This positively reviewed work gives a picture of country's economic path in the 1990s.

Reed, John. *Ten Days That Shook the World.* New York, NY: Boni & Liveright, 1919. An American journalist's first-hand account of the October Revolution of 1917 has been repeatedly reprinted and is now available as a Penguin Classics paperback.

Remnick, David. *Lenin's Tomb: The Last Days of the Soviet Empire.* New York, NY: Vintage Books, 1994. This seminal work about the collapse of the Soviet Union won the Pulitzer Prize for Non-Fiction in 1994.

Richmond, Yale. *From Nyet to Da, 4th Ed: Understanding the New Russia.* Boston, MA: Intercultural Press, 2008. A useful introduction to the culture for first-time visitors.

Von Bremzen, Anya. *Please to the Table: The Russian Cookbook.* New York, NY: Workman Publishing, 1990. A good introduction to the local cuisine, describing many of the most popular dishes of the former Soviet Union, with recipes showing how to make them using ingredients available in the United States.

Ward, Chris. *Stalin's Russia.* London, UK: Oxford University Press, 1999. A thorough text book, not only on Stalinism but on the literature about it.

LITERATURE AND FICTION

Bulgakov, Mikhail. *The Master and Margarita.* Ann Arbor, MI: Ardis, 1995. Written in the 1930s and published in the 1960s, this is a fantastical multi-layered novel about the Devil and his entourage wreaking havoc on the 1930s Moscow literary elite; it's seen as a satirical critique of Soviet society and politics, but it's still the ideal novel to read while visiting the Russian capital. This translation by Diana Burgin and Katherine Tiernan O'Connor is the aficionados' favorite.

Dostoyevsky, Fyodor. *Crime and Punishment.* London, England: Penguin Books, 2006. This is the ultimate Petersburg novel, a 19th-century masterpiece and the perfect accompaniment to a visit to the city.

Gogol, Nikolay. *Dead Souls.* New York, NY: Knopf Publishing, Everyman's Library, 2004. Another 19th-century classic, and a comic masterpiece. This translation by Richard Pevear and Larissa Volokhonsky has won high acclaim.

Pelevin, Viktor. *Homo Zapiens.* New York, NY: Penguin Group (USA), 2002. Also published as "Generation P," and "Babylon," this pop-culture novel, first published in 1999, about a poet-turned-advertising copywriter in 1990s Moscow.

Petrov, Yevgeny, and Ilf, Ilya. *The Twelve Chairs.* Evanston, IL: Northwestern University Press, 1997. This satirical novel about a con man in the 1920s is a very popular and much-quoted work.

Robski, Oksana. *Casual: A Novel.* New York, NY: Regan Books, 2006. Fun-to-read chick-lit about Moscow's 21st-century nouveaux-riches, with the action taking place in recognizable locales around the city—actual restaurants and elite residential districts. Despite all that, it's a murder mystery.

Yerofeyev, Venedikt. *Moscow Stations.* London, England: Faber & Faber, 1998. Also known as "Moscow—Petushki," "Moscow Circles," and "Moscow to the End of the Line," this is an amusing story written in 1969-70, about an alcoholic's drunken train ride to visit his beloved. Enjoy with a shot of vodka and a pickle.

Internet Resources

Expat.ru
www.expat.ru

The original English-language forum board for expats and Russians with sections dealing with just about every aspect of living in Rusia. Queries are usually answered promptly and the searching the archives can provide answers immediately.

ITAR-TASS
www.itar-tass.com/eng/

Another Russian wire news service providing similar coverage to that RIA Novosti. Like at RIA Novosti, here you'll find stories obscure stories from around Russia that would never make it into the Western press.

Menu.ru
http://eng.menu.ru

A massive catalog of Moscow restaurants that allows you to search using various criteria. It's regularly updated using information provided by the restaurants themselves.

Multitran
www.multitran.ru

This is the leading online dictionary—if you can't find the word you're looking for on this site it probably doesn't exist. It offers various other languages besides just English and Russian.

Promt Translator
www.online-translator.com

This site translates not just individual words, but entire expressions. If you keep the sentences simple it does a decent enough job, just don't expect it to translate poetry.

Redtape.ru
www.redtape.ru

A rival splinter group formed this alternative to expat.ru. The forum's community is probably a little tighter as it seems that most posters seem to know one another.

Restaurant.ru
http://en.restoran.ru

Similar to menu.ru, this site's English-language version also provides information about St. Petersburg, Yekaterinburg and other Russian cities, in addition to Moscow. As with menu.ru, it often provides restaurants' complete menus online.

Ros Business Consulting
www.rbcnews.com

This news service provides all you could want to know about financial issues in Russia. It also offers regular news and weather.

Russian News and Information Agency Novosti
http://en.rian.ru

This website offers the state wire service's comprehensive coverage of events in Russia as well as from around the rest of the world.

Russia Today
www.russiatoday.com/en

Russia's answer to CNN and the like, this is the website of the 24-hour Russian state-owned cable news channel that broadcasts in English. Besides news you'll find various other colorful feature stories as well.

WayToRussia
http://waytorussia.net

A huge resource-rich travel guide to Russia with its own forum board, tons of articles and numerous commercial services, including visa invitation support.

Yellow Pages
www.yellow-pages.ru

An online telephone directory and guide to cities around Russia. Probably not as comprehensive as similar services you might find in the West, but worth a try if you looking for a certain business' phone number.

Index

Restaurants Index

Nightlife Index

Shops Index

Hotels Index

MOSCOW

ST. PETERSBURG

Acknowledgments

We'd like to thank the Kalashnikova household in St. Petersburg—the chapter on the northern capital and its excursions wouldn't have been possible without their warm and generous hospitality. Also, a thank you must go to Alyona Kucherova for feeding our hungry newt while we were away on our travels researching the book. And finally, we thank our editor, Naomi Adler Dancis, for her wise suggestions and expert coordination of the project.

www.moon.com

DESTINATIONS | ACTIVITIES | BLOGS | MAPS | BOOKS

MOON.COM is all new, and ready to help plan your next trip! Filled with fresh trip ideas and strategies, author interviews, informative blogs, a detailed map library, and descriptions of all the Moon guidebooks, Moon.com is all you need to get out and explore the world—or even places in your own backyard. As always, when you travel with Moon, expect an experience that is uncommon and truly unique.

MAP SYMBOLS

▦ Expressway	◖ Highlight	✗ Airfield	⚑ Golf Course
Primary Road	○ City/Town	✈ Airport	🅿 Parking Area
Secondary Road	◉ State Capital	▲ Mountain	▰ Archaeological Site
Unpaved Road	⊛ National Capital	✦ Unique Natural Feature	Church
Trail	★ Point of Interest		
Ferry	• Accommodation	⌇ Waterfall	Gas Station
Railroad	▾ Restaurant/Bar	▲ Park	Glacier
Pedestrian Walkway	■ Other Location	▣ Trailhead	Mangrove
Stairs	Λ Campground	Skiing Area	Reef
			Swamp

CONVERSION TABLES

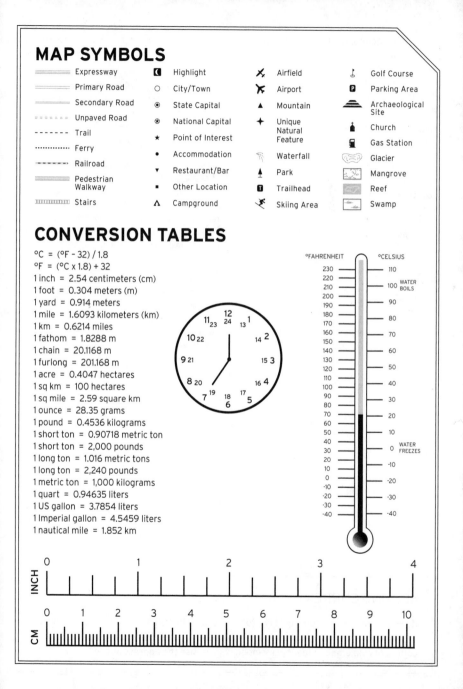

°C = (°F – 32) / 1.8
°F = (°C x 1.8) + 32
1 inch = 2.54 centimeters (cm)
1 foot = 0.304 meters (m)
1 yard = 0.914 meters
1 mile = 1.6093 kilometers (km)
1 km = 0.6214 miles
1 fathom = 1.8288 m
1 chain = 20.1168 m
1 furlong = 201.168 m
1 acre = 0.4047 hectares
1 sq km = 100 hectares
1 sq mile = 2.59 square km
1 ounce = 28.35 grams
1 pound = 0.4536 kilograms
1 short ton = 0.90718 metric ton
1 short ton = 2,000 pounds
1 long ton = 1.016 metric tons
1 long ton = 2,240 pounds
1 metric ton = 1,000 kilograms
1 quart = 0.94635 liters
1 US gallon = 3.7854 liters
1 Imperial gallon = 4.5459 liters
1 nautical mile = 1.852 km

MOON MOSCOW & ST. PETERSBURG

Avalon Travel
a member of the Perseus Books Group
1700 Fourth Street
Berkeley, CA 94710, USA
www.moon.com

Editor: Naomi Adler Dancis
Series Manager: Erin Raber
Copy Editor: Amy Scott
Graphics Coordinator: Stefano Boni
Production Coordinator: Tabitha Lahr
Cover Designer: Kathryn Osgood
Map Editor: Albert Angulo
Cartographers: Chris Markiewicz, Lohnes & Wright,
   and Jon Twena

ISBN-13: 978-1-59880-171-2
ISSN: 92-42317

Printing History
1st Edition — May 2009
5 4 3 2 1

KEEPING CURRENT

If you have a favorite gem you'd like to see included in the next edition, or see anything
that needs updating, clarification, or correction, please drop us a line. Send your
comments via email to feedback@moon.com, or use the address above.